ANDERSON'S
Law School Publications

Administrative Law Anthology
Thomas O. Sargentich

Administrative Law: Cases and Materials
Daniel J. Gifford

An Admiralty Law Anthology
Robert M. Jarvis

Alternative Dispute Resolution: Strategies for Law and Business
E. Wendy Trachte-Huber and Stephen K. Huber

The American Constitutional Order: History, Cases, and Philosophy
Douglas W. Kmiec and Stephen B. Presser

American Legal Systems: A Resource and Reference Guide
Toni M. Fine

Analytic Jurisprudence Anthology
Anthony D'Amato

An Antitrust Anthology
Andrew I. Gavil

Appellate Advocacy: Principles and Practice, *Third Edition*
Ursula Bentele and Eve Cary

Arbitration: Cases and Materials
Stephen K. Huber and E. Wendy Trachte-Huber

Basic Accounting Principles for Lawyers: With Present Value and Expected Value
C. Steven Bradford and Gary A. Ames

A Capital Punishment Anthology (and Electronic Caselaw Appendix)
Victor L. Streib

Cases and Materials on Corporations
Thomas R. Hurst and William A. Gregory

Cases and Problems in California Criminal Law
Myron Moskovitz

Cases and Problems in Criminal Law, *Fourth Edition*
Myron Moskovitz

The Citation Workbook: How to Beat the Citation Blues, *Second Edition*
Maria L. Ciampi, Rivka Widerman, and Vicki Lutz

Civil Procedure Anthology
David I. Levine, Donald L. Doernberg, and Melissa L. Nelken

Civil Procedure: Cases, Materials, and Questions, *Second Edition*
Richard D. Freer and Wendy Collins Perdue

Clinical Anthology: Readings for Live-Client Clinics
Alex J. Hurder, Frank S. Bloch, Susan L. Brooks, and Susan L. Kay

Commercial Transactions Series: Problems and Materials
Louis F. Del Duca, Egon Guttman, Alphonse M. Squillante, Fred H. Miller,
 Linda Rusch, and Peter Winship
   Vol. 1: Secured Transactions Under the UCC
   Vol. 2: Sales Under the UCC and the CISG
   Vol. 3: Negotiable Instruments Under the UCC and the CIBN

Communications Law: Media, Entertainment, and Regulation
Donald E. Lively, Allen S. Hammond, Blake D. Morant, and Russell L. Weaver

A Conflict-of-Laws Anthology
Gene R. Shreve

Constitutional Conflicts
Derrick A. Bell, Jr.

A Constitutional Law Anthology, *Second Edition*
Michael J. Glennon, Donald E. Lively, Phoebe A. Haddon, Dorothy E. Roberts,
 and Russell L. Weaver

Constitutional Law: Cases, History, and Dialogues, *Second Edition*
Donald E. Lively, Phoebe A. Haddon, Dorothy E. Roberts, Russell L. Weaver,
and William D. Araiza

The Constitutional Law of the European Union
James D. Dinnage and John F. Murphy

The Constitutional Law of the European Union: Documentary Supplement
James D. Dinnage and John F. Murphy

Constitutional Torts
Sheldon H. Nahmod, Michael L. Wells, and Thomas A. Eaton

A Contracts Anthology, *Second Edition*
Peter Linzer

Contract Law and Practice
Gerald E. Berendt, Michael L. Closen, Doris Estelle Long, Marie A. Monahan,
 Robert J. Nye, and John H. Scheid

Contracts: Contemporary Cases, Comments, and Problems
Michael L. Closen, Richard M. Perlmutter, and Jeffrey D. Wittenberg

A Copyright Anthology: The Technology Frontier
Richard H. Chused

Corporate Law Anthology
Franklin A. Gevurtz

Corporate and White Collar Crime: An Anthology
Leonard Orland

A Criminal Law Anthology
Arnold H. Loewy

Criminal Law: Cases and Materials
Arnold H. Loewy

A Criminal Procedure Anthology
Silas J. Wasserstrom and Christie L. Snyder

Criminal Procedure: Arrest and Investigation
Arnold H. Loewy and Arthur B. LaFrance

Criminal Procedure: Trial and Sentencing
Arthur B. LaFrance and Arnold H. Loewy

Economic Regulation: Cases and Materials
Richard J. Pierce, Jr.

Elder Law: Readings, Cases, and Materials
Thomas P. Gallanis, A. Kimberley Dayton, and Molly M. Wood

Elder Law: Statutes and Regulations
Thomas P. Gallanis, A. Kimberley Dayton, and Molly M. Wood

Elements of Law
Eva H. Hanks, Michael E. Herz, and Steven S. Nemerson

Ending It: Dispute Resolution in America
  Descriptions, Examples, Cases and Questions
Susan M. Leeson and Bryan M. Johnston

An Environmental Law Anthology
Robert L. Fischman, Maxine I. Lipeles, and Mark S. Squillace

Environmental Law Series
  Environmental Decisionmaking, *Third Edition*
  Robert L. Fischman and Mark S. Squillace

  Water Pollution, *Third Edition*
  Jackson B. Battle and Maxine I. Lipeles

  Air Pollution, *Third Edition*
  Mark S. Squillace and David R. Wooley

  Hazardous Waste, *Third Edition*
  Maxine I. Lipeles

Environmental Protection and Justice
  Readings and Commentary on Environmental Law and Practice
Kenneth A. Manaster

European Union Law Anthology
Karen V. Kole and Anthony D'Amato

An Evidence Anthology
Edward J. Imwinkelried and Glen Weissenberger

Family Law in Action: A Reader
Margaret F. Brinig, Carl E. Schneider, and Lee E. Teitelbaum

Federal Antitrust Law: Cases and Materials
Daniel J. Gifford and Leo J. Raskind

Federal Income Tax Anthology
Paul L. Caron, Karen C. Burke, and Grayson M.P. McCouch

Federal Rules of Civil Procedure
Publisher's Staff

Federal Rules of Evidence Handbook
Publisher's Staff

Federal Rules of Evidence: Rules, Legislative History, Commentary and Authority
Glen Weissenberger

Federal Wealth Transfer Tax Anthology
Paul L. Caron, Grayson M.P. McCouch, Karen C. Burke

First Amendment Anthology
Donald E. Lively, Dorothy E. Roberts, and Russell L. Weaver

The History, Philosophy, and Structure of the American Constitution
Douglas W. Kmiec and Stephen B. Presser

Individual Rights and the American Constitution
Douglas W. Kmiec and Stephen B. Presser

International Environmental Law Anthology
Anthony D'Amato and Kirsten Engel

International Human Rights: Law, Policy, and Process, *Second Edition*
Frank C. Newman and David Weissbrodt

Selected International Human Rights Instruments and Bibliography for Research on International Human Rights Law, *Second Edition*
Frank C. Newman and David Weissbrodt

International Intellectual Property Anthology
Anthony D'Amato and Doris Estelle Long

International Law Anthology
Anthony D'Amato

International Law Coursebook
Anthony D'Amato

International Taxation: Cases, Materials, and Problems
Philip F. Postlewaite

Introduction to the Study of Law: Cases and Materials
John Makdisi

Judicial Externships: The Clinic Inside the Courthouse, *Second Edition*
Rebecca A. Cochran

A Land Use Anthology
Jon W. Bruce

Law and Economics Anthology
Kenneth G. Dau-Schmidt and Thomas S. Ulen

The Law of Disability Discrimination, *Second Edition*
Ruth Colker and Bonnie Poitras Tucker

The Law of Disability Discrimination Handbook: Statutes and Regulatory Guidance
  Second Edition
Ruth Colker and Bonnie Poitras Tucker

Lawyers and Fundamental Moral Responsibility
Daniel R. Coquillette

Mediation and Negotiation: Reaching Agreement in Law and Business
E. Wendy Trachte-Huber and Stephen K. Huber

Microeconomic Predicates to Law and Economics
Mark Seidenfeld

Natural Resources: Cases and Materials
Barlow Burke

Patients, Psychiatrists and Lawyers: Law and the Mental Health System, *Second Edition*
Raymond L. Spring, Roy B. Lacoursiere, and Glen Weissenberger

Preventive Law: Materials on a Non Adversarial Legal Process
Robert M. Hardaway

Principles of Evidence, *Third Edition*
Irving Younger, Michael Goldsmith, and David A. Sonenshein

Problems and Simulations in Evidence, *Second Edition*
Thomas F. Guernsey

A Products Liability Anthology
Anita Bernstein

Professional Responsibility Anthology
Thomas B. Metzloff

A Property Anthology, *Second Edition*
Richard H. Chused

Public Choice and Public Law: Readings and Commentary
Maxwell L. Stearns

Readings in Criminal Law
Russell L. Weaver, John M. Burkoff, Catherine Hancock, Alan Reed, and Peter J. Seago

Science in Evidence
D.H. Kaye

A Section 1983 Civil Rights Anthology
Sheldon H. Nahmod

Sports Law: Cases and Materials, *Third Edition*
Ray L. Yasser, James R. McCurdy, and C. Peter Goplerud

A Torts Anthology, *Second Edition*
Julie A. Davies, Lawrence C. Levine, and Edward J. Kionka

Trial Practice
Lawrence A. Dubin and Thomas F. Guernsey

Unincorporated Business Entities
Larry E. Ribstein

FORTHCOMING PUBLICATIONS

Basic Themes in Law and Jurisprudence
Charles W. Collier

Cases and Materials on the Law Governing Lawyers
James E. Moliterno

First Amendment Law: Cases, Comparative Perspectives, and Dialogues
Donald E. Lively, Phoebe A. Haddon, John C. Knechtle, and Dorothy E. Roberts

Introduction to the Study of Law: Cases and Materials, *Second Edition*
John Makdisi

The Question Presented: Model Appellate Briefs
Maria L. Ciampi and William H. Manz

Secured Transactions Under the Uniform Commercial Code and International Commerce
Louis F. Del Duca, Egon Guttman, William H. Henning, Fred H. Miller, and Peter Winship

Principles of Evidence, *Fourth Edition*
Irving Younger, Michael Goldsmith, and David A. Sonenshein

ELDER LAW
Readings, Cases, and Materials

ELDER LAW
READINGS, CASES, AND MATERIALS

THOMAS P. GALLANIS
Assistant Professor of Law
Ohio State University College of Law

A. KIMBERLEY DAYTON
Professor of Law
University of Kansas School of Law

MOLLY M. WOOD
Managing Attorney, Legal Aid Society of Topeka
Visiting Professor Directing the Elder Law Clinic
University of Kansas School of Law

ANDERSON PUBLISHING CO.
CINCINNATI, OHIO

ELDER LAW: READINGS, CASES, AND MATERIALS
THOMAS P. GALLANIS, A. KIMBERLEY DAYTON, AND MOLLY M. WOOD

© 2000 by Anderson Publishing Co.

All rights reserved. No part of this book may be reproduced in any form or by any electronic or mechanical means including information storage and retrieval systems without written permission from the publisher.

Anderson Publishing Co.
2035 Reading Road / Cincinnati, Ohio 45202
800-582-7295 / e-mail andpubco@aol.com / Fax 513-562-5430
World Wide Web http://www.andersonpublishing.com

ISBN: 0-87084-430-X

Library of Congress Cataloging-in-Publication Data
Gallanis, Thomas P.
    Elder law : readings, cases, and materials / Thomas P. Gallanis, A. Kimberley Dayton, Molly M. Wood
      p. cm.
   Includes bibliographical references.
   ISBN 0-87084-430-X
   1. Aged--Legal status, laws, etc.--United States. I. Dayton, A. Kimberley. II. Wood, Molly M. III. Title.
   KF390.A4 G35 1999
   346.7301'3--dc21

99-15998
CIP

Dedication

For my great-aunt, Ona Bross
T.P.G.

For my late grandparents, Dock Ballard, Myrtle Johnson Ballard,
Robert P. Dayton, and Rhoda Yoder Dayton Gross
A.K.D.

For my parents, Julia Belle Tucker Wood and Harold Pope Wood, Jr.
M.M.W.

Table of Contents

Preface xix

Chapter 1. Aging in America 1
A. Aging in America: An Overview 2
B. Interdisciplinary Aspects of Aging 13
C. Social Policy and Aging: Selected Issues 17
   1. Crime and Fraud 17
   2. Mobility, Transportation, and Housing 36
   3. Ethical Issues 42
D. The Practice of Elder Law 47

Chapter 2. Special Ethical Problems When Representing the Elderly 53
A. Joint or Multiple Representation 53
   1. The Spouse 54
   2. Adult Children 55
   3. Caregivers and Other Unrelated Third Parties 59
B. The Disabled Client 76
   1. Evaluating Client Competence 76
   2. MRPC 1.14: Client Under a Disability 79
   3. Section 35 of The Restatement of the Law Governing Lawyers 81
   4. Taking Protective Action 83
   5. Withdrawal 84

Chapter 3. Discrimination 87
A. Introduction 88
B. Age Discrimination 90
   1. Federal Law 90
   2. State Law 113
C. Disability Discrimination 120
   1. Federal Law: The Americans with Disabilities Act 120
   2. State Law 135

Chapter 4. Planning for Retirement 147
A. Government Programs 148
   1. Old Age, Survivors, and Disability Insurance 148

xiv   ELDER LAW: READINGS, CASES, AND MATERIALS

		a. Origins	148
		b. Mechanics	154
		c. Eligibility	159
		d. Retirement Planning	160
		e. Alienation of Benefits	163
		f. Spousal and Survivor Benefits	164
		g. The Future of Social Security	165
	2.	Supplemental Security Income	171
	3.	Veterans' Pension Benefits	172
		a. Eligibility	172
		b. Dependent Benefits	173
	4.	State Retirement Benefits	173
B.	Employer-Based Pension Plans		177
	1.	A Brief History of Pensions and Pension Regulation	177
	2.	Pension Coverage	186
	3.	Types of Pension Plans	188
	4.	The Taxation of Pension Investments When Made	194
	5.	Pension Distributions: Mechanics and Taxation	194
		a. Annuities	195
		b. Lump Sum Distributions	196
		c. Early Distributions: A Note by the Editors	199
		d. Delayed Distributions: A Note by the Editors	199
	6.	Rollovers	201
C.	Private Savings: The Individual Retirement Account		202
	1.	Traditional and Roth IRAs	202
	2.	Education IRAs	207

Chapter 5. Property Management 209
A. Powers of Attorney 209

	1.	Background	209
	2.	Preparing the Power: The Use of Statutory Forms	211
	3.	Capacity to Execute or Revoke	211
	4.	Formalities of Execution	213
	5.	Taking Effect: The Special Case of the Springing Power	214
	6.	Scope of the Power	215
	7.	Gift-Giving: A Potential Tax Trap	217
	8.	Durable Powers and Ademption by Extinction	222
	9.	Lawyers as Agents	226
B.	Joint Ownership and Joint Accounts		229
	1.	Forms of Joint Ownership	229
	2.	Joint Bank Accounts: What Form of Ownership?	230
		a. Rights During Lifetime: Theory versus Practice	230
		b. Rights at Death: Presumptions and Their Rebuttal	230
	3.	The Reach of Third Parties: Creditors	231
	4.	The Reach of Third Parties: Gift Taxes	232

	5. The Reach of Third Parties: Estate Taxes	233
	6. Joint Accounts: An Evaluation	233
C.	Agency Accounts	234
D.	Revocable Inter Vivos Trusts	236
	1. Parties to the Trust Arrangment	236
	2. Trust Creation	237
	3. Revocability	239
	4. The Tax Treatment of Inter Vivos Trusts: A Brief Introduction	242
	5. The Reach of Creditors	244
	a. During the Settlor's Lifetime	244
	b. After the Settlor's Death	244
	6. Revocable Trusts and Medicaid	246
	a. Using Revocable Trusts to Shield Assets During the Lifetime of the Medicaid Recipient	246
	b. Governmental Claims on the Assets of the Medicaid Recipient After the Recipient's Death: The Case of Assets in a Revocable Trust	248
	7. The Revocable Trust as an Alternative to Guardianship	249
	8. The Revocable Trust as an Alternative to the Durable Power of Attorney	250
	9. The Revocable Trust as a Will Substitute	251
E.	Custodial Trusts Under the Uniform Custodial Trust Act	254

Chapter 6. Guardianship and Protection ... 259

A.	Adult Guardianship	259
	1. Background and Terminology	259
	2. Statistics on Guardianship	261
	3. The Standard of Incapacity	262
	4. The Process of Petitioning for Guardianship	265
	a. Background on UPC Article V and on the UGPPA	265
	b. The Procedures for Petitioning for Guardianship Under Article V of the 1990 UPC and Under the 1997 UGPPA	267
	5. The Use of Alternative Dispute Resolution ("ADR")	268
	6. The Guardian's Powers and Duties: The Statutory Language	271
	7. The Guardian's Powers and Duties: The Standard of Decisionmaking	271
	8. The Guardian's Powers and Duties: The Rise of Limited Guardianship	273
	9. The Guardian's Powers and Duties: Monitoring by the Court	275
	10. Professional Responsibility: Who Is the Client?	277
	11. Terminating the Guardian(ship)	279
B.	Elder Abuse	280
	1. The "Discovery" of Elder Abuse	280
	2. Definitions: Types of Elder Abuse	281
	3. Institutional Abuse: Information and Statistics	282

4. Noninstitutional Abuse (Except Consumer Fraud):
   Information and Statistics 285
5. Consumer Fraud Against the Elderly: Information and Statistics 288
6. Self-Neglect: Information and Statistics 290
7. Federal Responses to Elder Abuse 291
   a. The Older Americans Act of 1965 and
      Its Subsequent Amendments 291
   b. "A Decade of Shame and Inaction": 1978-1987 293
   c. The Older Americans Act Amendments of 1987 294
   d. The Nursing Home Reform Act of 1987 295
   e. The Older Americans Act Amendments of 1992 296
8. State Responses to Elder Abuse 297
   a. Adult Protective Services: Background 297
   b. Mandatory Reporting 301
   c. Liability for Failure to Report 304
   d. Remedies Against Abusers 305
      i. The Pre-Existing Criminal Law 305
      ii. The Use of Tort Law Against Institutional Abusers 306
      iii. Criminal and Tortious Conduct Outside of Institutions:
           To What Extent is There a Duty of Care? 310
      iv. Examples of New Remedies Against Elder Abuse 317
   e. Protection Against Self-Neglect 318

Chapter 7. Health Care 321
A. The U.S. Health-Care System: An Overview 321
B. Managing and Paying for Health Care 323
   1. Medicare 323
      a. Traditional Fee-for-Service 327
      b. Medicare Managed Care 330
   2. Supplemental Health Insurance 344
      a. "Medigap" 344
      b. Long-Term Care Insurance 346
   3. Medicaid and Long-Term Care 358
      a. Assistance for Low-Income Seniors 359
      b. Nursing Facility Care 364
      c. Estate Recovery 367
C. Health-Care Decisionmaking (Short of Ending Life) 372
   1. The Need for Substitute Decisionmaking 373
   2. The Common-Law Background:
      The Doctrine of Informed Consent 374
   3. The Common-Law Background: Medical Decisionmaking in the
      Years Before Advance Directives 377
   4. The Rise of Advance Medical Directives 379
      a. The Three Types of Advance Directives 379
      b. Luis Kutner and the Birth of the Living Will 379

			c.	The *Quinlan* Case and Its Aftermath..	381
			d.	The Living Will Today...	382
			e.	The Rise of Health-Care Proxies	383
			f.	Health-Care Proxies Today	384
	5.	Drafting Written Directives: The Use of Statutory Forms			384
	6.	The Uniform Health-Care Decisions Act			385
	7.	Encouraging the Use of Advance Directives: The Patient Self-Determination Act			387
	8.	Alternatives to Written Directives			392
	9.	Decisionmaking in the Absence of an Advance Directive: Surrogacy Statutes			395
	10.	The Standard(s) for Substitute Decisionmaking			396

Chapter 8. Housing 401
A. Home Ownership and "Aging in Place" 402
   1. Adaptations 407
   2. Home Equity Conversion Mortgages 408
B. The Elderly Tenant 417
   1. Protection from Discrimination 417
   2. Rental Subsidies 419
   3. Legal Remedies 420
C. Retirement Communities and Assisted Living 424
D. Nursing Facilities 433
   1. Nursing Home Residents' Rights 433
      a. Nursing Home Reform Act of 1987 433
      b. Other Remedies 441
   2. Involuntary Transfer and Discharge 458

Chapter 9. End of Life Issues 465
A. Viatical Settlements 465
   1. Introduction 466
   2. Regulatory Issues 471
B. The Right to Die 472
   1. Introduction: Constitutional Considerations 472
   2. Statutory Considerations 476
   3. Advance Directives, Living Wills, and Health Care Powers of Attorney 480
   4. Physician Assisted Suicide 496
C. Anatomical Donations 505
   1. Introduction 506
   2. The Uniform Anatomical Gift Act 509
      a. Counseling the Client 509
      b. Problems of Interpretation 510

    3. The National Organ Transplant Act 527
        a. Allocation of Donated Organs 527
        b. Problems of Interpretation 530
    4. Defining Death 533

Chapter 10. Estate Planning: An Overview 535
A. State Property Law 536
    1. Intestacy 536
        a. Terminology 536
        b. Purposes Behind Intestacy Statutes 537
        c. Sample Intestacy Laws 538
    2. Wills and Will Substitutes 538
        a. Wills: Formalities of Execution 538
            i. Formal Requirements 538
            ii. Purposes of Wills Act Formalities 539
            iii. Loosening the Formal Requirements 540
        b. Wills: Grounds for Contest 541
            i. Lack of Testamentary Intent 541
            ii. Lack of Testamentary Capacity 543
            iii. Undue Influence 544
            iv. Fraud 546
        c. Will Substitutes and the Distinction Between Probate and
           Nonprobate Transfers 547
    3. Protecting the Surviving Spouse Against Disinheritance 548
        a. Background on Elective Share Statutes 548
        b. The Elective Share:
           Incorporating Nonprobate Transfers and Spousal Assets 548
        c. The Elective Share:
           Responding to a Multiple-Marriage Society 549
    4. The Probate Process 550
        a. Terminology 550
        b. Functions of Probate 551
        c. Summary of the Probate Process 552
B. The Law of Federal Transfer Taxation 552
    1. The Federal Estate Tax 553
    2. The Federal Gift Tax 555
    3. The Federal Generation-Skipping Transfer Tax 557
C. A Note on State Death Taxes 559

Preface

Introduction. This book is designed to serve as the main textbook for courses and seminars on the intersection of law and aging. This area of the law is of rapidly-increasing significance because of the demographic changes affecting the United States and, indeed, the rest of the world. The percentage of Americans aged 65 or older has more than tripled since the beginning of the twentieth century, and this percentage will rise even more as the so-called "Baby Boomers" begin to join the ranks of the elderly. As people age, they often face a bewildering array of legal issues, ranging from age discrimination to retirement planning, from elder abuse to assisted suicide.

Coverage. The chapters in this book explore these topics in a systematic fashion. We begin in Chapters 1 and 2 with a general introduction to the legal and ethical issues facing the elderly and their lawyers. We then turn in Chapter 3 to the problem of age and disability discrimination. Chapter 4 addresses retirement planning and contains material on government programs (such as Social Security and SSI), private pensions, and Individual Retirement Accounts. Some elderly people need help in managing their assets, so Chapter 5 deals with the legal devices designed to assist with property management: powers of attorney, joint ownership, agency accounts, and inter vivos trusts. Chapter 6 then addresses two issues affecting both property and personal matters: guardianship, which can be of the person or of the estate, and elder abuse, which can be physical, emotional, or financial. Chapter 7 then turns to health care, which is a major concern for most older people; the chapter examines the relevant government programs (such as Medicare and Medicaid), the need for Medigap or long-term care insurance, and the use of living wills, powers of attorney, and surrogacy statutes to preserve or delegate medical decisions in the face of incapacity. Chapter 8 then covers issues pertaining to housing, including the regulation of nursing homes and the rise of assisted living facilities. Chapter 9, which we expect will be the last chapter to be covered in the typical semester, addresses end-of-life issues: viatical settlements, anatomical donations, and the right to die. There is also a Chapter 10, which provides a summary of estate planning basics for students who have not yet taken courses in trusts and estates or in federal transfer taxation.

Division of Responsibility. We have worked largely independently, focusing on our respective areas of expertise. Professor Gallanis has prepared the materials on pensions, IRAs, property management, guardianship, elder abuse, health-care decisionmaking, and estate planning (Chapters 4B, 4C, 5, 6, 7C, and 10). Professor

Dayton has prepared the introductory chapter and the units on discrimination and the end of life (Chapters 1, 3, and 9). Professor Wood has prepared the materials on ethical issues, public benefits, health care, and housing (Chapters 2, 4A, 7A, 7B, and 8).

Code Book. This book of readings is designed to be used with a companion code book, ELDER LAW: STATUTES AND REGULATIONS. Rather than reproduce statutes and regulations in a piecemeal fashion among our readings, we believe that it is better and easier to study legislative materials in a separate volume.

Acknowledgments. First and foremost, we would like to thank Sean Caldwell, the Managing Editor of Anderson Publishing, for his encouragement and support during the development and execution of this project. For financial support and invaluable library assistance, we would like to thank our respective institutions, the Ohio State University College of Law, the University of Michigan Law School (where Professor Gallanis taught during Fall 1998, when much of this book was prepared), the University of Kansas School of Law, and Kansas Legal Services, Inc., a private, non-profit corporation providing legal assistance to low-income, disabled, and elderly Kansans. A special word of thanks should also be given to the law students and secretaries who worked diligently and with good humor to help us compile these materials and obtain the necessary copyright permissions: Hope Evans ('99), Marci Love ('00), and Trina Lott of the Ohio State University College of Law, Fran Hewitt of the University of Kansas School of Law, and Madeline C. VanSickle of Kansas Legal Services. Finally, Professor Dayton and Ms. Wood would like to thank all of the students who have been enrolled in the University of Kansas Elder Law Clinic since its inception in Fall 1995; the dedication of these students to their clients and to the Kansas Elder Law Network has been invaluable.

THOMAS P. GALLANIS
Columbus, Ohio
A. KIMBERLEY DAYTON
MOLLY M. WOOD
Lawrence, Kansas

July, 1999

CHAPTER 1
Aging in America

A. Aging in America: An Overview 2
B. Interdisciplinary Aspects of Aging 13
C. Social Policy and Aging: Selected Issues... 17
D. The Practice of Elder Law.. 47

The senior boom is one of the central challenges of the coming century. . . . [O]ne of the central worries of my generation is that, as we age, we will impose unsustainable burdens on our children and undermine their ability to raise our grandchildren. We must use this time now to do everything in our power, not only to lift the quality of life and the security of the aged and disabled today, and the baby boom aged and disabled, but to make sure that we do not impose that intolerable burden on our children.

–President Bill Clinton, January 4, 1999

The phenomenon of "the aging of America" has begun. The first of the post-war "baby boomers" are now in their fifties, and the population of persons over age sixty five is expected to rise by over 70% between 2010 and 2030. This major demographic shift presents both challenges and opportunities for our society and the legal system. Among the policy challenges suggested by the aging of America are increasing stresses on so-called entitlement programs such as government retirement and health benefit programs, housing and transportation issues stemming from aging-related disabilities that may compromise an older person's ability to remain in a familiar environment without assistance, and a host of ethical problems relating to individual autonomy respecting financial, health care, and end of life issues.

The growth of the senior population has affected profoundly the legal infrastructure. Because of their numbers, older Americans represent a powerful political constituency. The past decade has produced much legislation aimed at addressing the needs of this demographic group. Moreover, the complexity of the sociolegal issues that impact on seniors has spawned an entirely new legal practice specialty known as "elder law." The elder law attorney must be cognizant not simply of such matters as estate planning, wills, and probate, but as well of such varied substantive legal and quasi-legal areas as public benefits (including social security, Medicare and Medicaid, and veterans' benefits), employment and retirement law, elder abuse, bioethics, and housing and long term care. Nor can the elder law attorney expect a practice confined either to state or federal law, for the legal texts that govern this area comprise a complex web of federal, state, and sometimes local regulations.

In this chapter, we offer an overview of the phenomenon of the aging of America and its consequences. Parts A and B include materials that document the "senior boom" about which President Clinton spoke and provide details about its nature, including cultural differences that affect how aging within particular groups of American society is regarded. Part C provides selected examples of social and legal matters that are or will be affected by this boom. Finally, Part D contains readings on the nature and practice of elder law.

A. Aging in America: An Overview

ECONOMICS AND STATISTICS ADMINISTRATION, U.S. DEPARTMENT OF COMMERCE
Statistical Brief, Sixty-five Plus in the United States (May 1995)
<http://www.census.gov/socdemo/www/agebrief.html>

America's elderly population is now growing at a moderate pace. But not too far into the future, the growth will become rapid. So rapid, in fact, that by the middle of the next century, it might be completely inaccurate to think of ourselves as a Nation of the young: there could be more persons who are elderly (65 or over) than young (14 or younger)! . . . During the 20th century, the number of persons in the United States under age 65 has tripled. At the same time, the number aged 65 or over has jumped by a factor of 11! Consequently, the elderly, who comprised only 1 in every 25 Americans (3.1 million) in 1900, made up 1 in 8 (33.2 million) in 1994. Declining fertility and mortality rates also have led to a sharp rise in the median age of our Nation's population—from 20 years old in 1860 to 34 in 1994.

According to the Census Bureau's "middle series" projections, the elderly population will more than double between now and the year 2050, to 80 million. By that year, as many as 1 in 5 Americans could be elderly. Most of this growth should occur between 2010 and 2030, when the "baby boom" generation enters their elderly years. During that period, the number of elderly will grow by an average of 2.8 percent annually. By comparison, annual growth will average 1.3 percent during the preceding 20 years and 0.7 percent during the following 20 years. . . .

The "oldest old"—those aged 85 and over—are the most rapidly growing elderly age group. Between 1960 and 1994, their numbers rose 274 percent. In contrast, the elderly population in general rose 100 percent and the entire U.S. population grew only 45 percent. The oldest old numbered 3 million in 1994, making them 10 percent of the elderly and just over 1 percent of the total population. Thanks to the arrival of the survivors of the baby boom generation, it is expected the oldest old will number 19 million in 2050. That would make them 24 percent of elderly Americans and 5 percent of all Americans.

We're living longer. Back when the United States was founded, life expectancy at birth stood at only about 35 years. It reached 47 years in 1900, jumped to 68 years in 1950, and steadily rose to 76 years in 1991. In 1991, life expectancy was higher for women (79 years) than for men (72 years). Once we reach age 65, we can expect to live 17 more years. During the 1980s, post-65 life expectancy improved for all race/sex groups. The biggest improvement (a rise of over 1 year) belonged to White men.

The elderly are becoming more racially and ethnically diverse. In 1994, 1 in 10 elderly were a race other than White. In 2050, this proportion should rise to 2 in 10. Similarly, the proportion of elderly who are Hispanic is expected to climb from 4 percent to 16 percent over the same period.

Our most populous States are also the ones with the largest number of elderly. In 1993, nine States had more than 1 million elderly. California, with 3.3 million, led the way, followed by Florida, New York, Pennsylvania, Texas, Ohio, Illinois, Michigan, and New Jersey.

Meanwhile, the States with the greatest proportion of elderly are generally different from those with the greatest number. Two exceptions, however, were Florida, where 19 percent of residents were elderly, and Pennsylvania, where 16 percent were. These 2 States led the Nation percentage-wise and, as just mentioned, ranked in the top 4 numerically. In-migration of the elderly contributed to Florida's high rankings. Joining Florida and Pennsylvania in having high proportions of elderly (14 percent or more) were 10 other States, including several sparsely populated Farm Belt States, such as North Dakota and Nebraska. Out-migration of the young contributed to the high proportions in these States and in Pennsylvania. During the 1980s, the greatest percent increases in elderly population were mostly in Western States and Southeastern coastal States.

Elderly women outnumber elderly men. Men generally have higher death rates than women at every age. As a result, elderly women outnumbered elderly men in 1994 by a ratio of 3 to 2—20 million to 14 million. This difference grew with advancing age. At ages 65 to 69, it was only 6 to 5. However, at age 85 and over, it reached 5 to 2. As more men live to older ages over the next 50 years, these differences may narrow somewhat. In 1993, noninstitutionalized elderly men were nearly twice as likely as their female counterparts to be married and living with their spouse (75 percent versus 41 percent). Elderly women, on the other hand, were more than three times as likely as elderly men to be widowed (48 percent versus 14 percent). The remaining men and women were either separated, divorced, had never married, or had absent spouses. Thus, while most elderly men have a spouse for assistance, especially when health fails, most elderly women do not.

Many elderly live alone. Another consequence of the relative scarcity of elderly men is the fact that elderly women were much more likely than men to live alone. So much more likely, in fact, that 8 in 10 noninstitutionalized elderly who lived alone in 1993 were women. Among both sexes, the likelihood of living alone increased with age. For women, it rose from 32 percent for 65- to 74-year-olds to 57 percent for those aged 85 years or more; for men, the corresponding proportions were 13 percent and 29 percent.

Dependency. Many assume health among the elderly has improved because they, as a group, are living longer. Others hold a contradictory image of the elderly as dependent and frail. The truth actually lies somewhere in between. Poor health is not as prevalent as many assume. In 1992, about 3 in every 4 noninstitutionalized persons aged 65 to 74 considered their health to be good. Two in three aged 75 or older felt similarly.

On the other hand, as more people live to the oldest ages, there may also be more who face chronic, limiting illnesses or conditions, such as arthritis, diabetes, osteoporosis, and senile dementia. These conditions result in people becoming dependent on others for help in performing the activities of daily living. With age comes increasing chances of being dependent. For instance, while 1 percent of those aged 65 to 74 years lived in a nursing home in 1990, nearly 1 in 4 aged 85 or older did. And among those who were noninstitutionalized in 1990-91, 9 percent aged 65 to 69 years, but 50 percent aged 85 or older, needed assistance performing everyday activities such as bathing, getting around inside the home, and preparing meals. . . . .

[*I*]*ncreasing numbers of people will have to care for very old, frail relatives.* As more and more people live long enough to experience multiple, chronic illnesses, disability, and dependency, there will be more and more relatives in their fifties and sixties who will be facing the concern and expense of caring for them. The parent-support ratio gives us an approximate idea of things to come. This ratio equals the number of persons aged 85 and over per 100 persons aged 50 to 64. Between 1950 and 1993, the ratio tripled from 3 to 10. Over the next six decades, it could triple yet again, to 29. Heart disease, cancer, and stroke are the leading causes of death among the elderly.

Of the 2.2 million Americans who died in 1991, 1.6 million (or 7 in 10) were elderly. Seven in 10 of these elderly deaths could be attributed to either heart disease, cancer, or stroke. Though death rates from heart disease have declined for the elderly since the 1960s, this malady remains the leading cause of death among them. Death rates from cancer, on the other hand, have increased since 1960.

Poverty Rates. The perception of "elderly" and "poor" as practically synonymous has changed in recent years to a view that the noninstitutionalized elderly are better off than other Americans. Both views are simplistic. There is actually great variation among elderly subgroups. For example, in 1992, the poverty rate, 15 percent for those under age 65, rose with age among the elderly, from 11 percent for 65 to 74-year-olds to 16 percent for those aged 75 or older. Elderly women (16 percent) had a higher poverty rate than elderly men (9 percent). The rate was higher for elderly Blacks (33 percent) and Hispanics (22 percent) than for Whites (11 percent). . . . [P]overty became less prevalent during the 1980s for every elderly sex/race/ethnic group. In addition, within each race/ethnic group, poverty was more common for women than for men at both the decade's beginning and end.

Median Income. In constant 1992 dollars, the median income for elderly persons more than doubled between 1957 and 1992 (from $6,537 to $14,548 for men, from $3,409 to $8,189 for women). [I]ncome disparities persist among various elderly subgroups. Age, sex, race, ethnicity, marital status, living arrangements, educational attainment, former occupation, and work history are characteristics associated with significant income differences. For instance, elderly White men had much higher median incomes than other groups. In 1992, their income was more than double that of elderly Black and Hispanic women ($15,276 versus $6,220 and $5,968, respectively). The difference in median income between Black and Hispanic women was not statistically significant.

Education. The elderly of the future will be better educated. Research has shown that the better educated tend to be healthier longer and better off economically. In 1993, noninstitutionalized elderly were less likely than those aged 25 to 64 to have completed at least high school (60 percent versus 85 percent) and more likely to have only an eighth grade education or less (24 percent versus 6 percent). The percent with less than a 9th-grade education rose with age for the elderly.

Fortunately, the proportion of elderly with at least a high school education will increase in the coming decades. That's because nearly 8 in 10 persons aged 55 to 59 in 1993 had at least a high school education; the same was true for nearly 9 in 10 persons aged 45 to 49. Additionally, while only 12 percent of the elderly had college degrees, 20 percent of 55- to 59-year-olds and 27 percent of 45- to 49-year-olds did.

DEPARTMENT OF HEALTH AND HUMAN SERVICES, ADMINISTRATION ON AGING
A Profile of Older Americans: 1998 (November 1998)
<http://www.aoa.dhhs.gov/aoa/stats/profile/default.htm>

The Older Population

The older population—persons 65 years or older—numbered 34.1 million in 1997. They represented 12.7% of the U.S. population, about one in every eight Americans. The number of older Americans increased by 2.8 million or 9.1% since 1990, compared to an increase of 7.0% for the under-65 population.

In 1997, there were 20.1 million older women and 14.0 million older men, or a sex ratio of 143 women for every 100 men. The sex ratio increased with age, ranging from 119 for the 65-69 group to a high of 248 for persons 85 and over.

Since 1900, the percentage of Americans 65+ has more than tripled (4.1% in 1900 to 12.7% in 1997), and the number has increased eleven times (from 3.1 million to 34.1 million).

The older population itself is getting older. In 1997 the 65-74 age group (18.5 million) was eight times larger than in 1900, but the 75-84 group (11.7 million) was 16 times larger and the 85+ group (3.9 million) was 31 times larger.

In 1997, persons reaching age 65 had an average life expectancy of an additional 17.6 years (19.0 years for females and 15.8 years for males). A child born in 1997 could expect to live 76.5 years, about 29 years longer than a child born in 1900. The major part of this increase occurred because of reduced death rates for children and young adults. Life expectancy at age 65 increased by only 2.4 years between 1900 and 1960, but has increased by 3.3 years since 1960.

Almost 2 million persons celebrated their 65th birthday in 1997 (5,335 per day). In the same year, over 1.7 million persons 65 or older died, resulting in a net increase of 214,000 (587 per day).

Figure 1
NUMBER OF PERSONS 65+: 1900 TO 2030
(numbers in millions)
Year (as of July 1)

Year	Number
1900	3.1
1920	4.9
1940	9.0
1960	16.7
1980	25.7
1997	34.1
2000	34.7
2010	39.4
2020	53.2
2030	69.4

Note: Increments in years are uneven.
(Based on data from the U.S. Bureau of the Census)

Future Growth

The older population will continue to grow significantly in the future. This growth slowed somewhat during the 1990s because of the relatively small number of babies born during the Great Depression of the 1930s. But the older population will burgeon between the years 2010 and 2030 when the "baby boom" generation reaches age 65.

By 2030, there will be about 70 million older persons, more than twice their number in 1997. People 65+ are projected to represent 13% of population in the year 2000 but will be 20% by 2030.

Minority populations are projected to represent 25% of the elderly population in 2030, up from 15% in 1997. Between 1997and 2030, the white nonhispanic population 65+ is projected to increase by 79% compared with 238% for older minorities, including Hispanics (368%) and nonhispanic blacks (134%), nonhispanic American Indians, Eskimos, and Aleuts (159%), and nonhispanic Asians and Pacific Islanders (354%).

Marital Status

In 199[5], older men were much more likely to be married [than] older women—74% of men, 42% of women (figure 2).

Almost half of all older women in 199[5] were widows (46%). There were four times as many widows (8.5 million) as widowers (2.1 million).

Although divorced older persons represented only 7% of all older persons in 199[5], their numbers (2.2 million) had increased five times as fast as the older population as a whole since 1990 (2.8 times for men, 7.4 times for women).

Figure 2
MARITAL STATUS OF PERSONS 65+: 1995*

	Women	Men
Married	42%	74%
Widowed	46%	16%
Single (never Married)	4%	4%
Divorced	7%	6%

(Based on data from the U.S. Bureau of the Census. See "Marital Status and Living Arrangements: March 1997 (Update), Current Population Reports, PPL-90)

* Principal sources of data for the Profile are the U.S. Bureau of the Census, the National Center of Health Statistics, and the Bureau of Labor Statistics.

Living Arrangements

The majority (66%) of older noninstitutionalized persons lived in a family setting in 1997. Approximately 10.7 million or 80% of older men, and 10.5 million or 57% of older women, lived in families (Figure 3). The proportion living in a family setting decreased with age. Only 47% of those 85+ years old lived in family setting. About 13% of older persons (8% of men, 17% of women) were not living with a spouse but were living with children, siblings, or other relatives. An additional 3% of men and 2% of women, or 776,000 older persons, lived with non-relatives. About 31% (9.9 million) of all noninstitutionalized older persons in 1997 lived alone (7.6 million women, 2.3 million men). They represented 41% of older women and 17% of older men. Living alone correlates with advanced age. Among women aged 85 and over, for example, three of every five lived outside a family setting.

Figure 3
LIVING ARRANGEMENTS OF PERSONS 65+: 1995**

Men		Women	
living with spouse	72%	living with spouse	40%
living with other relatives	8%	living with other relatives	17%
living alone or with non-relatives	20%	living alone or with non-relatives	43%

(Based on data from U.S. Bureau of the Census. See "Household and Family Characteristics: March 1997," Current Population Reports, P20-509)

** Excludes persons of Hispanic origin.

While a small number (1.4 million) and percentage (4%) of the 65+ population lived in nursing homes in 1995, the percentage increased dramatically with age, ranging from 1% for persons 65-74 years to 5% for persons 75-84 years and 15% for persons 85+.

Racial and Ethnic Composition

In 1997 about 15.3% of persons 65+ were minorities—8.0% were Black, 2.0% were Asian or Pacific Islander, and less than 1% were American Indian or Native Alaskan. Persons of Hispanic origin (who may be of any race) represented 4.9% of the older population. Only 7.1% of minority race and Hispanic populations were 65+ in 1997 (8.4% of nonhispanic blacks, 7.2% of Asians and Pacific Islanders, 7.0% of American Indians and native Alaskans, 5.7% of Hispanics), compared with 14.8% of nonhispanic whites.

Geographic Distribution

In 1997, about half (52%) of persons 65+ lived in nine states. California had over 3.5 million, Florida (2.7) and New York (2.4) million, Texas and Pennsylvania had almost 2 million, and Ohio, Illinois, Michigan, and New Jersey each had over 1 million (Figure 4). Person 65+ constituted 14.0% or more of the total population in 10 states in 1997 (Figure 4): Florida (18.5%); Pennsylvania and Rhode Island (15.8%); West Virginia (15.1%); Iowa (15.0%); North Dakota and Connecticut (14.4%); Arkansas and South Dakota (14.3%); and Massachusetts (14.1%).

In thirteen states, the 65+ population increased by 14.0% or more between 1990 and 1997(Figure 5): Nevada (49%); Alaska (43%); Hawaii and Arizona (25% each); Utah and Colorado (19% each); Delaware (17%); North Carolina and Wyoming (15 % each); South Carolina, Florida, and Texas (14% each).

The ten states with the highest poverty rates for elderly over the period 1994-1996 were: the District of Columbia (20%); South Carolina (17.9%); Louisiana (17.8%); Tennessee (17.7%); Mississippi (17.4%); Arkansas (17.0%); New Mexico (15.9%); Georgia (15.1%); Texas (14.6%); and Alabama (14.0%).

Persons 65+ were slightly less likely to live in metropolitan areas in 1997 than younger persons (77% of the elderly, 81% of persons under 65). About 29% of older persons lived in central cities and 48% lived in the suburbs.

The elderly are less likely to change residence than other age groups. In 1997 only 5% of persons 65+ had moved since 1996 (compared to 18% of persons under 65). A large majority of those elderly (81%) had moved to another home in the same state.

Figure 4
THE 65+ POPULATION BY STATE: 1997

State	Number of Persons	Percent of all Ages	% Increase 1990-97	Percent below poverty level 1994-1996*
U.S. Total	34,075,611	12.7%	9.1%	11.0%
Alabama	560,974	13.0%	7.5%	14.0%
Alaska	32,041	5.3%	42.7%	5.4%
Arizona	602,409	13.2%	25.3%	10.7%
Arkansas	359,909	14.3%	3.0%	17.0%
California	3,571,964	11.1%	13.9%	9.2%
Colorado	393,602	10.1%	18.9%	6.7%
Connecticut	469,600	14.4%	5.4%	6.8%
Delaware	94,371	12.9%	16.7%	9.8%
District of Columbia	73,375	13.9%	-4.8%	20.2%
Florida	2,708,804	18.5%	14.1%	10.1%
Georgia	738,154	9.9%	12.8%	15.1%
Hawaii	156,701	13.2%	25.3%	8.6%
Idaho	136,867	11.3%	12.6%	7.4%
Illinois	1,481,303	12.5%	3.3%	8.6%
Indiana	733,847	12.5%	5.3%	8.2%
Iowa	429,264	15.0%	0.6%	9.6%
Kansas	351,595	13.5%	2.6%	11.1%
Kentucky	488,893	12.5%	4.8%	11.4%
Louisiana	496,789	11.4%	6.0%	17.8%
Maine	173,264	13.9%	6.0%	11.0%
Maryland	583,854	11.5%	12.7%	9.2%
Massachusetts	862,493	14.1%	5.5%	9.0%
Michigan	1,214,010	12.4%	9.4%	9.1%
Minnesota	577,744	12.3%	5.5%	10.9%
Mississippi	332,982	12.2%	4.1%	17.4%
Missouri	740,595	13.7%	3.2%	9.4%
Montana	116,143	13.2%	9.0%	10.1%
Nebraska	227,538	13.7%	2.0%	10.3%
Nevada	192,645	11.5%	49.2%	7.1%
New Hampshire	141,454	12.1%	13.0%	8.4%
New Jersey	1,105,688	13.7%	7.3%	9.1%
New Mexico	192,941	11.2%	18.2%	15.9%
New York	2,427,365	13.4%	3.5%	12.3%
North Carolina	927,739	12.5%	15.1%	13.6%
North Dakota	92,545	14.4%	1.6%	11.4%
Ohio	1,494,482	13.4%	6.1%	10.6%
Oklahoma	444,453	13.4%	4.7%	12.6%
Oregon	430,276	13.3%	9.7%	6.2%
Pennsylvania	1,904,822	15.8%	4.1%	10.4%
Rhode Island	156,103	15.8%	3.9%	12.5%
South Carolina	453,825	12.1%	14.4%	17.9%
South Dakota	105,198	14.3%	2.8%	11.5%
Tennessee	670,142	12.5%	8.3%	17.7%
Texas	1,959,722	10.1%	14.0%	14.6%
Utah	180,029	8.7%	19.4%	5.1%
Vermont	72,213	12.3%	9.2%	10.6%
Virginia	755,546	11.2%	13.5%	13.7%
Washington	647,348	11.5%	12.3%	6.9%
West Virginia	274,333	15.1%	2.1%	13.4%
Wisconsin	683,357	13.2%	4.8%	7.9%
Wyoming	54,300	11.3%	14.8%	10.5%

* Calculated on the basis of the official poverty definitions for the years 1994-1997.

Income

The median income of older persons in 1996 was $17,768 for males and $10,062 for females. In terms of real median income (after adjusting for inflation), these figures represent an increase in real income from 1996 for men (+4.2%) and women (+2.2%).

Households containing families headed by persons 65+ reported a median income in 1997 of $30,660 ($31,167 for Whites, $23,420 for Blacks, and $22,677 for Hispanics). Approximately one of every seven (14.2%) family households with an elderly head had incomes less than $15,000 and 42.3% had incomes of $35,000 or more (figure 5).

Figure 5
PERCENT DISTRIBUTION BY INCOME: 1997

Family households with head 65+		Persons 65+ Reporting Income	
Under $10,000	5%	Under $5,000	9%
$10,000 - $14,999	9%	$5,000 - $9,999	28%
$15,000 - $24,999	24%	$10,000 - $14,999	21%
$25,000 - $34,999	19%	$15,000 - $24,999	21%
$35,000 - $49,999	18%	$25,000 - $34,999	9%
$50,000 - $74,999	12%	$35,000 - $49,999	6%
$75,000 and over	12%	$50,000 and over	6%
$30,660 median for 11.3 million family households 65+		*$13,049 median for 31.4 million persons 65+ reporting income*	

Based on data from Current Population Reports, "Consumer Income," P60-200, issued September, 1998, by the U.S. Bureau of the Census

For all older persons reporting income in 1997 (31.4 million), 37% reported less than $10,000. Only 21% reported $25,000 or more. The median income reported was $13,049. The major sources of income as reported by the Social Security Administration for older persons in 1996 were Social Security (reported by 91% of older persons), income from assets (reported by 63%), public and private pensions (reported by 41%), earnings (reported by 21%), and public assistance (reported by 6%).

Older households were less likely than younger households in 1994 to have received public assistance income (8% vs. 9%), food stamps (6% vs. 10%), or to have members covered by Medicaid (12% vs. 14%). About one-third (31%) of older renter households lived in publicly owned or subsidized housing in 1994 (14% for younger renters).

The median net worth (assets minus liabilities) of older households ($86,300), including those 75+ years ($77,700), was well above the U.S. average ($37,600) in 1993. Net worth was below $10,000 for 16% of older households but was above $250,000 for 17%.

Poverty

About 3.4 million elderly persons were below the poverty[*] level in 1997. The poverty rate for persons 65+ was 10.5%, slightly less than the rate for persons 18-64 (10.9%). Another 2.1 million or 6.4% of the elderly were classified as "near-poor" (income between the poverty level and 125% of this level). In total, one of every six (17.0%) older persons was poor or near-poor in 1997. One of every eleven (9.0%) elderly Whites was poor in 1997, compared to (26.0%) of elderly Blacks and (23.8%) of elderly Hispanics.

Older women had a higher poverty rate (13.1%) than older men (7.0%) in 1997. Older persons living alone or with nonrelatives were much more likely to be poor (21.0%) than were older persons living with families (6.0%).

Two-fifths (40.0%) of older black women who lived alone were poor in 1997. The poverty rate in 1997 for people 65+ was also high for those who lived in the South (13.1%).

Housing

Of the 20.8 million households headed by older persons in 1995, 78% were owners and 22% were renters. The median family income of older homeowners was $21,627. The median family income of older renters was $10,151.

About 53% of homes owned by older persons in 1995 were built prior to 1960 (35% for younger owners) and 6% had physical problems.

The percentage of income spent on housing (including maintenance and repair) in 1995 was higher for older persons than for the younger consumer population (34% vs. 27%). In 1995, the median value of homes owned by older persons was $81,956 ($56,15 for Blacks and $85,521 for Hispanics). About 80% of older homeowners in 1995 owned their homes free and clear.

Employment

About 3.9 million older Americans (12%) were in the labor force (working or actively seeking work) in 1997, including 2.3 million men (17%) and 1.6 million women (9%). They constituted 2.9% of the U.S. labor force. About 3.3% of them were unemployed. Labor force participation of older men decreased steadily from 2 of 3 in 1900 to 15.8% in 1985, and has stayed at 16%-17% since then. The participation rate for older females rose slightly from 1 of 12 in 1900 to 10.8% in 1956, fell to 7.3% in 1985, and has been around 8%-9% since 1988. Approximately half (53%) of the workers over 65 in 1997 were employed part-time: 46% of men and 63% of women.

About 680,000 or 18% of older workers in 1997 were self-employed, compared to 6% for younger workers. Two-thirds of them (67%) were men.

---

[*] Calculated on the basis of the official poverty definitions for the years 1994-1997.

Education

The educational level of the older population is increasing. Between 1970 and 1997, the percentage who had completed high school rose from 28% to 66%. About 15% in 1997 had a bachelor's degree or more. The percentage who had completed high school varied considerably by race and ethnic origin among older persons in 1997: 68% of Whites, 44% of Blacks, and 30% of Hispanics.

Health and Health Care

In 1995, 28.3% of older persons assessed their heath as fair or poor (compared to 9.4% for all persons). There was little difference between the sexes on this measure, but older Blacks were much more likely to rate their health as fair or poor (43%) than were older Whites (28%). Limitations on activities because of chronic conditions increase with age. In 1995, over one-third (37.2%) of older persons reported they were limited by chronic conditions. Among all elderly, 10.5% were unable to carry on a major activity. In contrast, only 13.9% of the total population were limited in their activities, and only 4.3% had a major restriction.

In 1994-95 more than half of the older population (52.5%) reported having at least one disability. One-third had a severe disability(ies). The percentages with disabilities increase sharply with age (Figure 6). Over 4.4 million (14%) had difficulty in carrying out activities of daily living (ADLs) and 6.5 million (21%) reported difficulties with instrumental activities of daily living (IADLs). [ADLs include bathing, dressing, eating, and getting around the house. IADLs include preparing meals, shopping, managing money, using the telephone, doing housework, and taking medication].

Figure 6
PERCENT WITH DISABILITIES, BY AGE: 1994-95

Age Group	% with any disability	% with severe disability
65+	52.5%	33.4%
15-64	18.7%	8.7%
0-14	9.1%	1.1%

Source: Current Population Reports, "Americans with Disabilities, 1994-95," P70-61, August, 1997

Most older persons have at least one chronic condition and many have multiple conditions. The most frequently occurring conditions per 100 elderly in 1994 were: arthritis (50), hypertension (36), heart disease (32), hearing impairments (29), cataracts (17), orthopedic impairments (16), sinusitis (15), and diabetes (10).

Older people accounted for 40% of all hospital stays and 49% of all days of care in hospitals in 1995. The average length of a hospital stay was 7.1 days for older people, compared to only 5.4 days for people under 65. The average length of stay for older people has decreased 5.0 days since 1964. Older persons averaged more contacts with doctors in 1995 than did persons under 65 (11.1 contacts vs. 5 contacts).

In 1995, 33.1 million persons aged 65 and over were enrolled in Medicare. Four out of every five (82.6%) received health and medical services covered by Medicare at an average annual payment of $15,074. (Data excludes HMO enrollees).

Over 11 million older persons received services under the Medicaid Program in 1995. While the average vendor payment for all Medicaid recipients was $3,311, that for persons aged 65 and over was $8,868.

Questions

1. Of what significance, if any, is the fact that as age increases, the percentage of women in a particular age group climbs?

2. How might race, gender, and ethnicity affect the development of legal and social remedies for the particular problems faced by seniors?

B. Interdisciplinary Aspects of Aging

Jeffrey L. Light
International Center for Education About Aging, Inc.
LinkAge 2000, *Image of Aging*
<http://library.advanced.org/10120/cyber/extended/what_image.html>[*]

What is the Image of Aging?

Images of aging can be both personal (our own) and societal (opinions of many people in our society). Our personal opinions can influence what the larger society things about the elderly, and what the larger society thinks can influence our personal views. If we believe that being old inevitably means being sick, disabled and unhappy, then we may become afraid that large numbers of elderly will somehow "use up" medical and social services and want to limit their use of these services. On the other hand, if we were to see only images of the retired young-old living in luxury then we might think that the elderly do not need any societal support because they are rich. Of course, neither of these two beliefs [is] true. The elderly are a diverse group in terms of their mental and physical health, their economic resources and their social lives.

We all have images of ourselves. These images includes both knowledge of our chronological age and our "subjective age" (how old we feel). While society may consider people to be old at sixty or sixty-five, many people at this age or older do not feel that they are old (similarly there are many people in their thirties or forties who do feel old). Even when individuals are in their seventies or eighties—and consider others in this group to be old—they may think of themselves as being young or middle-aged.

For some people, changes in physical health (heart disease, stroke, change in physical function) or changes in social role (widowed, retirement) signal a transition

---

[*] Reprinted with permission.

to old age and to a new lifestyle. But this is not always the case. There are many older adults who feel "younger" at retirement than they did while working and there are those older adults whose young, subjective image is not changed by illness or disability. If someone develops a disability in their teens, twenties or thirties, they do not think of themselves as being old because of their disability; similarly an older adult can separate illness or disability from how they feel inside.

Just like you have an image of yourself (i.e., friendly, fun-loving, funny, open-minded) older adults also have self-images. There is evidence that self-image is pretty stable throughout life. Older people may feel that they have changed in terms of health as they have gotten older, but they generally do not feel that they have changed in terms of personal characteristics. When you look at the images of older people on this web page, or when you see older people in your family or neighborhood, how do you think they feel about themselves? Do you think that if you talked to an older person about themselves their feelings are a lot different than yours?

Since we all live within a society, we have an image of the way the rest of society perceives us. Older people may feel that they are well-treated or that they are poorly treated. This varies from society to society, and even within societies. Sometimes older people feel that society has more than one attitude. For example, it is not uncommon for older people to feel that they have experienced a lack of respect, loss of authority and social standing but are treated well by society in other ways. A study in Norway found that the majority of elderly Norwegians felt that life had improved in terms of their material and economic status and that more care and assistance was available to them, but that their social standing and esteem had deteriorated. Interestingly, in this same study younger Norwegians believed that they would have fewer resources available to them when they are old. What do you think might cause this attitude?

Ageism is a type of discrimination that many people are not aware of. Ageism can include denying older people medical care because they are "too old to benefit," even though care could save lives or reduce disability.

Stereotypes are generally the result of a lack of correct information or misinformation. Some of the most commonly held negative stereotypes about the elderly include:

- The elderly are all alike
- Old people are sad and "lose their minds"
- Elderly people are isolated and lonely
- Being old means being physically disabled
- The elderly don't enjoy life
- Someone has to take care of the elderly—they just cannot take care of themselves
- The elderly are a burden, they don't do anything worthwhile
- Old people have stopped learning new things

Throughout this web page there is enough information to show that these stereotypes are not true for the elderly as a group. There may be some older adults who do not enjoy life, are sick or who are a burden—but the same can be said about people of all ages.

Negative stereotypes can influence our thoughts about the elderly. They may cause us to consider the elderly different and separate from everyone else. They may cause us to think of the elderly as less worthy than other groups of people. They may cause us think that we do not enjoy the company of the elderly. They may cause us to feel afraid of our own aging. They may cause us to see resources as for "them" or for "us."

Our negative thoughts may cause us to behave differently towards the elderly. They may cause us to ignore the elderly or treat them as sickly when they are not. They may cause us to agree to policies and practices that we would not agree to if we didn't hold these stereotypes. They may cause us to exclude the elderly from activities or force people to retire before they would like.

Studies of intergenerational programs show that participation not only improves knowledge and attitudes of children and teenagers about the elderly, but that they also change behaviors. Students who participate are more likely to be willing to share, help and cooperate with elderly persons. Studies also report that both young and old find these programs rewarding.

Administration on Aging Update
The Hispanic Elderly: A Cultural Mosaic (September 1997)
<http://www.aoa.dhhs.gov/update/update9-97.html#Mosaic>

Hispanics make up a cultural mosaic that, in many respects, is as varied as the rest of America's population. The Hispanic elderly, while sharing a common language, differ from each other in terms of their history, religion, economic status, educational attainment, political views and a host of other characteristics.

Hispanics may trace their roots on American soil for at least 600 hundred years or they may have come only recently. They may be of European (usually Spanish) or African ancestry, or they may trace their ancestry to one of the great civilizations of the Americas—Mayan, Aztec or Inca, or, very often, be a mixture of these races. Nearly two-thirds of Hispanics in this country trace their origins to Mexico or areas of the United States that once belonged to Mexico.

The second largest group of Hispanics—11 percent—come from Puerto Rico, while 7 percent come from Cuba. The remainder—many of whom are the most recent immigrants—come from Nicaragua, El Salvador, Guatemala, Peru, Bolivia, Colombia, Venezuela and the other nations of Central and South America. The majority of Hispanics have immigrated to the United States seeking better economic opportunities and/or because of political upheavals or oppression in their own countries.

The Hispanic Elderly—Growing in Numbers and Diversity

Over the years, the elderly Hispanic population has not only increased, but has become more racially diverse due to the influx of people from different Latin American countries. Compared to other Americans, however, a smaller percentage of Hispanics—6 percent in 1990, or 1.2 million—are elderly. Nevertheless, they are the fastest growing segment of the 65+ population. The Hispanic elderly population is projected to almost double as a percent of the total elderly population to 11.7 percent, or 7.9 million, in 2050.

Sixty-four percent of the Hispanic elderly are native-born Americans. They are concentrated in Arizona, California, Colorado, Illinois, Texas, Florida, and New York. An overwhelming majority live in urban areas. Hispanics generally have the least amount of formal education of any elderly group, with an average of 4 years of schooling.

Income

In 1990, the poverty rate for the Hispanic elderly was 22.5 percent—more than twice that for white Americans but less than the rate for African Americans, which stood at 33.8 percent. The Hispanic elderly are least likely to receive social security, public and private pensions or veterans benefits.

As a result of their low incomes and limited participation in Social Security and retirement plans, the Hispanic elderly are more likely than other older Americans to benefit from public assistance and, while their labor force participation rate is similar to that of older white and African Americans, they are more than twice as likely as white Americans to be underemployed (5.3 percent versus 2.3 percent).

Caring for the Elderly

Due to strong traditions of extended family ties and caring for one another, the Hispanic elderly are less likely to reside in long-term care facilities than white or African American elderly. They also are more likely to live with family members. In fact, over 75 percent live with their families, which tend to be multigenerational.

The Hispanic elderly face many of the problems encountered by other minority groups. Service providers report that the most serious problems facing the Hispanic elderly are lack of transportation, substandard housing, and inadequate health care. Their ability to locate and access needed services and assistance is often compounded by service providers' limited knowledge of Spanish.

Questions

1. Given the nature of the aging process, should lawyers who wish to practice elder law be encouraged or required to educate themselves in such areas as the biology, sociology, and psychology of aging?

2. How can an attorney working with older clients avoid "ageism"?

3. How might different cultural perceptions of aging affect the lawyer-client relationship?

C. Social Policy and Aging: Selected Issues

1. Crime and Fraud

U.S. Department of Justice, Bureau of Justice Statistics
Elderly Crime Victims: National Crime Victimization Survey (March 1994)
<http://www.ojp.usdoj.gov/bjs/pub/ascii/ecv.txt>

In 1992, persons 65 or older experienced about 2.1 million criminal victimizations. The National Crime Victimization Survey (NCVS) asks about 100,000 people every 6 months about the crimes they sustained. By interviewing a large sample of households selected to represent the U.S. population, BJS is able to draw accurate conclusions about crime in the Nation. The NCVS includes the violent crimes of rape, robbery, and assault; personal theft; and crimes that occur in households such as burglary, household larceny, and motor vehicle theft. Persons age 65 or older comprise about 14% of persons age 12 or older interviewed in the NCVS but report less than 2% of all victimizations. Unless otherwise noted, the data presented here are from a special analysis of the NCVS for elderly victims that aggregated data from 1987 to 1990. Trend data and information on the current rates of elderly victimizations are from the 1992 NCVS.

Crime victimization rates among the elderly have generally been declining.

- Over 20 years, the lowest rate of violent crime against the elderly was recorded in 1990, 3.5 per 1,000 persons age 65 or older. This was 61% lower than the 9 crimes per 1,000 persons in 1974, the peak year.
- The rates for personal theft and household crime among the elderly in 1992 were the lowest ever recorded in the 20-year history of NCVS. Persons age 65 or older are the least likely of all age groups in the Nation to experience crime.

Figure 7
NUMBER OF VICTIMIZATIONS
(per 1,000 persons or households)

Age	Violent Crime	Personal Theft	Household Crime
12-24	64.6	112.7	309.3
25-49	27.2	71.2	200.2
50-64	8.5	38.3	133.0
65 or older	4.0	19.5	78.5

Persons between the ages of 12 and 24 have the highest victimization rates for all types of crime, while those age 65 or older have the lowest (Figure 7).

- The violent crime rate is nearly 16 times higher for persons under age 25 than for persons over 65 (64.6 versus 4 victimizations per 1,000 persons in each

age group). The rate for robbery, one of the crimes of violence, for those under 25 is nearly 6 times higher than for those age 65 or older.
- According to the FBI, 5% of the murder victims in 1992 were age 65 or older.
- Just as for personal crime victimizations, persons over the age of 65 are significantly less likely to become victims of all forms of household crime than younger age groups.
- Personal larceny with contact (purse snatching and pocket picking) is an exception. Those who are 65 or older were about as likely as those under age 65 to be victims of personal larceny with contact.

The elderly appear to be particularly susceptible to crimes motivated by economic gain. Crimes motivated by economic gain include robbery and personal theft, as well as the household crimes of larceny, burglary, and motor vehicle theft. Like the general population, the elderly are most susceptible to household crimes and least susceptible to violent crimes. Unlike younger victims of violence, elderly victims of violence are about as likely to be robbed as assaulted. Robberies are 38% of the violent crimes against the elderly but 20% of the violence experienced by persons younger than age 65.

Injured elderly victims of violent crime are more likely than younger victims to suffer a serious injury (Figure 8). Violent offenders injure about a third of all victims. Among the violent crime victims age 65 or older, 9% suffer serious injuries like broken bones and loss of consciousness. By comparison, 5% of younger victims suffer serious injuries. In addition, when injured, almost half the older victims but a fourth of the younger ones receive medical care in a hospital.

Figure 8
PERCENT OF VIOLENT CRIME VICTIMS

Outcome	Under 65	65 or older
Injured	31%	33%
Serious	5	9
Minor	26	24
Received medical care	15	19
Hospital care	8	14

Note: Serious injuries are broken bones, loss of teeth, internal injuries, loss of consciousness, rape or attempted rape injuries, or undetermined injuries requiring 2 or more days of hospitalization. Minor injuries are bruises, black eyes, cuts, scratches, swelling, or undetermined injuries requiring less than 2 days of hospitalization.

Elderly violent crime victims are more likely than younger victims to face assailants who are strangers (Figure 9). Most victims of violent crime are attacked by a stranger rather than by a relative or someone whom the victim knows. Robbery victims age 65 or older are more likely than younger victims to be particularly vulnerable to offenders whom they do not know.

Figure 9
PERCENT OF VIOLENT CRIME VICTIMS WHOSE OFFENDERS ARE:

	Relatives	Acquaintances	Strangers	Relationship unknown
Crimes of violence				
Under 65	8%	33%	56%	3%
65 or Older	8%	20%	64%	8%
Robbery				
Under 65	5%	7%	74%	4%
65 or older	3%	5%	83%	9%
Assault				
Under 65	9%	36%	52%	3%
65 or older	13%	32%	47%	8%

Elderly victims of violent crime are almost twice as likely as younger victims to be raped, robbed, or assaulted at or near their home (Figure 10). Half of the elderly victims of violence and a quarter of those under age 65 are victimized at or near their home.

Figure 10
PLACE OF OCCURRENCE

	Total	At Home	Near Home	On the Street	In Public or Business Facility	Elsewhere
Crimes of Violence						
Under 65	100%	14%	11%	39%	21%	15%
65 or older	100%	25%	25%	31%	9%	10%
Robbery						
Under 65	100%	13%	9%	52%	16%	10%
65 or older	100%	20%	21%	37%	13%	10%
Assault						
Under 65	100%	14%	12%	36%	21%	15%
65 or older	100%	27%	29%	27%	7%	10%

The vulnerability of the elderly to violent crime at or near their home may reflect their lifestyle. Often living alone and not working away from home, persons age 65 or older are also less likely than younger persons to go out after dark to social gatherings. Public opinion surveys conducted over the last 20 years among national samples of persons age 50 or older consistently show that about half of those persons feel afraid to walk alone at night in their own neighborhood.

About 38% of elderly victims of violent crime and 35% of younger victims report facing an armed offender (Figure 11). When facing an armed offender, older victims are somewhat more likely to face an offender with a gun (41% versus 36%).

Figure 11
PERCENT OF VIOLENT CRIME VICTIMS

	Under 65	65 or older
Unarmed offenders	65%	62%
Armed offenders	35%	38%
Type of weapon used		
Guns	36%	41%
Knives or sharp instruments	30%	29%
Blunt objects	19%	18%
Other weapons	15%	12%

Most victims of violent crime, regardless of age, face lone assailants, but the likelihood of encountering multiple offenders varies by type of crime.

About half the robbery victims age 65 or older are accosted by multiple robbers; more than half of the robbery victims under 65 face single offenders. For aggravated assault, the reverse is true. Younger victims of aggravated assault are more likely than older victims to face multiple offenders (29% versus 20%).

Elderly victims, less often than younger victims, act to protect themselves during a violent crime. Victims age 65 or older take self-protective measures in 58% of their victimizations, compared to 73% of the younger victims. Moreover, the older victims are less likely to use physical action such as attacking or chasing the offender or resisting in some other way. Those persons age 65 or older who do protect themselves use nonphysical action, including arguing or reasoning with the offender, screaming, or running away.

Elderly victims of robbery and personal theft are more likely than younger victims to report those crimes to the police. Seven out of ten elderly victims and just over 5 out of 10 victims under age 65 report a robbery or attempted robbery to the police. No measurable difference, however, distinguishes older from younger victims in reporting aggravated assault or household crimes to the police.

Among the elderly, certain groups were generally more likely to experience a crime than others (Figure 12).

Figure 12
NUMBER OF VICTIMIZATIONS
(per 1,000)

Victim characteristics	Persons 65 or older Violence	Theft	Households headed by a person 65 or older Household Crime
Sex			
Male	4.9	19.8	82.2
Female	3.4	19.4	74.3
Age			
65 to 75	4.7	22.9	82.2
75 and over	3.0	14.2	74.3
Race			
White	3.6	19.5	70.9
Black	7.6	19.6	154.1
Family Income			
Less than $7,500	12.0	29.1	76.3
$7,500-$14,999	8.4	30.4	70.2
$15,000-$24,000	6.5	40.3	81.3
$25,000 or more	6.1	60.8	96.0
Marital Status			
Never married	3.0	18.2	77.6
Widowed	4.2	4.2	75.1
Married	7.6	26.3	71.1
Divorced/Separated	11.3	35.4	110.4
Place of Residence			
Urban	7.1	26.4	112.6
Suburban	2.9	19.6	61.2
Rural	2.2	11.4	64.5
Form of Tenure			
Own	3.1	17.8	82.0
Rent	7.7	26.7	66.8

- Elderly men generally have higher victimization rates than elderly women. Elderly women, however, have higher rates of personal larceny with contact such as purse snatching.
- The elderly age 65 to 74 have higher rates of victimization than those age 75 or older.
- Elderly blacks are more likely than elderly whites to be crime victims. However, rates of personal larceny that did not involve contact between the victim and offender were greater for whites.

- The elderly with the lowest incomes experience higher violence rates than those elderly with higher family incomes. Those elderly with the highest family income have the highest rates of personal theft or household crime.
- Elderly persons who are either separated or divorced, from among all marital statuses, have the highest rates of victimization for all types of crime.
- Elderly residents in cities have the highest rates of victimization for all types of crime, compared to suburban or rural elderly.
- Elderly renters are more likely than owners to experience both violence and personal theft. However, elderly homeowners are more likely than renters to be victims of household crime.

Figure 13
NUMBER OF VICTIMIZATIONS
(per 1,000 persons age 12 or older)

Violence			
Teenage black males	113	Adult black males	35
Teenage black females	94	Adult white males	18
Teenage white males	90	Adult white females	15
Young adult black males	80	Adult black females	13
Young adult black females	57	Elderly black males	12
Teenage white females	55	Elderly black females	10
Young adult white males	52	Elderly white males	6
Young adult white females	38	Elderly white females	3

Note: Teenage = age 12-19, Young adult = age 20-34, Adult = age 35-64, Elderly = age 65 and older
(White women age 65 or older have the lowest violent crime rates)

Figure 14
NUMBER OF VICTIMIZATIONS
(per 1,000 persons age 12 or older)

Personal theft			
Teenage white males	106	Adult black males	52
Young adult black males	105	Adult white females	48
Teenage white females	92	Adult white males	44
Young adult white males	89	Adult black females	43
Teenage black males	84	Elderly white females	18
Young adult white females	78	Elderly white females	15
Young adult black females	69	Elderly black males	13
Teenage black females	66	Elderly black females	9

Note: Teenage = age 12-19, Young adult = age 20-34, Adult = age 35-64, Elderly = age 65 and older
(Black women age 65 or older have the lowest personal theft rates)

Statement of Bruce C. Vladeck, Administrator
Health Care Financing Administration
Prevalence of Health Care Fraud and Abuse
Senate Committee on Government Affairs
Permanent Subcommittee on Investigation, June 26, 1997
<http://www.hcfa.gov/testmony/fraud1.htm>

Introduction

Mr. Chairman and Members of the Subcommittee, I am very pleased to have this opportunity to describe the Health Care Financing Administration's programs to fight fraud and abuse in Medicare and Medicaid. As we stand on the threshold of the twenty-first century, we are faced with the formidable task of ensuring the solvency of the Trust Fund, and preserving Medicare for future generations. In order to do this, we must begin by making sure that every dollar we spend for our beneficiaries is well-spent, and that our goals of efficiency and cost-effectiveness do not compromise the quality of their health care.

The annals of medicine are replete with case histories demonstrating that prevention is the best antidote to illness. This is equally true in the area of fiscal well-being: in order for our Medicare and Medicaid programs to remain both solvent and strong, we need to prevent improper or fraudulent claims which strain the fiscal and personnel resources of the system. By guaranteeing the initial accuracy of both claims and payments, we avoid having to "pay and chase," and we can prevent opportunities for fraud and abuse.

Incorrectly billed claims can stem not only from fraud, but from confusion and misinformation about the proper billing procedures. For example, if there is a payer primary to Medicare, the Medicare contractor will reject the claim and submit it to the appropriate primary payer. Where Medicare is primary, the Medicare contractor will make payment, then send the paid claims data to the supplemental insurer. HCFA uses many pre-payment mechanisms to determine the primary payer for benefits for a Medicare beneficiary and to ensure Medicare pays in the right order of payers. These mechanisms are part of our Medicare as a Secondary Payer (MSP) Activity, which I will describe in detail later in this testimony. Currently, we are seeking legislation that would improve our ability to verify whether Medicare is the primary or secondary payer.

Overview: The Issues

The sheer complexity of the health care delivery system virtually guarantees that there will be instances of unscrupulous claims billing. While some high-profile examples of fraud and waste are well-known to the public because of media attention, there are many less visible areas of concern. Some of these include:

Abusive Billing in Nursing Homes—Aside from the typical kind of fraud that occurs in charging patients for services they have not received, there are other, more difficult-to-detect abuses to which beneficiaries of nursing homes are vulnerable. These include inappropriate designation of nursing home patients as hospice patients, false patient census reports, improper billing of supplies and services for patients eligible for both Medicare and Medicaid ("dual eligibles"), unnecessary or inappropriate services being prescribed for nursing home patients, and billing as therapy services for services paid in the nursing home rate. Unnecessary medical supplies may be ordered for the unsuspecting patient, such as several cases found by the DHHS Inspector General (IG), in which thousands of dollars of surgical tape, hydrogel wound filler, and orthotic devices were inappropriately ordered and made available to other patients. Also, it has been estimated that as much as 32% of mental health services ordered for Medicare nursing home residents were unnecessary or inappropriate. Part of the problem stems from the fact that the nursing home itself is not responsible to coordinate the services, which may be initiated and billed by an outside entity.

Home Health Fraud—The "invisibility" of the home health setting invites profiteers to prey on disabled and elderly patients who may often be isolated, uninformed, and lacking the support of friends or family. We are finding continuous problems with unnecessary home health services, especially those provided to beneficiaries who are not homebound. Because of the difficulty in monitoring these situations, the patient may be at the mercy of an unethical provider or supplier. Overprescription and overcharging of oxygen and tube feeding supplies for home health patients have been found in bills submitted to Medicare and Medicaid. Through HCFA's Operation Restore Trust (ORT), we have located and penalized fraudulent home health agency owners across the Nation, and saved millions of dollars.

The 1981 report issued by the Senate's Permanent Subcommittee on Investigations identified several areas of Medicare and Medicaid home health care needing better oversight, and recommended that HCFA notify home health intermediaries in a timely fashion of any regulatory changes. We have acted on this recommendation, and we have developed checks and balances that ensure that this is done. Current HCFA procedures require that intermediaries have at least 90 days to carry out any program actions that may be required of them. Therefore, any legislative/statutory, regulatory, policy, or electronic system changes that directly affect the contractors are published in a quarterly release of HCFA's Task Management Plan, which is then distributed, along with pertinent materials, to intermediaries with a minimum 90 days' implementation deadline. This process alerts intermediaries that they must notify providers of new or revised program procedures or requirements. Intermediaries are also required to communicate program changes to their providers in a communique, usually in the form of a bulletin or similar form of notification. These checks and balances ensure accountability—of both intermediaries and HCFA.

Durable Medical Equipment—There is widespread concern that Medicare's payments for durable medical equipment are excessive. Medicare payments for DME are based on a fee schedule methodology established by Congress in Omnibus Budget Reconciliation Act (OBRA) 1987, and these fee schedule amounts were based on supplier's "reasonable charges" in the mid-1980s. Unless otherwise specified by Congress, these amounts have been increased annually by the Consumer Price Index-Urban (CPI-U) as required by statute. This statutorily prescribed payment methodology does not consider changes in technology or any other factors impacting suppliers' costs and as a result HCFA's payments for DME are often excessive.

Problems with the durable medical equipment (DME) industry have resulted in stricter controls over who can apply for, and receive, a license as a DME provider. A Notice will be issued this summer by HCFA that will require that DME providers meet certain criteria, including putting up a surety bond for licensure, and greater proof of the bona fide existence of the business. This will prevent abuses such as the case of the Florida man who received a DME license, despite the fact that the only actual supplies he had in stock were stuffed alligator heads and other souvenirs he sold from his garage. He had applied for a DME certification to sell wheelchairs to complement his brother-in-law's business of installing wheelchair lifts in cars. Examples like this are a good argument for DME bonding.

Fraudulent Billing Practices—Complex claims billing procedures offer multiple ways of cheating the system, from overt inflation and exaggeration of the level of services provided ("upcoding") to blatantly false cost reports submitted for reimbursement. A Maryland nursing home operator was prosecuted for adding his personal entertaining and decorating expenses to the facility's Medicaid bill, including a charge for services rendered by the operator's relative who was actually in jail at the time. In another case reported by the GAO, a supplier for a long-term care facility was forging physicians' signatures on certificates of medical necessity, and then billing for items that were either unnecessary, had already been provided to the patient, or were in fact never delivered. The President's FY98 Budget includes provisions to develop prospective payment systems for several services in Medicare. PPS pays a set rate according to the characteristics of the patient, and removes many of the incentives for providers to provide excessive services or submit fraudulent cost reports to receive high reimbursement.

Kickbacks—Providers such as laboratories, ambulance companies, and pharmacies may enter into unethical agreements with nursing home owners and clinical psychologists that may include kickbacks in exchange for being allowed to provide services to the nursing home residents. HCFA's State Medicaid Fraud Control Units have found cases of nursing home owners authorizing unnecessary services because they receive kickbacks from these ancillary services, such as ambulance companies, and laboratory and therapy services.

3-Day Payment Window—Current law prohibits providers from billing for pre-admission outpatient tests and services performed within 3 days of the time a patient is admitted to a hospital, if the tests and services are diagnostic services or other services related to the admission. This precludes the potential for double-billing medical services which should properly be provided as part of inpatient services. This 3-day payment window applies only to hospitals under the prospective payment system, since 1994 SSA legislation reduced the window to 1 day for non-PPS hospitals. Most improper billing relating to pre-admission services results from a misunderstanding of the law, which was originally instituted to curb further "unbundling" of services, i.e., separating of the various pre-admission tests in order to obtain additional payments.

Inpatient Mental Health Services—As the occupancy rates of psychiatric hospital inpatient beds have dropped, many hospitals have attempted to find ways to fill the void, often by hospitalizing patients who should be cared for in other, non-psychiatric, facilities. This is a temptation because diagnostic-related groups (DRGs) are not imposed on care in psychiatric hospitals, as they are in short-term acute care hospitals. Hospitalization of patients in psychiatric facilities can be extremely lucrative, with charges as high as $1000 per day. Also, patients hospitalized in psychiatric facilities are sometimes billed for unnecessary and unordered services. The President's FY98 budget has a provision to make Medicare payments less lucrative for these situations; ceilings would be established on reimbursements, so that facilities could not be reimbursed for these costs, if they were much more expensive than other psychiatric hospitals.

This is a particular area of concern for HCFA because of the potential for coercive hospitalization under some State laws, such as a case recently reported in Massachusetts. A child who had been taken to a hospital for a medication adjustment for his epilepsy was forcibly hospitalized, against his parents' wishes, in a psychiatric hospital. Although this situation was due in part to Section 12 of Massachusetts State law, it raises disturbing questions about lack of oversight in psychiatric hospitalizations.

Marketing Abuses—Questionable sales techniques are sometimes used in the marketing of health insurance, especially when the potential customers are elderly and may be ill-equipped to make informed choices. Some marketing representatives may use fear tactics to persuade beneficiaries to sign up for benefits they don't need and can sometimes ill afford. In response to these abuses, HCFA will be issuing National Managed Care Marketing Guidelines this summer, to assure that marketing materials present balanced and accurate information to beneficiaries and to discourage fraudulent or deceptive representation of health plans or services.

HCFA's Current Initiatives Against Fraud and Abuse

This Administration is seriously committed to aggressively prosecuting and preventing all forms of waste, fraud, and abuse. Toward this goal, we worked on a bi-partisan basis with the Congress to develop the necessary legislation. The Health Insurance Portability and Accountability Act of 1996 (HIPAA), which was enacted last year, contained important provisions to aid us in our war on waste, fraud and abuse in the Medicare program. Two of the most significant provisions for the Health Care Financing Administration (HCFA) were the implementation of the Medicare Integrity Program (MIP) and the Fraud and Abuse Control Program.

Medicare Integrity Program (MIP)—This program authorizes the Secretary to promote the integrity of the Medicare program by entering into contracts with eligible entities to carry out program integrity activities such as audits of cost reports, medical and utilization review, and payment determinations. MIP provided a stable source of funding for HCFA's program integrity activities, and provided us with the authority to contract for these activities with any qualified entity, not just those insurance companies who are currently our fiscal intermediaries or carriers.

The Medicare Integrity Program (MIP) was enacted to strengthen the Secretary's ability to deter fraud and abuse in the Medicare program in a number of ways. First, it created a separate and stable long-term funding mechanism for program integrity activities. Historically, Medicare contractor budgets had been subject to fluctuations of funding levels from year to year. Such variations in funding did not have anything to do with the underlying requirements for program integrity activities. This instability made it difficult for HCFA to invest in innovative strategies to control fraud and abuse. Our contractors also found it difficult to attract, train, and retain qualified professional staff, including clinicians, auditors, and fraud investigators. A dependable funding source allows HCFA the flexibility to invest in new and innovative strategies to combat fraud and abuse. It will help HCFA shift emphasis from post-payment recoveries on fraudulent claims to pre-payment strategies designed to ensure that more claims are paid correctly the first time.

Second, by permitting the Secretary to use full and open competition rather than requiring that we contract only with the existing intermediaries and carriers to perform MIP functions, the government can seek to obtain the best value for its contracted services. Prior law limited the pool of contractors that could compete for contracts, thus, we were not always able to negotiate the best deal for the government or take advantage of new ways to deter fraud and abuse. Using competitive procedures, as established in the Federal Acquisition Regulations System (FARS), we expect to attract a variety of offerors who will propose innovative approaches to implement MIP.

Third, MIP permits HCFA to address potential conflict of interest situations. We will require our contractors to report situations which may constitute conflicts of interest, thus minimizing the number of instances where there is either an actual, or an apparent, conflict of interest. By invoking the FARS in establishing multi-year contracts with an expanded pool of contractors, we will be able to avoid potential conflicts of interest and obtain the best value. Also, by permitting us to develop methods to identify, evaluate and resolve conflicts of interest, we can create a process to ensure objectivity and impartiality when dealing with our contractors. This is a concern particularly when intermediaries and carriers are also private health insurance companies processing Medicare claims.

To ensure that our resources are used as wisely as possible, we will also gradually reduce the number of contractors performing payment safeguard activities. Prior to the passage of HIPAA, all 72 contractors performed all aspects of program integrity work. With highly specialized contractors focusing solely on fraud and abuse prevention and detection, we will gain a cost-effective and efficient pool of contractors. We plan to focus contractors on program integrity activities for a geographic area, rather than by provider type, as is current practice. That way, contractors will have a more comprehensive picture of activity, and will be able to monitor whether doctor bills match hospital bills, in terms of procedures performed and dates of service. Furthermore, the reduction in the number of contractors performing activities such as medical and fraud review as well as audit does not mean that local presence will be eliminated. Medical directors will continue to play an important role in benefit integrity activities, and we intend to retain locally-based Medical directors as well as to continue our relationship with local physicians by using groups like Carrier Advisory Committees.

We are currently developing regulations to implement MIP, and we are also working on a scope of work for competitive contracts. As we transition work from one of our contractors, Aetna (which is terminating its Medicare work), we are testing a new contracting relationship in several Western States that will separate out (and consolidate) payment integrity activities from claims processing. This will give us valuable experience as we prepare to implement MIP.

Operation Restore Trust (ORT)—The Operation Restore Trust (ORT) project was the first comprehensive effort at collaboration between HCFA and law enforcement agencies. This two-year demonstration project, which was launched by the President in May 1995 and concluded on March 31, 1997, was designed to demonstrate new partnerships and new approaches in finding and minimizing fraud in Medicare and Medicaid. As a demonstration project, ORT targeted four areas of high spending growth: home health agencies, nursing homes, DME suppliers, and hospices. Since more than a third of all Medicare and Medicaid beneficiaries are located in New York, Florida, Illinois, Texas, and California, ORT efforts were targeted at these five states.

Fraud and Abuse Control Program—The program integrity activities of the Medicare contractors initiated many of the cases subsequently developed by the Office of Inspector General and Federal Bureau of Investigation, and support their prosecution by the Department of Justice. Using monies made available through the Fraud and Abuse Control Fund, established in HIPAA, we expanded our successful ORT efforts using the State survey agencies to be our "eyes and ears" in the field and to report back to the contractors whether providers are meeting Medicare billing as well as quality requirements. We have used this model successfully with our expanded home health surveys in the 5 Operation Restore Trust (ORT) States.

Through HCFA's expanded efforts, approximately $1.8 million has been allocated to HCFA for "Project ORT" through HIPAA's Fraud and Abuse Control Program, to enhance the program integrity activities that involve collaboration with State certification agencies. Eighteen States will participate in a total of 26 HIPAA funded projects, allowing us to survey approximately 300 providers for both certification and reimbursement issues. These enhanced surveys will be made of providers of home health services, skilled nursing services, outpatient physical therapy services, and laboratory services, as well as psychiatric services in both hospitals and community mental health centers. Many of these surveys will be modeled after the home health agency and skilled nursing facility surveys conducted during ORT. This collaboration, which is being institutionalized through the Fraud and Abuse Control Program established in HIPAA, establishes a funding stream for health care fraud and abuse activities, and requires DoJ and HHS to establish priorities jointly.

Medicare as a Second Payer (MSP)—This "front end" activity takes a proactive approach to identifying the correct payer before the claim is processed, so that Medicare does not pay inappropriately or unnecessarily. There are multiple areas that are scrutinized to ensure that the appropriate payer is billed:

Initial Enrollment Questionnaire (IEQ)—The IEQ is used to gather Medicare Secondary Payer (MSP) information for most new beneficiaries approximately three months before they become entitled to Medicare. For beneficiaries who do not apply for Medicare entitlement until after becoming eligible, HCFA conducts MSP development at the time the Medicare application is filed. This function is currently performed by an independent contractor.

First Claim Development—For all claims, the individual completing the Medicare claim for payment should indicate if there is other insurance that is primary to Medicare. If the beneficiary has not responded to the IEQ, and MSP information is not included on the first claim submitted for that beneficiary, the Medicare contractor submitting the first claim is responsible for mailing a questionnaire to the beneficiary or the provider to gather the required information. This function is currently performed by all Medicare fiscal intermediaries (FIs) and carriers.

Trauma Code Development—When a claim is received for Medicare primary payment and the claim contains one of certain specific trauma codes (which could indicate Worker's Compensation, automobile accidents, or other liability situations), the claim is scrutinized to determine if another insurer is the correct primary payer. Currently, this function is performed by the Medicare FIs and carriers.

MSP Litigation Settlement—HCFA has entered into agreements to settle MSP litigation with several health insurance companies. As part of these settlements, the affected private health care plans are required to periodically submit MSP information on their enrollees to HCFA. This activity is estimated to result in additional $540 million in MSP savings for Fiscal Year 1997. The settlement agreements require this mandatory reporting for 5 years. GHI, a Medicare Part B carrier, is currently processing this information to the Common Working File (CWF).

Internal Revenue Service (IRS)/Social Security Administration (SSA)/HCFA Data Match—Information on employers and employees provided by the IRS and SSA is analyzed by HCFA for use in contacting employers concerning possible insurance coverage of Medicare beneficiaries.

Voluntary Insurer/Employer Reporting for MSP—As an alternative to responding to the IRS/SSA/HCFA data match employer questionnaires, employers may enter into a voluntary agreement with HCFA to report primary payer information on a current basis. Likewise, other health insurance companies are encouraged to report on their insured who are Medicare eligible on a current basis. HCFA Central Office is currently negotiating its first such voluntary agreement.

Hospital Admissions Procedures Review—Institutional providers such as hospitals, as part of their Medicare participation agreements, are required to conduct admissions interviews to determine if another primary payer exists. FIs are required to review a sample of their hospitals annually to determine if their admissions procedures are complete and are routinely followed. MSP information thus acquired during hospital intake ensures that Medicare pays in the appropriate order of financial liability.

Claims Submission—Medicare claims submission instructions require that the existence of a primary payer other than Medicare be indicated on the claim. This information is also checked with HCFA's own insurance information obtained from other sources.

Data Systems to Fight Fraud and Abuse

Single Integrated Database System—HCFA is in the process of developing an automated Medicare claims processing and information system, which will, among other things, assist in our program integrity and provider exclusion efforts. This integrated system is being designed to consolidate the currently fragmented Medicare claims processing into one standardized system. Although we are currently re-examining the specific implementation strategy for this system, we believe a fully operational integrated system will assist us in preventing fraud. A significant advancement for HCFA will be the use of advanced technology to detect fraud and abuse at the outset—before Medicare pays health care providers. The single system will facilitate identification of data files containing aberrant patterns and data discrepancies, and alert Medicare contractors to review more cautiously selected Medicare claims.

Full implementation of an integrated database will aid us in preventing fraud and abuse because it will greatly improve HCFA's ability to profile data on a National or regional basis by type of service. We plan to use these profiles to identify and review aberrant billing patterns and to prevent inappropriate claims from being paid in the first place, thus avoiding the need to chase down those fraudulent claims that have already been paid. The single system will integrate data from Medicare Part A, Part B, and managed care and provide the opportunity to have a comprehensive view of billing practices and to incorporate new technology to facilitate innovative investigative techniques. We plan to use artificial intelligence in an analysis of patterns of care, auto-adjudication, and other analytic tools that will permit improved identification of payments that should not be made—prior to payment.

One way in which the new system will provide an enhanced ability to fight fraud is through the use of the National Provider Identifier, which is an industry wide unique identifier for providers and suppliers created under the authority of the Health Insurance Portability and Accountability Act of 1996 (HIPAA). This identifier will be used to create an integrated database that will contain a record of all providers and suppliers who are certified to bill Medicare for medical supplies or equipment provided to our beneficiaries. Our legislative proposal for authorization to require social security numbers from Medicare providers will enhance our ability to identify fraudulent providers and keep them from further defrauding the program. If a provider is excluded from the Medicare program, or has been identified as fraudulent, that provider will be flagged in the database, which must be accessed before the claim is paid. A single system will also enable us to flag providers who are excluded from Medicaid and other Federal health programs as well.

An integrated information system will improve our ability to assure proper payment. When a bill or claim is entered into the database from an excluded provider or supplier, payment will be denied. Additionally, the OIG can develop a civil monetary penalty case tracking system, which will use the claim submission information from the database to assist in identifying excluded providers and ensuring that they do not continue to bill.

HCIS Database—An important building block for HCFA's integrated information system is the HCFA Customer Information System (HCIS). This database supports multiple capabilities including program integrity initiatives, evaluation of policy and procedural changes, medical review studies, and dissemination of customer information. HCIS allows the user to view provider or service utilization data initially at the National level, and subsequently . . . through the various levels, from the State, contractor, provider type, or individual provider, to the beneficiary. This capability allows the rapid identification and analysis of factors contributing to aberrant data. As a result, audits or reviews can be focused, rapidly and inexpensively, on a particular level.

HCIS is currently limited to inpatient hospitals, outpatient providers, home health agencies, hospices, skilled nursing facilities and physicians. By the end of fiscal year 1997, these provider types will be augmented by DME suppliers and clinical laboratories. We are also planning to incorporate additional program data, such as cost report and enrollment data.

Los Alamos National Laboratories—In September 1996, HCFA signed an interagency agreement with the Los Alamos National Laboratory (LANL) to develop mathematical models which identify potentially fraudulent and abusive patterns. The agreement, which arose out of Operation Restore Trust, is for the two-year period, FY96 through FY97. Its purpose is to provide analytical and computer support to develop improved approaches to operating the Medicare program. The ultimate goal is the development of prepayment software to detect and deter fraudulent and improper claims. To date, LANL has made considerable progress. By the end of 1998, we will be able to better assess if their initial work with specific beneficiary and provider populations can be repeated and applied more broadly to other beneficiary and provider populations. LANL is also exploring new ways their technology can assist in our fight against Medicare fraud and abuse. Within the next few months, they will submit for our consideration a proposal for future fraud detection work. LANL is also under contract with HCFA to determine when the contractors and the computer systems should transition into the integrated database environment.

Fraud Investigation Database—One of HCFA's most promising initiatives in excluding fraudulent providers is the Fraud Investigation Database (FID). We began implementing the FID in May 1996, and we have been pleased with the success of the system. The FID is a case-tracking system to record and disseminate information regarding exclusions, and contains extensive national Medicare and Medicaid fraud data as well as comprehensive information on all excluded providers. The database is intended to assist HCFA and our partners in identifying excluded providers, as well as those who are allegedly defrauding the programs. For example, a Medicare contractor in one area can use this information to ensure that the providers it is reimbursing have not been excluded through the actions of another contractor.

In an effort to enhance coordination of the exclusion process, the FID is also accessible to the Medicaid anti-fraud agencies such as the Medicaid Fraud Control Units and the Surveillance and Utilization Review Systems. We expect very soon to be able to obtain data from these Medicaid entities on cases and information related to the providers that they suspect to be fraudulent. The FID is also designed to ensure the coordination of anti-fraud activities undertaken by our law enforcement partners and to facilitate the monitoring of cases referred to the OIG, the FBI or the U.S. Attorneys. As other Federal government agencies acquire access to the FID, we will be able to prevent a provider who defrauds one Federal program from ever repeating the fraud in another program.

Utilizing the combined forces of all of the programs and technology cited thus far, HCFA has succeeded in preventing millions of dollars in Medicare and Medicaid losses due to fraud and abuse. However, there are still some areas where we can become more effective in these efforts, with the help of additional legislation proposed by the President's Budget.

The President's Legislative Proposals

HIPAA provided a solid foundation on which to build program integrity activities. The President is proposing a number of additional fraud and abuse proposals in his FY98 Budget and the Medicare and Medicaid Fraud, Abuse, and Waste Prevention Amendments of 1997.

The President's FY98 Budget

The President's budget contains a number of proposals to reduce waste, fraud and abuse in the Medicare program. They include provisions to require insurance companies to report the insurance status of beneficiaries to ensure that Medicare pays appropriately. Private insurance is the primary payer when Medicare beneficiaries have such coverage and Medicare is required to be the secondary payer. Having insurance companies report information on Medicare beneficiaries they insure would greatly reduce the costly "pay and chase" method that we are forced to use.

In addition, we have several proposals to prevent excessive and inappropriate billing for home health services. We are proposing to close a loophole in the current payment calculation by linking payments to the location where care is actually provided, rather than the billing location. When we implement a home health prospective payment system (PPS), we are proposing to eliminate home health agency (HHA) periodic interim payments, which were originally established to encourage HHAs to join Medicare by providing a smooth cash flow. Since over 100 new agencies join Medicare each month, such financial inducements are no longer needed. We also propose to work with the medical community to develop more objective criteria for determining the appropriate number of visits for specific conditions, so that we can prevent excessive utilization.

Medicare and Medicaid Fraud, Abuse and Waste Prevention Amendments of 1997

In March, the President presented an additional set of legislative proposals titled the "Medicare and Medicaid Fraud, Abuse, and Waste Prevention Amendments of 1997." Some of these proposals build on the provisions enacted in HIPAA. Others seek to close loopholes or weaknesses in the Medicare statute that allow providers to take advantage of Medicare payment. Some of the provisions in the bill include:

Improving the Provider Enrollment Process—We propose to clarify the provider enrollment process, and strengthen HCFA's ability to combat fraud and abuse by not allowing "bad actors" to become Medicare providers or suppliers. These provisions would provide the Secretary the authority to deny Medicare entry for those provider applicants who have been convicted of a felony, and the authority to collect a fee for all Medicare and Medicaid applicants when they apply for enrollment or re-enrollment. The fee would cover administrative costs in processing applications and administering the HIPAA National Provider Identification program requirements. If an application is denied, a six-month waiting period must be completed before the provider could reapply.

This Subcommittee recommended in its 1981 Home Health Report that HCFA develop a data bank of owners, principals, and related organizations. We responded to this recommendation by developing a National provider enrollment application (HCFA 855) that captures that specific data for all Medicare providers, and the application will be available and effective on July 1, 1997. In conjunction with this data collection, we also intend to implement an electronic system (Provider Enrollment, Chain, and Ownership System) that will consolidate data collected by the enrollment application from fiscal intermediaries, carriers, and the National Supplier Clearinghouse. This system will maintain all existing provider data in one National repository.

Value of Capital When Ownership of an Institution Changes—This proposal, which would apply to all providers, would deem the sales price of an asset to be its net book value. There have been instances in which SNFs or hospitals currently game the system by creating specious "losses" in order to be eligible for additional Medicare payments. For example, a seller might claim that a significant portion of the purchase price of a hospital is attributable not to the value of the hospital building and other capital assets, but to the value of the certificate of need, the already assembled hospital staff, or some other intangible asset. By minimizing the value attributable to the capital assets, the seller is able to record a lower sales price, and a greater "loss" on the sale. The seller is then entitled to partial reimbursement for the loss from Medicare. This existing loophole is especially problematic in the case of hospitals paid under PPS for capital because the prospective capital payments to the new owner are unaffected by the low valuation of the hospital (prior to PPS, the new owner would be somewhat disadvantaged by the gaming because their cost-based capital payments would have been lower because of the low sales price). Further, this proposal would eliminate the need for any payment adjustments for gains or losses.

Bankruptcy Provisions—These proposals would protect the public's interests in bankruptcy situations. A provider would still be liable to refund overpayments and pay penalties and fines even if it filed for bankruptcy. Quality of care penalties could be imposed and collected, and Medicare suspensions and exclusions (including educational loan defaults) would still be in force even if a provider files for bankruptcy. Bankruptcy courts would not be able to re-adjudicate our coverage or payment decisions.

Clarify the Definition of Skilled Service for the Purposes of Home Health Eligibility—Venipuncture, which currently qualifies as skilled nursing care and therefore meets the eligibility criterion for intermittent skilled nursing services under the home health benefit, would be excluded. Under current law, if the other criteria are met (homebound, etc.), then a beneficiary who only requires venipuncture for the purpose of obtaining a blood sample as his/her qualifying skilled need would be entitled to all of the other covered home health services including home health aide services.

Hospice Benefit Modifications—This proposal would revise Medicare hospice coverage and payment policies in certain cases. First, after the two initial 90-day periods, this proposal would replace the current unlimited fourth hospice benefit period with an unlimited number of thirty-day periods. This change would help HCFA ensure that the hospice benefit is used for those beneficiaries with a terminal illness, but it would not end hospice care for those fortunate to survive longer than expected. Thirty-day re-certifications would, in fact, help ensure that only terminally ill patients continue to receive hospice care. Second, as the President's FY98 budget bill proposed for home health, this proposal would link payment for hospice services provided in the home to the geographic location of the site where the service was furnished. Third, this proposal would also limit beneficiary liability under hospice care. Currently, the major cause for denial of hospice claims is the fact that the beneficiary was not terminally ill within the meaning of the law (i.e., did not have a prognosis of six months or less of life expectancy at the time the services were rendered). If a hospice claim is denied because the patient was not terminally ill, the patient's liability for payment would be waived and the hospice would be liable for the overpayment unless it could prove that it did not know or have reason to know the claim would be disallowed. The standard of proof would be high since both the law and HCFA instructions are explicit as to the requirement and there are well established protocols for documentation of medical prognosis. Fourth, this proposal would create a new civil money penalty for physicians who certify that an ineligible individual meets Medicare requirements for hospice services eligibility, while knowing that the individual does not meet the requirements.

Rural Health Clinic (RHC) Benefit Reforms—Recognizing the importance of the rural health clinics, reforms are needed to strengthen Medicare policy and better target assistance. It should be emphasized that the inclusion of RHC proposals in the Fraud and Abuse Prevention bill is not meant to imply that we believe these providers are engaged in fraudulent or abusive activities. We do believe, however, that the RHC program could be better targeted to serve truly under-served rural areas, and as such, we have included several proposals to address this issue. These proposals would hold provider-based RHCs to the same payment limits as independent RHCs. The Secretary would also develop a prospective payment system for RHCs no later than December 31, 2000. Under such a system, beneficiary cost sharing would be based on 20 percent of the PPS amount. Prior to the development of a PPS system, beneficiary cost sharing would not be allowed to exceed 20 percent of Medicare's payment limit. The proposal would also include provisions to better target the placement of RHCs in under-served areas and still provide access to clinic services.

Clarify the Partial Hospitalization Benefit—A partial hospitalization program uses a multi-disciplinary team to provide coordinated services within an individualized treatment plan to severely mentally ill individuals; partial hospitalization may occur in lieu of an inpatient psychiatric hospitalization or continued psychiatric hospitalization. These intensive outpatient day programs include individual and group therapy, family counseling, occupational and activity therapy, diagnostic services, and drugs that cannot be self-administered. These programs are intended for patients who would be likely to be hospitalized without these services.

This proposal would establish Medicare coverage requirements and limitations to minimize program abuse, and would also preclude providers from furnishing partial hospitalization services in an individual's home or in an inpatient or residential setting. It would provide the Secretary broad authority to establish through regulation a prospective payment system for partial hospitalization services that reflects appropriate payment levels for efficient providers of service and payment levels for similar services in other delivery systems. The current cost reimbursement system would stay in place until the Secretary exercises this payment authority. In addition, this proposal would provide authority for the Secretary to establish (through regulation) Medicare participation requirements, such as health and safety requirements and provider eligibility standards for community mental health centers (CMHCs). Additionally, it would provide authority for CMHCs to be surveyed upon request by state agencies to determine compliance with Federal requirements or investigate complaints. It would also prohibit Medicare-only CMHCs. Finally, the bill includes a provision (which parallels the authority created in HIPAA for false certification of home health services) to penalize physicians for inappropriate admissions to partial hospitalization programs; this provision would create a strong incentive for physicians to certify need for partial hospitalization services only for those individuals who meet Medicare requirements.

Future Challenges

Health care delivery systems, like every other aspect of society, evolve over time. The current trend toward managed care as an alternative to the traditional fee-for-service system is a phenomenon which promises to change the face of the health care environment. This is because the type of integrated health care network that managed care provides can be a boon—or a bane—to elderly Medicare and Medicaid beneficiaries. Currently, we have only 12% of our beneficiaries in managed care, but in the future we will need to take a fresh look at our strategy to fight fraud and abuse, because the incentives are different in this type of delivery system. The emphasis on cost-effectiveness prevalent in managed health care delivery systems ensures fiscal soundness and value for the customer, but in some instances, unethical plans and providers may discourage or withhold needed care from beneficiaries.

In the same way, the growth spurt we are witnessing in the home health care industry indicates that as innovative new health care arrangements flourish, so will new opportunities for fraud and abuse. Growing numbers of the elderly, and especially of dual eligibles, also means increasing opportunities for those who seek to defraud Medicare and Medicaid patients, providers, and health plans. In home health settings, the physical isolation of the beneficiary is often an open invitation to unethical providers seeking ways to provide care based on financial incentives, rather than care that is actually needed. Not surprisingly, this problem also exists in nursing homes. The vulnerability of home health and nursing home patients suggests that very ill or elderly patients may be targeted because they may not be able to monitor their own bills for fraudulent charges. There is evidence that wherever there are concentrations of the frail elderly, there are providers seeking to provide unnecessary services.

Another area in which the elderly may be especially vulnerable is the services provided to beneficiaries with no roots in the community, such as recent immigrants or "snowbirds" who may be unable to ascertain the qualifications or credibility of the provider or supplier. Particularly in areas with high concentrations of elderly retirees from other States, profiteers can re-locate from city to city, often operating under aliases or fraudulent identification numbers. With the authority to collect Social Security numbers, we would be able to substantially reduce this threat.

Health care mega-corporations also pose challenges for fraud detection and prevention. New mergers and acquisitions are resulting in ever-larger health care corporations, which will be more difficult to monitor for fraud and abuse. On the other end of the spectrum, small walk-in "urgent care" facilities that are proliferating nationwide are difficult to monitor and also offer opportunities for fraud and waste. The challenge for HCFA and the Medicare program will be to understand the relationships between health care entities in order to understand the potential for kickbacks and other illegal relationships. When business relationships become complex and convoluted, they are hard to track; more time is needed to identify and confirm relationships and billing abuses.

Finally, mental health benefits and their potential misuse are a particular area of concern in fraud and waste detection. There have been numerous cases of mental health benefits ordered for individuals who are unable to benefit from them, or conversely, necessary mental health benefits are often being prescribed but not adequately provided. We need to be a step ahead of corrupt providers and suppliers who seek to defraud Medicare and Medicaid's allocated funds, which are essentially investments by taxpayers and which must be safeguarded for future generations.

Conclusion

The implementation of HIPAA has given us powerful weapons against waste, fraud, and abuse. The work of this Committee and other Members of Congress on HIPAA has been vital to this important legislation, which will increase our ability to protect the integrity of the Medicare program, and to safeguard the interests of our beneficiaries. Most importantly, the lessons and experience gained from our efforts in the past few years will guide us as we put our new legislative and administrative tools to use. By effectively utilizing the solid partnerships between State and Federal agencies, the public, and private health care organizations, we will preserve Medicare and Medicaid for future generations.

2. Mobility, Transportation, and Housing

National Aging Information Center, Administration on Aging
Limitations in Activities of Daily Living Among the Elderly: Data Analyses from the 1989 National Long-Term Care Survey (1996)
<http://www.aoa.gov/aoa/stats/adllimits/httoc.htm>

Introduction

The tables presented in this report are based on the 1989 National Long-Term Care Survey (NLTCS), a national sample of Medicare-enrolled persons 65 years of age and older who were asked to report on any chronic disabilities lasting 3 months or longer. A disability was defined as the inability to perform, or to perform without assistance, an Activity of Daily Living (ADL) or an Instrumental Activity of Daily Living (IADL). ADLs included eating, getting in and out of bed, getting around inside, dressing, bathing and using the toilet. IADLs included the ability to do heavy housework, laundry, meal preparation, grocery shopping, getting around outside, getting to places outside of walking distance, money management, using the telephone, and taking medications.

The 1989 NLTCS collected data on elderly persons who were functionally impaired or institutionalized and had received a detailed community resident survey in 1982 or 1984, as well as persons who had passed their 65th birthday since the 1984 NLTCS survey. Using a complex sample design of Medicare recipients, elderly from the 1982 and 1984 surveys were selected to provide national prevalence estimates of disability and institutionalization rates. Approximately 22,150 elders were screened in order to identify eligible community residents or institutional residents. Nearly 6,100 people met selection criteria and were chosen for a detailed interview.

* * *

Highlights

- Overall, nearly 84 percent of persons 65 years of age or older had no IADL or ADL limitations lasting 3 months or longer. Even among the oldest category, persons 85 or older, the majority (51 percent) reported they had neither ADL nor IADL limitations, though almost one-half (48.7 percent) had at least one limitation and more than one-third (38.1 percent) had both.
- Men were more likely (88 percent) than women (81 percent) to have neither an IADL nor an ADL limitation.
- Nearly 89 percent of persons 65 years of age and older who lived in the community had no ADL limitations lasting 6 months or longer. In the 65 to 74 age category, 93.8 percent had no ADL limitations.
- By contrast, 97 percent of institutional residents had ADL limitations lasting 6 months or longer, reflecting the admission policies of most institutions, i.e., that only persons with chronic ADL limitations are eligible for admission.
- Among community residents, 6.7 percent of those aged 65 and over had 1 to 2 ADL limitations, and 6.1 percent had 3 to 6 limitations lasting 3 months or longer. At ages 85 and over, 18.4 percent had 1 to 2 and 22 percent had 3 to 6 ADL limitations. In contrast, over 81 percent of those living in institutions over the age of 65 had 3 to 6 ADL limitations.
- The most frequently reported ADL limitations, lasting 3 months or longer, for community residents aged 65+ were bathing (9.4 percent); getting around inside (8.8 percent); and getting in and out of a bed or chair (5.9 percent). Women reported more ADL limitations than men in every age group and ADL category, with their distributions most like men for dressing and eating and least alike for using the bathroom or toilet and getting around inside.
- The most frequently reported ADL limitations, lasting 3 months or longer, among institutional residents aged 65 years or older were bathing (95.6 percent); getting around inside (81.8 percent); and getting in and out of a bed or

chair (77.9 percent). There is a relatively small difference across age categories in the distribution by ADL limitations for those in institutions.
- While the percentage with ADL limitations is far higher among institutional residents, the rank order of ADL limitations is the same for both community and institutional residents.

NLTCS findings and comparable numbers published by the U.S. Census Bureau are similar. Data for the Bureau's Special Tabulations on Aging show that in 1990, 88.1 percent of noninstitutionalized people nationwide aged 65 and over had no ADL limitation lasting 6 months or longer. In the age groups 65 to 74, 75 to 84, and 85+, the percentages were 91.6, 85.3, and 72.1 percent, respectively. Estimates from the NLTCS of elderly community residents with no ADL limitations lasting 6 months or longer . . . are several percentage points higher in each age category (91.3 percent community residents, overall; 94.4 percent at ages 65 to 74; 88.2 percent at ages 75 to 84; and 72.7 percent at ages 85+).

U.S. Department of Transportation
Improving Transportation for a Maturing Society (January 1997)
<http://www.volpe.dot.gov/opsad/mature.html>

Background

The older adult population (defined here as those over 65) increased in the United States eleven-fold during this century compared to a threefold increase for those under 65. We are all aware that Americans are living longer and many of us can look forward to an extended period of health and activity beyond age 80. The older adult group, which numbered 33.5 million in 1995, or 12.8 percent of the population, will grow to 36.2 million by 2005. By the year 2020 it will be 53.2 million, or 16.5 percent of the population. This population aging will impact all aspects of our society and represents a unique challenge to the community of transportation officials. The actions we can take now to prepare for this change will have a profound effect on the lives of future older Americans.

The Department of Transportation (DOT) has for years been extensively engaged in work to support the safety and mobility needs of older adults. The National Highway Traffic Safety Administration (NHTSA) has had an older driver program since 1988. The Federal Highway Administration (FHWA) embarked on a major program in 1989 for improving highway travel for an aging population. Federal Transit Administration (FTA) grant programs for older adults and persons with disabilities for rural transportation, and for paratransit, all provide benefits to older adults. . . .

In December 1995, Secretary Peña directed the Department to develop a long range overview, and draw up a preliminary, proactive strategy to determine the actions needed to accommodate the growing cohort of older adults who will be transportation providers and consumers in the 21st century. This overview was to encompass the perspective of older adults in all modes, operating commercially and privately. A full report on the issues analyzed, and some of the recommendations of the five expert panels that were convened follows. Specific recommendations, relative priorities, and budget estimates that would be part of a definitive long term strategic plan are the next step. The following elaborates on issues of safety and mobility, and then describes a number of components that would be integral to formulating such a plan.

Safety

The aging process affects individuals in many ways, resulting in a broad range of capabilities and extensive differences among older adults. The increased incidence of disease and decline in capabilities, that are part of the normal aging process, gradually impair the cognitive, sensory, or psychomotor capabilities needed for the operation of all transportation vehicles. Some diseases, such as strokes, cause sudden impairments. Generally, however, there is a slow decline of capabilities, at rates that vary widely among individuals. Most people, as their capacities diminish, withdraw gradually and responsibly from operating vehicles. Consequently, there is not at present a sufficient number of crashes associated with older users and operators to define a serious safety problem, although the changing demographics could lead to serious problems in the decades ahead.

Automobile Drivers—The perception of an older driver safety problem comes about when the crash and fatality rates per mile driven are examined. The fatality rate per 100 million vehicle miles traveled stays reasonably level for drivers up to age 75, and then begins to rise, climbing steeply for persons over 80. The much higher fatality rate for those over 80 is partly attributable to their greater fragility, compared with younger persons.

By 2020 there will be an additional 20 million more older adults in the population. Of particular concern are those aged 75 and above, and applying today's fatality rates to that group indicates that for them, traffic deaths could increase 45 percent (and possibly higher based on other trends), unless the efforts of the safety community can dramatically lower their crash rate or increase their crash protection.

Pedestrians—The safety of older pedestrians presents a significant challenge to the Department. Pedestrians aged 70 and over represented almost 9 percent of the population, but accounted for 19 percent of all pedestrian fatalities in 1994. The fatality rate for this group was higher than for any other age group—4.36 per 100,000 (vs. 2.1 for the overall population).

Commercial Operators—Older operators of trucks, buses, general aviation airplanes or ships do not appear to present a significant safety problem at this time. Typically, they maintain their performance levels by using their experience, automation of some activities, streamlining of tasks, and accommodation. The vast majority of older commercial operators retire responsibly, before medical conditions or diminishing capacities become an issue.

Safe Mobility, For Life

One vibrant force in this country is its high degree of personal mobility. Most of us are conditioned to go where we please, how we please, on our own schedule.

This is part and parcel of the quality of American life. We now have more cars than licensed drivers, more than 11.4 million documented water craft, and 170,000 airplanes, all for personal mobility (necessity or recreation) in one form or another. Except for persons living in our largest cities, and those with low incomes, the primary constraint on full mobility in the personal lives of most Americans comes with the erosion of the capacities necessary for the safe operation of a vehicle. There comes a time for most older adults when a difficult adjustment must be made, to find alternative means to get to such necessary destinations as grocery stores, medical appointments, places of worship, family, and social engagements. If safe, affordable mobility alternatives are not available, as can often be the case for those who retire to or live in rural areas or the outlying suburbs, the quality of life is clearly diminished.

It is in the national interest to keep people operating their personal vehicles as late in years as possible for quality of life reasons; yet we do not want that operation to unnecessarily endanger the individual or the public. It is also in the public interest to maintain the productivity and value added to our national economy of those older adults who operate vehicles commercially, as long as it is safe, yet we must recognize that more stringent screening and evaluating measures have been required to account for the higher public risks presented by those operating commercial vehicles.

These three policy objectives: safety, individual personal mobility, and facilitating the eventual transition to mobility alternatives define a strategic planning goal for the Nation's transportation system, Safe Mobility, For Life. This would be achieved through new extensions of the department's research, and improved coordination of funds and programs already available at the state and community level. The following precepts would characterize this goal:

1. keep people operating cars as late in life as possible, as long as they can do so safely;
2. promote technology and training that support those with functional or cognitive deficits so they can continue to operate vehicles safely;
3. improve screening and evaluation techniques to detect when people should no longer be operating;
4. bring new emphasis to the provision of non-driving alternatives for older adult transportation needs; and
5. educate the public on how to maintain safety and what to prepare for in older age.

A proposed series of Departmental initiatives that could contribute to this goal are outlined below. They must be added to a selected set of ongoing programs, that should continue to receive enhanced priority.

Recommended New Initiatives

The following initiatives are needed to assure that the whole spectrum of concerns for older adults are comprehensively addressed.

Added Emphasis on Mobility Alternatives for Older Adults—Mobility for older adults should be integrated into planning at all levels: individual, community, state and Federal. At the community level, metropolitan planning organizations (MPO) and state planning agencies should consider the special needs of older adults. The following actions are proposed:

- Inventory best planning practices to assure mobility alternatives for older adults.
- Evaluate the most effective mobility services and systems, and provide the means to stimulate their replication.
- Better coordinate Departmental and other Federal efforts by upgrading the DOT/HHS Coordinating Council on Human Services Transportation.
- Increase the focus of the FTA Technical Assistance program to improve mobility alternatives for older adults.
- Use the ISTEA reauthorization process to assure planning for the mobility of older adults.
- Enlarge powers for DOT and HHS Secretaries to grant waivers and exceptions for funding community providers, where they would lead to more cost effective transportation service and higher system use rates.

Countermeasures for Fragility of Older Adults—Place new emphasis on research to develop countermeasures to compensate for the fragility of older adults, recognizing the growing level of older adult injuries and fatalities expected over the next 25 years.

Develop Medical Practice Parameters and Guidelines—Develop a set of guidelines and training modules for use by physicians and health care professionals as an authoritative source when conducting evaluations required for commercial licensure, as well as personal licenses in instances where medical examinations are required.

Policy Studies—Initiate selected studies to support public policy decisions, covering such areas as Security in Transportation, Linkage of Mobility to Health Care Costs, Influence of Mobility Alternatives on Driver Cessation, and research to improve our understanding of the effects of certain medical conditions, functional disabilities, and behavioral limitations on operator performance and crash involvement.

* * *

Conclusions

Secretary Peña, concerned about the quality of life of the growing older population, initiated a comprehensive, forward looking overview of what improvements must be made to accommodate the changing demographic demands on the Nation's transportation system. These demographics will find us with a large population of older operators, who are more widely dispersed, and more accustomed to full mobility. Safety problems for older adults are anticipated in some areas and warrant continued attention. The effectiveness and productivity of our testing, evaluation and rehabilitation programs need to be improved. Countermeasures need to be developed to deal with the fragility and higher fatality rate of older adults. New forms of mobility alternatives need to be developed and tested. This will be an ongoing process, requiring continuous monitoring and innovative policy making. How the Department meets this challenge can have far ranging impacts on the quality of life for today's older adults and ultimately all of us.

3. Ethical Issues

Bruce A. Green & Nancy Coleman
Ethical Issues in Representing Older Clients: Foreword
62 FORDHAM L. REV. 961, 962-71 (1994)[*]

In recent years, the number of older persons receiving legal services has increased dramatically. This has occurred for at least three reasons. First, the older population has itself increased. Second, there is an ever increasing number of issues confronting older persons which call for the assistance of a lawyer. Third, and perhaps most importantly, legal services are now available more widely to older clients who in the past could not otherwise afford lawyers. This is true notwithstanding that there remains a great unmet need for legal services for older clients.

The expansion of the older client population in recent years has led to the identification of "elder law" as a discrete area of professional practice. Although elder law draws on many other areas of law, and although the particular legal problems confronting older clients generally are not unique to them, the recognition of elder law as an area of practice draws needed attention to the special challenge of adequately and ethically serving the legal needs of the older population. At the same time, a new breed of legal specialist has emerged: the elder law attorney. This is a lawyer who specializes in representing older clients in the range of legal issues they encounter.

* * *

Not only is the range of legal problems affecting older clients vast, but often older clients face multiple legal problems. Older people as a group are the greatest beneficiaries of administrative services and government programs, and often a lawyer's assistance is needed to enable an older client to understand and satisfy the various requirements and regulations governing the services and programs for which she or he may be eligible. A lawyer may also provide important assistance to an older client in planning for the possible problems of failing health and diminishing capacity; by addressing legal, financial, and health care problems in advance, older clients assisted by counsel may avoid having courts and administrative agencies intervene against their will through guardianship or commitment proceedings.

* * *

The recognition of older persons as an identifiable client population, of elder law as a discrete area of practice, and of the elder law attorney as a legal specialist with an identifiable philosophy of practice . . . [has led to] increasing concern about problems in counseling older clients—problems of the kind that lawyers typically think of as involving legal ethics or professional responsibility. These problems raise questions such as: To what extent is it proper to enter into an attorney-client relationship with more than one member of the same family? Who makes decisions in the

---

[*] Copyright © 1994. Reprinted with permission.

course of the attorney-client relationship and how are they to be made? How should clients be counseled in the course of the professional relationship and, in particular, to what extent is it appropriate for the lawyer to interpose his or her own views about what is in the client's best interest? And, when is it appropriate to disclose information learned from the client to someone else?

Lawyers have expressed concern that although these questions may arise in the course of representing virtually any client, they may be particularly vexing in the context of serving older clients.[8] Representing older clients may be different or more difficult for any of several reasons. Older clients may be particularly vulnerable. Because of failing health, they may have difficulty making considered decisions, or may be completely unable to articulate decisions. The matters in which they seek representation typically touch them in the most personal ways. In many cases, these matters may affect the interests of close family members as well.

Consider, for example, the older client[9] . . . who is on the verge of losing her home in litigation but who is confused and unsure about whether she even wants the lawyer's help. Legal Services lawyers say that this is not an unusual scenario. Yet it is a difficult one. A lawyer, respecting the client's autonomy, would feel uncomfortable making the decision for the client whether or not to proceed in litigation. At the same time, however, the client's autonomy might seem like an abstraction not worth preserving at the expense of a roof over her head. A lawyer who could protect the client against losing her home would feel very uncomfortable standing by and doing nothing.

Or consider the type of problem raised . . . [w]hen an older couple comes to the lawyer for help in estate planning or other financial planning: may the lawyer represent both spouses? Although they come to the lawyer's office as a couple, experience tells us that a husband and wife will often have different views about what is

---

[8] Not surprisingly, most of the writings devoted to ethical issues in representing older clients as a definable client group are of recent vintage. *See, e.g.,* Jacqueline Allee, *Representing Older Persons: Ethical Dilemmas,* PROB. & PROP., Jan./Feb. 1988, at 36; Ralph M. Cagle, *The Legal Ethics of Elder Law Practice: 5 Key Issues,* WIS. LAW., Aug. 1991, at 38; Maria M. Das Neves, *The Role of Counsel in Guardianship Proceedings of the Elderly,* 4 GEO. J. LEGAL ETHICS 855 (1991); John E. Donaldson, *The Ethical Considerations of Representing the Elderly,* TR. & EST., July 1991, at 18; Mark Falk, *Ethical Considerations in Representing the Elderly,* 36 S.D. L. REV. 54 (1991); Marshall B. Kapp, *Representing Older Persons: Ethical Challenges,* FLA. B.J., June 1989, at 25; John R. Murphy, *Older Clients of Questionable Competence: Making Accurate Competency Determination Through the Utilization of Medical Professionals,* 4 GEO. J. LEGAL ETHICS 899 (1991); Nancy C. Nawrocki, *Ethical Challenges in Serving the Elderly Client,* MICH. B.J., Jan. 1993, at 24; Sharon R. Rudy, *Practical and Ethical Aspects of Serving Elderly Clients,* 79 ILL. B.J. 410 (1991); Jay J. Sangerman, *Ethical Issues in Elder Law,* N.Y. ST. B.J., Sept./Oct. 1993, at 35; Linda F. Smith, *Representing the Elderly Client and Addressing the Question of Competence,* 14 J. CONTEMP. L. 61 (1988).

[9] *See* Jan E. Rein, *Client's with Destructive and Socially Harmful Choices—What's an Attorney to Do?: Within and Beyond the Competency Construct, in Ethical Issues in Representing Older Clients,* 62 FORDHAM L. REV. 1101 (1994). The basic problem that Professor Rein raises has been considered in the past, yet defies easy solution. As Paul R. Tremblay notes in his article for this Conference, *Impromptu Lawyering and De Facto Guardians, in Ethical Issues in Representing Older Clients,* 62 FORDHAM L. REV. 1429, 1430 n.4 (1994), the hypothetical borrows in part from one he discussed several years earlier in his article, *On Persuasion and Paternalism: Lawyer Decisionmaking and the Questionably Competent Client,* 1987 UTAH L. REV. 515.

important to them. They may even hesitate to be completely open with each other about what they consider important. Can the lawyer represent the husband and wife at the same time, when they may have differing interests or desires? That they come to the lawyer together suggests they approach the matter as a family; it might seem strange to suggest that a husband and wife need separate lawyers, as if they were adversaries in litigation. Yet the tradition of the legal profession is that lawyers must represent individual clients with undivided loyalty; thus, it may seem contrary to this important tradition for lawyers to represent individuals whose interests differ—even if those individuals are husband and wife.

Furthermore, the very philosophy of serving older clients "holistically" may pose additional challenges from the perspective of one's responsibilities as a member of the legal profession. For example, is it appropriate for the lawyer to enlist the assistance of doctors, social workers, or other professionals—and in the process, to disclose confidences of the older client—when it seems to be in the client's interest to do so, but the client seems unwilling or unable to give assent? Would doing so breach the attorney's duty to preserve the client's confidences?

For lawyers seeking guidance about how to proceed in situations like these, the point of departure has generally been the prevailing professional standards. In most states, the governing standards are based on the ABA Model Rules of Professional Conduct,[10] which were adopted in 1983.[11] In other states, including New York, the governing standards are based on the earlier ABA Model Code of Professional Responsibility,[12] which dates from 1969. Not surprisingly, however, both sets of rules provide only limited assistance.

This is not surprising for several reasons. First, the principal purpose of these rules is to serve as disciplinary standards, the violation of which will justify professional sanction. Thus, the rules "state the *minimum* level of conduct" for lawyers. Well-intentioned lawyers, however, are concerned not simply with understanding the *least* that is expected, but also with finding the right thing to do in those areas in which disciplinary rules afford discretion.

Second, the lawyers' codes are of limited utility because of their narrow scope. They are not intended to give complete guidance and, concerning some of the hardest questions of professional responsibility, they do not do so. As explained at the outset of the ABA Model Rules: "The Rules do not . . . exhaust the moral and ethical considerations that should inform a lawyer, for no worthwhile human activity can be

---

[10] California is one exception. California follows its own Rules of Professional Conduct, the first set of which was drafted in 1924. *See* California Rules of Professional Conduct (1992). California courts and ethics committees do, however, frequently turn to the ABA Model Code on questions about which the California Rules are "silent or obscure." *See* CHARLES W. WOLFRAM, MODERN LEGAL ETHICS 64 (1986).

[11] The Model Rules were adopted by the ABA in 1983 and have been amended on several occasions since then. *See* Model Rules of Professional Conduct (1983) [hereinafter Model Rules]; THOMAS M. MORGAN & RONALD D. ROTUNDA, PROFESSIONAL RESPONSIBILITY: PROBLEMS AND MATERIALS 12 (5th ed. 1992).

[12] *See* Model Code of Professional Responsibility (1981) [hereinafter Model Code].

completely defined by legal rules. The Rules simply provide a *framework* for the ethical practice of law."

And, finally, the guidance provided by the Model Code or the Model Rules is incomplete. Even though the legal profession is aware of the increasing diversity of the law, of modes of practice, and of legal needs, its professional standards remain deeply rooted in the nineteenth-century mode of practice out of which they emerged: the representation of sophisticated individuals and businesses, on a retained basis, typically in business transactions or in litigation. The result is that problems facing lawyers for older clients may not be addressed by the professional standards. Or, in the case of generally-worded standards that were drafted primarily with other situations in mind, it may be unclear how they should apply to these situations, or whether their application to any particular situation is in fact appropriate. Thus as [two commentators have noted] . . . "[I]n many areas of legal practice, and in particular those areas that most often affect the older client (such as domestic relations, estate planning, and life and health care planning), the lawyer may . . . act as counselor, intermediary, and fiduciary [rather than as a litigator]. In such roles the lawyer often must function without clear guidance from the profession's ethical standards."[19]

Lawyers have other places to look for guidance beyond the professional standards. These sources of guidance, like the professional standards themselves . . . are also incomplete. For example, many bar associations have committees that advise lawyers how the professional standards apply to their particular problems. These committees typically publish some of their opinions, to provide guidance to other lawyers. But the opinions are few in number and they suffer from many of the same limitations as the rules that they are interpreting.

Judicial decisions may also provide some guidance. But courts are typically more concerned with deciding the legal rights of the parties who appear before them than they are with elaborating upon the professional duties of the lawyers. And, while the American Law Institute is now preparing the first Restatement of the Law Governing Lawyers, the subject of this important contribution will be limited to the law as it applies in, for example, malpractice and disqualification proceedings. The Restatement will not give guidance on "sound professional practice," and although it may to some extent "inform the interpretation of the lawyer codes," that also is not its purpose.

How, then, should lawyers for older clients go about resolving the problems of professional responsibility that the professional standards do not answer clearly, do not answer to their satisfaction, or do not address at all? One possibility is for lawyers to resolve these problems for themselves. Many do. But it is common wisdom that in the area of legal ethics, as in ethics generally, the more viewpoints and

---

[19] Edward D. Spurgeon & Mary Jane Ciccarello, *The Lawyer in Other Fiduciary Roles: Policy and Ethical Considerations*, in *Ethical Issues in Representing Older Clients*, 62 FORDHAM L. REV. 1357 (1994). *Cf.* Stanley Sporkin, *The Need for Separate Codes of Professional Conduct for the Various Specialties*, 7 GEO. J. LEGAL ETHICS 149, 149 (1993) ("The [] existing ethics codes merely espouse certain general principles that apply to all lawyers, such as you don't co-mingle a client's funds with your own. They do not provide enough fact-specific provisions that apply directly to many of the various legal specialties.").

the more discourse we hear, the more likely we are to arrive at satisfactory, balanced answers. Thus, to widen the range of viewpoints, professional associations of lawyers who face common problems sometimes try to provide more considered guidance to their members. The work of [such] groups is an important step toward providing needed guidance to trust-and-estates lawyers. Yet these interpretations of the existing professional codes also have several limitations that naturally would lead the organizations that drafted them to collaborate with others as a further step toward developing the best answers to the ethical problems that their members face.

First, these collective efforts are mainly intended to interpret existing standards, and to do so against the background of existing doctrine or authority. That is because practitioners must adhere to the present standards, even if they require a lawyer to act in ways that seem inappropriate in a situation that was not adequately considered by the drafters of those standards. It is an important function to ask what the professional standards now require. But it is equally important to ask: if a lawyer were not bound by the existing standards, what would be the best thing to do in a given situation? In other words, what should the proper standards be? These are important questions because their answers suggest not only how the existing rules might be interpreted, but also how they ought to be amended.

A second concern about the collective efforts of specialized groups is that, if taken no farther, they may leave the conscientious practitioner more confused than when he or she began. The interpretations proposed by individual organizations are not authoritative. They provide just one more source of guidance—although obviously a very helpful one. These interpretations may be inconsistent with views rendered by others—including other specialized organizations. Imagine, for example, a lawyer whose general practice includes some work for older clients in the estate area. Should the lawyer look for guidance to the work of the ABA Section on Real Property, Probate and Trust Law? To the work of ACTEC, which might take a different approach? To the work of the National Academy of Elder Law Attorneys, which, as an organization committed to a "holistic" philosophy, might take yet another approach?

The existence of different groups with possibly different perspectives on the same set of issues suggests the third concern—that no single group has a sufficiently broad perspective on these professional responsibility issues.

* * *

The fact that individual groups tend to be defined by a similarity of interest or experience among their members would make any one group particularly hesitant to make such a claim. In looking for answers to the hard questions facing lawyers, it is critical to consider the widest variety of perspectives—to seek the views of lawyers who represent older clients, lawyers who practice in other areas, non-lawyer representatives of older persons, academics, health-care professionals, and others with valuable insights.

Questions

1. Do you think the elderly are more susceptible to crime, fraud, and abuse than the general population, or just more often targeted as victims? Does it make a difference in how the public and private sectors address these problems?

2. Is the federal government better able than the states to protect the older population from crime, fraud, and abuse? Why?

3. What is the importance to national, state, and local transportation planning efforts of the housing and mobility patterns of persons fifty-five and older?

4. Should the legal profession develop a separate or supplemental code of ethics for attorneys who practice elder law?

D. The Practice of Elder Law

Bureau of Labor Statistics
1998-99 Occupational Outlook Handbook (1998)
<http://stats.bls.gov/oco/ocos053.htm>

Lawyers. Employment of lawyers grew very rapidly from the early 1970s through the early 1990s, but has started to level off in the last several years. Employment is expected to grow about as fast as the average for all occupations through the year 2006. Continuing demand for lawyers will result from growth in the population and the general level of business activities. Demand will also be spurred by growth of legal action in such areas as health care, intellectual property, international law, *elder law*, sexual harassment, and the environment. The wider availability and affordability of legal clinics and prepaid legal service programs should result in increased use of legal services by middle-income people [emphasis added—Eds.].

Walter T. Burke
The Emergence of Elder Law
8 EXPERIENCE 4-7 (Winter 1998)[*]

While the question, "What is elder law?," has not echoed through the ages, it is a question that has been asked more frequently over the past ten years. As the American population grows older, a number of issues have become more relevant to seniors and their attorneys, leading them to focus on legal problems confronting this group and bringing into being the specialty known as elder law.

Elder law is often confused with Medicaid planning. It is much broader in that it encompasses a number of sub-specialties ranging from long-term care planning to

---

[*] Copyright © 1998 American Bar Association. All rights reserved. Reprinted with permission of the American Bar Association.

traditional trusts and estates. Unlike contracts or criminal law, elder law is not devoted to one substantive area of practice. Now, issues requiring the attention of specialists emerge almost daily as, for example, when elder citizens are victimized by domestic abuse or when legislation shifts the cost of long-term care to the consumer.

From guardianship issues to health care decision-making and from housing options to managed health care, the elder law practitioner must have a firm grasp on a number of areas under the general heading of this emerging specialty. In addition, perhaps most importantly, the lawyer must have compassion and patience.

No Age Limit

When should a client seek advice from an elder law attorney? At age 40? At age 50? At age 65? Or when it becomes necessary to enter a retirement community or be admitted to a nursing home? The answer is that the services of an elder law attorney may become necessary at any age depending upon the services sought. Often clients are in their thirties or forties seeking counsel on how best to help aging parents.

An elder law attorney must be able to assist younger clients in dealing with future costs associated with retirement and health care, since financial planning for one's retirement should begin as soon as one is employed. The government's attempts to shift the cost of long-term health care to the consumer makes this planning even more important.

It has been projected that by the year 2000 there will be 47.2 million people receiving Social Security benefits, an increase from 35.6 million in 1980 and from 3.5 million in 1950. As the pool of retirees grows, private investment becomes an integral part of financial planning. Also, as one advances in age, the investment strategies change. A younger individual currently investing in growth funds may need to switch to more conservative funds as retirement approaches or sometimes senior clients should be advised not to become too conservative, given that their savings may have to meet expenses for a generation or more.

Estate planning is also an integral part of elder law. The attorney practicing in this field must have knowledge of federal and state tax law in assisting clients during will preparation, account titling, designating beneficiaries, as well as estate administration. Elder law attorneys must know when credit shelter trusts and other estate planning vehicles may be appropriate. In addition to traditional trust and estate concerns, elder law attorneys will routinely discuss with clients issues such as advanced directives and durable powers of attorney. While those issues and documents are important to an individual at any age, their relevance and priority are obviously more significant to an elder person than one in his or her thirties . . . .

Housing alternatives for seniors pose their own set of challenges, including congregate housing (adult homes), adult foster homes and adult day care. At one end of the spectrum, assisted living may be appropriate for a senior desiring a residential setting but not needing a medical or skilled nursing facility. At the other end, nursing homes provide intermediate care and skilled nursing for those who need nursing care but not acute care associated with a hospital.

And then there is the issue of financing the decision. Medicare and Medicaid may pay for certain medical services offered by skilled nursing facilities but will not reimburse for most care received in an intermediate care or assisted living facility. Only Medicaid, and not Medicare, will pay for long-term custodial services.

Elder law encompasses more than calculating the mechanics of Medicaid eligibility and often involves administrative proceedings to assure proper benefits. Frequently, the elderly and frail need advice and assistance in this area. The elder law attorney must speak for those unable to speak for themselves . . . .

Enhancing the Quality of Life

Long-term care insurance has been developed to meet some of the costs associated with home care and nursing home care not covered by government programs. Elder law attorneys help clients understand the restrictions and options in their insurance contracts. This is another area of growth and concern for many seniors. Some states, such as New York and Connecticut, for example, also have approved contracts with provisions impacting their residents only, so that if a senior moves to another state, what may have been a good choice in one may become inappropriate in the other.

Elder law attorneys also assist the state and federal government in addressing budgetary issues regarding long-term care costs. They may make suggestions on how health care dollars may be more appropriately spent, or they may be advocates for maintaining or increasing expenditures of health care dollars. The elder law attorney will also assist clients in becoming financially able either independently or through government assistance to help pay for institutional care.

Elder law attorneys may provide counsel to seniors in discrimination actions in employment, health care and housing. In an era of corporate "downsizing" seniors face potential discrimination and loss of job security. The decisions regarding age discrimination have led to increased protection of the employment of older Americans.

With the integration of managed care into the health care market, the elder law attorney must have a grasp on the alphabet soup of managed care and how seniors are affected by the decisions of such organizations. While physicians and health maintenance organizations (HMOs) are competing for consumers, the development of new health care delivery systems from IPAs (Independent Physician Associations) to MSOs (Medical Service Organizations) affect the cost and type of medical care. Because seniors consume a major percentage of health care dollars, elder law attorneys are necessarily concerned with the health care consumer protection movement . . . .

The Supreme Court's recent decision in *Washington v. Glucksberg* (1997) regarding physician-assisted suicide presents elder law attorneys with many unanswered questions. The Court declared that there is no constitutionally protected right to hasten one's death, thus leaving it to the states to permit or prohibit physician-assisted suicide. Presently, only Oregon has a statutory plan for its legalization. The full impact of the Supreme Court decision cannot be ascertained, therefore, until we see how the other state legislatures react.

Currently, people over age 50 control 70% of the total net worth of households in the United States. Further, by the year 2030, people over age 65 will represent 22% of the U.S. population. According to the 1995 Census Bureau, 81% of individuals between ages 65 and 69 own their own homes, as do 80.9% of people between ages 70 and 74, and 74.6% of those over age 75. This amount of wealth and property will be transferred to the next generation in the coming decades. The legal, financial and tax implications of this enormous transfer of wealth to the next generation will severely impact the nation's economy.

Elder law attorneys must be capable of more than drafting trust agreements and testamentary documents. They also must be able to assist clients faced with depression, shock and loneliness, providing them not only with legal support but also empathy and moral support. Because many older clients do not seek legal advice on an ongoing basis, it is often a catastrophic illness or the loss of a spouse that causes a client to meet with an elder law attorney. It is imperative that the elder law attorney not only have the requisite legal knowledge but also the patience, compassion and understanding to help the client through such difficult times . . . .

Amelia E. Pohl
What Is Elder Law Anyway?
19 Nova L. Rev. 459, 459-63 (1995)[*]

Many of us who now consider ourselves "Elder Law" attorneys were practicing elder law long before it had a name. We were a group of attorneys concerned with problems unique to the elderly who worked as their advocates. Through various publications by agencies such as the Center for Social Gerontology, the American Association of Retired Persons, the Center for Public Representation, and the Legal Counsel for the Elderly, we became aware that other attorneys and agencies had similar interests and concerns. Because of the concern for the unique legal problems facing the elderly during the 1970s, the Department of Health, Education and Welfare awarded grant monies to provide direct legal services to the elderly in 1975.

The legal profession's involvement with the elderly began in 1978 when the American Bar Association formed the Commission on Legal Problems of the Elderly ("Commission"). Since 1988, the Commission has published a quarterly newsletter, BIFOCAL, and a bimonthly bulletin to various bar committees on the elderly. Attorney participation in elder law on the national level began with the formation of the National Academy of Elder Law Attorneys ("NAELA"). The initial group of twenty-six founding members decided to form NAELA while they were attending a joint conference on Law and Aging held in Washington, D.C. The term, "Elder Law," was coined by Michael Gilfix, Esquire, one of NAELA's founding members. The NAELA headquarters were established in Tucson, Arizona in 1987. NAELA grew rapidly to 1150 members in forty-eight states and the District of Columbia by 1991.

It is not surprising that the practice of elder law organized on a national level since much of elder law relates to federal programs that benefit the elderly in general, such as the Medicaid program. Many elder law attorneys join NAELA to meet with

---

[*] Copyright © 1995. Reprinted with permission.

other attorneys throughout the United States at the various symposia and institutes offered by NAELA, to exchange information and to determine how government benefit programs are administered in different states of the union . . . .

Other benefits were realized by elder law attorneys through their association with NAELA. By 1992, the express mission of NAELA was to "ensure delivery of quality legal services for the elderly and to advocate for their rights." Its stated purpose was to "provide information, education, networking, and assistance to attorneys, Bar organizations, and other individuals or groups advising elderly clients and their families." NAELA also seeks to promote "technical expertise and ethical awareness among attorneys, Bar organizations . . . [and t]o develop awareness of the issues surrounding legal services for the elderly."

The prominence of NAELA has helped to establish and to define the practice of elder law. At the first NAELA annual institute, held in November 1991 in San Antonio, Texas, a survey was taken of the attorneys attending the institute to determine how those attorneys defined elder law. NAELA found the three major categories to be:

1) Estate planning and administration, including tax questions;
2) Disability, Medicaid, and other long-term care issues; and
3) Guardianship, conservatorship, and commitment matters, including fiduciary administration. Other areas cited by NAELA included retirement benefits, Medicare, disability benefits, litigation in the areas of elder abuse, and elder fraud.

. . . One cannot practice elder law for any period of time without understanding that the needs of the clients extend beyond their legal problems. The clients may be frail or ill and require home health care or placement in an institutional facility. The clients may be well but fearful that future illness may deplete financial resources, and thus may need to consider a long-term care insurance policy. If a client is a caretaker and is overwhelmed with the demands of caring for a person who is suffering from some form of dementia, the client may need other support services offered by various religious organizations or nonprofit organizations, such as the Alzheimer's Association. Peter J. Strauss, author of many elder law publications, notes in his book, AGING AND THE LAW, that meeting the needs of the client(s) depends on moving beyond conventional legal work to offering practical assistance. Quite often, the attorney is the right person to provide information about home care, nursing homes, special geriatric health programs, adult day care, and respite care; handling even a few elder-law cases quickly leads to an accumulation of such information and contacts with the right people . . . .

There is no elder law certification in the State of Florida. However, the National Academy of Elder Law Foundation ("NAELF"), an organization created by the Board of Directors of NAELA, is, for the first time, offering, board certification upon meeting of the requirements set by NAELF. One of these requirements is successful completion of an examination covering the following topics:

1) Health and Personal Care Planning (including advance medical directives and living wills);
2) Pre-Mortem Legal Planning (wills and trusts);
3) Fiduciary Representation (including guardianship, trustees and personal representatives);
4) Legal Capacity Counseling (advising how capacity is determined and the level of capacity required for various legal activities);
5) Individual Representation (of those who are or who may be the subject of guardianship or conservatorship procedures);
6) Public Benefits Advice (including Medicaid, Medicare, social security, and veterans' benefits);
7) Advice on Insurance (including health, life, long-term disability, and burial/funeral policies);
8) Resident Rights Advocacy (including advising patients of their rights and remedies in matters such as admission, transfer, discharge policies, and quality of care);
9) Housing Counseling (reviewing options and financing of options such as mortgage alternatives, life care contracts, and home equity conversion);
10) Employment and Retirement Advice (pensions, retiree health benefits, and unemployment benefits);
11) Income, Estate, and Gift Tax Advice;
12) Counseling about Tort Claims Against Nursing Homes;
13) Age and/or Disability Discrimination Counseling (including employment and housing, and Americans with Disabilities Act); and
14) Litigation and Administrative Advocacy (including will contests, contested capacity issues, and elder abuse).

Then what is elder law? Is it all of the fourteen areas identified above? Or is it better understood as described in NAELA's brochure, *Elder Law: A Legal Practice Coming of Age*? Rather than being defined by technical distinctions, the brochure defines elder law by the client to be served . . . .

Questions

1. What areas of pre-law education would best serve someone interested in practicing elder law?

2. In view of population demographics and the market outlook of practitioners of elder law, should law schools expand their elder law curricula and encourage interdisciplinary education among law students who anticipate a career in this area?

CHAPTER 2

Special Ethical Problems When Representing the Elderly

A. Joint or Multiple Representation 53
B The Disabled Client.. 76

    Conduct of one's law practice in accordance with the rules of professional ethics is a burden borne by all lawyers regardless of their clientele. This chapter will, therefore. emphasize the particular problems which arise perhaps more frequently when working with the elderly both because of age-related impairments and family dynamics related to the transfer of wealth from one generation to the next.

    These materials are hardly exhaustive nor do they provide definitive answers to the elder law practitioner's most intractable problems. Many of the questions presented would be answered differently, yet fairly, by different lawyers. The following materials are offered for your consideration, in the hope that you will bring your values and life experience to bear on the application of the rules of our profession to your professional life.

A. Joint or Multiple Representation

    Although joint representation is not recommended, it is practiced routinely. The literature on legal ethics is replete with cautionary tales of parties who seemed to have the same interests at the beginning of the representation, but who, when their interests diverged, left the lawyer stranded. The following materials will focus on the common situations which arise when representing senior citizens whose spouses, children, and caregivers get involved.

1. The Spouse

Molly M. Wood
Who's the Client?: Competency and the Lawyer-Client Relationship
<http://www.ink.org/public/keln/ethicsmmw.html>*

I. When Someone Other Than The Senior Citizen Requests Representation

   A. The Spouse

It is common for spouses, particularly in long-lasting marriages, to become accustomed to acting for one another. It comes as a shock, therefore, when one of the marriage partners encounters barriers when attempting to handle legal matters for the other. Although it is important to handle the contacting spouse diplomatically, it is incumbent upon intake personnel and the responsible attorney to deal directly with the person whose legal problem is prompting the contact if at all possible.

   1. Joint Representation (*See*, [Model] Rules [of Professional Conduct] 1.7 *Conflict of Interest*, & 2.2 *Intermediary*)

Joint representation is potentially at odds with the lawyer's duty of loyalty to a client, but a client may consent to representation notwithstanding a conflict. Subparts (a)(1) and (b)(1) of Model Rule 1.7 contemplate a two-part test: The lawyer must reasonably believe that the client will not be adversely affected, and the client must consent after consultation. Thus, the lawyer must disclose that multiple representation is sought and must disclose the implications of common representation, including its risks and advantages. When more than one client is involved, the question of conflict must be resolved as to each client. Moreover, there may be circumstances where it is impossible to make the disclosure necessary to obtain consent. (*See Comment* to Model Rule 1.7).

The key issue in joint representation with respect to married people is the likelihood that effective representation of one spouse precludes effective representation of the other. Ideally, both marriage partners should have individual representation. As noted by example earlier, however, in marriages of long-standing the potential conflict of interest is more theoretical than real. In the estate planning context, for example, marriage partners who have never been married to another, share the same children, own all their property jointly, and want their children to share equally in their property after the death of the survivor must be counseled that that survivor could alter his or her disposition of the jointly held property at will. It would be common practice to counsel both parties regardless of the potential conflict after consultation.

Division of Assets counseling also implicates a potential conflict of interest which may be academic. The Medicaid applicant, that is, the institutionalized spouse, is likely to be incompetent and unable to consent to joint representation. When the

---

* Copyright © 1996. Reprinted with permission.

community spouse is seeking protection against impoverishment and is pursuing Medicaid assistance for the institutionalized spouse, however, it is proper to characterize the community spouse as the client. The institutionalized spouse is unrepresented, but is unlikely to be adversely affected by the lawyer's representation of his or her spouse. Moreover, the Division of Assets process is not typically adversarial. If it becomes so, the lawyer may be forced to withdraw or take other remedial action.

    2. Scope of Representation (*See* Rules 1.2 *Scope of Representation* & 2.1 *Advisor*)

If a lawyer perceives that the client expects assistance that would be improper or illegal for the lawyer to provide, the lawyer has duty to clarify the limitations on the scope of the lawyer's conduct. Such a duty to inform the client protects the client and ensures that the client's decisions regarding whether and how to proceed are knowledgeable.

"A lawyer may limit the objectives of the representation if the client consents after consultation." Rule 1.2(c). The lawyer should outline the scope of representation on the representation agreement or employment contract in as much detail as practicable, and provide a signed copy to the client.

Questions

1. Besides the problem areas suggested above, what other types of legal issues would be particularly sensitive to conflicts arising out of joint representation?

2. Wouldn't you be afraid of losing both clients if you suggested that one of the marriage partners should get separate counsel? How could you avoid this problem?

2. Adult Children

Walter T. Burke
Avoiding Pitfalls When Counseling the Elderly
THE COMPLEAT LAWYER—GEN. PRAC., SOLO, AND SMALL FIRM SECTION,
AMERICAN BAR ASSOCIATION (Spring 1998)
<http://www.abanet.org/genpractice/lawyer/complete/sp98burke.html>[*]

Before you begin to analyze the legal issues surrounding your client, you must make a basic decision: who is the client? Is it the adult child who calls you and asks you to prepare mom's will? Or is the mom your client? Determining who your client is can present an ethical dilemma that you should confront as early as possible when establishing the attorney-client relationship.

---

[*] Copyright © American Bar Association. All rights reserved. Reprinted with permission.

Who Is Your Client?

For instance, the adult child calls you to schedule an initial consultation with his parent to discuss the parent's will. At the initial meeting, the adult child comes with his parent and expects to be included in your discussion regarding the parent's wishes regarding her will. What do you do? Do you request time alone to speak with the parent, or do you simply permit the adult child to remain in the meeting?

Ethically, you should consider the facts and circumstances of the elderly individual and her family situation. In some situations, the elderly individual has discussed her plan with the adult child and is comfortable discussing her testamentary plan in front of the child. In other situations, the adult child may be in conflict with other siblings and is attempting to influence or control the disposition of his parent's estate. It is important to remember your state's ethical rules regarding the protection of the attorney-client privilege when determining who is your client.

In order to best protect a prospective or current elderly client from undue influence by family members or friends, you may choose to contact and communicate directly with the client alone and send drafts of any prepared legal documents to the client so that he or she may review and thoughtfully consider its contents outside the presence of anyone who may be exerting influence. Taking the time to decide who is your client at the beginning of the relationship may halt a later problem should the question arise as to whom you represent and with whom the attorney-client privilege attaches.

Questions

1. If the client expresses the desire to have the adult children or others present in the interview, does that absolve the lawyer of the duty of loyalty to the client?

2. Can you discuss the client's legal matters with the others outside the presence of the client?

Molly M. Wood
Who's the Client?: Competency and the Lawyer-Client Relationship
<http://www.ink.org/public/keln/ethicsmmw.html>[*]

I. When Someone Other Than The Senior Citizen Requests Representation

* * *

B. Adult Children & Other Relatives

Generally, the child or other relation must have a Durable Power of Attorney which is broad enough to encompass the scope of the representation sought. A child who has been appointed Guardian/Conservator, either limited or otherwise, would

---

[*] Copyright © 1996. Reprinted with permission.

have the authority to engage a lawyer on behalf of the Ward/Conservatee. Particularly in the case of married seniors who have adult children from prior marriages, children and other relatives can have subtle (or not so subtle) conflicts of interest with respect to the proposed client. Absent a surrogate decisionmaker or the client's informed consent, it is improper for the lawyer to discuss the legal affairs of a client or proposed client with anyone other than the client.

* * *

III. Confidentiality

    A.   The Attorney-Client Privilege

Unlike Rule 1.6, the Attorney-Client Privilege is an evidentiary rule which prevents the client or the lawyer from being compelled to disclose communications between lawyer and client in the course of their professional relationship. The client should be cautioned against conduct which impliedly waives the privilege, however, such as allowing others to participate in attorney-client meetings.

    B.   Rule 1.6: Confidentiality of Information

Rule 1.6 encompasses the duty of loyalty to the client and serves to protect the client's privacy interests. The obligation extends to all information about a client acquired in the course of the representation, regardless of whether disclosure would be embarrassing or detrimental. Thus, the obligation of confidentiality encompasses more than the attorney-client privilege since it can include the client's confidences and secrets even if the same information may be discoverable from other sources. The obligations of loyalty and confidentiality continue after the agency relationship has been concluded. (*See also* Rules 1.8 *Conflict of Interest: Prohibited Transactions,* and 1.9 *Conflict of Interest: Former Client.*)

        1.   Authorized Disclosures

An exception to confidentiality applies to disclosures to which the client has given informed consent. Rule 1.6(a) also recognizes that client consent may be implied as well as express as to disclosures necessary to effect the representation. A common application of this rule is the lawyer who seeks guidance from an appropriate diagnostician about a disabled client's condition. In such a case, the lawyer is disclosing confidential information for the client's own benefit and may do so even without the client's consent. (*See* Rule 1.14 *Client under a Disability.*)

Walter T. Burke
Avoiding Pitfalls When Counseling the Elderly
THE COMPLEAT LAWYER—GEN. PRAC., SOLO, AND SMALL FIRM SECTION
AMERICAN BAR ASSOCIATION (Spring 1998)
<http://www.abanet.org:80/genpractice/lawyer/complete/sp98burke.html>[*]

Defensive Will and Trust Drafting

Will drafting has been the traditional role for lawyers counseling elderly clients. Since people over the age of 50 presently control 70 percent of the total net worth in the United States, defensive estate planning may be necessary to protect a client's financial interests. The probability of a will contest should be considered before the lawyer begins to draft the client's will. A great percentage of will contests are merely for nuisance value, so it is best to confront the possibility of such a contest before drafting the will. Ask the following questions:

- Who made the initial contact, scheduled the appointment, or brought the client to your office?
- Does the proposed testamentary plan favor or disinherit one or more relatives?
- What are the client's reasons for favoring or disinheriting relatives?
- Who—the client or someone else—is promoting favoritism or disinheritance?
- Did the client's prior will, if any, follow a similar pattern of favoritism or disinheritance?

If you find that someone is attempting to influence your client, you should take proactive steps to ensure that the client's testamentary plan is of his own free volition. In order to further insulate against will contests, the lawyer drafting a will should consider using a standard procedure or checklist during the will execution ceremony. . . . In the event that the will is contested, evidence establishing that the lawyer always uses the same procedure in executing wills may be effectively used to defeat a will contest.

Other methods to combat a claim of incapacity include having the client write, in her own handwriting, a letter expressing her testamentary plan; routinely drafting notes to the file describing the client's mental capacity at meetings and during phone conversations; and audiotaping or videotaping the will execution ceremony.

What if your client wants to nominate you to act as executor of her will or wishes to leave you a bequest in her will. Depending on the state in which you practice, such a nomination or bequest may be forbidden either by statute or case law. In New York, case law dictates that where a lawyer or draftsperson is nominated as executor, he must disclose, in writing, to the client that he will be entitled to statutory commissions.

Where the client wishes to leave a bequest to a lawyer, it is best that the lawyer inform the client that another lawyer, not within the same firm, should prepare the will. Doing so will negate any inference of impropriety. In some states, the courts will disregard a gift to the lawyer unless the lawyer is related to the testator.

---

[*] Copyright © American Bar Association. All rights reserved. Reprinted with permission.

Questions

1. Would it be proper for you to draft a testamentary will for your grandparents? What ethics rules, court rules, or state laws are implicated?

2. What standard procedures, beyond the "testamentary formalities," would you implement to protect your client's estate from a will contest?

3. Caregivers and Other Unrelated Third Parties

Molly M. Wood
Who's the Client?: Competency and the Lawyer-Client Relationship
<http://www.ink.org/public/keln/ethicsmmw.html>*

I. When Someone Other Than The Senior Citizen Requests Representation

* * *

C. Social Workers, Health Care Professionals, and Others

Although the nature of our work implicates collaboration with social workers, health care professionals, and service organizations devoted to meeting the needs of senior citizens, these professionals do not have the authority to enter into the attorney-client relationship or seek any but the most general legal advice on behalf of senior citizens. They should be encouraged to refer potential clients to us directly.

In re Brantley
920 P.2d 433 (Kan. 1996)

* * *

FINDINGS OF FACT

1. Respondent, Keen K. Brantley, is a licensed Kansas attorney who has engaged in the general practice of law in Scott City, Kansas, since 1970. . . .

2. The complainant is Carla Hendrix, granddaughter of Mary Storm, a ninety-one year old resident of Anchorage, Alaska, who formerly resided in Scott City, Kansas. Following the death of her personal attorney, Charles Fleming, Mary Storm became a client of the Respondent in 1983. During the time in question, Mary Storm had done most of her banking business at the First National Bank of Scott City but had done some business at the Security State Bank in Scott City. At no time has Mary Storm ever been found to be incompetent, incapacitated or disabled by any medical person or court in Kansas or Alaska.

---

* Copyright © 1996. Reprinted with permission.

3. In 1977, Mary Storm's husband, R.E. Pfenninger, died leaving his entire estate to her under a joint and mutual will. The estate was valued at some $77,000.00. Under the terms of the will, any property remaining at Mary Storm's death was to be divided equally between the surviving children of Mr. Pfenninger by a previous marriage and Mary Storm's only child, Wayne Hendrix, by a prior marriage.

4. In 1985, Mary's brother, Leo Scott McCormick, died leaving his entire estate to Mary Storm, the only surviving McCormick sibling. The McCormick estate was valued at approximately $193,000.00. The First National Bank of Scott City was the executor and was represented by Respondent Brantley and his firm.

5. In February 1986, Mary Storm wrote a letter to her son, Wayne Hendrix, and his wife Delores stating, among other things, that her brother's estate would be settled soon and that most of the estate would go to Wayne as she did not need it. She further observed that she and Wayne were the only surviving family members.

6. Following the distribution of the McCormick estate, during the period April 1986, through July 1987, Mary Storm, from time to time, deposited sums of money in a savings account that her son and daughter-in-law had opened at Security State Bank in Scott City, Kansas. Mary Storm wrote seven different checks for deposit to their account over the fifteen month period totalling $191,425.00. Mary Storm's name was not on the Hendrix account, and at no time did Wayne or Delores Hendrix transfer any of Mary Storm's money into their account. During this period of time, Mary Storm, with the assistance of Respondent Brantley, caused Wayne Hendrix's name to be added as a joint tenant to several of her certificates of deposit and parcels of inherited real estate. At no time has Wayne or Delores Hendrix attempted to exercise any right of ownership to the certificates of deposit or the several parcels of real estate or the income therefrom.

* * *

Brantley admitted assisting Mary Storm in placing her three real estate installment contracts in joint tenancy with Wayne, but denied involvement in placing Wayne's name on any of Mary Storm's certificates of deposit as a joint owner.

7. From October 1986, through January 1988, the Hendrixes authorized wire transfers in the total amount of $85,000.00 from their Scott City account to their credit union account in Alaska, where they then resided.

8. In December 1986, Mary Storm fell and fractured her hip, which injury required a period of hospitalization followed by nursing home care. Prior to such injury Mary Storm had lived in her own home, had driven her own car, and had been self-sufficient.

9. Mary Storm continued to reside in a nursing home, and in July 1989, she was visited by her step-son, Ralph Pfenninger, who resided in Oklahoma. During this visit, Mr. Pfenninger states that he was advised by the nursing home administrator that Mary Storm was giving all of her money away and would soon have nothing to live on. As a matter of fact, Mary Storm had more than $100,000.00 in liquid assets and a comfortable income.

10. Ralph Pfenninger also visited with an officer of the Security State Bank of Scott City [Louise Wendler], who advised him that there had been some large transfers of funds from Mary Storm to her son, Wayne Hendrix.

11. Ralph Pfenninger then met with Respondent Brantley and expressed his concerns relative to the feared dissipation of Mary Storm's assets. Respondent Brantley was informed that the Security State Bank of Scott City had indicated a willingness to serve as conservator, and he thereupon conferred with Louise Wendler, a Vice President of Security State Bank, who further confirmed to him confidential information that Wayne and Delores Hendrix had made transfers from their Kansas account to their Alaska account totalling $85,000.00. Ms. Wendler further volunteered that, in her opinion, Mary Storm's deposits into the Hendrixs' account could not possibly be gifts due to their large amount. She admitted, however, that she had never consulted Mary Storm about this assumption.

12. Respondent Brantley never met personally with Mary Storm regarding the voluntary conservatorship but recalls that he talked by telephone with her at the nursing home and inquired if she was aware that Wayne Hendrix was in town withdrawing large amounts from her bank accounts. Understandably, Mary Storm replied that she knew nothing about any recent withdrawals from her accounts. Bank records in evidence reflect that she was correct in her reply.

* * *

13. Without further investigating the reported transfers of Mary Storm's assets, and without further personal conversation with Mary Storm, Respondent Brantley caused voluntary conservatorship proceedings to be prepared and sent the same to the nursing home for Mary Storm's signature with an office employee. The Security State Bank was appointed conservator under the voluntary conservatorship proceeding on July 11, 1989. Respondent Brantley candidly admits that, at this time, he was representing the conservatee, Mary Storm; her step-son, Ralph Pfenninger; and the conservator, Security State Bank, all in the same proceeding.

14. The conservatorship operated without event until September 21, 1989, when Respondent Brantley filed a Petition for Sale of Personal Property at Public Auction. Respondent Brantley prepared such pleadings for his client Security State Bank. The Petition was set for hearing on September 29, 1989, and copy of notice of hearing was reportedly mailed to Mary Storm. On September 22, 1989, Respondent Brantley filed a Petition for Appointment of Guardian ad Litem. The proposed guardian ad litem, William Wright, was not known to Mary Storm. As in the case of the Petition for Sale, Mary Storm was not consulted in connection with the Petition for Appointment of Guardian ad Litem.

15. Prior to the hearing on the Petition to Sell Personal Property and without court authorization or Mary Storm's knowledge, the Security State Bank contacted an auction company in early September and caused Mary Storm's personal property to be boxed and inventoried. Further, auction handbills were caused to be posted in Scott City and advertisements for sale placed in the local newspaper. Without court approval of the sale, the Security State Bank paid the auction company $450.00 out of Mary Storm's conservatorship funds on September 28, 1989, a day before the hearing.

16. The above mentioned Petition for Sale of Personal Property at Public Auction, prepared by Respondent Brantley, contained an allegation, "It is necessary to sell said personal property to pay taxes and expenses of the conservatorship." The alle-

gation, which is untrue, was verified on behalf of the conservator, Security State Bank.

17. Mary Storm's grandson, Richard Hendrix of WaKeeney, Kansas, was alerted by one of Mary Storm's neighbors a week before the proposed auction. He contacted WaKeeney attorney Paul Oller in regard to representing Mary Storm in having the sale halted. Mary Storm subsequently retained Paul Oller to represent her and instructed him to have the sale stopped and the conservatorship terminated.

18. At the September 29, 1989, hearing on Mary Storm's Petition for Termination of Conservatorship, the voluntary conservatorship was terminated and the Petition to Sell Personal Property was denied.

19. Later, on the same day, Respondent Brantley presented to the magistrate judge, ex parte, a Temporary Order restraining the disposition of the estate of the "conservatee" until the "petition" could be heard and further orders issued. No notice was given to Mary Storm or her attorney, Paul Oller. The Temporary Order was filed at 4:20 o'clock p.m. on September 29, 1989.

20. The above noted Temporary Order contained the caption of the previously terminated voluntary conservatorship proceeding. The order contained no explanation or justification for having been filed in a closed case. The Temporary Order was also silent as to the identity of the client being represented by Respondent Brantley in such matter.

21. The Temporary Order stated that there should no further disposition or depletion of the estate of the conservatee at a time when there was no conservatee and no conservatee estate. The Temporary Order prepared by Respondent Brantley further provided that the Temporary Restraining Order would continue in effect until the petition could be heard and further orders of the court issued, all at a time when there was no petition on file. In preparing and filing such order, Respondent Brantley was not following the direction of his purported client Mary Storm, and was acting adversely to her.

22. On October 2, 1989, Respondent Brantley filed an Involuntary Petition for Appointment of Conservator, on which petition he shows himself as attorney for the Petitioner, Ralph Pfenninger. At no time did Respondent consult with his purported client Mary Storm, or obtain her consent to his materially adverse representation of her step-son.

23. The Petition for Involuntary Conservatorship, prepared by Respondent Brantley for his client Ralph Pfenninger, stated that Mary Storm was "completely disoriented as to person, place and time as noted in the letter of Daniel R. Dunn, M.D. marked Exhibit A attached hereto and made a part hereof." In fact, there was no Exhibit A attached to the petition, there was not in existence any letter from Dr. Dunn, Respondent Brantley never contacted Dr. Dunn to request such a letter, and Respondent Brantley candidly admitted that he made up the language supposedly "noted in the letter." At no time during any of the conservatorship proceedings did the Respondent ever meet personally with Mary Storm to determine for himself her state of mind or knowledge of her financial affairs, and his false statements contained in said petition have never been corrected.

CHAPTER 2: SPECIAL ETHICAL PROBLEMS   63

24. On October 3, 1989, Respondent Brantley obtained Preliminary Orders which he had prepared on behalf of his client Ralph Pfenninger. On October 10, 1989, Mary Storm, through her attorney, Paul Oller, filed Answer of Proposed Conservatee, which answer raised multiple objections to Respondent Brantley's continued representation adverse to Mary Storm and listed numerous violations of the Model Rules of Professional Conduct. The answer further requested an accounting of all funds received by and spent by the conservator and requested disqualification of Respondent Brantley and discharge of the court appointed attorney. Respondent Brantley did not file a response or withdraw from the adverse representation.

25. Purportedly at the request of the court appointed attorney for Mary Storm, William Wright, the magistrate judge undertook to interview Mary Storm at the nursing home without any notice to interested parties. Later, he undertook to interview Mary Storm a second time in a Garden City hospital where she was recovering from recent cancer surgery. At the hospital visitation, the magistrate was accompanied by a court reporter. Again, the visitation was without notice to Mary Storm's family or her retained attorney of record. On October 12, 1989, the day following her cancer surgery, the magistrate judge dismissed Mary Storm's granddaughter from the hospital room and proceeded to interrogate Mary Storm. While not within the purview of the panel, the panel is shocked that a magistrate judge would undertake to interrogate an elderly person on the day following major surgery. Mary Storm was recovering from a mastectomy and was not in a position to answer questions about the conservatorship. She did not deny having talked with Paul Oller, but could not say one way or the other. Even in her condition, Mary Storm expressed her opposition to the proposed sale. She also expressed dislike for the Security State Bank officer she believed was responsible for the sale effort.

26. On October 16, 1989, hearing was had before the magistrate judge on Ralph Pfenninger's Petition for Involuntary Conservatorship and Mary Storm's Motion for Disqualification of Brantley. Apparently based upon his interview with Mary Storm, the magistrate judge ordered her attorney, Paul Oller, discharged from her representation and the motions filed by Oller were denied. No decision was reached in connection with the Petition for Involuntary Conservatorship, which matter was continued to November 14, 1989.

27. On October 25, 1989, Mary Storm's attorney, Paul R. Oller, filed an Attorney and Client Agreement with the court followed with the filing of a renewed answer on behalf of Mary Storm raising issues earlier asserted. Mary Storm again requested that Respondent Brantley be disqualified because of a conflict of interest, but the Respondent continued his representation of the step-son in the adversarial involuntary conservatorship proceeding.

28. At a court hearing on November 6, 1989, Respondent Brantley; Louise Wendler from the Security State Bank; Mary Storm's attorney, Paul Oller; and court appointed attorney, Bill Wright, appeared and agreed to a partial conservatorship of Mary Storm's assets which would not include her home, any of her personal property and her personal bank account for her own spending. Security State Bank was discharged and a new conservator appointed. No conservatorship bills were presented at the November 6, 1989, hearing when all of the parties were represented. Instead,

Respondent Brantley, representing the discharged conservator, prepared an order for the magistrate's approval for the discharged conservator to pay claims of $1,802.41 including $575.00 to Respondent Brantley. Respondent Brantley gave no notice of such order for proceedings thereon. His bill for services was never furnished to Mary Storm or her attorney, Paul Oller. As a result of the order for approval of claims of the conservator, Mary Storm paid for Respondent Brantley's representation of the Security State Bank and the step-son, Ralph Pfenninger, which services included efforts to sell her personal property and place her in an involuntary conservatorship, both against her expressed wishes.

29. In November 1989, Mary Storm was returned to possession of her home where she continued to reside with minimal outside assistance until the Spring of 1993, at which time she moved to Anchorage, Alaska, to live with her son, Wayne Hendrix, and his wife.

30. In July 1993, Mary Storm executed affidavits and powers of attorney empowering her granddaughter, Carla Hendrix, to return to Kansas, gather her assets, terminate the conservatorship and transfer Mary's assets to Alaska. As an alternative the conservatorship could be transferred to Alaska for court supervision.

31. A hearing was had on Mary Storm's request at which hearing Respondent Brantley appeared on behalf of the step-son in opposition to Mary Storm's expressed wishes. Mary Storm's request was denied by the court for the stated reason that she was not represented at the hearing and needed to be represented in order for a full adjudication to be rendered. Later, however, on October 13, 1993, the Mary Storm conservatorship was transferred to Anchorage, Alaska, to be supervised by the probate court in that jurisdiction. Since such transfer both the step-son, Ralph Pfenninger, and the Respondent Brantley have continued to attempt to monitor said proceedings and to obtain confidential information from the Alaska conservatorship.

32. In ex parte meetings with the magistrate judge and in scheduled hearings in the Storm case, Respondent justified the need for a conservatorship for Mary Storm by stating that the evidence would prove that her son, Wayne Hendrix, was an alcoholic, was financially irresponsible, and was guilty of wrongfully misappropriating some $85,000.00 of her funds. In fact, Respondent did not have evidence to support such claims and had not made a reasonable investigation in such regard.

33. While never medically or judicially determined, Mary Storm's ability to make adequate considered decisions in connection with Respondent's representation was, from time to time, apparently impaired, particularly during her nursing home stay and her post-cancer surgery period.

CONCLUSIONS

1. A majority of the Hearing Panel concluded that the following noted violations of the Model Rules of Professional Conduct, Supreme Court Rule 226 [1995 Kan. Ct. R. Annot. 245], were established by clear and convincing evidence.

2. MRPC 1.1 Competence [1995 Kan. Ct. R. Annot. 251]—Respondent failed to provide competent representation to his clients in the following particulars: (a) failure to fully investigate the claims of improper transfers from the account of Mary Storm and the threatened dissipation of her assets prior to initiating conservatorship

proceedings; (b) failure to personally interview a client for whom a conservatorship proceeding was proposed; (c) permitting his client conservator to proceed with sale related activities in regard to Mary Storm's personal property before a court order had been entered directing such sale, which activity resulted in unwarranted expense to Mary Storm; (d) obtaining an ex parte order in a closed involuntary conservatorship proceeding, all in connection with a planned involuntary conservatorship proceeding not yet filed; (e) preparing and causing to be filed a Petition for Involuntary Conservatorship relying on a non-existent medical report, which is herein characterized as incompetence only because there is insufficient evidence to establish a violation of MRPC 3.3 Candor Toward the Tribunal [1995 Kan. Ct. R. Annot. 311].

3. MRPC 1.2 Scope of Representation [1995 Kan. Ct. R. Annot. 255]—Respondent failed to abide by his client Mary Storm's decisions concerning the representation.

4. MRPC 1.4—Communication [1995 Kan. Ct. R. Annot. 263]—Respondent failed to keep his client, Mary Storm, reasonably informed.

5. MRPC 1.5 Fees [1995 Kan. Ct. R. Annot. 268]—Respondent failed to communicate the basis or rate of the fee to the client, Mary Storm, who was ultimately responsible therefore, and caused her estate to be charged for legal services rendered to adversarial persons.

6. MRPC 1.7 Conflict of Interest [1995 Kan. Ct. R. Annot. 275]—Respondent represented Security State Bank and Ralph Pfenninger in matters adverse to his client, Mary Storm, without consulting and without consent.

7. MRPC 1.9 Conflict of Interest [1995 Kan. Ct. R. Annot. 281]—Respondent, after undertaking to represent Mary Storm, later represented others in substantially related matters in which interests were materially adverse to her, all without her consent after consultation.

8. MRPC 1.14 Client Under Disability [1995 Kan. Ct. R. Annot. 293]—Respondent failed to reasonably maintain a normal client-lawyer relationship with Mary Storm when he believed her to be under a disability.

9. MRPC 3.3 Candor Toward the Tribunal [1995 Kan. Ct. R. Annot. 311]—Respondent made statements and allegations to the magistrate court which he knew, or should have known, to be false. In addition, he made false statements to the magistrate court without making reasonable and diligent inquiry, as above noted, into the true facts.

10. MRPC 8.4 Misconduct [1995 Kan. Ct. R. Annot. 340]—As a result of the foregoing conclusions, Respondent has violated the rules of professional conduct and has engaged in conduct prejudicial to the administration of justice.

The Disciplinary Administrator recommended to the panel a sanction for a definite period of time, such as 6 months, conditioned upon restitution and taking and passing the Multistate Professional Responsibility Examination.

In a split decision, the panel recommended published censure with costs assessed to Brantley. One panel member dissented, agreeing with Brantley's position.

DISCUSSION

A threshold observation in beginning our analysis relates to our standard of review. Rule 212(f) (1995 Kan. Ct. R. Annot. 215) provides:

The recommendations of the panel or the Disciplinary Administrator as to sanctions to be imposed shall be advisory only and shall not prevent the Court from imposing sanctions greater or lesser than those recommended by the Panel or the Disciplinary Administrator.

We now turn to the panel's findings of Brantley's rule violations

MRPC 1.1—Competence

MRPC 1.1 (1995 Kan. Ct. R. Annot. 251) provides:

A lawyer shall provide competent representation to a client. Competent representation requires the legal knowledge, skill, thoroughness and preparation reasonably necessary for the representation.

The Comment provides in part:

> In determining whether a lawyer employs the requisite knowledge and skill in a particular matter, relevant factors include the relative complexity and specialized nature of the matter, the lawyer's general experience, the lawyer's training and experience in the field in question, the preparation and study the lawyer is able to give the matter and whether it is feasible to refer the matter to, or associate or consult with, a lawyer of established competence in the field in question. . . .
>
> . . . .
>
> Competent handling of a particular matter includes inquiry into and analysis of the factual and legal elements of the problem, and use of methods and procedures meeting the standards of competent practitioners. It also includes adequate preparation.

1995 Kan. Ct. R. Annot. 251-52.

Brantley has been practicing law in Scott City since 1970. He was the attorney for the executor of the estate of Scott McCormick, Mary Storm's brother, with Mary Storm being the sole heir of that estate. Brantley prepared a codicil for Mary Storm's will (naming him as her executor) and in 1986, at her request, prepared assignments by which Mary Storm created joint tenancy ownership in three real estate installment contracts with her son, Wayne. Brantley was an experienced attorney well acquainted with Mary Storm and her legal affairs.

(a) Failure to Fully Investigate Claims of Improper Transfers

According to Brantley, the driving force behind this whole unfortunate scenario was Brantley's belief that Wayne Hendrix had misappropriated $85,000 from Mary Storm. After Ralph Pfenninger and Louise Wendler told him of the supposedly suspicious transfers by Wayne Hendrix in 1986 and 1987, Brantley called Mary Storm at the nursing home in July 1989 and asked her if she knew about them. Brantley did not provide sufficient information to Mary Storm for her to respond to his inquiry. She could not have made an informed decision about transactions that occurred some two years earlier, based on the scant information Brantley provided her over the telephone. There is no indication that Brantley ever asked Mary Storm if she wanted him to investigate the bank records on this matter, or that Brantley (with Mary Storm's permission) ever obtained or showed the documentation or specific information on these transfers to Mary Storm to confirm whether she knew or approved of them.

The subject wire transfers were from the Hendrix account at Security State Bank in Scott City to the Hendrix account in Alaska and all occurred from October 1986 (prior to Mary's broken hip) to January 1988. Those transfers, by themselves, should not have aroused suspicion. There were several large deposits into the Hendrix account at Security State Bank from April 1986 to July 1987, totalling $191,425.62. All but $69,862.88 of those deposits took place prior to December 1986, before Mary Storm broke her hip.

The panel's finding of incompetence based on Brantley's failure to investigate the circumstances of the supposedly improper transfers is amply supported in the record.

(b) Failure to Interview Mary Storm Before Proposing the Conservatorship

Establishment of a conservatorship, even a voluntary one, is a drastic step. *See In re Conservatorship of Marcotte*, 243 Kan. 190, Syl. ¶ 1, 756 P.2d 1091 (1988) ("A voluntary conservatee may not dispose of personal property by inter vivos conveyance during the conservatorship without court approval."). Yet Brantley took this drastic step without even a face-to-face interview with Mary Storm, choosing instead to rely on a brief telephone conversation and the statements of Ralph Pfenninger, her stepson, and Louise Wendler from Security State Bank.

(c) Permitting Sale-Related Activities Prior to Court Approval

As Brantley emphasized, there is no evidence in the record that Brantley knew Security State Bank engaged an auction company and incurred advertising expenses before the sale was approved by the court. The bank's actions were improper, but there was no evidence that Brantley permitted those actions.

The panel's conclusion that Brantley permitted the Bank's actions does not appear to be supported by the evidence in the record. Other conduct by Brantley, however, established his violations of MRPC 1.1.

(d) Obtaining Ex Parte Order Prior to Filing Petition for Involuntary Conservatorship

The record indicates that after Judge Goering terminated the voluntary conservatorship, Brantley represented to the judge that he had evidence Wayne Hendrix had misappropriated $85,000 of Mary Storm's funds and that Mary Storm's assets were at risk without a conservatorship in place. Not surprisingly, Judge Goering then suggested that an involuntary conservatorship should be filed, issued the temporary restraining order against Mary Storm's assets, and directed William Wright, as guardian ad litem to lock up her house. Judge Goering acted upon Brantley's inaccurate, incomplete, and unsupported representations. Brantley demonstrated incompetence by making those representations to the judge.

(e) Filing Involuntary Petition Containing Allegation as to Non-Existent Medical Report

Brantley excuses this mishap because the allegation was taken from a standardized form and left in the petition by mistake. Also, Judge Goering had already stated he would not rely on a doctor's letter and intended a complete evaluation of Mary Storm by Area Mental Health Center.

The fact that Judge Goering would not rely on a doctor's letter does not excuse Brantley's incompetence in leaving this untrue allegation in the petition. If Brantley knew at the time the petition was drafted that Judge Goering was not going to rely on a doctor's letter, then why was the allegation included? Even if this allegation was taken from a standardized form, it specifically referred to both Mary Storm and Dr. Dunn. The involuntary petition was a two-page document easy to proofread.

MRPC 1.2—Scope of Representation

MRPC 1.2 (1995 Kan. Ct. R. Annot. 255) provides:

> (a) A lawyer shall abide by a client's decisions concerning the lawful objectives of representation, subject to paragraphs (c), (d), and (e), and shall consult with the client as to the means which the lawyer shall choose to pursue.

The Comment provides in part:

> The client has ultimate authority to determine the purposes to be served by legal representation, within the limits imposed by law and the lawyer's professional obligations. . . .
>
> In a case in which the client appears to be suffering mental disability, the lawyer's duty to abide by the client's decisions is to be guided by reference to Rule 1.14.

1995 Kan. Ct. R. Annot. 255-56.

Failure to Abide by Mary Storm's Decisions Concerning Representation

Brantley never consulted with Mary Storm as to whether she wanted to have her household property auctioned off. Instead, he relied on Louise Wendler's and the guardian ad litem's statements that Mary Storm had agreed to the sale. At the September 29, 1989, court appearance, when he learned that Paul Oller had filed an objection to the sale on behalf of Mary Storm and the conservatorship had been terminated, Brantley represented to Judge Goering that Hendrix was misappropriating Mary Storm's funds and convinced the judge that a temporary restraining order needed to be issued. Brantley followed that representation by filing the petition for involuntary conservatorship signed by Ralph Pfenninger. Brantley's authority to act on behalf of Mary Storm ended when the voluntary conservatorship was terminated.

Brantley contends that the parties' settlement agreement in November 1989 allowing the conservatorship to continue somehow cures this ethical violation. Brantley ignores the fact that before the settlement agreement was reached, Mary

Storm had to retain her own attorney to represent her interests and oppose the involuntary conservatorship.

MRPC 1.4—Communication

MRPC 1.4 (1995 Kan. Ct. R. Annot. 263) states:

> (a) A lawyer shall keep a client reasonably informed about the status of a matter and promptly comply with reasonable requests for information.
>
> (b) A lawyer shall explain a matter to the extent reasonably necessary to permit the client to make informed decisions regarding the representation.

The Comment provides in part:

> The client should have sufficient information to participate intelligently in decisions concerning the objectives of the representation and the means by which they are to be pursued, to the extent the client is willing and able to do so. . . .
>
> . . . The guiding principle is that the lawyer should fulfill reasonable client expectations for information consistent with the duty to act in the client's best interests, and the client's overall requirements as to the character of representation.
>
> Ordinarily, the information to be provided is that appropriate for a client who is a comprehending and responsible adult. However, fully informing the client according to this standard may be impracticable, for example, where the client is a child or suffers from mental disability. *See* Rule 1.14.

1995 Kan. Ct. R. Annot. 263.

Mary Storm has not been determined to be mentally incompetent or disabled, so she should have been entitled to appropriate communication from Brantley. Brantley breached his ethical obligation to Mary Storm when, prior to the conservatorship, he failed to provide her sufficient information (and get her permission to do so) to make an informed decision concerning the purported suspicious fund transfers by Wayne Hendrix. Thereafter, he failed to communicate at all with Mary Storm, though he claims to have done so through the conservator and the guardian ad litem.

Mary Storm obviously was not given sufficient information about the proposed sale of her household property to make an informed decision. She voiced to Judge Goering during his ex parte hospital visit her opposition to the sale.

MRPC 1.5—Failure to Communicate Fees and Charging for Services Rendered to Adversaries

MRPC 1.5 (1995 Kan. Ct. R. Annot. 268-69) provides in part:

> (a) A lawyer's fee shall be reasonable. The factors to be considered in determining the reasonableness of a fee include the following:
>
> . . . .
>
> (4) the amount involved and the results obtained.

Brantley never sent any fee statements to Mary Storm in connection with the conservatorship. He sent those to the conservator for payment. Mary Storm should have been advised of Brantley's fees. Brantley claims that he did not render any services to adversarial persons in connection with the conservatorship because neither Security State Bank nor Ralph Pfenninger "had any other thought than to help Mary Storm." However, fees generated by Brantley in pursuing the proposed sale, temporary restraining order, and the involuntary petition were adversarial to Mary Storm. Those fees were paid by the conservator.

MRPC 1.7—Conflict of Interest

MRPC 1.7 (1995 Kan. Ct. R. Annot. 275) provides in part:

> (a) A lawyer shall not represent a client if the representation of that client will be directly adverse to another client, unless:
> (1) the lawyer reasonably believes the representation will not adversely affect the relationship with the other client; and
> (2) each client consents after consultation.

The Comment provides in part:

> Loyalty is an essential element in the lawyer's relationship to a client. An impermissible conflict of interest may exist before representation is undertaken, in which event the representation should be declined. If such a conflict arises after representation has been undertaken, the lawyer should withdraw from the representation.

1995 Kan. Ct. R. Annot. 275.

Brantley faced a conflict of interest from the beginning. Ralph Pfenninger saw Brantley in July 1989 and wanted a conservatorship for Mary Storm after Louise Wendler told Ralph that she had suspicions that Wayne Hendrix was misappropriating Mary's funds. Ralph was named as a residuary legatee under the mutual will of Mary and Ralph's father, R.E. Pfenninger. R.E. Pfenninger died in 1977. The residuary clause of this mutual will, obligated Mary, as survivor, to devise her residue in equal shares to her natural child, Wayne, and her husband R.E. Pfenninger's four natural children (or their issue, if not then living). Ralph may have believed that he would be entitled to a share of Mary's estate upon her death under this residuary clause. If so, Ralph had an obvious incentive to keep Mary Storm's assets intact until her death and restrict her ability to make inter vivos gifts. Brantley had assisted Mary Storm in placing her interests in three real estate installment contracts in joint tenancy with Wayne. Brantley handled Mary's brother's estate (Scott McCormick), which made a substantial distribution to Mary in 1986. It would be no surprise if Ralph Pfenninger harbored some jealousy and resentment toward Mary's son Wayne and would be anxious to stop Mary from giving her property to Wayne. During oral argument, Brantley stated he was unaware that Ralph Pfenninger was a residuary legatee under Mary's will, but indicated he would not have acted any differently if he had known that fact.

After Mary Storm retained Paul Oller to file an objection to the proposed sale of her household goods and obtain termination of the voluntary conservatorship, Brantley should have withdrawn from the case. Even if Brantley was unaware of Ralph's status as a residuary legatee under Mary's will, the adversarial relationship was clear by that point. He never obtained Mary Storm's consent to represent Security State Bank, Ralph Pfenninger, or both in seeking an involuntary conservatorship.

Brantley demonstrated mixed loyalties by failing to adequately investigate and relying on unsubstantiated suspicions of Ralph Pfenninger and Louise Wendler that Wayne Hendrix was misappropriating Mary Storm's funds. Brantley's pursuit of the involuntary conservatorship after Mary Storm retained her own attorney to oppose the sale and conservatorship confirmed this, as did his representation of Ralph Pfenninger in opposing Carla Hendrix's request for funds from the conservatorship to pay for moving expenses of Mary Storm's belongings to Alaska in 1993.

Brantley argues that his representation of Security State Bank or Ralph Pfenninger in the conservatorship matter was never adverse to Mary Storm because she ultimately needed a conservatorship. He contends that the fact she retained Paul Oller to oppose the conservatorship should be disregarded, because Judge Goering struck Oller's pleadings after interviewing Mary Storm ex parte at the hospital. Aside from Judge Goering's own conduct, his interview with Mary Storm made one thing very plain: Mary opposed the efforts to sell her household property.

Brantley cites two cases from other jurisdictions, *Hillman v. Stults*, 263 Cal. App. 2d 848, 70 Cal. Rptr. 295 (1968), and *American Nat. Bank v. Bradford*, 28 Tenn. App. 239, 188 S.W.2d 971 (1945), to support his argument that his simultaneous representation of Mary Storm, Security State Bank, and Ralph Pfenninger was not adverse to Mary Storm.

Both cases are distinguishable. *Bradford* involved a ward initially adjudged insane. Mary Storm has never been adjudged incompetent or disabled in any sense. In *Hillman*, the court determined the attorneys' and conservators' prior isolated representation of the conservatee's sister did not present any conflicts or involve confidential information, so disqualification for conflict of interest was not appropriate in a proceeding adversarial to the then-deceased sister. 263 Cal. App. 2d at 879-80. Brantley obtained confidential information concerning Mary Storm's and her son's banking transactions and used that information to advance the interests of Mary Storm's stepson, who wanted an involuntary conservatorship for Mary so that her assets could be preserved.

MRPC 1.9—Conflict of Interest: Former Client

MRPC 1.9 (1995 Kan. Ct. R. Annot. 281) states in part:

A lawyer who has formerly represented a client in a matter shall not thereafter:

(a) represent another person in the same or a substantially related matter in which that person's interests are materially adverse to the interests of the former client unless the former client consents after consultation; or

(b) use information relating to the representation to the disadvantage of the former client except as Rule 1.6 would permit with respect to a client or when the information has become generally known.

The Comment states in part:

When a lawyer has been directly involved in a specific transaction, subsequent representation of other clients with materially adverse interests clearly is prohibited. . . .

Information acquired by the lawyer in the course of representing a client may not subsequently be used by the lawyer to the disadvantage of the client.

1995 Kan. Ct. R. Annot. 282.

Brantley's representation became "materially adverse" to Mary Storm when she retained Paul Oller to stop the proposed sale and terminate the voluntary conservatorship. Thereafter, Brantley sought the temporary restraining order and involuntary conservatorship on behalf of Ralph Pfenninger and Security State Bank. The involuntary conservatorship petition satisfies the elements of a MRPC 1.9(a) violation. Mary Storm, the former client, did not consent to, nor was she consulted about, Brantley's continued involvement in the case after she retained Paul Oller.

Brantley's representation of Pfenninger in opposition to Carla Hendrix's request in 1993 for funds to move Mary Storm's personal property to Alaska was "materially adverse" to Mary Storm. Again, Brantley did not request or receive consent from Mary Storm for this adverse representation.

MRPC 1.14—Client Under Disability

MRPC 1.14 (1995 Kan. Ct. R. Annot. 293) states:

(a) When a client's ability to make adequately considered decisions in connection with the representation is impaired, whether because of minority, mental disability or for some other reason, the lawyer shall, as far as reasonably possible, maintain a normal client-lawyer relationship with the client.

(b) A lawyer may seek the appointment of a guardian or take other protective action with respect to a client, only when the lawyer reasonably believes that the client cannot adequately act in the client's own interest.

The Comment provides in part:

The normal client-lawyer relationship is based on the assumption that the client, when properly advised and assisted, is capable of making decisions about important matters. When the client . . . suffers from a mental disorder or disability, however, maintaining the ordinary client-lawyer relationship may not be possible in all respects. In particular, an incapacitated person may have no power to make legally binding decisions. Nevertheless, a client lacking legal competence often has the ability to understand, deliberate upon, and reach conclusions about matters affecting the client's own well-being. Furthermore, to an increasing extent the law recognizes intermediate degrees of competence. . . . It is recognized that some persons of advanced age can be quite capable of handling routine financial matters while needing special legal protection concerning major transactions.

The fact that a client suffers a disability does not diminish the lawyer's obligation to treat the client with attention and respect. If the person has no guardian or legal representative, the lawyer often must act as de facto guardian. Even if the person does have a legal representative, the lawyer should as far as possible accord the represented person the status of client, particularly in maintaining communication.

If a legal representative has already been appointed for the client, the lawyer should ordinarily look to the representative for decisions on behalf of the client.

1995 Kan. Ct. R. Annot. 293.

The record indicates that Brantley totally disregarded this rule. He had one telephone call with Mary Storm before filing the voluntary conservatorship and failed to provide her with adequate information in that call. Thereafter, he had no direct communication with Mary Storm.

MRPC 3.3—Candor Toward the Tribunal

MRPC 3.3 (1995 Kan. Ct. R. Annot. 311-12) states:

(a) A lawyer shall not knowingly:
(1) make a false statement of material fact or law to a tribunal. . . .
. . . .
(d) In an ex parte proceeding, a lawyer shall inform the tribunal of all material facts known to the lawyer which will enable the tribunal to make an informed decision, whether or not the facts are adverse.

The Comment provides in part:

An advocate is responsible for pleadings and other documents prepared for litigation, but is usually not required to have personal knowledge of matters asserted therein, for litigation documents ordinarily present assertions by the client, or by someone on the client's behalf, and not assertions by the lawyer. . . . However, an assertion purporting to be on the lawyer's own knowledge, as in an affidavit by the lawyer or in a statement in open court, may properly be made only when the lawyer knows the assertion is true or believes it to be true on the basis of a reasonably diligent inquiry.

1995 Kan. Ct. R. Annot. 312. The Comment indicates that a lawyer making an assertion in open court without a belief that the assertion is true, based on reasonably diligent inquiry, may violate the rule.

As described in the panel's Findings of Fact Nos. 16 and 23, Brantley made untrue allegations in pleadings filed in the court. Also, in obtaining the ex parte temporary restraining order, Brantley represented to Judge Goering after termination of the voluntary conservatorship that Wayne Hendrix had misappropriated $85,000 of Mary Storm's funds and her assets were at risk. Brantley continued to make this representation to the court at the 1993 hearing when Carla Hendrix sought funds from the conservator to pay for moving Mary Storm's belongings to Alaska, where Mary Storm lived.

Brantley contends that he made no knowingly false statements to the court and his representation that Hendrix had misappropriated $85,000 of Mary Storm's funds had a reasonable basis.

There does not appear to be any evidence in the record that Brantley made knowingly false statements to the court. However, according to the Comment, Brantley's failure to make a reasonable investigation regarding the Hendrix fund transfers before accusing Hendrix in court of misappropriating funds may be considered a violation of the rule. Making such accusations in an ex parte setting violates MRPC 3.3(d). The record does not show that Brantley provided the judge complete information about these transfers, such as the dates of the transfers (the last one well over a year before the conservatorship) and the fact that they involved only Hendrix's own account.

MRPC 8.4—Misconduct

MRPC 8.4 (1995 Kan. Ct. R. Annot. 340) states in part:

> It is professional misconduct for a lawyer to:
> (a) Violate or attempt to violate the rules of professional conduct, knowingly assist or induce another to do so, or do so through the acts of another.

Brantley has violated numerous rules of ethical conduct.

Aggravating and Mitigating Factors

The panel found the following aggravating and mitigating factors in the report:

Aggravating factors:

1. A pattern of misconduct is established throughout the Mary Storm conservatorship matter involving multiple offenses.

2. Respondent steadfastly refuses to acknowledge the wrongful nature of his conduct, and expresses remorse only if found to be in violation of the Model Rules of Professional Conduct.

3. The victim in this matter, Mary Storm, was quite vulnerable to the abuses and violations noted herein.

4. The Respondent has substantial experience in the practice of law.

Mitigating factors:

1. The Respondent has no prior disciplinary offenses.

2. While Respondent's actions are subject to the perception that he could financially benefit from a conservation of Mary Storm's assets in Scott City, should he someday handle the probate of her estate, the panel does not find any dishonest or selfish motive.

Brantley takes exception to aggravating factor No. 1 and mitigating factor No. 2. All factors were amply supported by the record.

Restitution

The Disciplinary Administrator requests that this court reconsider the issue of restitution. At the hearing, the Disciplinary Administrator submitted exhibits of fees and expenses, and Carla Hendrix testified as to the expenses and legal fees incurred in connection with the conservatorship, both in Scott City and Alaska. These included, among other things, Brantley's fees charged to the conservatorship totalling $1,180 in 1989. She also listed certain travel expenses she had incurred in making trips between Alaska and Scott City in connection with the conservatorship proceedings, additional attorneys' fees incurred in Alaska, and other miscellaneous expenses totalling approximately $11,000 all attributed to the dispute over the conservatorship.

The panel did not recommend restitution. We order restitution to include Brantley's fees in the sum of $1,180.

Conclusion

The panel recommended that Respondent be publicly censured under Supreme Court Rule 203(a)(3) (1995 Kan. Ct. R. Annot. 191) and that costs be assessed against Respondent. We find in the record clear and convincing evidence sustaining the panel's conclusions that Brantley violated MRPC 1.1, 1.2, 1.4, 1.5, 1.7, 1.9, 1.14, 3.3, and 8.4 and that he be sanctioned by published censure. We accept the report of the panel. We concur in the findings, conclusions, and recommendations of the panel with the additional imposition of restitution of attorney fees received by Brantley. Restitution is ordered in the sum of $1,180.

IT IS ORDERED THAT Keen K. Brantley be subject to published censure for his violations of the Model Rules of Professional Conduct.

IT IS FURTHER ORDERED THAT this order be published in the official Kansas Reports and that the costs of the proceeding, including the sum of $1,180 as restitution, be assessed against Respondent, to be paid to the office of the Disciplinary Administrator within 60 days from the date of this opinion.

B. The Disabled Client

While meeting an applicant or representing a client, a lawyer may discern that the client's "ability to make adequately considered decisions in connection with the representation is impaired." Rule 1.14(a). The degree and duration of impairment will vary widely, but the lawyer's fundamental ethical problem is that of approach: should the lawyer act in accordance with the client's expressed wishes, if any (the "advocacy" model)? Or, should the lawyer act in what the lawyer considers the client's best interests (the "best interests" model)? Or, should the lawyer do what the lawyer thinks the client would direct if the client were capable of instructing counsel competently (the "substituted judgment" model)?

For practical assistance, see Paul R. Tremblay, *On Persuasion and Paternalism: Lawyer Decisionmaking and the Questionably Competent Client*, 1987 UTAH L. REV. 515, 519-20 (1987), describing the range of choices available to the lawyer whose client's competency is in serious doubt as follows:

- withdraw;
- seek a guardian for the client, with the lawyer either serving as the petitioner or recruiting a third party to do so;
- seek unofficial consent from a family member or close friend;
- seek to persuade the client to make different or "better" choices;
- proceed as de facto guardian; or
- continue to presume competence irrebuttably.

The article goes on the suggest "that pursuing guardianship is legitimate in extreme cases, that reliance on family may be appropriate, that noncoercive persuasion is justified in less extreme cases, and that unilateral usurpation of client autonomy is never appropriate except in emergencies." *Id.* at 584.

1. Evaluating Client Competence

It is axiomatic that a person who has reached the age of majority is presumed competent. Moreover, a competent person is always able to make his or her own decisions. But what about when this "black-letter" principle breaks down? As the scrivener and advisor to your clients, when will you begin to doubt the propriety, and reliability, of the legal work you do?

Walter T. Burke
Avoiding Pitfalls When Counseling the Elderly
THE COMPLEAT LAWYER—GEN. PRAC., SOLO, AND SMALL FIRM SECTION
AMERICAN BAR ASSOCIATION (Spring 1998)
<http://www.abanet.org:80/genpractice/lawyer/complete/sp98burke.html>*

There was a time when "counseling the elderly" simply meant drafting wills for clients. Now, it means so much more, including estate tax planning, health care decision making, Medicaid planning, and guidance through the emotional tragedy of losing a spouse.

* * *

Before the Legal Work Begins

When scheduling both the initial consultation and subsequent meetings with an elderly client, be aware of the physical health and mental well-being of the client. It is probable that the client will have a routine medication regimen that you may be required to plan around.

For instance, in situations where the client is medicated, the client may be alert and lucid after her breakfast and medication; but after lunchtime and before the next scheduled medication, she may be groggy and confused. Where the client's capacity may be an issue, and in instances where the client has severe physical problems or signs of early dementia, knowing the client's medication schedule will be important in both helping the client as much as possible and combating a will contest or malpractice suit later.

Paul S. Appelbaum
The Medicalization of Judicial Decision-Making
ELDER LAW REP. (February 1999)**

The medicalization of judicial decision-making takes two forms. First, some courts sometimes permit moral issues to be transformed into medical issues. Consider the example of the adjudication of decision-making competence. Competence, of course, is a threshold requirement for persons to be able to exercise their decision-making rights, to make medical decisions, to manage their property, and in extreme cases even to marry. Persons found incompetent are deprived of those decision-making rights and someone else is appointed to make those decisions for them. In this process, for obvious reasons, psychiatrists are often called upon to examine the allegedly incompetent persons and to testify as to their capacities. Psychiatrists and other mental health professionals are experts in the diagnosis of pathological states affecting the mind. Psychiatrists can be expected to detect abnormalities that layper-

---

* Copyright © American Bar Association. All rights reserved. Reprinted by permission.
** Copyright © 1999 ELDER LAW REPORTER. Reprinted with permission.

sons might not, to determine their extent, and to describe their effects on relevant aspects of mental functioning. Expert testimony in these areas is perfectly appropriate, indeed, and probably essential to the process in many cases. In practice, however, psychiatrists are often asked to take one additional step: to offer an opinion as to whether a person is or is not competent. Why is this a problem? One might in fact say, if a psychiatrist doesn't know who is mentally competent, then who does?

The problem stems from the confusion that is generated between medical or scientific questions that a psychiatrist can legitimately address and legal issues with a moral underpinning that a psychiatrist cannot legitimately address. Examples of medical or scientific question include the degree of a person's impairment in functions as they relate to decision-making. Also, the subject's understanding of the facts of a given situation and appreciation of the implications of these facts and the consequences of a situation are all questions for the medical profession. Finally, the subject's ability to reason rationally, to weigh the risks and benefits, about a situation is clearly a medical issue. But there is a distinction between addressing these functions and addressing legal issues with intrinsic moral underpinnings that flow from this information.

The question of when a person is sufficiently impaired that he or she can fairly be deprived of the power to make decisions for himself or herself is a legal matter, not a medical one. Other examples of legal questions that psychiatrists should not answer are whether a person is competent to stand trial or is criminally responsible. For psychiatrists to assume this function implies the ability on their part to make moral judgments in an expert fashion. In fact, they have no more of that ability than any layperson does. In effect, the judge who asks for or tolerates psychiatric testimony about the ultimate issue in a hearing in which a legal-moral determination lies at the core of what the court must do is acquiescing in the medicalization of a profoundly moral question.

Unfortunately, my experience leads me to believe that the practice is not rare. Some years ago I testified at the competence hearing of a man whose son was petitioning to be appointed guardian of his estate. The son's attorney had called me and asked if I would examine the alleged incompetent to evaluate his competence to manage his financial affairs. On my examination, the indicia of moderate dementia were fairly evident. I noted memory loss, difficulty finding words, and a general sense of confusion, and, specific to the legal issue at hand, functional impairments were fairly evident as well. He could not perform even the simplest calculations. He could not describe to me what his assets were or how much he had. He could not characterize expenditures that might need to be made in order to sustain him, where his money came from for rent or groceries, or how much that cost, nor could he or would he account to me for significant amounts of money that he had withdrawn from the bank.

I prepared a written report detailing all of this information for the court. I testified to my observations, laying them out in detail, focusing on the description of the symptoms and the functional impairments, and carefully avoiding conclusions about the man's competence in the technical sense of the word or the need for a guardian in the case. From my own legal layperson's point of view, I imagined few more straightforward cases for a judge to adjudicate. But, when my testimony was complete, the judge leaned forward, peered at me, and asked, "But doctor, is he competent or not?" In asking me that question, the judge was requesting my collusion with him in turning a legal issue with moral roots, the question of when someone should be denied the right to control his or her assets, into a medical issue, the sort of question one might ask a doctor. That is, I think, the first way in which medicalization begins to permeate the judicial decision-making process—the turning of a moral, legal issue into a medical issue.

Question

How can the lawyer seek professional guidance informing the lawyer's opinion regarding the client's mental status without violating his or her duty of confidentiality?

2. MRPC 1.14: Client Under a Disability

Molly M. Wood
Who's the Client?: Competency and the Lawyer-Client Relationship
<http://www.ink.org/public/keln/ethicsmmw.html>*

II. The Impaired Client (*See* Rule 1.14 *Client Under a Disability*)

* * *

A. Duty to Maintain Normal Attorney-Client Relationship (*See* Rule 2.1 *Advisor*)

The resolution of a legal problem may involve such nonlegal considerations as social responsibility, morality, and economic, political or emotional consequences. It may be difficult, and often inappropriate, for a lawyer to limit advice to the narrow confines of compliance with procedural and substantive law. Advice that apprises the client of the full implication of a proposed course of action is ordinarily proper and desirable. Of course, a lawyer should not, under the guise of legal service, exploit the role of counselor.

1. Competency (*See* Rule 1.4 *Communication*)

Some of the most difficult ethical issues in the practice of law arise in representing marginally competent clients. The threshold question is whether the client has the capacity to retain the attorney. The next question is whether he or she sufficiently understands and can therefore make the decisions required. For estate planning purpose, for example, [most jurisdictions have] a relatively lenient standard—the testator

---

* Copyright © 1996. Reprinted with permission.

must know the scope of his or her property and "the natural objects of his or her bounty." For most other transactions a higher standard is required. For instance, to sell a house the owner must have a good idea of its market value.

It would be inappropriate to turn away any client exhibiting some mental deficiency, but it would also be inappropriate to move ahead with representation without taking any precautions. Although it would be advisable to require the applicant to produce medical support for a claim that his or her guardianship and conservatorship should be terminated, to send all such clients to a physician or social worker for an evaluation is not practical. Many clients would resist this move. In addition, taking such overt action might violate the attorney's obligation to act in the best interest of the client.

The alternative is for the attorney to document his or her informal assessment of the client's mental capacity. The attorney should take notes to create a record in case the client's capacity to understand the legal action he or she takes is ever challenged. If the result of this informal and nonprofessional evaluation demonstrates a lack of capacity, then the attorney should consider referring the client to appropriate medical and social services for further diagnosis, treatment, and care.

Ethically sensitive problems often arise when the well spouse or adult child of a senior with a degenerative disease, perhaps Alzheimer's or other dementia-type illness, seeks to become the attorney-in-fact of the proposed client or seeks to enter into some type of transaction which requires the proposed client to exert his or her legal authority to act. Although one's impulse may be to be anxious to assist, an incompetent person is unable to undertake to act for himself or delegate his authority under a Durable Power of Attorney. You must, therefore, make contact with the person who presumably wants to delegate that authority to determine that person's wishes and whether he or she is legally competent to undertake the proposed action.

This is a judgment call based upon the lawyer's appraisal of the functionality of the applicant and the complexity of the proposed legal action. For example, in the context of a Durable POA delegating the client's authority to his wife to handle their property and affairs, and all the property of the marriage is jointly owned, it is unnecessary for the client to understand much more than that his wife could sell the family home and, if she would, make off with the proceeds. Does the client believe his wife is trustworthy, that is, will she exercise her grant of authority for his best interests? Does the client understand that his grant of authority will increase his vulnerability to his attorney-in-fact's misdeeds?

3. Section 35 of The Restatement of the Law Governing Lawyers

Sheila Reynolds
Ethical Considerations in Representing an Impaired Client
Kansas Long-Term Care Handbook (1999)[*]

C. The Guidance of § 35 of The Restatement of the Law Governing Lawyers

The American Law Institute gave final approval to The Restatement of Law Third: Law Governing Lawyers in May of 1998, after a ten year drafting process. (Publication of the final approved volume is scheduled for late 1999.) Even before this Restatement received final approval, it was used by lawyers to answer or argue ethical questions and by judges to decide ethical issues. The Restatement will become an important source of guidance on ethical issues because it provides more substance and authority than the Model Rules of Profession Conduct.

The Model Rules of Professional Conduct are adopted by state supreme courts to govern the lawyer disciplinary process. The preliminary material found in the scope section of the Model Rules specifically states that "violation of a Rule should not give rise to a cause of action nor should it create any presumption that a legal duty has been breached. The Rules are designed to provide guidance to lawyers and to provide a structure for regulating conduct through disciplinary agencies." In contrast, the Restatement is intended to serve as a guide of the law of lawyering in all contexts, including the inherent power of the court to control litigation, malpractice actions, and the interpretation of lawyer ethics codes.

A section of the Restatement relevant to this discussion is § 35, Client Under Disability. . . . There are several differences between § 35 and [M]RPC 1.14. Overall, § 35 gives more specific guidance to lawyers representing impaired clients and provides more direct authorization for intervention than [M]RPC 1.14.

1. *Act in the Best Interests of the Client*

Subsection (1) parrots the language of [M]RPC 1.14(a) in requiring lawyers to maintain a normal client-lawyer relationship, as far as reasonably possible, with a client whose "ability to make adequately considered decisions in connection with the representation is impaired." This subsection additionally provides that the lawyer must act in the best interests of the client.

2. *Use Substituted Judgment*

Subsection (2) contains a concept not found in the Model Rule, requiring a lawyer representing an impaired client who has no guardian or other legal representative to use substituted judgment in pursuing a matter within the scope of the representation.

A lawyer representing a client impaired as described in Subsection (1) and for whom no guardian or other representative is available to act, must, with respect to a

---

[*] Copyright © 1999. Reprinted with permission.

matter within the scope of the representation, pursue the lawyer's reasonable view of the client's objectives or interests as the client would define them if able to make adequately considered decisions on the matter, even if the client expresses no wishes or gives contrary instructions.

3. *Possible Duty to Act*

The above section seems to create a duty for the lawyer to take over decision making whenever the lawyer determines the client meets the given definition of "impaired." Such a duty does not exist in the Model Rules or other bodies of law. The language in Rule 1.14 is discretionary, providing that the lawyer "may" take protective action. Although the Comment to Rule 1.14 states, "If the person has not guardian or legal representative, the lawyer often must act as *de facto* guardian," the word "must" here does not create a duty, because it is not part of the black-letter rule and because it is modified by "often."

If a lawyer has a duty to use substituted judgment on behalf of an impaired client, then a lawyer who fails to exercise that duty may be liable to the client who is damaged thereby. A saving grace of the RESTATEMENT on this issue is found in Comment d, which provides, "It is often difficult to decide whether the conditions of this Section have been met. A lawyer who acts reasonably and in good faith in perplexing circumstances is not subject to professional discipline or malpractice or similar liability." The language in the comment supports the view that the drafters did not intend to create legal liability for a lawyer who chooses not to use substituted judgment in representing a client the lawyer believes is impaired.

4. *Exceptions to Following Directions of the Client's Guardian*

Subsection (3) is also different from the Model Rule in that it addresses the relationship between the lawyer and the client's legal representative, providing that although usually the lawyer must follow the direction of the representative, there are exceptions when (1) the lawyer is representing the client in a matter against the interests of the representative or (2) the representative is violating his or her legal duties towards the client.

5. *When to Take Protective Action*

The last difference is found in subsection (4), which provides that a lawyer may seek the appointment of a guardian for the client or take other protective action when doing so is "practical" and will advance the client's objectives or interests. This language gives some basis for deciding when to take protective action, which is lacking in the Model Rule.

4. Taking Protective Action

Molly M. Wood
Who's the Client?: Competency and the Lawyer-Client Relationship
<http://www.ink.org/public/keln/ethicsmmw.html>*

II. The Impaired Client (*See* Rule 1.14 *Client Under a Disability*)

* * *

2. Protective Action (*See* Rule 1.14(b))

The lawyer's duty as an advisor to exercise "independent professional judgment" in representing a client is particularly compelling when the client may be incompetent. That independent judgment must be informed by the duty to protect a client's rights. If a lawyer finds that the client's condition makes it impossible to continue the representation, the lawyer may take protective action. Rule 1.14(b).

The first problem the lawyer considering protective action faces is that the information which leads the lawyer to question the client's competency is usually privileged under Rule 1.6, *Confidentiality.* "Protective action" within the meaning of the rule perforce entails the disclosure of "information gained with respect to the representation." So disclosure, to the extent necessary to serve the client's best interest, therefore, may be "impliedly authorized" within the meaning of Rule 1.6. (ABA Comm. on Ethics and Professional Responsibility, Informal Op. 89-1530 (1989)). Thus, the lawyer in this position may properly consult a physician concerning the suspected disability.

The next problem the lawyer faces, if a guardianship is to be sought, is the role the lawyer is to play in the proceedings, because appointment of a guardian is a drastic deprivation of civil rights and fundamentally inconsistent with the lawyer's duty of loyalty to the client. The statutory requirement of appointed counsel for the proposed ward in guardianship proceedings at least partly addresses this problem. . . . It is generally not desirable, therefore, for the lawyer to participate in the imposition of a guardianship upon a person to whom the attorney-client privilege may have attached, except as appointed counsel.

Finally, when the lawyer is acting on behalf of a disabled person through a court-appointed guardian or attoney-in-fact, but believes that the guardian or agent is acting contrary to the ward's best interests, the lawyer's authority to take "protective action" may come into play.

C. Abuse, Neglect and Exploitation (*See* Rule 2.3 *Evaluation for Use by Third Persons*)

A lawyer may only undertake an evaluation for third parties if the lawyer "reasonably believes that making the evaluation is compatible with other aspects of the lawyer's relationship with the client." Rule 2.3(a)(1). Typically, it is a lawyer's past relationship with a client which casts into question the "compatibility" of an evaluation. The most obvious incompatibility is that created by the tension between a

---

[*] Copyright © 1996. Reprinted with permission.

lawyer's duty to maintain the confidentiality of information relating to representation of a client and a lawyer's duty not to provide fraudulent or misleading information to third persons who will be relying on the lawyer's evaluation. (*See* Rules 1.6 *Confidentiality* and 4.1 *Truthfulness in Statements to Others.*)

Client Under a Disability
ABA Formal Ethics Op. 96-404 (August 2, 1996)[*]

When a client is unable to act adequately in his own interest, a lawyer may take appropriate protective action including seeking the appointment of a guardian. The lawyer may consult with diagnosticians and others, including family members, in assessing the client's capacity and for guidance about the appropriate protective action. The action taken should be the least restrictive of the client's autonomy that will yet adequately protect the client in connection with the representation. Withdrawal from representation of a client who becomes incapacitated is disfavored, even if ethically permissible under the circumstances.

The lawyer may recommend or support the appointment of a particular person or other entity as guardian, even if the person or entity will likely hire the lawyer to represent it in the guardianship, provided the lawyer has made reasonable inquiry as to the suggested guardian's fitness, discloses the self-interest in the matter, and obtains the court's permission to proceed. In all aspects of the proceeding, the lawyer's duty of candor to the court requires disclosure of all pertinent facts, including the client's view of the proceedings.

5. Withdrawal

Molly M. Wood
Who's the Client?: Competency and the Lawyer-Client Relationship
<http://www.ink.org/public/keln/ethicsmmw.html>[**]

II. The Impaired Client (*See* Rule 1.14 *Client Under a Disability*)

* * *

D. Withdrawal from Representation (*See* Rule 1.16 *Declining or Terminating Representation*)

A client can discharge a lawyer with or without cause, and no lawyer can continue to represent a client who does not wish to be represented. In the case of a disabled client, however, a client's severe mental impairment may operate to suspend or

---

[*] Copyright © American Bar Association. All rights reserved. Reprinted by permission of the American Bar Association. Copies of ABA Ethics Opinions are available from Service Center, American Bar Association, 750 North Lake Shore Drive, Chicago, IL 60611, 312-988-5522.

[**] Copyright © 1996. Reprinted with permission.

terminate a pre-existing attorney-client relationship. Because withdrawal from representation, though depending on the degree of impairment and the status of the proceedings may be necessary, is *not* favored, absent other cause, the client's refusal to accept a lawyer's advice regarding the resolution of a policy question is not sufficient grounds for withdrawal where termination will prejudice the client. (*But see* Rule 3.1 *Meritorious Claims and Contentions.*)

Client Under a Disability
ABA Formal Ethics Op. 96-404 (August 2, 1996)[*]

In the absence of Rule 1.14, a lawyer whose client becomes incompetent would have no choice but to withdraw, not only because a lawyer who continues the representation would be acting without authority, but also because the lawyer would be unable to carry out his responsibilities to the client under the Rules. *See* Rule 1.16(a)(1) (withdrawal required where "the representation will result in violation of the rules of professional conduct"). While Rule 1.14 permits a lawyer to take protective action in such situations, it does not compel the lawyer to do so, and many lawyers are uncomfortable with the prospect of having to so act. The Committee considers that withdrawal is ethically permissible as long as it can be accomplished "without material adverse effect on the interests of the client." Rule 1.16(b).

On the other hand, while withdrawal in these circumstances solves the lawyer's dilemma, it may leave the impaired client without help at a time when the client needs it most. The particular circumstances may also be such that the lawyer cannot withdraw without prejudice to the client. For instance, the client's incompetence may develop in the middle of a pending matter and substitute counsel may not be able to represent the client effectively due to the inability to discuss the matter with the client. Thus, without concluding that a lawyer with an incompetent client may never withdraw, the Committee believes the better course of action, and the one most likely to be consistent with Rule 1.16(b), will often be for the lawyer to stay with the representation and seek appropriate protective action on behalf of the client.

Further Reading. Alison Barnes et al., Counseling Older Clients ch. 3 (1997); Peter J. Strauss et al., Aging and the Law, ch. 3 (1996); Symposium, *Ethical Issues in Representing Older Clients*, 62 Fordham L. Rev. 961-1583 (1994)

---

[*] Copyright © 1996 American Bar Association. Reprinted by permission of the American Bar Association.

CHAPTER 3

Discrimination

A.	Introduction	88
B.	Age Discrimination	90
C.	Disability Discrimination	120

During the past quarter century, legislative and judicial activity at both the state and federal levels has resulted in the creation of a broad array of civil rights enforceable against private and public entities. Comprehensive statutory schemes such as the Age Discrimination in Employment Act, the Americans with Disabilities Act, and their state counterparts, contemplate a society in which age or handicap do not limit an individual's ability fully to participate in all spheres of public and private activity. The broadening and strengthening of civil rights laws has, not surprisingly, had significant costs. Litigation statistics compiled by the Administrative Office of the United States Courts show that in 1998, almost 24,000 workplace discrimination lawsuits were filed in federal court, a figure that has doubled since 1992. Age and disability discrimination suits comprise a substantial and increasing share of these cases. Government and private entities are now required to make public accommodations, broadly defined, accessible to all but the most severely impaired. Although both employment law and disability law each comprise their own practice specialties, it is important for the elder law practitioner to understand some of the basic principles associated with these important substantive areas. In this chapter, we introduce discrimination law as it relates primarily to the senior population.

A. Introduction

National Academy of Elder Law Attorneys
Law & Aging Series: Age Discrimination
<http://www.naela.com/naela/agediscrim.htm>*

The Issue

Since the 1960s, the federal government has enacted many laws prohibiting discrimination against persons based upon their age. Such laws apply in all states and many states have enacted additional laws that enhance the federal protections. The laws prohibit age discrimination in employment, in housing options, in the delivery of services and benefits from federally-assisted programs and services, and in the granting of credit.

The laws involved are the Age Discrimination in Employment Act of 1967 (ADEA), the Age Discrimination Act of 1975, the Rehabilitation Act of 1973, the Fair Housing Amendments Act of 1988, the Americans with Disabilities Act of 1990, the Equal Credit Opportunity Act of 1974 and the Truth in Lending Act of 1968. Each of these federal laws has specific provisions that address the question of discrimination based upon age. All of these laws are complex and lengthy, but each also provides relatively easy access to the agencies charged with enforcement.

In the Age Discrimination in Employment Act, employees and job applicants over the age of 40 are protected from age discrimination in respect to any employment practice or decision including hiring and discharge, promotion, layoffs, compensation, and other terms, conditions and rights of employment. Age may not be used in advertising employment positions either specifically or by [implication].

The Age Discrimination Act of 1975 prohibits age discrimination in the delivery of federal or federally-assisted services and benefits. Such programs may include health services, educational programs, housing, welfare, food stamps, and rehabilitation programs.

The Rehabilitation Act protects persons with handicaps from discrimination in housing programs, employment and other federally-assisted programs.

The Fair Housing Amendments protect older handicapped adults from discrimination in the sale or rental of housing. Another housing statute recognizes the physical and mental benefits of pets to older persons and prohibits unreasonable rules barring pets in housing that receives federal assistance.

The Americans with Disabilities Act is a sweeping law requiring reasonable access to places of public accommodation and public entities. The Act further protects persons with disabilities in employment, transportation and communications programs and assures that such programs will be usable and reachable by such persons.

The statutes relating to credit issues require that information about credit be readily available and subject to challenge, that the actual costs of credit be promi-

---

* Reprinted with permission.

nently disclosed and make it unlawful to discriminate against any applicant for credit on the basis of age. The act protects persons 62 and older.

What You Need To Know

Each of the laws prohibiting discrimination based upon age has specific enforcement provisions. While the laws are indeed complex, all of them provide for governmental assistance in protecting your rights. At the same time, some of the laws allow an individual to bring a private lawsuit for damages resulting from prohibited discrimination.

Actions taken will depend upon the result wanted. If someone is denied credit and believes the denial was wrongfully based upon age, the goal then is probably [simply to] get a loan. If, on the other hand, someone is denied a promotion or discharged from employment because of one's age, then you may want to be promoted, reinstated and perhaps paid for the loss of income you would have earned. In some cases, it is also possible to obtain punitive damages where there has been willful discrimination.

There are certain exceptions that permit an employer to act based upon age considerations. Firefighters and law enforcement officers, for example, are not covered by the ADEA for public safety reasons. Tenured university employees have been excluded from coverage as are certain executives and policy making employees. In addition, there are certain defenses that are available to employers charged with age discrimination; these include such things as age-specific qualifications for the job itself such as a model for children's clothing. An employer can always discharge or pass over an employee for poor performance or other job related problems other than age.

In determining whether you may be a victim of age discrimination, it is important to look at all of the circumstances surrounding your employment, credit or housing problem and gather as much information as possible about what has occurred. It will be important that you keep records concerning any events that make you believe that age was the reason for your problem—such records include copies of letters, employment reviews and forms.

Finally, there are time limits (statutes of limitations) governing how long you can wait before making a complaint. If you suspect you have been discriminated against, you should take action promptly.

Where To Go For Help

If you suspect that you have been discriminated against in programs of assistance, in your employment (obtaining or keeping a job or getting a promotion), in matters involving your housing or in credit matters, there are several places you can obtain assistance.

In many of the laws prohibiting discrimination, the federal government has placed the responsibility of enforcement on federal agencies. In employment matters, you can contact the Equal Employment Opportunity Commission (EEOC); the EEOC has offices throughout the country. The state's Attorney General's Office or the Office of the U.S. Attorney are also good resources.

The U.S. Attorney and the state Attorney General are also helpful in assisting with discrimination claims concerning housing, credit or in other matters. The Federal Trade Commission is also able to assist with credit matters.

In addition, the private elder law attorney who has experience in Age Discrimination matters, may provide invaluable help. Some of the laws prohibiting age discrimination also permit a person to initiate a private lawsuit for payment of damages as a result of the discrimination.

The Role Of The Elder Law Attorney

Age discrimination is one of the areas that elder law attorneys have focused on in their work, since it is an important area of protecting the rights of older persons. Elder law attorneys are able to work with clients to select the best route in enforcing the claim of illegal discrimination and are able to effectively assist clients in determining their goals in the matter.

Elder law attorneys are particularly sensitive to the concerns of older persons and their families and are able to address these specific issues. Elder law attorneys are also able to provide information about other areas affecting the elderly.

Questions

How would you begin to counsel a client whom you believe to have been the victim of unlawful age or disability discrimination? Is it inevitably in such a client's interest to litigate her claim?

B. Age Discrimination

1. Federal Law

In connection with the following excerpts, read the Age Discrimination in Employment Act (incorporating the Older Workers Benefit Protection Act) in the statutory supplement.

Rene E. Thorne & Howard Shapiro
The Age Discrimination in Employment Act: Protection for Older Workers
THE COMPLEAT LAWYER **(Spring 1998)**[*]

Although all federal labor and employment laws apply to older employees, the Age Discrimination In Employment Act (ADEA) in particular protects older workers. As the baby boomers age, and companies continue to experience layoffs, down-

---

[*] Copyright © American Bar Association. All rights reserved. Reprinted by permission of the American Bar Association.

sizing, and reductions in force, there will continue to be a surge of age discrimination lawsuits under the ADEA and corresponding state laws.

Who Is Covered?

The ADEA applies to private employers engaged in an industry affecting commerce who have 20 or more employees for each working day in each of 20 or more calendar weeks during the current or preceding calendar year. The ADEA also applies to employment agencies and to labor organizations (i.e., unions) if the organization maintains or operates a hiring hall, or has 25 or more members, and

(1) is a certified bargaining agent under the NLRA [National Labor Relations Act], or
(2) is otherwise recognized as a bargaining agent, or
(3) has one of the specified relationships with a covered union.

The ADEA also applies to states and their political subdivisions, but not to state military departments.

Who Is Protected?

Age limits. The ADEA protects individuals who are at least 40 years of age. Generally, there is no upward cap on ADEA coverage under federal law. However, many state age discrimination statutes still provide an upward cap of 70 years of age.

Employees. The ADEA defines an "employee" simply as "an individual employed by any employer." Over the years, courts used a variety of tests to determine whether an individual is an employee for purposes of the ADEA. Some circuits use the "economic realities" test. Other circuits use the "hybrid test."

Today, most courts have adopted a test that focuses on the control the putative employer exercises over the alleged employee, and may include as many as 11 other factors:

(1) the kind of occupation;
(2) the skill required in the particular occupation;
(3) whether the "employer" or the individual in question furnishes the equipment used and the place of work;
(4) the length of time during which the individual has worked;
(5) the method of payment;
(6) the manner in which the work relationship is terminated;
(7) whether annual leave is afforded;
(8) whether the work is an integral part of the business of the "employer";
(9) whether the worker accumulates retirement benefits;
(10) whether the "employer" pays social security taxes; and
(11) the intention of the parties.

Bona fide executives. The ADEA allows the forcible retirement of an individual who is 65 years old and in "a bona fide executive or a high policymaking position" for the two-year period immediately before retirement, if that individual is entitled to a non-forfeitable annual pension benefit equaling $44,000.

What Is Prohibited under the ADEA?

Prohibitions for employers. Employers cannot discriminate in any way against employees because of their age. Specifically, the act makes it unlawful for an employer: (1) to fail or refuse to hire or to discharge any individual or otherwise discriminate against any individual with respect to his compensation, terms, conditions, or privileges of employment, because of such individual's age; (2) to limit, segregate, or classify his employees in any way which would deprive or tend to deprive any individual of employment opportunities or otherwise adversely affect his status as an employee, because of such individual's age; or (3) to reduce the wage rate of any employee in order to comply with [the Act].

Retaliation. Employers, employment agencies, and labor organizations are prohibited from taking adverse employment action against any individual because he opposed practices prohibited by the ADEA; or because the individual made a charge, testified, assisted, or participated in an investigation, proceeding, or litigation under the ADEA.

Vacancy publishing restrictions. Employers, employment agencies, and labor organizations may not publish advertisements or notices seeking employment that contain age preferences, specifications, or discrimination.

Notice posting requirements. Employers have a duty to post conspicuously a notice informing employees of their rights under the ADEA.

What Is Not Prohibited under the ADEA?

Good cause. Of course, it is not unlawful "to discharge or otherwise discipline an individual for good cause." Among other things, "good cause" may consist of work rule violations or documented poor performance.

Bona fide occupational qualification. Distinguishing among employees is not unlawful "where age is a bona fide occupational qualification reasonably necessary to the normal operation of the particular business." The Supreme Court has held that the exception is narrow. This principle is illustrated by the case of *Williams v. Hughes Helicopters, Inc.* There, the court held the defendant could rely on the FAA's Age 60 Rule as a bona fide occupational qualification to validate its "stop flying" policy at ages 55 and 60 for test pilots.

Reasonable factors other than age. Distinguishing among employees is not unlawful "where the differentiation is based on reasonable factors other than age." The Supreme Court has held that "a decision . . . to fire an older employee solely because he has nine-plus years of service and therefore is "close to vesting would not constitute discriminatory treatment on the basis of age," although such conduct may be a violation of ERISA. The Supreme Court explained that the prohibited stereotyping (that is, "Older employees are likely to be _____") did not come into play in such a decision. The Court cautioned, however, that "target[ing] employees with a particular pension status on the assumption that these employees are likely to be older" may constitute age discrimination.

The case of *EEOC v. Insurance Co. of North America* is also illustrative. There, the court held that an employer had not discriminated against the plaintiff on the basis of age when it declined to hire him on the basis of his "overqualification" for a loss-control position. The employer argued that based on his 30 years of experience in the field, the plaintiff might delve too deeply into—and spend an inordinate amount of time examining—accounts. Agreeing with the employer, the court concluded that the employer acted for a legitimate business purpose and not pursuant to the plaintiff's age. The court cautioned, however, that rejecting an applicant based on overqualification might constitute age discrimination, where, for example, the job qualifications are not defined by objective criteria.

Bona fide seniority system. To the extent that terminations or layoffs are pursuant to a bona fide seniority system, the practice is lawful under the provisions of § 623(f)(2) of the ADEA: "It shall not be unlawful for an employer . . . (2) to observe the terms of a bona fide seniority system. . . ."

The Older Workers' Benefit Protection Act

The Older Workers Benefit Protection Act (OWBPA) of 1990 was passed to amend the ADEA in several important respects. First, OWBPA defines the terms under which employers may observe the terms of a bona fide employee benefit plan:

> It shall not be unlawful . . . to observe the terms of a bona fide employee benefit plan—
> (i) where, for each benefit or benefit package, the actual amount of payment made or cost incurred on behalf of an older worker is no less than that made or incurred on behalf of a younger worker . . . ; or
> (ii) that is a voluntary early retirement incentive plan consistent with the relevant purpose of [the ADEA]. Notwithstanding [the above], no such employee benefit plan or voluntary early retirement incentive plan shall excuse the failure to hire any individual, and no such employee benefit plan shall require or permit the involuntary retirement of any individual [age 40 or older] because of the age of such individual. An employer, employment agency, or labor organization . . . shall have the burden of proving that such actions are lawful in any civil enforcement proceeding brought under this chapter . . . .

It is not unlawful under an ERISA plan to condition eligibility for normal or early retirement benefits on attainment of a minimum age. In addition, there are detailed sections concerning the legality of various provisions in pension plans.

Waiver of rights under the ADEA. Another important concept under the OWPBA is that an employee can only waive his rights under the ADEA when the waiver is knowing and voluntary. The OWBPA defines the terms under which waiver is permitted:

(1) It must be written in understandable English as part of an employer-individual agreement;
(2) It must specifically refer to rights or claims arising under the ADEA;
(3) It may not waive the individual's rights or claims arising after its execution;
(4) There must be consideration exchanged for the waiver in addition to something to which the individual already is entitled;

94   ELDER LAW: READINGS, CASES, AND MATERIALS

(5) The individual must be advised in writing to consult with an attorney before entering the agreement;
(6) The individual has at least 21 days to consider the agreement, and
   (a) This period is extended to at least 45 days if the waiver is sought in connection with an exit incentive or other termination program offered to a group; . . .
(7) The agreement must allow at least 7 days after execution for its revocation by the individual and not become effective until then;
(8) If the waiver is sought in connection with an exit incentive or other termination program offered to a group, the employer must inform the individual, in writing understandable to the average participant, of
   (a) What group is covered, the eligibility factors, and applicable time limits, and
   (b) The ages and job titles of all potential participants, and the ages and job titles of all noneligible persons in the same job classification or organizational unit; and
(9) If the waiver is sought in settlement of an EEOC charge or a lawsuit brought under the ADEA, items 1-5 above must be met, and the individual must have reasonable time to consider the settlement.

The burden of proving that a waiver is knowing and voluntary, in compliance with those standards, falls upon the party asserting its validity, and is an affirmative defense. No waiver will affect the EEOC's rights to enforce the ADEA, however.

In dealing with releases under the ADEA and OWBPA, practitioners need to be aware that the Supreme Court recently ruled that a release that does not fully comply with the OWBPA cannot be enforced by the employer even if the departing employee fails to tender back the consideration to the employer prior to instigating a lawsuit against the employer.

Burdens of Proof and Defenses

Burden of proof in an ADEA case. It is a rare case in which the plaintiff will have direct evidence of discrimination. As such, in *McDonnell Douglas Corp. v. Green*, the Supreme Court set forth a detailed method of proof of intentional discrimination where there is no direct evidence of discriminatory intent. An employee must show the following:

   a.   Membership in a protected class (i.e., 40 or older).
   b.   Adverse personnel action (termination, failure to promote, etc.).
   c.   A younger employee was treated more favorably.
   d.   The plaintiff was as good or as qualified as the younger employee, or some other evidence of age discrimination.

Once the plaintiff proves these four elements, and creates an inference of discrimination, the burden of going forward with evidence shifts to the defendant to articulate a legitimate, nondiscriminatory reason for the decision. If the employer successfully meets this burden, the plaintiff must then demonstrate that the proffered reason was merely a pretext for discrimination. The ultimate burden of proof of intentional discrimination, however, always remains with the plaintiff.

In recent years, the Supreme Court has modified the *McDonnell Douglas* model somewhat in age discrimination cases based on failure to hire or rehire. In *O'Connor v. Consolidated Caterers Corp.*, the Court held that the ADEA prohibits age discrimination even among persons within the protected group, so that the plaintiff need not demonstrate that the favored applicant or employee was outside the protected group.

Disparate treatment standards. The "disparate treatment" theory applies when "the employer simply treats some people less favorably than others." Liability in a disparate treatment case "depends on whether the protected trait (under the ADEA age) actually motivated the employer's decision." An employer may be liable under the ADEA where the employment decision at issue was based on a formal, facially discriminatory policy, requiring adverse treatment of all employees with that trait, or where the employment decision was motivated by the protected trait on an ad hoc, informal basis.

There are three ways a plaintiff can prove a prima facie case of disparate treatment:

(1) direct evidence of intent;
(2) statistical evidence; and
(3) proof in accordance with the formula originally set out in *McDonnell Douglas*.

Enforcing the ADEA

Filing an EEOC charge. Under 29 U.S.C. § 626(d), "No civil action may be commenced by an individual under [the ADEA] until 60 days after a charge alleging unlawful discrimination has been filed with the [EEOC]."

Statute of limitations. A charge of age discrimination shall be filed with the EEOC: (1) within 180 days after the alleged age discrimination occurred, or (2) within 300 days of the alleged discrimination if the state in which the discrimination occurred provides a law prohibiting age discrimination and empowering a "state authority" to grant or seek relief from the employment discrimination.

Tolling of the charge filing period. As a general rule, an employer's failure to post the required notice may toll, or suspend, the charge filing periods unless the employer can show other employee knowledge of the statute.

Filing a lawsuit. The Civil Rights Act of 1991 amends the procedure for filing suit under the ADEA to comport with Title VII requirements. The ADEA requires the EEOC to notify complainants when a charge is dismissed or terminated. The charging party thereafter has 90 days from receipt of the notice to file suit. The ADEA also gives employees the right to trial by jury.

Arbitration. In *Gilmer v. Interstate/Johnson Lane Corp.*, the Supreme Court required a securities dealer on the New York Stock Exchange to arbitrate his ADEA claim against his employer. The employee had signed an agreement stating he would arbitrate any such claim. The Supreme Court held arbitration of an ADEA claim, pursuant to an arbitration agreement, does not contravene the purposes of the ADEA.

What Relief Is Available to Employees?

The ADEA provides remedies that include unpaid wages, reinstatement, promotion, liquidated damages in the case of willful violations, and "such legal or equitable relief as may be appropriate to effectuate the purposes of" the act.

Back pay. Back pay awards may include lost wages, pension benefits, insurance benefits, profit sharing, and other benefits that the employee would have earned "but for" the discrimination. The claimant is obligated to mitigate damages. It is the defendant's burden to establish that the plaintiff failed to mitigate his damages in order to limit successfully a plaintiff's back pay award. To cut off a back pay award, defendants must prove that the plaintiff did not exercise "reasonable" diligence in seeking employment substantially equivalent to the position he lost. To limit a back pay award, an employer may make an unconditional offer of employment, i.e., offer a terminated employee a full and unconditional return to work.

Liquidated damages. If an employer's violation of the act is "willful," the employee is entitled to double the amount of wages/salary due to her. The standard for proving a willful violation is set forth in *Hazen Paper Co. v. Biggins, McLaughlin v. Richland Shoe Co.*, and *Trans World Airlines, Inc. v. Thurston*. A "willful" violation occurs when an employer "either knew or showed reckless disregard for the matter of whether its conduct was prohibited by the ADEA."

In determining whether a "willful" violation occurred, it is irrelevant whether the employment decision was based on a formal, facially discriminatory policy, affecting all employees with that trait, or was based on an ad hoc, informal basis. Once an employee demonstrates a "willful" violation, the employee need not, as some appellate courts have required, additionally show that an employer's conduct was outrageous, or provide direct evidence of the employer's motivation, or prove that age was the predominant rather than a determinative factor in the employment decision.

The Supreme Court has ruled that awards of back pay and liquidated damages are taxable under I.R.C. § 104(a)(2).

Reinstatement or front pay. As an equitable remedy, a terminated age discriminatee can seek full reinstatement to her job. Where reinstatement is not feasible, front pay may be awarded to compensate an employee for future lost compensation. However, a court may not consider front pay unless it first determines that reinstatement is "not feasible."

Compensatory and punitive damages. Courts have held that compensatory damages are not an available remedy under the ADEA. Also, punitive damages are not an available remedy under the ADEA.

Attorney fees and costs. The ADEA incorporates the attorney fees provision of the Fair Labor Standards Act, and allows fees and court costs to a prevailing plaintiff.

Injunction. Although a broad injunction barring any future discrimination of all similarly-situated employees may be an abuse of discretion, a narrow injunction protecting one individual—who had been subject to "widespread continuous antagonism" by the employer—may not constitute an abuse of discretion.

Questions

1. How can an employer protect itself from workplace litigation?

2. Does the prospect of obtaining attorney's fees in civil rights litigation suggest any ethical dilemmas for the elder law attorney?

O'Connor v. Consolidated Coin Caterers Corporation
517 U.S. 308 (1996)

JUSTICE SCALIA delivered the opinion of the Court.

Petitioner James O'Connor was employed by respondent Consolidated Coin Caterers Corporation from 1978 until August 10, 1990, when, at age 56, he was fired. Claiming that he had been dismissed because of his age in violation of the ADEA, petitioner brought suit in the United States District Court for the Western District of North Carolina. After discovery, the District Court granted respondent's motion for summary judgment, and petitioner appealed. The Court of Appeals for the Fourth Circuit stated that petitioner could establish a prima facie case under *McDonnell Douglas* only if he could prove that (1) he was in the age group protected by the ADEA; (2) he was discharged or demoted; (3) at the time of his discharge or demotion, he was performing his job at a level that met his employer's legitimate expectations; and (4) following his discharge or demotion, he was replaced by someone of comparable qualifications outside the protected class. Since petitioner's replacement was 40 years old, the Court of Appeals concluded that the last element of the prima facie case had not been made out.[2] Finding that petitioner's claim could not survive a motion for summary judgment without benefit of the *McDonnell Douglas* presumption (*i.e.*, "under the ordinary standards of proof used in civil cases"), the Court of Appeals affirmed the judgment of dismissal. We granted O'Connor's petition for certiorari.

In *McDonnell Douglas*, we "established an allocation of the burden of production and an order for the presentation of proof in Title VII discriminatory treatment cases." *St. Mary's Honor Center v. Hicks*, 509 U.S. 502, 506 (1993). We held that a plaintiff alleging racial discrimination in violation of Title VII of the Civil Rights Act of 1964, 42 U.S.C. §2000e *et seq.*, could establish a prima facie case by showing "(i) that he belongs to a racial minority; (ii) that he applied and was qualified for a job for which the employer was seeking applicants; (iii) that, despite his qualifications, he was rejected; and (iv) that, after his rejection, the position remained open and the employer continued to seek applicants from persons of [the] complainant's qualifications." Once the plaintiff has met this initial burden, the burden of production shifts to the employer "to articulate some legitimate, nondiscriminatory reason for the employee's rejection." If the trier of fact finds that the elements of the prima facie

---

[2] The court also concluded that even under a modified version of the *McDonnell Douglas* prima facie standard which the Fourth Circuit applies to reduction in force cases, see *Mitchell v. Data General Corp.*, 12 F.3d 1310, 1315 (1993), petitioner could not prevail. We limit our review to the Fourth Circuit's treatment of this case as a non reduction in force case.

case are supported by a preponderance of the evidence and the employer remains silent, the court must enter judgment for the plaintiff.

In assessing claims of age discrimination brought under the ADEA, the Fourth Circuit, like others,[3] has applied some variant of the basic evidentiary framework set forth in *McDonnell Douglas*. We have never had occasion to decide whether that application of the Title VII rule to the ADEA context is correct, but since the parties do not contest that point, we shall assume it. On that assumption, the question presented for our determination is what elements must be shown in an ADEA case to establish the prima facie case that triggers the employer's burden of production.

As the very name "prima facie case" suggests, there must be at least a logical connection between each element of the prima facie case and the illegal discrimination for which it establishes a "legally mandatory, rebuttable presumption." The element of replacement by someone under 40 fails this requirement. The discrimination prohibited by the ADEA is discrimination "because of [an] individual's age," 29 U.S.C. § 623(a)(1), though the prohibition is "limited to individuals who are at least 40 years of age," § 631(a). This language does not ban discrimination against employees because they are aged 40 or older; it bans discrimination against employees because of their age, but limits the protected class to those who are 40 or older. The fact that one person in the protected class has lost out to another person in the protected class is thus irrelevant, so long as he has lost out *because of his age*. Or to put the point more concretely, there can be no greater inference of *age* discrimination (as opposed to "40 or over" discrimination) when a 40 year old is replaced by a 39 year old than when a 56 year old is replaced by a 40 year old. Because it lacks probative value, the fact that an ADEA plaintiff was replaced by someone outside the protected class is not a proper element of the *McDonnell Douglas* prima facie case.

Perhaps some courts have been induced to adopt the principle urged by respondent in order to avoid creating a prima facie case on the basis of very thin evidence— for example, the replacement of a 68 year old by a 65 year old. While the respondent's principle theoretically permits such thin evidence (consider the example above of a 40 year old replaced by a 39 year old), as a practical matter it will rarely do so, since the vast majority of age discrimination claims come from older employees. In our view, however, the proper solution to the problem lies not in making an utterly irrelevant factor an element of the prima facie case, but rather in recognizing that the prima facie case requires "evidence *adequate to create an inference that an employment decision was based on a[n] [illegal] discriminatory criterion* . . . ." *Teamsters v. United States*, 431 U.S. 324, 358 (1977) (emphasis added). In the

---

[3] *See, e.g., Roper v. Peabody Coal Co.*, 47 F.3d 925, 926-27 (7th Cir. 1995); *Rinehart v. Independence*, 35 F.3d 1263, 1265 (8th Cir. 1994), *cert. denied*, 514 U.S. 1096 (1995); *Seman v. Coplay Cement Co.*, 26 F.3d 428, 432, n.7 (3d Cir. 1994); *Roush v. KFC Nat. Mgt. Co.*, 10 F.3d 392, 396 (6th Cir. 1993), *cert. denied*, 513 U.S. 808 (1994); *Lindsey v. Prive Corp.*, 987 F.2d 324, 326, n.5 (5th Cir. 1993); *Goldstein v. Manhattan Industries, Inc.*, 758 F.2d 1435, 1442 (11th Cir.), *cert. denied*, 474 U.S. 1005 (1985); *Haskell v. Kaman Corp.*, 743 F.2d 113, 119, and n.1 (2d Cir. 1984); *Cuddy v. Carmen*, 694 F.2d 853, 856-57 (D.C. Cir. 1982); *Douglas v. Anderson*, 656 F.2d 528, 531-32 (9th Cir. 1981); *Loeb v. Textron, Inc.*, 600 F.2d 1003, 1014-16 (1st Cir. 1979); *Schwager v. Sun Oil Co. of Pa.*, 591 F.2d 58, 60-61 (10th Cir. 1979).

age discrimination context, such an inference can not be drawn from the replacement of one worker with another worker insignificantly younger. Because the ADEA prohibits discrimination on the basis of age and not class membership, the fact that a replacement is substantially younger than the plaintiff is a far more reliable indicator of age discrimination than is the fact that the plaintiff was replaced by someone outside the protected class. The judgment of the Fourth Circuit is reversed, and the case is remanded for proceedings consistent with this opinion.

It is so ordered.

Questions

1. Do you agree with the outcome of this case? Why or why not?

2. Does the plain language of the ADEA or its underlying purposes suggest a preference for older to younger workers within the protected age group?

3. Soon after *O'Connor* was decided, the EEOC issued enforcement guidelines interpreting this decision for its investigators and others interested in compliance with the ADEA as interpreted in *O'Connor*. See EEOC Notice No. 915.002 (9-18-96), www.eeoc.gov/docs/oconnor.txt. Review these guidelines. Do you agree with the EEOC's interpretation of *O'Connor*?

Scott v. The Goodyear Tire and Rubber Co.
160 F.3d 1121 (6th Cir. 1998)

NATHANIEL R. JONES, Circuit Judge. Plaintiff Albert J. Scott appeals the grant of summary judgment in favor of Defendant Goodyear Tire and Rubber Company ("Goodyear") in this age discrimination case brought under the Age Discrimination in Employment Act ("ADEA"), 29 U.S.C. §§ 621 *et seq.* and Ohio's counterpart statute.[4] Specifically, Scott contends that Goodyear constructively discharged him when it eliminated his position following company restructuring and offered him early retirement instead of redeployment[5] to a comparable position within the company. Upon consideration of the record and applicable law, we reverse the grant of summary judgment and remand for proceedings consistent with this opinion.

I.

Albert Scott began his employment with Goodyear on June 6, 1952 and continued working for the company until December 1993—the date of his decision to retire. During his 41 years of uninterrupted service to Goodyear, Scott held many positions including stockman, gas man, general service man, delivery and sales person of Tires, Batteries and Accessories, credit sales manager, store manager, retail

---

[4] Although Scott brought his claim under section 4101.17, the Ohio age discrimination statute has since been recodified at Ohio Rev. Code Ann. § 4112.14 (Anderson 1988).

[5] "Redeployment" and its derivatives are the parties' choice terms for "reassignment."

store operations representative, division inventory coordinator and, finally, Operations Manager. Scott received satisfactory reviews throughout his employment with Goodyear.

In his final position as Operations Manager, Scott bore responsibility for administering, implementing, and coordinating policy and procedures dictated by the company to its eastern region district managers and retail stores. Although Goodyear centered its operations managers within its headquarters in Akron, Ohio, Scott's duties sometimes required him to travel to store locations to handle administrative matters directly with store managers.

In May of 1993, Goodyear began a comprehensive restructuring of its upper-level management structure, which resulted in the elimination of the five Operations Manager positions maintained by the company, including the position held by Scott.[6] The other four positions were held by John Cox (63 years old), Rodney Gwinn (51 years old), Greg Wahrle (35 years old) and Shayon Smith (32 years old). Scott, who was 61 years old when his position was eliminated, was told that he had not been redeployed because others could better meet the experience, skill, educational and other characteristic needs of the company. Redeployed employees, as Gordon Hewitt, a Goodyear executive described it, would need, among other things, a "high energy level."

With the elimination of the operations manager position, Goodyear created the new position of Retail Administrator. Where, according to Goodyear management, the former position had fed the "heavily paperwork oriented system" and bred "inefficiency between Akron and the regions," Goodyear intended the new position to help improve management efficiency and customer relations. Under the new structure, the retail administrator position demanded a familiarity with computer technology, as the prevailing paper-based data recording system had become a major source of inefficiency.

Sometime around early December 1993, Ken Gable and Rob Morris, both subordinates of Goodyear's Manager of Human Resources Paul Evert, were instructed by Evert to travel to Cleveland, Ohio and inform Scott that his position had been eliminated. Evert also requested that Gable cover the options available to Scott in the wake of his job loss. According to Gable's deposition testimony, he inquired into the decision to eliminate Scott's position, but was "advised that the decision had been made and that [informing Scott of the elimination and decision not to redeploy him] was [his] assignment and that [Evert] was not going to discuss how the decision was arrived at [sic]." With Evert having closed off that discussion, Gable and Morris traveled to Cleveland the next day, and informed Scott that his job had been eliminated. Scott questioned Gable about the reasons for the decision, and Gable responded that he was not in a position to tell him because he did not know.

Gable then presented Scott with three options in lieu of continuing on as an operations manager. First, Scott could accept layoff status and receive no benefits at all and no possibility of recall. Second, Scott could accept layoff status, receive sup-

---

[6] The company only maintained five operations manager positions. Each operations manager took responsibility for a particular region of Goodyear's national business.

plemental unemployment compensation benefits on a regular basis and remain under consideration for recall to a new position, if such a position became available at a later date.[7] Finally, Scott could opt for retirement and receive a lump sum payment of $114,500.86, as well as monthly retirement checks and continued health benefits into retirement. Scott ultimately chose retirement.

As it turns out, some of the other former operations managers were retained and redeployed within the company. Shayon Smith was redeployed into a newly created retail administrator position based on his ability to "look at the overall process and then to get other people to cooperate with him that were not his peers" and his electronics background, as was Greg Wahrle, because his "programming skills" and his "team player" approach were highly rated among executives. Rodney Gwinn accepted a district manager position in Phoenix. Goodyear officials stated in deposition testimony that Gwinn's previous experience as a district manager made him a natural fit for the Phoenix position. Thus, of the five former operations managers, only Scott and John Cox, the two oldest managers, were not offered definite redeployment opportunities within the company.[8]

After his retirement, Scott brought this age discrimination action under the ADEA and a corresponding Ohio anti-discrimination statute on May 12, 1995, alleging that Goodyear's decision to eliminate his position was impermissibly motivated by age considerations. During the subsequent discovery phase, Scott compiled a number of suspicious facts. First, as noted above, he uncovered the irregular manner with which the decision to eliminate his position was handled. According to the undisputed deposition testimony of Evert and Gable, the latter was instructed to inform Scott of the elimination of his operations manager position without asking further questions. Consequently, Gable entered the discussion with Scott unable to answer questions about why the company had decided not to redeploy him. According to Gable, this occurrence deviated from normal practice, since he, as human resources representative, was generally given latitude to inquire into the basis for a given employment decision and to assess for the adversely-treated worker his or her prospects for future employment with the company. On occasion, in fact, Gable was given permission to find other employment within the company for a dismissed employee.

In addition to the unusually vague response given to Scott, various statements of two of the three managers responsible for the decision to eliminate Scott's position indicated age bias. According to Edward Ercegovich,[9] a Goodyear employee at the time of the reorganization, Ed Gallagher, who was then Vice President of the

---

[7] Under this second option, Scott risked losing medical benefits after 18 months of taking lay-off status.

[8] The operations manager positions were not the only positions eliminated as a result of the corporate reorganization. In all, forty-eight positions were eliminated as part of this restructuring, including regional secretaries, operations staff persons, administrative managers and district administrators.

[9] Ercegovich himself brought a substantively identical age discrimination suit against Goodyear after Goodyear eliminated his position and failed to redeploy him. We reversed the district court's grant of summary judgment to Goodyear because we found that material issues of fact existed as to whether Ercegovich was denied a transfer because of his age. *Ercegovich v. Goodyear Tire & Rubber Co.,* 154 F.3d 344 (6th Cir. 1998).

Retail Sales Division, made statements in 1993 such as "this company is run by white haired old men, waiting to retire" and "this must change." Ercegovich similarly attested that he heard Hewitt state in August 1995 in reference to Goodyear's upcoming Budget planning: "Some people will lose their jobs, but in time, we will replace them with young college graduates at less money."[10] Further, Scott presented deposition testimony from two of the three redeployed operations managers, Shayon Smith and Greg Wahrle, indicating that they had not been told that they were being laid off. Finally, Scott presented statistical evidence showing the average age of eliminated employees at 47.35 years old and that of non-eliminated employees at 40.47 years old. In reviewing these statistical findings, Drs. Harvey Rosen and John Burke, both economists, performed a chi-square test[11] to determine whether the age of an employee was a non-factor in determining whether his or her position was eliminated. After conducting further statistical analysis using a chi-square testing model, the economists concluded that the "data marginally *fail to reject* the null hypothesis that employee age is insignificant in explaining whether or not an employee's position was eliminated."

---

[10] The affidavit states in full substantive part:

Edward E. Ercegovich, after being duly sworn, according to law deposes and states that he is of legal age, sound mind, and has personal knowledge of the following:
1. That he was employed by the Goodyear Tire and Rubber Company in its Retail Stores Division from February 7, 1962, until October 28, 1994;
2. That from or about January, 1992, through the end of his employment with Goodyear he served as Quality Systems Coordinator;
3. That while functioning in that position in or about late 1993, he had the opportunity to hear and did hear Edward Gallagher, then Vice President of the Retail Stores Division, substantively state in a meeting on the seventh floor that "This company is being run by white haired old men, waiting to retire", and "This must change"; and
4. That while still functioning in the same position with the Retail Stores Division in or about August 25, 1995, I heard Gordon Hewitt, Director of Finance for the Retail Stores Division, substantively state in his 1995 Budget/Business Plan presentation to the group that "Some people will lose their jobs, but in time, we will replace them with young college graduates at less money."

J.A. at 202. While Ercegovich's affidavit seems in order, we note that Scott, in his brief, also attributes quotes to Hewitt through deposition testimony of Gable to the effect that Goodyear "needs to hire younger men." However, a closer look at the deposition in question suggests that Gable was actually quoting former Goodyear Executive Mel Morrison, not Hewitt. *See* J.A. at 549. Morrison left Goodyear in 1990, several years before the relevant temporal period regarding Goodyear's allegedly discriminatory acts. Hence, we have serious doubts of any probative value that the quotes from the Gable deposition may have in this case.

[11] In *King v. General Electric Co.,* 960 F.2d 617 (7th Cir. 1992), the Seventh Circuit explained:

A chi-square test evaluates the disparity between the expected and observed frequency of a certain outcome. For example, suppose that of the individuals terminated at a given time, a greater percentage of them are within the protected age class. We want to determine whether the disparity in termination rates can be attributed to chance, or whether the disparity is so large, that some factor other than chance probably influence[s] the selection of the individuals terminated. . . . A [c]hi-square test will determine whether the chance or other factors influenced the outcome.

Id. at 626 n.5 (citing Walter Connolly, Jr. et al. *Use of Statistics in Employment Opportunity Litigation* § 10.05[2] (1991)).

CHAPTER 3: DISCRIMINATION   103

Prior to trial, however, Goodyear submitted a summary judgment motion on May 3, 1996, which the district court granted. Inexplicably, in the face of the economist's conclusions, the district court stated that no evidence supported Scott's contention that Goodyear managers forced him into retirement due to his age and thereby created an actionable instance of discrimination. Further, the district concluded that, even if Scott had raised a genuine factual question regarding a constructive discharge theory, he failed to provide additional evidence to support an inference that age-related bias motivated the adverse redeployment decision. Moreover, the district court determined that Scott failed to establish a prima facie case of age discrimination because he voluntarily accepted early retirement. Scott then filed this timely appeal.

II.

Summary judgment is proper "if the pleadings, depositions, answers to interrogatories, and admissions on file, together with the affidavits, if any, show that there is no genuine issue as to any material fact and that the moving party is entitled to a judgment as a matter of law." Fed. R. Civ. P. 56(c). This court exercises *de novo* review of a grant of summary judgment below.

Under the ADEA, a plaintiff is typically required to proffer evidence of the following to make out a prima facie case of age discrimination: (1) that plaintiff was between 40 and 65 years old; (2) that he was qualified for the particular position; (3) that he was subjected to adverse employment action; and (4) that he was replaced by a younger individual. Once a prima facie case has been established, this court applies the shifting burden framework of *McDonnell Douglas v. Green,* 411 U.S. 792 (1973), to age discrimination cases as well. Thus, upon presentation of a prima facie case, the defendant must submit a legitimate, nondiscriminatory reason motivated the adverse employment action. The plaintiff is then required to demonstrate that the reason proffered by the defendant was pretextual. In the words of the Supreme Court, the pretext inquiry considers whether "the legitimate reasons offered by the defendant were not its true reasons, but were a pretext for discrimination."

The district court found, and parties appear to concede, that the law applicable to work force reduction cases is appropriate here. In such cases, this court takes account of the fact that the employer may not replace the plaintiff with a single worker. "Where, as here, there is a reduction in force, a plaintiff must either show that age was a factor in eliminating his position, or, where some employees are shifted to other positions, that he was qualified for another position, he was not given a new position, and that the decision not to place him in a new position was motivated by plaintiff's age." Consequently, the fourth prong of the prima facie age discrimination showing is supplanted by a requirement that the plaintiff proffer "additional direct, circumstantial, or statistical evidence tending to indicate that the employer singled out [the plaintiff] for discharge for impermissible reasons." For purposes of our review of the summary judgment grant below, this case turns on two issues: whether the actions taken against Scott by Goodyear can be construed as constructive termination and, if so, whether Scott has provided sufficient evidence of discriminatory intent regarding the alleged adverse actions to create a factual question on the pretext issue. We answer in the affirmative as to both issues.

A.

The first two prima facie elements appear to be established on the record. There is no dispute that Scott was 61 years old at the time his position was eliminated. Further, Scott maintained satisfactory marks throughout his 41 years of employment with the company and presented deposition testimony indicating that he took advantage of company-provided career development computer training. Thus, in common with the district court, we find that sufficient evidence exists on record to indicate that Scott was qualified for his position as operations manager.

Turning to the third prong, Scott alleges two theories of adverse treatment by Goodyear. First, Scott claims that he was constructively terminated by Goodyear due to his age. Second, Scott claims that Goodyear management intentionally decided against redeploying him on the basis of his age. We discuss each theory in turn.

The discriminatory termination to which Scott alleges to have fallen victim must overcome a significant hurdle—the menu of options given to him at the time his position was eliminated, all of which involved either accepting lay-off status or retiring, and his ultimate decision to retire. Scott maintains that he was laid off by Goodyear, even though he accepted the retirement option. Given this circumstance, Scott cannot prevail on a theory of actual discharge but must rely on the constructive discharge doctrine. As Scott phrased the issue in his brief in opposition to summary judgment below, he alleges to have been "forced to accept a lay-off without the likelihood of recall at the expense of much-needed medical benefits[.]"

"The law in this circuit is clear that a constructive discharge exists if working conditions are such that a reasonable person in the plaintiff's shoes would feel compelled to resign." *Bruhwiler v. University of Tennessee*, 859 F.2d 419, 421 (6th Cir. 1988) (citing *Henry v. Lennox Industries, Inc.*, 768 F.2d 746, 752 (6th Cir. 1985)). In the typical discriminatory constructive discharge case, the employer does not overtly seek a discontinuation in the employment relationship but the employee claims to be subjected to intolerable working conditions due to discriminatory behavior. *See, e.g., id.* at 420 (research toxicologist hired by University possessing more seniority than her male supervisors and paid much less than her less experienced male supervisors resigned after receiving an "unsatisfactory" evaluation and being given names of possible job contacts by a superior when she did not asked for them); *Henry v. Lennox Industries, Inc.*, 768 F.2d 746, 751-52 (6th Cir. 1985) (constructive discharge occurred where employee was required to train the person who would supervise her, refused an explanation for her demotion, and never was seriously considered for a supervisory position). However, in the instant case, Scott alleges that the offer of layoff with possible recall amounted to a choice between voluntary and involuntary retirement. According to Scott's view, Goodyear had no intention of recalling him had he accepted layoff status.

The district court addressed the constructive discharge issue by analyzing this court's decisions in *Ackerman v. Diamond Shamrock Corp.*, 670 F.2d 66 (6th Cir.

1982), and *Wilson v. Firestone Tire & Rubber Co.*, 932 F.2d 510 (6th Cir. 1991), to find that the constructive discharge doctrine should not apply to this case:

> There is no evidence that Gable coerced Scott into accepting retirement. On the contrary, the record indicates that Gable fully explained Scott's available options. Although Scott contends that the "evidence is clear" that Goodyear never intended to recall him and that this rendered the layoff option illusory, there is no evidence to substantiate this allegation.

We disagree.

The *Ackerman* court considered an instance in which the plaintiff, Edward Ackerman, at age 59, was informed that his director of communications job was being eliminated in the wake of corporate reorganization. Ackerman was offered an early retirement package which gave him "much more than the benefits to which he would be entitled if he were simply terminated." Although the record conflicted over whether Ackerman consulted an attorney before signing the early retirement agreement, he testified that he signed the agreement "of his own free will, that he understood the terms of the agreement, and that his employer complied with the agreement."

Finding no evidence of discriminatory intent, other than the conclusory allegations of Ackerman that he could "think of no reason for his discharge other than his age," we determined that Ackerman voluntarily signed the early retirement offer and thus was not constructively discharged. The court determined that Ackerman had not upheld his prima facie burden. *Ackerman*, therefore, stands for the proposition that a mere allegation that improper motives led an employer to offer early retirement benefits is insufficient to prove that the employee who accepted those benefits was constructively discharged.

In *Wilson*, this court considered whether the plaintiff in that case presented adequate evidence indicating that age considerations motivated the decision to (1) eliminate his position and (2) offer him a choice of a lesser position or early retirement. The plaintiff in that case, Ival Wilson, had presented circumstantial evidence of illicit motivation on the part of Firestone management in its determination to offer Wilson early retirement benefits, which this court found unpersuasive. Wilson offered the following three facts to support his claim: (1) that management had referred to his 33 years of employment with the company in a memo written by a manager at the time Wilson's severance package was being developed; (2) a conversation with his immediate supervisor a few months prior to the decision to eliminate his position in which his immediate supervisor stated that he hoped that older employees would accept the new company-wide early retirement option so that younger workers would not be displaced and; (3) the personnel documents kept by Firestone that included the birthdates and years of service of its employees. On this record, we concluded that an inference of discriminatory motivation in an adverse employment decision had not been proven.

Additionally, the *Wilson* court determined that the plaintiff did not demonstrate that he was actually or constructively discharged. A key factor in the decision to find against discharge was that Firestone had offered Wilson "legitimate opportunities for continued employment." Since Wilson had, among other choices, the option to replace any of three of his former subordinates or accept early retirement, the court found that he was not forced to resign from the company.

Wilson and *Ackerman*, while similar to the facts of the instant case, both differ by the evidence presented by the plaintiff and, at least with respect to *Wilson*, on the facts surrounding the alleged discharge. In its reliance on these two cases, the district court overlooked some vitally important evidence submitted by Scott at the summary judgment phase indicating that the retirement decision was less than voluntary.

First, we note the odd directives given to Gable, the Goodyear Human Resources executive. Gable was informed by Paul Evert that the position held by Scott would be eliminated and was told to travel to the Cleveland field office to report that fact to Scott. Gable, who testified that he had participated in at least three corporate reorganizations with Goodyear, had informed other Goodyear employees of such job eliminations in the past and many times received instructions to offer such employees lower level positions in lieu of lay-off. However, in this case, it appears that Evert cut off any further discussion regarding the decision to eliminate Scott's position.

Additionally, Scott recalled in deposition testimony that Gable and Morris, the other Goodyear executive present at the meeting with Scott in Cleveland, used the term "laid off" to describe the elimination of his position. Consequently, when Scott attempted to query Gable about the reasons for the elimination of his position and the possibility of future employment, Gable could not provide any answers. While the record does not reflect whether Gable made a formal or informal practice of informing other persons subjected to job elimination of their likelihood of being recalled, his inability to address the reasons for the elimination and decision not to redeploy Scott seem substantial enough reason for Scott to entertain the subjective belief that he would not be recalled if he chose lay-off status. Further, it seems that Wahrle and Smith may not have been told that they were being "laid off," and, more significantly, both were redeployed.

Scott thus chose retirement having no definite prospect of continued employment with the company. Therefore, where ordinary charges of constructive discharge typically entail a decision on the part of the employee to resign in light of an intolerable working environment or some such allegation, Scott decided upon the option best suited to his needs with the understanding that he did not have the option of continued employment. For that reason, we find that the doctrine of constructive discharge applies in this case.

In addition to the constructive termination theory, Scott charges that the decision not to redeploy him serves as an actionable basis for going forward with his case. We note that, while this court has never recognized a right to redeployment under the ADEA, a decision made by an employer to redeploy younger employees while not redeploying older ones is a recognized form of adverse employment action.

Examining the pertinent facts, we first note that the two oldest operations managers, Scott, at age 61, and Cox, at age 63, were not redeployed by the company at the time those positions were eliminated. Further, Scott has presented statistical evidence suggesting that the average age of employees whose positions were eliminated (47.35 years old) was significantly higher than the average age of employees whose positions remained intact through the corporate restructuring (40.47 years old). The district court took exception to the probative value of these statistics because 66 employees included in the redeployed comparison group "were never considered for redeployment since their positions were not in jeopardy [and therefore] the presumption that the sample was representative of all candidates for redeployment is false." After reviewing the statistical findings, however, we conclude that the district court hastily cast them aside for the following reasons.

First, while the statistics were not as probative as they perhaps may have been, they do reveal some startling age comparisons between persons occupying positions that were eliminated and those unaffected by the reorganization. In addition to showing a nearly seven-year age disparity between the two groups, the statistical evidence, which was compiled by two economists, Drs. Harvey Rosen and John Burke, pointed to a less than 1% chance that the discrepancy arose due to randomness. Not only does this evidence increase the likelihood that the decisions to eliminate certain positions were based on age but it also makes more likely the possibility that age played a part in redeployment decisions.

Second, the district court, borrowing language from *Chappell v. GTE Products Corp.*, 803 F.2d 261, 268 n.2 (6th Cir. 1986), deemed the seemingly inculpatory comments attributed to Goodyear managers Gallagher and Hewitt as "too abstract, in addition to being irrelevant and prejudicial, to support a finding of age discrimination." However, it would seem that a statement that the company "is run by white haired old men, waiting to retire," and "[t]his must change," both of which are attributed to Gallagher, as well as a statement that those who lose their jobs through reorganization will be replaced with "young college graduates at less money," which was attributed to Hewitt, read in a light most favorable to Scott, would be deemed relevant and probative by the district court. Such statements may have been "abstract, irrelevant and prejudicial" had they been made well-after the operative events or some other such occurrence. But these statements appear to have been made in and around the time of the corporate reorganization. In addition, the statements are consistent with what took place—Cox and Scott, the two oldest operations managers were not redeployed. We thus agree with the *Ercegovich* panel that "[b]oth remarks on their face strongly suggest that the speaker harbors a bias against older workers."

B.

Having found Scott to have presented a prima facie case of discrimination, we turn to the question of whether "the legitimate reasons offered by the defendant were not its true reasons, but were a pretext for discrimination." We find that a jury question pertains to this issue, as there is conflicting evidence on the record. On the one hand, Goodyear has proffered an ostensibly legitimate motive to reduce its management layers for greater efficiency. On the other hand, however, as has been indicated, statements indicating bias against older workers have been attributed to Goodyear managers Gallagher and Hewitt. Both managers played a role in the decision to eliminate the position held by Scott. Evert ordered Gable not to answer routine questions from Scott regarding his position's elimination. The two oldest operations managers, Scott and Cox, were not redeployed. Further the statistical evidence seems to suggest that age considerations factored into the job elimination decisions and, by consequence, the redeployment determinations.

III.

Because we find that Scott has presented sufficient evidence to support a prima facie case, we find that the district court ruling to the contrary should be reversed. Additionally, we further conclude that the district court had sufficient evidence of pretext to create a jury question on that issue. Accordingly, we reverse the district court's grant of summary judgment to Goodyear and remand this case for proceedings consistent with this opinion.

[Judge Alan E. Norris dissented on the ground that the plaintiff/appellant had failed to come forward with circumstantial or statistical evidence of discriminatory intent.]

Questions

1. Does the Sixth Circuit's decision in this case "open the door" to a flood of unwarranted age discrimination litigation?

2. Should a company-wide restructuring that results in the retirement or severance of a large number or proportion of older employees be presumed to be motivated by discriminatory intent?

Oubré v. Entergy Operations, Inc.
522 U.S. 422 (1998)

JUSTICE KENNEDY delivered the opinion of the Court.

An employee, as part of a termination agreement, signed a release of all claims against her employer. In consideration, she received severance pay in installments. The release, however, did not comply with specific federal statutory requirements for a release of claims under the Age Discrimination in Employment Act of 1967 (ADEA). After receiving the last payment, the employee brought suit under the ADEA. The employer claims the employee ratified and validated the nonconforming release by retaining the monies paid to secure it. The employer also insists the release bars the action unless, as a precondition to filing suit, the employee tenders back the monies received. We disagree and rule that, as the release did not comply with the statute, it cannot bar the ADEA claim.

Petitioner Dolores Oubré worked as a scheduler at a power plant in Killona, Louisiana, run by her employer, respondent Entergy Operations, Inc. In 1994, she received a poor performance rating. Oubré's supervisor met with her on January 17, 1995, and gave her the option of either improving her performance during the coming year or accepting a voluntary arrangement for her severance. She received a packet of information about the severance agreement and had 14 days to consider her options, during which she consulted with attorneys. On January 31, Oubré decided to accept. She signed a release, in which she "agree[d] to waive, settle, release, and discharge any and all claims, demands, damages, actions, or causes of action . . . that I may have against Entergy . . . ." In exchange, she received six installment payments over the next four months, totaling $6,258.

The Older Workers Benefit Protection Act (OWBPA) imposes specific requirements for releases covering ADEA claims. OWBPA, 29 U.S.C. §§ 626(f)(1)(B), (F), (G). In procuring the release, Entergy did not comply with the OWBPA in at least three respects: (1) Entergy did not give Oubré enough time to consider her options, (2) Entergy did not give Oubré seven days after she signed the release to change her mind, and (3) the release made no specific reference to claims under the ADEA.

Oubré filed a charge of age discrimination with the Equal Employment Opportunity Commission, which dismissed her charge on the merits but issued a right-to-sue letter. She filed this suit against Entergy in the United States District Court for the Eastern District of Louisiana, alleging constructive discharge on the basis of her age in violation of the ADEA and state law. Oubré has not offered or tried to return the $6,258 to Entergy, nor is it clear she has the means to do so. Entergy moved for summary judgment, claiming Oubré had ratified the defective release by failing to return or offer to return the monies she had received. The District Court agreed and entered summary judgment for Entergy. The Court of Appeals affirmed, 112 F.3d 787 (CA5 1996) (per curiam), and we granted certiorari.

II

The employer rests its case upon general principles of state contract jurisprudence. As the employer recites the rule, contracts tainted by mistake, duress, or even fraud are voidable at the option of the innocent party. See 1 RESTATEMENT (SECOND) OF CONTRACTS § 7, and Comment b (1979); *e.g., Ellerin v. Fairfax Sav. Assn.*, 78 Md. App. 92, 108-09, 552 A.2d 918, 926-27 (Md. Spec. App.), *cert. denied,* 316 Md. 210, 557 A.2d 1336 (1989). The employer maintains, however, that before the innocent party can elect avoidance, she must first tender back any benefits received under the contract. *See, e.g., Dreiling v. Home State Life Ins. Co.*, 213 Kan. 137, 147-48, 515 P.2d 757, 766-67 (1973). If she fails to do so within a reasonable time after learning of her rights, the employer contends, she ratifies the contract and so makes it binding. RESTATEMENT (SECOND) OF CONTRACTS, *supra,* § 7, Comments d, e; *see, e.g., Jobe v. Texas Util. Elec. Co.,* No. 05-94-01368CV (Tex. App.–Dallas, Aug. 14, 1995) (unpublished). The employer also invokes the doctrine of equitable estoppel. As a rule, equitable estoppel bars a party from shirking the burdens of a voidable transaction for as long as she retains the benefits received under it. *See, e.g., Buffum v. Peter Barceloux Co.*, 289 U.S. 227, 234 (1933) (citing state case law from Indiana and New York). Applying these principles, the employer claims the employee ratified the ineffective release (or faces estoppel) by retaining all the sums paid in consideration of it. The employer, then, relies not upon the execution of the release but upon a later, distinct ratification of its terms.

These general rules may not be as unified as the employer asserts. *See generally* Annot., 76 A.L.R. 344 (1932) (collecting cases supporting and contradicting these rules); Annot., 134 A.L.R. 6 (1941) (same). And in equity, a person suing to rescind a contract, as a rule, is not required to restore the consideration at the very outset of the litigation. *See* 3 RESTATEMENT (SECOND) OF CONTRACTS, *supra,* § 384, and Comment b; RESTATEMENT OF RESTITUTION § 65, Comment d (1936); D. Dobbs, LAW OF REMEDIES § 4.8, p. 294 (1973). Even if the employer's statement of the general rule requiring tender back before one files suit were correct, it would be unavailing. The rule cited is based simply on the course of negotiation of the parties and the alleged later ratification. The authorities cited do not consider the question raised by statutory standards for releases and a statutory declaration making nonconforming releases ineffective. It is the latter question we confront here.

In 1990, Congress amended the ADEA by passing the OWBPA. The OWBPA provides: "An individual may not waive any right or claim under [the ADEA] unless the waiver is knowing and voluntary. . . . [A] waiver may not be considered knowing and voluntary unless at a minimum" it satisfies certain enumerated requirements, including the three listed above. 29 U.S.C. § 626(f)(1).

The statutory command is clear: An employee "may not waive" an ADEA claim unless the waiver or release satisfies the OWBPA's requirements. The policy of the Older Workers Benefit Protection Act is likewise clear from its title: It is designed to protect the rights and benefits of older workers. The OWBPA implements Congress' policy via a strict, unqualified statutory stricture on waivers, and we are bound to take Congress at its word. Congress imposed specific duties on employers who seek releases of certain claims created by statute. Congress delineated these duties with precision and without qualification: An employee "may not waive" an ADEA claim unless the employer complies with the statute. Courts cannot with ease presume ratification of that which Congress forbids. The OWBPA sets up its own regime for assessing the effect of ADEA waivers, separate and apart from contract law. The statute creates a series of prerequisites for knowing and voluntary waivers and imposes affirmative duties of disclosure and waiting periods. The OWBPA governs the effect under federal law of waivers or releases on ADEA claims and incorporates no exceptions or qualifications. The text of the OWBPA forecloses the employer's defense, notwithstanding how general contract principles would apply to non-ADEA claims.

The rule proposed by the employer would frustrate the statute's practical operation as well as its formal command. In many instances a discharged employee likely will have spent the monies received and will lack the means to tender their return. These realities might tempt employers to risk noncompliance with the OWBPA's waiver provisions, knowing it will be difficult to repay the monies and relying on ratification. We ought not to open the door to an evasion of the statute by this device.

Oubré's cause of action arises under the ADEA, and the release can have no effect on her ADEA claim unless it complies with the OWBPA. In this case, both sides concede the release the employee signed did not comply with the requirements of the OWBPA. Since Oubré's release did not comply with the OWBPA's stringent safeguards, it is unenforceable against her insofar as it purports to waive or release her ADEA claim. As a statutory matter, the release cannot bar her ADEA suit, irrespective of the validity of the contract as to other claims.

In further proceedings in this or other cases, courts may need to inquire whether the employer has claims for restitution, recoupment, or setoff against the employee, and these questions may be complex where a release is effective as to some claims but not as to ADEA claims. We need not decide those issues here, however. It suffices to hold that the release cannot bar the ADEA claim because it does not conform to the statute. Nor did the employee's mere retention of monies amount to a ratification equivalent to a valid release of her ADEA claims, since the retention did not comply with the OWBPA any more than the original release did. The statute governs the effect of the release on ADEA claims, and the employer cannot invoke the employee's failure to tender back as a way of excusing its own failure to comply.

We reverse the judgment of the Court of Appeals and remand for further proceedings consistent with this opinion.

It is so ordered.

[The Appendix, which sets out the text of 29 U.S.C. § 626(f), is omitted.]

JUSTICE BREYER, with whom JUSTICE O'CONNOR joins, concurring.

This case focuses upon a worker who received a payment from her employer and in return promised not to bring an age-discrimination suit. Her promise failed the procedural tests of validity set forth in the OWBPA, 29 U.S.C. § 626(f)(1). I agree with the majority that, because of this procedural failing, the worker is free to bring her age-discrimination suit without "tendering-back" her employer's payment as a precondition. As a conceptual matter, a "tender-back" requirement would imply that the worker had ratified her promise by keeping her employer's payment. For that reason, it would bar suit, including suit by a worker (without other assets) who had already spent the money he received for the promise. Yet such an act of ratification could embody some of the same procedural failings that led Congress to find the promise not to sue itself invalid. For these reasons, as the majority points out, a tender-back precondition requirement would run contrary to Congress' statutory command. *Cf.* 1 RESTATEMENT (SECOND) OF CONTRACTS § 85, Comment b (1979) (a promise ratifying a voidable contract "may itself be voidable for the same reason as the original promise, or it may be voidable or unenforceable for some other reason"); D. Dobbs, LAW OF REMEDIES 982 (1973) (hereinafter Dobbs) ("[C]ourts must avoid allowing a recovery that has the effect of substantially enforcing the contract that has been declared unenforceable, since to do so would defeat the policy that led to the . . . rule in the first place.").

I write these additional words because I believe it important to specify that the statute need not, and does not, thereby make the worker's procedurally invalid promise totally void, i.e., without any legal effect, say, like a contract the terms of which themselves are contrary to public policy. See 1 RESTATEMENT (SECOND) OF CONTRACTS, §7, Comment a; 2 *id.*, § 178. Rather, the statute makes the contract that the employer and worker tried to create voidable, like a contract made with an infant, or a contract created through fraud, mistake or duress, which contract the worker may elect either to avoid or to ratify. *See* 1 *id.*, § 7 and Comment b .

To determine whether a contract is voidable or void, courts typically ask whether the contract has been made under conditions that would justify giving one of the parties a choice as to validity, making it voidable, *e.g.,* a contract with an infant; or whether enforcement of the contract would violate the law or public policy irrespective of the conditions in which the contract was formed, making it void, *e.g.,* a contract to commit murder. *Compare* 1 *id.,* § 7, Comment b (voidable) with 2 *id.,* § 178 and Comment d (void). The statute before us reflects concern about the conditions (of knowledge and free choice) surrounding the making of a contract to waive an age-discrimination claim. It does not reflect any relevant concern about enforcing the contract's substantive terms. Nor does this statute, unlike the Federal Employers' Liability Act, 45 U.S.C. § 51 et seq., say that a contract waiving suit and thereby avoiding liability is void. § 55. Rather, as the majority's opinion makes clear, the OWBPA prohibits courts from finding ratification in certain circumstances, such as those presented here, namely, a worker's retention of a employer's payment for an invalid release. That fact may affect ratification, but it need not make the contract void, rather than voidable.

That the contract is voidable rather than void may prove important. For example, an absolutely void contract, it is said, "is void as to everybody whose rights would be affected by it if valid." 17A AM. JUR. 2d, CONTRACTS § 7, p. 31 (1991). Were a former worker's procedurally invalid promise not to sue absolutely void, might it not become legally possible for an employer to decide to cancel its own reciprocal obligation, say, to pay the worker, or to provide ongoing health benefits-whether or not the worker in question ever intended to bring a lawsuit? It seems most unlikely that Congress, enacting a statute meant to protect workers, would have wanted to create-as a result of an employer's failure to follow the law-any such legal threat to all workers, whether or not they intend to bring suit. To find the contract voidable, rather than void, would offer legal protection against such threats.

At the same time, treating the contract as voidable could permit an employer to recover his own reciprocal payment (or to avoid his reciprocal promise) where doing so seems most fair, namely, where that recovery would not bar the worker from bringing suit. Once the worker (who has made the procedurally invalid promise not to sue) brings an age-discrimination suit, he has clearly rejected (avoided) his promise not to sue. As long as there is no "tender-back" precondition, his (invalid) promise will not have barred his suit in conflict with the statute. Once he has sued, however, nothing in the statute prevents his employer from asking for restitution of his reciprocal payment or relief from any ongoing reciprocal obligation. *See* RESTATEMENT OF RESTITUTION § 47, Comment b (1936) ("A person who transfers something to another believing that the other thereby comes under a duty to perform the terms of a contract . . . is ordinarily entitled to restitution for what he has given if the obligation intended does not arise and if the other does not perform"); Dobbs, *supra,* at 994 (restitution is often allowed where benefits are conferred under voidable contract). A number of older state cases indicate, for example, that the amount of consideration paid for an invalid release can be deducted from a successful plaintiff's damages award. *See, e.g., St. Louis-San Francisco R. Co. v. Cox*, 171 Ark. 103, 113-15, 283 S.W. 31, 35 (1926) (amount paid for invalid release may be taken into consideration in setting remedy); *Koshka v. Missouri Pac. R. Co.*, 114 Kan. 126, 129-30, 217 P. 293, 295 (1923) (the sum paid for an invalid release may be treated as an item of credit against damages); *Miller v. Spokane Int'l R. Co.*, 82 Wash. 170, 177-78, 143 P. 981, 984 (1914) (same); *Gilmore v. Western Elec. Co.*, 42 N.D. 206, 211-12, 172 N.W. 111, 113 (1919).

My point is that the statute's provisions are consistent with viewing an invalid release as voidable, rather than void. Apparently, five or more Justices take this view of the matter. As I understand the majority's opinion, it is also consistent with this view, and I consequently concur in its opinion.

[JUSTICE SCALIA dissented on the ground that the OWBPA did not abrogate the common-law doctrines of "tender back" and ratification, and, because no "tender back" was made, the judgment of the lower court should have been affirmed. JUSTICES THOMAS, with whom CHIEF JUSTICE REHNQUIST joined, dissented on the ground that the OWBPA does not clearly and explicitly abrogate the doctrines of ratification and tender back, and the lower court had determined that petitioner had ratified her release.]

Questions

1. Does the majority's interpretation of the ADEA's waiver provision imply a paternalistic view of older workers?

2. In July 1998, the EEOC promulgated final regulations intended to implement this decision. Read 22 C.F.R. §1625.22 (1998) in the statutory supplement. Do you think the regulations fairly capture the substance of *Oubré*?

2. State Law

Although many lawyers assume that federal law provides the most effective means of redressing age-related employment discrimination, most states have also enacted laws that provide older workers from workplace discrimination. In many circumstances, state remedies, which may include administrative or informal procedures can sometimes provide more speedy justice and effective relief to the client. In some circumstances, however, resort to such remedies may foreclose a subsequent lawsuit based on federal law. The elder law attorney thus must balance carefully the legal and strategic consequences of pursuing a state remedy for age-based discrimination in lieu of or concurrently with a federal claim.

Memorandum of Understanding Between the National Association of Attorneys General and the Equal Employment Opportunity Commission
(Nov. 10, 1997)
<http://www.eeoc.gov/docs/naagmem.txt>

The enforcement of laws against employment discrimination and the eradication of unfair employment practices is a national priority. State and federal officials' strong interest in enforcement and elimination of employment discrimination crosses regional lines as well as particular Administrations. The signatories to this Memorandum of Understanding agree that it is critical to develop effective and lasting mechanisms for communication and cooperation among state Attorneys General and the Equal Employment Opportunity Commission (EEOC) responsible for the enforcement of federal and state employment discrimination laws. It is also agreed that those mechanisms should continue through changes in administration at the national and state levels. Accordingly, the signatories to this Memorandum of Understanding agree to establish the following institutional mechanisms for communication, cooperation and joint work on affirmative enforcement of employment discrimination laws:

1. The EEOC will designate a district office liaison to each state Attorney General office that chooses to participate in the program who will be responsible for ensuring communication and cooperation with the participating state Attorneys General. The EEOC will also designate headquarters liaison(s) to state Attorneys General for amicus requests and for other specified purposes. Each participating state Attorney General will designate an employment discrimination liaison who will be responsible for ensuring communication and cooperation with other state Attorneys General and the EEOC. The co-chairs of the permanent Working Group described in paragraph 6 below will be responsible for circulating a list of liaisons and for notifying the liaisons of any changes in designations that are made. The liaisons' responsibilities will include: sharing information about pending or proposed litigation or projects which are likely to contribute significantly to the development of employment discrimination laws or which involve significant pattern and practice violations; identifying technical assistance and training needs; providing pleadings and briefs to each other; bringing important judicial decisions and other emerging issues to the attention of other liaisons; notifying each other of pending legislation concerning employment laws and practices; making requests for amicus assistance or intervention or other types of legal assistance; and otherwise ensuring the timely and effective dissemination of significant information related to employment discrimination.

2. The EEOC will provide informational reports (limited to information of public record) to the National Association of Attorneys General (NAAG) for circulation to each participating state Attorney General. State Attorneys General offices will submit reports to NAAG for a quarterly report on important employment discrimination developments in their states which will be shared with all signatories to this agreement.

3. Representatives of state Attorneys General and the EEOC will participate in regular conference calls and will meet annually to, as appropriate: discuss national, regional and state employment discrimination issues; share investigative techniques and information regarding effective methods of enforcement; identify potential joint enforcement efforts; identify and initiate joint litigation and policy enforcement efforts; organize and coordinate training activities; and bring important judicial decisions and emerging issues to the attention of each other. The representatives will also share information about fair employment initiatives and coordinate and combine efforts to address employment discrimination in a manner that most effectively utilizes the expertise and resources of the represented offices. Any sharing of informa-

tion shall be consistent with applicable confidentiality provisions. NAAG's staff, in consultation with representatives of state Attorneys General, and a representative of the EEOC, will be responsible for coordinating the annual meetings and the conference calls.

4(a). In order to effectively address common concerns, the EEOC and the state Attorneys General intend to develop joint enforcement initiatives in one or more areas of mutual concern. The signing of this Memorandum does not obligate the EEOC or any state Attorney General to participate in any joint initiative. A state Attorney General that desires to participate in a joint initiative with the EEOC will supply a letter of participation to the EEOC.

(b) The signatories direct the establishment of an Employment Task Force to report on the most effective means practicable for carrying out the joint initiatives referenced in paragraph 4(a) and to coordinate the implementation of the joint initiatives. The Task Force will consider, among other things, joint initiatives in which each participating agency commits personnel and resources to policy initiatives and investigation and litigation efforts. The Task Force will make recommendations about which agencies should lead the enforcement efforts in a particular subject area and geographic location, taking into account the relative expertise of the participants, the extent of resources each agency commits to the project, the nature of the remedies or sanctions for the violation of law available in a state or federal forum, and similar criteria. Problems in the implementation of joint initiatives will be brought to the attention of the Working Group described in paragraph 6, below, for resolution.

5. The EEOC and the state Attorneys General will continue to enforce laws independently of one another. EEOC and participating state Attorneys General will notify in writing each other's offices functioning in their jurisdiction of their enforcement efforts whenever an office commences a civil enforcement action in an administrative agency or court, which it believes is likely to contribute significantly to the development of employment discrimination law. Notifications will be made to the relevant liaison(s) designated pursuant to paragraph 1 above within two business days of the event triggering the notification requirement, if possible. Notifications will not be made if any office determines that such notification is inappropriate under the circumstances.

6. The signatories to this Agreement direct the establishment of an Employment Working Group which will continue as a permanent body. It will consist of representatives designated by the EEOC and representatives of state Attorneys General designated by the President of the National Association of Attorneys General. The Working Group will be co-chaired by a representative of the EEOC and representatives of two state Attorneys General. The Working Group will serve as a clearinghouse for information and complaints about the implementation of this agreement, investigate whether improvements in the mechanisms for communication and cooperation are needed, identify common training requirements and plan training events, assist in the resolution of conflicts arising in joint initiatives or enforcement efforts, and otherwise make recommendations for ways to advance the objective of joint enforcement of employment discrimination laws. Each co-chair of the Employment Working Group will be available to receive information from employment discrim-

ination liaisons about problems in the implementation of this agreement. The Working Group will communicate with each other regularly, but not less than once a year.

Question

Read the Kansas Act Against Discrimination, KSA 44-1001 to -11013 (1998), in the statutory supplement. In what ways does the substance of this statute differ from federal age discrimination law? In what ways do procedures for enforcement differ?

Pozzobon v. Parts for Plastics, Inc.
770 F. Supp. 376 (N.D. Ohio 1991)

SAM H. BELL, United States District Judge.

Currently pending before the court in the above-captioned matter is a motion to dismiss the third and fourth counts of plaintiff Orlando J. Pozzobon's complaint under Fed.R.Civ.P. 12(b)(6) filed by defendant Parts for Plastic, Inc. The underlying complaint, filed on March 5, 1991, alleges age discrimination in violation of the Age Discrimination in Employment Act (ADEA), 29 U.S.C. § 621 et seq. (Counts One and Two), and Ohio Revised Code § 4112.02(A) (Count Three); wrongful discharge in violation of Ohio public policy (Count Four); and intentional infliction of emotional distress (Count Five). The claim of age discrimination under Ohio law is brought pursuant to O.R.C. §§ 4112.02(N) and 4112.99. Plaintiff seeks a declaration that the policies and practices of defendant are in violation of the ADEA, a permanent injunction, and $500,000 in compensatory and punitive damages.

When considering a motion to dismiss for failure to state a claim pursuant to Federal Rule of Civil Procedure 12(b)(6), the court is constrained to accept as true the allegations of a complaint. The motion to dismiss under 12(b)(6) should be denied unless it can be established beyond a doubt that the plaintiff can prove no set of facts in support of his claim which would entitle him to relief.

The court's analysis begins with a consideration of plaintiff's third count, the allegation of age discrimination under Ohio law. Plaintiff claims a violation of O.R.C. § 4112.02(A), which provides as follows:

> It shall be unlawful discriminatory practice:
> (A) For any employer, because of the race, color, religion, sex, national origin, handicap, age, or ancestry of any person, to discharge without just cause, to refuse to hire, or otherwise to discriminate against that person with respect to hire, tenure, terms, conditions, or privileges of employment, or any matter directly or indirectly related to employment.

Plaintiff's asserted basis for a private cause of action under this section is twofold, O.R.C. §§ 4112.02(N) and 4112.99. The former section provides as follows:

(N) An aggrieved individual may enforce his rights relative to discrimination on the basis of age as provided for in this section by instituting a civil action, within one hundred eighty days after the alleged unlawful practice occurred, in any court of competent jurisdiction for any legal or equitable relief that will effectuate his rights. A person who files a civil action under this division is, with respect to the practices complained of, thereby barred from instituting a civil action under section 4101.17 of the Revised Code or from filing a charge with the Ohio civil rights commission under section 4112.05 of the Revised Code.

Section 4112.99 provides that "whoever violates this chapter is subject to a civil action for damages, injunctive relief, or any other appropriate relief." Prior to 1987, § 4112.99 only provided for criminal sanctions. In 1987, an amendment was enacted which resulted in the section in its present form.

Defendant argues that O.R.C. § 4112.08 expressly bars plaintiff's claim of age discrimination under Ohio law in this case. This section provides as follows:

The provisions of section 4112.01 to 4112.08 of the Revised Code, shall be construed liberally for the accomplishment of the purposes thereof and any law inconsistent with any provision hereof shall not apply. Nothing contained in section 4112.01 to 4112.08 and 4112.99 of the Revised Code, shall be deemed to repeal any of the provisions of any law of this state relating to discrimination because of race, color, religion, sex, national origin, age, or ancestry; *except that any person filing a charge under section 4112.05 of the Revised Code is, with respect to the practices complained of, thereby barred from instituting a civil action under section 4101.17 or division (N) of section 4112.02 of the Revised Code.*

O.R.C. § 4112.08 (emphasis added). Section 4112.05 provides for the filing of a grievance with the Ohio Civil Rights Commission in order to redress alleged unlawful discriminatory practices. § 4112.05(B). The complaint herein states that plaintiff has filed such a grievance, and plaintiff does not controvert this in his brief in opposition to the motion to dismiss. Consequently, according to defendant, plaintiff is precluded from bringing this suit due to the explicit and unambiguous language of § 4112.08.

In response, plaintiff argues that the Code expressly allows the bringing of the instant cause, citing to § 4112.99. According to plaintiff's logic, while the language of § 4112.08 may bar an aggrieved party from bringing a private action under § 4112.02(N) if that person has already filed a claim with the Civil Rights Commission under § 4112.05, it does not also bar one from bringing such an action under § 4112.99, which is not mentioned in § 4112.08. Having filed the instant cause under § 4112.99 as well as § 4112.02(N), plaintiff contends that § 4112.08 thus cannot be utilized to bar his claim.

In support of the proposition that the language of § 4112.99 allows the filing of a private action in the instant cause, plaintiff cites to three cases: *Elek v. Huntington National Bank*, 1989 Ohio App. LEXIS 3299, 50 Fair Empl. Prac. Cas. (BNA) 1396 (Ohio App. Franklin Cty. 1989); *Eyerman v. Mary Kay Cosmetics*, 1990 U.S. Dist.

LEXIS 618, 51 Fair Empl. Prac. Cas. (BNA) 1594 (S.D. Ohio 1990); and *Grant v. Monsanto Co.*, 1989 U.S. Dist. LEXIS 16015, 51 Fair Empl. Prac. Cas. (BNA) 1593 (S.D. Ohio 1989). *Elek* and *Grant* stand for the proposition that § 4112.99 provides for a private right of action for any violation of Chapter 4112, notwithstanding the fact that other parts of the chapter create overlapping private causes of action for specific types of discrimination. The *Grant* court specifically held that § 4112.99 creates an entirely new, separate private cause of action, and that an aggrieved person may bring an age discrimination in employment suit under either § 4112.99 or § 4112.02(N). On June 12, 1991, the Ohio Supreme Court affirmed the court of appeals decision in *Elek. See Elek v. Huntington National Bank*, 60 Ohio St. 3d 135, 573 N.E.2d 1056 (1991). The case involved a handicap discrimination claim brought as a private civil action pursuant to § 4112.99. In rejecting the defendant's argument that § 4112.99 does not create a new, independent private right of action, the Supreme Court found, inter alia, that the language of this section is unambiguous and that the legislative history supports such an interpretation. *Id.*, 60 Ohio St. 3d at 137. Due to this recent Supreme Court holding, we are constrained to hold that an age discrimination claimant may utilize either § 4112.02(N), § 4112.99, or both in pursuing an action for age discrimination.

The Supreme Court in *Elek*, however, did not face the more narrow issue before this court, viz., whether § 4112.99 allows a private right of action for age discrimination where the plaintiff-employee has previously filed a claim with the Civil Rights Commission under § 4112.05. This court does not believe that *Elek* could reasonably be read to stand for such a proposition. If the legislature had desired that § 4112.99 would so modify the language of § 4112.08 in cases of age discrimination, we believe that it would have done so in a less ambiguous fashion, either by changing the language of § 4112.08 or by more clearly stating its intent in § 4112.99. In holding as we do, we are guided by the caveat contained in § 4112.08 that "nothing contained in sections 4112.01 to 4112.08 and 4112.99 of the Revised Code shall be deemed to repeal any of the provisions of law of this state relating to discrimination . . . ." The court takes this language to mean that the 1987 amendment to § 4112.99 creating an independent private right of action was not intended to and does not alter the final sentence of § 4112.08, nor does it alter the detailed, comprehensive legislative scheme created for age discrimination suits, *see infra*.

The holding of this court, thus, has no bearing upon the efficacy of *Elek*. The court there was not faced with issues regarding the effect of § 4112.99 on § 4112.08 in age discrimination suits. *Elek*, rather, stands for the proposition that both § 4112.99 and § 4112.02(N) create independent private rights of action in age discrimination suits. With this holding we are in complete agreement. The court does not believe, however, that the amendment to § 4112.99 nullifies the effect of § 4112.08 in age discrimination suits. Thus, while an employee is permitted to bring a private action for age discrimination under § 4112.99, he should not be allowed to circumvent Ohio's detailed legislative scheme for bringing age discrimination suits, including the mandate of § 4112.08.

In closing this portion of the opinion, and holding that Count Three of the complaint is barred, the court adopts the following reasoning:

Protection against age discrimination is provided under Ohio law by three statutory sections: (1) O.R.C. § 4101.17(B), which permits a civil action for violation of subsection (A) of that section; (2) O.R.C. § 4112.02(N), which permits a civil action to be brought against those who violate the other subsections of that section; and (3) O.R.C. § 4112.05, which permits a complaint to be brought with the Ohio Civil Rights Commission for violations of §§ 4112.02 and 4112.021.

Each of these statutory remedies is exclusive—the choice of one remedy precludes recourse to other remedies. See O.R.C. §§ 4101.17(B), 4112.02(N) and 4112.08. This exclusivity of remedies, however, causes a conflict in the context of the joinder of an Ohio age discrimination suit with one brought under the ADEA. The ADEA requires, in states with administrative procedures for resolution of age discrimination claims, that proceedings under those state procedures be brought at least 60 days before the filing of a claim under federal law. See 29 U.S.C. § 633. Thus, in order to fulfill the prerequisite to a suit under the federal law in Ohio, a plaintiff must file a complaint with the OCRC pursuant to O.R.C. § 4112.05, and thus, by the terms of that section, waive his or her right to bring a civil action under either O.R.C. § 4101.17(B) or § 4112.02(N).

However, simply because Ohio's age discrimination law has the effect of requiring a litigant to choose between his or her state and federal remedies does not invalidate the law or require the Court to construe the terms of that law inconsistently with its plain meaning. *Keister v. Delco Products*, 680 F. Supp. 281, 282 (S.D. Ohio 1987). We recognize that this decision, issued prior to the amendment of § 4112.99, did not discuss the effect of that statute. However, we do not deem it reasonable to conclude that the single, broadly worded sentence contained in § 4112.99 could possibly have been intended to eradicate the detailed legislative scheme discussed in *Keister* and still in existence in the Ohio Revised Code.

The fourth count of plaintiff's complaint alleges that defendant's actions, i.e., the alleged wrongful discharge, "violate public policy in that all of the above-named statutes prohibit discipline and/or discharge against plaintiff for unlawful reasons." Complaint at para. 22.

In its motion to dismiss, defendant contends that Ohio does not recognize a tort cause of action for wrongful discharge in violation of public policy. In response, plaintiff relies upon *Greeley v. Miami Valley Maintenance Contractors, Inc.*, 49 Ohio St. 3d 228, 551 N.E.2d 981 (1990), for the proposition that a tort cause of action for wrongful discharge in violation of public policy is available in Ohio.

In *Greeley*, the court held that public policy warrants an exception to the employment-at-will doctrine where the employee is discharged for a reason which is prohibited by statute. *Id.*, 49 Ohio St. 3d at 234. Due to the fact that the statute at issue, O.R.C. § 3113.213(D),[12] did not itself provide plaintiff with a private cause of action, but rather only imposed a fine upon the employer, the court held that a common law tort action for wrongful discharge in violation of public policy was available to plaintiff.

---

[12] This statute prohibits employers from discharging or disciplining an employee to whom a wage garnishment order applies.

Plaintiff would have this court read *Greeley* as holding that, where an employer is alleged to be in violation of an Ohio statute, the employee may bring a wrongful discharge tort action even where the statute at issue itself provides for a comprehensive private right of action. *Greeley* does not stand for such a proposition. In *Greeley*, the aggrieved plaintiff had no other recourse, due to the fact that the statute only provided that the employer be fined. The Ohio Supreme Court thus deemed it necessary to create an exception to the employment-at-will doctrine and allow employees a tort wrongful discharge action for violations of § 3113.213(D).

In the case at bar, an exception to the at-will doctrine already exists in the statutes themselves. Victims of age discrimination are entitled to bring civil actions under §§ 4101.17(B), 4112.02(N), 4112.05, or 4112.99, regardless of whether the employer-employee relationship is deemed as one "at-will." There is certainly no reason here to carve out another exception to the employment-at-will doctrine, as was the case in *Greeley*, and permit a tort action.[13]

For the foregoing reasons, the court finds that the third and fourth counts of plaintiff's complaint fail to state claims for which relief can be granted. As such, defendant's motion to dismiss these portions of the complaint is hereby granted pursuant to Fed.R.Civ.P. 12(b)(6).

It is so ordered.

Question

Is the result in *Pozzobon* consistent with the purposes that underlie the ADEA and its state counterparts?

C. Disability Discrimination

1. Federal Law: The Americans with Disabilities Act

The passage of the Americans with Disabilities Act of 1990 (ADA) marked a major paradigm shift in public policy concerning the treatment of the disabled. For the first time in history, virtually all public and private entites were charged with an obligation to make facilities accessible, provide job accomodations, and otherwise allow those with physical and mental impairments full, or nearly full, participation the full range of human activity. The ADA is of special import to the senior population, as persons age 55 and older make up a majority of the severely disabled, and a majority of persons over the age of 65 have at least some kind of disability that interferes with one or more activities of daily living. (See below.) Thus, disability discrimination is a major concern for many older clients. In this section, we introduce some basic principles of disability law as it pertains to the aging population.

---

[13] In so holding, the court is in agreement with the reasoning of Judge Aldrich in *Emser v. Curtis Industries, Inc.*, 774 F. Supp. 1076 (N.D. Ohio 1991), a case factually similar to the one at bar.

U.S. Census Bureau, *Americans with Disabilities: 1994-95—Table 1D: Disability Status of Persons 65 Years Old and Over by Race and Hispanic Origin: 1994-95 Data from the Survey of Income and Program Participation*
<http://www.census.gov/hhes/www/disable/sipp/disab9495/ds94t1d.html>

TABLE 1D
DISABILITY STATUS OF PERSONS 65 YEARS OLD AND OVER BY RACE AND HISPANIC ORIGIN
1994-95 Data from the Survey of Income and Program Participation

	Number (thousands)	Percent distribution
Age 65 years and over	31,256	100.0
With any disability	16,420	52.5
Severe	10,426	33.4
Not severe	5,994	19.2
Uses a wheelchair	995	3.2
Does not use a wheelchair, has used a cane, crutches, or a walker for 6 months or more	3,547	11.4
Difficulty with one or more functional activities	14,679	47.0
Unable to perform one or more functional activities	8,270	26.5
Difficulty with one or more ADL's*	4,429	14.2
Needs personal assistance with one or more ADL's	2,219	7.1
Difficulty with one or more IADL's**	6,490	20.8
Needs personal assistance with one or more IADL's	4,929	15.8
Needs personal assistance with one or more ADL's or IADL's	5,126	16.4

* Activities of daily living (ADLs) include bathing, dressing, eating, and getting around the house.

** Instrumental activities of daily living (IADLs) include preparing meals, shopping, managing money, using the telephone, doing housework, and taking medication.

DISABLED PERSONS WITH WHITE ORIGINS
(Not Hispanic Origin)

	Number (thousands)	Percent distribution
White, not Hispanic origin	26,881	100.0
With any disability	13,717	51.0
Severe	8,530	31.7
Not severe	5,187	19.3
Uses a wheelchair	793	3.0
Does not use a wheelchair, has used a cane, crutches, or a walker for 6 months or more	2,887	10.7
Difficulty with one or more functional activities	12,223	45.5
Unable to perform one or more functional activities	6,784	25.2
Difficulty with one or more ADL's	3,591	13.4
Needs personal assistance with one or more ADL's	1,753	6.5
Difficulty with one or more IADL's	5,299	19.7
Needs personal assistance with one or more IADL's	3,981	14.8
Needs personal assistance with one or more ADL's or IADL's	4,165	15.5

Disabled Persons with Black Origins

	Number (thousands)	Percent distribution
Black	2,584	100.0
With any disability	1,703	65.9
Severe	1,249	48.3
Not severe	455	17.6
Uses a wheelchair	156	6.0
Does not use a wheelchair, has used a cane, crutches, or a walker for 6 months or more	460	17.8
Difficulty with one or more functional activities	1,571	60.8
Unable to perform one or more functional activities	999	38.7
Difficulty with one or more ADL's	592	22.9
Needs personal assistance with one or more ADL's	341	13.2
Difficulty with one or more IADL's	823	31.9
Needs personal assistance with one or more IADL's	640	24.8
Needs personal assistance with one or more ADL's or IADL's	650	25.2

Disabled Persons with American Indian, Eskimo, or Aleut Origins

	Number (thousands)	Percent distribution
American Indian, Eskimo, or Aleut	100	100.0
With any disability	63	(B)
Severe	52	(B)
Not severe	11	(B)
Uses a wheelchair	2	(B)
Does not use a wheelchair, has used a cane, crutches, or a walker for 6 months or more	26	(B)
Difficulty with one or more functional activities	53	(B)
Unable to perform one or more functional activities	41	(B)
Difficulty with one or more ADL's	19	(B)
Needs personal assistance with one or more ADL's	14	(B)
Difficulty with one or more IADL's	28	(B)
Needs personal assistance with one or more IADL's	20	(B)
Needs personal assistance with one or more ADL's or IADL's	20	(B)

Disabled Persons with Asian or Pacific Islander Origin

	Number (thousands)	Percent distribution
Asian or Pacific Islander	509	100.0
With any disability	257	50.5
Severe	161	31.7
Not severe	96	18.9
Uses a wheelchair	15	2.9
Does not use a wheelchair, has used a cane, crutches, or a walker for 6 months or more	47	9.3
Difficulty with one or more functional activities	230	45.2
Unable to perform one or more functional activities	114	22.4
Difficulty with one or more ADL's	63	12.4
Needs personal assistance with one or more ADL's	35	7.0
Difficulty with one or more IADL's	88	17.4
Needs personal assistance with one or more IADL's	74	14.5
Needs personal assistance with one or more ADL's or IADL's	74	14.5

Disabled Persons with Hispanic Origin

	Number (thousands)	Percent distribution
Hispanic Origin	1,448	100.0
With any disability	854	59.0
Severe	551	38.1
Not severe	303	20.9
Uses a wheelchair	65	4.5
Does not use a wheelchair, has used a cane, crutches, or a walker for 6 months or more	157	10.9
Difficulty with one or more functional activities	775	53.5
Unable to perform one or more functional activities	438	30.2
Difficulty with one or more ADL's	217	15.0
Needs personal assistance with one or more ADL's	105	7.3
Difficulty with one or more IADL's	338	23.4
Needs personal assistance with one or more IADL's	287	19.8
Needs personal assistance with one or more ADL's or IADL's	289	19.9

Question

What might account for the fact that a larger percentage of African-American and Hispanic-origin seniors are disabled as compared to white seniors?

In connection with the following excerpts, read titles I, IIA, and III of the Americans With Disabilities Act in the statutory supplement.

The U.S. Equal Employment Opportunity Commission
Enforcement Guidance: Reasonable Accommodation and Undue Hardship Under the Americans with Disabilities Act (March 1999)
<http://www.eeoc.gov/docs/accommodation.html>

Reasonable Accommodation

Title I of the Americans with Disabilities Act of 1990 (the "ADA") requires an employer to provide reasonable accommodation to qualified individuals with disabilities who are employees or applicants for employment, unless to do so would cause undue hardship. "In general, an accommodation is any change in the work environment or in the way things are customarily done that enables an individual with a disability to enjoy equal employment opportunities." There are three categories of "reasonable accommodations":

(i) modifications or adjustments to a job application process that enable a qualified applicant with a disability to be considered for the position such qualified applicant desires; or

(ii) modifications or adjustments to the work environment, or to the manner or circumstances under which the position held or desired is customarily performed, that enable a qualified individual with a disability to perform the essential functions of that position; or

(iii) modifications or adjustments that enable a covered entity's employee with a disability to enjoy equal benefits and privileges of employment as are enjoyed by its other similarly situated employees without disabilities.

The duty to provide reasonable accommodation is a fundamental statutory requirement because of the nature of discrimination faced by individuals with disabilities. Although many individuals with disabilities can apply for and perform jobs without any reasonable accommodations, there are workplace barriers that keep others from performing jobs which they could do with some form of accommodation. These barriers may be physical obstacles (such as inaccessible facilities or equipment), or they may be procedures or rules (such as rules concerning when work is performed, when breaks are taken, or how essential or marginal functions are performed). Reasonable accommodation removes workplace barriers for individuals with disabilities.

Reasonable accommodation is available to qualified applicants and employees with disabilities. Reasonable accommodations must be provided to qualified employees regardless of whether they work part-time or full-time, or are considered "probationary." Generally, the individual with a disability must inform the employer that an accommodation is needed.

There are a number of possible reasonable accommodations that an employer may have to provide in connection with modifications to the work environment or adjustments in how and when a job is performed. These include:

- making existing facilities accessible;
- job restructuring;
- part-time or modified work schedules;
- acquiring or modifying equipment;
- changing tests, training materials, or policies;
- providing qualified readers or interpreters; and
- reassignment to a vacant position.

There are several modifications or adjustments that are not considered forms of reasonable accommodation. An employer does not have to eliminate an essential function, i.e., a fundamental duty of the position. This is because a person with a disability who is unable to perform the essential functions, with or without reasonable accommodation, is not a "qualified" individual with a disability within the meaning of the ADA. Nor is an employer required to lower production standards—whether qualitative or quantitative—that are applied uniformly to employees with and without disabilities. However, an employer may have to provide reasonable accommodation to enable an employee with a disability to meet the production standard. While an employer is not required to eliminate an essential function or lower a production standard, it may do so if it wishes.

An employer does not have to provide as reasonable accommodations personal use items needed in accomplishing daily activities both on and off the job. Thus, an employer is not required to provide an employee with a prosthetic limb, a wheelchair, eyeglasses, hearing aids, or similar devices if they are also needed off the job. Furthermore, an employer is not required to provide personal use amenities, such as a hot pot or refrigerator, if those items are not provided to employees without disabilities. However, items that might otherwise be considered personal may be required as reasonable accommodations where they are specifically designed or required to meet job-related rather than personal needs.

A modification or adjustment satisfies the reasonable accommodation obligation if it is "effective." In the context of job performance, this means that a reasonable accommodation enables the individual to perform the essential functions of the position. Similarly, an effective accommodation will enable an applicant with a disability to have an equal opportunity to participate in the application process and to be considered for a job. Finally, a reasonable accommodation will be effective if it allows an employee with a disability an equal opportunity to enjoy the benefits and privileges of employment that employees without disabilities enjoy.

Example A: An employee with a hearing disability must be able to contact the public by telephone. The employee proposes that he use a TTY to call a relay service operator who can then place the telephone call and relay the conversation between the parties. This is a reasonable accommodation because it is effective. It enables the employee to communicate with the public.

Example B: A cashier easily becomes fatigued because of lupus and, as a result, has difficulty making it through her shift. The employee requests a stool because sitting greatly reduces the fatigue. This reasonable accommodation is effective because it removes a workplace barrier—being required to stand—and thus gives the employee the opportunity to perform as well as any other cashier.

The term "reasonable accommodation" is a term of art that Congress defined only through examples of changes or modifications to be made, or items to be provided, to a qualified individual with a disability. The statutory definition of "reasonable accommodation" does not include any quantitative, financial, or other limitations regarding the extent of the obligation to make changes to a job or work environment. The only statutory limitation on an employer's obligation to provide "reasonable accommodation" is that no such change or modification is required if it would cause "undue hardship" on the employer. Undue hardship addresses quantitative, financial, or other limitations on an employer's ability to provide reasonable accommodation.

Undue Hardship

"Undue hardship" means significant difficulty or expense and focuses on the resources and circumstances of the particular employer in relationship to the cost or difficulty of providing a specific accommodation. Undue hardship refers not only to financial difficulty, but to reasonable accommodations that are unduly extensive, substantial, or disruptive, or those that would fundamentally alter the nature or operation of the business. An employer must assess on a case-by-case basis whether a particular reasonable accommodation would cause undue hardship. The ADA's "undue hardship" standard is different from that applied by courts under Title VII of the Civil Rights Act of 1964 for religious accommodation.

U.S. Department of Justice, Civil Rights Division, Disability Rights Section
A Guide to Disability Rights Laws (October 1, 1996)
<http://www.usdoj.gov/crt/ada/cguide.htm>

This guide provides an overview of Federal civil rights laws that ensure equal opportunity for people with disabilities. To find out more about how these laws may apply to you, contact the agencies and organizations listed below.

Americans With Disabilities Act (ADA)

The ADA prohibits discrimination on the basis of disability in employment, State and local government, public accommodations, commercial facilities, transportation, and telecommunications. It also applies to the United States Congress.

To be protected by the ADA, one must have a disability or have a relationship or association with an individual with a disability. An individual with a disability is defined by the ADA as a person who has a physical or mental impairment that substantially limits one or more major life activities, a person who has a history or record of such an impairment, or a person who is perceived by others as having such an impairment. The ADA does not specifically name all of the impairments that are covered.

ADA Title I: Employment

Title I requires employers with 15 or more employees to provide qualified individuals with disabilities an equal opportunity to benefit from the full range of employment-related opportunities available to others. For example, it prohibits discrimination in recruitment, hiring, promotions, training, pay, social activities, and other privileges of employment. It restricts questions that can be asked about an applicant's disability before a job offer is made, and it requires that employers make reasonable accommodation to the known physical or mental limitations of otherwise qualified individuals with disabilities, unless it results in undue hardship. Religious entities with 15 or more employees are covered under Title I.

Title I complaints must be filed with the U. S. Equal Employment Opportunity Commission (EEOC) within 180 days of the date of discrimination, or 300 days if the charge is filed with a designated State or local fair employment practice agency. Individuals may file a lawsuit in Federal court only after they receive a "right-to-sue" letter from the EEOC.

Charges of employment discrimination on the basis of disability may be filed at any U.S. Equal Employment Opportunity Commission field office. Field offices are located in 50 cities throughout the U.S. and are listed in most telephone directories under "U.S. Government."

* * *

ADA Title II: State and Local Government Activities

Title II covers all activities of State and local governments regardless of the government entity's size or receipt of Federal funding. Title II requires that State and local governments give people with disabilities an equal opportunity to benefit from all of their programs, services, and activities (e.g. public education, employment, transportation, recreation, health care, social services, courts, voting, and town meetings).

State and local governments are required to follow specific architectural standards in the new construction and alteration of their buildings. They also must relocate programs or otherwise provide access in inaccessible older buildings, and communicate effectively with people who have hearing, vision, or speech disabilities. Public entities are not required to take actions that would result in undue financial and administrative burdens. They are required to make reasonable modifications to policies, practices, and procedures where necessary to avoid discrimination, unless they can demonstrate that doing so would fundamentally alter the nature of the service, program, or activity being provided.

Complaints of Title II violations may be filed with the Department of Justice within 180 days of the date of discrimination. In certain situations, cases may be referred to a mediation program sponsored by the Department. The Department may bring a lawsuit where it has investigated a matter and has been unable to resolve violations.

* * *

Title II may also be enforced through private lawsuits in Federal court. It is not necessary to file a complaint with the Department of Justice (DOJ) or any other Federal agency, or to receive a "right-to-sue" letter, before going to court.

ADA Title II: Public Transportation

The transportation provisions of Title II cover public transportation services, such as city buses and public rail transit (e.g. subways, commuter rails, Amtrak). Public transportation authorities may not discriminate against people with disabilities in the provision of their services. They must comply with requirements for accessibility in newly purchased vehicles, make good faith efforts to purchase or lease accessible used buses, remanufacture buses in an accessible manner, and, unless it would result in an undue burden, provide paratransit where they operate fixed-route bus or rail systems. Paratransit is a service where individuals who are unable to use the regular transit system independently (because of a physical or mental impairment) are picked up and dropped off at their destinations.

ADA Title III: Public Accommodations

Title III covers businesses and nonprofit service providers that are public accommodations, privately operated entities offering certain types of courses and examinations, privately operated transportation, and commercial facilities. Public accommodations are private entities who own, lease, lease to, or operate facilities such as restaurants, retail stores, hotels, movie theaters, private schools, convention centers, doctors' offices, homeless shelters, transportation depots, zoos, funeral homes, day care centers, and recreation facilities including sports stadiums and fitness clubs. Transportation services provided by private entities are also covered by Title III.

Public accommodations must comply with basic nondiscrimination requirements that prohibit exclusion, segregation, and unequal treatment. They also must comply with specific requirements related to architectural standards for new and altered buildings; reasonable modifications to policies, practices, and procedures; effective communication with people with hearing, vision, or speech disabilities; and other access requirements. Additionally, public accommodations must remove barriers in existing buildings where it is easy to do so without much difficulty or expense, given the public accommodation's resources.

Courses and examinations related to professional, educational, or trade-related applications, licensing, certifications, or credentialing must be provided in a place and manner accessible to people with disabilities, or alternative accessible arrangements must be offered.

Commercial facilities, such as factories and warehouses, must comply with the ADA's architectural standards for new construction and alterations.

Complaints of Title III violations may be filed with the Department of Justice. In certain situations, cases may be referred to a mediation program sponsored by the Department. The Department is authorized to bring a lawsuit where there is a pattern or practice of discrimination in violation of Title III, or where an act of discrimination raises an issue of general public importance. Title III may also be enforced through private lawsuits. It is not necessary to file a complaint with the Department of Justice (or any Federal agency), or to receive a "right-to-sue" letter, before going to court.

ADA Title IV: Telecommunications

Title IV addresses telephone and television access for people with hearing and speech disabilities. It requires common carriers (telephone companies) to establish interstate and intrastate telecommunications relay services (TRS) 24 hours a day, 7 days a week. TRS enables callers with hearing and speech disabilities who use text telephones (TTY's or TDD's), and callers who use voice telephones, to communicate with each other through a third party communications assistant. The Federal Communications Commission (FCC) has set minimum standards for TRS services. Title IV also requires closed captioning of Federally funded public service announcements.

Questions

1. What fundamental changes in workplaces, public spaces, and educational institutions do you think the ADA requires?

2. Does the ADA create too much potential liability for employers who wish to terminate the employment of incompetent older workers?

3. Some older persons suffer from psychiatric disabilities, for example, Alzheimer's disease, that may severely compromise their ability to act "normally." How can such persons be accommodated under the ADA—or can they be?

**Settlement Agreement Between the United States of America
and Moon River Enterprises, Inc., Branson, Missouri
re: Moon River Theater, Branson, Missouri
(removal of architectural barriers in a live performance theater) (June 2, 1998)
<http://www.usdoj.gov/crt/ada/moonrivr.htm>**

Background

1. This matter was initiated by a complaint filed with the United States Department of Justice ("the Department") against Moon River Enterprises, Inc., the owner and operator of Andy Williams' Moon River Theatre ("Respondent"). The complaint was investigated by the Department under the authority granted by Section 308(b) of the Americans with Disabilities Act of 1990 ("ADA"), 42 U.S.C. § 12188.

The Parties

2. The parties to this Settlement Agreement ("Agreement") are the United States of America and Moon River Enterprises, Inc.

3. Andy Williams' Moon River Theatre is a theater located at 2500 W. Highway 76, Branson, Missouri 65616.

4. Respondent, the owner and operator of Andy Williams' Moon River Theatre, is a public accommodation as defined by Title III of the ADA because respondent is

the owner or operator of a "theater . . . or other place of exhibition or entertainment." 42 U.S.C. § 12181; 28 C.F.R. § 36.104(3).

5. The subject of this Agreement is readily achievable barrier removal at the Andy Williams' Moon River Theatre.

6. The Department conducted a site visit of the Moon River Theatre that identified a number of architectural barriers to access in and around the theater. The Department believes that the failure to remove barriers violates Title III of the ADA.

Accordingly, it is hereby agreed that:

7. Moon River Enterprises, Inc. is a private entity that owns and operates the Andy Williams' Moon River Theatre, a place of public accommodation as defined by title III of the ADA, 42 U.S.C. § 12181, and 28 C.F.R. § 36.104. The theater is subject to the "readily achievable" barrier removal provisions of the ADA at 42 U.S.C. § 12184 and 28 C.F.R. § 36.304 because it is a place of public accommodation as defined in § 36.104.

8. This Agreement is final and binding on all parties to this action, including all principals, agents, and successors in interest of Andy Williams' Moon River Theatre and the United States Department of Justice.

9. Respondent has cooperated fully towards the removal of barriers to access where readily achievable to do so since it was first notified of the complaint filed with the Department. This Agreement does not constitute an admission of a violation of the ADA on the part of Moon River.

Actions to be taken by Moon River Enterprises, Inc.

10. In the time since Respondent was first notified of violations at the theater and the date of this Agreement, Respondent has corrected many of the problems identified in the Department's site survey, paragraph 6 above, including adding additional signage, making the public telephones accessible, installing visual alarms in the mens' and womens' rooms, and improving accessibility in the restrooms. In order to fully resolve this matter, Respondent agrees to take the following additional steps to remove barriers to access by April 15, 1998:

(a) Provide a designated area adjacent to an accessible route where persons with disabilities may be dropped off and picked up if all designated accessible parking spaces are filled;

(b) Install additional vertical signage at the accessible parking spaces closest to the main entrance of the theater that complies with the ADA Accessibility Guidelines for Buildings and Facilities ("Standards") §§ 4.1.2(5), 4.6.4;

(c) Ensure that the accessible route from the designated accessible parking spaces to the designated accessible entrance has no change in level at the walkway joints, Standards §§ 4.1.2(1), 4.3.8, 4.5.2, and is regularly inspected;

(d) Convert the existing designated accessible stall into an alternate toilet stall in the mens' and womens' room in the upper and lower lobbies; the stall is to be 36 inches wide with parallel grab bars complying with Figures 30(b) and (d) and Standards §§ 4.1.3(11), 4.17.3, 4.26, and 4.22.4.

(e) Provide grab bars in all alternate stalls (see paragraph 10(d) above) that are mounted in the required location and at the required height in accordance with Standards §§ 4.1.3(11), 4.17.6, 4.22.4, and Figure 30(d).

(f) Ensure that the centerline of the toilet is exactly 18 inches in all mens' and women's room alternate stalls. Standards §§ 4.1.3(11), 4.17.3, 4.22.4.

(g) Relocate the toilet paper dispenser so that it does not obstruct the grab bar in both the mens' and women's room alternate stalls. Standard §§ 4.1.3(11), 4.16.6, 4.22.4.

(h) Provide the required number of accessible wheelchair locations in the theater area. Standards §§ 4.1.3(19)(a), 4.33.1.

11. Nothing herein shall require Respondent to invalidate, refuse to honor, modify and/or exchange any tickets already sold for the 1998 holiday season as of the date of this Agreement which are for seats that ultimately will become designated as accessible wheelchair locations pursuant to paragraph 10(h) herein.

12. Prior to commencement of work, but no later than March 29, 1998, Respondent shall provide the United States with a detailed dimensioned sketch or drawing of the proposed barrier removal work. The United States shall have 15 days from receipt of Respondent's list to notify Respondent in writing of its approval of the plans or of its objections.

Implementation and Enforcement of the Settlement Agreement

13. The Attorney General is authorized, pursuant to 42 U.S.C. § 12188(b)(1)(B), to bring a civil action under Title III, enforcing the ADA in any situation where a pattern or practice of discrimination is believed to exist or a matter of general public importance is raised. In consideration of the terms of this Agreement, the Attorney General agrees to refrain from filing civil suit under Title III in this matter regarding the specific issues discussed herein, so long as Respondent complies with the terms of this Agreement.

14. The Department may review compliance with this agreement at any time. If the Department believes that this agreement or any requirement thereof has been violated, it agrees to notify Respondent in writing of the specific violation(s) alleged. Respondent shall have forty-five (45) days from its receipt of the notice to cure the violation(s) and provide written certification, and photographs if appropriate, to the Department. If Respondent fails to cure the violation(s) or provide written certification within the forty-five (45) day period, the Department may institute a civil action for relief in Federal district court, and the Department is authorized to seek civil penalties for any violation of this agreement, pursuant to 42 U.S.C. § 12188(b)(2)(C).

15. A violation of this Agreement that is not cured pursuant to paragraph 14 above shall be deemed a subsequent violation of the ADA. 42 U.S.C. § 12188(b)(3) and 28 C.F.R. § 36.504(b).

16. By April 30, 1998 the Respondent shall certify to the Department, in writing, that they have fulfilled all of their obligations under this Agreement. The certification shall describe the steps that have been taken to fulfill those obligations and shall be accompanied by photographs depicting the completed barrier removal work.

The parties expressly agree that providing such certification is essential to the enforcement of this agreement, and that a failure to provide the certification required by this paragraph constitutes a breach of this agreement sufficient to warrant the penalties set out in paragraph 14.

17. The United States agrees that Respondent's completion of the steps set forth in this Agreement has fully resolved the complaint submitted to the United States and the issues detailed in paragraphs 6 and 10, above. The United States further agrees that the complaint and the investigation in this matter shall be administratively closed upon completion of the steps set forth in this Agreement.

18. This Agreement is a public document. A copy of this document or any information contained in it, may be made available to any person. Respondent or the United States shall provide a copy of this Agreement to any person on request.

19. The effective date of this Agreement is the date of the last signature below. This Agreement shall be binding on Respondent and its successors in interest, and Respondent has a duty to so notify all such successors in interest.

20. Failure by the Department of Justice to enforce this entire Agreement or any provision thereof with regard to any deadline or any other provision herein shall not be construed as a waiver of its right to do so with regard to other deadlines and provisions of this Agreement.

21. This Agreement constitutes the entire agreement between the parties on the matters raised herein, and no other statement, promise, or agreement, either written or oral, made by either party or agents of either party, that is not contained in this written Agreement, shall be enforceable. This Agreement is limited to the facts set forth herein and it does not purport to remedy any other potential violations of the Americans with Disabilities Act, including violations of the alterations or new construction provisions of the Act, or any other Federal law. This Agreement does not affect the continuing responsibility of Respondent to comply with all aspects of the Americans with Disabilities Act, including readily achievable barrier removal.

22. A signor of this document in a representative capacity for a partnership, corporation, or other such entity, represents that he or she is authorized to bind such partnership, corporation or other entity to this Agreement.

Questions

Does the Moon River consent agreement adequately protect the interests of persons with physical disabilities? Is it likely that persons who attend performances at the Moon River Theatre have other disabilities that this agreement does not address?

U.S. Department of Justice, Civil Rights Division, Disability Rights Section
How to File a Title III Complaint
<http://www.usdoj.gov/crt/ada/t3compfm.htm>

This is in response to your request for information on how to file a complaint under Ttitle III of the Americans with Disabilities Act.

Title III prohibits discrimination based on disability in public accommodations. Private entities covered by Title III include places of lodging, establishments serving food and drink, places of exhibition or entertainment, places of public gathering, sales or rental establishments, service establishments, stations used for specified public transportation, places of public display or collection, places of recreation, places of education, social service center establishments, and places of exercise or recreation. Title III also covers commercial facilities (such as warehouses, factories, and office buildings), private transportation services, and licensing and testing practices.

If you feel you or another person have been discriminated against by an entity covered by Title III, send a letter to the Department of Justice, at the address below, including the following information:

- Your full name, address, and telephone number, and the name of the party discriminated against;
- The name of the business, organization, or institution that you believe has discriminated;
- A description of the act or acts of discrimination, the date or dates of the discriminatory acts, and the name or names of the individuals who you believe discriminated; and
- Other information that you believe necessary to support your complaint. Please send copies of relevant documents. Do *not* send original documents. (Retain them.)

Sign and send the letter to [this address]: Disability Rights Section, Civil Rights Division, U.S. Department of Justice, Post Office Box 66738, Washington, D.C. 20035-6738.

The Disability Rights Section will consider your complaint and inform you of its action. The office will investigate the complaint and determine whether to begin litigation. We will not necessarily make a determination on each complaint about whether or not there is an ADA violation. If we believe there is a pattern or practice of discrimination, or the complaint raises an issue of general public importance, we may attempt to negotiate a settlement of the matter or we may bring an action in U.S. District Court. Any such action would be taken on behalf of the Unites States. We do not act as an attorney for, or representative of, the complainant. You also have the option of filing your own case in U.S. District Court.

Depending on the nature of your complaint, other information would also be helpful to our investigation:

1. Small businesses have limited protection from lawsuits. Except with respect to new construction and alterations, no lawsuit can be filed concerning acts or omissions that occur before—
   1) July 26, 1992, by businesses with 25 or fewer employees and gross receipts of $1,000,000 or less.
   2) January 26, 1993, by businesses with 10 or fewer employees and gross receipts of $500,000 or less.
2. The name or names of the individuals or entities who have an ownership and/or managerial interest in each facility or business that is the subject of your complaint, with phone numbers and addresses, including zip codes, if you have them.
3. Information specifying whether the facility is owned and/or operated by a private entity or a state or local government.
4. The nature of the activity or service provided by the business.
5. If you are alleging failure to remove architectural barriers, a description, including as much detail as possible, of the barriers. If possible, please provide pictures, videotapes, diagrams, or other illustrations that accurately set forth the alleged violation.
6. Any suggestions for remedying the alleged violations of the ADA.
7. Information about whether you have filed a related complaint with a U.S. Attorneys Office, or any other Federal, State, or local agency, or any court, or whether you intend to file such a complaint.

Privacy Act Statement

The authority for collecting this information is contained in 42 U.S.C. § 12188(b). We need this information in order to investigate your complaint. The personal information will be used primarily for authorized civil rights compliance and enforcement activities conducted by the Department of Justice. The Department will not disclose the name of, or other identifying information about, an individual unless it is necessary for enforcement activities against an entity alleged to have violated federal law, or unless such information is required to be disclosed under the Freedom of Information Act, 5 U.S.C. § 552, or as is allowed through the publication of a routine use in accordance with the Privacy Act of 1974, 5 U.S.C. § 552a. To further the Department's enforcement activities, information we have about you may be given to appropriate Federal, State, or local agencies. Additional disclosures of information may be made: to Members of Congress or staff; to volunteer student workers within the Department of Justice so that they may perform their duties; to the news media when release is made consistent with the Freedom of Information Act and 28 C.F.R. § 40.2; and to the National Archives and Records Administration and General Services Administration to perform records management inspection functions in accordance with their statutory responsibilities. Furnishing of the requested information is voluntary except that the failure to provide such information may result in our being unable to process your complaint.

Question

The Department of Justice document above is intended to guide the layperson on how to proceed pro se in connection with a claim under Title III of the ADA. Do you believe it accomplishes its purpose? Do you think that the attorney has a role to play even at the administrative level?

2. State Law

Question

Reread the Kansas Act Against Discrimination in the statutory supplement. In what ways does the protection against disability discrimination available under this law differ from that guaranteed by the ADA?

City of Moorpark v. Superior Court
959 P.2d 752 (Cal. 1996)

Labor Code section 132a (section 132a) prohibits employers from discriminating against employees "who are injured in the course and scope of their employment." When an injury of this kind results in disability, we have held that section 132a prohibits discrimination based on the disability. In addition, the California Fair Employment and Housing Act (Gov. Code, § 12900 et seq. (FEHA)) prohibits various types of employment discrimination, including discrimination based on a disability. (Gov. Code, § 12921.) Finally, we have recognized a common law protection against certain types of discriminatory or retaliatory termination of employment. This common law remedy for wrongful discharge arguably extends to disability discrimination, though we have not addressed the issue.

Several Court of Appeal decisions have held that section 132a provides the exclusive remedy for discrimination based on a work-related disability, precluding FEHA or common law wrongful discharge claims. More recent decisions have reached this conclusion despite a 1993 amendment to the FEHA that plaintiff argues repealed section 132a, at least in part. Before the 1993 amendment, the FEHA provided: "Nothing contained in [the FEHA] shall be deemed to repeal any of the provisions of . . . any . . . law of this state relating to discrimination because of . . . physical disability [or] mental disability . . . ." (Gov. Code, former § 12993, subd. (a); Stats. 1992, ch. 913, § 25, p. 4325.) The 1993 amendment added the phrase: "unless those provisions provide less protection to the enumerated classes of persons covered under this part." (Gov. Code, § 12993, subd. (a).)

In this case, we consider whether FEHA and common law wrongful discharge remedies are available to an employee who has suffered discrimination based on a work-related disability, meaning, for present purposes, a disability resulting from an injury "arising out of and in the course of the employment" that gave rise to the discrimination. (Lab. Code, § 3600.) We conclude that section 132a does not provide the exclusive remedy for this type of discrimination and that FEHA and common law remedies are available.

Factual and Procedural Background

Theresa L. Dillon's complaint alleges that the City of Moorpark employed her as an administrative secretary from May 1990 until February 28, 1994. After she recovered from knee surgery and her doctor released her to return to work, City Manager Steve Kueny terminated her employment, informing her that her residual disability prevented her from performing her essential job functions. Dillon told Assistant City Manager Richard Hare that she could perform her job and that she wanted to return to work, but Hare told her she could not have her job back. Dillon also objected in writing to Kueny, again to no avail. Dillon then filed a charge of disability discrimination with the California Department of Fair Employment and Housing and received notice of a right to sue under Government Code section 12965, subdivision (b). On February 22, 1995, Dillon sued the City of Moorpark, Kueny, and Hare, alleging causes of action for discrimination in violation of the FEHA, wrongful termination in violation of public policy (common law wrongful discharge), breach of contract, and intentional and/or negligent infliction of emotional distress. She sought both compensatory and punitive damages.

Defendants demurred to all causes of action, arguing in part that, because Dillon's disability was work related, section 132a provided her exclusive remedy. Defendants asked the court to take judicial notice of Dillon's section 132a petition, which alleged essentially the same disability discrimination as part of a workers' compensation proceeding. The superior court disagreed that section 132a provided Dillon's exclusive remedy and overruled the demurrers to the FEHA and common law wrongful discharge causes of action. The court sustained the demurrers to the breach of contract and emotional distress causes of action on grounds not relevant here. Dillon then amended her complaint, dropping the breach of contract cause of action and restating the emotional distress cause of action.

On July 7, 1995, defendants petitioned the Court of Appeal for a writ of mandate, again arguing that section 132a provided Dillon's exclusive remedy and that the trial court therefore had erred in overruling the demurrers to Dillon's first two causes of action. The Court of Appeal denied the petition, citing the 1993 amendment to the FEHA, which it found to be "clear and intelligible." According to the Court of Appeal, the 1993 amendment meant "simply this: should any provision of state law offer less protection than does the FEHA, then such provision is inoperable and effectively preempted by the FEHA." The court concluded that section 132a offered "less protection" than the FEHA to victims of disability discrimination because it did not offer as many remedial options, did not provide a right to a jury trial or a right to appeal, and resulted in smaller overall awards. Because section 132a offered "less protection," the court concluded that the FEHA implicitly repealed section 132a. Without explanation, however, the court held that the FEHA only repealed the exclusivity aspect of section 132a. The court stated that section 132a remained an "alternative mechanism[]" for resolving disability discrimination claims.

We granted review in order to consider the interrelationship between section 132a and other statutory and common law remedies for disability discrimination in the workplace.

Discussion

1. Exclusivity of section 132a remedy.

Section 132a provides: "It is the declared policy of this state that there should not be discrimination against workers who are injured in the course and scope of their employment. (1) Any employer who discharges, or threatens to discharge, or in any manner discriminates against any employee because he or she has filed or made known his or her intention to file a claim for compensation with his or her employer or an application for adjudication, or because the employee has received a rating, award, or settlement, is guilty of a misdemeanor and the employee's compensation shall be increased by one-half, but in no event more than ten thousand dollars . . . , together with costs and expenses not in excess of two hundred fifty dollars . . . . Any such employee shall also be entitled to reinstatement and reimbursement for lost wages and work benefits caused by the acts of the employer."

On its face, section 132a's remedies apply only when employers retaliate against employees for pursuing their rights under the workers' compensation law. In *Judson Steel Corp. v. Workers' Comp. Appeals Bd.*, 586 P.2d 564 (1978), however, we focused on the first sentence of section 132a, which declares a general policy barring discrimination against injured employees. We concluded that section 132a's remedies are available whenever an employee suffers "discrimination incurred as the result of his injury," including discrimination based on disability.

In *Portillo v. G.T. Price Products, Inc.*, 131 Cal. App. 3d 285 (1982), the court held that, in cases where section 132a applied, it provided an employee's exclusive remedy. The plaintiff in *Portillo* brought a common law wrongful discharge action, alleging her employer discharged her in retaliation for filing a workers' compensation claim. Defendant demurred, arguing that section 132a provided the plaintiff's exclusive remedy, and the trial court sustained the demurrer.

The Court of Appeal affirmed. Noting that the Workers' Compensation Appeals Board had "'full . . . jurisdiction'" to resolve section 132a claims, the court found applicable the exclusive remedy provisions that apply to other workers' compensation remedies. The court emphasized the legislative compromise underlying the workers' compensation law:

> "The Workers' Compensation Act is designed to afford workers quick determination of their claims for injury without regard to the common law questions of liability, negligence or fault on the part of and other common law defenses available to the employer. *The Legislature has balanced this imposition or burden on the employer by limiting the employee to seek redress in a single forum, the Workers' Compensation Appeals Board.* On balance, the fact that the *exclusivity of remedy* before the Workers' Compensation Appeals Board is for the benefit of workers generally outweighs any occasional disadvantage that could be argued."

The court also quoted Labor Code section 5300, which provides that proceedings "[f]or the recovery of compensation, or concerning any right or liability arising out of or incidental thereto" "shall be instituted before the [Workers' Compensation] [A]ppeals [B]oard *and not elsewhere* . . . ." Finally, the court emphasized that section 132a addressed the precise wrong that the plaintiff alleged and that courts should not, by enforcing a common law remedy, "say that a different rule for the particular facts should have been written by the Legislature" (*id.* at p. 290). Accordingly, the court held that section 132a provided the plaintiff's exclusive remedy and affirmed the judgment of dismissal.

In *Pickrel v. General Telephone Co.*, 205 Cal. App. 3d 1058 (1988), the court extended *Portillo* to a case specifically involving disability discrimination. The plaintiff in *Pickrel* brought a FEHA cause of action alleging termination of her employment based on a "physical handicap." The trial court sustained a demurrer, and the Court of Appeal affirmed. Citing and following much of its reasoning, the court held that section 132a provided the exclusive remedy for an employee claiming discrimination based on a work-related disability. The court stated that the result in *Portillo* was "consonant with the trend of recent decisions '. . . to narrow the range of exceptions to exclusivity, [thus] benefit[ing] both employers and employees within the system, by . . . preserving the low cost, efficiency and certainty of recovery which characterizes workers' compensation.'"

After the *Pickrel* decision, we addressed the scope of workers' compensation exclusivity in *Shoemaker v. Myers*, 801 P.2d 1054 (1990) and *Gantt v. Sentry Insurance*, 824 P.2d 680 (Cal. 1992). Both cases considered what remedies are available to an employee who suffers a physical or psychological injury as a result of wrongful termination of employment, but neither case involved termination based on a work-related injury or disability. Therefore, neither case implicated section 132a directly.

In *Shoemaker*, the employee alleged wrongful termination and related causes of action, including termination in violation of a "whistleblower" protection statute (Gov. Code, former § 19683). We concluded "that disabling injuries, whether physical or mental, arising from termination of employment are generally within the coverage of workers' compensation and subject to the exclusive remedy provisions, unless the discharge comes within an express or implied statutory exception or the discharge results from risks reasonably deemed not to be within the compensation bargain." By referring to the "compensation bargain," we recognized the same legislative compromise that the *Portillo* court cited: "[T]he employer assumes liability for industrial personal injury or death without regard to fault in exchange for limitations on the amount of that liability. The employee is afforded relatively swift and certain payment of benefits to cure or relieve the effects of industrial injury without having to prove fault, but, in exchange, gives up the wider range of damages potentially available in tort."

Though we stated that most injuries arising from termination of employment fall within the compensation bargain, we noted that "the exclusive remedy provisions are not applicable [to injuries arising from] 'conduct where the employer or insurer stepped out of their proper roles' [citations] . . . ." Therefore, we concluded that an injury resulting from a wrongful termination in violation of a whistleblower statute "lies well outside the compensation bargain," and the exclusive remedy provisions do not apply. We reasoned that, by enacting the whistleblower statute, "[t]he Legislature clearly intended to afford an *additional* remedy to those already granted under other provisions of the law; otherwise [the whistleblower statute] would be rendered meaningless."

The decision in *Shoemaker* turned in part on the fact that the whistleblower statute constituted a specific declaration of the Legislature's intent to create a new, additional remedy. The same could not be said about common law remedies, and we expressly did not decide in *Shoemaker* whether, in addition to a claim under the whistleblower statute, the plaintiff could also pursue a common law wrongful discharge claim. We addressed that unresolved question in *Gantt*, concluding that "the . . . 'compensation bargain' cannot encompass conduct, such as sexual or racial discrimination, 'obnoxious to the interests of the state and contrary to public policy and sound morality.'" Accordingly, we held that workers' compensation exclusivity did not preclude a common law wrongful discharge claim: "we decline the invitation to retreat from our long-held view that employees discharged in violation of fundamental public policy may bring an action against their employers sounding in tort."

In *Angell v. Peterson Tractor, Inc.*, 21 Cal. App. 4th 981 (1994), the court considered whether *Pickrel*'s holding remained valid in light of *Shoemaker* and *Gantt*; that is, whether wrongful termination in violation of section 132a "could be considered "a risk reasonably encompassed within the compensation bargain" for which workers' compensation is the exclusive remedy. The court seemed to accept without discussion that disability discrimination could form the basis of a common law wrongful discharge claim. The court also acknowledged our holding in *Gantt* that these claims do not fall within the compensation bargain. Nevertheless, the court concluded that, by enacting section 132a, ". . . the Legislature specifically placed this type of discriminatory termination within the scope of the compensation bargain." Accordingly, the court held that section 132a provided an employee's exclusive remedy for discrimination based on a work-related disability, precluding claims under both the FEHA and the common law.

In rejecting the conclusion of *Portillo, Pickrel, Angell*, and related cases, the Court of Appeal in this case focused on the 1993 amendment to the FEHA, reading it as repealing by implication all antidiscrimination laws that provide "less protection" than the FEHA, including section 132a. Notably, the Court of Appeal did not find an outright repeal of section 132a, but merely a repeal of its exclusivity, thus permitting employees to pursue FEHA and common law remedies in addition to section 132a remedies. We agree with the Court of Appeal that section 132a does not preclude Dillon's FEHA and common law causes of action, but, unlike the Court of Appeal, we reach this conclusion without relying on the 1993 amendment to the FEHA. Accordingly, we do not decide what effect, if any, the 1993 FEHA amendment had on section 132a.

Though the Court of Appeal decided *Portillo* 16 years ago, and though other Court of Appeal decisions have affirmed its holding, we have never addressed its validity. We do so now.

As noted, the *Portillo* court held that, when section 132a applies, it provides an employee's exclusive remedy. In reaching this conclusion, the court applied the exclusive remedy provisions that apply to other workers' compensation remedies. (*See* Lab. Code, §§ 3600, 3602, subd. (a).) But section 132a is quite different from other workers' compensation remedies. Most workers' compensation remedies compensate an employee for a medical injury. Section 132a, however, addresses a breach of an employee's civil rights and applies regardless of whether that breach causes a medical injury. Because of this distinction, we see no compelling reason to treat section 132a like other workers' compensation remedies.

Moreover, the existence of a workers' compensation remedy does not by itself establish that the remedy is exclusive. Rather, the scope of workers' compensation exclusivity depends on the terms of the exclusive remedy provisions. Section 132a does not itself contain an exclusive remedy clause, and, as explained below, the general exclusive remedy provisions of the workers' compensation law expressly do not apply to section 132a.

Labor Code section 3600, subdivision (a), provides: "Liability for the compensation provided *by this division*, in lieu of any other liability whatsoever . . . , shall . . . exist against an employer for any injury sustained by his or her employees arising out of and in the course of the employment . . . ." (Italics added.) When section 3600 refers to "this division," it refers to division 4 of the Labor Code. Section 132a, on the other hand, is in division 1 of the Labor Code. Similarly, Labor Code section 3602, subdivision (a), provides: "Where the conditions *of compensation* set forth in Section 3600 concur, the right to recover *such compensation* is . . . the sole and exclusive remedy of the employee . . . ." (Italics added.) Labor Code section 3207 defines "'[c]ompensation'" as "compensation under Division 4 . . . includ[ing] every benefit or payment conferred by Division 4 upon an injured employee . . . ." Again, section 132a is in division 1 of the Labor Code, not division 4. Thus, the plain language of the exclusive remedy provisions of the workers' compensation law apparently limits those provisions to division 4 remedies. Remedies that the Legislature placed in other divisions of the Labor Code are simply not subject to the workers' compensation exclusive remedy provisions.

The *Portillo* court also relied on the "compensation bargain" underlying the workers' compensation law, whereby "[t]he Workers' Compensation Act . . . afford[s] workers quick determination of their claims" but "limit[s] the employee to . . . a single forum, the Workers' Compensation Appeals Board." The court reasoned that this same "compensation bargain" applied implicitly to section 132a. In other words, section 132a affords workers an inexpensive and quick remedy for discrimination based on a work-related disability, but that remedy is exclusive.

Again, the *Portillo* court erred. Though the compensation bargain, and in particular the exclusive remedy principle, applies to most workers' compensation proceedings, we recognized in *Shoemaker* and *Gantt* that certain employer conduct falls outside the compensation bargain. Specifically, we held in *Shoemaker* that an injury resulting from a wrongful termination in violation of a whistleblower protection statute "lies well outside the compensation bargain," and the exclusive remedy provisions do not apply. In *Gantt*, we reaffirmed *Shoemaker* and extended its holding to a case involving a common law wrongful discharge cause of action. We concluded that "the . . . 'compensation bargain' cannot encompass conduct, such as sexual or racial discrimination, 'obnoxious to the interests of the state and contrary to public policy and sound morality.'" Termination in violation of section 132a is just as "'obnoxious to the interests of the state and contrary to public policy and sound morality'" as sexual or racial discrimination. Therefore, a section 132a violation, like sexual and racial discrimination, falls outside the compensation bargain, and workers' compensation is not the exclusive remedy.

In addition, the *Portillo* court relied in part on Labor Code section 5300, which provides that proceedings "[f]or the recovery of compensation, or concerning any right or liability arising out of or incidental thereto" "shall be instituted before the [Workers' Compensation] [A]ppeals [B]oard *and not elsewhere* . . . ." (Lab. Code, § 5300, subd, (a), italics added.) But, even assuming an employee's rights under section 132a are "right[s] . . . incidental" to "the recovery of compensation," Labor Code section 5300 merely establishes the Workers' Compensation Appeals Board as the exclusive *forum* for pursuing a section 132a claim; it does not establish that the section 132a claim is the employee's exclusive remedy. Therefore, Labor Code section 5300 provides weak support for the *Portillo* court's conclusion.

Finally, the *Portillo* court emphasized that section 132a addressed the precise wrong that the plaintiff alleged (*Portillo, supra,* 131 Cal. App. 3d at pp. 288-89) and that courts should not "say that a different rule for the particular facts should have been written by the Legislature." This argument, however, fails to recognize that the Legislature sometimes enacts a new remedy, intending to *supplement* other remedies. When courts enforce a common law remedy despite the existence of a statutory remedy, they are not "say[ing] that a different rule for the particular facts should have been written by the Legislature." They are simply saying that the common law "rule" coexists with the statutory "rule."

Accordingly, we find *Portillo*'s reasoning unpersuasive. Moreover, the Court of Appeal cases that followed *Portillo* do not persuade us that section 132a is exclusive. In *Pickrel*, the court simply cited *Portillo* and followed much of its reasoning. The court noted that the result in *Portillo* was "consonant with the trend of recent decisions," but of course we do not decide cases based on trends. In *Angell*, as in *Portillo*, the court failed to recognize that the Legislature sometimes intends statutory remedies to supplement, not supplant, common law remedies.

The provisions of the FEHA and our decisions interpreting it further support our conclusion that section 132a is not exclusive. The FEHA broadly announces "the public policy of this state that it is necessary to protect and safeguard the right and opportunity of all persons to seek, obtain, and hold employment without discrimination or abridgment on account of . . . physical disability [or] mental disability . . . ." (Gov. Code, § 12920.) The FEHA further provides that "[i]t shall be an unlawful employment practice . . . [f]or an employer, because of the . . . physical disability [or] mental disability . . . of any person, to . . . discriminate against the person . . . ." (Gov. Code, § 12940, subd. (a).) Nothing in these provisions suggests that the FEHA only applies to physical or mental disabilities that are unrelated to work. Moreover, the FEHA declares that its "provisions . . . shall be construed liberally for the accomplishment of the purposes thereof." (Gov. Code, § 12993, subd. (a).) A construction of section 12940, subdivision (a), that narrows the term "disability" to disabilities unrelated to work seems inconsistent with the principle of liberal construction.

Furthermore, our decisions have consistently emphasized the breadth of the FEHA. In *State Personnel Bd. v. Fair Employment & Housing Com.* (1985) 39 Cal. 3d 422, we considered whether the FEHA covered state civil service employees despite similar antidiscrimination provisions in the Civil Service Act. (See Gov. Code, § 19702, subd. (a).) We concluded that "[t]he FEHA was meant to supplement, *not . . . be supplanted by*, existing antidiscrimination remedies, in order to give employees the maximum opportunity to vindicate their civil rights against discrimination. . . ." (*State Personnel Bd. v. Fair Employment & Housing Com., supra,* 39 Cal. 3d at p. 431, italics added.) Similarly, in *Rojo*, we considered whether victims of sex discrimination could bring common law wrongful discharge claims in addition to FEHA claims. We concluded that the Legislature intended the FEHA "to amplify" (*Rojo, supra*, 52 Cal. 3d at p. 75) other remedies and "to expand" (*id.* at p. 80) the rights of persons who are victims of employment discrimination. (*See also Jennings v. Marralle* (1994) 8 Cal. 4th 121, 135 [The Legislature intended "to create new rights within the FEHA statutory scheme while leaving existing rights intact . . . ."].) None of these cases suggests that non-FEHA remedies circumscribe the scope of the FEHA.

Finally, the public education provisions of the workers' compensation law support our conclusion that section 132a is not exclusive. Labor Code section 139.6 provides: "(a) The administrative director shall establish and effect within the Division of Workers' Compensation a continuing program to provide information and assistance concerning the rights, benefits, and obligations of the workers' compensation law to employees and employers subject thereto. The program shall include, but not be limited to, the following: . . . . (2) The preparation, publishing, and as necessary, updating, of a pamphlet advising injured workers of their basic rights under workers' compensation law, *and informing them of rights under . . . the provisions of the Fair Employment and Housing Act relating to individuals with a disability*." (Italics added.) This legislative mandate to inform "injured workers" of their FEHA rights would make little sense if section 132a provided an injured worker's exclusive remedy for disability discrimination.

In conclusion, we hold that section 132a does not provide an exclusive remedy and does not preclude an employee from pursuing FEHA and common law wrongful discharge remedies. We disapprove any cases that suggest otherwise. Nevertheless, we emphasize that not every instance of disability discrimination in violation of section 132a gives rise to a valid FEHA claim. The term "disability" has a specific meaning in the context of the workers' compensation law that it has in no other context. On the other hand, the FEHA includes detailed definitions of "'Physical disability'" and "'Mental disability'" that make no reference to the workers' compensation law. (Gov. Code, § 12926, subds. (i), (k).) Because the standards for establishing disability discrimination may well be different under the FEHA than under section 132a, a decision in an employee's favor on a section 132a petition would not establish a FEHA violation. Moreover, to the extent section 132a and the

FEHA overlap, equitable principles preclude double recovery for employees. For example, employees who settle their claims for lost wages and work benefits as part of a section 132a proceeding could not recover these damages as part of a subsequent FEHA proceeding.

2. Dillon's common law wrongful discharge cause of action.

In the case of Dillon's common law wrongful discharge cause of action, our conclusion that section 132a does not provide an exclusive remedy is only half the analysis. We must also decide whether disability discrimination can form the basis of a common law action of this type.

In *Tameny*, we reaffirmed "that when an employer's discharge of an employee violates fundamental principles of public policy, the discharged employee may maintain a tort action . . . ." (*Tameny, supra,* 27 Cal. 3d at p. 170.) In that case, the plaintiff alleged that his employer terminated him because he refused to participate in an illegal scheme to fix gasoline prices. (*Id.* at p. 169.) The trial court sustained the defendants' demurrer to the plaintiff's tort cause of action for wrongful discharge, and the plaintiff appealed. (*Id.* at p. 171.) We reversed, noting the long-standing rule "that a wrongful act committed in the course of a contractual relationship may afford both tort and contractual relief . . . ." (*Id.* at pp. 174-175.) We reasoned that "an employer's obligation to refrain from discharging an employee who refuses to commit a criminal act . . . reflects a duty imposed by law upon all employers in order to implement the fundamental public policies embodied in the state's penal statutes. As such, a wrongful discharge suit exhibits the classic elements of a tort cause of action." (*Id.* at p. 176.) In subsequent cases applying *Tameny*, we recognized tort causes of action for wrongful discharge based on sex (*Rojo, supra,* 52 Cal. 3d at pp. 90-91), age (*Stevenson, supra,* 16 Cal. 4th at pp. 897, 909), and retaliation for testifying truthfully (*Gantt, supra,* 1 Cal. 4th at pp. 1086-1087). We have not, however, addressed whether disability discrimination, like sex and age discrimination, can form the basis of a common law wrongful discharge claim.

In *Stevenson*, we articulated a four-part test for determining whether a particular policy can support a common law wrongful discharge claim. The policy "must be: (1) delineated in either constitutional or statutory provisions; (2) 'public' in the sense that it 'inures to the benefit of the public' rather than serving merely the interests of the individual; (3) well established at the time of the discharge; and (4) substantial and fundamental." (*Stevenson, supra,* 16 Cal. 4th at p. 894; see also *Jennings v. Marralle, supra,* 8 Cal. 4th at p. 130; *Gantt, supra,* 1 Cal. 4th at pp. 1090, 1095; *Rojo, supra,* 52 Cal. 3d at pp. 89-90.) "'[P]ublic policy' as a concept is notoriously resistant to precise definition, and . . . courts should venture into this area, if at all, with great care . . . ." (*Gantt, supra,* 1 Cal. 4th at p. 1095.) Therefore, when the constitutional provision or statute articulating a public policy also includes certain substantive limitations in scope or remedy, these limitations also circumscribe the common law wrongful discharge cause of action. Stated another way, the common law cause of action cannot be broader than the constitutional provision or statute on which it depends, and therefore it "presents no impediment to employers that operate within the bounds of law." (*Ibid.*) For example, in *Jennings*, we noted that the

FEHA does not apply to employers of fewer than five employees (Gov. Code, § 12926, subd. (d)), and therefore we found no fundamental public policy against age discrimination by these employers. (*Jennings v. Marralle, supra,* 8 Cal. 4th at pp. 135-136; *see also Reno v. Baird* (1998) 18 Cal. 4th 640, 663-664.)

As in *Stevenson,* "[t]hree of the[] four requirements [of a policy that can support a common law wrongful discharge claim] are not reasonably subject to dispute in this case." (*Stevenson, supra,* 16 Cal. 4th at p. 894.) First, the FEHA clearly delineates a policy against disability discrimination in employment—at least in the case of employers of five or more employees. (Gov. Code, §§12940, subd. (a), 12926, subd. (d).) Moreover, the FEHA is just one expression of a much broader policy against disability discrimination that appears in a variety of legislative enactments. (See, e.g., Civ. Code, §§ 51, 54 [barring disability discrimination in public accommodations]; Gov. Code, §§ 11135 [barring disability discrimination in state-funded programs], 19230, subd. (a) [declaring state policy to encourage disabled persons to participate in the social and economic life of the state], 19230, subds. (b), (c), 19702 [barring disability discrimination in state civil service employment].) Second, the policy "'inures to the benefit of the public'" (*Stevenson, supra,* 16 Cal. 4th at p. 894) because (1) any member of the public may develop a disability and become the victim of disability discrimination, (2) the public at large benefits from the productivity of disabled employees, and (3) any type of invidious discrimination "'foments . . . strife and unrest.'" (*Id.* at p. 895.) Third, the policy against disability discrimination has been included in the FEHA since July 1, 1974, and therefore is well established. (Stats. 1973, ch. 1189, §§ 6, 9, pp. 2501-2502.)

Accordingly, we turn to whether the policy against disability discrimination is "substantial and fundamental." Disability discrimination is indistinguishable in many ways from race and sex discrimination. Specifically, it can "attack[] the individual's sense of self-worth in much the same fashion as race or sex discrimination." (*Stevenson, supra,* 16 Cal. 4th at p. 896.) Nevertheless, an employer may have valid reasons to treat disabled employees differently than nondisabled employees, and the FEHA recognizes this fact by expressly providing that it does not "subject an employer to any legal liability resulting from the refusal to employ or the discharge of an employee with a physical or mental disability, where the employee, because of his or her physical or mental disability, is unable to perform his or her essential duties even with reasonable accommodations . . . ." (Gov. Code, § 12940, subd. (a)(1).)

But this caveat does not lead us to conclude that the policy against disability discrimination is not "substantial and fundamental." Even in the case of race, sex, and age discrimination, the FEHA does not prohibit discrimination that is "based upon a bona fide occupational qualification." (Gov. Code, § 12940.) Similarly, our opinions articulating "substantial and fundamental" policies against sex and age discrimination use the term "discrimination" only in the pejorative sense to refer to arbitrary judgments about individuals based on group stereotypes. (*Stevenson, supra,* 16 Cal. 4th at p. 896.)

Disability sometimes impacts a person's ability to perform a particular job, in which case the employer may treat a disabled employee differently than a nondisabled employee. Nevertheless, if disabled employees can prove that they can perform the job duties as effectively as nondisabled employees, taking into consideration the possibility, if any, that their condition will change, as well as the employer's short and long-term needs, then we think discrimination based on disability, like sex and age discrimination, violates a "substantial and fundamental" public policy and can form the basis of a common law wrongful discharge claim. Nevertheless, this remedy must be "carefully tethered to fundamental policies that are delineated" in the FEHA on which it is based. (*Gantt, supra*, 1 Cal. 4th at p. 1095.) Accordingly, just as disability discrimination in violation of section 132a does not alone establish a valid FEHA claim, it also does not alone establish a valid common law wrongful discharge claim. Furthermore, to the extent section 132a, the FEHA, and the common law remedies overlap, equitable principles preclude multiple recoveries for the same injury.

We conclude that disability discrimination can form the basis of a common law wrongful discharge claim. Because section 132a does not provide the exclusive remedy for discrimination based on a work-related disability, the trial court was correct to overrule the demurrer to Dillon's common law wrongful discharge cause of action.

3. Dillon's intentional infliction of emotional distress cause of action.

We held in *Cole v. Fair Oaks Fire Protection Dist.* (1987) 43 Cal. 3d 148, 160, that the exclusive remedy provisions of the workers' compensation law preclude a civil claim for intentional infliction of emotional distress if the employer's actions giving rise to the claim were "a normal part of the employment relationship." The Court of Appeal did not decide whether *Cole* applies here, and defendants did not raise this issue in their petition for review. Accordingly, we also do not reach the issue.

Conclusion

Section 132a does not provide an exclusive remedy precluding FEHA and common law wrongful discharge claims. In addition, disability discrimination can form the basis of a common law wrongful discharge claim. Accordingly, the trial court was correct to overrule defendants' demurrer to Dillon's FEHA and common law wrongful discharge claims, and the Court of Appeal was correct to deny defendants' petition for a writ of mandate. We affirm the judgment of the Court of Appeal.

[The concurring and dissenting opinions have been omitted.—Eds.]

Questions

1. The premise of workers' compensation is that it provides protection for employers from multiple claims for workplace related injuries. Is *City of Moorpark* consistent with that premise?

2. The Equal Employment Opportunity Commission has said that employers may ask job applicants about any state workers' compensation claims that they may have filed in the past. What would be the purpose of such a question? Doesn't the ADA cover disabilities that are due to workplace injuries?

FURTHER READING. RUTH COLKER & BONNIE POITRAS TUCKER, THE LAW OF DISABILITY DISCRIMINATION (2d. ed. 1998); PETER J. STRAUSS & NANCY M. LEDERMAN, THE ELDER LAW HANDBOOK CH. 16 (1996); PETER J. STRAUSS ET AL., AGING AND THE LAW, ch. 6 (1996).

CHAPTER 4

Planning for Retirement

Part A. Government Programs... 148
Part B. Employer-Based Pension Plans 177
Part C. Private Savings: The Individual Retirement Account....................... 202

The aging and retirement of the Baby Boomers has been characterized by some as nothing short of apocalyptic. Will the Social Security system remain financially viable as fewer workers contribute to support the retirement of the elderly population bulge? Will the predicted shortfall be made up in personal savings—savings which the Boomers have notoriously neglected? Will we continue to protect low income elderly with Supplemental Security Income? Many current retirees have pensions, but most current workers don't have that option. Will the gap created by the lack of conventional pensions be filled adequately by voluntary contributions to retirement savings vehicles? This chapter will provide a brief outline of the current sources of retirement income for the elderly as well as stimulate the reader's interest and concern over the financial security of future generations of workers.

Government programs have been the bulwark protecting the elderly from poverty since the depression. Part A surveys the mechanics of Social Security benefits, Old Age, Survivors, and Disability Insurance and its companion welfare program, Supplemental Security Income. It also explores some of the problems and possibilities of this most popular of social safety nets. The disability, medical, and retirement programs available to veterans of U.S. military service deserve a mention in the context of retirement planning because such a significant number of Americans and their dependents are affected. Finally, many states offer retirement benefits in the form of pensions, annuities, and the like which help retired state workers meet their needs.

Part B examines the employer-based pension plan: its history and its modern operation. Among the topics considered are the growth of pensions in the 20th century, the different types of plans, the tax treatment of contributions and distributions, and the use of rollovers from one plan to another or from a pension plan to an individual retirement account.

Part C concerns private savings. Savings take many forms, ranging from checking accounts to real estate investments; instead of canvassing them all, this chapter concentrates on one form of savings that is particularly keyed to retirement: the individual retirement account, or IRA. IRAs now come in three varieties—traditional, Roth, and Education—and the chapter examines their characteristics, purposes, and relative merits.

A. Government Programs

1. Old Age, Survivors and Disability Insurance (OASDI)

The Social Security Act was signed into law by President Roosevelt on August 14, 1935. In addition to several provisions for general welfare, the new Act created a social insurance program designed to pay retired workers age 65 or older a continuing income after retirement.

> *We can never insure one hundred percent of the population against one hundred percent of the hazards and vicissitudes of life, but we have tried to frame a law which will give some measure of protection to the average citizen and to his family against the loss of a job and against poverty-ridden old age.*
> —*President Roosevelt upon signing the Social Security Act*

a. Origins

Since Social Security became law in 1935, millions of American families have depended on this far reaching, complex social insurance program to take the sharp financial edge off disability, retirement, and the loss of the family breadwinner. In 1997, one out of every six Americans received some assistance from one or more of the many benefits available from Social Security Administration (SSA) programs. No group of citizens has more contact with SSA than the elderly. In 1996, persons 65 and over accounted for 81% of all OASDI benefits recipients.

Social Security Administration
Pre-Social Security History
<http://www.ssa.gov/history/early.html>

The "Miracle" of the Market

In the heady days of the Roaring Twenties another idea arose for providing economic security to average Americans—the presumed ever-upward march of the stock market.

From 1927 to 1929 the volume of shares traded on the stock market doubled, with much of it bought on "margin" where investors actually had to pay as little as 10% of the full price of a stock. By late 1929 the amount of stock debt outstanding was nearly three times larger than the total federal budget for that year. And in the 1920s it was not just the prosperous who invested their futures and fortunes in the stock market, many small investors bet their meager incomes on dreams of future riches.

In the spirit of the times people believed that the stock market could only go up. A week before the stock market crash a Yale University economist would say that the stock market had reached "what looks like a permanently high plateau." A major Wall Street financier published an article in the Ladies Home Journal entitled "Everybody Ought to Be Rich" in which he told the Journal's readers that they could be worth $80,000 in ten years by investing only $15 a week in the stock market (this was at a time when the average worker's take-home pay was $1,300 per year). As one historian described the resulting era: ". . . such figures were extraordinary, magical, intoxicating. What was more, any number could play, and as many as a million did. They were, most of them, amateurs. . . . On their lunch hours, they crowded into the customer's rooms of the brokerage houses to watch their money, 'feverish young men and heated elders, eyes intent upon the ticker tape.'"

Despite all the promises of unlimited wealth, all the expectations of an endless upward spiral in national income, and despite all those eyes intently watching the ticker tapes, the stock market would crash, and with it the "roaring twenties" would come to a screeching halt, and the economic security of millions of Americans would disappear overnight.

The Stock Market Crash & The Great Depression

When the New York Stock Exchange opened on the morning of Thursday, October 24, 1929, nervous traders sensed something ominous in the trading patterns. By 11:00 a.m. the market had started to plunge. Shortly after noon a group of powerful bankers met secretly at J.P. Morgan & Co. next door to the Exchange and pledged to spend $240 million of their own funds to stabilize the market. This strategy worked for a few days, but the panic broke out again the following Tuesday, when the market crashed again, and nothing could be done to stop it.

Before three months had passed, the Stock Market lost 40% of its value; $26 billion of wealth disappeared. Great American corporations suffered huge financial losses. AT&T lost one-third of its value, General Electric lost half of its, and RCA's stock fell by three-fourths within a matter of months.

As America slipped into economic depression, unemployment exceeded 25%; nine thousand banks failed; the Gross National Product declined from $105 billion in 1929 to only $55 billion in 1932. Compared to pre-Depression levels, net new business investment was a minus $5.8 billion in 1932. Wages paid to workers declined from $50 billion in 1929 to only $30 billion in 1932.

* * *

Radical Calls to Action

The decade of the 1930s found America facing the worst economic crisis in its modern history. Millions of people were unemployed, two million adult men ("hobos") wandered aimlessly around the country, banks and businesses failed and the majority of the elderly in America lived in poverty. These circumstances led to many calls for change.

Every Man a King

Huey Long was Governor of Louisiana from 1928 to 1932 and was elected to the U.S. Senate in 1930. A nominal Democrat, Huey Long was a radical populist. He wanted the government to confiscate the wealth of the nation's rich and privileged. He called his program Share Our Wealth. It called upon the federal government to guarantee every family in the nation an annual income of $5,000, so they could have the necessities of life, including a home, a job, a radio and an automobile. He also proposed limiting private fortunes to $50 million, legacies to $5 million, and annual incomes to $1 million. Everyone over age 60 would receive an old-age pension. His slogan was "Every Man A King."

The Share Our Wealth program immediately became a movement. Clubs were formed in every state in the nation. By 1935 the movement claimed 27,000 local clubs with 7.7 million members.

The Townsend Movement

Francis E. Townsend was a lean, bespectacled doctor from Long Beach, California. In 1933 he found himself unemployed at age 66 with no savings and no prospects. This experience galvanized him to become the self-proclaimed champion of the cause of the elderly. He devised a plan known as the Townsend Old Age Revolving Pension Plan, or Townsend Plan for short.

The basic idea of the Townsend Plan was that the government would provide a pension of $200 per month to every citizen age 60 and older. The pensions would be funded by a 2% national sales tax. There were three eligibility requirements:

- the person had to be retired;
- "their past life is free from habitual criminality;"
- the money had to be spent within the U.S. by the pensioner within 30 days of receipt.

Dr. Townsend published his plan in a local Long Beach newspaper in early 1933 and within about two years there were 7,000 Townsend Clubs around the country with more than 2.2 million members actively working to make the Townsend Plan the nation's old-age pension system.

Fire & Brimstone

Another influence on Depression-era public policy was the Social Justice Movement led by a radio preacher by the name of Father Charles E. Coughlin. Father Coughlin had a weekly radio program with 35-40 million listeners which he used to mix a little religion with a lot of politics. His enemies, in addition to the devil himself, were Roosevelt, international bankers, communists and labor unions, and he was not shy in describing them in interchangeable terms. At the height of his popularity, Father Coughlin had a greater share of the weekly broadcast audience than Howard Stern, Rush Limbaugh, Paul Harvey and Larry King combined . . . .

A Writer & his EPIC

Upton Sinclair was a famous novelist and social crusader from California, and an avowed Socialist, who in 1933 was asked by a dissident group of Los Angeles Democrats to help them draft a platform proposal for dealing with the state's economic problems. They were so impressed by Sinclair's plan—which he christened the End Poverty in California, or EPIC plan—that they persuaded him to change his registration to Democratic and to run for the party's nomination for governor in 1934.

Sinclair's EPIC scheme was a 12-point program to remake the Californian economy . . . . Point 10 of the plan was a proposal to give pensions of $50 a month to all needy persons over 60 who had lived in California for at least three years. There was a state pension plan in operation in California at the time, but its benefits were very low, and the eligibility requirements were so severe that most elderly Californians could not qualify. (This was true of many of the state pension programs around the country.) Sinclair's pension proposal was very popular because in one fell swoop it reduced the minimum age for pensions by 10 years, almost doubled their value, and eliminated restrictive eligibility requirements.

Sinclair's EPIC program, and especially its pension proposal, had a great appeal in Depression-weary California. Sinclair and his supporters organized EPIC clubs, published newsletters, formed ad hoc organizations and found a large chorus of supporters with unlimited enthusiasm for his ideas. In short order, Upton Sinclair's EPIC movement captured the Democratic party and Sinclair became the Democratic nominee for governor in the election of 1934. The party's platform became the EPIC program, including the pension plan.

When the votes were counted, Upton Sinclair got 37% of the vote, the Republican candidate got 48% and a third-party progressive candidate took another 13%. Had it been a two-man race, Upton Sinclair might have become Governor of California and the EPIC pension plan might well have become the California model.

* * *

The Establishment Response

If America was to avoid the siren songs of the "radical calls to action," responsible political leaders would need to offer some persuasive alternatives. As the Depression grew, three general approaches emerged: do nothing; rely on voluntary charity; and expand welfare benefits for those hardest hit by the Depression.

The Do Nothing Response

It seemed to many politicians and leading public figures that the Depression was just another dip in the economic cycle and that it would right itself soon enough. These voices counseled a restrained response, or no response at all. In the early aftermath of the stock market crash such views were especially common. On New Year's Day 1930, Secretary of the Treasury Andrew Mellon stoically observed: "I can see nothing in the situation which warrants pessimism." President Herbert Hoover defiantly stated: "Any lack of confidence in the economic future or the basic strength of business in the United States is foolish." And publisher Arthur Brisbane confidently predicted that "All the really important millionaires are planning to continue prosperity."

This view that nothing very much was wrong, and nothing very much needed to be done, began to fade quickly as the Depression deepened. Even so, it held considerable sway in the early years after The Crash. President Hoover's own innate optimism would also cause him to make several statements about the economic crisis that seemed at considerable variance with the day-to-day experience of most Americans, which undermined the persuasiveness of this viewpoint.

Hoover's "Volunteerism"

President Hoover had a distinguished career in international volunteer relief work, and as an engineer, before becoming president. This gave him two firm convictions: that the economy was a mechanism like any other, that it operated according to principles not unlike the engineering principles behind any machine; and that the most effective way to combat economic insecurity was through voluntary relief. The first view, what we might call Hoover The Engineer, inclined him toward the "do nothing" response because he believed the economy would correct itself, just as any well-designed mechanical device would do. The second view, what we might call Hoover The Volunteer, shaped his other response to the Depression.

Hoover made a name for himself in international relief efforts before and after World War I. He helped feed millions of starving people, through the efforts of voluntary partnerships of government, business and private giving. He knew this kind of "volunteerism" worked, on a massive scale, and he saw no reason why it should not work to solve the problems of the Depression. So although he engaged in some limited federal relief efforts, his main response to the Depression was to advocate voluntary efforts, which never materialized.

The main problem with this strategy was that America was able to help rebuild Europe in the aftermath of World War I because America's economy was basically sound. In the Depression the total wealth of the nation was cut in half during the first three years after The Crash. This made voluntary charity an impossible ideal.

Expand Welfare

Even before the Depression hit, the States had been forced to deal with the problems of economic security in a wage-based, industrial economy. Workers Compensation programs were established at the state level before Social Security, and there were state welfare programs for the elderly in place before Social Security. Prior to Social Security, the main strategy for providing economic security to the elderly, in the face of the demographic changes discussed above, was to provide various forms of old-age "pensions." These were welfare programs, eligibility for which was based on proof of financial need. By 1934, most states had such "pension" plans. Even at the state level, however, these plans were inadequate. Some had restrictive eligibility criteria which resulted in many of the elderly being unable to qualify. The most generous plan paid a maximum of $1 per day.

In the Congress, the consensus of conventional wisdom was for more old-age assistance like that available in the states. This was an attitude widely shared in both major political parties. Conservatives preferred this approach because it restricted government aid to the smallest possible number of people (the truly needy) thus restricting the role of government in the provision of economic security. And because it fit with the idea that the Depression was a temporary problem that would soon go away, and when it went away the old-age pensions could go away too—again, reducing the role of government. This became the conservative viewpoint on economic security for the elderly . . . .

The problem with this strategy was that the Depression didn't go away, and the underlying challenges to the traditional approaches to economic security were being driven by factors much larger and more permanent than the economic crisis of the 1930s. That is, this approach was based on the belief that nothing fundamental had changed about America and that the old tried and true approaches would continue to work . . . .

The "New" Alternative

With the coming to office of President Roosevelt in 1932, and the introduction of his economic security proposal based on social insurance rather than welfare assistance, the debate changed. It was no longer a choice between radical changes and old approaches that no longer worked. The "new" idea of social insurance, which was already widespread in Europe, would become an innovative alternative.

Social insurance, as conceived by President Roosevelt, would address the permanent problem of economic security for the elderly by creating a work-related, contributory system in which workers would provide for their own future economic security through taxes paid while employed. Thus it was an alternative both to reliance on welfare and to radical changes in our capitalist system. In the context of its time, it can be seen as a conservative, yet activist, response to the challenges of the Depression.

The Social Insurance Movement

The Social Security program that would eventually be adopted in late 1935 relied for its core principles on the concept of "social insurance." Social insurance was a respectable and serious intellectual tradition that began in Europe in the 19th century and was an expression of a European social welfare tradition. It was first adopted in Germany in 1889 at the urging of the famous Chancellor, Otto von Bismarck. Indeed, by the time America adopted social insurance in 1935, there were 34 European nations already operating some form of social insurance program . . . .

Although the definition of social insurance can vary considerably in its particulars, its basic features are: the insurance principle under which a group of persons are "insured" in some way against a defined risk, and a social element which usually means that the program is shaped in part by broader social objectives, rather than being shaped solely by the self-interest of the individual participants.

* * *

One of the earliest American advocates of a plan that could be recognized as modern social insurance was Theodore Roosevelt. In 1912, Roosevelt addressed the convention of the Progressive Party and made a strong statement on behalf of social insurance: "We must protect the crushable elements at the base of our present industrial structure . . . it is abnormal for any industry to throw back upon the community the human wreckage due to its wear and tear, and the hazards of sickness, accident, invalidism, involuntary unemployment, and old age should be provided for through insurance." TR would succeed in having a plank adopted in the Progressive Party platform that stated: "We pledge ourselves to work unceasingly in state and nation for: . . .The protection of home life against the hazards of sickness, irregular employment, and old age through the adoption of a system of social insurance adapted to American use."

b. Mechanics

Richard L. Kaplan
Top Ten Myths of Social Security
3 ELDER L.J. 191, 196-98 (1995)[*]

One of the myths that makes the Social Security program so politically untouchable is the belief that current retirees are simply recovering their own contributions. If this were true, one would indeed be hard pressed to suggest reducing Social Security benefits. If people do not recover their own investments, after all, Social Security might be seen as just another tax-like government imposition. Social Security, in fact, is partially a program of social insurance and partially a program of ensuring retirement income. Yet many, if not most, retirees seem to believe that its retirement income function is its overwhelmingly predominant, if not sole, characteristic. Accordingly, they view the monthly payments that they receive as a return of the taxes that they paid to the system during their working lives.

During much of Social Security's existence, its taxes were imposed at much lower rates and on a much lower wage base than is currently the case. For example, from 1937 through 1949, the Social Security tax rate was only 2% rather than the present 12.4%, which continues to be split between the employer and employee. Rates were increased after that date, but on an irregular schedule—sometimes once every four years, sometimes every year. But the total tax rate was only half of the current rate as recently as 1962, and did not reach 10% until 1978. Similarly, the wage base on which this tax was imposed was only $3,000 through 1950, and was then raised on an irregular schedule until it reached $7,800 in 1968. The wage base was then raised again in 1972 and every year thereafter. Even so, it did not rise above $30,000 until 1982. Due to these low rates and low wage base during many of the years in which current retirees were working, their maximum Social Security tax—including their employer's portion—was only $60. As recently as 1972, in fact, the maximum amount paid in was only $828. And of course, during those years, persons who did

---

[*] Reprinted by permission. Copyright to the *Elder Law Journal* is held by the Board of Trustees of the University of Illinois.

not earn the maximum wage cap paid in even smaller amounts. Consequently, when current retirees relate their payments of Social Security taxes—both their own and their employer's share—to current benefits, a low-wage earner retiring in 1995 at age sixty-five recovers all of the Social Security taxes paid in forty months. Even a maximum-wage earner who paid tax on whatever wage cap was in effect, recovers the cumulative investment in less than seven years. In other words, after four and one-half years of receiving Social Security benefits, an average-wage-earning retiree is collecting welfare. That is, *all* of that worker's money has been repaid, including the employer's portion paid on the worker's behalf. Even if one includes interest earned during that interval, at some point most current retirees are receiving funds in excess of what they had put into the system.

On the other hand, the relationship between payments to, and benefits received from, Social Security is changing over time. As noted above, the Social Security tax rate has increased dramatically in the past twenty years or so. The wage base on which those Social Security taxes are collected, moreover, has risen dramatically since 1972, and has more than tripled since 1978. As a result, people who retire in the future may not, in fact, recover all of their investments in the form of retirement benefits. Some computations involving unmarried men earning maximum earnings and having average life expectancies indicate that they may not recover all of the Social Security taxes when they retire. Another way of describing this phenomenon is that the number of years needed to recover the much-greater Social Security taxes paid into the system in recent years may exceed the person's anticipated life expectancy upon attaining retirement age. On the other hand, huge categories of beneficiaries will not face this predicament for many years—namely, married men (whose spouses receive additional Social Security benefits and who have longer life expectancies generally), women (who have longer life expectancies generally), and workers who earned less than the wage cap (whose taxes paid into the system were necessarily lower).

To summarize, in the future, some retirees will be simply recovering their own funds. But *at the present time*, and for many years to come, almost all retirees will have long since recovered their tax payments into the Social Security program, often many times over.

Question

Is it accurate for Professor Kaplan to characterize some retirees' receipt of benefits as "welfare?"

Social Security Administration
History: Frequently Asked Questions
<http://www.ssa.gov/history/hfaq.html>

Q4: Is it true that Social Security was originally just a retirement program?
A: Yes. Under the 1935 law, Social Security only paid retirement benefits to the primary worker. A 1939 change in the law added survivors benefits and benefits for the retiree's spouse and children. In 1956 disability benefits were added.

Q5: How was age 65 chosen as the age for full retirement?
A: Generally, it was chosen to conform to contemporary practice during the 1930s.

> By the time America moved to social insurance in 1935 the German system was using age 65 as its retirement age. But this was not the major influence on the Committee on Economic Security (CES) when it proposed age 65 as the retirement age under Social Security. This decision was not based on any philosophical principle or European precedent. It was, in fact, primarily pragmatic, and stemmed from two sources. One was a general observation about prevailing retirement ages in the few private pension systems in existence at the time and, more importantly, the 30 state old-age pension systems then in operation. Roughly half of the state pension systems used age 65 as the retirement age and half used age 70. The new federal Railroad Retirement System passed by Congress earlier in 1934 also used age 65 as its retirement age. Taking all this into account, the CES planners made a rough judgment that age 65 was probably more reasonable than age 70. This judgment was then confirmed by the actuarial studies. The studies showed that using age 65 produced a manageable system that could easily be made self-sustaining with only modest levels of payroll taxation. So these two factors, a kind of pragmatic judgment about prevailing retirement standards and the favorable actuarial outcome of using age 65, combined to be the real basis on which age 65 was chosen as the age for retirement under Social Security. <http://www.ssa.gov/history/age65.html>.

Q6: Is it true that life expectancy was less than 65 back in 1935?
A: Not really. Life expectancy at birth was less than 65, but this is a misleading measure. A more appropriate measure is life expectancy after attainment of adulthood, which shows that most Americans could expect to live to age 65 once they survived childhood.

Q7: When did COLAs (cost-of-living allowances) start?
A: COLAs were first paid in 1975 as a result of a 1972 law. Prior to this, benefits were increased irregularly by special acts of Congress.

* * *

Q14: What does FICA mean and why are Social Security taxes called FICA contributions?

A: Social Security payroll taxes are collected under authority of the Federal Insurance Contributions Act (FICA). The payroll taxes are sometimes even called "FICA taxes." But what is FICA? Is it a separate law, apart from the Social Security Act? In the original 1935 law the benefit provisions were in Title II of the Act (which is why we sometimes call Social Security the "Title II" program). The taxing provisions were in a separate title, Title VIII . . . . As part of the 1939 Amendments, the Title VIII taxing provisions were taken out of the Social Security Act and placed in the Internal Revenue Code. Since it wouldn't make any sense to call this new section of the Internal Revenue Code "Title VIII," it was renamed the "Federal Insurance Contributions Act." The payroll taxes collected for Social Security are of course taxes, but they can also be described as contributions to the social insurance system that is Social Security. Hence the name "Federal Insurance Contributions Act." So FICA is nothing more than the tax provisions of the Social Security Act, as they appear in the Internal Revenue Code.

* * *

Q18: Was the original Social Security program designed to be self-supporting?
A: Yes. In fact the actuaries estimated the program would have a $47 billion reserve by 1980, and the Trust Fund balance hit $46 billion in 1974. However, the reserve declined after that so that the balance stood at only $26 billion in 1980. (Today the Trust Fund reserves are over $700 billion.)

Q19: Has Social Security ever been financed by general tax revenues?
A: Not to any significant extent.

> Since military wages were not covered employment until 1957, spending several years in the military would result in reduced Social Security benefits. Even after military service became a form of covered employment, the low cash wages paid to servicemen and women meant that military service was also a financial sacrifice. As a special benefit for members of the armed forces the Congress decided to grant special noncontributory wage credits for military service before 1957 and special deemed military wage credits to boost the amounts of credited contributions for service after 1956. These credits were paid out of general revenues as a subsidy to military personnel. So, each year since 1966 the Social Security Trust Funds have in fact received some relatively small transfers from the general revenues as bonuses for military personnel.
>
> In 1966 Congress also identified another "disadvantaged" group: elderly individuals (age 72 before 1968) who had not been able to work long enough under Social Security to become insured for a benefit. People in this group were granted special Social Security benefits paid for entirely by the general revenues of the Treasury . . . . Over time, of course, these beneficiaries will disappear as Father Time claims members of the group.
>
> Finally, as part of the 1983 Amendments, Social Security benefits became subject to federal income taxes for the first time, and the monies generated by this taxation are returned to the Trust Funds from general rev-

enues—the third and last source of general revenue financing of Social Security.

All three of these general revenue streams are so small relative to the payroll tax funding that for most practical purposes we could still accurately describe the Social Security program as "self-supporting." <http://www.ssa.gov/history/genrev.html>.

Q20: How much has Social Security paid out since it started?
A: Regular monthly benefit payments began in January 1940. Since then, more than 12 billion payments worth more than $4 trillion have been issued.

Q21: Has Social Security always taken in more money each year than it needed to pay benefits?
A: No. So far there have been 11 years [1959, 1961, 1962, 1965, 1975-81—Eds.] in which the Social Security program did not take enough in FICA taxes to pay the current year's benefits. During these years, Trust Fund bonds in the amount of about $24 billion made up the difference.

Q22: When was Social Security taken "off-budget"?
A: The current "off-budget" status of Social Security has been in effect since 1986.

Since the Social Security Trust Funds have a dedicated source of revenue apart from general taxation [i.e., the payroll tax collected under FICA], one could argue that the transactions involving Social Security are a separate function of government which should be accounted for outside the government's general budget ledger. And in fact, from 1937 until 1969 this is how the Social Security Trust Funds were viewed. Beginning in fiscal year 1969 (during the final months of the Johnson Administration) a change was introduced to make the Trust Funds part of what is called the "unified Federal budget." The idea of the unified budget is to show all transactions involving the Federal government in one combined budget.

Under the accounting procedures adopted in 1969, assets in any government-managed trust fund, such as Social Security, are considered assets of the government. So the balance in the Social Security Trust Funds in 1969 (approximately $34 billion) was considered as an offset to the general budget deficit the government otherwise would have experienced in 1969. This accounting procedure stayed in place until 1986 when the Social Security Trust Funds were once again taken "off-budget." This is the rule even today, although when the Federal budget is presented it often is described in both ways, with and without the Social Security Trust Funds, and different commentators choose which description they prefer. <http://www.ssa.gov/history/offbudget.html>.

Question

What attributes of an insurance program does the Old Age, Survivors, and Disability Insurance program have?

c. **Eligibility**

Patrick H. Donahue
Social Security
KANSAS LONG-TERM CARE HANDBOOK 8-9 (1999)*

1. *Insured status.*

To be eligible for Social Security retirement benefits, an individual must meet the requirements for "fully insured" status. Insured status requires the accumulation of a lifetime minimum number of OASDI quarters of coverage. Individuals born in 1929 or later need 40 quarters of coverage. Fewer quarters of coverage are needed for persons born prior to 1929. An individual earns one quarter of coverage for earning a specified amount of taxable income—in 1998 one quarter of coverage was earned for each $700 of earnings. A maximum of four quarters of coverage can be earned each year. Individuals who have not earned the required number of credits may return to work and do so.

2. *Retirement age.*

Full retirement age is the age at which individuals receive full retirement benefits. Because of longer life expectancies, Social Security is increasing the retirement age in gradual steps. The present retirement age is 65. This applies to persons born in 1937 or earlier. The following chart shows how the increase to age 67 in full retirement age has been phased-in:

Birth Year	Full Retirement Age
1938	65 and 2 months
1939	65 and 4 months
1940	65 and 6 months
1941	65 and 8 months
1942	65 and 10 months
1943-54	66
1955	66 and 2 months
1956	66 and 4 months
1957	66 and 6 months
1958	66 and 8 months
1959	66 and 10 months
1960 and later	67

Persons can retire as early as 62, but the reduction in benefits for retiring at 62 is 20%. Benefits are reduced 6 2/3% for each year prior to full retirement age. *Early retirement is contrasted by delayed retirement.* There is no requirement that an individual receive retirement benefits at full retirement age. In fact, SSA encourages delayed retirement. Individuals gain approximately 8% more benefits for each year of retirement delay after full retirement age.

---

* Copyright © 1999. Reprinted with permission.

3. Bona fide *retirement*.

With self-employed or partially self-employed individuals it is often unclear when work stops and retirement really begins. Social Security has a procedure for investigating questionable retirement cases. Individuals who continue to carry on work-like activity may be disqualified from receiving retirement benefits. To determine whether retirement is *bona fide*, SSA uses the "substantial services test." Work-like activity more than 45 hours per month is presumed to be substantial services. This defeats retirement. The presumption, however, is rebuttable. On the other hand, work-like activity totaling less than 15 hours per month is presumed *not* to be a substantial service. Again, the presumption is rebuttable. SSA will challenge "sham" retirements. *Bona fide* retirement cases usually arise in the context of small, closely held businesses in which the principal wants to maintain some control over day-to-day operations. Similarly situated persons who often carry on some work-like activity after retirement, including lawyers, ministers, farmers, insurance agents and consultants, may also be the subject of questionable retirement reviews.

Questions

1. Is increasing "full retirement age" fair? Why or why not?

2. Why would it be necessary for SSA to monitor a beneficiary's *bona fides* with respect to retirement status?

d. Retirement Planning

David M. English
What Estate Planners and Their Clients Should Know About Social Security
EST. PLAN. 90, 94-96 (February 1998)[*]

How are a worker's contributions calculated? Social Security is funded principally by FICA withholding on wages and by taxes on self-employment income. Almost all workers are subject to FICA withholding. The employer pays 7.65%, and an additional 7.65% is withheld from the worker's paycheck. From this 15.3% total, 12.4% is allocated to Social Security and 2.9% for Part A Medicare hospital benefits. The 15.3% maximum applies to the first $68,400 of wages or self-employment income (in 1998). Only the 2.9% Medicare tax is assessed on the excess above $68,400.

The computations become more complicated for workers holding more than one job during the year. For such workers, each employer must withhold FICA on the first $68,400 in wages paid by that employer. If this results in withholding on more than $68,400 in wage income, the excess withheld on the worker's, but not the employer's, portion of the tax may be claimed as a credit on the worker's income tax return for the year.

---

[*] Copyright © 1998. Reprinted with permission.

Self-employed individuals must pay both portions of the tax: a 15.3% levy on the first $68,400 in self-employment income subject to the tax, and a tax of 2.9% on the excess. To place self-employed persons on an equal footing with those who are employed, the tax is assessed on only 92.35% (100% - 7.65%) of the taxpayer's self-employment income, and the self-employed individual may deduct half of the tax payable as an adjustment to gross income. In addition, for self-employed persons who also hold regular jobs, the maximum tax rate applies to only the first $68,400 of combined wage and self-employment income. Self-employment tax is computed on Schedule SE to the Form 1040.

* * *

What happens if a recipient takes a part-time job? With the exception of persons receiving disability benefits, who are covered by separate work rules, Social Security recipients are subject to what is know as the "earnings test." The Social Security benefits of a worker or beneficiary under age 65 are reduced $1 for each $2 of earned income above a minimum floor. For workers and other recipients age 65 through 69, the offset is $1 for each $3 of earned income above the floor.

A worker under age 65 may earn up to $9,120 ($760 per month) in 1998 without reduction of benefits, a figure adjusted annually for cost of living increases. The earnings test for workers age 65 through 69 is far more generous, and has been scheduled by Congress to increase at a much more rapid rate. Set at $12,500 for 1996, the earnings limit for this age group increased to $13,500 for 1997 and $14,500 for 1998, and will increased to $15,500 for 1999, after which it will rise sharply, reaching $30,000 in 2002 ($17,000 in 2000 and $25,000 in 2001). The earnings limit does not apply to Social Security recipients age 70 and older, who may earn unlimited amounts without a reduction of benefits.

To what extent are Social Security benefits subject to income tax? Code Section 86 subjects up to 85% of a recipient's Social Security benefits to income tax. As originally enacted, Section 86 taxed no more than 50% of Social Security benefits, and the benefits of lower income individuals retained their former exemption. In 1993, Congress, in need of yet additional revenue for the Trust Fund (to which the tax on Social Security benefits is allocated), increased the maximum to 85%, but only for those with higher income. The result is a three-tier system: recipients with lower incomes whose benefits are exempt, a middle group for whom no more than 50% of benefits are subject to tax, and a higher income group for whom up to 85% of benefits may be included in gross income.

The starting point in computing the benefits includable in gross income is to determine the taxpayer's "modified adjusted gross income" (MAGI). MAGI equals the taxpayer's adjusted gross income (AGI) increased by the amount of tax-exempt interest received or accrued. The next step is to add to MAGI one-half of the Social Security benefits received during the year. Then, the total of MAGI and half the Social Security benefits received is compared to a "base amount" determined by the taxpayer's filing status: $32,000 for taxpayers filing a joint return, and $25,000 for taxpayers filing as single individuals or heads of households. A severe penalty is exacted against married taxpayers filing separately. Their base amount is zero.

Because of their zero base amount, they may sidestep much of the computational process. A minimum of 42 1/2% (1/2 of 85%) of their Social Security benefits are includable in gross income.

For taxpayers whose MAGIs plus half the Social Security benefits received exceed the respective $25,000 and $32,000 base amounts, a portion of their Social Security benefits are included in gross income. To determine how much, the next step is to compare the sum of MAGI plus half the benefits received to yet another figure, the "adjusted base amount." The adjusted base amount is $44,000 for taxpayers filing a joint return, $34,000 for taxpayers filing as single taxpayers and heads of household, and once again an unfavorable zero for married taxpayers filing separately.

What results from completion of this next step are the second and third tiers. For joint filers whose MAGI plus half the benefits received is between $32,000 and $44,000, up to 50% of benefits are included in gross income. For those above $44,000, the maximum possible percentage is 85%. For single taxpayers and heads of households, the 50% maximum applies to persons whose MAGIs plus half the benefits received are between $25,000 and $34,000; up to 85% of benefits are included in gross income for those above $34,000.

The final step is to actually compute the portion of benefits includable in gross income. The computation is relatively straight-forward for those in the second or middle tier. For those in the second tier, the Social Security benefits includable in gross income equal the lesser of (1) one-half of the benefits received or (2) one-half of the amount by which the MAGI plus half the Social Security benefits received exceeds the base amount.

The computation is more complicated for those in the third or highest tier. For higher earners, the amount of benefits includable in gross income is the lesser of two figures. The first of these figure is 85% of the benefits received. The second figure equals one-half of the second tier spread (1/2 times $44,000 less $32,000, or $6,000 for joint filer; 1/2 times $34,000 less $25,000, or $4,500 for single taxpayers and heads of households) plus 85% of the excess by which the taxpayer's MAGI plus half the benefits received exceeds the adjusted base amount ($44,000 for joint filers, $34,000 for single taxpayers and heads of households). For taxpayers with the highest incomes, this computation will always result in 85% of the Social Security benefits being included in gross income.

What planning can be done to reduce this tax bite? For individuals with very low or very high incomes, planning to reduce or avoid the tax on Social Security benefits is either unnecessary or unrealistic. Either none or 85% of benefits will be includable in gross income. Planning is more beneficial for those in the large middle group—those in the second tier and those not too far into the third tier. The key to planning is income deferral, not necessarily income avoidance. Purchasing tax-exempt securities does nothing to avoid the tax on Social Security benefits because tax-exempt interest is added to AGI for purposes of calculating MAGI. But income that is deferred is excluded from consideration.

Popular methods for creating deferred income include the purchase of Series EE bonds, on which the interest income need be reported only when the bonds are redeemed, and the purchase of single-premium annuities, on which tax is avoided until withdrawals begin. A decision to take a qualified plan benefit in the form of an immediate lump sum can be advantageous at least as far as the taxation of Social Security benefits is concerned. Lump-sum distributions eligible for capital gains treatment or five- or ten-year averaging are excluded from AGI and hence do not make their way into MAGI.

Given the earnings test and tax on benefits, what is the true cost of taking a part-time job? When the possible loss of benefits due to taking part-time work is combined with the income tax that will be assessed on the additional income earned plus the possibility that the extra earned income will result in a greater percentage of the remaining Social Security being included in gross income, a decision to return to work can result in what is in effect a marginal tax rate of close to 100%. Consider the following example.

Example. A single individual, age 63, receives in 1998 a $10,000 pension, $10,000 in Social Security, and $10,000 from a part-time job; she does not itemize her deductions. Her base income for purposes of computing the tax on Social Security benefits is $25,000 (i.e., the sum of MAGI plus half her Social Security benefits, which equals $20,000 from the pensions and part-time job plus one-half her Social Security benefits). Her taxable income is $13,050 ($10,000 pension plus $10,000 part-time job less $4,250 standard deduction and $2,700 personal exemption), and her tax bill is $1,958. None of her Social Security benefits are includable in gross income. She decides to take a second part-time job that will pay her an additional $10,000.

This decision will cost her at least $7,666 in reduced benefits and additional taxes, or what amounts to an effective tax rate of 77%. Her Social Security benefits will be reduced by $5,000—that is, by half of her additional earned income. Her taxable income will increase by $12,500, consisting of the $10,000 in additional earnings plus $2,500 or 50% of the remaining $5,000 in Social Security benefits. This will increase her taxable income to $25,550, on which she will pay a tax of $3,859 or an increase of $1,901. Finally, her second employer will withhold a total of 7.65% or $765 in FICA taxes. Should the $10,000 in extra income be derived from self-employment, the results will be even worse. Instead of FICA withholding of $765, she would have to pay self-employment tax of $1,530.

e. Alienation of Benefits

Philpott v. Essex County Welfare Board
409 U.S. 413 (1973)

The Essex County Welfare Board sued its welfare recipient and his trustee in the Essex County Court, New Jersey, to reach a bank account in which the recipient's trustee had deposited a check for six months' retroactive disability benefits paid to the recipient under the Social Security Act.

On certiorari, the United States Supreme Court reversed. In an opinion by Douglas, J., expressing the unanimous view of the court, it was held that all claimants, including a state, are subject to the provision of 42 U.S.C. §407 exempting social security payments from all legal process.

f. Spousal and Survivor Benefits

Richard L. Kaplan
Top Ten Myths of Social Security
3 ELDER L.J. 191, 204-05 (Fall 1995)[*]

Social Security is often described as a program that rewards the "traditional" marital relationship, sometimes called "Ozzie and Harriet" after a popular 1950s television program, of a working man married his entire adult life to a woman who does not work in the compensated work force. Indeed, . . . married couples receive greater benefits when only one spouse is employed than when both spouses produce the equivalent earnings. Nevertheless, it is not true that Social Security favors lifelong marital partners.

Social Security provides a derivative benefit not only to the spouse of a worker who has retired, but also to the ex-spouse of a worker, if that ex-spouse was married at least ten years to the worker and has not remarried. In certain circumstances, subsequent remarriages are ignored—namely, when the remarriage occurs after reaching age sixty. But in any case, a person who is a divorced spouse can collect benefits based on the worker's work history without affecting benefits that are paid to that worker, to that worker's current spouse, or to any other recipients (for example, children) who may be collecting derivative benefits from that worker's account. Their marriage, however, must have lasted at least ten years. So if, for example, Hank was married to Alice for eleven years, then to Betty for twelve years, and then to Carol for ten years, all three of this ex-wives could collect benefits equal to one-half of his worker's retirement benefit. Once a person has been married at least ten years, in other words, that person's spouse has become vested in that person's Social Security record, and further years of marriage do not increase the amount of that spouse's Social Security benefit. In effect, Social Security provides no incentive to stay married once a marriage has lasted ten years.

For example, assume that Ozzie and Hank both qualify for a worker's retirement benefit of $1,000. Ozzie and Harriet (Ozzie's wife) will receive Social Security benefits of $1,500 per month—assuming that Harriet would not receive more than $500 based upon her own work record, and assuming that both Ozzie and Harriet have reached "full retirement age." Using the same assumptions about spousal work records and age, Hank would receive his $1,000 per month, and his former wives (Alice, Betty, and Carol) would each receive $500, as would his current spouse, Deborah—a grand total of $3,000 per month, compared to Ozzie and Harriet's $1,500.

---

[*] Reprinted by permission. Copyright to the *Elder Law Journal* is held by the Board of Trustees of the University of Illinois.

Moreover, when a retired worker dies, his or her surviving spouse succeeds to the retired worker's *entire* benefit. Therefore, if Ozzie dies, Harriet's benefit would rise from $500 to $1,000 per month, ignoring intervening cost-of-living adjustments. This stepped-up benefit rule, however, also applies to surviving former spouses—once again, assuming that the marriage lasted at least ten years, and that the spouse's own work record does not provide a greater benefit. As a result, Hank's three surviving ex-wives and his surviving spouse will each receive $1,000 after Hank dies, producing a grand total of $4,000 from Hank's account compared to $1,000 for Harriet from Ozzie's account.

Question

Why shouldn't former spouses share equally in one benefit amount rather than having the total amount paid from one worker's account limited only by the number of marriages lasting 10 years?

g. The Future of Social Security

In January, 1998, Social Security Commissioner Kenneth Apfel addressed the National Academy of Social Insurance. Among the points he made were:

- Over the last twenty years, Social Security has played a central role in reducing poverty among the elderly.
- Social Security is an insurance program, providing not just retirement benefits, but also disability, survivor, and dependent benefits for impaired or deceased wage earners.
- Social Security has an intergenerational financial basis, with current retiree benefits being paid by current workers.
- Social Security, while an important factor in reducing poverty, was never meant as the source for all retirement income.
- Change is needed in the Social Security system as a result of changing generational demographics: fewer younger workers funding the system and more older workers receiving benefits from the system.

See National Senior Citizens Law Center, *The Clinton Administration Addresses the Long-Term Solvency of Social Security,* NSCLC WASHINGTON WEEKLY, February 13, 1998, at 26.

Robert Eisner
Don't Sock the Elderly, Help Them: Old Age Is Hard Enough
5 ELDER L.J. 181, 189-93 (1997)[*]

... [T]he intermediate projection of the Social Security trustees would have the Old Age and Survivors and Disability trust funds short of funds in thirty-three years. Some would cut benefits or raise payroll taxes or both to keep the funds fully solvent for at least seventy-five years. Others would combine this with "privatization," risking some of the guaranteed benefits of Social Security in the stock market. And some, embracing various elements of these prescriptions, focus on encouraging private saving.

Lawrence R. Jacobs & Robert Y. Shapiro
Public Support for Social Security and Medicare, AARP WEBPLACE (1998)
<http://www.aarp.org/focus/ssecure/part_3/view_1jrs.htm>[**]

In September 1994, Third Millennium sponsored a poll that journalists eagerly reported as finding that young Americans considered UFOs more likely than the prospect of collecting Social Security. The survey is still widely cited as evidence of Americans sinking confidence in Social Security. According to the reports by journalists, Americans had weighed the relative likelihood of UFOs existing and collecting Social Security, and found extraterrestrial life more probable. The reality, however, is that the actual survey never offered respondents a direct comparison. Instead, it offered two separate questions at opposite ends of the survey. Americans may well have offered different responses if they were actually asked to compare UFOs and Social Security's future.

The media's reporting of the Third Millennium survey is an instructive warning about some of the common misperceptions of public opinion toward Social Security, Medicare, and entitlements more generally.

Journalists use polls like Third Millennium's to harp on the public's sinking confidence in Social Security as the baby boomers head for retirement. The recurrent message is change—Americans are losing confidence in Social Security's future.

The truth is that there is no clear trend of eroding confidence; it has risen and fallen in recent years. A more complicated question is explaining why confidence remains low, with generally less than half of Americans confident in the program's future since 1975, when pollsters began tracking it. Weak confidence appears to be related to Americans' general distrust in government and media coverage of Social Security. When media coverage of the program peaked at its height in the early 1980s, public confidence bottomed out. When coverage fell off, confidence recovered and reached its highest point in a dozen years by 1990 and 1991 (with about 50%

---

[*] Copyright © 1997 by the Board of Trustees of the University of Illinois. Reprinted with permission.

[**] Copyright © 1998. Reprinted with permission.

expressing confidence in Social Security's future). The uptick in news reporting on Social Security in 1993 coincided with another drop in public confidence.

Another favorite topic of journalists is the war between the young and old. Younger Americans are portrayed as harboring deep doubts about whether their generation is being ripped off by seniors and baby boomers heading for retirement. The truth is that seniors are more sensitive to threats to Social Security and Medicare such as extending the age of eligibility or cutting cost of living adjustments. But, fear over immediate threats does not translate into a pitched war. The fact is that young Americans have consistently been just as supportive (if not more so) of spending on Medicare and Social Security as older Americans. Young Americans' support for these programs may spring from an appreciation that their parents rely on them.

Journalists have also reported that Americans support privatization of Social Security. For example, Anne Willette opened her October 1, 1996 story for USA Today by heralding a poll that purports to show public support for privatizing Social Security. "Almost six in 10 people," she informs us, "want to invest some of their Social Security taxes themselves—even though they might end up with less money at retirement." Missing is any reference to alternative surveys that have shown public uneasiness with privatization. For instance, a December 1996 Time/CNN poll reported that 36% favored privatization and 56 opposed it. (The poll asked: "Some people favor investing a portion of their Social Security tax funds in the stock market because this might lead to higher investment returns. Other people oppose this idea because this is too risky. What is your opinion?") The truth is that Americans are deeply ambivalent about privatizing Social Security.

Journalists are also fond of claiming that Americans are caught in a dilemma of whether to protect entitlements or to balance the budget. For instance, CNN's Donna Kelly kicked off her story of the Senate vote on the balanced budget amendment on February 28, 1995 by highlighting the "mixed messages" of Americans who simultaneously supported a balanced budget and opposed cuts in Social Security and Medicare. The take home point was that politicians were tied in knots by the contradictory preferences of Americans.

Framing the debate in these terms fits the battle lines in Washington, but it distorts public opinion. Americans support approaches to deficit reduction that avoid cutting social programs; polls suggest that the public favors reducing defense spending, forgoing tax reduction, limiting net benefits received by the rich (including even Medicare and Social Security), and raising taxes on the rich and on tobacco and alcohol. The problem was that the public's preferred approaches to the budget were ruled out by elites.

The bottom line is that Americans of all ages remain loyal—if nervous—supporters of Social Security.

Question

Some people favor investing a portion of their Social Security tax funds in the stock market because this might lead to higher investment returns. Other people oppose this idea because this is too risky. What is your opinion?

Steven C. Wilber
Social Security Reform: A Comparison of Alternative Proposals
TAX NOTES, at 1667-74 (December 28, 1998)[*]

I. Introduction

The issue of social security reform is under consideration by the Clinton administration as well as in the U.S. Congress, and for good reason. According to a recent U.S. General Accounting Office study, the social security system faces a revenue shortfall of approximately $3 trillion over the next 75 years. While program revenues should continue to exceed expenditures until 2013, the substantial size of the anticipated shortfall highlights the need for reform in the near future. In the absence of such reform, the program will be unable to meet its obligations by 2032. Experts agree that this would have a grave impact on both workers and beneficiaries, as well as society as a whole.

The social security program is the cornerstone of America's retirement system. For nearly 60 years social security has provided benefits to retired workers and their families. For 15 percent of this population, social security is the only source of cash income. The program also provides benefits for many disabled Americans. Social security was originally designed as a pay-as-you-go system in which the payroll taxes of current workers are used to pay the benefits of current beneficiaries. Under this system, any excess revenues are credited to a social security trust fund to serve as a reserve for future benefits. Currently these reserves are invested in interest-bearing government securities, providing additional revenues for the program.

This financing system made sense during the program's early years, when benefits were low and the number of workers per beneficiary was high. However, as the program matured, more beneficiaries were added at higher average benefit levels. Thus, over the years a number of legislative actions have been taken to maintain the long-term solvency of the social security system. For example, the social security payroll tax was increased 20 times between 1937 and 1990, when it reached its current combined rate of 12.4 percent of covered earnings.

II. Congressional Proposals

Traditional approaches to resolving social security's long-term financing problems include increasing program revenues, decreasing program expenditures, or both, while maintaining the program's pay-as-you-go structure. Program revenues are typically increased by raising the payroll tax, increasing the tax base, or increasing the taxation of benefits. Expenditures have been decreased by cutting benefits and increasing the retirement age.

However, given the current political climate, it is unlikely that Congress will be willing to raise taxes or cut benefits. This has led members of Congress to consider new ways of reforming social security. Some recent proposals seek to maintain the current structure but increase revenues by allowing the government to invest the trust fund in higher-earning assets, such as corporate stocks and bonds. Other proposals

---

[*] Copyright © 1999 Tax Analysts. Used with permission.

suggest moving to a fully funded system by privatizing social security, at least to some degree. This would be accomplished by establishing personal retirement accounts for all covered workers. The various proposals differ as to the size of the accounts and degree of individual control, but all would allow some private market investment. Many of the recent proposals include provisions to raise the retirement age. The major congressional proposals to reform the social security system, introduced in the 105th Congress, are compared in Appendix A [not reproduced here due to its length—Eds.].

III. Other Proposals

A. The 1994-1996 Advisory Council Plan

The Report of the 1994-1996 Advisory Council on Social Security outlined three options for social security reform. The first option seeks to maintain the current system's basic benefit structure by increasing revenues and reducing outlays. Specifically, the plan seeks to increase program revenues by extending coverage to state and local government employees hired after 1997, extending and increasing the taxation of benefits to all recipients, and increasing the payroll tax by a combined 1.6 percent. The plan also calls for an extension of the benefit computation period from 35 to 38 years by 1999, thereby reducing benefits by an average of 3 percent. Since these revenue and expenditure measures do not completely solve the long-term solvency problem, the panel members recommended that Congress consider investing up to 40 percent of the trust fund in the stock market.

The second option seeks to restore program solvency mainly through reductions in outlays. Such reductions would be achieved by accelerating the increase in the retirement age to 67 by 2011 and to 70 by 2083, reducing the growth of basic benefits, and extending the benefit computation period. This option would also establish a system of mandatory individual accounts to be funded by employee contributions. Specifically, workers would be required to contribute an additional 1.6 percent of covered earnings into a personal saving account. Individuals would have limited choices on how these accounts would be invested.

The third option would replace the current social security system with a new two-tiered system. The first tier would provide a flat-rate benefit based on a worker's length of service. Workers with 35 or more years of covered employment would receive a monthly benefit equal to $410 (or 65 percent of the current poverty level). The second tier would supplement this basic benefit by creating a system of Personal Saving Accounts, funded by 5 percentage points of the current 6.2 percent payroll tax on employees. These accounts would be individually owned and managed. Workers would be able to invest in a wide range of investment options.

B. The Ball Plan

Since the release of the Advisory Council's report, former Social Security Commissioner Robert Ball has made a number of proposals that attempt to maintain the program's current structure. His most recent proposal would supplement social security with a system of voluntary personal savings accounts. These accounts, which would be similar to Individual Retirement Accounts, would be funded by additional payroll deductions of up to 2 percent of covered wages. In addition to the creation of personal accounts, Ball proposes to restore long-term solvency to the social security program by investing up to 50 percent of the trust fund in stocks, extending coverage to newly hired state and local government employees, and increasing the maximum amount of a worker's earnings subject to social security taxation.

C. The Feldstein Plan

Another proposal, which has received considerable attention recently, was developed by Professor Martin Feldstein of Harvard University. Under the Feldstein plan, workers would be required to deposit an additional 2 percent of covered earnings into a personal retirement account. Income taxes would be reduced dollar-for-dollar for contributions made to personal accounts. The reduction in the income tax would be financed by federal budget surpluses. At retirement, for every dollar withdrawn from a personal account, the retiree's social security benefits would be reduced by $0.75.

D. The Kotlikoff Plan

Professor Laurence Kotlikoff of Boston University has proposed a plan to replace the retirement portion of the current system with a mandatory system of Personal Social Security Accounts. Under the Kotlikoff plan, 8 percentage points of the current 12.4 percent combined payroll tax would be diverted to a personal account to be invested in a single market-weighted global index fund composed of stocks, bonds, and real estate. Contributions to personal accounts would be tax deferred.

A similar plan, authored by David Altig and Jagadeesh Gokhale of the Federal Reserve Bank of Cleveland, would create a voluntary system of personal accounts. Under the Altig/Gokhale plan, workers under the age of 32 would be allowed to divert 46 percent of their payroll tax into personal savings accounts, similar to IRAs. The remaining 54 percent of the payroll tax would be used to pay benefits under the current system. Workers joining the new system would not receive any benefits under the current system.

Questions

1. Of the possible solutions to "fixing" Social Security—reducing benefits to workers or their dependents, increasing full retirement age, increasing maximum taxable wages, increasing the percentage contributed by workers and employers, creating individual investment accounts for each worker, investing the Social Security trust fund partially or wholly in the stock market—or some combination, what approach would you support? Why?

2. If workers have their own separate accounts, how will dependent benefits be paid?

2. Supplemental Security Income

National Association of State Budget Officers
The Supplemental Security Income Program
<http://www.nasbo.org/pubs/infobrf/v05n01.htm>[*]

SSI is a federal welfare program that provides monthly cash payments to needy aged, blind, and disabled persons in accordance with uniform, nationwide eligibility requirements. One of the largest cash assistance programs for low income individuals, SSI is a means-tested, federally administered program that was established in October of 1972 and began making payments in January of 1974. The SSI program provides "flat grants" based on a uniform federal income support level. In addition to the federal SSI payment, both a mandatory and an optional state supplementation was authorized for SSI.

Social Security benefits are the single highest source of income for SSI recipients. The SSI program was envisioned as a guaranteed minimum income for the aged, blind, and disabled which would supplement the Social Security Program. An income-related program, SSI provides for those who were not covered under Social Security or who had earned only minimal entitlement under the program. In other words, the program was intended to build on the Social Security program as a basic national income maintenance system for the aged, blind and disabled.

Approximately 38 percent of recipients receive Social Security benefits (63 percent of the aged, 31 percent of the disabled, and 36 percent of the blind) and about 13 percent receive some other type of unearned income. The SSI program is funded by general revenues of the U.S. Treasury, while Social Security benefits are funded by the Social Security taxes paid by workers, employers, and self-employed persons. The federal SSI benefits are indexed to the Consumer Price Index (CPI) and by the same percentage as Social Security benefits.

The federal monthly benefit standard for 1998 is $494 for an individual and $741 for a couple. In addition, SSI eligibility is restricted to qualified persons who have resources/assets of not more than $2,000, or $3,000 in the case of a couple. SSI law requires that SSI applicants file for all other benefits for which they may be entitled. Since its inception, SSI has been viewed as the "program of last resort." In other words, after evaluating all other income, SSI pays what is necessary to bring an individual to the statutorily prescribed income "floor."

SSI beneficiaries are categorically eligible for food stamps and do not have to meet the net income eligibility standard of the Food Stamp program. Only those SSI beneficiaries living in households where other household members do not receive SSI benefits must apply for food stamps and meet the income eligibility standards.

---

[*] Reprinted with permission.

Social Security Administration
1999 Social Security Changes
<http://www.ssa.gov/press/1999fact.htm>

SSI Federal Payment Standard:

	1998	1999
Individual	$494/mo.	$500/mo.
Couple	$741/mo.	$751/mo.

SSI Resources Limits:

	1998	1999
Individual	$2,000	$2,000
Couple	$3,000	$3,000

3. Veterans' Pension Benefits

VA History in Brief
VA PAMPHLET VA 80-97-2 (September 1997)

The Department of Veterans Affairs (VA) administers billions of dollars annually in federal benefits for military veterans and their dependents.... When eligible dependents and survivors are included, about one-third of the nation is eligible for benefits and services from VA.... Approximately 2.7 million veterans received disability compensation or pensions from VA in fiscal 1996. Another 682,000 surviving spouses, children and parents received similar benefits.

The veteran population of 25.6 million, estimated as of July 1997, is expected to decline to 24.3 million by 2000 and then to 20 million by 2010. At the same time, the number of elderly veterans is expected to increase substantially. The population of veterans age 65 and older is expected to increase from 8.6 million in July 1994 to a peak of 9.3 million in 2000.

a. Eligibility

Department of Veterans Affairs
FEDERAL BENEFITS FOR VETERANS AND DEPENDENTS (1996)

Veterans may be eligible for support if they have limited income when they have 90 days or more of active military service, at least one day of which was during a period of war. Their discharge from active duty must have been under conditions other than dishonorable. They must be permanently and totally disabled for reasons traceable neither to military service nor to willful misconduct. Payments are made to qualified veterans to bring their total income, including other retirement or Social Security income, to an established support level. Countable income may be reduced by unreimbursed medical expenses. Pension is not payable to those who have assets that can be used to provide adequate maintenance. . . .

b. Dependent Benefits

Department of Veterans Affairs
FEDERAL BENEFITS FOR VETERANS AND DEPENDENTS (1996)

Surviving spouses and unmarried children of deceased veterans with wartime service may be eligible for a nonservice-connected pension based on need. Children must be under age 18, or up to age 23 if attending a VA-approved school. Pension is not payable to those with estates large enough to provide maintenance. The veteran must have been discharged under conditions other than dishonorable and must have had 90 days or more of active military service, at least on day of which was during a period of war, or a service-connected disability justifying discharge for disability. If the veteran died in service not in line of duty, benefits may be payable if the veteran had completed at least two years of honorable service. Children who became incapable of self-support because of a disability before age 18 may be eligible for a pension as long as the condition exists, unless the child marries or the child's income exceeds the applicable limit. A surviving spouse who is a patient in a nursing home, is in need of regular aid and attendance of another person or is permanently housebound may be entitled to higher income limitations or additional benefits.

Questions

What features distinguish the VA pension system from Social Security's OASDI benefits? In what ways is the VA pension system more like SSI?

4. State Retirement Benefits

National Conference of Commissioners on Uniform State Laws
Management of Public Employee Retirement Systems Act
Draft Approved at 1997 Annual Meeting
<http://www.law.upenn.edu/library/ulc/mopepf/retirsy2.htm>*

Section 2. Definitions. In this [Act]:
    (1) "Administrator" means a person primarily responsible for the management of a retirement system or, if a person is not clearly designated, the trustee of the system who has the ultimate authority to manage the system.

---

    * Copyright © 1997. Reprinted with permission.

174   ELDER LAW: READINGS, CASES, AND MATERIALS

(2) "Agent group of programs" means a group of retirement programs which shares administrative and investment functions but maintains a separate account for each retirement program so that assets accumulated for a particular program may be used to pay benefits only for that program's participants and beneficiaries.

(3) "Appropriate grouping of programs" means:
  (A) for defined benefit plans, a cost-sharing program or an agent group of programs; and
  (B) for defined contribution plans, a group of retirement programs which shares administrative and investment functions.

(4) "Beneficiary" means a person, other than the participant, who is designated by a participant or by a retirement program to receive a benefit under the program.

(5) "Code" means the federal Internal Revenue Code of 1986, as amended.

(6) "Cost-sharing program" means a retirement program for the employee of more than one public employer in which all assets accumulated for the payment of benefits may be used to pay benefits to any participants or beneficiaries of the program.

(7) "Defined benefit plan" means a retirement program other than a defined contribution plan.

(8) "Defined contribution plan" means a retirement program that provides for an individual account for each participant and for benefits based solely upon the amount contributed to the participant's account, and any income, expenses, gains, and losses credited or charged to the account, and any forfeitures of accounts of other participants that may be allocated to the participant's account.

(9) "Employee" includes an officer of a public employer.

(10) "Fair value" means the amount that a willing buyer would pay a willing seller for an asset in a current sale, as determined in good faith by a fiduciary.

(11) "Fiduciary" means a person who:
  (A) exercises any discretionary authority to manage a retirement system;
  (B) exercises any authority to invest or manage assets of a system;
  (C) provides investment advice for a fee or other direct or indirect compensation with respect to assets of a system or has any authority or responsibility to do so; or
  (D) is a trustee or a member of a trustee board.

(12) "Furnish" means:
  (A) to deliver personally, to mail to the last known place of employment or home address of the intended recipient, or, if reasonable grounds exist to believe that the intended recipient would receive it in ordinary course, to transmit by any other usual means of communication; or
  (B) to provide to the intended recipient's public employer if reasonable ground exist to believe that the employer will make a good faith

effort to deliver personally, by mail, or by other usual means of communication.
(13) "Governing law" means state and local laws establishing or authorizing the creation of a retirement program or system and the principal state and local laws and regulations governing the management of a retirement program or system or assets of either.
(14) "Guaranteed benefit policy" means an insurance policy or contract to the extent the policy or contract provides for benefits in a guaranteed amount. The term includes any surplus in a separate account, but excludes any other portion of a separate account.
(15) "Insurer" means a company, service, or organization qualified to engage in the business of insurance in this State.
(16) "Nonforfeitable benefit" means an immediate or deferred benefit that arises from a participant's service, is unconditional, and is enforceable against the retirement system.
(17) "Participant" means an individual who is or has been an employee enrolled in a retirement program and who is or may become eligible to receive or is currently receiving a benefit under the program, or whose beneficiaries are or may become eligible to receive a benefit. The term does not include an individual who is no longer an employee of a public employer and has not accrued any nonforfeitable benefits under that employer's retirement program.
(18) "Public employer" means this State or any political subdivision, or any agency or instrumentality of this State or any political subdivision, whose employees are participants in a retirement program.
(19) "Qualified public accountant" means:
  (A) An auditing agency of this State or a political subdivision of this State which has no direct relationship with the functions or activities of a retirement system or its fiduciaries other than:
    (i) function relating to this [Act]; or
    (ii) a relationship between the system and the agency's employees as participants or beneficiaries on the same basis as other participants and beneficiaries; or
  (B) a person who is an independent certified public accountant, certified or licensed by a regulatory authority of a State.
(20) "Related person" or an individual means:
  (A) the individual's spouse or a parent or sibling of the spouse;
  (B) the individual's descendant, sibling, or parent, or the spouse of the individual's descendant, sibling, or parent;
  (C) another individual residing in the same household as the individual;
  (D) a trust or estate in which an individual described in subparagraph (A), (B), or (C) has a substantial interest;
  (E) a trust or estate for which the individual has fiduciary responsibilities; or

(F) an incompetent, ward, or minor for whom the individual has fiduciary responsibilities.
(21) "Retirement program" means a program of rights and obligations which a public employer establishes or maintains and which, by its express terms or as a result of surrounding circumstances:
 (A) provides retirement income to employees; or
 (B) results in a deferral of income by employees for periods extending to the termination of covered employment or beyond.
(22) "Retirement system" means an entity established or maintained by a public employer to manage one or more retirement programs, or to invest or manage the assets of one or more retirement programs.
(23) "Trustee" means a person who has ultimate authority to manage a retirement system or to invest or manage its assets.

* * *

Section 4. Establishment of Trust.
 (a) Except as otherwise provided in subsection (b), all assets of a retirement system are held in trust. The trustee has the exclusive authority, subject to this [Act], to invest and manage those assets.
 (b) Assets of a retirement system which consist of insurance contracts or policies issued by an insurer, assets of an insurer, and assets of the system held by an insurer need not be held in trust.
 (c) If an insurer issues a guaranteed benefit policy to a retirement system, assets of the system include the policy but not assets of the insurer.
 (d) If a retirement system invests in a security issued by an investment company registered under the Investment Company Act of 1940 (15 U.S.C. § 80a-1 *et seq.*), the assets of the system include the security, but not assets of the investment company.

* * *

Section 21. Alienation of Benefits.

Benefits of a retirement program may not be assigned or alienated and shall be exempt from claims of creditors, except [to the extent expressly permitted by another law of this State].

Question

Why should a state employee retirement benefit plan have an "anti-alienation" provision?

B. Employer-Based Pension Plans

1. A Brief History of Pensions and Pension Regulation

Patricia E. Dilley
The Evolution of Entitlement: Retirement Income and the Problem of Integrating Private Pensions and Social Security
30 LOYOLA L.A. L. REV. 1063, 1085, 1087-88, 1112-19, 1137 (1997)[*]

Retirement—the extended period of leisure after the end of a working life expected by most workers in the late twentieth century—is a recent phenomenon. While every human culture has some experience of supporting older members who live past the age of productive labor, it was not until widespread industrialization and the development of industrial-laboring and middle classes in Europe and the United States in the twentieth century that retirement became a relatively common occurrence.

* * *

The notion of retirement necessarily rests on the ability of an economy to produce enough surplus wealth to support older nonworkers. In agrarian societies generally up until the mid-to-late nineteenth century, advancing age was not automatically associated with cessation of work, which occurred only if and when actual physical incapacity set in. The pattern of frequent famine and plagues that characterized Europe from the thirteenth through eighteenth centuries probably ensured that few of the poor survived to great ages; life past age sixty was largely reserved for the well-off bourgeoisie and the nobility who guaranteed comfort in old age through continued control of their wealth and families. In the absence of such accumulated wealth, the incapacity brought on by advancing age necessitated dependency on family, church, or local organized poor relief.

* * *

Private pensions have never been the principal or even major source of income in old age for United States workers. Nonetheless, limited pension and profit sharing plans existed in the United States long before the federal retirement program [known as Social Security—Eds.] was pushed through the New Deal Congress in 1935. Employer-sponsored group savings plans, and eventually pension plans, seem to have been an outgrowth of the "private social welfare" efforts begun in the late-nineteenth century by American businesses as employers began to perceive the advantages of pension trusts and stock purchase plans, first as a source of capital and later as a way of easing their older and more highly paid employees off the payroll.

* * *

Private employers in the United States began establishing annuity pension plans for their employees late in the nineteenth century, years before the enactment

---

[*] Copyright © 1997. Reprinted with permission.

of the federal income tax and the possibility of sheltering income from tax through deferring compensation. The first United States pension plan appears to have been established by the American Express Company in 1875 when American Express was principally associated with the railroad industry. The plan was not a true retirement plan, but rather paid benefits to disabled employees who had twenty years of service with the company, had reached age sixty, and were recommended for the pension by company management.

This type of plan was put into place by many United States and Canadian railroads in the years following 1875, but those plans seem to have been more a response to the occupational hazards presented by railroad employment than an anticipation of retirement pensions. However, most developed into straight retirement plans during the 1900 to 1930 period when the greatest number of industrial pension plans were established. The most widely accepted estimate of pension plans and participation is that between 1875 and 1929 around 400 industrial pension plans were established, with about that number still in operation on the eve of the Depression.

The companies establishing these plans employed about 10% of the industrial labor force—a force substantially less than the entire work force including agricultural and casual labor. It is not clear, however, how many of those employees were eligible to participate in the plan or would eventually qualify for benefits. According to a recent estimate, although industrial pensions were not uncommon by 1935, no more than 4% of male workers and 3% of female workers met the requirements for receipt of pensions at that time.

* * *

Most early pension plans were noncontributory. That is, the plans were financed completely by the employer who generally interpreted the obligation to pay benefits as voluntary. Perhaps the earliest case exploring the nature of the promise made to the employee in an industrial pension plan was *McNevin v. Solvay Process Company* [1898, *affirmed* 1901—Eds.] in which the court analyzed pensions on the theory that they were a gift from employer to employee. In that case the ruling turned on the authority of the company's directors to refuse to pay a pension claim under the plan. Since the pension payment itself was viewed as a gratuity, there was no automatic obligation to pay even though an amount was "credited" under the employee's name in the bookkeeping for the plan.

The "gratuity" theory of pensions matched employers' views of their obligations under pension plans at least until after the inception of the income tax—the plans were written to be strictly discretionary, with payments made out of current income and usually no advance funding for future obligations. Another early case decided a year or two after *Solvay Process* reinforced the gratuity theory by holding that the employer had created no implication of employee vesting in amounts credited under employee names and that upon the bankruptcy of the employer, the employees had no rights as creditors. Even though these cases found no legal entitlement and no employee vesting in the absence of a plan provision specifically providing for it, employers nevertheless stopped the practice of crediting amounts to employee bookkeeping accounts for fear of creating any possible admission of liability under the pension plan.

While the gratuity theory was cited by the courts well into the 1950s, in the 1920s some courts apparently began to uphold employee claims on noncontributory funds on the grounds that the pension was part of a contractual agreement between employer and employee, not simply a gift. Perhaps as a result, employers began to cut back on noncontributory plans: "After 1923, new pension plans were overwhelmingly contributory and insured, and many employers pared back their programs or simply stopped notifying workers or their dependents of pension eligibility."

* * *

The modest expansion of employer-sponsored pension plans from 1900 into the 1920s coincided with increasing use of labor management practices designed to limit employee turnover and fend off union organization. Unions in general opposed establishment of employer-provided plans. They viewed the plans as an interference with bargaining rights although they occasionally set up their own benefit plans, frequently covering sickness, disability, and unemployment, and less frequently old age, payable only if sufficient funds were available.

Employers saw pension plans as a means to an end: workers would trade a pay increase or right to strike for the promise of a pension. Moreover, pensions could be used to "purge the payroll" of older workers who were probably more highly paid and had begun to be perceived as less productive. Since the pension promise itself was so tenuous and required no current funding or payment of benefits except to those who retired immediately after a plan was established with benefits substantially lower than their salaries had been, current employment costs theoretically could be reduced along with turnover of valued employees.

* * *

The very modest use of employer-provided pensions coincided with other labor management practices such as seniority, a fact that both aided and impeded older workers. Workers who "caught on" with a company when they were relatively young could benefit from seniority practices that gave preference in salary and job protection to longer-service workers. Henry Ford's innovation of the wage ladder, an artificial hierarchy of pay based on length of service that encouraged workers to stay with the company, was just one example of the many kinds of employee benefits, including pensions, that were increasingly tied to longevity after 1900. The seniority system probably worked to the disadvantage of those older workers attempting to find new employment in middle age, since they could not offer a long period of service and high youthful productivity, characteristics that seniority and benefit plans were developed to encourage.

The concept of mandatory retirement took hold in American business during this period as well, particularly in industries such as the railroads, which had already established employer-provided pensions and organized their compensation and benefits around longevity of employment. In 1900 the Pennsylvania Railroad established a maximum hiring age of thirty-five and retirement age of seventy, with a company pension, as a way of controlling the costs of expensive older workers while at the same time reducing employee turnover.

Of course, pension promises that appear quite inexpensive when made often turn out to be much more expensive when they actually have to be fulfilled. While employers limited the likelihood of eligibility for pensions with long service requirements and requirements that the worker be employed at the time of disability or retirement, pension liabilities still became a major cost issue for employers in the late 1920s.

* * *

Many employers in the 1920s attempted to mitigate the impact of these rising costs by insuring their pension liabilities, but even the insurers began to be alarmed by the size of future costs.

* * *

Thus, even before the advent of the deep economic crisis in the 1930s, companies were attempting to retrench on retirement commitments they had already made. Some larger employers, perhaps recognizing the link between seniority, employee management, and retirement income, began to support calls for federalization of retirement programs. Most businesses, however, resisted any suggestion of federal intervention and instead continued to cut back on plan promises.

This brief history reveals the limited aspirations of employer-sponsored private pension plans in the pre-World War II era. The goal of most employers was control of their labor forces, not retirement income security. Funded plans were seen as vehicles for capital formation, not income replacement in old age. The continuing pressure from workers for pension plans, and their willingness to accept an extremely insecure pension promise as a tradeoff for current wages, reflects the general insecurity created by industrialization and dislocation of traditional trade occupations. Nonetheless, private pension plans, which were almost always unfunded and benefited almost exclusively long-term—thirty years or more in many cases—high-wage workers, could not be expected to, and did not, underwrite mass retirement.

* * *

Of particular importance to the coordination of Social Security with private pensions is the rejection in 1935 and later of suggestions that workers covered by a private pension should be excluded from Social Security. The original proposal was to cover all manual and nonmanual laborers earning less than $250 per month, with the exception of government and railroad employees who had fairly complete retirement plans already in place. Private employer-provided pensions were not viewed as the equivalent of federal civil service or railroad pensions, and with good reason. Both of the latter systems had more or less government-guaranteed sources of financing, and workers with long service were virtually assured of receiving their pensions. Private plans, on the other hand, were few in number, and many, if not most, had failed or gone bankrupt during the economic collapse earlier in the decade; private plans could not be considered any sort of alternative to a government-sponsored plan.

W. Greenough & F. King
Pension Plans and Public Policy 38-44, 59-63, 66-67 (1976)[*]

As noted earlier, the railroads were among the first of the industrial employers to establish pension plans, starting with the B&O and the Pennsylvania. This was consistent with the fact that the early pension plans tended to appear in the more prosperous industries and the larger concerns, among which were the railroads—new, growing, and able to attract massive amounts of capital.

* * *

The later decline of the railroads illustrates the problems pension plans encounter if they have not made sound financial arrangements to back up their pension promises. Until the late 1920s the railroads continued to flourish and to represent attractive employment opportunities. Beginning with the Great Depression, railroad revenues declined sharply and at the same time the number of railroad workers expecting to be retired because of age or years of service was increasing.

* * *

With virtually no pension reserves established to meet pension liabilities, and with many of the roads operating in the red in the late 1920s and early '30s, companies resorted to various expediencies to ease the financial pressures.

* * *

These emergency measures were not enough. Without sufficient pension reserves, with a declining capacity to sustain a pay-as-you-go retirement system amidst the economic shambles of the Great Depression, and with growing competition from the trucking industry, the railroads' benevolent and optimistic pension promises were turning into a financial monster.

* * *

There was little prospect that the troubled railroads could make good on their pension promises for the quarter-million older employees due to retire within three or four years. Strong pressure developed for some kind of legislative action to bail the railroads out.

* * *

The federal government responded with a plan to take over and administer the pension promises of the railroads. The government approach was to inject substantial federal appropriations to cover immediate obligations, and for the future to develop a plan incorporating employee and employer contributions under a federally run plan . . . . The system now operates something along the lines of Social Security and functions as a substitute Social Security system for railroad employees.

* * *

---

[*] From *Pension Plans and Public Policy* by W. Greenough and F. King © 1976 Columbia University Press. Reprinted with the permission of the publisher.

Unfortunately, the catastrophic failure of the railroads' pension plans did not at the time lead to any movement for pension reform.

* * *

While the larger industrial employers were establishing their pension plans in the early years of the 20th century, the trade unions, independently of employers, were attempting their own programs of member benefits.

* * *

The first union plan to provide for periodic old-age payments, as distinct from lump-sum or periodic benefits for permanent disability, was established by the Patternmakers in 1900. The plan was not funded and depended on the union treasury. The first plan with a degree of funding for old-age payments was established in 1905 by the Granitecutters.

* * *

The first union plan offering old-age benefits as a matter of right rather than as gratuities was established by the Brotherhood of Locomotive Engineers in 1912.

* * *

By 1928, it was estimated that about 40 percent of trade union membership belonged to national unions offering one form or another of old age and permanent and total disability benefits. But the funds for the benefits necessarily had to be derived from assessments on union members. As the numbers of older union members increased, the assessments on all members had to be increased . . . . To increase union dues became more difficult, and within a few years after the Great Depression began almost all of the union welfare plans had collapsed.

* * *

The Great Depression seriously shook American confidence in the virtues of individual thrift and in personal savings as a way to prepare for old age. With 13 million people out of work, savings erased, and long-standing traditions of self-reliance undermined, the 1930s were becalmed years for both union welfare plans and employer-sponsored pension plans. In this atmosphere the passage of the Social Security Act of 1935, America's first national social insurance legislation, was virtually inevitable. This was to be the main pension development until after World War II.

* * *

At the close of the 1940s the stage was set for a renewal of union interest in pension plans, not in mutual assistance or fraternal benefits, but in the negotiation of pension plans with employers through collective bargaining. Conditions were ready for the next phase of union welfare activity. The Internal Revenue Act of 1942 had placed the tax treatment of pension plans in a clearer light . . . . Combined with the sharp increases in corporate and excess-profits tax rates of the 1940s, the special tax treatment that was accorded pension plans under the 1942 act enhanced employer receptiveness to union pension demands.

* * *

The first struggle of a large union for a negotiated pension plan was that of John L. Lewis and the United Mine Workers of America [in 1945-46]. Although the plan that came out of this struggle had spectacular weaknesses, it focused attention on the question of pensions for union members.

* * *

[Greenough and King then go on to discuss demands for pensions in the steel and automotive industries. It is worth noting that, while the preceding excerpts have focused on the development of pensions in the unionized workplace, pensions also developed over the course of the 20th century in other sectors: for example, for public employees (federal, state, and municipal) and for nonprofit employees, such as professors at private universities. For more details, *see* Greenough & King at 49-59.—Eds.]

* * *

Federal regulation of private pension plans dates from the early 1920s in an amalgam of taxation principles and social principles. The Internal Revenue Code and Treasury regulations have had a considerable influence on private pension plans in the United States, and the evolution of the code as applied to pensions and profit-sharing plans is a significant part of the history of American pension plans.

The 1920s. The first industrial pension plans were usually paid out of current company earnings as a current business expense—a pay-as-you-go basis—but it was not too long before it became evident that at there were advantages in establishing at least some reserves and separate trust or insurance arrangements. By the early 1920s many of the pay-as-you-go plans had been transformed into trusts, although by no means fully funded, and new plans were being initially established as trusts.

Almost immediately a question arose as to the taxability of the income of such trusts and of the status of employer contributions under the relatively new U.S. income tax laws. In 1926, pension trusts created by employers for the exclusive benefit of some or all employees were made exempt from federal income tax. It was also provided that employer contributions to such trusts, and the income therefrom, would not be taxable to the beneficiaries until actually distributed.

* * *

The 1942 Revisions. By 1942 it had become apparent that the existing laws and regulations were too simple and needed refinement. Under the earlier legislation, pension trusts on behalf of "some or all employees" . . . had been utilized to develop trusts that included as participants only small groups of officers and favored key employees in the higher income brackets, apparently as a means of tax avoidance (or deferment) for persons in a position to create a trust in the first place.

* * *

The new tax code of 1942 brought further into view and placed in statutory form the public policy principle that federal tax laws could and should be used as a means of requiring employers to meet certain expressed standards in voluntarily established private pension plans.... To qualify for the statutory tax treatment of employer contributions... under the new code, a plan was required to be: (1) for the exclusive benefit of the employer's employees or their beneficiaries; (2) for the purpose of distributing the corpus and income to the employees; (3) impossible for the employer to use or divert the fund before satisfying the plans' liabilities to the employees and their beneficiaries; and (4) nondiscriminatory as to extent of coverage—a large percentage of regular employees must be eligible to participate, and neither contributions nor benefits were to discriminate in favor of officers, stockholders, or highly compensated employees or supervisory employees.

Amendments to the pension sections of the code between 1942 and 1974 were not fundamental in nature.

* * *

The Employee Retirement Income Security Act of 1974. Little significant change took place in U.S. legislation regarding private pension plans in the three decades following the 1942 changes in the Internal Revenue Code. But by the mid-1960s a change in atmosphere could be detected. In 1964, heavy losses in pension expectations were occasioned by a widely publicized shutdown of the South Bend, Indiana, Studebaker Corporation plant. In the same year, Professor Merton C. Bernstein published a comprehensive and influential analysis of private pension plans and their possible future directions.... In 1965 a pension policy study group appointed by President Kennedy issued a report... offer[ing] numerous recommendations for legislation.

* * *

The 1974 Pension Reform Act [known as ERISA—Eds.] established basic new requirements in virtually every area of pension administration and funding, including rules of participation and eligibility, minimum vesting standards, reporting and disclosure to government and to plan participants, funding standards, actuarial standards, fiduciary conduct, and past service liability amortization rules. It established a Pension Benefit Guaranty Corporation within the Labor Department to protect plan participants through insurance in the event of plan termination. The Act's standards are applied to private plans, except for church or church-related plans, but not to public employee plans.

J. Langbein & B. Wolk
Pension and Employee Benefit Law 89-90 (2d ed. 1995)[*]

ERISA has been considerably modified since the statute came into force in 1974, and pension taxation has experienced annual legislative tinkering. Following is a list of major post-1974 legislation, with thumbnail sketches of the substance of the changes.

* * *

1. *Revenue Act of 1978.* The Act created the SEP-IRA as a pension alternative for small employers. The Act added IRC § 401(k) . . . making employee contributions to employer-sponsored thrift plans tax deferred.

* * *

3. *Economic Recovery Tax Act of 1981 (ERTA).* ERTA emphasized tax deferral incentives to promote saving. It increased the contribution ceiling on Keogh plans . . . [and] on IRA accounts . . . and allowed employees already covered by other pension plans to establish IRAs.

* * *

6. *Retirement Equity Act of 1984 (REA or REAct).* REAct was meant to address a variety of issues thought to be of special concern to women. ERISA originally allowed a plan to set a minimum age of 25 for plan participation; REAct lowered the age to 21. REAct made the rules for reckoning a break in service more benign, including a protected period for maternity or paternity leave. . . . REAct made express provision for enforcing certain state domestic relations decrees touching pension assets [called qualified domestic relations orders (QDROs)] . . . . REAct introduced mandatory spousal rights in pension plans [known as qualified joint and survivor annuities (QJSAs) and qualified preretirement survivor annuities (QPSAs)].

7. *Consolidated Omnibus Budget Amendment Act of 1985 (COBRA).* COBRA added ERISA Title I, Part 6, requiring that the sponsor of a group health plan make continuation coverage available to certain employees, spouses, ex-spouses, dependents, and others for periods up to three years after coverage might otherwise cease.

* * *

8. *Tax Reform Act of 1986 (TRAC).* TRAC reduced the top-bracket rates of personal income taxation from 50 percent to as low as 28 percent, but the 1993 Clinton tax package restored a top bracket of 39 percent. Lower tax brackets reduce the incentive to defer taxation, whether through qualified pension plans or otherwise. TRAC largely repealed the provision of ERTA that allowed persons covered by another pension plan to make tax-deductible contributions to an IRA account.

* * *

---

[*] Copyright © 1995. Reprinted with permission.

11. *Americans with Disabilities Act (ADA)*. The ADA prevents discrimination against disabled persons in the provision of pension or health insurance benefits.

Note on Recent Legislation Affecting Retirement Assets

The following legislation should be added to the list complied by Professors Langbein and Wolk:

1. *The Taxpayer Relief Act of 1997 (TRA '97)*. This Act created a new type of IRA, known as a Roth IRA. (It was named for Senator William Roth of Delaware, the Chairman of the Senate Finance Committee.)

2. *The Internal Revenue Service Restructuring and Reform Act of 1998.* This Act clarified some of the rules governing IRAs.

Questions

1. Why did pensions develop when they did, and not earlier?

2. The history of pensions and pension regulation can be divided into four stages: 19th century origins, slow growth in the early decades of the 20th century, rapid growth in the years after World War II, and the post-1974 "age of ERISA." What characterizes and explains each of these stages?

3. Why are pensions employment-based?

2. Pension Coverage

Paul Fronstin
Employee Benefits, Retirement Patterns, and Implications for Increased Work Life, 3-4
(EBRI Issue Brief No. 184, April 1997)[*]

Between 1940 and 1970, the percentage of workers participating in a private pension plan increased from 15 percent to 45 percent, and it has remained at roughly 40 percent through the 1980s and 1990s (chart 2 [reproduced below—Eds.]). However, private wage and salary workers ages 51-61 have a higher likelihood of participating in a pension plan, and the trend has been increasing over time. In 1995, 54 percent of private wage and salary workers ages 51-61 were participating in a pension plan, up from 51 percent in 1988. This increases to 59.3 percent among full-time workers ages 51-61 and 72.7 percent among full-time workers ages 51-61 working for firms with 100 or more employees. As a result, pension income as a share of total income is increasing for retirees. In 1979, pension income accounted for 15 percent

---

[*] Copyright © 1997. Reprinted with permission.

of the income of the elderly, while in 1995 it accounted for 19 percent. In addition, Social Security income as a share of total income remained fairly constant during this time period.

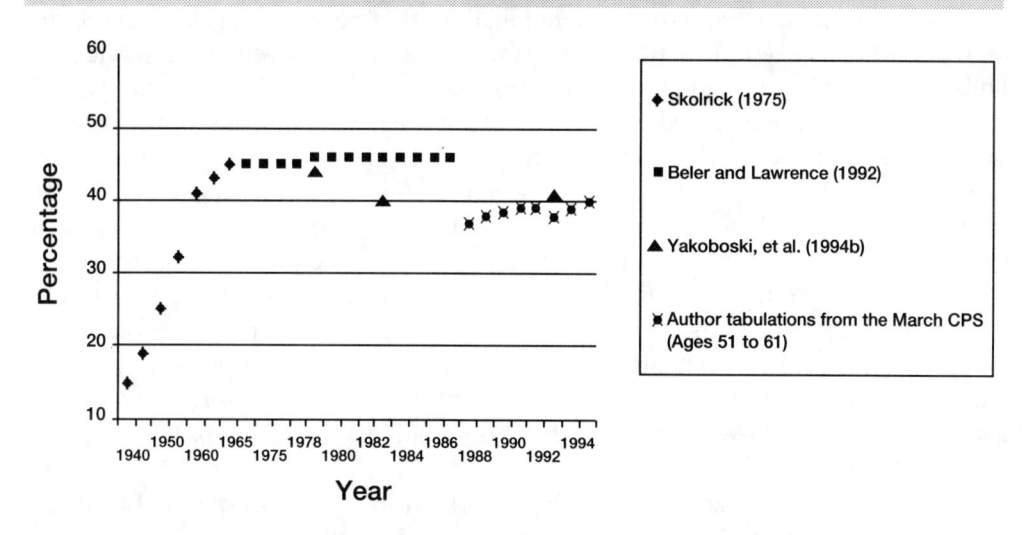

Chart 2
PRIVATE PENSION PLAN PARTICIPATION RATES
1940-1995

♦ Skolrick (1975)
■ Beler and Lawrence (1992)
▲ Yakoboski, et al. (1994b)
✳ Author tabulations from the March CPS (Ages 51 to 61)

Source: Employee Benefit Research Institute
CPS = Current Population Survey

Questions

1. Why did pension coverage increase so rapidly between the 1940s and the 1970s?

2. Why has pension coverage stabilized in the years after the mid-1970s?

3. Who is likely to be covered by a pension? Who is *not* likely to be covered?

3. Types of Pension Plans

EMPLOYEE BENEFIT RESEARCH INSTITUTE
FUNDAMENTALS OF EMPLOYEE BENEFIT PROGRAMS 69-71, 173-74 (5th ed. 1997)[*]

Defined Benefit Plans

In a defined benefit plan, each employee's future benefit is determined by a specific formula, and the plan provides a nominal level of benefits on retirement. Usually, the promised benefit is tied to the employee's earnings, length of service, or both. For example, an employer may promise to pay each participant a benefit equal to a percentage of the employee's final five-year average salary times number of years of service at retirement, or the employer may pay a flat dollar amount per year of service. A defined benefit plan is typically not contributory—i.e., there are no employee contributions. And there are usually no individual accounts maintained for each employee. The employer makes regular contributions to the plan to fund the participants' future benefits. The employer bears the risk of providing the guaranteed level of retirement benefits. In 1993, 56 percent of full-time employees of medium and large private establishments were covered by defined benefit plans. [Note: this number declined to 52 percent in 1995, according to Department of Labor statistics available on the World Wide Web at <stats.bls.gov:80/news.release/ebs3.t01.htm>—Eds.]

Defined benefit plan sponsors may choose from several formulas for determining final retirement benefits. These include:

Flat-Benefit Formulas—These formulas pay a flat-dollar amount for every year of service recognized under the plan.

Career-Average Formulas—There are two types of career-average formulas. Under the first type, participants earn a percentage of the pay recognized for plan purposes in each year they are plan participants. The second type of career-average formula averages the participant's yearly earnings over the period of plan participation. At retirement, the benefit equals a percentage of the career-average pay multiplied by the participant's number of years of service.

Final-Pay Formulas—These plans base benefits on average earnings during a specified number of years at the end of a participant's career (usually five years); this is presumably the time when earnings are highest. The benefit equals a percentage of the participant's final average earnings, multiplied by the number of years of service. This formula provides the greatest inflation protection to the participant but can represent a higher cost to the employer.

Defined Contribution Plans

In a defined contribution plan, employers generally promise to make annual or periodic contributions to accounts set up for each employee. (Sometimes defined contribution plans are referred to as individual account plans.) The current contribution

---

[*] Copyright © 1997. Reprinted with permission.

is guaranteed but not a level of benefits at retirement, as in a defined benefit plan. In 1993, 49 percent of full-time employees in medium and large private establishments participated in one or more defined contribution plans, up from 45 percent in 1988. [Note: in 1995, this number increased to 55 percent, according to Department of Labor statistics available at <stats.bls.gov:80/news.release/ebs3.t01.htm>.—Eds.]

The contribution to a defined contribution plan may be stated as a percentage of the employee's salary and/or may be related to years of service. Sometimes there are only employer contributions, sometimes only employee contributions, and sometimes both. The benefit payable at retirement is based on money accumulated in each employee's account. The accumulated money will reflect employer contributions, employee contributions (if any), and investment gains or losses. The accumulated amount may also include employer contributions forfeited by employees who leave before they become fully vested, to the extent such contributions are reallocated to the accounts of employees who remain.

There are several types of defined contribution plans, including money purchase plans, profit-sharing plans, 401(k) arrangements, savings plans, and employee stock ownership plans (ESOPs). These are described briefly below.

Savings, or Thrift, Plan—A savings, or thrift, plan is essentially an employee-funded savings plan. An employee generally makes contributions on an after-tax basis to an account set up in his or her own name. The contributions are often stated as a percentage of pay. The contributions may be matched (in full or in part) by the employer, but there is no statutory obligation for employer contributions.

Profit-Sharing Plan—A profit-sharing plan provides for contributions to the plan sometimes based on annual profits for the previous year. However, profits are not required for contributions, and a company is under no obligation to make contributions on a regular basis. Contributions are typically divided among participants in proportion to their respective earnings.

Money Purchase Pension Plan—Employer contributions are mandatory in a money purchase plan. They are usually stated as a percentage of employee salary. Retirement benefits are equal to the amount in the individual account at retirement.

Employee Stock Ownership Plan—An ESOP is a tax-qualified employee benefit plan that provides shares of stock in the sponsoring company to participating employees. An ESOP is required to invest primarily in employer stock and is permitted to borrow money on a tax-deductible basis to purchase this stock.

401(k) Arrangement—A qualified cash or deferred arrangement ["CODA"] under sec. 401(k) of the Internal Revenue Code allows an employee to elect to have a portion of his or her compensation (otherwise payable in cash) contributed to a qualified profit-sharing, stock bonus, or . . . money purchase pension plan. The employee contribution is most commonly treated as a pretax reduction in salary. [Note: section 401(k) does not apply to employees of organizations that are tax-exempt; such organizations can set up plans that are somewhat similar but regulated under section 403(b).—Eds.]

* * *

[Note: before 1962, self-employed individuals could not participate in qualified pension plans.—Eds.]

Since 1962, federal policy has encouraged the provision of pensions for the self-employed. . . through the Self-Employed Individuals Tax Retirement Act. This law created Keogh plans, named for U.S. Rep. Eugene J. Keogh of New York, who sponsored the original legislation . . . .

Keogh plans may be classified as either defined contribution or defined benefit plans.

U.S. Department of Labor
Employee Benefits in Medium and Large Private Establishments 1995
<http://stats.bls.gov:80/news.release/ebs3.toc.htm>

Table 1. Percent of full-time employees participating in selected employee benefit programs, medium and large private establishments, 1995

Category	Percent
All retirement [plans]	80
Defined benefit	52
Defined contribution	55
Types of [DC] plans:	
Savings and thrift.	41
Deferred profit sharing	13
Employee stock ownership	5
Money purchase pension.	7
401(k) plans:	
With employer contribution	45
Without employer contribution	9

Note on the Changing Balance Between Defined Benefit and Defined Contribution Plans

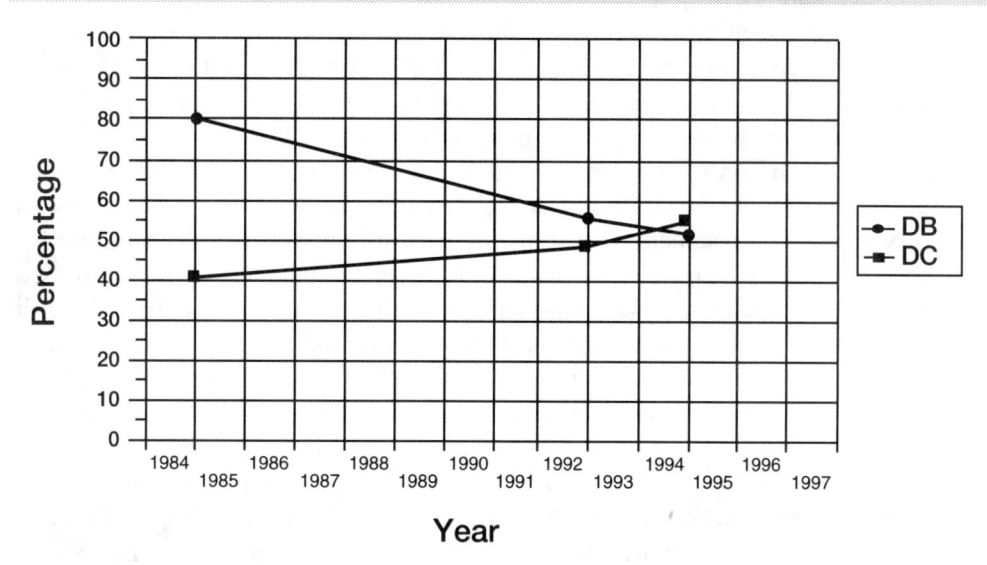

Percent of full-time employees participating in employee benefit programs in medium and large private establishments: 1985, 1993 and 1995.
(DB = defined benefit, DC = defined contribution)

[Chart: Percentage vs. Year showing DB declining from ~80% in 1985 to ~52% in 1995, and DC rising from ~40% in 1985 to ~55% in 1995.]

Prepared by TPG based on data from the Department of Labor's Employee Benefits Survey.

Jeffrey N. Gordon
Employees, Pensions, and the New Economic Order
97 COLUM. L. REV. 1519, 1547-50 (1997)[*]

One very powerful recent trend has been the declining percentage of workers covered by defined benefit plans and the increasing importance of defined contribution plans, especially 401(k) plans. This is not so much because of the termination of defined benefit plans (although some smaller firms have terminated these plans), but because of the diminishing importance of the heavily unionized, manufacturing industries that typically have provided defined benefit coverage. For example, over the 1980-1995 period, the number of private industry workers covered by defined benefit plans declined by 21% (from 30.1 million to an estimated 23.9 million), but the coverage ratio declined by 41% (from 41% of all private industry workers to an estimated 24%). This indicates that the declining significance of defined benefit plans shows up not only in the number of participants, but, even more importantly, through reduced workforce penetration. By contrast, over the same period, the number of private industry workers covered by defined contribution plans has increased by 211%

---

[*] This article originally appeared at 97 Colum. L. Rev. 1519 (1997). Reprinted by permission.

(from 18.9 million to an estimated 40 million) and the coverage ratio has increased by 227% (from 18% to an estimated 41%). The growth in the number of workers covered by 401(k) plans has been explosive since the IRS issued regulations in the early 1980s that clarified the terms "cash or deferred accounts" added by statutory amendment in 1978. In 1995, an estimated 26.5 million workers or 27% of the private industry workforce had 401(k) plans.

Growth in the number of 401(k) plans seems not to have directly replaced defined benefit coverage, because the firms with defined benefit plans were the quickest to offer 401(k) plans as an add-on and the existence of a defined benefit plan is highly correlated with the offering of a 401(k) plan. There is also significant, though not uncontroverted, evidence that at least a substantial amount of employee savings in 401(k) plans is additional savings, not in substitution for other financial assets. Nevertheless, for many firms 401(k) plans might well have substituted for defined benefit plans that otherwise would have been adopted as the firm increased in size, thereby reducing the per-employee administrative costs of a defined benefit plan to a feasible level. Also, during the 1980-1993 period, the percentage of compensation outlays going to pension and retirement plans declined from 6.2% to 4.1%, suggesting that the defined contribution plans put in place may have been less rich than the defined benefit plans that had previously been the dominant pension form. Moreover, there is evidence that the present value of employer pension contributions for workers in defined benefit plans is roughly double the comparable value for employees in defined contribution environments, 14% of salary versus 7.5%.

Finally, the increasing importance of defined contribution plans is reflected in the dramatic shift in the relative share of pension fund assets. Over the 1980-1995 period, the ratio of assets in private defined benefit plans to assets in defined contribution plans fell from 2.5 to 1 at the beginning of the period to 1 to 1 in 1995. By 1995, 401(k) plan assets were nearly 50% of the estimated defined contribution total (approximately $650 billion of a total defined contribution pool of $1.4 trillion), quite a remarkable statistic for a retirement category that was at $0 in 1983. Moreover, the difference in residual ownership of plan assets means that the growth in defined contribution assets is likely to outstrip growth in defined benefit assets at an ever-increasing rate. The growth in defined benefit assets will be constrained by the increase in pension obligations, since firms can recapture gains that exceed funding requirements. The growth in defined contribution assets, on the other hand, will be constrained primarily by the rate of investment return.

Questions

1. Compare the State Teachers Retirement System of Ohio (described at <www.strsoh.org>) with TIAA-CREF (described at <www.tiaa-cref.org>). How would you characterize these plans?

2. Why are the advantages of defined benefit plans? What are the advantages of defined contribution plans?

3. What explains the rapid growth in defined contribution plans?

Note on Pension Plans Aimed at Small Businesses: SEPs and SIMPLE Plans

Employee Benefit Research Institute
Fundamentals of Employee
Benefit Programs 125, 485 (5th ed. 1997)*

The U.S. Congress . . . [enacted] the Revenue Act of 1978, which established a new tax-favored retirement plan aimed primarily at small employers—the simplified employee pension (SEP).

SEPs are arrangements under which an individual retirement account (IRA) is established for each eligible employee. The employee is immediately vested in employer contributions and generally directs the investment of the money. These arrangements are sometimes called SEP-IRAs.

A principal difference for individuals between a SEP and an employer-sponsored IRA is the larger annual contribution available for a SEP. SEPs must also meet some qualified retirement plan rules for eligibility, coverage, vesting, and contributions that do not exist for employment-based IRAs.

SEPs offer employers an alternative to more complex and costly qualified pension plans. Paperwork, recordkeeping, and reporting requirements are kept to a minimum.

SEPs may be set up by corporations, unincorporated businesses and partnerships, and self-employed persons. Although companies of any size may create SEPs, the simplicity of the arrangment is designed to interest small businesses.

* * *

The Small Business Job Protection Act of 1996 created a simplified retirement plan for small businesses called the savings incentive match plan for employees (SIMPLE) retirement plan. SIMPLE plans can be adopted by employers who employ 100 or fewer employees on any day during the year and who do not maintain another employer-based retirement plan.

Question

Why did Congress consider it necessary to create SEP-IRAs and SIMPLE plans?

---

* Copyright © 1997. Reprinted with permission.

4. The Taxation of Pension Investments When Made

Peter M. Van Zante
*Rollover of Retirement Plan Distributions:
A Proposal to Eliminate the Dual Rollover Structure*
86 KY. L.J. 31, 42-43 (1997-1998)[*]

In contrast [to most forms of savings], retirement savings are not included in the taxpayer's income tax base for so long as the savings are held as identifiable retirement savings, that is, held in a tax-qualified retirement plan. The exclusion from the income tax base for retirement savings is implemented by a trilogy of Code provisions. The employer, which pays the contribution to its retirement trust, is allowed an income tax deduction for the contribution [citing IRC § 404]. A participating employee need not include in her gross income any amount attributable to the employer's contribution nor to any increase in the value of the participant's vested accrued benefit [citing IRC § 402(a)]. And the retirement trust is exempt from income tax, so the investment earnings on the contributions are accumulated tax-free [citing IRC § 501]. This exclusion of retirement savings from the income tax base continues as long as the savings are held as identifiable retirement savings.

Questions

What are the tax advantages offered by pension plans? (Read, by way of example, Internal Revenue Code § 402(a) in the statutory supplement. What statutory language offers the tax advantage mentioned by Professor Van Zante?)

5. Pension Distributions: Mechanics and Taxation

EMPLOYEE BENEFIT RESEARCH INSTITUTE
FUNDAMENTALS OF EMPLOYEE
BENEFIT PROGRAMS 60 (5th ed. 1997)[**]

Pension plans generally offer retiring participants a choice between two payment options: an annuity, in which the benefit is paid out in a stream of regular payments, usually monthly and usually over the life of the participant (or lives of the participant and spouse) but sometimes over some other specified period; or in a lump sum. The type of distribution and when it is taken determines the tax treatment.

---

[*] Copyright © 1998. Reprinted with permission.
[**] Copyright © 1997. Reprinted with permission.

a. Annuities

Gail Levin Richmond
Taxes and the Elderly: An Introduction
19 NOVA L. REV. 587, 618-19 (1995)[*]

Most retirement benefits can be traced to the following funding sources: employer contributions that were not included in the employee's gross income; employee contributions made on a pre-tax basis; and income earned on funds invested in the retirement plan. Prior to receiving a distribution, the employee has not reported these amounts as gross income. In addition, the employee may have contributed nondeductible funds, generally referred to as contributions made on an after-tax basis. Although the employee is taxed on the initial investment, earnings attributable to these contributions also escape taxation until withdrawn from the plan. When funds are withdrawn from one of these plans, the recipient is entitled to recover his or her contributions without additional income tax. Remaining benefits are included in gross income.

* * *

Payment of benefits generally takes one of two forms: lump sum or annuity. If the employee receives the entire benefit in a lump sum, his or her gross income includes amounts received in excess of after-tax contributions. If the benefit is taken as a stream of payments, any tax-free amount is recovered on a pro rata basis.

Questions

1. Why might an employee want to receive his or her pension benefits in the form of annuity, rather than in a lump sum?

2. Read Internal Revenue Code §§ 72(a)-(d) in the statutory supplement, focusing on subsection (d). Then answer the following questions.

(a) After a distinguished career at the bar, Perry is about to retire at age 60. He has elected to receive his pension in the form of an annuity—$5000 per month—and the relevant actuarial tables suggest that he should expect to live until the age of 75. Assuming that his pension was funded purely with employer contributions, how much of each month's payment is taxable income to Perry?

(b) Would your answer change—and if so, how—if while he was working Perry had contributed $310,000 of his pre-tax earnings to his pension account?

(c) Would your answer change—and if so, how—if while he was working Perry had contributed $310,000 of his after-tax earnings to his pension account?

---

[*] Copyright © 1995. Reprinted with permission.

3. (a) Suppose the same facts as in Question 2(a) except that, instead of electing a single-life annuity, Perry instead elected a joint and 50% survivor annuity that would pay Perry $4000 per year for his life, then $2000 per year to his faithful secretary, Della, for her remaining life. When Perry retires, Della will also be 60, but her life expectancy is 80. Assuming that Perry's pension was funded purely with employer contributions, how much of each month's payment is taxable to Perry and, after his death, to Della? Would your answer change—and if so, how—if while he was working Perry had contributed $450,000 of his pre-tax earnings to his pension account?

(b) Would your answer change—and if so, how—if while he was working Perry had contributed $450,000 of his after-tax earnings to his pension account?

b. Lump Sum Distributions

Gail Levin Richmond
Taxes and the Elderly: An Introduction
19 Nova L. Rev. 587, 619 (1995)

Special rules apply to lump-sum distributions from qualified retirement plans. Without special treatment, a lump-sum distribution might be seriously depleted by income taxes assessed at federal rates as high as 39.6%, as well as any applicable state income tax. A five-year averaging provision results in treating the lump sum as if it was actually received in five taxable years. Employees born before 1936 are entitled to additional computation benefits involving a special 20% capital gains rate and a ten-year averaging election.

Internal Revenue Service
Instructions for Form 4972
[Tax on Lump-Sum Distributions] at 1-2, 4 (1998)

What is a Qualified Lump-Sum Distribution?

It is the distribution or payment in 1 tax year of a plan participant's entire balance from all of the employer's qualified plans of one kind (i.e., pension, profit-sharing, or stock bonus plans) in which the participant had funds.

* * *

In addition, the distribution must have been made after the participant reached age 59$^{1}/_{2}$.

* * *

CHAPTER 4: PLANNING FOR RETIREMENT

Distributions That Do Not Qualify for the 20% Capital Gain Election or for the 5- or 10-Year Tax Option

The following distributions are not qualified lump-sum distributions and *do not* qualify for the 20% capital gain election or the 5- or 10-year tax option:

1. Any distribution that is partially rolled over to another qualified plan or an IRA.

2. An distribution if an earlier election to use either the 5- or 10-year tax option had been made after 1986 by the same plan participant.

* * *

4. Any distribution made during the first 5 tax years that the participant was in the plan, unless it was paid because the participant died.

* * *

7. A distribution from an IRA.

8. A distribution from a tax-sheltered annuity (section 403(b) plan).

* * *

10. A distribution from a qualified pension or annuity plan when the participant or his or her surviving spouse received an eligible rollover distribution from the same plan (or another plan of the employer required to be aggregated for the lump-sum distribution rules), and the proceeds of the previous distribution were rolled over tax free to an eligible retirement plan (including an IRA).

* * *

20% capital gain election. If the plan participant was born before 1936 and there is an amount shown in Form 1099-R, box 3 [reflecting pre-1974 participation in the plan—Eds.], you can use Part II of Form 4972. You are electing to apply a 20% tax rate to the capital gain portion [meaning the portion of the lump sum distribution that reflects pre-1974 participation.—Eds.].

* * *

5- or 10-year tax option. If the plan participant was born before 1936, you can use Part III [of the form] to choose the 5- or 10-year tax option to figure your tax on the lump-sum distribution. You can choose either option whether or not you make the 20% capital gain election described earlier. . . . [Once you make the 20% capital gain election with respect to a portion of the distribution, however, the 5- or 10-year treatment can only apply to the remaining, non-capital-gain portion.—Eds.] If the plan participant was born after 1935 but the distribution was made on or after the date the participant reached age $59^1/2$, you can choose the 5-year tax option to figure your tax on the lump-sum distribution. You cannot use either the 10-year tax option or the 20% capital gain election.

Tax Rate Schedule for the 5-Year Tax Option

If the amount [of the distribution] is:		Enter [the following tax due] . . .		Of the amount over:
Over	But not over			
$-0-	$25,350		15%	-0-
25,350	61,400	$3,802.50	+28%	25,350
61,400	128,100	13,896.50	+31%	61,400
128,100	278,450	34,573.50	+36%	128,100
278,450	- - - - -	88,699.50	+39.6%	278,450

Tax Rate Schedule for the 10-Year Tax Option

If the amount [of the distribution] is:		Enter [the following tax due] . . .		Of the amount over:
Over	But not over			
-0-	1,190		1%	-0-
1,190	2,270	130.90	+12%	1,190
2,270	4,530	260.50	+14%	2,270
4,530	6,690	579.90	+15%	4,530
6,690	9,170	900.90	+16%	6,690
9,170	11,440	1,297.70	+18%	9,170

Questions

1. Why might an employee choose to receive his or her pension benefits in the form of a lump sum?

2. After an uninspiring career at the bar, Perry has decided to retire on February 1, 1999, which will be his 62nd birthday. He has decided to receive his pension benefits in a lump sum of $100,000, rather than in the form of an annuity. Assuming that 1998 tax rates are in effect for 1999 and that he will have $100,000 of other taxable income for 1999 (with only the personal exemption plus standard deduction of $6,950), how much tax will Perry owe on the lump-sum distribution?

3. What if February 1, 1999, was Perry's 66th birthday? (Assume that $90,000 of the $100,000 lump-sum payment is attributable to Perry's pre-1974 participation in the plan.)

c. Early Distributions: A Note by the Editors

The general rule is that a 10% excise (meaning "additional") tax is imposed on distributions that are made before the plan participant reaches age 59$^{1}/_{2}$. IRC § 72(t)(1), § 72(t)(2)(A)(i). This tax applies to the portion of the distribution that is includible in gross income. IRC § 72(t)(1). The "investment in the contract" is not includible, and thus is not subject to the excise tax.

There are exceptions to the general rule, meaning that there are instances in which early distributions do not attract the 10% excise tax. The most important of these exceptions are:

1. The plan participant has died before the age of 59$^{1}/_{2}$. IRC § 72(t)(2)(A)(ii).
2. The plan participant is "disabled" within the meaning of IRC § 72(m)(7). IRC § 72(t)(2)(A)(iii).
3. The distribution is in the form of an annuity. IRC § 72(t)(2)(A)(iv).
4. The participant is at least 55 years old and has stopped working for his or her employer. IRC § 72(t)(2)(A)(v).
5. The distribution is for amounts paid for medical care and does not exceed the allowable medical-expense deduction (currently 7$^{1}/_{2}$% of adjusted gross income). IRC § 72(t)(2)(B). It does not matter whether the taxpayer actually itemizes his or her deductions; the exception applies even if the taxpayer simply takes the standard deduction.
6. The recipient is receiving the payment pursuant to a qualified domestic relations order (QDRO), which is a court order relating to a divorce decree. IRC § 72(t)(2)(C).
7. The distribution is "rolled over" into another qualified plan or IRA. IRC § 72(t)(1).

d. Delayed Distributions: A Note by the Editors

As a general rule, a pension plan participant must begin receiving plan benefits, either in a lump sum or in the form of an annuity, no later than his or her "required beginning date." Failure to do so results in a 50% excise tax on the following amount: (1) the "minimum required distribution" minus (2) the actual distribution. IRC §§ 4974(a), (b) and 401(a)(9).

Thus, two definitions are important: the "required beginning date" and the "minimum required distribution."

As defined in IRC § 401(a)(9)(C), the required beginning date (RBD) for most employees is April 1 following the later of: (a) the calendar year in which the participant reaches age 70$^{1}/_{2}$ or (b) the calendar year in which the participant retires.[3]

---

[3] This option was inserted by the Small Business Job Protection Act of 1996 (P.L. 104-188). Under prior law, the required beginning date for most qualified plan participants was April 1 following the calendar year of reaching 70$^{1}/_{2}$; the possibility of later retirement only applied to participants in governmental and church pension plans. The 1996 Act extended the option to all qualified plan par-

The principal exception to this rule is that, if the participant owns more than 5% of the sponsoring employer, the RBD is April 1 following the calendar year in which the employee reaches age $70^{1}/_{2}$ (in other words, the same as what is option (a) for most employees).

As defined in IRC § 401(a)(9)(A)(ii), the minimum required distribution is the distribution necessary to ensure that the pension assets will be distributed (a) over the life of the employee; or (b) over the lives of the employee and a designated beneficiary; or (c) over a term certain not longer than the life expectancy of the employee or the life expectancy of the employee and a designated beneficiary. Think about why option (c) is drafted as it is.

On the calculation of life expectance for the purpose of determining the minimum required distribution, read the following excerpt.

> Both the Code and proposed regulations permit recomputation of the participant's, and where the designated beneficiary is the participant's spouse, such spouse's life expectancy on an annual basis. If the plan language is silent regarding recalculation, such recalculation will occur unless the participant or spouse elects otherwise. Recalculation of life expectancy is advantageous if the individual whose life expectancy is being recalculated continues to live. For example, where the payout is over the joint lives of a husband and wife, annual life expectancy recalculation will slow the decrease in the life expectancy factors, hence, increase the distribution period. However, there is a trap. If the individual whose life expectancy is being recalculated dies, the factor with respect to such individual is reduced to zero. Thus, the planner must play roulette where the maximum deferral period is sought. If the participant and spouse are in relatively good health and can be expected to outlive their life expectancies, a distribution period extending for the participant and spouse's life expectancy, as recalculated annually, might produce the longest distribution period. However, if there is a likelihood that death will occur before expiration of the life expectancies, the planner might wish to limit the distribution period to a number of years equal to the joint life expectancy of the participant and the spouse as of the required beginning date, without recalculation.

Gair Bennett Petrie, *Estate and Income Tax Planning for Retirement Plans and IRAs*, 32 IDAHO L. REV. 253, 295-96 (1996). Why might annual recalculation be a good idea? Why might it be ill-advised?

If the plan participant dies before reaching the required beginning date, then the general rule is that the benefits must be distributed by December 31 of the fifth calendar year following the year in which the participant's death occurred. IRC § 401(a)(9)(B)(ii).

---

ticipants other than those owning more than 5% of the sponsoring employer. Note that the definition of "retires" within the meaning of this subsection remains a source of ambiguity. *See* Louis A. Mezzullo, *Planning for Distributions from Qualified Retirement Plans*, TR. & EST. 36, 39 (July 1998).

Two exceptions to this rule should be noted, however. (1) If the participant has named someone *other than his or her spouse* as a designated beneficiary, then payments may be made: (a) over the life of the designated beneficiary, or (b) over a term certain not extending beyond the life expectancy of the designated beneficiary. But the payments must begin no later than December 31 of the year after the year in which the participant died. IRC § 401(a)(9)(B)(iii). (2) If the participant has named *his or her surviving spouse* as a designated beneficiary, then payments need not begin until the later of (a) December 31 of the year after the year in which the participant died, or (b) December 31 of the calendar year in which the participant would have reached 70^1/$_2$. IRC § 401(a)(9)(B)(iv).

The final point to be made concerns what happens when the participant dies after the required beginning date but before the pension assets have been fully distributed. In such a case, the remaining portion of the benefit must be distributed at least as rapidly as under the method of distribution in effect on the day of the participant's death. IRC § 401(a)(9)(B)(i)(II).

6. Rollovers

Internal Revenue Service
Pensions and Annuity Income
Publication No. 575, at 30 (1998)

A rollover is a withdrawal of cash or other assets from a qualified retirement plan or IRA that is reinvested into another qualified retirement plan or IRA. Do not include the amount rolled over in your income and do not take a deduction for it. The amount rolled over is taxable later as the new retirement plan or IRA pays that amount to you. If you roll over amounts into an IRA, subsequent distributions of these amounts from the IRA do not qualify for the capital gain treatment or 5- or 10-year tax option discussed earlier.

* * *

Eligible rollover distributions. An eligible rollover distribution is any distribution of all or any part of the balance . . . in a qualified retirement plan *except*:

1) The nontaxable part of a distribution (such as your after-tax contributions)
. . . .

2) Any of a series of substantially equal distributions paid at least once a year over: a) your lifetime or life expectancy, b) the joint lives or life expectancies of you and your beneficiary, or c) a period of 10 years or more,

3) A required minimum distribution at the required beginning date.

* * *

Withholding requirements. If an eligible rollover distribution is paid to you, the payer must withhold 20% of it. This applies even if you plan to roll over the distribution to another qualified retirement plan or to an IRA. However, you can avoid withholding by choosing the *direct rollover option*, discussed later.

* * *

Direct rollover option. You can choose to have any part or all of an eligible rollover distribution paid directly to another qualified retirement plan that accepts rollover distributions or to an IRA.

No tax withheld. If you choose the direct rollover option, no tax will be withheld from any part of the distribution that is directly paid to the trustee of the other plan. If any part of the eligible rollover distribution is paid to you, the payer must generally withhold 20% of it for income tax.

Payment to you option. If an eligible rollover distribution is paid to you, 20% generally will be withheld for income tax. However, the full amount is treated as distributed to you even though you actually receive only 80%. You must include in income any part (including the part withheld) that you do not roll over within 60 days to another qualified retirement plan or IRA.

Questions

1. What is a rollover, and under what circumstances is it permitted?

2. Which option should a taxpayer choose: the direct rollover or the "payment to you"? Why?

C. Private Savings: The Individual Retirement Account

1. Traditional and Roth IRAs

Elizabeth R. Salasko
Beyond Plain Vanilla: The New Flavors of IRAs
PROB. & PROP. 22, 22-24 (May/June 1998)[*]

An IRA is a savings vehicle that allows an individual to make contributions to an account that he or she manages. Earnings on the contributions are not subject to income tax until the individual withdraws amounts from the account. The contributions may be deductible, subject to certain income and other limitations. Individuals generally have until April 15 to make a contribution to an IRA for the previous calendar year. The Code generally limits an individual's contribution to $2,000 per year and imposes an excise tax of 6% on excess contributions. Withdrawals before age $59^{1}/_{2}$ generally trigger an excise tax of 10% of the withdrawn amount, which is in

---

[*] Copyright © 1988 by the American Bar Association. Reprinted by permission.

addition to the income tax payable on the withdrawn amount. Mandatory distributions generally begin after the individual reaches age 70^1/$_2$.

* * *

Traditional IRAs

Contributions. Before TRA 97, a taxpayer could contribute an amount equal to his or her earned income, up to $2,000 per year, to a traditional IRA. Code § 408(a)(1). If neither the taxpayer nor his or her spouse participated in a qualified retirement plan, the taxpayer could deduct the full $2,000. If the taxpayer or his or her spouse participated in a qualified plan, the taxpayer could deduct the contribution only if the taxpayer's adjusted gross income (AGI) did not exceed certain limits.

Limits on Deductibility. Before TRA 97, Congress phased out the deductibility of IRA contributions at relatively low AGI levels. For married taxpayers filing jointly, if one or both spouses participated in a qualified plan, the couple could deduct an IRA contribution only if the couple's AGI was less than $40,000. Congress ratably reduced the deduction if the couple's AGI was $40,000-50,000 and eliminated the deduction for couples with AGIs above $50,000. A single taxpayer who participated in a qualified plan could deduct an IRA contribution only if the taxpayer's AGI was below $25,000. Congress phased out the deduction for such single taxpayers with AGI between $25,000 and $35,000 and eliminated the deduction if the taxpayer had an AGI above $35,000. Code § 219(g).

TRA 97 changed the rules regarding participation by a spouse in a qualified plan and the phaseout limits for deductibility of IRA contributions. Both changes will make deductible IRAs more widely available to taxpayers. Under TRA 97, a spouse's participation in a qualified plan does not count against a nonparticipating spouse, for whom an IRA contribution is now fully deductible, as long as the couple's AGI does not exceed $150,000. Congress phased out the deduction for couples with AGIs between $150,000 and $160,000 and eliminated the deduction for couples with AGIs above $160,000.[1]

For married or single taxpayers who participate in a qualified plan, the phaseout range for single taxpayers is now $30,000-40,000 and is $50,000-60,000 for married taxpayers. The phaseout range for single taxpayers will increase each year until 2005, when it will be $50,000-60,000. For married taxpayers, the phaseout range will increase each year until 2007, when the range will be $80,000-100,000.

The following example illustrates the foregoing rules. Abigail is a participant in a qualified plan. Benjamin, her husband, does not participate in a qualified plan. Their AGI for 1997 was $140,000. Before TRA 97, neither Abigail nor Benjamin could make a deductible IRA contribution because their combined AGI exceeded the 1997 phaseout limit of $50,000. Assume that Abigail and Benjamin again have an AGI of $140,000 for 1998. Abigail may not make a deductible IRA contribution

---

[1] [Note that these amounts apply only to married taxpayers filing jointly. For married individuals filing separately, the deduction is phased out between $0 and $10,000 of AGI. *See* JOINT COMMITTEE ON TAXATION, GENERAL EXPLANATION OF TAX LEGISLATION ENACTED IN 1998 161 (1998).—Eds.]

because she is a participant in a qualified plan and their joint AGI exceeds the 1998 phaseout limit of $60,000. Benjamin, however, may make a $2,000 deductible IRA contribution because he is not a participant in a qualified plan and their joint AGI is below the $150,000 limit. If Abigail and Benjamin's AGI increases to $250,000 in 1999, neither of them may make a deductible IRA contribution because their joint AGI will exceed $160,000.

Withdrawals. Withdrawals from a traditional IRA before the IRA owner attains age 59$^{1}/_{2}$ generally result in a 10% penalty. Code § 72(t)(1). Before TRA 97 the penalty did not apply to certain withdrawals, such as withdrawals following the death or disability of the IRA owner or for the payment of medical expenses or health insurance premiums for unemployed individuals. Code § 72(t)(2). TRA 97 added two more exceptions to the penalty rules for withdrawals for certain higher education expenses and first-time homebuyer expenses.[2]

Withdrawals to fund higher education. No penalties will apply to withdrawals if the taxpayer uses the withdrawn amounts to pay for certain higher education expenses for the taxpayer, the taxpayer's spouse or the taxpayer's or spouse's children or grandchildren. Code § 72(t)(2)(E)(7). Qualified expenses include tuition, room and board, fees, books, supplies and equipment required for enrollment or attendance at qualified post-secondary eligible educational institutions (including graduate courses). The Code does not limit the amount of the withdrawals a taxpayer may make for qualified higher education expenses, although a taxpayer cannot use withdrawals to pay expenses for which the taxpayer takes a Hope Scholarship credit.

The Hope Scholarship credit is available only to students who cannot be claimed as a dependent by another taxpayer. Congress limited the Hope credit to $1,500 per year (100% of the first $1,000 plus 50% of the next $1,000 of qualified tuition paid) during a taxpayer's first and second year of post-secondary education. Code § 25A(b). Congress phased out the Hope credit for single taxpayers with AGIs between $40,000 and $50,000 and for married taxpayers filing jointly with AGIs between $80,000 and $90,000. Code § 25A(d).

Although penalties will not apply, withdrawals from an IRA to fund higher education will be taxable. Accordingly, relying on withdrawals from a traditional IRA to fund higher education may be less appealing than a loan from a 401(k) or other qualified plan that permits plan loans. A loan generally results in no income tax or penalty tax consequences, although the participant must usually repay a loan from a qualified plan over five years. By contrast, the taxpayer need not repay an IRA withdrawal.

Withdrawals to fund first-time homebuyer expenses. A taxpayer may now make penalty-free withdrawals from a traditional IRA to finance up to $10,000 of "qualified first-time homebuyer expenses." Code § 72(t)(2)(F). The first-time homebuyer may be the taxpayer, his or her spouse or a child, grandchild or ancestor of the taxpayer or spouse. The taxpayer must use the withdrawn funds within 120 days to pay "qualified acquisition expenses" for his or her principal residence, including a down payment, construction costs, mortgage financing expenses (e.g., points) and other

---

[2] [Note that these exceptions apply only to early withdrawals from IRAs, not to early withdrawals from qualified pension plans.—Eds.]

closing costs. Code § 72(t)(8). The "first-time" requirement is not what it seems. TRA 97 defines a first-time homebuyer as any taxpayer who has not had an ownership interest (severally or jointly with his or her current spouse) in a principal residence for the two year period before signing a purchase agreement or beginning construction of a new home. As under prior law, amounts withdrawn are taxable as ordinary income.

Nondeductible IRAs

Taxpayers who cannot take full advantage of deductible contributions to traditional IRAs because of participation in qualified retirement plans or AGI limitations may nevertheless make nondeductible contributions to IRAs. These contributions may not exceed earned income up to $2,000 per year less any contributions made to traditional or Roth IRAs (described below). Code § 408(o). Distributions of earnings are taxable and subject to a 10% penalty under the same rules that govern traditional IRAs. Distributions of previously taxed contributions are tax free. Code §§ 72, 408(d). TRA 97 changed none of these provisions.

Jolie Howard
The Roth IRA: A Viable Savings Vehicle for Americans?
35 HOUS. L. REV. 1269, 1279-81, 1283-84 (1998)[*]

The 1997 [Taxpayer Relief] Act created a new IRA vehicle named for the Senator who introduced it. The Roth IRA differs from the traditional IRA in that contributions made to it are nondeductible. However, income generated in the Roth IRA will build up tax-free similar to the traditional IRA, but unlike the traditional IRA, distributions from the Roth IRA are tax-exempt.

Qualified individuals may make a maximum annual contribution of $2,000 to a Roth IRA. The amount of the contribution allowed is reduced by any deductible contributions made to other types of IRAs for the applicable tax year. Although the taxpayer may not take a deduction for the contribution, the incentive for contributing to this type of IRA is two-fold. First, the earnings in the account can accumulate tax-free; second, any qualified distributions will not be included in the taxpayer's income. A husband and wife can each contribute up to $2,000 to a Roth IRA provided that the combined compensation of the couple is equal to at least the total contributed amount. An individual may continue to make contributions to a Roth IRA account even after he or she reaches age $70^1/_2$.

Like the traditional IRA, the ability to make contributions to a Roth IRA is subject to limitations based on one's AGI. However, the income phase-out levels are much higher for the Roth IRA than for the traditional IRA. The available contribution limit for the Roth IRA begins to phase-out ratably for single taxpayers with an AGI of $95,000 and for married taxpayers filing jointly with an AGI of $150,000.

---

[*] Copyright © 1998. Reprinted with permission.

Qualified distributions from Roth IRA accounts are not includible in gross income, nor subject to the ten percent penalty on early withdrawals. To reach qualified status, however, an individual may not take a distribution within the first five years of the account's creation. A qualified distribution is one made: after the taxpayer reaches age $59^{1}/_{2}$; at the death of the individual; due to the individual's disability; or for a qualified special purpose. A qualified special purpose pertains to the first-time homebuyer exception mentioned above. All other distributions are includible in income to the extent the distribution is attributable to earnings in the account and, therefore, are subject to the ten percent early withdrawal penalty unless an exception applies.

* * *

The main difference between the two IRAs is the timing of the tax benefit to the individual. With a traditional IRA, the taxpayer receives the benefit up-front with a tax deduction for the contribution, accumulates income tax-free, and pays taxes on the distributions when taken at retirement. In contrast, with the Roth IRA, the taxpayer does not receive a tax deduction when the contribution is made, but still accumulates tax-free income, and does not pay taxes when distributions are taken.

One important distinction between the two IRAs is that although Congress raised the level of income eligibility for individuals with respect to the traditional IRA, the income ceilings for the Roth IRA are much higher. For higher income individuals, therefore, "the new Roth IRA wins hands down." Another important distinction between the two IRAs is that the Roth IRA, unlike the traditional IRA, has "no required beginning date for distributions." An individual can open a Roth IRA even after he reaches age $70^{1}/_{2}$ and can leave the money in the account, untouched, until he dies.

* * *

An individual also must consider the amount of the taxpayer's contributions, the return on IRA investment, and his or her current and future tax status. With the Roth IRA, a taxpayer effectively locks in his or her tax rate, meaning that he or she knows the amount of taxes to be paid in the year in which the contribution is made. With the traditional IRA, the individual is betting that the tax rate will be lower after retirement so that he or she receives a benefit by taking the deduction up-front and paying taxes in the future. If the taxpayer's rate increases at the time of retirement, he or she will, in effect, pay more taxes with the traditional IRA because he or she pays the tax when distributions are taken during retirement.

Questions

1. What are the principal differences between traditional and Roth IRAs?
2. For which taxpayers is the Roth IRA a good investment?

2. Education IRAs

Elizabeth R. Salasko
Beyond Plain Vanilla: The New Flavors of IRAs
PROB. & PROP. 22, 26-27 (May/June 1998)[*]

TRA 97 created a new tax deferred savings vehicle for funding higher education for individuals under age 18, the "Education IRA." Though called an IRA, an Education IRA is not technically an individual retirement account within the meaning of Code § 7701(a)(37).

Contributions. Married taxpayers with "modified" AGIs below $150,000 and single taxpayers with modified AGIs below $95,000 may contribute up to $500 per beneficiary to an Education IRA. Modified AGI is adjusted gross income increased by certain excludable non-U.S. income. Code § 530(c) phases out contributions in the same manner as for the Roth IRA. An individual may be a beneficiary of multiple Education IRAs, and beneficiaries need not be dependents of or related to the contributors. The IRS is taking the position, however, that the total contribution per beneficiary per year cannot exceed $500. Contributions, which are not tax deductible, are in addition to the $2,000 combined limit for traditional, nondeductible and Roth IRAs. Contributions will qualify for the $10,000 per donee annual gift tax exclusion under Code § 2503(b), though not for the educational expense exclusion of Code § 2503(e). See Code §§ 530(d)(3), 529(c)(2). A taxpayer may not make contributions to an Education IRA in any amount in the same year that the taxpayer contributes to a Code § 529 qualified state tuition program. Contributions in excess of the allowable limit are subject to a 6% excise tax unless returned, with earnings, before filing of the contributor's tax return. Code § 4973(a).

Withdrawals. A beneficiary of an Education IRA may withdraw contributions from the IRA tax free. A withdrawal of earnings from the Education IRA will be tax free to the extent that the beneficiary uses the withdrawn amounts to pay for post-secondary education expenses. Qualified expenses include tuition, books, supplies for students enrolled at least half-time and the minimum room and board allowance applicable for a full-time student as determined by the institution under guidelines for determining financial aid. Code § 530(b)(2)(A) reduces qualified education expenses by nontaxable scholarships, fellowship grants and educational assistance allowances.

A taxpayer cannot take either a Hope Scholarship credit or a Lifetime Learning credit in a year in which the taxpayer makes withdrawals from an Education IRA. Code § 25A(e). The Lifetime Learning credit is available to students who are not claimed as dependents by another taxpayer and is equal to 20% of up to $5,000 in qualifying post-secondary education, including graduate courses, after June 30, 1998. The $5,000 limit increases to $10,000 in 2003. Code § 25A(c). The Lifetime Learning credit phases out for single taxpayers with AGIs between $40,000 and $50,000 and $80,000 and $90,000 for married taxpayers filing jointly. Code § 25A(d).

---

[*] Copyright © 1998 by the American Bar Association. Reprinted with permission.

To the extent the amounts withdrawn from an Education IRA exceed qualified education expenses, a pro rata share of the earnings will be taxable to the beneficiary and a 10% penalty will apply to the taxable amount (unless made on account of death or disability). Code § 530(d)(2), (4).

When the beneficiary of an Education IRA reaches age 30, he or she may roll over unused assets within 60 days to an Education IRA for another member of the beneficiary's family. Code §§ 530(d)(5), 529(e)(2), 2032A(e)(2). . . .

To the extent that the new beneficiary is in the same generation as the prior designated beneficiary, the rollover will have no gift tax consequences. If the new beneficiary is a generation below the first beneficiary, the transfer will be a taxable gift, although the annual exclusion will apply. Code §§ 530(d)(3), 529(c). Funds may also be rolled over before age 30 to another member of the beneficiary's family, but no more than once in a 12 month period. A named beneficiary may be redesignated at any time to a different member of the named beneficiary's family without tax consequences. Code § 530(d)(5), (6). Funds remaining in an Education IRA when the beneficiary reaches age 30 must be distributed to the beneficiary as taxable income subject to a 10% penalty.

If a beneficiary dies before age 30 with assets still in an Education IRA, his or her gross estate will include the remaining assets. Code § 530(b)(1)(E). Earnings accumulated in an Education IRA at death are not subject to the 10% penalty. A disabled beneficiary may withdraw assets from an Education IRA without a penalty tax. Code § 530(d)(4). An Education IRA may be transferred to a spouse or former spouse under the terms of a divorce decree without tax consequences. Like traditional IRAs, if a taxpayer uses an Education IRA as security for a loan, Code § 408(e)(4) treats the amount used as security as a taxable distribution. Code § 408(e)(4).

Questions

1. Why is the Education IRA not technically an IRA?
2. For which taxpayers is the Education IRA a good investment?

FURTHER READING. ALISON BARNES ET AL., COUNSELING OLDER CLIENTS ch. 6 (1997); LOUIS A. MEZZULLO, AN ESTATE PLANNER'S GUIDE TO QUALIFIED RETIREMENT PLAN BENEFITS (2d ed. 1998); PETER J. STRAUSS & NANCY M. LEDERMAN, THE ELDER LAW HANDBOOK, ch. 17 (1996); PETER J. STRAUSS ET AL., AGING AND THE LAW, ch. 7 (1996).

CHAPTER 5

Property Management

A. Powers of Attorney 209
B. Joint Ownership and Joint Accounts 229
C. Agency Accounts 234
D. Revocable Inter Vivos Trusts 236
E. Custodial Trusts under the Uniform Custodial Trust Act 254

This chapter examines the principal mechanisms—short of guardianship, which is discussed in Chapter 6—for managing the property of elderly persons who are not entirely able to handle their own affairs. These mechanisms are, in order of presentation: powers of attorney; joint ownership (including joint bank accounts); agency accounts; revocable inter vivos trusts; and custodial trusts under the Uniform Custodial Trust Act.

Each of these arrangements has its advantages and disadvantages. As you read the material in each section, try to imagine the circumstances for which the particular arrangement under discussion would be best suited.

A. Powers of Attorney

1. Background

Carolyn L. Dessin
Acting as Agent Under a Financial Durable Power of Attorney:
An Unscripted Role
75 Neb. L. Rev. 574, 576-81 (1996)[*]

A power of attorney is an instrument by which a principal empowers an agent to act on the principal's behalf. At common law, a power of attorney was revoked by the incompetency or incapacity of the principal. Thus, having a power of attorney provided no protection from the difficulties of becoming incompetent or incapacitated

---

[*] Copyright © 1996. Reprinted with permission.

because the power of attorney would cease to be effective at the exact moment that the principal needed it most.

The notion of durability had its genesis in this deficiency of a common-law power of attorney. Two approaches to durability are possible: 1) a power of attorney can be immediately effective and survive the incapacity of the principal (the "immediately effective" power) or 2) the power of attorney can become effective only when the principal becomes incapacitated (the "springing" power).

In 1954, Virginia enacted the first statute that allowed an agent to continue to act as empowered by a power of attorney even after the principal became disabled, incompetent, or incapacitated. Ten years later, the National Conference of Commissioners on Uniform State Laws promulgated the Model Special Power of Attorney for Small Property Interests Act ("the 1964 Act"). The 1964 Act was designed to be a less expensive alternative to guardianship or conservatorship proceedings. Designed to be used only in situations involving limited assets, the act was fairly comprehensive, and included a number of safeguards. For example, the Act required that powers executed under it had to be approved by a judge of a court of record to be valid. Interestingly, the 1964 Act offered three standards relating to the liability of the agent. Alternative one made the agent liable only in the case of "intentional wrongdoing, [gross negligence], or fraud." The second alternative held the uncompensated agent liable only for "intentional wrongdoing, gross negligence, or fraud" but held the compensated agent to the standard applied to other fiduciaries. Alternative three held all agents to the standard applied to other fiduciaries. The three alternatives were the result of a divergence of opinion among the Commissioners on Uniform State Laws. Originally, the drafting committee suggested the lowest standard, alternative one, because they thought that small amounts of assets would be involved and relatives or close friends would be serving as agents "without compensation and as a labor of love." The 1964 Act received limited acceptance, although a number of states may have borrowed provisions from it to use in enactments of the later Uniform Probate Code or Uniform Durable Power of Attorney Act.

When the National Conference of Commissioners on Uniform State Laws approved and promulgated the Uniform Probate Code ("U.P.C.") in 1969, it included sections 5-501 and 5-502. These sections provided that the authority of an agent to act under a power of attorney could continue beyond the incompetence of the principal. In addition to the idea of durability, the U.P.C. altered the common-law rule that the death of the principal ended the authority of an agent under a durable power of attorney and voided any acts performed by the agent after the death. After the promulgation of the U.P.C., the durable power of attorney gained rapid acceptance.

In 1979, the National Conference amended and expanded the sections of the U.P.C. dealing with durable powers of attorney and approved the Uniform Durable Power of Attorney Act ("U.D.P.A.A."), a free-standing act paralleling the language of and designed to act as an alternative to sections 5-501 to 5-505 of the U.P.C. All fifty states and the District of Columbia have enacted statutes authorizing durability of powers. Thus, the financial durable power of attorney is an available planning tool throughout the United States. . . .

In most states, the principal must express the intention that the power be durable. It is possible, however, that even an instrument that does not contain an express durability provision can be interpreted to create a durable power of attorney.

Question

Examine, in the statutory supplement, the Illinois short form power of attorney (755 Illinois Compiled Statutes 45/3-3). What makes this a *durable* power?

2. Preparing the Power: The Use of Statutory Forms

Many states have a statutory power-of-attorney form. This means that the form has been approved by the state government and that a copy of it can be found in the state's legislative code. Lawyers drafting powers of attorney in these states must be attentive to whether the statutory form is presented merely as a model, or whether substantially the same language must be used. In either case, tracking the language of the statutory form (to the extent that it reflects the wishes of the particular principal) will ensure a document's validity.

To answer the following questions, read in the statutory supplement: (a) Oklahoma Statutes Annotated 15 §§ 1003 and 1019; and (b) New Mexico Statutes Annotated §§ 45-5-602 and 45-5-617.

Questions

Is the statutory form in Oklahoma merely a suggested model, or should all forms track the language of the statute? What about the statutory form in New Mexico?

3. Capacity to Execute or Revoke

Carolyn L. Dessin
Acting as Agent Under a Financial Durable Power of Attorney:
An Unscripted Role
75 NEB. L. REV. 574, 581 (1996)[*]

Although the durable power of attorney is designed to survive the incompetency of the principal, the principal must, of course, be competent when he executes the durable power of attorney for the power to be valid. Further, if a person loses competency, he or she cannot revoke a durable power of attorney while incompetent.

---

[*] Copyright © 1996. Reprinted with permission.

In re Guardianship of Ray
No. 657, 1991 Ohio App. LEXIS 4308, at *11 (September 16, 1991)

The creation of a power of attorney requires that the principal be mentally competent at the time the power is executed. Derived from contracts law, the test to be used to determine mental capacity is the ability of the principal to understand the nature, scope and the extent of the business she is about to transact.

In re Rick
C.M. No. 6920, 1994 Del. Ch. LEXIS 49, at *14 (March 23, 1994)

On the question of [the principal's] capacity to execute the 1993 power of attorney, the parties refer to the legal standards for evaluating a claim of lack of testamentary capacity. . . . The standard is that one who makes a will must, at the time of execution, be capable of exercising thought, reflection and judgment, and must know what he or she is doing and how he or she is disposing of his or her property. The person must also possess sufficient memory and understanding to comprehend the nature and character of the act.

Hilbert v. Benson
917 P.2d 1152, 1156 (Wyo. 1996)

In comparing the governing standards of testamentary capacity for executing wills and of contractual capacity for executing inter vivos conveyances, we agree . . . that a higher degree of mental capacity is required to execute an inter vivos conveyance or contract or to transact business generally, than is required in executing a will.

Restatement (Second) of Property (Donative Transfers)
§ 34.5(1)-(4) and comment*

§ 34.5 *Donor Mentally Incompetent*

(1) A mentally incompetent person cannot make a valid will or a valid inter vivos donative transfer.

(2) The legal guardian of a mentally incompetent person may make valid inter vivos donative transfers of the incompetent's property only to the extent authorized by a court.

(3) A person before becoming mentally incompetent may give another person a power of attorney to act for him or her during any incompetency, including the power to make inter vivos donative transfers.

---

* Copyright © American Law Institute. Reprinted with permission.

(4) A person before becoming mentally incompetent may transfer property to a trustee to hold in trust with an authorization to the trustee to make valid inter vivos donative transfers of the trust property in the event of the incompetency of the creator of the trust. Such authorized donative transfers cannot be prevented by a legal guardian or any other representative of the mentally incompetent person.

(5) A trustee to whom property is transferred by another for the benefit of a person who is or becomes mentally incompetent may be authorized by the trust instrument to make inter vivos donative transfers of the trust property to others. Such authorized donative transfers cannot be prevented by a legal guardian or any other representative of the mentally incompetent person.

Comment on Subsection (1):

a. *Who is mentally incompetent.* A person is mentally incompetent to make a donative transfer if such person is unable to understand fully the significance of such transfer in relation to such person's own situation. Stated another way, to be mentally competent a person must know and understand the extent of his or her property, comprehend to whom he or she is giving his or her property, and know the natural objects of his or her bounty. A slightly different statement of what constitutes mental capacity is that the person must understand the nature and extent of his or her property, know and recall the natural objects of his or her property, and be able to determine and understand how he or she wishes to dispose of his or her property.

A person who is mentally incompetent part of the time but who has lucid intervals during which he or she comprehends fully the significance of a donative transfer can, in the absence of an adjudication or statute that has contrary effect, make a valid will or a valid inter vivos donative transfer, provided such will or transfer is made during a lucid interval.

Questions

1. Is the required level of capacity for executing a durable power of attorney the same as for executing a contract? For executing a will?

2. What level(s) of capacity *should* be required for these actions?

4. Formalities of Execution

Carolyn L. Dessin
Acting as Agent Under a Financial Durable Power of Attorney:
An Unscripted Role
75 NEB. L. REV. 574, 581-82 (1996)[*]

With respect to execution formalities, durable powers of attorney are generally easier to execute than wills. Typically, the only execution requirements are that the

---

[*] Copyright © 1996. Reprinted with permission.

power be in writing and signed by the principal. A few states impose additional execution requirements, none of which are particularly oppressive.

William M. McGovern, Jr.
Trusts, Custodianships, and Durable Powers of Attorney
27 REAL PROP., PROB. & TR. J. 21 (1992)[*]

UPC section 5-501 requires only that durable powers be "in writing," meaning that even an unsigned writing will suffice. However, some states require durable powers to be signed and witnessed like a will, and others require the same formalities as for a deed.

In California, a printed form durable power sold "for use by a person who does not have the advice of legal counsel" must contain a warning that states: "This is an important legal document. . . . If there is anything about this form that you do not understand, you should ask a lawyer to explain it to you."

Question

Examine the Illinois short form power of attorney in the statutory supplement, 755 Illinois Compiled Statutes 45 § 3-3. What formalities are required for its execution?

5. Taking Effect: The Special Case of the Springing Power

Marc S. Beckerman
Practice Considerations in Estate and Disability Planning
PROB. & PROP. 62, 63 (May/June 1998)[**]

If the power does not take effect immediately, it is a "springing" power, and the client and the drafting lawyer must determine what events will make the power effective. Local law may propose or require language to establish this effectiveness. In New York, for instance, the statutory form of springing power of attorney allows the client to define the event that activates the power and allows the client to name specific persons to certify that such an event has occurred. Similarly, California law provides that a person executing a springing power of attorney "may designate one or more persons who, by a written declaration under penalty of perjury, have the power to determine conclusively that the specified event or contingency has occurred."

---

[*] Copyright © 1992 American Bar Association. Reprinted by permission.
[**] Copyright © 1998 by the American Bar Association. Reprinted with permission.

Ramona C. Rains
Planning Tools Available to the Elderly Client
19 AM. J. TRIAL ADVOCACY 599, 604-05 (1996)*

Another problem associated with the springing durable power of attorney is the difficulty inherent in determining when a person has become incapacitated. If it becomes necessary to have a court determine the mental capacity of the principal, part of the benefit of the durable power of attorney over conservatorship proceedings will be defeated. Some commentators suggest designating an attorney or relative to decide whether the individual has become incapacitated, thus triggering the springing durable power of attorney. Another technique is to state in the durable power of attorney that the agent's affidavit will serve as conclusive proof that the springing durable power of attorney has been triggered. If the client is concerned that the agent will abuse the durable power of attorney, the attorney may want to advise his client to choose another agent. Not all states recognize the springing durable power of attorney [here, the author cites the law of South Carolina—Eds.], thus, the attorney should be aware of the current law in the jurisdiction in which he practices.

Questions

1. Examine the Illinois short form power of attorney in the statutory supplement. How would you use this form to create a springing power? What events might be used to trigger the power, and what language would you use to describe these events?

2. Now evaluate your proposed language. How likely is it that what you have drafted will lead to litigation?

6. Scope of the Power

Carolyn L. Dessin
Acting as Agent Under a Financial Durable Power of Attorney:
An Unscripted Role
75 NEB. L. REV. 574, 582-83 (1996)**

With respect to breadth of powers, there are a few restrictions on the acts that can be delegated to agents under durable powers of attorney. The restrictions may come from statutes, common law, public policy limitations, or contract provisions that curtail the delegation of duties or assignment of rights. Although few courts have considered the limits of delegability, the existing decisions suggest that the range of nondelegable acts is fairly narrow. Even if a restriction exists, its validity might be subject to challenge. Thus, the breadth of a durable power is virtually limitless.

---

* Copyright © 1996. Reprinted by permission
** Copyright © 1996. Reprinted with permission.

Additionally, a court has fairly limited supervisory power over an agent under a durable power of attorney. Court approval for the agent's acts is generally not required.

Daniel S. Brennan
*Durable Power of Attorney:
An Ethical Option When Planning for Elderly Clients*
3 GEO. J. LEGAL ETHICS 751, 755 (1990)[*]

The scope of the durable power of attorney is restricted only by the intent of the principal. The document may be broad and sweeping, or it may confer limited powers. To avoid potential disputes regarding the breadth of the durable power of attorney, it may be advisable to include specific grants of authority in the document. Among the powers that should be considered are: power of access to safe deposit boxes, ability to sign tax returns, the power to settle tax disputes, the power to deal with retirement plans, the power to fund inter-vivos trusts, the power to deal with life insurance, the power to borrow money, and the power to settle or pursue litigation on behalf of the principal. Because the durable power of attorney may potentially encompass many powers, the lawyer drafting the document should take special care to explain to the elderly client the exact duties that are being conferred. The lawyer should be especially aware of the fears and concerns of the elderly client who may be particularly suspicious about the loss of control.

Mallory v. Mallory
450 N.Y.S.2d 272, 273-74 (1982)

The plaintiff and the defendant were married on August 16, 1959. On February 29, 1980, a default judgment of divorce was granted against the defendant [Elizabeth Mallory] and in favor of the plaintiff [Shelton Mallory]. Thereafter, by order dated April 7, 1981, the default judgment was vacated upon the consent of the attorneys for both parties. It is this order, vacating the default, which Ethel Aikens, the movant, seeks to vacate. In support of this motion, Ms. Aikens attaches a copy of a general statutory short form power of attorney executed by the plaintiff on March 8, 1980, naming her as plaintiff's attorney in fact.

* * *

A careful examination of the affidavits in support of the motion makes it clear that the relief requested could not ultimately be granted to the movant under any circumstances. In making its determination, the court is convinced that Ethel Aikens lacks standing to bring this application. The fact that the movant possesses a power

---

[*] Reprinted with permission of the publisher, Georgetown University and Georgetown Journal of Legal Ethics © 1990.

of attorney is of no assistance to her. It appears that on this motion Ethel Aikens is relying on the portion of the power which gives the donee the power to act in "all other matters." This, however, does not give the donee carte blanche.

* * *

While a principal might very well be bound by the acts of his agent if the agent were to purchase a car on behalf of the principal, or if the agent were to sell certain goods on behalf of the principal, such is not the case where an agent seeks to obtain a divorce for the principal.

Questions

1. What powers are given to agents under the Illinois short form power of attorney in the statutory supplement? If an Illinois resident wanted to create a power of attorney that was more restrictive, how would he or she accomplish this?

2. Why are agents prevented from exercising powers of the kind described in *Mallory*?

7. Gift-Giving: A Potential Tax Trap

In connection with the following excerpts, read Internal Revenue Code §§ 2511 and 2038(a)(1) in the statutory supplement.

Hans A. Lapping
License to Steal: Implied Gift-Giving Authority and Powers of Attorney
4 ELDER L.J. 143, 143-46 (1996)[*]

As America ages, more people are realizing that they may some day need assistance with their financial affairs should they become incapacitated. Consequently, attorneys are increasingly being called upon by their clients to draft powers of attorney as part of the elderly person's estate plans. Often these general powers authorize the attorney-in-fact to do everything the principal could do if personally present and capable of acting.

In addition to the implementation of a power-of-attorney, prudent estate planning frequently involves a program of estate reduction by making gifts within the limit of the annual $10,000 per donee gift tax exclusion. This gift-giving technique used in estate planning is common and is contemplated by the Internal Revenue Code (Code).

Because these two approaches to estate planning often intersect, it becomes advisable for an attorney-in-fact to make gifts of the principal's assets by taking

---

[*] Reprinted by permission. Copyright to the *Elder Law Journal* is held by the Board of Trustees of the University of Illinois.

advantage of the annual gift tax exclusion. Despite the fact that a general grant of power-of-attorney would seemingly include the ability to make gifts, the Internal Revenue Service (IRS or Service) has consistently challenged the authority of those attorneys-in-fact who attempt to make gifts by arguing that the agents are acting ultra vires. According to the IRS, because the attorney-in-fact is acting without authority, the gifts are actually "revocable transfers" and, consequently, are includable in the decedent's estate. Although most courts have agreed with the IRS's position, several recent Tax Court and court of appeals decisions have interpreted broad grants of power to include the authority to make gifts. Furthermore, both Alabama and Virginia have enacted legislation that specifically recognizes that a general grant of power to an attorney-in-fact includes implied authority to make gifts, thereby denying the IRS the ability to challenge powers-of-attorney on this ground in these two states.

Estate of Rosa B. Neff v. Commissioner of Internal Revenue
73 T.C.M. (CCH) 2606 (1997)

VASQUEZ, Judge:

Respondent determined a deficiency in petitioner's Federal estate tax in the amount of $61,381.... The sole issue for decision is whether transfers of decedent's property shortly before her death were incomplete gifts, the value of which should be included in her estate....

Findings of Fact

Rosa B. Neff (decedent) died on September 13, 1992, at the age of 97. Decedent was a resident of Keyes, Oklahoma, most of her adult life and at the time of her death. Decedent executed her last will and testament on January 18, 1980.

A Federal estate tax return was filed on behalf of petitioner on June 9, 1993. The Federal estate tax return was signed by Chris Hunt, the estate's executor. On May 1, 1993, a Federal gift tax return for the 1992 tax year was filed on behalf of the estate by Chris Hunt.

The 1992 Federal gift tax return showed gifts to 19 relatives of decedent made on August 27 or 28 or September 12, 1992. These gifts included 19 separate annuities, 3 Series E bonds, and $4,000 in cash, with a total reported value of $293,249. The estate claimed nineteen $10,000 exclusions under section 2503(b), in the total amount of $190,000, resulting in a net taxable gift of $103,249. After the gifts in issue were made, the total gross estate, as reported on the estate tax return, exceeded $973,000.

Rosa Neff purchased the 19 separate annuities in 1987 from Delta Life and Annuity Co. (Delta Life). The 19 annuitants were decedent's nephews and nieces, a sister-in-law, and a former brother-in-law (Chris Hunt). On each of the annuities, decedent was listed as the owner, and the annuitant was listed as the contingent owner. The contingent owner would become the owner at the death of decedent. Jess Murphy was the selling agent on behalf of Delta Life with respect to the 19 annuities. The 19 annuities were transferred to their respective "annuitants" on or about August

27, 1992, according to the schedules attached to the Federal estate and gift tax returns. The three Series E bonds were transferred on August 28, 1992. The $4,000 in cash was transferred on September 12, 1992.

These gifts of annuities, bonds, and cash were executed by Chris Hunt, Melvin Hammontree, and Mildred Williams, who at the time jointly held a durable power of attorney on behalf of decedent. Mr. Hunt, Mr. Hammontree, and Ms. Williams were each recipients of one of the annuities in issue. The durable power of attorney contained broad grants of authority which stated, inter alia:

> My attorneys-in-fact shall have all of the powers, discretions, elections, and authorities granted by statute, common law, and under any rule of court.
>
> * * *
>
> My attorneys-in-fact may sell, convey, lease, exchange, mortgage, pledge, release, hypothecate, or otherwise deal with, dispose of, exchange, or encumber any of my property, either real or personal.
>
> * * *
>
> My attorneys-in-fact may act in all matters with respect to all powers described herein as freely, fully, and effectively as I could or might do personally if present and of sound and disposing mind.

The power of attorney did not, however, contain an explicit grant of gift-giving authority. Decedent executed the durable power of attorney by her own hand on July 17, 1992, and her signature was notarized. Prior to initiating the transfer of the 19 annuities, Mr. Murphy consulted the attorney who had drafted the durable power of attorney regarding whether the attorneys in fact had the power to make the transfers under the durable power of attorney. Mr. Murphy was told that the attorneys in fact did have the power to make such transfers.

The Rosa Neff Living Trust (the trust), a revocable trust, was created on August 27, 1992, by Mr. Hunt, Mr. Hammontree, and Ms. Williams, acting as decedent's attorneys in fact. Decedent did not personally sign the trust documents; they were executed by her attorneys in fact on August 27, 1992. Decedent's property was distributed according to the provisions of the trust rather than the provisions of decedent's will.

During the period August 16 through September 1, 1992, decedent was hospitalized due to a fall which resulted in a broken hip. On September 1, 1992, decedent returned to her home, where she was under the care of home health care nurses and family members until her death on September 13, 1992. Decedent died of acute heart failure as a result of chronic cardiovascular hypertensive disease and bronchitis from which she had suffered for approximately 10 years. Decedent's death was not unexpected.

Rosa Neff did not file any Federal gift tax returns during the 10-year period preceding her death in 1992. The only gifts made by Rosa Neff to relatives during this 10-year period which can be shown by documents bearing her signature are checks of small amounts, with respect to which gift tax returns were not required to be filed. Decedent also made several gifts of bonds and certificates of deposit during the 10-year period preceding her death, the amounts of which did not require the filing of Federal gift tax returns. Decedent was mentally competent to manage her affairs at all times.

Decedent was concerned about retaining control of her property at the time that she was considering executing a power of attorney. Decedent was present when the power of attorney was discussed with the attorney who drafted the document. Decedent was capable of signing her name in spite of failing eyesight if directed where to sign.

Prior to her injury and hospitalization, decedent informed several individuals that she was considering making a gift of the 19 annuities. Sometime during the summer of 1992, decedent told Betty Aaron, her accountant, that she was considering giving the annuities to the respective annuitants presently rather than after her death. Decedent also talked to Mr. Murphy about the possibility of giving the annuities to the annuitants. Prior to meeting with the attorney regarding the drafting of a durable power of attorney, decedent indicated to Chris Hunt that she wanted to give the 19 annuities to the annuitants.

Prior to her last illness, decedent cashed in two Delta Life annuities whose contingent owners had died. These annuities are not included in the 19 in issue. At the time that decedent cashed in the two annuities, she told Mr. Murphy that she intended to pay the taxes resulting from the transaction and give a portion of the proceeds of the annuities, in the amount of the principal or face amount of $10,000 each, to the heirs of the deceased annuitants/contingent owners.

Ultimate Finding of Fact

Decedent intended to make a present inter vivos gift of the 19 annuities in issue to the respective recipients.

Opinion

Section 2038(a)(1) provides that a decedent's gross estate includes any interest in property transferred by the decedent for less than full consideration if, at the time of the decedent's death, the transferred interest was subject to the decedent's power to revoke, alter, amend, or terminate. Section 2033 provides that the gross estate includes the value of all property to the extent that the decedent had an interest in it at the time of her death. State law determines the extent of a decedent's interest in property. We will follow the decisions of the highest State court, but in the absence of a decision by that court, we may look to the State's lower courts' rulings and holdings.

Respondent contends that because the durable power of attorney did not specifically grant the attorneys in fact the authority to make gifts of decedent's property, such gifts were incomplete, invalid, or revocable by decedent and thus includable in decedent's gross estate. We disagree.

The elements of a completed gift under Oklahoma law are: (1) intention to give, (2) complete delivery, and (3) acceptance by the donee. In order to establish an inter vivos gift after the death of the alleged donor, "the evidence must be clear, explicit, and convincing in support of every element necessary to constitute a gift." There does not seem to be any dispute that the annuities were delivered and accepted by the donees. Thus, if petitioner can prove donative intent, the transfers will be considered to be completed gifts which are not includable in decedent's gross estate. Respondent claims that the required donative intent cannot be supplied by a written durable power of attorney absent an express written gift authorization. Petitioner contends that the required donative intent is present because decedent authorized her attorneys in fact to make the gifts, because decedent ratified the gifts after the transfers, and because a written durable power of attorney, even absent an express gift authorization, is adequate to allow decedent's attorneys in fact to make effective inter vivos gifts. In order to determine whether the requisite donative intent existed, we must first look to the record as a whole to determine whether decedent possessed the requisite intent, taking into account the authority granted to decedent's attorneys in fact.

Decedent's Intent To Make Gifts

The transfers of property which are in issue in this case were executed shortly before decedent's death by decedent's attorneys in fact. Chris Hunt testified that in the summer of 1992 decedent specifically instructed him and Melvin Hammontree to transfer the annuities in question to the respective annuitants. We found Mr. Hunt's testimony to be credible and supported by the record as a whole. Shortly before the gifts were made, some of decedent's nephews became sick, and they needed money. At that time, decedent decided to give all of the annuities to the annuitants. Mr. Hunt testified that after he completed the transfers and so informed decedent, she was "well pleased" that the transfers were taken care of.

The record provides additional reasons to believe Mr. Hunt's testimony. The annuities were transferred to the annuitants who had been chosen by decedent when she originally purchased the annuities. These 19 annuitants would have become the owners of their respective annuities upon the death of decedent.

Jess Murphy testified that when contingent owners of two annuities not in issue predeceased decedent, it was decedent's desire that a portion of the funds from the annuities go to the heirs of the contingent owners. Mr. Murphy described decedent as "generous in giving." Additionally, Betty Aaron, decedent's accountant since approximately 1984, testified that decedent had talked to her in the summer of 1992 about transferring the annuities in question to the annuitants at that time rather than waiting until her death. Mr. Murphy and Ms. Aaron were not contingent owners of any of the annuities. Lastly, even after the transfers in question, decedent was left with over $973,000 in assets.

We are cognizant that some States have a flat prohibition against attorneys in fact making gifts to themselves or to third parties absent express written authorization. Oklahoma, however, has not adopted such a rule. We believe that if the Oklahoma Supreme Court were to rule on this issue, it would look for "clear, explicit, and convincing" evidence of intent. . . . Given the facts and circumstances of this case, we conclude that under Oklahoma law, the transfers in question would be valid gifts.

* * *

The power of attorney which decedent executed does not restrict the attorneys in fact from making gifts. The power of attorney which decedent executed authorized her attorneys in fact to "convey . . . any of my property, either real or personal." The power of attorney authorizes the attorneys in fact to "act in all matters . . . as freely, fully, and effectively as I could or might do personally if present." This language evidences an intent to permit the attorneys in fact to make gifts of decedent's property.

Respondent argues that this Court should not allow decedent's intent to make a gift or decedent's ratification of a gift to be proved by the oral testimony of interested parties; namely Mr. Hunt. Respondent points to various factors which she contends show that decedent did not intend to make present inter vivos gifts at the time of the transfers. We disagree. As we have already found, petitioner's witnesses were credible, and their testimony was supported by the record . . . . Based on the record as a whole, we conclude that decedent, acting through her attorneys in fact, made completed inter vivos gifts of the annuities in question. Therefore, the value of the gifts is not includable in decedent's gross estate.

Questions

What does the Illinois short form power of attorney in the statutory supplement say about an agent's authority to give gifts? If you were representing a client who wanted to execute this form, what step(s) might you take to avoid future litigation with the Internal Revenue Service?

8. Durable Powers and Ademption by Extinction

In connection with the *Hegel* case, below, read the following in the statutory supplement: Ohio Revised Code § 2107.501, Pre-1990 Uniform Probate Code § 2-608, and 1990 Uniform Probate Code § 2-606.

In re Estate of Hegel
668 N.E.2d 474 (Ohio 1996)

FRANCIS E. SWEENEY, SR., Justice.

In this case, we must determine whether an ademption has occurred where specifically devised property was sold to a third party prior to the testator's death under a durable power of attorney. Since we find that the devise has been adeemed, we reverse the decision of the court of appeals. The principle of ademption refers to "a taking away" of a specific bequest or devise and occurs when the object of the legacy ceases to exist. In *Bool* [*v. Bool*, a case decided in 1956—Eds.], we held, at paragraph one of the syllabus, that "[w]here the subject of a specific bequest has been extinguished in the lifetime of a testator, such bequest is adeemed, and the designated beneficiary thereof is wholly deprived of it or any property in lieu of it, in the absence of a contrary expression in the will."

Since the *Bool* decision, the General Assembly has enacted R.C. 2107.501(B), which sets forth a narrow exception to the ademption doctrine for the sale of specifically devised or bequeathed property made by a guardian. According to this statute, "[i]f specifically devised or bequeathed property is sold by a guardian, ... the specific devisee or legatee has the right to a general pecuniary devise or bequest equal to the net proceeds of sale. . . ." Thus, the specific devisee or legatee's rights are protected and are not extinguished where the guardian sells specifically devised or bequeathed property.

R.C. 2107.501 was modeled after former Uniform Probate Code Section 2-608. However, this Uniform Probate Code section, amended in 1987 and in 1990, and renumbered as Section 2-606, was expanded to protect specifically devised or bequeathed property sold by attorneys-in-fact acting under a durable power of attorney. Thus, under current Uniform Probate Code Section 2-606(b), if specifically devised property is sold "by an agent acting within the authority of a durable power of attorney for an incapacitated principal, ... the specific devisee has the right to a general pecuniary devise equal to the net sale price. . . ."

To date, the General Assembly has not adopted Uniform Probate Code Section 2-606. Instead, R.C. 2107.501 is limited in its scope to specific devises or bequests sold by a guardian and does not apply to sales by attorneys-in-fact. Had the General Assembly intended for the statutory exception in R.C. 2107.501 to apply to agents acting under the authority of a durable power of attorney, in addition to guardians, it could have amended the statute to include reference to powers of attorney, similar to the language contained in amended Uniform Probate Code Section 2-606. However, it chose not to do so.

Despite the *Bool* decision and the clear language of R.C. 2107.501(B), the majority of the court of appeals focused on the testator's intent and held that the specific bequest had not been adeemed. Although the majority recognized that Ohio has not yet adopted Uniform Probate Code Section 2-606, it decided to treat those acting under powers of attorney the same as guardians. We disagree with this interpretation and are unwilling to read into the statute language that the General Assembly has decided not to specifically include. Furthermore, we do not view those acting under powers of attorney the same as guardians. Guardians are appointed by the probate court and are subject to the court's control, whereas attorneys-in-fact have much more freedom and can act without court approval as the principal's "alter ego."

The statutory language of R.C. 2107.501(B) is clearly limited to the sale of property by guardians and does not protect specifically devised property sold by attorneys-in-fact. Thus, as applied to this case, when Boettger, as attorney-in-fact, sold the testator's residence and its contents prior to the testator's death, Boettger adeemed her specific devise and lost her right to the devised property.

Accordingly, we reverse the judgment of the court of appeals and reinstate the decision of the probate court.

MOYER, C.J., and DOUGLAS and COOK, JJ., concur.
RESNICK and STRATTON, JJ., separately dissent.
PFEIFER, J., dissents.

ALICE ROBIE RESNICK, Justice, dissenting.
The incapacity of Helen Hegel is a crucial and distinguishing factor that makes this case different from a typical ademption case. Since the majority fails to recog-

nize or find that incapacity does indeed make a difference, I must dissent. The factual circumstances of this case illustrate in a compelling way that the majority decision is not only unfair but contrary to law. I would affirm the judgment of the court of appeals that no ademption occurred.

Of critical importance to this case are the undisputed facts that Patricia Boettger had no knowledge of the contents of Hegel's will until after Hegel's death, and that Hegel was suffering from an incapacity at the time of the sale of the property, with that incapacity continuing until the time of Hegel's death. Boettger was acting in good faith and in the best interests of Hegel (and ultimately of Hegel's estate) when she sold the residence and its contents. The majority's determination that the specific devise of the house and bequest of the contents to Boettger have been adeemed punishes Boettger for inadvertently acting inconsistently with the contents of the will when Boettger knew nothing about those contents.

In *Bool v. Bool*, at paragraph one of the syllabus, this court set down the bright-line rule that a specific bequest is adeemed when the subject of the bequest is extinguished before the testator's death. However, since *Bool* did not involve the complicating factor of a testator's incapacity, it is questionable whether a situation involving incapacity of the testator at the time of the extinguishment of the specific bequest or devise falls within the bright-line rule established by *Bool*.

In *Bishop v. Fullmer* (1960), the Court of Appeals for Defiance County considered this very question—whether the rule of *Bool* requires ademption when the testator was mentally incompetent at the time of the sale of the property specifically devised. The *Bishop* court stated that "[t]he factual situation in the case at bar was not before the Supreme Court in the *Bool* case," and that the *Bool* decision did not control the decision in the case before it, "which requires the application of a different principle of law." The appellate court in *Bishop* concluded that the mental competency of the testator was the "vital and controlling issue" to determine whether the specific devise had been adeemed.

Although in *Bishop* it was a guardian who had sold the property in question covered by the specific devise, no statute existed at the time to justify the court's decision to distinguish the factual scenario before it from that of *Bool*. R.C. 2107.501(B), establishing a statutory exception to the ademption doctrine when a guardian sells the specifically devised or bequeathed property, was not enacted until 1975, and took effect on January 1, 1976. Thus, the *Bishop* court, predating R.C. 2107.501(B) by approximately fifteen years, established a common-law exception to *Bool*'s bright-line ademption rule when the testator is incapacitated or incompetent at the time the specific devise or bequest is extinguished.

I see no reason why the common-law exception recognized in *Bishop* for sale of property by a guardian should not also apply to a sale by the holder of a durable power of attorney. The critical factor in *Bishop* was the testator's incapacity at the time of the sale, not that the one who conducted the sale was a guardian. Like the *Bishop* court, I conclude that the fact of the testator's incapacity at the time of the sale of the property in this case distinguishes the situation before us from that in *Bool*. That the General Assembly has not adopted Uniform Probate Code Section 2-606 to specifically address a sale by an attorney-in-fact should not deter us from recognizing that a common-law exception to *Bool*'s bright-line ademption doctrine exists.

Such a common-law exception should control our decision in this case. The court of appeals was correct in its determination that no ademption occurred here, given the undisputed facts of this case.

STRATTON, Justice, dissenting.

I join in Justice Resnick's dissent. I strongly agree that the incapacity of the testator is the key distinguishing issue here, not "guardian" vs. "attorney-in-fact." Attorneys-in-fact are a more recent occurrence and their use is now often encouraged by estate planners and counselors as a way to avoid "court interference" or supervision. Most testators have little appreciation of the difference in the roles of guardian and attorney-in-fact other than one seems less complicated to use than the other.

Today's decision gives a dangerous power to all attorneys-in-fact to change a will once their charge becomes incompetent. There is now no protection against the greedy or unscrupulous attorneys-in-fact. At least in Hegel's case, Boettger did what she believed was best for her charge, innocently depriving herself of her inheritance and providing an unintended windfall to the other heirs. But now, nothing prevents an attorney-in-fact from altering a will to his or her benefit. For example, a house, the main asset in the estate, may be left to Heir A. Heir B inherits the remaining cash. Heir B is appointed attorney-in-fact. The testator becomes incompetent. Heir B sells the house, claiming the cash is insufficient to pay debts. The bequest is adeemed; Heir B now inherits everything. Heir A is out in the cold. At least in a guardianship, a court can supervise an estate and prevent such injustice. Under this court's holding, there would be no recourse.

Ademption is a doctrine that means if a testator makes changes to his or her estate and does not alter his or her will to accommodate those changes, the results are deemed intended since the testator could have made the necessary adjustments. In a situation of incompetence, the testator no longer is accountable for changes in the estate as he or she lacks the capacity for intent and lacks the ability to execute a new will. To allow ademption because of another's action or intent, even though designated as an attorney-in-fact, can create a great potential for abuse. Legal counsel and estate planners should be cautioned to advise all their clients, past and present, who have executed an attorney-in-fact designation (assuming the client is still competent), that an attorney-in-fact now holds dangerous power to alter the effect of their wills if they become incompetent.

Questions

1. If you had been a member of the Ohio Supreme Court, how would you have decided this case? Why?

2. How would this case have been decided under the 1990 UPC? What explains the 1990 UPC's approach?

9. Lawyers as Agents

ABA Model Code of Professional Responsibility
Canons 5 and 9, and Ethical Consideration 5-6[*]

Canon 5

A Lawyer Should Exercise Independent Professional Judgment on Behalf of a Client

Canon 9

A Lawyer Should Avoid Even the Appearance of Professional Impropriety

EC 5-6 Interests of a Lawyer That May Affect His Judgment

A lawyer should not consciously influence a client to name him as executor, trustee, or lawyer in an instrument. In those cases where a client wishes to name his lawyer as such, care should be taken by the lawyer to avoid even the appearance of impropriety.

Linda J. Whitton
Durable Powers as a Hedge Against Guardianship: Should the Attorney-at-Law Accept Appointment as Attorney-in-Fact?
2 ELDER L.J. 39, 42, 62-65 (1994)[**]

When a client desires the benefits of a durable power of attorney but does not have a trusted family member or friend to serve as attorney-in-fact, the drafting lawyer is faced with the dilemma of how to assist the client with obtaining an appropriate agent. Authors of a comprehensive durable powers practice manual have suggested that one solution is to appoint the attorney-at-law as the client's attorney-in-fact. Likewise, a note writer has recommended advance delegation of durable powers to a client's lawyer as a means of avoiding the problems which could arise if a client loses competency during the course of legal representation. Despite these suggestions, the ethical propriety of a lawyer serving in the dual role of attorney-at-law and attorney-in-fact under a durable powers delegation has heretofore remained unexamined.

* * *

---

[*] Reprinted by permission. Copies of the ABA Model Code of Professional Responsibility (1981) are available from Member Services, American Bar Association, 750 North Lake Shore Drive, Chicago, Illinois 60611, 312-988-5522.

[**] Reprinted by permission. Copyright to the *Elder Law Journal* is held by the Board of Trustees of the University of Illinois.

Assuming arguendo that a lawyer agrees to accept delegation of durable powers as an accommodation to a client, two questions must be examined. First, would this arrangement pose ethical and practical difficulties for the lawyer when drafting the durable power of attorney? Second, would this arrangement compromise the attorney-client relationship or the services provided to the principal after the advent of incompetency?

To answer the first question, it is necessary . . . [to consider three] drafting considerations—scope of authority, time of commencement, and conditions on the agent's performance. Of the three, scope of authority would appear to be least affected by the dual attorney-at-law/ attorney-in-fact role. If the goal of the durable power of attorney is to prevent guardianship, the scope of authority will need to be comprehensive regardless of the identity of the agent. Likewise, any specialized powers included within this scope will be dictated by the principal's unique circumstances rather than those of the agent. The same is not true, however, for the remaining drafting considerations.

Choice of when a durable power of attorney is to commence, a matter of client preference, becomes particularly problematic when the attorney-at-law will also serve as attorney-in-fact. If the client prefers a springing power, should the attorney recommend an agent affidavit as proof of the client's incompetency, thereby accepting full responsibility for determining when the client has become incompetent? Or should the attorney recommend physician certification, which requires more effort to obtain, but which will probably better protect the attorney's exposure to liability?

Neither of the foregoing alternatives is totally satisfactory for the attorney or the client. In the first, the attorney breaches, at the very least, client loyalty by becoming the sole judge of the client's competency. In the second, the attorney must not only breach loyalty by questioning the client's competency, but must also breach confidentiality by divulging information about the client's condition in order to obtain the physician's certification of incompetence. The client, on the other hand, risks the attorney assuming control prematurely under the first alternative but faces certain invasion of privacy under the second.

Even more problematic is the issue of conditions on the agent's performance. How can the lawyer maintain independent professional judgment in advising the principal on negotiation of the agent's compensation when it is the lawyer who will be compensated as agent?

* * *

[T]he problems associated with accepting delegation of a client's durable powers go beyond the issue of compensation. Limitation of liability, the other primary inducement for agent performance, also raises a dilemma for the drafting attorney. One could argue that a lawyer who agrees to serve as attorney-in-fact is entitled to the same extent of liability limitation and indemnification from the principal as would be recommended if a nonlawyer were appointed. However, wearing both the hat of the draftsperson and the agent places the lawyer in a conflict of interest posture that precludes independent professional judgment about the proper extent of liability limitation.

* * *

Furthermore, objective advice with respect to placing limitations in the durable power of attorney for the purpose of monitoring the agent's activities is also impossible when the drafting attorney is the agent.

* * *

As the foregoing ethical problems demonstrate, the dual attorney-at-law/attorney-in-fact role would seriously impede the lawyer's independent professional judgment when advising the client with respect to the majority of durable power drafting considerations, thereby compromising the attorney-client relationship. In addition, consideration of the typical issues occasioned by the advent of client incompetency will demonstrate how dual representation would further erode the attorney-client relationship upon the advent of client incompetency, as well as negatively impact the services provided to the incompetent principal.

Upon the onset of client incompetency, the lawyer faces a dilemma similar to that faced by the attorney who institutes guardianship proceedings for a client . . . . First, the lawyer must breach client loyalty by questioning the client's competency and then client confidentiality either by stating, via affidavit, that the client is incompetent, or by revealing the client's condition to a physician to obtain a certification of incompetence. The disintegration of the attorney-client relationship, however, would not stop with breach of loyalty and confidentiality.

At the point when a client loses competency and the attorney-at-law becomes vested with the client's durable powers, the lawyer, in effect, loses a client. The lawyer can no longer communicate with the client about material aspects of the representation, and the client can no longer make the substantive decisions governing the representation. In reality the lawyer, as attorney-in-fact, also becomes the client. There is no longer accountability for any actions taken by the lawyer as attorney-at-law because there is no longer a competent principal to ask questions, make decisions, or file a complaint for malpractice or disciplinary action. This fusion of roles obliterates all of the essential characteristics of the attorney-client relationship: undivided loyalty, confidentiality, client-centered decision making, independent professional judgment, and accountability.

Questions

1. Do you agree with Professor Whitton that lawyers should always avoid being named as their clients' attorneys-in-fact?

2. If a client wanted to name you as his or her agent, what steps might you take to minimize any conflicts of interest or appearance of impropriety?

B. Joint Ownership and Joint Accounts

1. Forms of Joint Ownership

Edwin G. Fee, Jr.
New Disclaimer Regs. and Other Rules Affecting Jointly Owned Property
25 EST. PLAN. 117 (March/April 1998)*

The most common forms of ownership in which two or more persons may own property are joint tenancy, tenancy in common, and tenancy by the entirety. State law determines which type of ownership exists with respect to particular property. Because the definitions of these categories vary from state to state, the following discussion describes the most common features of these types of ownership.

Joint tenancy. Joint tenancy is a form of ownership by two or more persons pursuant to which each joint tenant owns an undivided interest in the entire property and has a right of survivorship. Depending on applicable state law, a joint tenant may transfer his joint interest to a third person, thus converting the joint tenancy into a tenancy in common (discussed below). A joint tenant might accomplish the same result by transferring his joint interest to himself as a tenant in common. A joint tenant also may seek judicial partition of the property, pursuant to which he would receive a proportionate part of the property.

When a joint tenant dies, his interest automatically passes in equal shares to the remaining joint tenant(s). Because an interest in a joint tenancy does not pass under a deceased owner's will, joint tenancy is a method of avoiding probate.

Tenancy in common. A tenancy in common is not subject to a right of survivorship. Instead, each tenant in common owns an undivided interest in a portion of the property. When one of the owners dies, his interest passes to his named beneficiaries (if the owner has a valid will) or heirs (if the owner dies without a will) according to state probate law. Furthermore, each tenant in common can sell his interest freely. Because tenancy in common is not really a form of joint ownership, this article focuses primarily on joint tenancy and a related form of ownership, tenancy by the entirety.

Tenancy by the entirety. Tenancy by the entirety is a form of joint ownership between spouses that is recognized by approximately half the states. Similar to joint tenancy, in tenancy by the entirety each spouse has a right of survivorship. Thus, tenancy by the entirety can be used to avoid probate on the death of the first spouse to die. Unlike joint tenancy, though, one spouse acting alone generally cannot partition or transfer his interest.

---

* Copyright © 1998. Reprinted with permission.

Question

Joint tenancy—or, where it exists, tenancy by the entirety—has been described as an "imperfect" will substitute. Why?

2. Joint Bank Accounts: What Form of Ownership?

To get an overview of the UPC's approach to multiple-party bank accounts, skim the excerpts from Article VI of the UPC in the statutory supplement.

a. Rights During Lifetime: Theory versus Practice

Read UPC § 6-211(b) (and the accompanying comment) and Ohio Revised Code § 1109.07(A) in the statutory supplement.

Question

Are funds in joint bank accounts truly held in joint tenancy?

b. Rights at Death: Presumptions and Their Rebuttal

In connection with the following excerpt, read UPC § 6-212(a) (and the accompanying comment) in the statutory supplement.

Ronald R. Volkmer
Problems Resulting from Joint Tenancies
21 EST. PLAN. 375, 377 (November/December 1994)*

The most nettlesome problem in the law of joint tenancy bank accounts involves whether to allow extrinsic evidence to rebut the presumption of survivorship contained in the standard form for a joint tenancy account. The most widely accepted approach . . . is that there is a presumption that the surviving joint tenants to a joint tenancy are entitled to the balance upon the death of one of the joint tenants. This presumption, however, may be rebutted by evidence of a contrary intent, showing that the depositor did not intend to have survivorship rights attach even though the account is placed in survivorship form. Opening the door to such evidence allows for proof of so-called convenience accounts—as for example, where the grandmother

---

* Copyright © 1994. Reprinted with permission.

placed the granddaughter's name on the joint account for the limited purpose of making withdrawals.

Allowing extrinsic evidence to be admitted is hazardous because the person whose intent is questioned is now deceased and the written language of the account (providing for survivorship) is being overridden. Almost every state has had to muddle through this difficult issue, with legislatures in some states taking the lead in establishing clear rules. More often than not, though, it is the state appellate courts that have had the unenviable task of sorting all this out. To say there has been much confusion in the law is an understatement.

Questions

1. Does the UPC adopt the majority approach described by Professor Volkmer?

2. If you were representing a client who wished to set up a multiple-party bank account with a survivorship feature, what steps might you take to avoid future litigation about survivorship?

3. The Reach of Third Parties: Creditors

Edwin G. Fee, Jr.
New Disclaimer Regs. and Other Rules Affecting Jointly Owned Property
25 EST. PLAN. 117, 117-118 (March/April 1998)*

[The rule that tenants by the entirety cannot be unilaterally partitioned by one spouse] creates an advantage in some instances, because creditors of only one spouse generally cannot force partition and sale of the property to satisfy the spouse's individual debt. In contrast, creditors often can satisfy an individual debt with an interest held as a joint tenant or a tenant in common. Creditors of both spouses usually can seek satisfaction of the joint debt from property held in any of the forms described above.

Question

How serious is the problem raised by the ability of creditors to reach property held in joint tenancy or tenancy in common?

---

* Copyright © 1998. Reprinted with permission.

4. The Reach of Third Parties: Gift Taxes

In connection with the following excerpt, read Treas. Reg. §§ 25.2511-1(a) and 25.2511-2(b) in the statutory supplement.

Edwin G. Fee, Jr.
New Disclaimer Regs. and Other Rules Affecting Jointly Owned Property
25 EST. PLAN. 117, 118 (March/April 1998)[*]

If a donor using his sole funds creates a joint bank account for himself and a donee (or a similar type of ownership by which the donor can regain the entire fund without the donee's consent), no gift occurs upon the creation of the account. Because the donor still has the ability to withdraw the entire amount in the account, he has not given up dominion and control over the deposited funds. Instead, a gift from the donor to the donee occurs when the donee draws on the account for his own benefit. The gift is the amount withdrawn to the extent the donee has no obligation to account for a part of the proceeds to the donor.

This general rule does not apply in the case of a so-called true joint tenancy. In some states, the creation of a joint bank account between two people "effects a present transfer to each tenant of an alienable one-half interest therein." In this situation, to the extent that one joint owner contributes more than half of the amount deposited in the account, the owner who contributes more makes a gift to the other owner.

* * *

[With respect to property other than bank accounts,] [a]ssume that a donor with his own funds purchases property and has the title conveyed to himself and a donee as joint owners, with rights of survivorship . . . but these rights may be defeated by either party severing his interest. In this situation, there is a gift to the donee of half of the value of the property[.]

Question

In a jurisdiction that has adopted the UPC, how can one tell whether the transfer of funds into a joint account will be considered a taxable gift? (Hint: see § 6-211 in the statutory supplement.)

---

[*] Copyright © 1998. Reprinted with permission.

5. The Reach of Third Parties: Estate Taxes

In connection with the following excerpt, read Internal Revenue Code §§ 2033 and 2040 in the statutory supplement.

Edwin G. Fee, Jr.
New Disclaimer Regs. and Other Rules Affecting Jointly Owned Property
25 EST. PLAN. 117, 120 (March/April 1998)[*]

Section 2040(a) generally provides that the gross estate includes the entire value of (1) a joint tenancy with right of survivorship; (2) a tenancy by the entirety; or (3) a deposit of money, bond, or other instrument in the name of the decedent and any other person and payable to either or the survivor. Nevertheless, there are several exceptions . . . that specifically address (1) property for which the decedent did not furnish all the consideration; (2) property acquired by gift, bequest, or inheritance; and (3) property held by spouses. The rules concerning joint interests do not apply to an interest held as a tenant in common (which is included in the gross estate under Section 2033). In addition, Section 2040(a) should not require inclusion in the decedent's estate of any property in which the decedent had only a nominal, rather than beneficial, joint interest.

Question

What estate tax consequences arise in the context of a typical joint bank account?

6. Joint Accounts: An Evaluation

Richard V. Wellman
New Types of Joint Bank Accounts Resolve Many Problems
22 EST. PLAN. 232, 232 (July/August 1995)[**]

Use of joint checking and savings accounts is perilous for others than happily married couples. Married persons often accept the risk that whatever one of them puts in the account may be lost due to the other's whim or bad luck. Married couples probably intend the survivor of them to enjoy the entire account on the death of the other. They view the joint account as an easily arranged, costless device for achieving mutual money management goals, including having funds accessible to either or to the survivor. The implicit risk that the entire account may be lost to creditors of either

---

[*] Copyright © 1998. Reprinted with permission.
[**] Copyright © 1995. Reprinted with permission.

coincides with the expectations of married couples with or without joint accounts. As a result, joint accounts are very popular.

The problem is that the advantages of a joint account make it attractive to unmarried persons, many of whom undoubtedly select this form of account without knowing the risks that attend it when used by others than spouses. For example, an account funded by one person as a means of passing to a surviving party any balance remaining at the depositor's death may cause the depositor to be treated as having made an immediate gift of a fraction of the deposited funds to others named as joint parties. This means that the depositor may have to account to the other person for part of a later withdrawal of more than his or her share. In addition, there is a risk that creditors or a spouse of the other party may have a right to reach some or all of the funds. Moreover, litigation over whether the survivor was intended to receive a gift of the balance on hand at death is a distinct possibility.

Questions

1. What are the advantages and disadvantages of joint bank accounts?
2. How would you evaluate the use of joint bank accounts? Is Professor Wellman's critique accurate, or is it overstated?

C. Agency Accounts

In connection with the following readings, skim the excerpts from Article VI of the UPC in the statutory supplement, paying particular attention to §§ 6-203(a), 6-204, 6-205, 6-211(d), 6-224, and 6-226.

David M. English
The UPC and the New Durable Powers
27 Real Prop., Prob. & Tr. J. 333, 354-58 (1992)[*]

A joint tenancy bank account can be one of the probate lawyer's biggest nightmares. The signature card states that the survivor takes the entire account, but following the depositor's death the attorney may discover that the depositor did not intend to create a true joint tenancy. Instead, the depositor created the account for purposes of "convenience." The other joint tenant was supposed to have authority to pay the depositor's bills but was not to receive the funds at the depositor's death. Litigation then ensues to determine whether the evidence of that intent is sufficient to rebut the presumption that the signature card controls.

This problem has persisted for decades despite continued calls for clarifying legislation and pleas to bankers to exercise care in handing out joint tenancy signature

---

* Copyright © 1992 American Bar Association. Reprinted by permission.

cards. The durable power is an excellent alternative for bankers to consider. A depositor may grant an agent authority to pay bills without granting the agent an ownership interest, and the agency may survive into incapacity, when it is most needed. The durable power option has yet to take hold, however. Perhaps that is because of a lack of readily available account forms and because banks fear potential liability for making payments after the principal's death, a concern that does not apply if a joint account is substituted.

Although durable power bank accounts are rarely used, that failure is not due to a lack of legislative attention. Wisconsin has authorized the device since 1974 and Washington since 1981. However, since 1988, the durable power bank account has come into its own, with the UPC and four additional states joining the list of enacting jurisdictions.

* * *

The most significant recent development in bank powers of attorney is the 1989 revision of Article VI of the UPC . . . . The UPC now authorizes a depositor to create an agency account that may survive incapacity . . . . The UPC provides an omnibus form that covers not only the creation of agency accounts, but also joint accounts, Totten trusts, and payable-on-death accounts, which are referred to by different terms. The form is complex, confusing, and, for all practical purposes, mandatory. The new UPC provisions do, however, respond to bankers' concerns about liability by providing that the bank cannot be held liable until it has (1) received written notice to stop payments and (2) had a reasonable opportunity to act upon the notice.

Richard V. Wellman
New Types of Joint Bank Accounts Resolve Many Problems
22 Est. Plan. 232, 236-37 (July/August 1995)[*]

Finally, and most importantly, the revised UPC form offers an agency account feature. It is triggered if the account form labels a person who is to have withdrawal authority as "agent" for another described as the owner. The label identifies an individual who has authority to make withdrawals but who cannot benefit personally from the position and is accountable to the account owner or the owner's estate for sums withdrawn. This arrangement is called a "convenience account" in at least two states [Florida and Texas], an "agency designation" in states that have enacted the 1989 revision of the UPC as well as in other states, and an account with an "additional authorized signatory" in Tennessee. The concept implicit in this form might be used (1) in a single-owner account without a death beneficiary, (2) in a p.o.d. account naming an owner and one or more death beneficiaries plus an agent for the owner, or

---

[*] Copyright © 1995. Reprinted with permission.

(3) in a joint account in which an agent is added to serve for all the parties. Under the best of this legislation, depository protection for payouts on the order of the agent continues until the depository receives written notice of the principal's death or other revocation of the agency. This last provision assures protection of the depository for payouts to the "agent" even though the owner for whom the agent was designated to act may have died, causing termination of the agency for all purposes other than protection of the bank. Without this provision, depositories would continue to have reason to avoid offering agency accounts.

The agency account feature improves the choice of accounts available to the elderly single parent . . . . This person usually chooses a child living nearby to have signature power merely for the parent's convenience, while other children living at a distance, together with the child nearby, are intended to be death beneficiaries of the account. Now, rather than making all the children parties with the parent on a joint account, the parent can designate the nearby child his agent on an account that names the parent as sole owner, and all the children, including the agent-child, as p.o.d. beneficiaries. On the parent's death, the agent will have the power, assuming no written notice terminating the apparent authority has been given to the bank, to withdraw the money and will become legally accountable to divide it as intended. The advantage of this arrangement over the old joint account naming all the children as parties is the absence of risk of loss during the parent's lifetime to creditors of any of the children, because an account agent has no beneficial interest in an account balance.

Questions

1. What are the advantages of agency accounts over the more traditional joint account?

2. Are there ways in which the UPC's approach to agency accounts might be improved?

D. Revocable Inter Vivos Trusts

1. Parties to the Trust Arrangement

Henry Hansmann & Ugo Mattei
The Functions of Trust Law: A Comparative Legal and Economic Analysis
73 N.Y.U. L. REV. 434, 438 (1998)[*]

In a prototypical Anglo-American trust, three parties are involved: the "settlor" transfers property to the "trustee," who is charged with the duty to administer the property for the benefit of the "beneficiary." Any of these three roles may be played by more than one person. Also, the same person may play more than one of the three

---

[*] Copyright © 1998. Reprinted with permission.

roles. In particular, the settlor and the beneficiary may be the same person, in which case the trust involves a simple delegation of responsibility for managing property from the settlor/beneficiary to the trustee.

Question

What happens if the settlor, the trustee, and the beneficiary are all the same person?

2. Trust Creation

Restatement (Third) of Trusts
Introductory Note to Part 2, Chapter 3
(Tent. Draft No. 1, 5 April 1996)[*]

There are numerous methods of disposing of property during life and at death .... The creation of a trust is another method—a particularly flexible and useful method—of making property dispositions, either inter vivos or by will. As appears from the rules and commentary in this Chapter, the requirements for the creation of a trust are quite simple, even if they sometimes give rise to difficult issues.

In order to create a trust, there must be a proper manifestation of the intention to do so, either by the settlor or in communications between the settlor and the intended trustee; and the settlor ordinarily must make an effective inter vivos or testamentary transfer of the trust property to the trustee, just as other means of disposition ordinarily require that the property owner make an effective transfer to create property interests in others. An important exception to the transfer requirement is that trust dispositions also may be accomplished by the property owner's declaration that certain of the declarant's own property is now held by the declarant in trust for one or more others or for both the declarant and others. In addition, trusts are occasionally created by contract even before the promised transfer occurs, or by transfers eventually made pursuant to promises or pursuant to insurance or retirement plan beneficiary designations, even after the settlor's death.

No consideration is required for the creation of a trust. In fact, most trusts are created by gratuitous transfer. Ordinarily, however, if the property owner does not manifest an intention immediately to create a trust, but only the intention to create a trust in the future, no trust is created. Nor is the property owner bound later to create the trust in such a case, unless the requirements for the formation of a contract are complied with. The result is the same (that is, no trust and no obligation later to create one) where, in the absence of consideration, although language of present transfer is used, the would-be settlor does not at the time own the property purportedly transferred in trust.

---

[*] Copyright © 1996. Reprinted with permission.

Thus, a trust is normally created by an effective disposition of property, either during life or at death, and not by a mere attempt or undertaking to make a disposition in the future. Although a settlor can gratuitously and effectively make a present disposition of property in trust by declaration, an attempt to make a present, outright gift inter vivos that is ineffective (for lack of delivery, for example) will not be treated as a declaration of trust. Similarly, an undertaking to make a disposition at some future date that is not binding as a contract will not be salvaged by treating it as a declaration of trust.

If the trust property is an interest in land, statutes of frauds in nearly all states require that the creation of an enforceable trust be manifested and proved by written instrument. If the trust is to be a testamentary trust, it is ordinarily necessary to satisfy the requirements of the state's statute of wills.

RESTATEMENT (THIRD) OF TRUSTS
§§ 10 and 20 (Tent. Draft No. 1, 5 April 1996)*

§ 10. *Methods of Creating a Trust*
A trust may be created by:

* * *

(b) a transfer inter vivos by a property owner to another person as trustee for one or more persons, at least one of whom is not the sole trustee; or

(c) a declaration by a property owner that he or she holds that property as trustee for one or more others or for the property owner and one or more others.

§ 20. *Validity of Oral Inter Vivos Trusts*

Except as required by a Statute of Frauds, a writing is not necessary to create an enforceable inter vivos trust, whether by declaration, by transfer to another as trustee, or by contract.

Comment:

a. *Common-law and statutory rules.* Most states have enacted statutory provisions like Section 7 of the English Statute of Frauds, specifically requiring a writing for the inter vivos creation of enforceable trusts of interests in land[.]

Questions

1. What formalities are required to create a trust of which the settlor is also the trustee?

2. What formalities are required to create a trust in which the settlor is not the trustee?

---

* Copyright © 1996. Reprinted with permission.

3. Revocability

Estate and Trust of Pilafas
836 P.2d 420 (Ariz. 1992)

McGregor, Judge.

The remainder beneficiaries (appellants) under an inter vivos trust agreement appeal the trial court's determination that Steve J. Pilafas (decedent) revoked his inter vivos trust and will and died intestate. Appellants raise two issues on appeal. The first is whether appellees presented sufficient evidence that decedent revoked his will. We find the evidence sufficient and affirm that part of the trial court's judgment. The second issue is whether the trial court erred in determining that decedent effectively revoked his inter vivos trust. We hold that the court did err and reverse.

I.

On August 30, 1982, decedent executed a trust agreement appointing himself trustee of certain described properties for the benefit of himself and other specified beneficiaries. Decedent immediately funded the trust by executing and recording a deed and an assignment that transferred a Phoenix residence and his interest in a note and deed of trust on a mobile home park to himself as trustee under the trust agreement. The trust corpus also included other real property, an agreement of sale, and, eventually, a promissory note payable to the trustee and secured by a deed of trust on real property that decedent acquired on June 2, 1988.

The trust agreement directed the trustee to pay decedent the trust income and any principal amounts that decedent requested in writing. The agreement directed that, upon decedent's death, a portion of the trust estate be distributed to the eight nonprofit organizations that are appellants in this case. The remaining portion was to be held in various trusts for decedent's wife, Geraldine P. Pilafas; brother, appellant Theodore J. Pilafas; sons, Steve J. Pilafas, Jr., and John S. Pilafas; and granddaughter, appellant Stephanie J. Pilafas. Decedent explicitly "omitted any provision for his children NICHOLAS S. PILAFAS, IRENE PILAFAS PAPPAS, and JAMES S. PILAFAS...."

Article X of the trust agreement, entitled "Revocation," provided:

> The Settlor may at any time or times during the Settlor's lifetime by instrument in writing delivered to the Trustee amend or revoke this Agreement in whole or in part.... This power is personal to the Settlor and may not be exercised by the Settlor's Personal Representative or others.

In accord with the revocation provision, decedent twice amended the trust agreement by instrument in writing. On September 16, 1982, decedent executed a "First Amendment to Trust Agreement" that substituted a new article VIII regarding trustee succession and added a new article XI regarding the sale of trust property. On January 19, 1987, after his divorce, decedent executed a "Second Amendment to Trust Agreement" that revoked article XI and added an amended article III, thereby deleting his former wife as a trust beneficiary and increasing the share to be distributed to the eight nonprofit beneficiary organizations.

Decedent simultaneously executed a will and the second trust amendment. The will explicitly excluded decedent's former wife, disposed of certain personal property, and directed that other personal property be distributed in accordance with a separate written statement. The will gave the residue of decedent's estate to the trust.

After executing the second amendment to his trust agreement and his new will, decedent apparently improved his relationships with appellees Irene Pappas, James S. Pilafas and Nicholas Pilafas. In communications with his attorney and his family during the last month of his life, decedent indicated an intention to revise his estate plan to include all his children.

Decedent's attorney prepared the trust agreement, the two amendments, and the will, and assisted decedent in executing them. The attorney did not retain decedent's original documents and, to the best of his knowledge, gave decedent the signed originals of the trust agreement, the amendments and the will immediately after they were executed.

Decedent died on September 28, 1988. Subsequently, decedent's son, appellee James S. Pilafas, unsuccessfully searched decedent's house and belongings for the original will and trust documents. No information of record indicates their possible whereabouts.

According to appellees James S. Pilafas and Nicholas S. Pilafas, decedent fastidiously saved important records and was unlikely to have lost his original will and trust. At his death, decedent had a room filled with important documents, including photographs, old divorce papers, his selective service card from 1945, and letters from his children. Appellees also testified that decedent was a man of direct action who sometimes acted impulsively, and who had been known to tear or discard papers that offended him.

On December 2, 1988, appellee James S. Pilafas commenced these proceedings by filing a petition for formal appointment of special administrator and special trustee. On March 8, 1989, he filed a petition for adjudication of intestacy, determination of heirs, determination of revocation of trust, and appointment of personal representative. The petition sought a determination that decedent had revoked his trust agreement and will and died intestate, leaving his five adult children as his lawful heirs. The petition asked the court to authorize James S. Pilafas to transfer all the trust assets to decedent's estate.

Appellants objected to the petition, seeking a determination that decedent had revoked neither his will nor his trust agreement, and asking that the will be admitted to probate. Appellees filed a response and motion for summary judgment that the trial court granted by its order of December 18, 1989. The court determined decedent revoked his trust agreement and his will and died intestate, leaving his five adult children as heirs. The court authorized James S. Pilafas, as special trustee, to transfer all trust assets to the decedent's estate. Appellants timely appealed.

* * *

III.

Appellees ask us to extend to revocable inter vivos trusts the common law presumption that a will last seen in the testator's possession that cannot be found after his death has been revoked. Appellees' reliance on this common law presumption is misplaced, however, if decedent's trust agreement was not susceptible to revocation by physical destruction.

Unlike the execution of a will, the creation of a trust involves the present transfer of property interests in the trust corpus to the beneficiaries. Even a revocable trust vests the trust beneficiary with a legal right to enforce the terms of the trust. The terms of the trust also limit the powers of the settlor and trustee over the trust corpus, even when the settlor declares himself trustee for the benefit of himself and others. The terms of decedent's trust agreement governing revocation provide:

> The Settlor may at any time or times during the Settlor's lifetime by instrument in writing delivered to the Trustee amend or revoke this Agreement in whole or in part . . . .

Appellants argue that under this provision decedent could exercise his power to revoke the trust only through an "instrument in writing delivered to the Trustee. . . ." We agree.

This court, when not bound by previous decisions or legislative enactments, follows the Restatement of the Law. Restatement (Second) of Trusts § 330 (1959) provides:

> (1) The settlor has power to revoke the trust if and to the extent that by the terms of the trust he reserved such a power.
> (2) Except as stated in §§ 332 and 333, the settlor cannot revoke the trust if by the terms of the trust he did not reserve a power of revocation.

Restatement § 330(2) makes it clear that, with two narrow exceptions, a trust is revocable only if the settlor expressly reserves a power to revoke, and the terms of the trust strictly define and limit the reserved power of revocation.

These general principles necessarily entail the more specific rule that when the settlor reserves a power to revoke his trust in a particular manner or under particular circumstances, he can revoke it only in that manner or under those circumstances.

* * *

Because appellees presented no evidence showing that decedent complied with the required method of revocation, the inter vivos trust was not revoked and remained valid.

IV.

For the foregoing reasons, we affirm the trial court's ruling that decedent revoked his will and died intestate, reverse the court's ruling that decedent revoked his trust agreement and the amendments thereto, and remand for proceedings consistent with this opinion.

GERBER, P.J., and MELVYN T. SHELLEY, Retired Judge, concur.

Questions

1. Do you agree with the outcome of *Pilafas*? Why or why not?

2. If you had been Mr. Pilafas' lawyer, what might you have done differently in order to avoid litigation?

4. The Tax Treatment of Inter Vivos Trusts: A Brief Introduction

In connection with the following excerpts, skim through the following in the statutory supplement: Internal Revenue Code §§ 671-678, 2036, 2038, 2501(a)(1), and 2511(a); and Treas. Reg. §§ 25.2511-2(b)-(d).

Howard B. Soloman
Revocable Trusts—A Contrarian's Viewpoint
68 N.Y. St. B.J. 34, 35 (February 1996)[*]

Revocable trusts (also known as "living trusts") have gained enormous popularity in recent years, often being advertised in seminars and literature as the cure all for estate and estate tax planning ills. While the technique has its virtues and place in the estate planner's arsenal of techniques, it is not always necessary.

* * *

(3) Perception: Revocable trusts save income taxes.

Reality: These trusts are "grantor trusts" under IRC Sections 671 *et seq.* and, as such, both items of ordinary income and capital gain are fully reportable on the Grantor's individual income tax return.

(4) Perception: Revocable trusts save estate taxes.

Reality: IRC Section 2038 provides that if the creator of a trust at the time of his or her death has the power to alter, amend or revoke the trust, the principal of the trust is fully includable in his or her estate. Thus, in and of itself, the revocable trust saves no estate taxes. Indeed, if the perception were the reality, everyone, including William Gates, Warren Buffett, and Ross Perot would create one for no purpose other than the avoidance of estate taxes, and the estate tax would be a nullity.

---

[*] Reprinted with permission from the *New York State Bar Journal*, February 1996, published by the New York State Bar Association, One Elk Street, Albany, New York 12207.

Darin N. Digby
What Powers Can a Donor Retain Over Transferred Property?
24 Est. Plan. 318, 318-19, 324 (August/September 1997)[*]

In order for a gratuitous transfer of property to be a completed gift for gift tax purposes, the donor must part with all dominion and control over the property so ". . . as to leave in him no power to change its disposition, whether for his own benefit or for the benefit of another. . . ."

* * *

For purposes of this article, assume that the reason for establishing an irrevocable trust is to make an effective transfer of property (or the value of the property) for federal transfer tax purposes. An effective transfer for transfer tax purposes means that the transfer to the trust will be a completed gift for federal gift tax purposes and that the value of the trust property will be excluded from the donor's gross estate for federal estate tax purposes.

* * *

Is the transfer a completed gift?

In order for a gratuitous transfer of property to be a completed gift for gift tax purposes, the donor must part with all dominion and control over the property so ". . . as to leave in him no power to change its disposition, whether for his own benefit or for the benefit of another. . . ."

Estate tax effects . . . .

Assuming that the donor successfully completes the gift, the next hurdle is to ensure that the property transferred to the trust is excluded from the donor's gross estate for estate tax purposes. There are many traps for the unwary that, if not avoided, will cause an otherwise effective transfer of property to be included in the donor's estate. Most of these pitfalls can be traced to Sections 2036 and 2038. The grantor's use, possession, right to income, or other enjoyment of the transferred property, whether direct or indirect, is generally treated as if the grantor had retained the property under Section 2036(a)(1).

* * *

Income tax considerations

Sections 671-677 provide the mechanism for taxing income to the grantor of a trust when the grantor has retained substantial control over trust income and principal. Unlike the estate tax provisions, the income tax provisions are supplemented by elaborate and detailed Regulations which, if precisely followed, will result in shifting the trust income to the trust or its beneficiary[.]

---

[*] Copyright © 1997. Reprinted with permission.

Dennis L. Belcher & James D. Bridgeman
Defective May Be More Effective:
The Tax Advantages of Intentional Grantor Trusts
PROB. & PROP. 24, 24 (March/April 1993)[*]

It has long been a truism that the federal income tax and transfer tax systems are separate and distinct systems that frequently conflict with each other. For this reason, tax planners traditionally have been concerned not only with ensuring that a lifetime gift is eliminated from the donor's estate for federal estate tax purposes but also with preventing the donor from continuing to be taxed on the income earned from the donated property under the grantor trust rules of the Internal Revenue Code.

Since enactment of the Tax Reform Act of 1986, however, what once was a pitfall has become a potential windfall for taxpayers. Because of the compressed income tax brackets and the substantially higher federal estate tax rate structure, what once was undesirable—application of the grantor trust rules—now may produce substantial reductions in the donor's ultimate estate and gift tax liability.

Question

Do revocable trusts provide any tax advantages?

5. The Reach of Creditors

a. During the Settlor's Lifetime

Clifton B. Kruse, Jr.
Revocable Trusts: Creditors' Rights After the Settlor-Debtor's Death
PROB. & PROP. 40, 40 (November/December 1993)[**]

The RESTATEMENT (SECOND) OF TRUSTS § 156 (1959) succinctly states the widespread, if not universal, rule that "where a person creates for his [or her] own benefit a trust with a provision restraining the voluntary or involuntary transfer of his [or her] interest, . . . creditors can reach [the trust estate]." This policy apparently has not been well understood because . . . many revocable trust settlors have tried to avoid their creditors during their lifetimes by transferring their personal wealth into revocable trusts.

Leach v. Anderson, 535 P.2d 1241, 1243 (Utah 1975), typifies the public policy favoring creditors of revocable trust settlors. A person may not use "a trust as a device [to avoid creditors] and enjoy substantially all of the advantages of ownership

---

[*] Copyright 1993 by the American Bar Association. Reprinted by permission.
[**] Copyright 1993 by the American Bar Association. Reprinted by permission.

[while] at the same time [placing the assets] beyond the legitimate [reach] of . . . creditors." *Leach* affirms that this rule applies to both the creditors with claims at the time the revocable trust is created and to creditors whose claims arise later. Whether the transferor-settlor intended to avoid or defraud his or her creditors is immaterial.

* * *

Whatever objectives a revocable trust might accomplish for its settlor, avoiding the legitimate claims of the settlor's creditors during the settlor's life is not one of them.

b. After the Settlor's Death

Clifton B. Kruse, Jr.
Revocable Trusts: Creditors' Rights After the Settlor-Debtor's Death
PROB. & PROP. 40, 40-42 (November/December 1993)[*]

[The author notes that older cases tend to favor the settlor's heirs.—Eds.] A decision in 1939 by the Supreme Court of Ohio held that a deceased settlor's creditors cannot invalidate the trust without proof that the conveyance into the trust was in violation of the state's fraudulent transfer laws. *Schofield v. Cleveland Trust Co.*, 21 N.E.2d 119 (Ohio 1939) . . . . A 1942 decision is no more generous to creditors. *Greenwich Trust Co. v. Tyson*, 27 A.2d 166, 173-174 (Conn. 1942). Although a settlor reserves the right to the trust's income for life, the settlor's creditors cannot attach the settlor's expired interest. The ownership of the trust estate passes to others at the settlor's death, and therefore the trust corpus is not available to satisfy the unpaid obligations of the deceased settlor.

* * *

More recent cases do not support the *Schofield* and *Greenwich* decisions and suggest a change in public policy . . . . A 1979 Massachusetts intermediate appellate court decision is [one of the newer cases] to [this] effect: *State Street Bank and Trust Co. v. Reiser*, 389 N.E.2d 768 (Mass. App. 1979). In *State Street*, a debtor left at his death a trust that he created during his life, funded with most of his wealth. A bank creditor sought to satisfy a debt owing to it by the settlor from the trust. "We conclude," the court wrote, "that the [creditor] can do so." The court recognized that the settlor's death terminated his retained power to amend or revoke the trust and further acknowledged that on the settlor's death, equitable title to the trust assets is vested in the trust's remainder beneficiaries. Notwithstanding these facts, the court observed that the possession of a general power of appointment over trust assets is similar to a right to revoke and noted that the holder can appoint the property to himself or herself or to his or her executors. "[T]he property could have been devoted to the pay-

---

[*] Copyright © 1993 by the American Bar Association. Reprinted by permission.

ment of [the power holder's] debts and, therefore, [the person's] creditors have an equitable right to reach that property. . . . [T]he same analysis and policy should . . . apply to trust property over which the settlor retains dominion. . . . [It is] at least as great as a power of appointment[,]" and should, therefore, be subject to the same result. "It is excessive obeisance to the form in which the property is held to prevent creditors from reaching property placed in trust . . . [following the settlor's death]." *State Street, supra,* at 771[.]

* * *

Several states have enacted legislation addressing creditors' rights following the death of a settlor of a fully funded revocable trust. [The author mentions statutes in Missouri, California, Massachusetts, and Michigan, as well as reform efforts underway in Florida and Washington state.—Eds.] The legislation permits creditors to reach the trusts.

Question

With respect to the avoidance of creditors, what advantages, if any, do revocable trusts possess?

6. Revocable Trusts and Medicaid

This topic will be covered in greater depth in Chapter 7. However, the following readings are presented by way of introduction to the use of trusts in Medicaid planning.

a. Using Revocable Trusts to Shield Assets During the Lifetime of the Medicaid Recipient

Hal Fliegelman & Debora C. Fliegelman
Giving Guardians the Power to Do Medicaid Planning
32 WAKE FOREST L. REV. 341, 362-63 (1997)[*]

Competent persons also frequently shelter assets for Medicaid eligibility purposes by transferring assets to trusts. In the case of a transfer of assets to a revocable trust, the corpus of the trust is considered a resource available to the individual for determining Medicaid eligibility; thus, the divestiture is not an effective strategy for sheltering the assets transferred. Similarly, that portion of the corpus of an irrevocable trust that could generate income payable to or for the benefit of the individ-

---

[*] Copyright © 1997. Reprinted with permission.

ual is also considered to be a resource available to the individual, which also defeats a sheltering strategy. However, any portion of the corpus of an irrevocable trust that could not be used to generate income payable to or for the individual will be considered to be a transfer for less than fair market value, subject to the transfer rules discussed [earlier in the article].

However, some transfers to trusts are effective sheltering devices. An individual can shelter his or her own assets and thus become eligible for Medicaid benefits—all other things being equal—by transferring the assets to an irrevocable trust for the sole benefit of the individual's spouse or disabled child to the extent that income from the trust corpus cannot be payable to the spouse or disabled child. Certain disabled individuals may also shelter their own assets or income in trusts and become eligible for Medicaid benefits if the trust agreement provides for repayment to the state, upon the individual's death, of Medicaid benefits paid for the individual.

Clifton B. Kruse, Jr.
Critical Differences in Estate Planning Strategies Between Revocable Trusts and Wills
23 ACTEC NOTES 145, 146 (1997)[*]

Transfer of otherwise exempt assets into revocable trusts may result in loss of their Medicaid exempt status.

* * *

Homesteads, otherwise treated as exempt resources of homeowners applying for or receiving Medicaid, may lose their exempt status, however, when transferred into their owners' revocable trusts. In Massachusetts, for example, ". . . the home is rendered countable as an asset if the [Medicaid] applicant holds title through a revocable trust rather than individually . . . ."

Similarly, in New Jersey, homesteads placed into revocable trusts lose their exempt-asset status and their value becomes countable.

* * *

In Arizona, the Bureau of Financial Eligibility . . . has similarly held that the homestead exemption, the right of a Medicaid recipient to retain his or her home and still receive state-federal long term care benefits, is sacrificed if the home is held in trust.

* * *

Colorado recently began treating the transfer of a home into the Medicaid applicant's or recipient's revocable trust as a Medicaid disqualifying transfer.

* * *

---

[*] Copyright © 1997. Reprinted with permission.

California's rules, however, are otherwise. Under the Medi-Cal Eligibility Procedures Manual, "No person shall be made ineligible [for Medi-Cal benefits] to the extent otherwise exempt income or property [such as the Medi-Cal beneficiary's home] is held in trust."

b. Governmental Claims on the Assets of the Medicaid Recipient After the Recipient's Death: The Case of Assets in a Revocable Trust

Jon M. Zieger
*The State Giveth and the State Taketh Away:
In Pursuit of a Practical Approach to Medicaid Estate Recovery*
5 ELDER L.J. 359, 360, 366-67 (1997)[*]

As the cost of providing medical assistance to Medicaid recipients has continued to increase dramatically in the decades since that program's inception, states have sought various methods of reducing Medicaid expenditures. Estate recovery programs, designed to recoup Medicaid assistance from a recipient's estate, represent one method states have implemented to reduce Medicaid costs. Under these programs, the cost of medical assistance provided to a recipient becomes a debt of the recipient's estate or the estate of the recipient's surviving spouse.

* * *

Because estate recovery programs are largely creatures of state law and vary from state to state, a single definition of an estate recovery program is implausible. However, certain common elements can be adduced . . . . Because certain classes of assets are exempted when determining eligibility for Medicaid, a deceased Medicaid recipient may have been sufficiently needy to qualify for Medicaid and yet still leave a substantial estate. An estate recovery program focuses on recovering the amount expended on the recipient's behalf from these exempt assets after the recipient's death.

---

[*] Reprinted by permission. Copyright to the *Elder Law Journal* is held by the Board of Trustees of the University of Illinois.

Clifton B. Kruse, Jr.
*Critical Differences in Estate Planning Strategies
Between Revocable Trusts and Wills*
23 ACTEC NOTES 145, 145 and n.2 (1997)*

Revocable trusts do not protect a Medicaid beneficiary's assets held in such a trust from estate recovery laws and regulations. Use of a revocable trust does not insulate assets . . . (including those [assets] that are exempt during a Medicaid beneficiary's life) from recovery by the states who have furnished Medicaid benefits to the settlor. [The author notes, however, that assets exempt during the life of a Medicaid beneficiary may remain exempt "for the life of the Medicaid recipient's spouse, until the beneficiary has no surviving child under age 21, or so long as the recipient's child is blind or disabled as defined in 42 U.S.C. §1382c(a)(3)(A)."—Eds.]

Question

With respect to the receipt of Medicaid benefits during life and the avoidance of estate recovery after death, what advantages, if any, do revocable trusts possess?

7. The Revocable Trust as an Alternative to Guardianship

William M. McGovern, Jr.
Trusts, Custodianships, and Durable Powers of Attorney
27 REAL PROP., PROB. & TR. J. 1, 3-5 (1992)**

Knowledgeable lawyers prefer a trust to a guardianship for managing property. Because guardians do not usually acquire title to the ward's property, their acts may be voidable for lack of authority. This possible lack of authority makes many outsiders reluctant to deal with guardians. In contrast, trustees hold legal title to the property and can convey it to bona fide purchasers, even if the conveyance is unauthorized. Furthermore, many states limit guardians to a restricted list of investments, and guardians often cannot make any investment without court approval. In stark contrast, the "prudent person" standard [governing trusts] allows trustees more flexibility in investment decisions.

The Uniform Probate Code (UPC) eliminates many of the differences between trusts and guardianships. It gives a conservator "title as trustee" to the property of the protected person. Bona fide purchasers are protected "as if the conservator properly exercised the power." The UPC also gives conservators the same investment powers as trustees and allows them to make investments "without court authorization or confirmation."

---

* Copyright © 1997. Reprinted by permission.
* Copyright © 1992 by the American Bar Association. Reprinted by permission.

Despite the UPC modifications, a trust is still preferable to a guardianship for a number of reasons.

* * *

Imposing a guardianship on incompetent adults is possible, but it requires burdensome court proceedings, which can be extremely expensive. The current trend to reduce court involvement in fiduciary administration does not extend to incompetency determinations. For example, to seek an incompetency determination the UPC stipulates an elaborate procedure involving attorney representation, visitor interviews, physician examinations, cross examination of witnesses, and a trial by jury. The UPC requires these procedures because an alleged incompetent "should be extended the same rights as any other person whose personal freedom may be restricted as a result of the proceedings." These proceedings also impose significant emotional costs on family members who are forced to produce evidence of a loved one's incapacity.

A trust, on the other hand, can eliminate most of the emotional and financial costs of a guardianship. For example, parents who think that their adult children can not handle property can put the property into a trust without having the children adjudicated incompetent. A trust can also provide for the settlor's own property without a judicial determination that the settlor has become incompetent.

Questions

For the management of property, what advantages do revocable trusts have over guardianships? Are there any advantages that guardianships have over revocable trusts?

8. The Revocable Trust as an Alternative to the Durable Power of Attorney

Carolyn L. Dessin
Acting as Agent Under a Financial Durable Power of Attorney: An Unscripted Role
75 Neb. L. Rev. 574, 584, 602, 619 (1996)[*]

Estate planners view the durable power of attorney as an important planning tool, and its use is widely recommended. It can be broad, and it is easy to execute. The cost of executing a durable power of attorney will probably be less than the cost of creating an inter vivos trust or instituting a guardianship. A person may not even need to consult an attorney to obtain a durable power of attorney because a state statute may provide a form durable power of attorney. Additionally, powers of attorney in printed form are widely available in stationery and office supply stores. In sum,

---

[*] Copyright © 1996. Reprinted with permission.

a durable power of attorney is an inexpensive, popular tool that creates a much more flexible arrangement than either a guardianship or a trust. With flexibility, however, comes the possibility for abuse.

* * *

In light of the popularity of the durable power of attorney as a planning tool, it is critically important that the role of the agent be better defined. This is particularly true because estate planning attorneys often market the durable power of attorney to clients as an alternative to a trust or guardianship. Without a clearly defined role, the agent may not perform the way the principal expects, and the principal may suffer financially by choosing to execute the durable power of attorney rather than to create a trust.

* * *

Aside from enhanced protection of incompetent principals, another salutary effect of a better-defined standard of behavior for agents under durable powers of attorney would be a likely increase in the willingness of third parties to deal with agents. Many have noted that third parties sometimes refuse to deal with agents under durable powers. Without a reasonable assurance that third parties will deal with the agent, the durable power of attorney is not an acceptable alternative to either the trust or a guardianship in the event of disability.

Questions

What advantages do durable powers of attorney have over revocable trusts? What advantages do revocable trusts have over durable powers?

9. The Revocable Trust as a Will Substitute

John H. Langbein
The Nonprobate Revolution and the Future of the Law of Succession
97 HARV. L. REV. 1108, 1109, 1113 (1984)[*]

Four main will substitutes constitute the core of the nonprobate system: life insurance, pension accounts, joint accounts, and revocable trusts. When properly created, each is functionally indistinguishable from a will—each reserves to the owner complete lifetime dominion, including the power to name and to change beneficiaries until death.

* * *

---

[*] Copyrighted © 1984 Harvard Law Review Association. Reprinted by permission.

Either by declaration of trust or by transfer to a third-party trustee, the appropriate trust terms can replicate the incidents of a will. The owner who retains both the equitable life interest and the power to alter and revoke the beneficiary designation has used the trust form to achieve the effect of testation. Only nomenclature distinguishes the remainder interest created by such a trust from the mere expectancy arising under a will. Under either the trust or the will, the interest of the beneficiaries is both revocable and ambulatory.

Jay D. Waxenberg & Henry J. Leibowitz
Comparing the Advantages of Estates and Revocable Trusts
22 EST. PLAN. 265, 265-69 (September/October 1995)[*]

Advocates of living trusts frequently contend that using them as will substitutes offers a number of advantages, including saving estate taxes and probate fees, minimizing legal and accounting fees, eliminating delays, and insuring privacy. Many of these claims are untrue or overrated but there are some situations in which a living trust may be useful. An examination of the pros and cons will help you decide whether this device is right for clients.

To be effective, a living trust must be funded during the settlor's lifetime. This involves the re-registration of all the client's assets in the name of the trust. The practitioner must prepare deeds and other transfer documents and beneficiary designations, as well as correspond with banks, transfer agents, brokers, and title companies. The client must pay any transfer or recording fees that may apply. In many cases, this process can be time-consuming and expensive.

* * *

Despite the claims (express or implied) of many advocates of living trusts, no estate tax savings can be achieved with a living trust that cannot as easily be accomplished with a traditional will. There are estate tax saving opportunities available through the use of irrevocable trusts created during life but such trusts are vastly different from the revocable living trust, and using them may involve incurring gift tax.

Living trusts do not save income tax either. Indeed, estates governed by traditional wills have available some income tax planning opportunities that are not available to estates governed by living trusts. Perhaps the most important of these is the fact that an estate under a will can select a fiscal year for income tax purposes but a trust must report on a calendar year basis. By choosing a fiscal year, the estate may be able to defer recognition of post-death income for as much as 11 months, almost always enabling the beneficiaries to postpone their tax payments on that income for an entire year.

---

[*] Copyright © 1995. Reprinted with permission.

In addition, an estate receives a $600 personal exemption each year while a trust receives only a $100 exemption unless the trust instrument requires that all income be distributed each year, in which case the exemption increases to $300.

* * *

Because property transferred to a living trust during the settlor's lifetime is not part of the probate estate, the costs directly associated with probating a will may be avoided through the use of a living trust. Nevertheless, since it is often necessary to have a pour-over will where there is a living trust, some probate fees may be unavoidable.

The probate fee structure is different in every jurisdiction, but the fees charged by most courts are modest and are deductible on the estate's tax return.

* * *

Except for the legal work involved in the probate proceeding itself, which usually is not significant, the legal and accounting services for an estate governed by a living trust are roughly the same as those for an estate governed by a traditional will. Moreover, the attorney's fees for preparing a living trust agreement, a pour-over will, and all the necessary transfer documents are frequently greater than the fee for preparing a traditional will.

* * *

Claims by supporters of living trusts that these entities avoid delays in distributing assets are often grossly exaggerated. Of course, the trustee of a living trust can continue to administer the assets without interruption by the settlor's death, but in most states, including Florida, a will can be admitted to probate after only a minimal delay—usually no more than a week or two. Even in New York, where the wait for probate can be longer, an executor acting under a traditional will can apply for preliminary letters testamentary and usually receive authority to perform all essential duties within a few days after death.

* * *

Advocates of living trusts often argue that such trusts afford greater privacy as to the disposition of assets than does a traditional will. Although a living trust may never need to be filed in court, in actual practice, many banks and brokerage firms require that a copy of the trust agreement be submitted to them for review before they will open an account, so that the contents of the agreement may never be entirely confidential.

* * *

The fact that a living trust is not filed in court does not prevent a challenge to the client's estate plan or to the validity of the governing instrument. A living trust can be contested for the same reasons as can a will (e.g., undue influence, incompetence, or fraud).

* * *

A living trust may be an excellent option to consider if the client owns real estate located in more than one state. In an estate governed by a traditional will, additional probate documents must be filed with each of the local probate courts. If the property is held in a living trust, the costs associated with these ancillary probate filings can be avoided.

Questions

Do you agree with Messrs. Waxenberg and Leibowitz? How would you evaluate the merits of a revocable trust as a substitute will?

E. Custodial Trusts under the Uniform Custodial Trust Act

In connection with the following excerpt, skim through the provisions of the Uniform Custodial Trust Act ("UCTA") in the statutory supplement.

Gerry W. Beyer
Simplification of Inter Vivos Trust Instruments: From Incorporation by Reference to the Uniform Custodial Trust Act and Beyond
32 S. Tex. L. Rev. 203, 213-14, 217-24, 229-30 (1991)[*]

The National Conference of Commissioners on Uniform State Laws began drafting the Uniform Custodial Trust Act in 1984. After three years of work, the Commissioners approved the UCTA at their 1987 conference. The ABA then approved it in February 1988. [So far, the UCTA has been adopted in 14 states: Alaska, Arkansas, Hawai'i, Idaho, Louisiana, Massachusetts, Minnesota, Missouri, Nebraska, New Mexico, North Carolina, Rhode Island, Virginia, and Wisconsin.—Eds.]

The UCTA authorizes the creation of a statutory custodial trust by delivering property to another person with a clear indication that the property is to be governed by the provisions of the UCTA. Using trust analogies, the drafters modeled the UCTA after the Uniform Transfers to Minors Act because "of its widespread use and the familiarity of third party financial institutions with the registration concept."

* * *

The UCTA was "designed to provide a statutory standby inter vivos trust for individuals who typically are not very affluent or sophisticated, and possibly represented by attorneys engaged in general rather than specialized estate practice." The

---

[*] Copyright © 1991. Reprinted with permission.

drafters anticipated that the primary users of the UCTA would be elderly individuals seeking to make arrangements for the future management of their property in the event they were to become incapacitated. Other users would include individuals needing to distribute funds to incapacitated persons without guardians or conservators, parents wishing to make gifts to adult children, military personnel and others temporarily residing outside of the United States, and those persons who have received property under the Uniform Gifts/Transfers to Minors Act and desire to continue the custodial trust arrangement into their adult years.

* * *

The UCTA provides a person with several methods with which to create a custodial trust. The methods make it relatively simple to effectuate one of the UCTA's goals of making the creation of custodial trusts an easy process that may be accomplished without legal advice.

* * *

The drafters expect the transfer in trust to be the most commonly used method for creating a custodial trust. The property owner simply makes a written transfer directing the transferee to hold the property as a custodial trustee under the UCTA. The transfer must designate a beneficiary, and the transferor is authorized to name himself or herself as the beneficiary.

* * *

A property owner may also create a custodial trust by executing a written declaration that describes the property, names a beneficiary, and indicates that the declarant holds the property as a custodial trustee under the UCTA. The property owner, however, cannot be the sole beneficiary of a self-declaration of trust.

* * *

The person with the right to designate the recipient of property contingent upon a future event may create a custodial trust effective upon the occurrence of that future event. The designation must be in writing, and it must clearly indicate that the property is to be held in a custodial trust for the named beneficiary.

* * *

The ... methods discussed above are not exclusive; if other methods satisfying UCTA requirements are used to create a custodial trust, they will be equally effective. For example, "[a] custodial trust could be created by the exercise of a valid power of attorney or power of appointment given by the owner of property." The UCTA was not designed to displace or restrict other methods of trust creation. Thus, if a trust fails to meet the requirements of the UCTA—for example where a non-beneficiary transferor reserves the power to revoke the transfer—the trust may still be enforceable under the state's normal trust law.

* * *

Acceptance of the custodial trust property triggers the trustee's duties under the UCTA.

* * *

The beneficiary of a custodial trust has only the beneficial interest in the property; legal title to the property is in the trustee.

* * *

The UCTA does not authorize successive interests in a trust. The only situation where the trust may continue beyond the original beneficiary's lifetime is when the at-death distributee is incapacitated. In such a case, the trust continues for the use and benefit of the distributee, but only until the distributee's incapacity is removed or the trust terminates.

* * *

As long as the beneficiary is not incapacitated, the trustee must follow the beneficiary's directions concerning the management, control, investment, and retention of trust property.

* * *

The trustee need not follow the directions of someone exercising a durable power of attorney given by a beneficiary who has become incapacitated. Accordingly, the incapacitated beneficiary's agent may neither terminate the trust nor direct the administration or distribution of custodial trust property.

* * *

A trustee is provided with very broad powers under the UCTA. The trustee has "all the rights and powers over custodial trust property which an unmarried adult owner has over individually owned property, but a custodial trustee may exercise those rights and powers in a fiduciary capacity only." Alternatively, a state could choose to substitute language which refers to its statutes supplying fiduciary powers.

* * *

If the beneficiary is not incapacitated, the trustee must follow the beneficiary's distribution instructions. In this situation, the trustee acts more like an agent than a traditional trustee.

* * *

The trustee's duties with respect to the distribution of trust property are considerably different if the beneficiary is or becomes incapacitated or if the transferor directs that the trust be administered as if the beneficiary were incapacitated. In this situation, the trustee is authorized to use trust property as the trustee considers reasonably prudent for the use and benefit of the beneficiary, as well as for individuals whom the beneficiary supported when the beneficiary became incapacitated or who are legally entitled to the beneficiary's support, even if such individuals have not been receiving any support (e.g., beneficiary failed to make child support payments). It is significant that the UCTA permits distributions for the benefit of the beneficiary without regard to whether the distributions are needed for the beneficiary's support, maintenance, education, or health care.

Questions

How do custodial trusts under the UCTA work? What are their advantages and weaknesses, in general and in comparison with the other methods of property management discussed in this chapter?

FURTHER READING. ALISON BARNES ET AL., COUNSELING OLDER CLIENTS chs. 7, 8 (1997); PETER J. STRAUSS & NANCY M. LEDERMAN, THE ELDER LAW HANDBOOK ch. 11 (1996); PETER J. STRAUSS ET AL., AGING AND THE LAW, chs. 25, 29 (1996).

CHAPTER 6

Guardianship and Protection

A. Adult Guardianship 259
B. Elder Abuse 280

In this chapter, we examine two areas of the law that protect the most vulnerable of the elderly. Part A explores the law of adult guardianship, which can be invoked when someone is not capable of making personal or financial decisions. Part B considers the ugly reality of elder abuse and the extent to which the legal system provides safeguards against it.

A. Adult Guardianship

1. Background and Terminology

Mark D. Andrews
The Elderly in Guardianship: A Crisis of Constitutional Proportions
5 ELDER L.J. 75, 79-80 (1997)[*]

Guardianship arises under the state power of *parens patriae*, a power "inherited from English law where the Crown assumed the 'care of those who, by reason of their imbecility and want of understanding, are incapable of taking care of themselves.'" As early as 1890, the U.S. Supreme Court recognized the doctrine as it was inherited from England, holding that the American Revolution gave the state the power previously vested in the British Parliament and king. The Court concluded that it is "indispensable that there should be a power in the legislature to authorize a sale of the estates of infants, idiots, insane persons and persons not known, or not in being, who cannot act for themselves." To care for persons unable to care for themselves, the state can appoint a guardian, often a relative. If no suitable guardian is available, the state itself becomes the guardian of the elderly ward.

Guardianship begins when a person asks the court to make a determination whether another person is able to handle her affairs. When this motion is filed, the

---

[*] Reprinted by permission. Copyright to the *Elder Law Journal* is held by the Board of Trustees of the University of Illinois.

court often will appoint a guardian ad litem to advise the court of the person in question's ability to manage her affairs or estate. If the guardian ad litem finds that the elderly person is not competent to handle her affairs, the guardian ad litem will recommend to the court how the alleged incompetent's affairs should be handled. If the person is judged incompetent, a court may appoint either a conservator to care for the incompetent's property or a guardian to care for the ward's person and property. The incompetent person is the ward of the guardian or conservator. The terms incompetency and incapacity are most often used to describe the condition that warrants appointment of a guardian. Current trends gravitate toward using incapacity, because it carries a less pejorative stigma and focuses more on the capacity to manage one's affairs, rather than the more blanket term incompetency, which suggests a stigmatizing mental deficiency.

Danielle Priola
Case Note, *Disability Law—Burden of Proof...*
In Re M.R., *135 N.J. 155, 638 A.2d 1274 (1994)*
26 SETON HALL L. REV. 407, 408 n. 4 (1995)[*]

[G]uardianship arrangements can be classified into four categories: plenary guardianship, guardianship of the person, guardianship of the estate, and limited guardianship. A plenary guardianship arrangement vests the guardian with the authority to make decisions on behalf of the ward at an incompetency adjudication. A guardianship of the estate appointment concerns the financial and property rights of the incompetent while a guardianship of the person arrangement encompasses the remaining rights involved with personal decision-making. The last arrangement, a limited guardianship, particularizes the decision making dynamics to the individual needs of the ward.

Jamie L. Leary
*A Review of Two Recently Reformed Guardianship Statutes:
Balancing the Need to Protect Individuals Who Cannot Protect Themselves
Against the Need to Guard Individual Autonomy*
5 VA. J. SOC. POL'Y & L. 245, 264 (1997)[**]

In cases where a guardianship is necessary, some state statutes now mandate that a limited guardianship be used unless it can be shown that a plenary guardianship is necessary. This allows the ward to maintain control over every area that she can until she no longer is able to do so. Such a change requires increased court involvement, however, because guardians have to seek a new court order whenever the ward's abilities change.

---

[*] Copyright © 1995. Reprinted with permission.
[**] Copyright © 1997. Reprinted with permission.

Questions

1. What is the distinction between guardianship and conservatorship? (Note that this book often uses "guardianship" to cover both terms.)

2. What is the distinction between plenary and limited guardianship?

2. Statistics on Guardianship

Paula L. Hannaford & Thomas L. Hafemeister
*The National Probate Court Standards:
The Role of the Courts in Guardianship and Conservatorship Proceedings*
2 ELDER L.J. 147, 154-56 (1994)[*]

A pervasive problem for organizations examining the use of guardianship for the elderly has been the lack of accurate or reliable information concerning the number of persons actually under the protection of a guardian in the United States. Much of the criticism of guardianship proceedings [in the late 1980s stemmed] from a few highly publicized, notorious, and particularly heinous examples of guardians' abuse and neglect of wards. Whether these examples constitute the exceptions or the rule of how guardianships actually function was unknown, however. To begin to address this problem, staff members from the National Probate Court Standards Project compiled statistical information about the number of guardianship cases filed in thirty-five states and the District of Columbia from 1990 through 1992.

The number of guardianship cases filed varies widely among the states, both in terms of absolute numbers and relative to the state's population. The total number of filings was 86,622 for twenty-two states and the District of Columbia in 1990; 114,882 for thirty-two states and the District of Columbia in 1991; and 133,005 for thirty-four states and the District of Columbia in 1992. Taking into account only those states reporting filings for all three years (twenty-one states and the District of Columbia), the number of filings increased twenty-five percent between 1990 and 1992. Seventeen states and the District of Columbia showed an increase in the number of filings during this period, with Alaska showing the largest percentage increase. The range of the average number of filings for the three-year period varies between a low of 122 in the District of Columbia to a high of 22,675 in Michigan. When adjusted for population, the average number of guardianship filings per 100,000 ranged from a low of 10.9 filings in Virginia to a high of 241.8 in Michigan. Based on the 1992 figures provided by the state courts, the total number of guardianship cases filed in state courts exceeds 300,000 annually, with an average per capita filing estimated at 121.3 per 100,000 of U.S. population.

---

[*] Reprinted by permission. Copyright to the *Elder Law Journal* is held by the Board of Trustees of the University of Illinois.

Guardianship cases appear to be highly concentrated in particular states. The filings in Florida, Indiana, Michigan, New York, and Ohio—the five states with the largest guardianship caseloads—account for more than sixty-four percent of the total for 1990, more than fifty-four percent in 1991, and more than sixty-eight percent in 1992. However, all five are among the ten most populous states in the country. When adjusted for population, the five states with the highest average filing rates per 100,000 were: Michigan (241.8), Vermont (175.4), Connecticut (142.8), Arkansas (119.3), and Indiana (115.2). The five states with the lowest average filing rates, when adjusted for population, were: Virginia (10.9), the District of Columbia (20.5), Colorado (36.6), Washington (49.7), and Hawaii (54.6). These results may be partially explained by the fact that the states with the highest per capita number of guardianship filings also had an above-average proportion of persons over age eighty-five. Similarly, with the exception of the District of Columbia, the states with the lowest guardianship filing rates had a below-average proportion of persons over age eighty-five. In other words, not surprisingly, states with a comparatively large proportion of elderly persons in their population have higher numbers of guardianship cases filed.

Question

How common is guardianship?

3. The Standard of Incapacity

In connection with the following excerpt, read §5-103(7) of the 1990 UPC and § 102(5) of the 1997 Uniform Guardianship and Protective Proceedings Act ("UGPPA") in the statutory supplement.

Phillip B. Tor & Bruce D. Sales
A Social Science Perspective on the Law of Guardianship: Directions for Improving the Process and Practice
18 LAW & PSYCHOL. REV. 1, 4-10 (1994)[*]

The chief purpose of a guardianship hearing is to make a legal determination about a subject's competency. Since determination of incompetency is a legal conclusion, each state spells out in its guardianship statute the legal requirements for making such a finding. The statutory standards can be categorized into three groups: the causal link approach, the Uniform Probate Code (UPC) approach, and the functional approach.

---

[*] Copyright © 1994. Reprinted with permission.

A. *Causal Link Approach*

The causal link approach refers to the traditional standards of incompetency where mental or physical conditions are linked to a generalized incapacity for self care. Under these statutes, the court could declare a person incompetent on the basis of a diagnostic label, such as aged or mentally retarded, if there is testimony that the subject is inadequately caring for himself or herself or his or her property. For example, a discontinued version of the Minnesota guardianship statute included the categories of "old age," "imperfection or deterioration of mentality," and "incompetent to manage his person." This type of statute is based on classifications. Incompetence and the general inability to care for one's self or manage one's responsibilities are viewed as inevitable consequences of that classification. If the petitioner (the party who initiates the guardianship action) can convince the court that the proposed ward has a disabling condition and is not taking proper care of himself or herself or his or her assets, the court could legally approve the guardianship.

* * *

Because causal link statutes offer only vague standards for incompetency, they give the judge wide discretion in deciding what evidence is admissible. In turn, broad judicial discretion gives rise to the likelihood of different outcomes of incompetency determinations for persons with similar disabilities who are adjudicated in the same jurisdiction. It also increases the likelihood of discrepant decisions by the same judge when hearing cases for defendants with similar conditions. Moreover, a person who fits into a statutory category but is capable of some degree of self-maintenance may still be forced to surrender to a plenary guardianship.

B. *Uniform Probate Code Approach*

In an effort to escape the stigmatic labels of the traditional causal link statutes, the Uniform Probate Code (UPC) approach defines "incapacity" as an impairment of cognitive and communicative abilities resulting from one of a number of mental or physical conditions. The operative wording for incapacity in UPC statutes is the lack of "sufficient understanding or capacity to make or communicate responsible decisions concerning his person." Most state legislatures have made changes to their guardianship statutes by incorporating this language.

* * *

This legislative desire to measure incompetency by the impairment of cognitive processes does not alleviate many of the problems with the causal link approach. UPC statutes perpetuate the use of causal categories and give the court too much discretion because the key cognitive processes upon which they focus (i.e., understanding or capacity to make or communicate responsible decisions) remain vague. In addition, although the UPC emphasizes the defendant's ability to make decisions, it allows the court to discount that ability if the decisions are not deemed responsible. This standard of incompetency fails to distinguish the capacity to make a decision, albeit a foolish one, from the capacity to make a socially or morally responsible decision. Thus, the court's finding of incapacity continues to turn on its own values, rather than on functional deficiencies. Finally, courts in UPC jurisdictions may seldom have sufficient information about the proposed ward's conduct to make an objective determination about the proposed ward's decision making abilities. For these reasons, judicial inconsistencies may continue to plague guardianship proceedings.

* * *

C. *Functional Approach*

The functional approach represents the most recent innovation in guardianship standards. It requires that the court look at objective behavioral evidence of functional limitations in the person's daily activities when determining an individual's need for assistance. These statutes list specific activities, such as securing food, clothing, and health care for oneself. Courts will thereby have useful guidelines for determining when and how much assistance is needed to protect the individual from that person's incapacity, without imposing unnecessary restrictions on the individual's autonomy.

The functional approach is familiar and useful to mental health professionals because it focuses on behavioral objectives in the care and treatment of people with mental and physical disabilities. [It has been] argued that the functional approach can aid judicial decision making by referring to the very same objective criteria used by geriatric nurses, social workers, psychologists, physicians, and related health workers to evaluate patients with mental, physical, and social disabilities. This information is expected to help the court in deciding when and to what degree intervention is called for.

A growing number of states have adopted the functional approach. The New Hampshire code, for example, defines "functional limitations" as:

> ... behavior or conditions ... which impair (one's) ability to participate in and perform minimal activities of daily living that secure and maintain proper food, clothing, shelter, health care or safety for himself or herself....
>
> "Incapacity" means a legal, not a medical, disability and shall be measured by functional limitations.... Inability to provide for personal needs or to manage property shall be evidenced by acts or occurrences, or statements which strongly indicate imminent acts or occurrences.

The statute also discusses the minimum frequency and duration of the observed limitations which evidence the need for guardianship.

* * *

It has been argued that legislatures should write statutes that not only mandate evidence of functional deficits, but also require prehearing standardized functional evaluations.... Both requirements would serve to screen out petitions that do not present a prima facie case worthy of judicial consideration, bring consistency to the determinations of legal incapacity, and create a more accurate and fair adjudicatory process.

Indeed, such evaluations are logically compelled because the functional approach requires that guardianship petitions include information about the prospective ward that only professional health care workers could provide.

* * *

Despite the compelling logic for applying the functional approach, the impact that changes in the statutory definitions of incompetency have had on the guardianship system needs to be empirically examined.

Questions

Into which of the categories described by Messrs. Tor and Sales would you put 1997 UGPPA §102(5)? How does this section differ from 1990 UPC § 5-103(7)?

4. The Process of Petitioning for Guardianship

Guardianship procedures vary considerably from state to state. In this section, we examine the procedures contained in two uniform laws: (a) Article V of the UPC, which was promulgated in 1969 and revised in 1982, and (b) the UGPPA, which was promulgated in 1982 and revised in 1997. We begin, however, with some background.

a. Background on UPC Article V and on the UGPPA

A. Frank Johns & Vicki Joiner Bowers
Guardianship Folly: The Misgovernment of Parens Patriae and the Forecast of Its Crumbling Linkage to Unprotected Older Americans in the Twenty-First Century—A March of Folly? Or Just a Mask of Virtual Reality?
27 STETSON L. REV. 1, 34-37, 40, 45 (1997)[*]

The Uniform Probate Code (UPC) is a creation of the National Conference of Commissioners on Uniform State Laws. Promulgated in 1969, the UPC resulted from a continuing review and study of probate laws.

* * *

Consistency and continuity of language is the hallmark of any uniform legislation or code. The UPC endeavored to remedy arcane and inconsistent language in guardianship statutes from state to state. UPC Article V applied the then-current language to the guardianship concept, thus eliminating the arcane and embarrassing terms brought into modern American jurisprudence from . . . previous ages.

---

[*] Copyright © 1997. Reprinted with permission.

* * *

Article V covers guardianships for both minors and adults, and protective proceedings for property. It provides terminology continuity in "typical" guardianship legislation, and addresses and incorporates many recommendations of concurrent empirical research and studies.

* * *

During the 1970s, the UPC, with its Article V on guardianship and conservatorship, gained acceptance.

* * *

During the mid-1970s, the ABA's Committee on the Mentally Disabled began an effort that promoted revision of the Uniform Probate Code Article V to include "limited guardianship" to avoid an asserted "overkill" implicit in standard guardianship proceedings. UPC spokespersons and the National Conference of Commissioners objected and temporarily barred recommended UPC revisions, contending "typical" guardianship legislation was sufficient.

However, many of the UPC states began amending statutes to include some form of limited guardianship, but the states utilized inconsistent language . . . . To not be left behind, the National Conference of Commissioners changed course, and developed what was to be the Uniform Guardianship and Protective Proceedings Act.

* * *

In 1982, the Commissioners produced a stand alone act entitled The Uniform Guardianship and Protective Proceedings Act (UGPPA). The UGPPA restructured UPC Article V to include explicit language relative to the concept of limited guardianship, and incorporated the limited guardianship philosophy into all other parts to provide internal consistency and accommodate the limited guardianship concept. Alternatively, with the modifications to Article V, it was offered as a component part to the UPC.

Jamie L. Leary
A Review of Two Recently Reformed Guardianship Statutes: Balancing the Need to Protect Individuals Who Cannot Protect Themselves Against the Need to Guard Individual Autonomy
5 VA. J. SOC. POL'Y & L. 245, 269-70 (1997)[*]

In the mid-1970s, the ABA Commission on the Mentally Disabled began reform work to expand Article V of the Uniform Probate Code to include limited guardianships. This effort culminated in the drafting of a "free-standing" act in 1982: the Uniform Guardianship and Protective Proceedings Act ("UGPPA" or "the Act"). The

---

[*] Copyright © 1997. Reprinted with permission.

1982 UGPPA focused on the concept of limited guardianship "so that the authority of the protector would intrude only to the degree necessary on the liberties and prerogatives of the protected person." The National Conference of Commissioners worked to incorporate the concept of the limited guardianship throughout the statute "to provide internal consistency."

The 1997 UGPPA makes an important change in the concept of limited guardianships, but has also been expanded to include other important procedural reforms. It ensures due process by providing for adequate representation for the respondent and requiring the respondent's presence at the hearing. It defines incapacity using a functional approach so that an individual who simply needs technological assistance can retain control over other areas of her life. Finally, it requires the court to monitor guardians.

b. The Procedures for Petitioning for Guardianship Under Article V of the 1990 UPC and Under the 1997 UGPPA

Answers to the following questions, and to subsequent questions posed in this unit on guardianship, will be found in the 1990 UPC, Article V, Part 3, and the 1997 UGPPA, Article 3, both of which deal with guardianship of the person.

Questions

Compare the answers to the following questions under Article V of the 1990 UPC and under the 1997 UGPPA. Which approach is better, and might a third approach be better than either?

1. *Procedural Matters Before the Hearing.* Who may file the guardianship petition? What information must the petition contain? What notice must be provided to the person alleged to be incapacitated?

2. *Procedural Matters at the Hearing.* Who is required or permitted to be present at the hearing? To what extent are lawyers and health-care professionals involved? What form does the hearing take, and what types of evidence may be presented? Who is the ultimate decision-maker? What standard of proof is required before a guardian may be appointed?

3. *Emergencies.* What happens in an emergency?

4. *Selecting the Guardian.* Who may be appointed as guardian? Must the guardian be a person, or may an entity or organization serve as guardian?

5. The Use of Alternative Dispute Resolution ("ADR")

Susan N. Gary
Mediation and the Elderly: Using Mediation to Resolve Probate Disputes Over Guardianship and Inheritance
32 WAKE FOREST L. REV. 397, 414-15, 424-31, 434 (1997)[*]

Disputes over guardianship can arise either before the guardian is named or after the appointment. One type of dispute occurs when the person who is alleged to be incapacitated does not want to have a guardian appointed. Susan Hartman, the Directing Attorney for the Center for Social Gerontology's Guardianship Mediation Program, has written that, despite law reforms, guardianship proceedings are still handled in a routine manner, with little attention given to the capacity issues and little exploration of alternatives to guardianship. The adult for whom the guardianship is sought may feel betrayed and demeaned by the process. An adversarial legal proceeding may exacerbate these feelings.

Another type of conflict may develop when two adult children each want to be appointed guardian of their mother or father. The conflict may have roots in differing views of appropriate care for the parent, it may hide concern over protecting an inheritance, or it may simply reflect a long-standing sibling rivalry.

Different opinions about decisions that have been made or that need to be made on behalf of the older adult may also lead to conflict before the appointment of a guardian. Family members may disagree about medical or financial decisions. They may disagree about where the older person should live and what type of living arrangement is appropriate. Although the older person may not be incapacitated, if the person is of somewhat limited capacity, failure to resolve a dispute about any of these issues may result in a guardianship proceeding as a last resort. Mediation may be useful as a means of resolving the dispute and eliminating the need for a guardianship proceeding.

After a court appoints a guardian, disputes may occur if other family members disagree with actions taken by the guardian. The conflict may be over the appropriateness of decisions and quality of care, or it may focus on whether the guardian is breaching his fiduciary duties and misusing the protected person's funds. Although the guardian may be acting under legal authority, family disagreements may escalate into adversarial battles that lead to continued fighting within the family.

In addition to conflicts among family members, conflicts may develop between the older person or family members and hospitals, nursing homes, or service agencies. In some situations, one of these care providers may bring a guardianship proceeding as a convenient—albeit inappropriate from the standpoint of the protected person—resolution of the problem.

* * *

---

[*] Copyright © 1997. Reprinted with permission.

In discussing the advantages of mediation, this article compares mediation with litigation, the form of legal dispute resolution most widely used to resolve probate disputes. Mediation's beneficial characteristics include the opportunity for privacy and confidentiality, the promotion of therapeutic effects for the parties, the expanded possibility that an ongoing relationship between parties can be maintained, the potential for creating solutions uniquely suited to the problem at hand, and the possible reduction of financial costs as compared with those incurred in litigation. Each of these characteristics makes mediation an appropriate form of dispute resolution for parties to a probate dispute to consider.

* * *

A. *Privacy and Confidentiality*

* * *

Privacy benefits probate disputants in two ways: first, by avoiding public discussion of a family's "dirty laundry," and second, by encouraging disputants to speak freely in an attempt to reach a resolution that deals with the messy relationship problems, as well as the legal property problems.

* * *

B. *Emotional Benefits*

* * *

In a guardianship proceeding, the older adult faces a potential loss of dignity, as well as the loss of legal and civil rights. The appointment of a guardian may assist the older adult with practical or financial needs, but by ignoring the emotional aspect of the proceeding, may leave the protected person confused, angry, or bitter. A mediation proceeding gives the older adult a voice. The process allows him to speak about his concerns and gives the family members a chance to explain the need for the guardianship. Regardless of whether the resolution is a less restrictive solution or a request that the court appoint a guardian, the older adult will benefit from the chance to hear and to be heard.

* * *

In addition to the potential emotional benefits of mediation, parties using mediation to resolve their dispute may avoid some of the emotional costs of litigation. The litigation process itself can be traumatic.

* * *

C. *Ongoing Relationships*

* * *

First, in the course of understanding each other's views of the problem, the process increases communication between the parties. Second, by participating in the process of problem solving, the parties may be better able to work with each other to solve future problems. Both of these aspects of mediation can contribute to a better long-term relationship between the parties.

Mediation may also further an ongoing relationship between the parties by what it does not do. Litigation, in contrast with mediation, encourages parties to become entrenched in their positions and to view a successful outcome as a win for one party and a loss for the other.

* * *

D. *Unique Solutions*

* * *

In a guardianship proceeding, the court will either appoint a guardian, usually significantly depriving the protected person of rights, or decide that a guardian is not necessary, leaving the older person to fend for herself. Mediation allows the older adult and the family members to work together to reach a solution, perhaps arranging for some assistance for the older person without the need to have a guardian appointed.

* * *

E. *Financial Costs*

* * *

Much has been written about the high financial cost of litigation. Although mediation is not necessarily less expensive than litigation, research in family law has shown that mediation costs less than litigation in resolving divorce cases. In addition to potential savings for the parties, a goal of mediation is to reduce societal costs by reducing the burden on the court system.

* * *

V. *Current Attempts to Encourage or Mandate Mediation in Probate*

Mediation in the probate context is still in its infancy; but increasingly legislatures, the judiciary, and attorneys are turning to mediation as an appropriate dispute resolution process for handling probate issues. No data exists on the extent to which probate courts are currently using mediation.

Questions

1. How would you evaluate the advantages of ADR? Does it have any disadvantages compared to the procedures used in the UPC and UGPPA?

2. Should parties be required to try some form of ADR before filing a formal guardianship petition?

6. The Guardian's Powers and Duties: The Statutory Language

Questions

1. *Authority.* What powers does the guardian have?

2. *Responsibility.* What duties must the guardian perform?

3. *Delegation.* To what extent may a guardian delegate his powers or duties to others?

7. The Guardian's Powers and Duties: The Standard of Decisionmaking

Hal Fliegelman & Debora C. Fliegelman
Giving Guardians the Power to Do Medicaid Planning
32 Wake Forest L. Rev. 341, 349-352 (1997)[*]

The standards by which courts decide whether a guardian may have certain powers and take certain actions have always been guided by one main principle: avoiding abuse and protecting the ward. What is best for the ward, however, is not always easy to ascertain. Interested parties may disagree over what is best. Judges may feel constrained by statute or common law. Wards may have left incomplete or incoherent instructions, or none at all. In the effort to give guardians the authority to do what is "best" for the ward while also guarding against potential abuse, courts have developed various standards, including the "continuing pattern" theory, "best interests of the ward," and "substituted judgment." In addition, courts have relied on constitutional concepts such as equal protection to permit guardians to take such actions as giving gifts and making transfers from the guardianship estate.

1. *Continuing pattern*

The continuing pattern theory is generally criticized. It requires a determination of what the incompetent would do, based on what he or she has already done. Evidence of the incompetent's prior intent . . . is the only factor given any weight. It is considered a purely subjective test. The subjective test, however, is not always appropriate. As [one] court . . . explained, the subjective test, "however meaningful," is entirely inapplicable in the case of a congenital incompetent:

> To so conclude [that subjective intent "must always stand as an indispensable prerequisite to relief"] would offer an individual as Brennan [a profoundly disabled child—Eds.] less opportunity in the law than persons who have come to know a disability in later life. Brennan has not had the opportunity to consider or formulate a lifetime or testamentary plan. He has been deprived of the opportunity to know and convey his personal

---

[*] Copyright © 1997. Reprinted with permission.

feelings for those who stand as the natural objects of his bounty. He has not had the opportunity to confer with business or legal advisors and reflect upon what meaning the imposition of inheritance taxes may have upon the plans he would make relative to the succession of his property. Brennan is deprived of these opportunities not by his own choice or inaction but rather by reason of multiple physical and mental disabilities brought upon him by the very event of his birth. In this day and these circumstances, it would be inappropriate to cling in dogmatic fashion to rules which are incapable of satisfaction. Rather, the court in pursuit of its equitable powers is called upon to do justice.

Many courts have abandoned subjective intent as the sole standard.... Some jurisdictions now combine the subjective test with other, more objective standards.

2. *Best interests of the ward*

The best interests doctrine allows the court to proceed based on what it believes would be most beneficial to the ward. The best interests model has been likened to a parent-child relationship. Like a parent, a "best interests" guardian is expected to intervene where a ward lacks the ability to act according to his own best interests, or lacks the appreciation of the consequences of his actions. "The intervention is not condoned because it suits the parent or the guardian, or because the intervention by guardianship serves some third party or societal interest, but only because the interests of the child or ward are thereby best served." The requirement that the court determine what is in the ward's best interest is "intended to substitute a judicial determination for the guardian's personal discretion in order to provide additional protection to the ward." Determination of a ward's best interests should involve some consideration of the ward's wishes, where they are ascertainable.

"Best interests" statutes usually enumerate factors for the court to consider in determining what is best for the ward.

* * *

The problem with the "best interests" standard is that "the interests of the individual depend upon who is defining them." The definition of "best" is vague and uncertain, even with statutory guidelines.

* * *

3. *Substituted judgment*

The substituted judgment doctrine [involves] .... essentially an objective, "reasonably prudent person" standard .... "The controlling principle is that the court will act with reference to the incompetent and for his benefit as he would probably have acted if [capable]." [Under this standard,] [a] guardian may not act contrary to the settled intention of the ward.

Questions

1. What are the advantages and disadvantages of the three approaches described by Mr. and Ms. Fliegelman?

2. Which of the three approaches has been adopted by the 1990 UPC? By the 1997 UGPPA?

8. The Guardian's Powers and Duties: The Rise of Limited Guardianship

Sally Balch Hurme
Current Trends in Guardianship Reform
7 MD. J. CONTEMP. LEGAL ISSUES 143, 160-64, 168, 170-71 (1995-1996)[*]

Because a grant of full or plenary powers to a guardian results in a drastic loss of legal rights, legislatures have paid substantial attention to the appropriateness of limiting the powers granted to the guardian. As one author has commented, "use of guardians who are limited in their powers would promote the values of autonomy, self-determination, and individual dignity, and discourage the overreach of societal interference and manipulation." Logic makes a compelling case for limiting the deprivation of rights through a tailored guardianship order that matches the particular disabilities of the individual rather than the wholesale removal of rights through plenary orders.

1. *Historical Call for Tailored Orders*—Advocates have called for limited guardianship for more than a decade. As early as 1979, the ABA Commission on the Mentally Disabled recommended that state laws be changed to avoid an asserted "overkill" implicit in standard guardianship proceedings.

A key reason the National Conference of Commissioners on Uniform State Laws adopted the Uniform Guardianship and Protective Proceedings Act (UGPPA) in 1982 to amend the Article V guardianship provisions of the Uniform Probate Code (UPC) was to include the concept of limited guardianships. Following the ABA Commission's recommendation, the UGPPA recognized the need for more sensitive procedures and for appointments fashioned so that the authority of the protector would intrude only to the degree necessary on the liberties and prerogatives of the protected person. In short, rather than permitting an all-or-none status, there should be an intermediate status available to the courts through which the protected person will have personal liberties and prerogatives restricted only to the extent necessary under the circumstances. The court should be admonished to look for a least-restrictive protection approach.

Seven years later the National Guardianship Symposium called for limited guardianship orders that are "as specific as possible with respect to the guardian's

---

[*] Copyright © 1996. Reprinted with permission.

powers and duties." The symposium reformers predicted that such specificity would help the courts limit guardianship and tailor orders to the incapacitated person's circumstances.

The newly issued National Probate Court Standards joins in directing probate judges to "detail the duties and powers of the guardian, including limitations to the duties and powers, and the rights retained by the respondent." The commentary to this standard notes that

> [b]ecause the preferred practice is to limit the powers and duties of the guardian to those necessary to meet the needs of the respondent, the court should specifically enumerate in its order the assigned duties and powers of the guardian. . . . By listing the powers and duties of the guardian, the court's order can serve as an educational road map to which the guardian can refer and use to help answer questions about what the guardian can or cannot do in carrying out the guardian's assigned responsibilities.

2. *Legislative Efforts*—Most state legislatures have taken major strides in recognizing the need for and appropriateness of limited orders. Limited orders, as used in this context, means more than just differentiating between a guardian of the person and a guardian (or conservator) of the estate. Every state that has implemented major guardianship reform in the past few years has incorporated provisions for limited orders or has mandated the issuance of limited orders enumerating the specific personal and financial powers given to the guardian and assigning the guardian only those duties and powers that the person is incapable of exercising. For example, Florida's comprehensive 1989 revision of its guardianship provisions requires that the order enumerate the guardian's specific powers and duties and state that "the guardian may exercise only those delegable rights which have been removed from the incapacitated person." Further, the order "must be consistent with the incapacitated person's welfare and safety, must be the least restrictive appropriate alternative, and must reserve to the incapacitated person the right to make decisions in all matters commensurate with his ability to do so."

The statute resulting from New York's massive revision requires that guardians have only those powers necessary to assist the incapacitated person to compensate for any limitations. The guardianship is to be "tailored to the individual needs of [an incapacitated] person, which takes into account the personal wishes, preferences and desires of the person, and which affords the person the greatest amount of independence and self-determination and participation in all the decisions affecting such person's life." This conception of limited guardianship is considered the cornerstone of both the Florida and New York statutory schemes.

Other states have followed the trend to provide for limited guardianship by stating a preference for limited guardianship, mandating specific findings of incapacity and providing the choice of the least restrictive intervention.

* * *

3. *Appellate Court Endorsement*—A review of reported decisions finds appellate courts approving the use of tailored orders and enforcing the legislative mandates

to limit the powers delegated to a guardian because of the serious deprivation of civil rights resulting from full guardianship.

* * *

4. *Self-Autonomy*—The overarching public policy to maintain the incapacitated person's self-autonomy to the highest degree possible in the new guardianship practices requires a combined emphasis on less restricted alternatives, functional assessment, and tailored orders. New York's guardianship laws clearly reflect an awareness of, and attention to, these interests. The statute states that guardianships should be "tailored to the individual needs of [an incapacitated] person, which takes into account the personal wishes, preferences and desires of the person, and which affords the person the greatest amount of independence and self-determination and participation in all the decisions affecting such person's life."

Questions

1. What explains the burgeoning interest in limited guardianship?

2. To what extent has the principle of limited guardianship been embodied in the provisions of the 1990 UPC? In the provisions of the 1997 UGPPA?

3. Are there any disadvantages to limited guardianship?

9. The Guardian's Powers and Duties: Monitoring by the Court

Sally Balch Hurme
Current Trends in Guardianship Reform
7 MD. J. CONTEMP. LEGAL ISSUES 143, 182-88 (1995-1996)[*]

The court practices following the guardian's appointment are widely divergent. Some states may require that guardians periodically report on the personal and financial well-being of the incapacitated person and routinely review the need to continue the guardianship. Other states may do little to provide ongoing oversight of the guardian's actions, reviewing the guardianship only if someone formally petitions the court.

The sources of this monitoring diversity are not clear, but a possible cause for a "hands off" policy is the philosophy behind the Uniform Probate Code (UPC). Its underlying premise is that the courts should not be involved in the day-to-day administration of a decedent's estate. The court's role is to be "wholly passive until some interested person invokes its power to secure resolution of a matter." For historical reasons guardianship was included in the probate code. Thus, under the original UPC, the guardian, like the probate administrator, received little supervision until filing the final accounting.

---

[*] Copyright © 1996. Reprinted with permission.

Unlike the administration of a decedent's estate, guardianship is for a living person whose needs can change over time. Not only should the court tailor the initial guardianship order to the immediate needs of the incapacitated person, but it should also establish routine procedures to supervise the guardian, to revise the guardianship order, and to resolve problems when the circumstances of the incapacitated person or the guardian change.

A 1991 study of guardianship monitoring by the American Bar Association's Commissions on Legal Problems of the Elderly and Mental and Physical Disability Law revealed that legislatures and courts are becoming more receptive of the need to monitor guardianship cases. The overwhelming legislative trend in the past decade has been to require guardians to report periodically on the incapacitated person's financial and personal status. To this end, all fifty states and the District of Columbia authorize courts to order financial accountings. In 1991, forty-three jurisdictions required guardians of the person to report on the incapacitated person's personal status and ten states require guardians of the property to report on both financial and personal status. All of the new statutes, with the exception of Delaware's, require the guardians of the person and of the estate to file annual financial and personal status reports.

Some states also require initial care reports or property management plans to be filed along with the more traditional inventories.

The South Dakota periodic report is typical of the type of information guardians must provide to the court. The report must state the current mental, physical, and social condition of the protected persons; their living arrangements; medical, educational, vocational, and other professional service provided to the protected persons; the guardian's opinion as to the adequacy of care; a summary of the guardian's visits with and activities on the protected person's behalf; whether the guardian agrees with the current treatment or habilitation plan if the protected person is institutionalized; and a recommendation as to the need to continue or change the guardianship's scope. Texas law requires guardians to file personal reports which include information such as when they most recently saw the incapacitated person and how frequently they see the incapacitated person. Additionally, the guardian must indicate whether the incapacitated person's mental and physical health has improved, deteriorated, or remained unchanged. The guardians also must evaluate whether the incapacitated person is content or unhappy with his or her living arrangements.

It must be emphasized that effective supervision of a guardian should include more than just receiving a periodic report. The court must establish procedures for reviewing and verifying the reports and for reconsidering the need to continue or modify the guardianship. Such procedures would promote more uniform review for all cases and provide up-to-date information on the location and status of the incapacitated person.

Based on the premise that a report is pointless if no one reviews it or acts on it, some legislatures have been fairly specific about the procedures a court must follow once such reports are filed. New York requires a court examiner to review the reports within thirty days of filing and authorizes various sanctions for failure to file.

It also establishes specific hours of training for guardians, court evaluators, and court examiners.

Texas has gone further than New York by creating a monitoring system to keep the court abreast of its guardianship cases. The court is directed to use reasonable diligence to determine whether a guardian is performing all required duties. The court is also required to examine the well-being of each incapacitated person, as well as the bond's sufficiency. Finally, the court must review each guardianship annually to see if it should be continued, modified, or terminated. Texas letters of appointment expire one year and 120 days after issuance. The letter can be renewed only if the accounting has been filed and approved. Additionally, the incapacitated person, or any other person, can request modification or termination of the guardianship through the submission of an informal letter.

Rhode Island requires the probate court to monitor each guardianship file and impose sanctions where necessary. In the case of a guardian over property, if the guardian fails to file an annual accounting, the guardian is accountable for the full value of the estate and can receive no compensation. Texas judges have the authority to imprison guardians for up to three days for any one offense, while New York judges can deny or reduce the compensation of the guardian or remove the guardian. Courts have become increasingly willing to impose various sanctions on guardians who have breached their fiduciay duty and misused funds. Guardians have been convicted of embezzlement, had judgments imposed against them, as well as having their gifts and sales set aside. The courts have held guardians liable for failure to segregate funds, denied their commissions, and have even removed guardians in certain situations. In addition, attorneys for guardians have been held liable for failing to discover and disclose their client's misappropriation of funds.

Questions

1. To what extent do the 1990 UPC and 1997 UGPPA provide for the monitoring of guardians?

2. What behavior(s) are these provisions attempting to prevent?

10. Professional Responsibility: Who Is the Client?

Fickett v. Superior Court of Pima County
558 P.2d 988 (Ariz. Ct. App. 1976)

HOWARD, Chief Judge.

Petitioners are defendants in a pending superior court action filed by the present conservator (formerly guardian) of an incompetent's estate against the former guardian and petitioners, attorneys for the former guardian. The gravamen of the complaint was that petitioner Fickett, as attorney for the former guardian, was negligent in failing to discover that the guardian had embarked upon a scheme to liquidate the guardianship estate by misappropriation and conversion of the funds to his own use and making improper investments for his personal benefit.

Petitioners filed a motion for summary judgment contending that, as a matter of law, since there was no fraud or collusion between the guardian and his attorney, the attorney was not liable for the guardian's misappropriation of the assets of the guardianship estate. In opposing the motion for summary judgment, the present conservator conceded that no fraud or collusion existed. His position, however, was that one could not say as a matter of law that the guardian's attorney owed no duty to the ward. The respondent court denied the motion for summary judgment and petitioners challenge this ruling by special action.

The general rule for many years has been that an attorney could not be liable to one other than his client in an action arising out of his professional duties, in the absence of fraud or collusion. In denying liability of the attorney to one not in privity of contract for the consequences of professional negligence, the courts have relied principally on two arguments: (1) That to allow such liability would deprive the parties to the contract of control of their own agreement; and (2) that a duty to the general public would impose a huge potential burden of liability on the contracting parties.

* * *

We cannot agree with petitioners that they owed no duty to the ward and that her conservator could not maintain an action because of lack of privity of contract. We are of the opinion that the better view is that the determination of whether, in a specific case, the attorney will be held liable to a third person not in privity is a matter of policy and involves the balancing of various factors, among which are the extent to which the transaction was intended to affect the plaintiff, the foreseeability of harm to him, the degree of certainty that the plaintiff suffered injury, the closeness of the connection between the defendant's conduct and the injuries suffered, the moral blame attached to the defendant's conduct, and the policy of preventing future harm.

We believe that the public policy of this state permits the imposition of a duty under the circumstances presented here.

* * *

We are of the opinion that when an attorney undertakes to represent the guardian of an incompetent, he assumes a relationship not only with the guardian but also with the ward. If, as is contended here, petitioners knew or should have known that the guardian was acting adversely to his ward's interests, the possibility of frustrating the whole purpose of the guardianship became foreseeable as did the possibility of injury to the ward. In fact, we conceive that the ward's interests overshadow those of the guardian .... We believe the following statement in *Heyer v. Flaig* ... as to an attorney's duty to an intended testamentary beneficiary is equally appropriate here:

> The duty thus recognized in Lucas stems from the attorney's undertaking to perform legal services for the client but reaches out to protect the intended beneficiary. We impose this duty because of the relationship between the attorney and the intended beneficiary; public policy requires

that the attorney exercise his position of trust and superior knowledge responsibly so as not to affect adversely persons whose rights and interests are certain and foreseeable.

Although the duty accrues directly in favor of the intended testamentary beneficiary, the scope of the duty is determined by reference to the attorney-client context. Out of the agreement to provide legal services to a client, the prospective testator, arises the duty to act with due care as to the interests of the intended beneficiary. We do not mean to say that the attorney-client contract for legal services serves as the fundamental touchstone to fix the scope of this direct tort duty to the third party. The actual circumstances under which the attorney undertakes to perform his legal services, however, will bear on a judicial assessment of the care with which he performs his services.

We, therefore, uphold the respondent court's denial of petitioners' motion for summary judgment since they failed to establish the absence of a legal relationship and concomitant duty to the ward.

* * *

HATHAWAY, J., and JACK G. MARKS, Superior Court Judge, concur.

Questions

1. Did the court reach the right result? Why or why not?

2. Are there any disadvantages to the imposition of attorney liability in such cases?

11. Terminating the Guardian(ship)

Questions

1. *Removal.* Under what circumstances may a court remove a previously-appointed guardian?

2. *Termination.* Under what circumstances may a guardianship be terminated?

B. Elder Abuse

1. The "Discovery" of Elder Abuse

Seymour Moskowitz
New Remedies for Elder Abuse and Neglect
PROB. & PROP. 52, 52-53 (January/February 1998)[*]

In the past 30 years, the popular image of an idealized and peaceful American family has been shattered. In 1962, in a pioneering article, C. Henry Kempe and his colleagues called the medical community's attention to the problem of physical child abuse, coining the term "battered child syndrome." Within a few years, volumes of research on child abuse surfaced . . . . In the 1970s a broad-based movement against spousal abuse and violence against women arose as a result of both public and professional attention.

Elder abuse, by contrast, received attention much later. Some early studies in the 1970s in Great Britain highlighted "granny bashing." By the early 1980s several American studies demonstrated that elder abuse was a serious problem in the United States as well.

Joann Blair
"Honor Thy Father and Thy Mother"—But For How Long?: Adult Children's Duty to Care for and Protect Elderly Parents
35 U. LOUISVILLE J. FAM. L. 765, 765 (1996-1997)[**]

Neglect of the elderly is a prevalent problem facing Americans that has only recently gained widespread attention. Child abuse and spousal abuse were addressed in the 1960's and 1970's, respectively, but in the past decade elder abuse has acquired a place in the spotlight of American politics . . . . In the United States, the House of Representatives Select Committee on Aging conducted the first major investigation of the elder abuse problem in 1981.

Question

Why did it take so long to discover the problem of elder abuse and bring it to the nation's attention?

---

[*] Copyright © 1998 by the American Bar Association. Reprinted by permission.
[**] Copyright © 1997. Reprinted with permission.

2. Definitions: Types of Elder Abuse

National Center on Elder Abuse
NCEA—*What is Elder Abuse?*
<www.gwjapan.com/NCEA/basic/index.html>*

Federal definitions of elder abuse, neglect, and exploitation appeared for the first time in the 1987 Amendments to the Older Americans Act. These definitions were provided in the law only as guidelines for identifying the problems and not for enforcement purposes. Currently, elder abuse is defined by state laws, and state definitions vary considerably from one jurisdiction to another in terms of what constitutes the abuse, neglect, or exploitation of the elderly. In addition, researchers have used many different definitions to study the problem. Broadly defined, however, there are three basic categories of elder abuse: (1) domestic elder abuse; (2) institutional elder abuse; and (3) self-neglect or self-abuse. In most cases, state statutes addressing elder abuse provide the definitions of these different categories of elder abuse, with varying degrees of specificity.

National Center on Elder Abuse
National Elder Abuse Incidence Study: Final Report, Executive Summary,
HTML Page 4 (September 1998)
<www.aoa.gov/abuse/report/Cexecsum-03.htm>

[In this study,] [*p*]*hysical abuse* was defined as the use of physical force that may result in bodily injury, physical pain, or impairment. Physical punishments of any kind were examples of physical abuse.

Sexual abuse was defined as non-consensual sexual contact of any kind with an elderly person.

Emotional or psychological abuse was defined as the infliction of anguish, pain, or distress.

Financial or material exploitation was defined as the illegal or improper use of an elder's funds, property, or assets.

Abandonment was defined as the desertion of an elderly person by an individual who had physical custody or otherwise had assumed responsibility for providing care for an elder or by a person with physical custody of an elder.

Neglect was defined as the refusal or failure to fulfill any part of a person's obligations or duties to an elder.

Self-neglect was characterized as the behaviors of an elderly person that threaten his/her own health or safety. The definition of self-neglect excludes a situation in which a mentally competent older person (who understands the consequences of his/her decisions) makes a conscious and voluntary decision to engage in acts that threaten his/her health or safety.

---

* Reprinted with permission.

Questions

1. Having read through these definitions, do you have a better appreciation for the "many faces" of elder abuse?

2. Do you know anyone who has experienced elder abuse as defined above—even if you did not previously think of it as abuse?

3. Institutional Abuse: Information and Statistics

Michael Moss
Many Elders Receive Care at Criminals' Hands
WALL ST. J., March 18, 1998, at B1[*]

When Carletos Bell applied to work at the San Antonio Convalescent Center, he didn't try to hide his violent criminal past. He disclosed his record of aggravated assault right on his application for nurse-assistant.

He got the job anyway, in June 1996. Six months later, Mr. Bell was charged with sexually assaulting a 71-year-old resident of the nursing home. He pleaded not guilty and is now in jail awaiting trial.

The case illustrates a growing problem for nursing-home patients and owners alike: People with serious rap sheets are landing jobs as care givers for the elderly.

* * *

. . . [C]rime against residents of nursing homes has been a growing concern among patient advocates. Efforts to draw attention to the problem have been stymied partly by the lack of good data. Advocates say there is severe underreporting of crimes—especially of rapes—because residents often fear retribution for leveling complaints.

Still, the U.S. Department of Health and Human Services' Office of Inspector General took disciplinary actions mostly related to nursing-home abuse in 382 cases in 1997, more than double a year earlier. The office received 1,613 reports of abuse allegations in that year, up 14% over a three-year period.

Lesser crimes abound as well. Four percent of nursing-home workers acknowledged they stole money, jewelry and other items from residents, in questionnaires completed as part of a soon-to-be published study by Diana Harris, a sociologist at the University of Tennessee, Knoxville. Ten percent of workers said they saw other staff steal.

---

[*] Republished by permission of Dow Jones, Inc. via Copyright Clearance Center, Inc. © 1998 Dow Jones and Company, Inc. All rights reserved worldwide.

Elizabeth B. Herrington
Strengthening the Older Americans Act's Long-Term Care Protection Provisions: A Call for Further Improvement of Important State Ombudsman Programs
5 ELDER L.J. 321, 322-23 (1997)*

Patrick Shane Williams, a young male nurse, was found in the room of a screaming, half-naked eighty-four-year-old Alzheimer's sufferer. An investigation by the nursing home ensued when Williams could offer no plausible explanation for the resident's agitated condition.

Confronted with incriminating evidence, Williams confessed his wrongdoing to receive a plea bargain from the state. During his employment as a night nurse, he had raped again and again victims ranging from 61 to 102 years old. For three years at the Meadow Manor nursing home in Taylorville, Illinois, Williams had raped several women, all of whom were confused or demented. Although several complaints had been made about him, no one listened to the victimized women's pleas for help. Until this final incident, Williams maintained the women were delusional and no further investigation had occurred.

Many complaints in nursing homes do not reach the outrageous abuse level of the Williams case, nor do the majority involve sexual abuse. According to recent data, however, the problem is extensive; the state-legislated Illinois Department on Aging Elder Abuse Program assisted nearly 5000 elder abuse victims in fiscal year 1995. The majority of these reports involved financial exploitation, which is highly associated with emotional abuse.

Seymour Moskowitz
New Remedies for Elder Abuse and Neglect
PROB. & PROP. 52, 53 (January/February 1998)**

[S]ome evidence indicates that mistreatment in institutions, such as nursing homes, is a serious problem. One recent study found that 40% of nursing home staff admitted committing at least one psychologically abusive act toward a resident in the preceding year and 10% admitted physically abusing residents [citing K. Pillemer & David W. Moore, *Abuse of Patients in Nursing Homes*, 29 GERONTOLOGIST 314 (1989)—Eds.].

---

* Reprinted by permission. Copyright to the *Elder Law Journal* is held by the Board of Trustees of the University of Illinois.

** Copyright © 1998 by the American Bar Association. Reprinted by permission.

George S. Ingalls et al.
Elder Abuse Originating in the Institutional Setting
74 N.D. L. Rev. 313, 313-14 (1998)[*]

The Older Americans Act (OAA) was passed by Congress in 1965 to provide for state area agencies on aging to assess the need for elder abuse prevention services. In 1987, the Omnibus Budget Reconciliation Act amended the OAA to reform the standards for nursing home facilities and to provide for the Long Term Care Ombudsman Program to investigate and resolve complaints at the facilities.

The Long Term Care Ombudsman Annual Report for Fiscal Year 1995 has recently been published. This report gives specific statistics of complaints leveled at long term care facilities and the resolution of these complaints. According to the report, about 72% of the facility complaints were either resolved or partially resolved. Over 85% of the complaints related to nursing home residents. The total number of complaints by the fifty-two national Ombudsmans' Offices reporting was 218,455 complaints filed by 162,338 complainants. Nursing home complaints amounted to 86.7% of the complaints.

Twenty-eight state Ombudsmans' Offices provided a detailed breakdown of complaints. Out of 54,305 total complaints, 47,343 pertained to nursing facilities, and 30% of these complaints were from the residents themselves. Twenty-nine states provided the most frequently cited complaints. Of the 82,442 complaints pertaining to nursing homes, 24,587 pertained to residents' rights. Of these residents' rights complaints, 6,128 were for abuse, gross neglect, and exploitation. There were also 17,780 complaints dealing with the quality of life, and 25,945 addressing residential care.

Questions

1. How serious is the problem of institutional abuse?

2. Is it a new problem, an increasing problem, or a constant problem that has only recently come to light?

---

[*] Copyright © 1998. Reprinted with permission.

4. Noninstitutional Abuse (Except Consumer Fraud): Information and Statistics

Billingslea v. State
780 S.W.2d 271 (Tex. Crim. App. 1989)

DUNCAN, J.

* * *

Appellant, his wife, and son lived with Hazel Billingslea (also referred to as the decedent), appellant's 94 year old mother, in a small two story frame house in Dallas. Hazel Billingslea's home had been her son's residence since approximately 1964. Appellant's only sibling was his sister, Katherine Jefferson, a resident of New Mexico. Virginia Billingslea (the decedent's granddaughter), Katherine Jefferson's daughter, lived approximately fifteen blocks from her grandmother's Dallas' home. Virginia Billingslea was raised by Hazel Billingslea and had a close relationship with her. Accordingly, she kept in regular contact by telephone and by occasional visits to her grandmother's house.

Unspecified frailties of old age affecting the elder Mrs. Billingslea forced her to become bedridden in March, 1984. Granddaughter Virginia, unaware of her grandmother's condition, made several attempts to visit her during the ensuing weeks. On each occasion her uncle (appellant) "testily" informed her that her grandmother was "asleep." Undaunted, Virginia attempted to reach her grandmother by telephone, only to be threatened by her uncle on at least two occasions to "keep [her] goddamned motherfucking ass out of him and his mother's business or he would kill [her]."

After all attempts to visit her grandmother failed, Virginia contacted her mother (appellant's sister), Katherine Jefferson, in New Mexico. Mrs. Jefferson in turn contacted the Dallas Social Security Office and requested a formal inquiry into her mother's welfare.

Velma Mosley with the Adult Protective Services section of the Texas Department of Human Resources testified that she received a report from the Social Security Office on April 20, 1984, requesting that she check on the elder Mrs. Billingslea. A few days later, Ms. Mosley, accompanied by two Dallas police officers and a police social service employee, proceeded to Mrs. Billingslea's house.

They came upon the appellant in the front yard. After some discussion, he reluctantly allowed them to enter the premises. Upon entering, they were assailed by the strong, offensive odor of rotting flesh permeating the household. While one of the police officers remained downstairs with the appellant, who wanted to know "what these motherfuckers were doing in his house," the social worker and police officer made their way upstairs. Upon entering the bedroom, they found Hazel Billingslea lying in bed, moaning and asking for help. Ms. Mosley testified that the stench was so overwhelming that she was forced to cover her face. Ms. Mosley pulled back the sheets to examine Mrs. Billingslea. Nude from the waist down, Mrs. Billingslea appeared weak and in a great deal of pain.

Ms. Mosley discovered that part of Mrs. Billingslea's heel was eaten away by a large decubitus (bedsore). Other decubiti on her hip and back appeared to have eaten through to the bone. When Ms. Mosley attempted to raise Mrs. Billingslea from the bed to continue her physical examination, "she moaned so much till I didn't look any further." Mrs. Billingslea was immediately transported to Parkland Hospital in Dallas.

Dr. Frase, at that time Chief Medical Resident at Parkland Hospital, examined Mrs. Billingslea. He testified that she was severely cachectic, i.e., that she had suffered severe muscle loss. Her mental state was one of near total disorientation, and she had apparently been unable to feed herself for some time. In addition to the decubiti, second degree burns and blisters were found on her inner thighs, caused by lying in pools of her own urine. Maggots were festering in her open bedsores.

Dr. Frase testified that weeping bedsores as severe as those he found on Hazel Billingslea would have taken anywhere from four to six weeks to develop. He further testified that until her death Mrs. Billingslea required large dosages of narcotics to relieve her pain. In his opinion, the bedsores, burns, blisters, and loss of muscle resulted in serious bodily injury indicative of overall neglect of Mrs. Billingslea in the months prior to her death.

Questions

1. The facts in *Billingslea* seem unusual, but how unusual are they?
2. Must abuse rise to this level in order to be considered "abuse"?

National Center on Elder Abuse
National Elder Abuse Incidence Study: Final Report
Executive Summary, HTML Pages 1-3 (September 1998)
<www.aoa.gov/abuse/report/Cexecsum.htm>

The National Elder Abuse Incidence Study (NEAIS) was conducted by the National Center on Elder Abuse at the American Public Human Services Association (formerly known as the American Public Welfare Association) and the Maryland-based social science and survey research firm, Westat. The Administration for Children and Families (ACF) and the Administration on Aging (AoA) in the U.S. Department of Health and Human Services jointly funded this research. The study asked the fundamental question: What is the incidence of domestic elder abuse and neglect in the United States today? In public health and social research, the term "incidence" means the number of new cases occurring over a specific time period. The NEAIS used a rigorous methodology to collect national incidence data on what has been a largely undocumented phenomenon, and it provides the basis to estimate the incidence of domestic elder abuse and neglect among those aged 60 and above in 1996.

The NEAIS originated in 1992 when Congress, through the Family Violence Prevention and Services Act of 1992 (P.L. 102-295), directed that a study of the national incidence of abuse, neglect, and exploitation of elderly persons be conducted under the auspices of the Administration for Children and Families.... Because the legislative mandate primarily was concerned with the prevention of violence in domestic settings, the study focused only on the maltreatment of non-institutionalized elderly. Elders living in hospitals, nursing homes, assisted-living facilities, or other institutional or group facilities were not included in the study.

In order to maximize the utility of the research, the study also collected and analyzed data about elder self-neglect in domestic settings, and these findings are reported separately from the findings for abuse and neglect. In the NEAIS, the phrase "elder maltreatment" generally refers to the seven types of abuse and neglect that are measured in the study—physical abuse, sexual abuse, emotional or psychological abuse, financial or material exploitation, abandonment, neglect, and self-neglect.

* * *

To arrive at the most accurate estimate of the national incidence of elder abuse and neglect in 1996, researchers added two numbers: (1) reports submitted to [adult protective services] agencies and substantiated (i.e., determined to have occurred or be occurring) by those agencies, and (2) reports made by sentinels and presumed to be substantiated. Consistent with three national incidence studies on child abuse and neglect, this methodology assumes the sentinel reports represent substantiated reports. Because the incidence estimate is statistically derived from the nationally representative sample, researchers also calculated the standard error to establish the range of the incidence estimate within a 95 percent confidence interval.

Using the identical methodology, researchers also separately calculated the estimated national incidence of elder abuse, neglect, and/or self-neglect in 1996. Both incidence estimates are for unduplicated elderly persons. In other words, individuals are counted only once, even if: (1) they were abused and neglected and/or self-neglecting, (2) more than one report were received about the same incident, or (3) different incidents were reported for the same elderly person during the study period.

* * *

The best national estimate is that a total of 449,924 elderly persons, aged 60 and over, experienced *abuse and/or neglect* [but not self-neglect] in domestic settings in 1996. Of this total, 70,942 (16 percent) were reported to and substantiated by APS agencies, but the remaining 378,982 (84 percent) were not reported to APS. From these figures, one can conclude that over five times as many new incidents of abuse and neglect were unreported than those that were reported to and substantiated by APS agencies in 1996. The standard error suggests that nationwide as many as 688,948 elders or as few as 210,900 elders could have been victims of abuse and/or neglect in domestic settings in 1996.

* * *

Data show that family members were the perpetrators in nine out of ten (89.7 percent) substantiated incidents of domestic elder abuse and neglect [reported by adult protective services agencies]. Adult children of elder abuse victims were the most likely perpetrators of substantiated maltreatment (47.3 percent). Spouses represented the second largest group of perpetrators (19.3 percent). In addition, other relatives and grandchildren, at 8.8 percent and 8.6 percent respectively, were the next largest groups of perpetrators. Non-family perpetrators included friends/neighbors (6.2 percent), in-home service providers (2.8 percent), and out-of home service providers (1.4 percent)

* * *

As with [protective services] reports, perpetrators reported by sentinels were most frequently family members (89.6 percent), including the adult children (30.8 percent), spouses (30.3 percent), and a parent (24.0 percent). Parents are possible abusers of elders because elders were defined as persons aged 60 and over, and some persons in their 60s and 70s had parents in their late 70s and 80s. Friends, neighbors, and service providers were believed to be responsible for the abuse and neglect 10 percent of the time.

Questions

1. What, if anything, about these statistics surprised you?

2. How accurate are these statistics? How much of a problem is noninstitutional elder abuse?

5. Consumer Fraud Against the Elderly: Information and Statistics

Richard A. Starnes
Consumer Fraud and the Elderly: The Need for a Uniform System of Enforcement and Increased Civil and Criminal Penalties
4 ELDER L.J. 201, 202, 205-10 (1996)[*]

The elderly population in the United States is the target of various types of consumer fraud in a much greater proportion than the rest of society. Currently, Americans over the age of sixty-five make up about twelve and a half percent of the nation's population (about thirty-one million people), and that figure is predicted to climb to eighteen percent by the year 2000. Yet, this population constitutes at least thirty percent of the nation's victims of fraud. Many operators of fraudulent schemes specifically target the elderly for a number of different reasons.

* * *

---

[*] Reprinted by permission. Copyright to the *Elder Law Journal* is held by the Board of Trustees of the University of Illinois.

Although the large number of different types of scams makes it difficult to categorize them, most can be placed in a few general areas which have the largest effect on the elderly. Those general areas include telemarketing fraud, health care fraud, and home repair fraud.

1. *Telemarketing fraud*

* * *

Although any product can be used in a fraudulent telemarketing sales scheme, the most common is some type of fake investment, resulting in an investment scam. These fake investments include the sale of coins, precious metals, gems, real estate, or oil and gas leases. The victim, assured of a safe and profitable investment, pays large amounts of money, often their entire savings, to purchase these investments before discovering, usually too late, that the investments were either nonexistent or worthless. The sweepstakes scam begins when a victim receives a letter stating that he or she has won a prize and gives a number to call to claim the prize. The catch is usually that the prize requires either a significant fee for "processing" or shipping, or the purchase of a high-priced product which overshadows the value of the prize. In some scams, the prize does not even exist, so the victim pays for nothing.

Many other telemarketing scams exist, including credit card scams, 900-number scams, and false charitable organizations.

* * *

2. *Health care fraud*

Health care fraud, which comes in a number of different forms, is one of the fastest growing areas of fraud against the elderly. Health care fraud can involve either physicians or salespeople representing health groups or companies selling medicine or medical equipment. Quackery, one of the most prevalent forms of health care fraud, involves the marketing of miracle cures by some kind of medicine, device, or procedure.

* * *

Another major area of health care fraud is misrepresentation of the services rendered and the cost of services performed. Often, this involves defrauding not only the patient, but also defrauding the provider of the patient's insurance coverage or other medical benefits. In these schemes, physicians will either charge for services they did not perform, overcharge for procedures, or misrepresent the services that they performed in order to place the procedure within the scope of insurance coverage.

* * *

3. *Home repair fraud*

Another area which attracts a number of consumer fraud schemers is home repair and improvements. These schemes are carried out in many different ways, but they all start basically the same way. A contractor approaches a victim, saying that his or her work crew was doing some work in the neighborhood and noticed some type of problem with the victim's home. The contractor will then offer a bargain for the repair service, often telling the victim not to mention it to anyone because the deal was not given to other customers. At this point, the scheme may take many different paths. The contractor may take a large down payment and then leave, never doing the work. If the crew actually does the work, it is often shoddy and will need to be repaired, costing the elderly victim even more money. Sometimes the workers will perform the work even if the victim turned down the offer and then demand payment for the services. Even worse, the perpetrators of these schemes often scan the obituaries looking for recent widows as targets, because they may not be knowledgeable about the types of repairs and the necessity of having them performed.

Questions

Do you agree that the elderly are particularly vulnerable to consumer fraud? Why or why not?

6. Self-Neglect: Information and Statistics

National Center on Elder Abuse
National Elder Abuse Incidence Study: Final Report
Executive Summary HTML Pages 1, 4 (September 1998)
<www.aoa.gov/abuse/report/Cexecsum.htm> and <. . . /Cexecsum-03.htm>

[From HTML Page 4] [In this study,] [s]*elf-neglect* was characterized as the behaviors of an elderly person that threaten his/her own health or safety. The definition of self-neglect excludes a situation in which a mentally competent older person (who understands the consequences of his/her decisions) makes a conscious and voluntary decision to engage in acts that threaten his/her health or safety.

* * *

[From HTML Page 1] The best national estimate is that a total of 449,924 elderly persons, aged 60 and over, experienced *abuse and/or neglect* in domestic settings in 1996. Of this total, 70,942 (16 percent) were reported to and substantiated by APS agencies, but the remaining 378,982 (84 percent) were not reported to APS. From these figures, one can conclude that over five times as many new incidents of abuse and neglect were unreported than those that were reported to and substantiated by APS agencies in 1996. The standard error suggests that nationwide as many as 688,948 elders or as few as 210,900 elders could have been victims of abuse and/or neglect in domestic settings in 1996.

* * *

The best national estimate is that a total of 551,011 elderly persons, aged 60 and over, experienced *abuse, neglect, and/or self-neglect* in domestic settings in 1996. Of this total, 115,110 (21 percent) were reported to and substantiated by APS agencies, with the remaining 435,901 (79 percent) not being reported to APS agencies. One can conclude from these figures that almost four times as many new incidents of elder abuse, neglect, and/or self-neglect were unreported than those that were reported to and substantiated by APS agencies in 1996. The standard error suggests that nationwide as many as 787,027 elders or as few as 314,995 elders could have been abused, neglected, and/or self-neglecting in domestic settings in 1996....

Questions

1. How serious is the problem of self-neglect?

2. One commentator has observed: "If the individual has the right to decide whether to refuse medical care even though that refusal may result in death, there is surely a right to make less life-threatening choices regarding personal eating habits, dress, appearance, cleanliness, and other elements of one's lifestyle." Katheryn D. Katz, *Elder Abuse*, 18 J. FAM. L. 695, 720 (1979-80). Do you agree? Does this undercut the existence of self-neglect as a category of elder abuse?

7. Federal Responses to Elder Abuse

a. The Older Americans Act of 1965 and its Subsequent Amendments

1 U.S. Senate Special Committee on Aging
Developments in Aging: 1996, at 259-60
(Report No. 105-36, 105th Cong., 1st Sess., June 24, 1997)

The Older Americans Act (OAA), enacted in 1965, is the major vehicle for the organization and delivery of supportive and nutrition services to older persons. It was created during a time of rising societal concern for the needs of the poor. The OAA's enactment marked the beginning of a variety of programs specifically designed to meet the social and human needs of the elderly.

The OAA was one in a series of Federal initiatives that were part of President Johnson's Great Society programs. These legislative initiatives grew out of a concern for the large percentage of older Americans who were impoverished, and a belief that greater Federal involvement was needed beyond the existing health and income-transfer programs. Although older persons could receive services under other Federal programs, the OAA was the first major legislation to organize and deliver community-based social services exclusively to older persons.

* * *

When enacted in 1965, the OAA established a series of broad policy objectives designed to meet the needs of older persons. Although the OAA then lacked both legislative authority and adequate funding, it did establish a structure through which the Congress would later expand aging services.

* * *

The Act authorizes a wide array of service programs through a nationwide network of 57 State agencies on aging and 660 area agencies on aging (AAAs).

* * *

The Act establishes the Administration on Aging (AOA) within the Department of Health and Human Services (HHS) which administers all of the Act's programs except for the Senior Community Service Employment Program administered by the Department of Labor (DOL), and the commodity or cash-in-lieu of commodities portion of the nutrition program, administered by the U.S. Department of Agriculture (USDA).

* * *

The Act has been amended 13 times since the original legislation was enacted. Major amendments included the creation of the national nutrition program for the elderly in 1972 and the network of area agencies on aging in 1973. Other amendments established the long-term care ombudsman program and a separate grant program for older Native Americans in 1978, and a number of additional service programs under the State and area agency on aging program in 1987, including in-home services for the frail elderly, programs to prevent elder abuse, neglect and exploitation, and health promotion and disease prevention programs, among others. The most recent amendments in 1992 created a new Title VII to consolidate and expand certain programs that focus on protection of the rights of older persons (which under prior law were authorized under Title III).

During the 1970s, Congress significantly improved the OAA by broadening its scope of operations and establishing the foundation for a 'network' on aging under a Title III program umbrella. In 1973, the area agencies on aging were authorized. These agencies, along with the State Units on Aging (SUAs), provide the administrative structure for programs under the OAA. In addition to funding specific services, these entities act as advocates on behalf of older persons and help to develop a service system that will best meet older Americans' needs. As originally conceived by the Congress, this system was meant to encompass both services funded under the OAA, and services supported by other Federal, State, and local programs.

Question

What effect did the 1973 amendments have on the original OAA?

b. "A Decade of Shame and Inaction": 1978-1987

Subcommittee on Health and Long-Term Care
House Select Committee on Aging
Elder Abuse: A Decade of Shame and Inaction, at 66-68
(Comm. Pub. No. 101-752, 101st Cong., 2d Sess., April 1990)

What follows is an analysis of the evolution of State and Federal policy in the recognition and prevention of elder abuse since that issue first received national attention in the late 70s.

* * *

The States have the primary responsibility for protecting the rights of all their citizens, young and old alike.

* * *

State advocates of Federal involvement in the area of protective services for elders suggest that one way to encourage States to make the [necessary] statutory and administrative changes would be to make Federal funding for elder abuse-related contingent on certain State level requirements . . . . The Prevention, Identification and Treatment of Elder Abuse Act (H.R. 7551), introduced by Reps. Mary Rose Oakar (D-Ohio) and Claude Pepper (D-Fla.) in the 96th Congress [1979-1980], used this method to encourage States to modify their elder abuse-related laws and procedures. Although this bill enjoyed wide bipartisan co-sponsorship and was supported by virtually all the States, it died in the 96th Congress before passage.

In subsequent Congresses, Reps. Oakar and Pepper introduced the measure again. H.R. 769 was referred in the 97th Congress to the House Education and Labor and Energy and Commerce Committees. By the end of the Congress it enjoyed the support of 84 cosponsors but did not pass. Again in the 98th Congress, the measure was again introduced as H.R. 3833. It too was referred to the Committees on Education and Labor and Energy and Commerce, but failed to pass the House. At the beginning of the 99th Congress, the 100th Congress, and the 101st Congress, H.R. 1674, H.R. 3899, and H.R. 220 were introduced respectively. All three failed to receive full consideration or House passage.

Aside from H.R. 1674, elder abuse prevention was the subject of legislation under two other bills enacted during the 98th Congress. The Child Abuse Amendments of 1984 (P.L. 98-457) contained authorization for support of demonstration grants to establish, maintain and expand programs to prevent incidents of family violence . . . . Regrettably, no appropriations were ever made available for these provisions.

* * *

The [other piece of legislation enacted during the 98th Congress was the] Older Americans Act Amendments of 1987.

Question

Why was so little accomplished between 1978 and 1987?

c. The Older Americans Act Amendments of 1987

Subcommittee on Health and Long-Term Care
House Select Committee on Aging
Elder Abuse: A Decade of Shame and Inaction, at 68
(Comm. Pub. No. 101-752, 101st Cong., 2d Sess., April 1990)

The Older Americans Act Amendments of 1987 . . . required Area Agencies on Aging to assess the need for elder abuse prevention services and the extent to which the need was being met within each planning and service area. In addition, the law added a new "State plan on aging" requirement to govern the conduct of elder abuse prevention activities when the State Agency on Aging opted to provide such services. Under this provision, the State plan would have to assure that any area agency carrying out elder abuse prevention activities would conduct its program consistent with State law and be coordinated with existing State adult protection services activities. The program was to provide public education to identify and prevent abuse; receive reports on incidence of abuse; provide outreach, conferences and referrals to other sources of assistance; and refer complaints to law enforcement or public protective service agencies . . . . While $5 million was authorized to be spent in 1988, 1989 and 1990 under the Act for this new elder abuse program, as of this writing no money has been appropriated for that purpose.

Molly D. Velick
*Mandatory Reporting Statutes:
A Necessary Yet Underutilized Response to Elder Abuse*
3 ELDER L.J. 165, 178-79 (1995)[*]

The 1990 report on elder abuse by the House Subcommittee on Health and Long-Term Care continually refers to government's "woefully inadequate" funding of [state-based] adult protective services. The report also notes that many states which passed mandatory reporting laws during the 1980s expected to receive federal funding for adult protective services. The states anticipated that eligibility for such funding would be based in part on the enactment of mandatory reporting requirements. The Elder Abuse and Prevention Act (House Bill 7551), a bill originally introduced in the Ninety-sixth Congress, promised funding for state adult protective services. When the bill failed to pass, however, states were hard pressed to actually carry out

---

[*] Reprinted by permission. Copyright to the *Elder Law Journal* is held by the Board of Trustees of the University of Illinois.

their new adult protective-services mandates. Congress did pass another piece of legislation aimed at helping the elderly, the Older Americans Act Amendments of 1987, but it did not appropriate any money to implement the Act until 1990.

Even then, Congress appropriated only a meager $3 million.

Question

What were the 1987 amendments designed to do?

d. The Nursing Home Reform Act of 1987

In connection with the following excerpt, read the Nursing Home Residents' Bill of Rights (42 U.S.C. §1395i-3(c)) in the statutory supplement, especially subsection (1)(A)(ii) and subsection (6).

George S. Ingalls et al.
Elder Abuse Originating in the Institutional Setting
74 N.D. L. Rev. 313, 316-17 (1998)[*]

[I]n order to combat the increase in nursing home abuse that came to light in the 1980s, Congress passed the Nursing Home Reform Act (included in the Omnibus Budget Reconciliation Act of 1987 [OBRA]).

This Act mandates that, for a facility to qualify for federal funding, "A skilled nursing facility must provide services to attain or maintain the highest practicable physical, mental, and psychological well-being of each resident in accordance with a written plan of care which" describes the resident's needs and how those needs will be met. This plan of care is to be prepared initially with the participation of the residents' families and is to be periodically reviewed and revised. "The resident has a right to a dignified existence, self determination, and communication with and access to persons and services inside and outside the facility." "The resident has the right to be free of interference, coercion, discrimination, and reprisal from the facility in exercising his or her rights." To achieve these goals, the law provides that a resident has certain rights that must be met by the nursing facility. The "facility must care for its residents in a manner and in an environment that promotes maintenance or enhancement of each resident's quality of life." "The facility must promote care for residents in a manner and in and environment that maintains or enhances each resident's dignity and respect in full recognition of his or her individuality."

OBRA 1987 includes a "Residents' Bill of Rights" which provides the basic requirements for the care of residents in skilled nursing facilities. This Bill of Rights is found in 42 U.S.C. § 1395i-3(c)-(h) and 42 C.F.R. § 483.10-483.15.

---

[*] Copyright © 1998. Reprinted with permission.

Questions

1. With respect to the topic of elder abuse, what rights does this legislation provide?

2. How effective is the legislation at guaranteeing these rights?

e. The Older Americans Act Amendments of 1992

Alison Barnes
The Policy and Politics of Community-Based Long-Term Care
19 NOVA L. REV. 487, 520 (1995)[*]

The 1992 amendments to the OAA . . . included a new provision, Title VII, authorizing programs for prevention of abuse and neglect and the provision of legal assistance. The administration of Title VII funds differs from [previous approaches under Title III] in that states can bypass administration by the network of federal administrative Area Agencies on Aging. States were also given permission to transfer funds between service and nutrition programs to maximize their ability to meet the needs of target groups.

U.S. Administration on Aging
Elder Abuse Prevention Fact Sheet
<www.aoa.gov/factsheets/abuse.html> (visited Nov. 19, 1998)

The State Elder Abuse Prevention Program, created by the 1987 Amendments to the OAA, was consolidated into the new Vulnerable Elder Rights Protection Activities, Title VII, when the OAA last was reauthorized in 1992. Title VII provides the states discretion in setting priorities for spending these moneys.

1 U.S. Senate Special Committee on Aging
Developments in Aging: 1996, at 261, 263
(Report No. 105-36, 105th Cong., 1st Sess., June 24, 1997)

Title III [of the Older Americans Act, as amended] authorizes grants to State and area agencies on aging to act as advocates on behalf of programs for the elderly and to coordinate programs for this group. This program supports 57 State agencies on aging, 660 area agencies on aging, and over 27,000 service provider organizations. This nationwide network of supportive, nutrition, and other social services programs receive most of the Act's total Federal funding (65 percent in fiscal year 1997).

---

[*] Copyright © 1995. Reprinted with permission.

* * *

Title VII [of the Older Americans Act, as amended] authorizes funds for activities that protect the rights of the vulnerable elderly. Programs authorized are—The Long-Term Care Ombudsman Program; programs to prevent elder abuse, neglect, and exploitation; elder rights and legal assistance, outreach, counseling, and assistance programs on insurance and public benefits. Title VII also authorizes an elder rights program for Native American elderly. Funds are distributed to State agencies on aging based on a formula which takes into account State population age 60 or over.

Questions

How does Title VII differ from Title III? Why?

Overall Questions on the Federal Role

1. How would you characterize the federal government's response to the problem of elder abuse?

2. Should the federal government's role in combating elder abuse be expanded? If so, how?

8. State Responses to Elder Abuse

a. Adult Protective Services: Background

Audrey S. Garfield
*Elder Abuse and the States' Adult Protective Services Response:
Time for a Change in California*
42 HASTINGS L.J. 859, 869-72, 874-75, 885-90, 892, 897-98, 904, 912-13 (1991)[*]

Between 1973 and January 1981, prior to publication of the House of Representatives first report on elder abuse, only sixteen states enacted legislation focusing on the problem of abuse of adults, and these laws addressed the problem of abuse of all adults eighteen and older; until 1979 none was specific to elders. By 1980, immediately before the first House Report, only five states had passed statutes specifically aimed at protecting elders. By 1985—and no doubt as a result of the congressional attention and national publicity that the problem finally received in the early 1980s—that number mushroomed to forty-four. Today fifty states, including California, have enacted some type of legislation that addresses the problem of elder abuse.

---

[*] © 1991 by University of California, Hastings College of the Law. Reprinted from Hastings Law Journal, Vol. 42, No. 3, by permission.

A. *A Starting Point: What Are Adult Protective Services?*

Adult protective services (APS) traditionally are defined as "a system of preventive, supportive, and surrogate services for the elderly living in the community to enable them to maintain independent living and avoid abuse and exploitation." An adult protective services law is a statute that establishes an APS system. Most states include elder abuse provisions in their already existing adult protective services legislation.

Although the content of APS laws varies from state to state, each adult protective services system typically includes two main components: coordinated provision of services for adults determined to be at risk of abuse, and the actual or potential power (of the state or a local governmental entity) to intervene legally in an individual's life and make decisions for him. This power usually is invoked when an elder is deemed incapable of making decisions for himself, is personally in danger, or is dangerous to others. In some states the power includes the ability to intervene when an elder refuses services or is deemed incapable of consenting.

In addition to these general categories, elder abuse APS statutes ordinarily contain any combination of more specific sections including but not limited to who is covered by the statute (i.e., elders only or elders and dependent adults); provisions for mandatory reporting of abuse; guidelines for investigation of abuse; provisions regarding involuntary as well as emergency intervention; and definitions of abuse, neglect, and exploitation.

A number of states' laws exclusively address the problem of elder abuse. Other states not only have these exclusive statutes but also have other laws that cover elder abuse. In conjunction with existing elder-abuse-specific or adult protective services laws, some states also use domestic violence statutes to protect elderly from abuse and yet others have provisions in their penal codes that provide for criminal prosecution of elder abusers. States' definitions of those protected under APS laws also vary. Some provide protection for all adults over eighteen who are impaired, incapacitated, or otherwise disabled. Other statutes refer only to "elderly" individuals, with "elderly" typically defined either as sixty years and older or sixty-five years and older.

B. *Adult Protective Services Statutes*

A background on the substance of APS laws in other states is crucial to a critical examination of California's APS response to elder abuse. The following sections discuss the general provisions found in state APS statutes that are applied in the context of elder abuse.

(1) *Definitions of Abuse, Neglect, and Exploitation*

The definitions of what constitutes elder abuse vary widely. Typically the broad categories include physical, psychological, fiduciary, and sexual abuse or exploitation as well as neglect; the definitions of each type of abuse vary within these respective categories.

* * *

(2) *Mandatory Reporting*

Mandatory reporting provisions were the first major laws enacted in response to the problem and continue today to be the mainstay of most state elder abuse laws. Almost all state APS laws mandate a wide variety of professionals to report known or suspected cases of elderly abuse. The "professionals" most often include health care and social service professionals including law enforcement officers, social workers, physicians, and nurses. Some states list in detail those persons required to report, and others mandate anyone with knowledge or reasonable cause to believe that abuse has occurred to report the incident.

* * *

(3) *Central Registries*

A number of statutes mandate the establishment and maintenance of a central registry, a centralized listing of all abuse reports and information regarding any subsequent investigations, to which certain statutorily authorized individuals may gain access. Broadly stated, the purpose of a registry is to receive and maintain reports of abuse in a manner that facilitates rapid access and recall of the information reported, of subsequent investigations based on those reports, and of other relevant information.

* * *

(4) *Confidentiality*

* * *

Almost all states restrict the access to elder abuse records in some manner. Most statutes stipulate that the report and all information gathered during the subsequent investigation are not public record. Some specifically list individuals who have a right of access; among these are the victim, certain agencies involved in the investigation such as local law enforcement and administrative agencies, the court, and (in some states) bona fide and approved researchers. A number of states mandate total confidentiality; others provide that information may be released with the victim's permission.

* * *

(5) *Expungement of Records*

The majority of APS statutes have few provisions designed to assure that the rights of alleged perpetrators or victims of abuse are protected. Other than the confidentiality provisions, only a few states with central registry systems provide additional means of protection for alleged abusers. Select states provide for amendment of reports or expungement of records from the registry if the reports are determined to be inaccurate or unsubstantiated.

* * *

(6) *Penalties for the Abuser*

The majority of state APS laws do not prescribe penalties against the perpetrator. [This is left to other state statutes, or to state common law.]

* * *

(7) *Investigations*

All state statutes provide for some type of initial investigation after a report of alleged abuse is received. The laws vary with respect to which agency has responsibility for conducting this investigation. The majority of statutes name the state human services, social services, or welfare department as the entity with primary esponsibility. A number of statutes assign this responsibility to the local welfare agency or law enforcement agency.

* * *

(8) *Provision of Services*

Once an investigation is completed or the elder requests assistance, provision of protective services may be recommended for the elder. APS statutes typically contain at least some provisions that are aimed at providing services to needy adults. These services are designed to assist elders in whatever way they require, while also permitting the elder to continue residing in the community.

* * *

The services component generally includes some combination of health, social, psychological, medical, and legal assistance. These services are not intended to function as random aids administered by unrelated agencies. Rather, the goal is to render coordinated services and assistance through a caseworker, usually a social worker, who can assess the individual's needs and combine the various programs and community resources to meet those needs. The services offered vary and often include visiting nurses, clinical services, special transportation, and hot home-delivered meals. These services are intended, among other things, to alleviate or prevent harm resulting from elder abuse. The availability of services depends on the funding allocated by the state to assist abused elders.

* * *

(9) *Involuntary or Nonconsensual Intervention*

The majority of state APS laws include an exception to the requirement of consent to services when the elder has been determined to be incapacitated.

* * *

Two procedures are used most widely to impose involuntary services on abuse victims in the nonemergency setting. The majority of states use the traditional guardianship or conservatorship mechanisms that already exist within their probate codes. Others have established a special procedure within their APS laws that operates independently of the guardianship or conservatorship sections of the probate code. For the most part these procedures function in the same manner as guardianships and conservatorships. Most proceedings result in an order by the court designating an individual, organization, or agency to act as the functional equivalent of a guardian or conservator.

* * *

(10) *Emergency Intervention*

One common exception to the rule that involuntary services may be provided only after formal guardianship or guardianship-like proceedings is the provision of short-term emergency services. Emergency provisions in APS laws most often constitute an exception to the rule that services only may be provided with the elder's consent although some state APS laws exclusively apply to elderly who are in the equivalent of an emergency situation. The New York APS laws, for example, only apply to "endangered adults," those individuals who are in a condition or situation that poses an imminent risk of death or serious physical harm and who lack the capacity to comprehend the consequences of remaining in the situation. Emergencies typically are defined as circumstances that "present a substantial risk of death or immediate and serious physical harm" to the elder.

b. Mandatory Reporting

Seymour Moskowitz
New Remedies for Elder Abuse and Neglect,
PROB. & PROP. 52, 53 (January/February 1998)*

Mandatory reporting of suspected abuse and neglect has been a significant legislative response to the problem of mistreatment of the elderly. Presently, 42 states and the District of Columbia have statutes requiring reporting. These laws require various groups (typically professionals such as doctors, nurses, psychologists and social workers) to report known and suspected incidents to prescribed public officials. Eight states—Colorado, Illinois, New Jersey, New York, North Dakota, Pennsylvania, South Dakota and Wisconsin—make reporting voluntary.

Most statutes require a state agency to conduct an investigation, including a visit to the allegedly abused elder, after it receives a report of abuse. State laws typically grant immunity from liability for making a report to persons obliged to report, and almost all states guarantee the reporter anonymity. The required content of the report typically includes names and addresses of the abused elderly citizen, the reporter, the alleged abuser, information relating to the nature and extent of the harm, the basis of the reporter's knowledge and similar information.

---

* Copyright © 1998 by the American Bar Association. Reprinted by permission.

Audrey S. Garfield
Elder Abuse and the States' Adult Protective Services Response: Time for a Change in California
42 HASTINGS L.J. 859, 877-82, 884-85 (1991)[*]

To date, much of the literature discussing elder abuse laws has focused on those provisions mandating reporting of elder abuse and has offered numerous criticisms of their requirements. One major criticism is that mandatory reporting provisions are inappropriately modeled after child abuse reporting laws. State intervention in the case of child abuse is based on the doctrine of parens patriae, which is the traditional role of the state to act as sovereign and guardian over persons who cannot care or speak for themselves . . . . Modern day guardianship proceedings, involuntary provision of medical services, and involuntary provision of elder abuse adult protective services all are based on the state's parens patriae obligation or power . . . . Critics argue that mandatory reporting laws presume, solely on the basis of advanced years, that the elderly are incompetent and unable to know when they need or want outside assistance. Requiring reporting of elder abuse infantilizes elders and encourages the already pervasive ageism in our society.

More broadly, mandatory reporting is one of a number of provisions in APS statutes that is criticized because it deprives elderly citizens of their rights to self-determination. The legitimacy of state intervention under parens patriae turns on a determination of mental incapacity. Intervention through mandatory reporting of suspected abuse cannot be justified or supported since the age of an individual is the only criterion considered before the reporter is mandated to override the individual's right to self-determination. To presume that every adult over the age of sixty-five is unable to decide what is best for himself is an absurd proposition. As one author put it, "once the age of majority is reached the decision-making power over one's life belongs to the individual; [and] that power is not lost by virtue of old age alone. The aged do not, by definition, become incompetents who need protection from themselves and others." Mandatory reporting laws, however, in effect assume that an abused elder does not seek assistance because he is unable or incompetent to do so. If an elderly individual will not report, laws dictate that someone else should do so. This assumption fails to recognize that an elder's seemingly irrational nonaction actually may reflect a reasoned decision that remaining in the abusive situation is preferable to facing alternatives such as eventual institutionalization.

The existence of mandatory reporting provisions is troublesome particularly because a number of courts, employing a variety of rationales, have recognized that a competent adult has the right to refuse medical treatment even if such refusal means imminent death. The individual's right to decide whether or not he wishes to remain in an abusive situation or seek assistance is, of course, not analogous to a competent individual's right to refuse medical treatment when such treatment is futile. Undoubtedly, an argument can be posited that state intervention in the former circumstance

---

[*] © 1991 by University of California, Hastings College of the Law. Reprinted from Hastings Law Journal, Vol. 42, No. 3, by permission.

is not as intrusive because the right to remain in an abusive situation implicates a far less significant interest, be it a liberty or privacy interest, than does the right to determine whether one will live or die. The analogy is useful, however, if only to illustrate the irony that a competent elder's right to self-determination and autonomy permits him to decide to end his life but, under mandatory reporting provisions, will not empower him to decide whether he wants or needs outside assistance to extricate himself from an abusive situation.

* * *

Mandatory reporting laws originally were enacted on the theory that to curb abuse, victims first had to be found and identified. The belief that cases needed to be "found" was based on early studies which indicated that abused elderly would not seek help for themselves. One study, for example, asserted that "[p]ride, embarrassment, fear, isolation, lack of access to services, and mental confusion are all obstacles to [elderly] acknowledging . . . abuse and seeking professional assistance." More recent commentaries, however, conclude that mandatory reporting actually is not "finding" cases that otherwise would not be reported. One Maryland study indicated that ninety-five percent of reported cases were already known to agencies and that in many states most reports of abuse come from nonmandated reporters.

One major assumption of any mandatory reporting system is that adequate services will exist within the community to assist the abused individual and to help find solutions for the problem of abuse. Unfortunately, the services available to aid victims of elder abuse are severely limited. . . . Without funding for services, mandatory reporting is meaningless and inappropriate. State intervention can be justified only if assistance is available to combat the reported abuse.

A final area of concern regarding mandatory reporting is its effect on privileged communications between professionals such as physicians and their clients or patients. Many mandated reporters are professionals who have an obligation to uphold their clients' statutory privilege to confidential communications. Specific provisions within reporting laws expressly abrogate many of these privileges. As a general principle, abrogation of the privileges alone is not necessarily offensive since often there are exceptions to these privileges. Incursions on the physician-patient privilege, for example, are justified if necessary to protect society from crime—by exposing criminal offenders—or to protect those who are unable to care for themselves—as in cases of child abuse. Any exception in the case of elder abuse, however, is not tailored to protect society from crime, but rather is based on the familiar assumption that because of their age elders cannot protect themselves. The incursions on these privileges ultimately are examples of yet another instance in which ageism is encouraged.

In addition to fears that such provisions promote ageism, critics also worry that abridgement of these privileges will discourage elders from seeking medical or other assistance from those professionals who are required to report believed instances of abuse. Elders often choose not to seek assistance against abuse because they legitimately fear eventual institutionalization. If an elder believes his doctor will report suspected abuse to the authorities and thereby set in motion a process that may end with his being removed from his home, the elder understandably is reluctant to seek much-needed medical attention. Others have voiced concern that abrogation of privileges will discourage the abuser from seeking professional help such as psychological counselling. Critics theorize that an abuser who knows that his treating physician is obliged to report abuse will be deterred from seeking the very assistance, such as in-home help caring for the elder and counseling for himself, that may help him end his abusive behavior.

Questions

Should the reporting of elder abuse be mandatory? Why or why not?

c. Liability for Failure to Report

Seymour Moskowitz
New Remedies for Elder Abuse and Neglect
PROB. & PROP. 52, 54-55 (January/February 1998)[*]

State laws typically make the failure to report suspected elder mistreatment to public authorities a criminal offense. Most states make these omissions a misdemeanor, but sanctions are often minor or unspecified. Statutes often require a mental state of willfulness to prove a violation. Criminal enforcement of these reporting law is almost nonexistent for a wide variety of reasons. Few actual cases of prosecution against doctors, nurses or other professionals exist. A computer search of published decisions in all states between 1994 and 1997 yielded only one prosecution based on these statutes, and even that case did not directly involve a failure to report.

* * *

In addition to criminal enforcement, lawyers can use mandatory reporting laws in civil actions. Tort suits for damages against professionals who fail to diagnose and report elder mistreatment can help compensate victims and change behavior of professionals. Elder abuse statutes typically require only "reasonable suspicion" or "reasonable belief" that abuse has occurred, not definitive proof. A few states explicitly provide civil liability for failure to report. When statutes are silent on civil liability, a malpractice claim may allow recovery. A professional's failure to diagnose obvious mistreatment or failure to report suspected physical abuse or neglect could constitute professional negligence, especially if the mistreatment is repeated with resulting injury. The standard of care in such suits may be based on protocols and assessment instruments. Expert testimony may also guide the judge or jury on the appropriate standard of care.

---

[*] Copyright © 1998 by the American Bar Association. Reprinted by permission.

* * *

[In addition to civil liability, there may be administrative sanctions for a failure to report.] All members of licensed professions are subject to some form of disciplinary control . . . . Some jurisdictions make the failure to file any report required by law grounds for revocation of professional licenses.

* * *

A few states (Michigan, Minnesota, Iowa, and Arkansas) have explicitly created a civil cause of action for damages against persons who intentionally or negligently fail to report elder abuse or neglect.

Question

If the reporting of elder abuse is mandatory, what sanctions, if any, should be administered to persons who fail to comply with the reporting requirements?

d. Remedies Against Abusers

i. The Pre-Existing Criminal Law

Seymour Moskowitz
New Remedies for Elder Abuse and Neglect
PROB. & PROP. 52, 52, 56 (January/February 1998)*

[C]riminal law has been the traditional tool to combat elder abuse.

* * *

The criminal justice system provides numerous possibilities for dealing with elder abuse. The state can prosecute physical abuse as assault or battery. Financial exploitation is typically theft, extortion or some other crime.

Question

To what extent is traditional criminal law a useful tool for preventing or remedying elder abuse?

---

* Copyright © 1998 by the American Bar Association. Reprinted by permission.

ii. The Use of Tort Law Against Institutional Abusers

Gail Diane Cox
End of Life Valued
NAT'L L.J., March 2, 1998, at A1, A26[*]

Lesley A. Clement was a business litigator in the Sacramento, Calif. Area when her "grandma" Dorothy, 83, suffering from Alzheimer's disease, changed her life. Dorothy Palmer, actually Ms. Clement's great-aunt, was found locked outside her nursing home one night with a broken rib, blood streaming down her face and a mango-sized bruise on her forearm.

No criminal charges were brought, but Ms. Clement, as the only family member with a law degree, filed a suit, though she'd never before read a medical chart. In the third week of trial, in February 1994, the suit settled confidentially, and state regulators ultimately revoked the license of the woman who ran the nursing home.

Ms. Clement was a lawyer transformed. She set up her own practice devoted to litigating nursing home abuse cases full-time on a contingency basis. Four years later, she enthuses, "Talk about feeling good about what you do!" And, she says, in 1997, she paid more in taxes than she ever grossed doing business law.

What's striking is that anyone could find elder abuse law lucrative. For years, personal injury and especially wrongful-death suits against nursing homes were the province of a few true believers with independent sources of income. Conventional wisdom had it that juries typically did not place a high cash value on lives already so diminished—not to mention on people who had already exceeded their life expectancies and had been left in the care of strangers. Or, as Ms. Clement calls it, the "he-used-to-be-a-vegetable, he's-still-a-vegetable, these-things-happen-and-who-cares?" defense.

Big Verdicts

But a glance at recent verdict reports shows the landscape has changed. Seven-figure settlements and awards are no longer rare. On Feb. 11, a West Palm beach jury awarded $6.3 million—$1.5 million in compensatory damages plus $4.8 million in punitives—to the widow of Charles Barnes, a man who was institutionalized after suffering seven strokes that left him with vascular dementia. He wandered away from the nursing home, fell in a pond and drowned. *Hamilton v. First Healthcare Corp.,* 97-1621.

Last year one of the largest verdicts nationwide was $83 million—reduced to $55 million—awarded to the niece and grandnephew of an 84-year-old Texas woman, Ruth Waites, who jurors came to believe was killed by an untreated bedsore. *Williams v. Beverly Enterprises,* 95-437 (Dist. Ct. Rusk Co., Texas).

---

[*] This article is reprinted with permission from the March 2, 1998 edition of *The National Law Journal.* © 1998 NLP IP Company.

What must be unnerving for the nursing home industry and its insurance carriers is that the facts in Mr. Barnes' and Ms. Waites' deaths are not unusual. Wandering and bedsores are two of the most common circumstances in wrongful-death suits against homes, says Steven M. Levin, of Chicago's Levin & Perconti. He is a former chair of the American Trial Lawyers Association's nursing home litigation group.

"Nursing home abuse is one of few growth areas left in litigation," he says. "Now you're getting my standard speech, but I tell lawyer groups that nursing home wrongful deaths are where we were 20 years ago with medical malpractice and product liability. You can argue today there are too many of those suits, but you have to admit those fields are much safer as a result."

Mr. Levin recalls nursing home litigation group meetings at the ATLA's annual conventions in the early 1990s. He says there were "maybe five or six guys wandering in." As of the 1997 gathering, the group boasted 140 members in 40 states.

"It's the tort of the 90s," agrees Arnold R. Gellman, who has represented plaintiffs in the past but today defends nursing homes as a partner at New York's Epstein Becker & Green P.C. Fresh from a trial in South Florida where, he says, he settled a bedsore death case for an amount in the high six figures, he observes, "These are very jury-friendly lawsuits."

The tide of healthy verdicts for the elderly is attributed by both the plaintiffs' and defense bars to baby boomers' concerns and to the growing waves of terror and guilt the public feels about institutions that take over what families, a few generations back, would have been forced to do themselves. Mr. Gellman adds that the trend toward corporations buying nursing home chains adds the element of corporate defendants and managed care plans. "It's a confluence of great targets," he says.

Plaintiffs' attorneys acknowledge that even in states where punitive damages aren't allowed formally, the cases have a large punitive element.

"A great deal does ride on the family, how close they were, how often they visited. So sure, you argue loss of love. But frankly, the main value of these cases isn't so much the loss, but the jury's perception of how badly the defendant acted," says Steven Levin.

That doesn't mean Mr. Levin and his colleagues concede the quality-of-life issue.

"You say, 'She had already lived longer than the average,' and I reply, 'That means her few remaining years were that much more precious,'" says Mr. Levin.

As Jules B. Olsman, of Detroit's Olsman, Ganos & Mueller, who has a general personal injury practice and is the current head of ATLA's nursing home litigation group, puts it, "I don't care if they're 140. I'll tell the jury, 'No one deserves to die this way. Look, multiple fractures. Unexplained.'"

Quality of Life

And these cases can be graphic. A jury, for instance, can be asked to look at an easel with a blow-up of a decubitous ulcer. In Ruth Waites' case, the hospital reported removing eight pounds of dead flesh while trying to save the woman's life. In some bedsores, a ball-and-socket hip joint is visible. Occasionally, there is caked feces or maggots.

"Ninety-nine percent of the photos are admissible, with the judge finding their probative value outweighing any effect they might have on the jurors," says Mr. Gellman.

Countering bedsore photos is a familiar educational challenge for defense attorneys, says Joseph F. Babiarz Jr., of Detroit's Plunkett & Cooney P.C., who estimates he has defended more than 30 wrongful-death cases during the past five years. "Bedsores look so horrendous that the lay juror's reaction is that someone must be to blame. But virtually any expert will testify that no matter how good care is, some bedsores are inevitable," Mr. Babiarz says. "I tell the jury that just as there can be heart failure or kidney failure due to age, and they can accept that, so, too, there can be skin failure. Why question that? Skin is the body's largest organ."

The Defense Research Institute of Chicago has printed a guide to defending nursing home cases, written by Davis Carr and his colleagues at Mobile, Ala.'s Carr, Alford, Clausen & McDonald L.L.C. It suggests the defense may be able to neutralize bedsore photos by presenting some of its own: "The wound should be as clean as possible. . . . You should not be able to identify that the wound is on a human body."

It's a tactic that Mr. Babiarz says he'd try only if he was lucky enough to have a bedsore photo taken by the nursing home at the time of the resident's admission—that is, a bedsore brought from home.

Ms. Clements volunteers, "I'll tell you what doesn't work for them. I've actually had defense attorneys say, 'That may look bad, but it isn't. It's like diaper rash.' You should see the female jurors recoil."

A state-of-the-art defense in wandering cases entails taking the high ground, arguing that patients have a right—often spelled out in state statutes passed in the first wave of nursing home legislation in the late 1970s—to be free of oppressive chemical or physical restraints.

"They say the patient was dirty. Well, you've got a right to refuse to bathe, and so do nursing home residents, unless they have had conservators appointed, and most haven't," says Mr. Babiarz.

When defense counsel argued that solicitude for Charles Barnes' remaining dignity and independence stopped the home from making him wear a "wander guard," his widow's attorney, Richard Schuler, was prepared. The nursing home had never asked Mr. Barnes about wearing an alarm and, his widow testified on the stand, when she brought it up that after an earlier wandering incident, her husband said he would wear one.

Mr. Schuler, of West Palm Beach, Fla.'s Schuler, Wilkerson, Halvorson & Williams, complains that the defense and its insurance adjustors were "behind the curve all the way" in their settlement offers. But he also underestimated the worth of the case, his first wrongful-death suit against a nursing home.

He says he would have settled for $2.5 million. And when the jury came in with compensatory damages after less than two hours of deliberation, he thought he'd lost. On the contrary, "because they found there was a statutory violation of Mr. Barnes' patients' rights, all right—his right to be cared for and supervised—the attorneys' fees and costs will be computed on top of the $6.3 million."

On the Defense

Some defense attorneys, when asked to describe a major victory, tend to cite cases with offbeat facts. In one, the decedent was a long-term, but ambulatory, resident who was running errands for staff to a convenience store across a four-lane highway at night when a car struck and killed him. The defense won by arguing that the driver, who had settled early, was primarily at fault.

Another defense attorney told of a woman with advanced AIDS dementia who had apparently drowned while taking a bath unattended. A coroner testified that the bite marks on her tongue and the lack of water in her stomach indicated she had, in fact, died of an end-stage convulsion. As the defense attorney reminded the jurors in closing arguments, it could have happened if she had been both in her bed and supervised.

Asked about the change in climate for nursing home cases, Mr. Babiarz maintains that for the great bulk of cases, the conventional wisdom still prevails, and plaintiffs' demands are unrealistic. "We settle a lot, where there is no value, in the $15,000 to $20,000 range," he says. "You write it off to nuisance value because the cases are so hard to try. And there's a simple reason why they're hard to try, besides the image of nursing homes. Your witnesses aren't usually the doctors and registered nurses you have testifying for you in [medical malpractice] cases. Typically, the aides are unsophisticated—if you can even find them, the turnover is so great—and it's easy for plaintiffs' counsel to intimidate people with minimal education, or to twist what they say."

But he won't deny that seven-figure awards are on the rise. "If this keeps up, the insurers will just refuse to cover the homes. They're going to be closing and sending residents back to their families, whether they can take them or not. Then you're going to see a legislative backlash."

But so far, plaintiffs' attorneys get safe passage through the tort-reform war zone when their targets are nursing homes. "Suddenly you've got [the American Association of Retired Persons] and the Grey Panthers and all these other advocacy groups on your side, and the 'reformers' aren't just up against nasty trial lawyers," says Mr. Levin.

For example, last year's tort reform caps in Ohio expressly excluded nursing homes from the bar against collecting punitive damages in statutory wrongful death claims. And a Florida appellate court in 1995 upheld a special statute for nursing home cases that allows the recovery of pain-and-suffering damages by the estate of the deceased. *Beverly Enterprises–Florida Inc. v. Spilman*, 661 So. 2d 287.

The reasoning behind these rulings is the same as that behind the private attorney general statutes in California, Illinois and a number of other states Mr. Levin explains. Lawmakers recognize the policing value of lawsuits and the ineffectiveness of state and federal regulation of nursing homes. It's not an accident, he adds, that a number of his colleagues—among them David Marks, of Houston, who won the Williams case—are former prosecutors.

Ms. Clement says she's looking forward to the day when an abuse suit is framed in such a way that it will provoke federal criminal action against a corporate officer of a nursing home. In the meantime, she says she's working to "get the word out" about the value today's jurors are placing on the lives of the institutionalized elderly. She has taught five continuing education courses in the past year, and she regularly secures from clients commitments that any settlements will not be kept confidential.

"Ben Gets Good Care"

The Ben Bretz case is her favorite example of what she calls defense attorneys' not getting it. She represented the man's daughter-guardian, who brought a personal injury suit on his behalf, alleging that the octogenarian had been so malnourished and dehydrated that he could no longer swallow. Opposing counsel brought a motion last April arguing that the daughter's refusal to accept a $150,000 immediate cash settlement on behalf of a man who had less than six months to live showed the daughter was interested only in enlarging her inheritance.

Ms. Clements substituted a new guardian, former California Supreme Court Justice Armand Arabian.

"It was a little hard for them to say he had a conflict of interest." The ultimate settlement with the nursing home's insurer was $1.5 million.

"Ben gets very good care these days," Ms. Clements brags. "He's put on 30 pounds."

Questions

1. What explains the large verdicts juries are willing to award in these cases?
2. What explains the hesitation of state legislators to apply tort-reform laws to suits against nursing homes?

iii. Criminal and Tortious Conduct Outside of Institutions: To What Extent is There a Duty of Care?

Joann Blair
"Honor Thy Father and Thy Mother"—But For How Long?:
Adult Children's Duty to Care for and Protect Elderly Parents
35 U. LOUISVILLE J. FAM. L. 765, 768 (1996-1997)[*]

In order to be criminally liable for a failure to act or for an omission, such as failing to care for an elderly parent, a corresponding legal duty to act must exist. A legal duty can be expressly provided for in a criminal statute itself, imposed by another statute, based upon a contract, or voluntarily assumed. Legal duties may also

---

[3] Copyright © 1997. Reprinted with permission.

arise via special relationships such as parent and child, husband and wife, employer and employee, landlord and licensee, or a supervisory relationship in which one individual is responsible for supervising the conduct of another who is deemed physically dangerous. A person must have notice that a legal duty to take affirmative action exists before liability for violating that duty can attach.

People v. Heitzman
886 P.2d 1229 (Cal. 1994)

LUCAS, Chief Justice.
Penal Code section 368, subdivision (a), is one component of a multi-faceted legislative response to the problem of elder abuse. The statute imposes felony criminal liability on

> [a]ny person who, under circumstances or conditions likely to produce great bodily harm or death, willfully causes or permits any elder or dependent adult, with knowledge that he or she is an elder or dependent adult, to suffer, or inflicts thereon unjustifiable physical pain or mental suffering, or having the care or custody of any elder or dependent adult, willfully causes or permits the person or health of the elder or dependent adult to be injured, or willfully causes or permits the elder or dependent adult to be placed in a situation such that his or her person or health is endangered. . . .

In this case, we must decide whether the statute meets constitutional standards of certainty. As we shall explain, we conclude initially that, on its face, the broad statutory language at issue here fails to provide fair notice to those who may be subjected to criminal liability for "willfully . . . permit[ting]" an elder or dependent adult to suffer pain, and similarly fails to set forth a uniform standard under which police and prosecutors can consistently enforce the proscription against "willfully . . . permit[ting]" such suffering. Under these circumstances, section 368(a) would be unconstitutionally vague absent some judicial construction clarifying its uncertainties.

We conclude that the statute may properly be upheld by interpreting its imposition of criminal liability upon "[a]ny person who . . . permits . . . any elder or dependent adult . . . to suffer . . . unjustifiable pain or mental suffering" to apply only to a person who, under existing tort principles, has a duty to control the conduct of the individual who is directly causing or inflicting abuse on the elder or dependent adult. Because the evidence in this case does not indicate that defendant had the kind of "special relationship" with the individuals alleged to have directly abused the elder victim that would give rise to a duty on her part to control their conduct, she was improperly charged with a violation of section 368(a). We therefore reverse the judgment of the Court of Appeal.

I. FACTS

The egregious facts of this case paint a profoundly disturbing family portrait in which continued neglect of and apparent indifference to the basic needs of the family's most vulnerable member, an elderly dependent parent, led to a result of tragic proportion. Sixty-seven-year-old Robert Heitzman resided in the Huntington Beach home of his grown son, Richard Heitzman, Sr., along with another grown son, Jerry Heitzman, and Richard's three sons. On December 3, 1990, police were summoned to the house, where they discovered Robert dead in his bedroom. His body lay on a mattress that was rotted through from constant wetness, exposing the metal springs. The stench of urine and feces filled not only decedent's bedroom, but the entire house as well. His bathroom was filthy, and the bathtub contained fetid, green-colored water that appeared to have been there for some time.

Police learned that Jerry Heitzman was primarily responsible for his father's care, rendering caretaking services in exchange for room and board. Jerry admitted that he had withheld all food and liquids from his father for the three days preceding his death on December 3. Jerry explained that he was expecting company for dinner on Sunday, December 2, and did not want his father, who no longer had control over his bowels and bladder, to defecate or urinate because it would further cause the house to smell.

At the time of his death, decedent had large, decubitus ulcers, more commonly referred to as bed sores, covering one-sixth of his body. An autopsy revealed the existence of a yeast infection in his mouth, and showed that he suffered from congestive heart failure, bronchial pneumonia, and hepatitis. The forensic pathologist who performed the autopsy attributed decedent's death to septic shock due to the sores which, he opined, were caused by malnutrition, dehydration, and neglect.

Twenty years earlier, decedent had suffered a series of strokes that paralyzed the left side of his body. Defendant, 31-year-old Susan Valerie Heitzman, another of decedent's children, had previously lived in the home and had been her father's primary caregiver at that time. In return, defendant's brother Richard paid for her room and board. Richard supported the household by working two full-time jobs, and supplemented this income with decedent's monthly Social Security and pension checks.

One year prior to her father's death, defendant decided to move away from the home. After she moved out, however, she continued to spend time at the house visiting her boyfriend/nephew Richard, Jr. Since leaving to live on her own, she noticed that the entire house had become filthy. She was aware that a social worker had discussed with Jerry the need to take their father to a doctor. When she spoke to Jerry about it, he told her he had lost the doctor's telephone number the social worker had given him. She suggested to Jerry that he recontact the social worker. She also discussed with Richard, Jr., the need for taking her father to the doctor, but she never made the necessary arrangements.

In the last six weekends before her father died, defendant had routinely visited the household. She was last in her father's bedroom five weeks prior to his death, at which time she noticed the hole in the mattress and feces-soiled clothing lying on the floor. Another of decedent's daughters, Lisa, also visited the house that same day.

Two weeks prior to her father's death, defendant spent the entire weekend at the house. On Sunday afternoon, she saw her father sitting in the living room, and noticed that he looked weak and appeared disoriented. A week later, during Thanksgiving weekend, and several days prior to decedent's death, defendant again stayed at the house. Decedent's bedroom door remained closed throughout the weekend, and defendant did not see her father. On the day decedent died, defendant awoke mid-morning and left the house to return to her own apartment. Around one o'clock in the afternoon, Jerry discovered decedent dead in his bedroom.

In a two-count indictment, the Orange County District Attorney jointly charged Jerry and Richard, Sr., with involuntary manslaughter, and Jerry, Richard, Sr., and defendant with violating section 368(a). At the preliminary examination, the magistrate determined that, although defendant did not have care or custody of decedent as did her brothers, there was probable cause to believe she owed a duty of care to her father and that she had been grossly negligent in failing to carry out that duty. She was therefore held to answer along with her brothers for willfully permitting an elder to suffer unjustifiable physical pain and mental suffering.

On November 4, 1994, an information was filed in superior court charging defendant with a violation of section 368(a). Thereafter, she moved to set aside the information pursuant to section 995 on the basis that the evidence presented at the preliminary hearing failed to establish probable cause she had committed a crime. In relevant part, defendant argued that the evidence that she knew of her father's deteriorating condition did not create a duty for her to act to prevent the harm suffered by him. In its opposition to her motion, the prosecution contended that defendant's duty of care was established by section 368(a) itself, which imposes a duty on every person to not permit any elderly or dependent adult to suffer unjustifiable pain.

* * *

The superior court agreed with defendant that the statutory language at issue was unconstitutionally vague, ... dismissed the case against her. The People appealed the court's order of dismissal, and the Court of Appeal reversed .... The court found that such a duty did exist, based on the special relationship between a parent and child codified in the financial support statutes, section 270c and Civil Code former sections 206 and 242, and thus rejected defendant's vagueness challenge.

* * *

II. DISCUSSION

A. *Criminal Liability for a Failure to Act*

* * *

Defendant here was charged under section 368(a) with willfully permitting her elder father to suffer the infliction of unjustifiable pain and mental suffering. It was thus her failure to act, i.e., her failure to prevent the infliction of abuse on her father, that created the potential for her criminal liability under the statute. Unlike the imposition of criminal penalties for certain positive acts, which is based on the statutory proscription of such conduct, when an individual's criminal liability is based on the failure to act, it is well established that he or she must first be under an existing legal duty to take positive action.

* * *

When a criminal statute does not set forth a legal duty to act by its express terms, liability for a failure to act must be premised on the existence of a duty found elsewhere . . . .

Whether the statute adequately denotes the class of persons who owe such a duty is the focus of the constitutional question presented here.

B. *Vagueness*

The Fourteenth Amendment to the United States Constitution and article I, section 7 of the California Constitution, each guarantee that no person shall be deprived of life, liberty, or property without due process of law. This constitutional command requires "a reasonable degree of certainty in legislation, especially in the criminal law. . . ."

* * *

For several reasons, we reject the People's contention that the statute itself imposes a blanket duty on everyone to prevent the abuse of any elder. The wide net cast by a statutory interpretation imposing such a duty on every person is apparent when we consider that it would extend the potential for criminal liability to, for example, a delivery person who, having entered a private home, notices an elder in a disheveled or disoriented state and purposefully fails to intervene.

Under general principles of tort law, civil liability is not imposed for the failure to assist or protect another, absent some legal or special relationship between the parties giving rise to a duty to act. In the absence of any indication, express or implied, that the Legislature meant to depart so dramatically from this principle, well established at the time section 368(a) was enacted, it would be unreasonable to interpret the statute as imposing a more serious form of liability, indeed, felony criminal liability, on every person who fails to prevent an elder from suffering abuse, absent some legal or special relationship between the parties.

* * *

[D]ecisions construing either section 368(a) or the felony child abuse statute on which it was modeled do not provide a clear definition of those under a duty to protect either elders or children, respectively. Under these circumstances, section 368(a) fails to provide adequate notice as to the class of persons who may be under an affirmative duty to prevent the infliction of abuse. Of equal, if not greater, constitutional significance, police and prosecutors may lack sufficient standards under which to determine who is to be charged with permitting such abuse.

* * *

Richard, Sr., and Jerry were not the only family members residing with decedent. Richard, Sr.'s three sons also lived in the home. One of these individuals, Richard, Jr., was defendant's boyfriend. For the last six weekends before her father's death, defendant had routinely been in the house visiting with Richard, Jr. Approximately one month before her father died, defendant discussed with Richard, Jr., the possibility of his helping her take decedent to the doctor. The record therefore would appear to support an inference that whatever defendant knew about her father's deteriorating condition, Richard, Jr., knew as well. Under the prosecutor's reading of the statutory language, the first part of section 368(a) would also appear to be applicable to decedent's grandson, Richard, Jr. He was, however, neither arrested nor charged.

Lisa, a fourth Heitzman sibling who, like defendant, did not reside in the same house as her father and brothers, had visited the home five weeks before decedent's death. She was present in the home when defendant entered their father's room for the last time and discovered the hole where the mattress had rotted through. The record also indicates that at one point Lisa contacted the Orange County Department of Social Services concerning her father's condition, but that the agency did not follow up on her call. It would thus appear that Lisa, like defendant, was well aware of decedent's situation. Unlike defendant, however, Lisa was neither arrested for nor charged with a violation of section 368(a).

* * *

We have determined that the portion of section 368(a) purporting to impose on any person the duty to prevent the infliction of pain or suffering on an elder fails to meet the constitutional requirement of certainty. Before declaring a statute void for vagueness, however, we have an obligation to determine whether its validity can be preserved by "giv[ing] specific content to terms that might otherwise be unconstitutionally vague."

* * *

The Restatement Second of Torts provides guidance as to both the nature and the scope of the special relationships that would give rise to a duty to prevent an individual from inflicting pain or suffering on an elder, pursuant to section 368(a). These special relationships are defined as those between (1) parent and minor child, (2) employer and employee, (3) landowner and licensee, and (4) "[o]ne who takes charge of a third person whom he knows or should know to be likely to cause bodily harm to others if not controlled."

* * *

From this it follows that one will be criminally liable for the abusive conduct of another only if he or she has the ability to control such conduct.

* * *

III. DISPOSITION

Based on their status as Robert Heitzman's caretakers, felony criminal liability was properly imposed on Richard, Sr., and Jerry pursuant to section 368(a) for the role they played in bringing about their father's demise.

* * *

Furthermore, given defendant's failure to intercede on her father's behalf under the egregious circumstances presented here, we can well understand the prosecution's decision to charge defendant under section 368(a). Because the People presented no evidence tending to show that defendant had a legal duty to control the conduct of either of her brothers, however, we reverse the judgment of the Court of Appeal with directions to reinstate the trial court's order dismissing the charges against defendant.

We emphasize that our disposition of this case in no way signifies our approval of defendant's failure to repel the threat to her father's well-being. The facts underlying this case are indeed troubling, and defendant's alleged indifference to the suffering of her father cannot be condoned. The desire to impose criminal liability on this defendant cannot be accomplished, however, at the expense of providing constitutionally required clarity to an otherwise vague statute.

The judgment of the Court of Appeal is reversed.

KENNARD, ARABIAN and GEORGE, JJ., concur.

BAXTER, Justice, dissenting.

I respectfully dissent. The majority essentially holds that even though defendant knew her aged and disabled father was living in her brothers' home under conditions that were painful, degrading, and ultimately fatal, she cannot be criminally prosecuted for her failure to act because she did not stand in a "special relationship" with either her father or her brothers under tort law.

* * *

Based on the preliminary hearing record in this case, there was ample evidence that defendant's failure to intervene in her father's behalf was criminally negligent, and thus violated section 368.

* * *

In brief, the preliminary hearing record indicates that defendant—formerly her father's caretaker—knew he was paralyzed, incontinent, and completely dependent upon others to feed, clean, and move him. For a period of at least six weeks before her father died, defendant repeatedly visited and spent the night in the home where her brothers and father lived. Defendant had actual knowledge during this time that her father required, but did not receive, medical attention; that his person and physical surroundings had become filthy from human waste and debris; that the mattress from which he could not move without assistance was damp and rotted through; and that he was confined alone in his room for long stretches of time.

Nevertheless, defendant did not take any steps to assist her father during this period. She did not attempt to obtain professional help (e.g., telephoning the doctor, social worker, or paramedics); to care for him while present in the home (e.g., feeding or cleaning him); or to discuss with other family members the possibility of making different care arrangements (e.g., hospitalization or professional caretaking assistance). The evidence further discloses that defendant's father died as a result of the deplorable conditions of which defendant was actually or presumably aware (septic shock from bed sores, malnutrition, and dehydration).

In light of the foregoing, I would affirm the judgment of the Court of Appeal insofar as it reversed the superior court's order sustaining defendant's demurrer and dismissing the case.

MOSK and WERDEGAR, JJ., concur.

Questions

1. With which do you agree: the majority opinion in *Heitzman*, or the dissent? Why?

2. To what extent should family members have a duty to care for their elderly parents or relatives?

iv. Examples of New Remedies Against Elder Abuse

Duane St. Clair
Bill Targets Those Who Prey On Elderly, Disabled
COLUMBUS DISPATCH, May 20, 1998, at 3B*

Bilking defenseless adults out of their life's savings would be a more serious crime under legislation passed by the Ohio House of Representatives yesterday and sent to the Senate.

House Bill 632, sponsored by Rep. Patrick J. Tiberi, R-Columbus, cleared the House unanimously.

Tiberi said the proposal is designed to punish anyone who, by deception or intimidation, defrauds elderly or disabled adults and takes their money, assets or property.

Tiberi said financial predators bilked $75,000 from a Grove City woman with Parkinson's disease and a combined $80,000 from a Columbus woman and a Hillard man, both with Alzheimer's disease.

Offenders now are punished by a maximum 18 months in prison. Under House Bill 632, they would draw one to five years in prison if the loss to the victim is between $5,000 and $25,000. Larger amounts would be punishable by a longer sentence.

---

* Copyright © 1998. Reprinted with permission.

Seymour Moskowitz
New Remedies for Elder Abuse and Neglect
PROB. & PROP. 52, 56 (January/February 1998)[*]

Recognizing the need for new statutory remedies, several states have become "laboratories" to test new remedies. In 1992 California enacted the Elder Abuse Protection Act to help victims engage lawyers to take their cases [citing Cal. Welf. & Inst. Code §§15657-15657.3]. The statute creates new remedies when a plaintiff proves by clear and convincing evidence that the defendant is capable of recklessness, oppression, fraud or malice in the commission of abuse of the elderly. These remedies include postmortem recovery for pain and suffering and mandatory attorney's fees and costs. The act allows fees for the services of a conservator litigating an elder's claim and continuation of a pending action by the elder's personal representative or successor.

Another innovative statute is Illinois' recent Financial Exploitation of the Elderly and Disabled Act, which provides for criminal penalties as well as treble damages and attorney's fees for a civil judgment for conversion of a senior citizen's property by threat or deception [citing Ill. Ann. Stat. ch. 320, para. 720 5/16-13]. These enhanced remedies are available regardless of the outcome of a criminal case. Statutes such as this make civil suits against the financial exploiter more feasible, and even attractive, for lawyers.

e. Protection Against Self-Neglect

Audrey S. Garfield
Elder Abuse and the States' Adult Protective Services Response:
Time for a Change in California
42 HASTINGS L.J. 859, 870, 897-900, 904, 912, 914-15 (1991)[**]

Although the content of APS laws varies from state to state, each adult protective services system typically includes two main components: coordinated provision of services for adults determined to be at risk of abuse, and the actual or potential power (of the state or a local governmental entity) to intervene legally in an individual's life and make decisions for him. This power usually is invoked when an elder is deemed incapable of making decisions for himself, is personally in danger, or is dangerous to others. In some states the power includes the ability to intervene when an elder refuses services or is deemed incapable of consenting.

* * *

---

[*] Copyright © 1998 by the American Bar Association. Reprinted by permission.

[**] © 1991 by University of California, Hastings College of the Law. Reprinted from Hastings Law Journal, Vol. 42, No. 3, by permission.

APS statutes typically contain at least some provisions that are aimed at providing services to needy adults.

* * *

The majority of state APS laws include an exception to the requirement of consent to services when the elder has been determined to be incapacitated.

* * *

The first and most fundamental problem with these provisions is that many of the statutes do not include a definition of "lacks capacity to consent" . . . . The absence of a definition leaves the door open to subjective and ad hoc determinations of capacity.

* * *

Of perhaps greater concern is the fact that some states do not even require a determination of "lack of capacity" before an elder may be required to receive services absent consent.

* * *

Even with respect to those states that define "incapacity," "lack of capacity," or "incompetence," the substance of these definitions is subject to criticism. These criticisms are the same as those that have been levied against the employment of similar definitions in guardianship statutes.

* * *

Two procedures are used most widely to impose involuntary services on abuse victims in the nonemergency setting. The majority of states use the traditional guardianship or conservatorship mechanisms that already exist within their probate codes. Others have established a special procedure within their APS laws that operates independently of the guardianship or conservatorship sections of the probate code.

* * *

One common exception to the rule that involuntary services may be provided only after formal guardianship or guardianship-like proceedings is the provision of short-term emergency services. Emergency provisions in APS laws most often constitute an exception to the rule that services only may be provided with the elder's consent although some state APS laws exclusively apply to elderly who are in the equivalent of an emergency situation.

* * *

States generally employ one of two procedures to administer emergency services. In the majority of states the agency must file a petition with the court and obtain an emergency court order before any emergency assistance may be provided. Other state codes permit emergency assistance to be administered without first obtaining a court order, but require that a petition be filed to obtain an emergency order within a mandated brief time period.

Questions

How would you evaluate the procedures described by Ms. Garfield? Are they too intrusive? If so, what procedures, if any, are appropriate to protect the elderly from self-neglect?

FURTHER READING. ALISON BARNES ET AL., COUNSELING OLDER CLIENTS ch. 27 (1997); WINSOR C. SCHMIDT JR., GUARDIANSHIP: THE COURT OF LAST RESORT FOR THE ELDERLY AND DISABLED (1995); PETER J. STRAUSS & NANCY M. LEDERMAN, THE ELDER LAW HANDBOOK ch. 13 (1996); PETER J. STRAUSS ET AL., AGING AND THE LAW, chs. 20, 21 (1996).

CHAPTER 7

Health Care

A. The U.S. Health-Care System: An Overview 321
B. Managing and Paying for Health Care 323
C. Health-Care Decisionmaking (Short of Ending Life) 372

In this chapter, we examine a range of medical issues confronting the elderly. We begin, in Part A, with an overview of the health-care system in the United States. In Part B, we evaluate the mechanisms, both governmental and private, by which elderly persons can manage and pay for their medical needs. And in Part C, we consider the methods by which the elderly can preserve their ability to make medical decisions, or can have this ability delegated to others, in the face of illness or incapacity.

A. The U.S. Health-Care System: An Overview

Mary Onnis Waid
Health Care Financing Administration
Brief Summaries of Medicare and Medicaid: Title XVIII and Title XIX of the Social Security Act as of June 25, 1998
<http://www.hcfa.gov/medicare/ormedmed.htm>[*]

Since early in this century, health care issues have continued to escalate in importance for our Nation. Beginning in 1915, various efforts to establish government health insurance programs have been initiated every few years. From the 1930s on, there was agreement on the real need for some form of health insurance to

---

[*] Copyright © 1997. Reprinted with permission.
NOTE: The following are very brief summaries of complex subjects. They do not yet reflect the changes made by the recently enacted Balanced Budget Act of 1997 (P.L. 105-33). These summaries are not legal documents nor are they intended to fully explain all of the relevant laws, regulations, and rulings of the Medicare and Medicaid programs. They should not be relied on in making specific decisions; original sources of authority should be researched and utilized. The views expressed herein are those of the author, and do not necessarily reflect the policy or legal positions of the Health Care Financing Administration or the Department of Health and Human Services. These summaries should be used only as brief overviews and general guides to the Medicare and Medicaid programs.

alleviate the unpredictable and uneven incidence of medical costs. The main health care issue at that time was whether health insurance should be privately or publicly financed.

Private health insurance coverage expanded rapidly during World War II, when fringe benefits were increased to compensate for government limits on direct wage increases. This trend continued after the war, in part due to the favorable tax treatment of providing compensation in the form of fringe benefits. Private health insurance (mostly group insurance financed through the employment relationship) was especially needed and wanted by middle-income people. Yet not everyone could obtain or afford private health insurance. Government involvement was sought. Various national health insurance plans, financed by payroll taxes, were proposed in Congress starting in the 1940s; however, none was ever brought to a vote.

In 1950, Congress acted to improve access to medical care for needy persons who were receiving public assistance. This permitted, for the first time, Federal participation in the financing of State payments to the providers of medical care for costs incurred by public assistance recipients. In 1960, the Kerr-Mills bill provided medical assistance for aged persons who were not so poor, yet still needed assistance with medical expenses. But a more comprehensive improvement in the provision of medical care, especially for the elderly, became a major congressional priority.

After consideration of various approaches, and after lengthy national debate, Congress passed legislation in 1965 establishing the Medicare and the Medicaid programs as Title XVIII and Title XIX of the Social Security Act. Medicare was established in response to the specific medical care needs of the elderly (and in 1973, the severely disabled and certain persons with kidney disease). Medicaid was established in response to the widely perceived inadequacy of welfare medical care under public assistance. In 1977, the Health Care Financing Administration (HCFA) was established under the Department of Health and Human Services to administer the Medicare and Medicaid programs.

National Health Care Overview

As a share of the gross domestic product (GDP), health care spending stabilized in 1993-96 at 13.6 percent. The GDP is the total value of goods and services produced in the United States. And although 1996 showed the slowest growth in more than 37 years of measuring health care spending, our nation's total spending for health care broke the $1.0 trillion mark in 1996. For the 275 million persons residing in the United States, the average expenditure for health care in 1996 was $3,759 per person.

Health care is funded through a variety of private payers and public programs. Private funds include individuals' out-of-pocket expenditures, private health insurance, philanthropy and non-patient revenues (e.g., gift shops, parking lots, etc.), as well as health services that are provided in industrial settings. For the years 1974 through 1991, these *private* funds paid for 58 to 60 percent of all health care expenditures. But by 1996, the private share of health expenditures had dropped to 53.3 percent of our Nation's total health care expenditures, while the share of health care provided by *public* spending increased correspondingly over this period.

Public spending represents expenditures by Federal, State, and local governments. Of the publicly funded health care expenditures for our Nation, each of the following account for a small percentage of the total: the Department of Defense health care programs for military personnel; the Department of Veterans Affairs health programs; non-commercial medical research; payments for health care under Workers Compensation programs; health programs under State-only general assistance programs; and the construction of public medical facilities. Other activities which are also publicly funded include: maternal and child health services; school health programs; public health clinics; Indian health care services; migrant health care services; substance abuse and mental health activities; and medically-related vocational rehabilitation services. The largest shares of public health expenditures, however, are for the Medicare and Medicaid programs.

Together, Medicare and Medicaid financed $351 billion in health care services in 1996—more than one-third of the nation's total health care bill and almost three-quarters of all public spending on health care. Since their enactment, both Medicare and Medicaid have been subject to numerous legislative and administrative changes designed to make improvements, with financial considerations, in the provision of health care services to our nation's aged, disabled and poor persons.

Questions

Do you agree that government involvement in the provision of health care is appropriate? Why or why not?

B. Managing and Paying for Health Care

1. Medicare

Mary Onnis Waid
Health Care Financing Administration
Brief Summaries of Medicare and Medicaid: Title XVIII and Title XIX of the Social Security Act as of June 25, 1998
<http://www.hcfa.gov/medicare/ormedmed.htm>[*]

Medicare Data Summary

The Medicare program covers 95 percent of our Nation's aged population, plus many of those eligible persons who are on Social Security because of disability. In CY 1997, HI covered about 38 million enrollees at a cost of $137.8 billion, and SMI covered 36 million enrollees at a cost of $72.8 billion in 1997. Administrative costs were 1.2 percent of HI and 1.8 percent of SMI disbursements for 1997. Of those

---

[*] Copyright © 1997. Reprinted with permission. *See* Disclaimer, *supra* p. 321 n.*.

persons who were entitled to Medicare in 1997, about 87 percent used Supplementary Medical Insurance services, while only 22 percent used the Hospital Insurance services. The combined HI and SMI benefit payments for all Medicare services in CY 1997 averaged about $6,300 per enrollee. Total disbursements for Medicare for 1997 was $213.575 billion.

* * *

Administration of Medicare

The Department of Health and Human Services (DHHS) has the overall responsibility for administration of the Medicare program, with the assistance of the Social Security Administration (SSA). The Health Care Financing Administration (HCFA) is a component of DHHS. HCFA has primary responsibility for Medicare, including: formulation of policy and guidelines; contract over-sight and operation; maintenance and review of utilization records; and general financing of Medicare. SSA is responsible for the initial determination of an individual's Medicare entitlement, and has the overall responsibility for maintaining the Medicare master beneficiary record.

A Board of Trustees, which is composed of two appointed members of the public and four ex-officio members, oversees the financial operations for the trust funds for both HI and SMI. The Secretary of the Department of Treasury is the managing trustee. The Board of Trustees reports the status and operation of the Medicare trust funds to Congress on or about the first day of April each year.

State agencies (usually State Health Departments under agreements with HCFA) assist by helping DHHS to identify, survey, and inspect provider and supplier facilities or institutions wishing to participate in the Medicare program. In consultation with HCFA, they then certify those that are qualified. The State agency also assists providers as a consultant, and coordinates the various State programs to assure effective and economical endeavors.

* * *

Program Financing, Beneficiary Liabilities, and Vendor Payments

All financial operations for Medicare are handled through two trust funds, one for the Hospital Insurance and one for Supplementary Medical Insurance. These trust funds—which are special accounts in the U. S. Treasury—are credited with all income receipts and charged with all Medicare expenditures for benefits and administration costs. Assets not needed for the payment of costs are invested in special Treasury Securities. The following sections describe Medicare's financing provisions, beneficiary cost-sharing requirements, and the basis for determining Medicare reimbursements to health care providers.

Program financing:

The Medicare Part A program (HI) financing is primarily through a mandatory payroll deduction (FICA tax). Almost all employees and self-employed workers in the U.S. work in employment covered by the Medicare HI program and pay taxes to support the cost of benefits for aged and disabled beneficiaries. The FICA tax is 1.45 percent of earnings (paid by each employee and by the employer for each), as well as 2.90 percent for self-employed persons. For 1994 and later, this tax is paid on all covered wages and self-employment income without limit. (Prior to 1994, the tax applied only up to a specified maximum amount of earnings.) The trust fund for the HI program also receives income from: (i) a portion of the income taxes levied on Social Security benefits paid to high-income beneficiaries, (ii) premiums from certain persons who are not otherwise eligible and choose to enroll voluntary, (iii) general funds reimbursements for the cost of certain other uninsured individuals, and (iv) interest earnings on the invested assets of the trust fund. The taxes paid each year are used mainly to pay benefits for current beneficiaries. Income not needed to pay current benefits and related expenses is invested in U.S. Treasury securities. The hospital insurance trust fund money is used only for the HI program, and the SMI trust funds cannot be transferred for HI use.

The Medicare Part B program (SMI) is financed through: (i) premium payments ($43.80 per month in 1998) which are usually deducted from the monthly Social Security benefit checks of those who are enrolled in the SMI program, and (ii) through contributions from general revenue of the U.S. Treasury. SMI benefits may also be bought for persons by a third party directly paying the monthly premium on behalf of the enrollee. Beneficiary premiums are currently set at a level that covers 25 percent of the average expenditures for aged beneficiaries. Except for a small amount of interest income, general revenues provide the balance of the financing for SMI.

The Medicare Part C program (Medicare+Choice) has rather complex financing, depending upon which plan is chosen. Basically, the funding for the Medicare+Choice program comes from the HI and SMI trust funds in proportion to the relative weights of HI and SMI benefits to the total benefits paid by the Medicare program.

Beneficiary payment liabilities:

For Parts A and B, beneficiaries are responsible for charges not covered by the Medicare program, and for various cost-sharing aspects of both HI and SMI. These liabilities may be paid: (1) by the Medicare beneficiary, (2) by a third party such as private medigap insurance purchased by the Medicare beneficiary, or (3) by Medicaid, if the person is eligible. The term medigap is used to mean private health insurance which, within limits, pays most of the health care service charges not covered by Parts A or B of Medicare. These policies—which must meet Federally-imposed standards—are offered by Blue Cross and Blue Shield, and various commercial health insurance companies.

For hospital care covered under HI, the beneficiary's payment share includes a one-time deductible amount at the beginning of each benefit period ($764 in 1998). This covers the beneficiary's part of the first 60 days of each spell of inpatient hospital care. If continued inpatient care is needed beyond the 60 days, additional coinsurance payments ($191 per day in 1998) are required through the 90th day of a benefit period. Medicare pays nothing after day 90, unless the beneficiary elects to use lifetime reserve days, for which a co-payment ($382 per day in 1998) is required from the beneficiary.

For skilled nursing care covered under HI, the first 20 days of SNF care are fully covered by Medicare. But for days 21 through 100, a co-payment ($95.50 per day in 1998) is required from the beneficiary. After 100 days of SNF care per benefit period, Medicare pays nothing for SNF care. Home health care has no deductible or co-insurance payment by the beneficiary. In any HI service, the beneficiary is responsible for fees to cover the first three pints or units of non-replaced blood per calendar year. The beneficiary has the option of paying the fee or of having the blood replaced.

There are no premiums for the HI portion of Medicare for most people aged 65 and over. Eligibility for HI is generally earned through the work experience of the beneficiary or that of a spouse. However, some persons who are otherwise unqualified for Medicare may purchase HI coverage if they also buy the SMI coverage. The cost is determined by a formula: if they have 30 to 39 quarters of coverage as defined by the Social Security Administration, the 1998 cost of HI is reduced to $170 per month; if not, the HI cost is $309 per month.

For SMI, the beneficiary's payment share includes: one annual deductible (currently $100); the monthly premiums; the co-insurance payments for SMI services (usually 20 percent of the medically-allowed charges); a deductible for blood; and payment for any services which are not covered by Medicare. These cost-sharing contributions are required of the beneficiaries for SMI services. For ESRD patients, Medicare SMI covers kidney dialysis and physician charges incurred by the patient and donor during the transplant and follow-up care. Regular SMI cost-sharing also applies for ESRD services.

For Part C, the beneficiary's payment share is based upon the cost-sharing structure of the specific Medicare+Choice plan selected by the beneficiary, as each plan has its own requirements.

Vendor payments:

For HI, prior to 1983, payment to vendors was made on a "reasonable cost" basis. Medicare payments for most inpatient hospital care are now paid under a plan known as the Prospective Payment System (PPS). Under the PPS, a hospital is paid a predetermined amount, based upon the patient's diagnosis within a diagnosis related group (DRG), for providing whatever medical care is required during that person's inpatient hospital stay. In some cases the payment received is less than the hospital's actual costs; in other cases it is more. The hospital absorbs the loss or makes a profit. Certain payment adjustments exist for extraordinarily costly cases. The BBA made some reductions in the amounts paid to hospitals, and to other payments for traditional fee-for-service programs. Payments for inpatient rehabilitation, psychiatric, home health, hospice and for skilled nursing care coverage continue to be paid under the reasonable cost methodology, with each service having some restrictions and limitations—although payment methods will be restructured as required by the BBA.

For SMI, prior to 1992, physicians were paid on the basis of "reasonable charge." This was initially defined as the lowest of (1) the physician's actual charge,

(2) the physician's customary charge, or (3) the prevailing charge for similar services in that locality. Starting January, 1992, allowed charges were defined as the lesser of: the submitted charges, or a fee schedule based on a relative value scale (RVS). Payments for durable medical equipment and clinical laboratory services are also based on a fee schedule. Hospital outpatient services and HHAs are currently reimbursed on a reasonable cost basis. The BBA provided for implementation of a Prospective Payment System for these services in the future. If a doctor or supplier agrees to accept the approved rate as payment in full (takes assignment), then payments provided must be considered as payments in full for that service. No added payments (beyond the initial annual deductible and co-insurance) may be sought from the beneficiary or insurer. If the provider does not take assignment, the beneficiary will be charged for the excess (which may be paid by medigap insurance). Limits now exist on the excess which doctors or suppliers can charge. Physicians are "participating" physicians if they agree before the beginning of the year to accept assignment for all Medicare services they furnish during the year. Since Medicare beneficiaries may select their doctors, they have the option to choose those who do participate.

For Part C, payments to the Medicare+Choice plans are based on a blend of local and national capitated rates, generally determined by the capitation payment methodology described in Section 1853 of the Social Security Act. Actual payments to plans vary based on characteristics of the enrolled population. New risk adjusters are scheduled to be implemented in January 2000.

a. Traditional Fee-for-Service

Mary Onnis Waid
Health Care Financing Administration
Brief Summaries of Medicare and Medicaid: Title XVIII and Title XIX of the Social Security Act as of June 25, 1998
<http://www.hcfa.gov/medicare/ormedmed.htm>[*]

Overview

Title XVIII of the Social Security Act, entitled "Health Insurance for the Aged and Disabled," is commonly known as "Medicare." As part of the Social Security Amendments of 1965, the Medicare legislation established a health insurance program for aged persons to complement the retirement, survivors and disability insurance benefits under Title II of the Social Security Act.

When first implemented in 1966, Medicare covered only most persons age 65 and over. By the end of 1966, 3.7 million persons had received at least some health care services covered by Medicare. In 1973, other groups became eligible for Medicare benefits: persons who are entitled to Social Security or Railroad Retirement

---

[*] Copyright © 1997. Reprinted with permission. *See* Disclaimer, *supra* p. 321 n.[*].

disability benefits for at least 24 months; persons with end-stage renal disease (ESRD) requiring continuing dialysis or kidney transplant; and certain otherwise non-covered aged persons who elect to *buy into* Medicare.

Medicare consists of two primary parts: Hospital Insurance (HI), also known as "Part A," and Supplementary Medical insurance (SMI), also known as "Part B." When Medicare began on July 1, 1966, there were 19.1 million persons enrolled in the program. A third part of Medicare, sometimes known as "Part C," is the Medicare+Choice program—which was established by the Balanced Budget Act of 1997 (Public Law. 105-33) and began to provide services on January 1, 1998. Beneficiaries must, however, have Medicare Part A and Part B in order to enroll in a Part C plan. In 1997, about 38 million persons were enrolled in one or both of parts A and B of the Medicare program. About 87 percent of all Medicare enrollees used some HI and/or SMI service in 1997.

Medicare Coverage

Hospital Insurance (HI) is generally provided automatically to persons age 65 and over who are entitled to Social Security or Railroad Retirement Board benefits. Similarly, individuals who have received such benefits based on their disability, for a period of at least 24 months, are also entitled to HI benefits. In 1997, the HI program provided protection against the costs of hospital and specific other medical care to about 38 million people (33 million aged and five million disabled enrollees). Approximately 22 percent of these individuals received services covered by HI during the year. The HI benefits totaled $137.8 billion in 1997 (an increase of 7.1 percent over the prior year), with an average expenditure per HI enrollee of $3,600 (an increase of 6 percent over 1996).

Health Care Financing Administration
Medicare and You (November 1998)
<http://www.medicare.gov/publications/handbook.html>

Medicare is a Health Insurance Program for:
- People 65 years of age and older;
- Certain younger people with disabilities;
- People with End-Stage Renal Disease (people with permanent kidney failure who need dialysis or a transplant).

What is the Original Medicare Plan?

The Original Medicare Plan is the traditional pay-per-visit arrangement. You can go to any doctor, hospital, or other health care provider who accepts Medicare. You must pay the deductible. Then Medicare pays its share, and you pay your share (coinsurance). The Original Medicare Plan has two parts: Part A (Hospital Insurance) and Part B (Medical Insurance). If you are in the Original Medicare Plan now, the way you receive your health care will not change unless you enroll in another Medicare health plan.

What is Part A (Hospital Insurance)?

Part A (Hospital Insurance) helps pay for care in hospitals and skilled nursing facilities, and for home health and hospice care. If you are eligible, Part A is premium free—that is, you don't pay a premium because you or your spouse paid Medicare taxes while you were working. Your Fiscal Intermediary can answer your questions on what Part A services Medicare will pay for and how much will be paid. You are eligible for premium-free Medicare Part A (Hospital Insurance) if:
- You are 65 or older. You are receiving or eligible for retirement benefits from Social Security or the Railroad Retirement Board, or
- You are under 65. You have received Social Security disability benefits for 24 months, or
- You are under 65. You have received Railroad Retirement disability benefits for the prescribed time and you meet the Social Security Act disability requirements, or
- You or your spouse had Medicare-covered government employment, or
- You are under 65 and have End-Stage Renal Disease.

If you don't qualify for premium-free Part A, and you are 65 or older, you may be able to buy it. (Contact Social Security Administration).

What is Part B (Medical Insurance)?

Part B (Medical Insurance) helps pay for doctors, outpatient hospital care and some other medical services that Part A doesn't cover, such as the services of physical and occupational therapists. Part B covers all doctor services that are medically necessary. Beneficiaries may receive these services anywhere (a doctor's office, clinic, nursing home, hospital, or at home). Your Medicare carrier can answer questions about Part B services and coverage. You are automatically eligible for Part B if you are eligible for premium-free Part A. You are also eligible if you are a United States citizen or permanent resident age 65 or older. Part B costs $45.50 per month in 1999. Part B is voluntary. If you choose to have Part B, the monthly premium is deducted from your Social Security, Railroad Retirement, or Civil Service Retirement payment. Beneficiaries who do not receive any of the above payments are billed by Medicare every 3 months.

If you didn't take Part B when you were first eligible, you can sign-up during 2 enrollment periods:

General Enrollment Period: If you didn't take Part B, you can only sign up during the general enrollment period, January 1 through March 31 of each year. Your Part B coverage is effective July 1. Your monthly Part B premium may be higher. The Part B premium increases 10% for each 12-month period that you could have had Part B but did not take it.

Special Enrollment Period: If you didn't take Part B because you or your spouse currently work and have group health plan coverage through your current employer or union, you can sign up for Part B during the special enrollment period. Under the special enrollment period, you can sign up at any time you are covered under the group plan. In addition, if the employment or group health coverage ends, you have 8 months to sign up. The 8-month period starts the month after the employment ends or the group health coverage ends, whichever comes first. Generally, your monthly Part B premium is not increased when you sign up for Part B during the special enrollment period.

What Are Your Out-of-Pocket Costs?

The Original Medicare Plan pays for much of your health care, but not all of it. Your out-of-pocket costs for health care will include your monthly Part B premium. In addition, when you get health care services, you will also have to pay deductibles and coinsurance or copayments. Generally, you will pay for your outpatient prescription drugs. You also pay for routine physicals, custodial care, most dental care, dentures, routine foot care, or hearing aids. Physical therapy and occupational therapy services, except for those you get in hospital outpatient departments, are subject to annual limits. The Original Medicare Plan does pay for some preventive care, but not all of it.

Your Out-of-Pocket Costs May Depend On:

- Whether your doctor accepts assignment.
- How often you need health care.
- What type of health care you need.

Questions

1. Would you characterize the traditional fee-for-service Medicare program as an insurance program or a public benefits program?
2. What significant gaps in coverage can you identify?
3. Why should enrollment at age 65 be restricted?

b. Medicare Managed Care

Mary Onnis Waid
Health Care Financing Administration
Brief Summaries of Medicare and Medicaid: Title XVIII and Title XIX of the Social Security Act as of June 25, 1998
<http://www.hcfa.gov/medicare/ormedmed.htm>*

Managed Care Plans

Prepaid health care plans known as managed care plans, such as competitive medical plans (CMPs) and health maintenance organizations (HMOs), are options for Medicare beneficiaries. Managed care plans function on a basis different from regular fee-for-service covered under Medicare. Under managed care plans, the

---

* Copyright © 1997. Reprinted with permission. *See* Disclaimer, *supra* p. 321 n.*.

Medicare beneficiary selects a specific HMO, CMP, or other approved plans within a service area for comprehensive health care services. It is central to the managed care concept that this selected plan coordinate all of the health care services for that person. Managed care plans function on a financial basis that is different from the traditional fee-for-service reimbursements to health care providers. Managed care plans receive a per-person payment from Medicare that is predetermined, based on a formula that is established by law and the demographic characteristics of the Medicare beneficiaries enrolled in their plan.

In addition to the regular services covered under Medicare, the managed care plans often cover services such as preventive care, prescription drugs, eyeglasses, dental care, or hearing aids. Electing to participate in a managed care plan may also serve as an alternative to purchasing medigap insurance (described later) which is often wanted if the beneficiary has traditional fee-for-service coverage. Although there are certain restrictions, limitations and differences from the fee-for-service plans, the managed care plan's fixed monthly premiums and cost-sharing structure helps to provide more predictability for out-of-pocket costs for the beneficiaries who do not have medigap insurance.

* * *

Medicare+Choice (Part C) is another option provided by the Balanced Budget Act of 1997 (BBA). Under the BBA, Medicare beneficiaries who have both Part A and Part B can choose to get their benefits through a variety of risk-based plans known as Part C of Medicare. To participate in this Part C, the beneficiaries must be entitled to HI and be enrolled in SMI (except for ESRD patients, who must be enrolled in Part C before they get ESRD; they cannot switch to Part C after they are diagnosed with ESRD). As is the case for risk plans, organizations that are seeking to contract as Medicare+Choice plans will have to meet specific organizational, financial, and other requirements. The primary Medicare+Choice plans are:

- Coordinated care plans, which includes Health Maintenance Organizations, Provider-Sponsored Organizations and Preferred Provider Organizations, and other certified public or private coordinated care plans and entities that meet the approved required standards as set forth in the law.
- The private, unrestricted fee-for-service plans, which allow beneficiaries to select certain private providers. For those providers who agree to accept the plan's payment terms and conditions, this option does not place the providers at risk, nor vary payment rates based upon utilization.
- The Medical Savings Account (MSA) plan allows beneficiaries (only a limited number for the first five years) to enroll in a plan with a high-deductible (maximum for 1999 = $6,000). The Federal government pays a prescribed portion of the capitation amount into an insurance fund for each enrollee. The difference between the Medicare capitation rate and the plan premium is deposited into the MSA account. Deposits for the entire year are made at the start of the year. After the deductible is paid, the MSA plan pays providers the lesser of 100% of specified expenses or 100% of amounts that would have

been payable under the original fee-for-service Medicare program. If extra money remains in the MSA, it can be used to pay for future medical needs (including some not covered by Medicare—e.g., dentures). Or, subject to certain requirements, the extra money can be used for non-medical purchases.

Except for MSA-plans, all Medicare+Choice plans are required to provide the current Medicare benefit package, excluding hospice services, and any additional health services required under the adjusted community rate process. There are some restrictions as to who may elect an MSA-plan, even when enrollment is no longer limited in number of participants.

It should be noted that some health care services are not provided under any part of Title XVIII. Non-covered services under Medicare include long term nursing care or custodial care, and certain other health care needs—such as dentures and dental care, eyeglasses, hearing aids, most prescription drugs, etc. These are not a part of the Medicare program unless they are a part of a managed care plan, or—after January 1, 1999—are selected as a part of the Medicare+Choice program.

Questions

1. What concerns might motivate someone to go outside the "Original" Medicare program?

2. What public policy concerns are implicated by the trend toward managed care?

Health Care Financing Administration
Medicare and You (November 1998)
<http://www.medicare.gov/publications/handbook.html>

Have you heard that Medicare now offers more health plan choices?

Different health plan choices may affect your:

>Cost: What you pay.
>Extra Benefits: What extra benefits you get, like prescription drugs.
>Providers: How much choice you have among doctors, and hospitals, and other health care providers.

Starting in 1999, Medicare offers more health plan choices. One of the new health plan choices might be right for you. The choice is yours. No matter what you decide, you are still in the Medicare program. All Medicare health plans must provide all Medicare covered services. To be eligible for the other Medicare health plan choices:

You must have Part A (Hospital Insurance) and Part B (Medical Insurance). You must not have End-Stage Renal Disease. (ESRD is permanent kidney failure that requires dialysis or a transplant.) However, ESRD beneficiaries currently in a health plan will be able to remain in the plan they are in. You must live in the service area of a health plan. The service area is the geographic area where the plan accepts enrollees. For plans that require you to use their doctors and hospitals, it is also the area where services are provided. The plan may disenroll you if you move out of the plan's service area. If you are disenrolled, you are automatically covered under the Original Medicare Plan. You can also choose to join a Medicare health plan in your new area.

All of the Medicare health plan choices are listed below. However, they may not all be available in your area.

- The Original Medicare Plan,
- The Original Medicare Plan with a Supplemental Insurance Policy,
- Medicare Managed Care Plans:
    Health Maintenance Organizations (HMOs),
    HMOs with Point of Service Options (POS),
    Provider sponsored Organizations (PSOs),
    Preferred Provider Organizations (PPOs),
- Private Fee-for-Service Plans,
- Medicare Medical Savings Account Plans (MSAs), and
- Religious Fraternal Benefit Society Plans (RFBs).

* * *

Remember: The Original Medicare plan doesn't pay for or cover everything. To get more coverage, you may purchase a Supplemental Insurance Policy, or you may consider joining a Medicare Managed Care Plan or Private Fee-for-Service Plan. Another choice is the Medicare Medical Savings Account (MSA) Plan. You should look at how all the health plan choices differ on cost, choice of doctors and hospitals, and benefits.

Cost—What you pay:

- All beneficiaries pay the Part B premium of $45.50 (in 1999).
- Monthly premiums tend to be lower in Medicare Managed Care Plans (if you follow the plan rules) than in most Supplemental Insurance Policies and some Private Fee-for-Service Plans.
- Your out-of-pocket costs (what you must pay) tend to be lower in most Managed Care Plan and the Original Medicare Plan with some Supplemental Insurance Policies. Costs often are higher in the Original Medicare Plan without a Supplemental Insurance Policy.
- In Medicare MSA Plans, there is no monthly premium. You pay for all the costs of services prior to meeting the high deductible for your plan. Your Medicare MSA can help pay the costs of services prior to your meeting the high deductible.
- In Private Fee-For-Service Plans and Medicare MSA Plans, you may be asked to pay extra charges by doctors, hospitals, and other providers who don't accept the plan's fee as payment in full.

Providers

The Original Medicare Plan, the Original Medicare Plan with a Supplemental Insurance Policy, Private Fee-for-Service Plans, and certain Medicare MSA Plans have the widest choice of doctors and hospitals. In most Medicare Managed Care Plans, and in some Medicare MSA Plans, you must choose your doctors and hospitals from a list provided by the plan. You may want to check if your current doctor is on the plan's list, and is accepting new Medicare patients under that plan. There is no guarantee that a particular doctor will stay with the plan. You can go to any specialist who accepts Medicare in the Original Medicare Plan, the Original Medicare Plan with a Supplemental Insurance Policy, Private Fee-for-Service Plans, and some Medicare MSA Plans. Most Medicare Managed Care Plans and some Medicare MSA Plans require a referral from your primary care doctor for you to see a specialist. In Private Fee-For-Service Plans and Medicare MSA plans, you may be asked to pay extra charges by doctors, hospitals, and other providers who don't accept the plan's fee as payment in full.

Extra Benefits—What Services You Get

In Medicare Managed Care Plans or Private Fee-For-Service Plans, you may get extra benefits, like vision or dental care beyond the benefits covered by the Original Medicare Plan or the Original Medicare Plan with a Supplemental Insurance Policy. In lieu of extra benefits, enrollees in Medicare MSA Plans receive a deposit in their Medicare MSA from Medicare.

Prescription Drugs—An Important Extra Benefit

In general, the Original Medicare Plan does not cover outpatient prescription drugs. Many Medicare Managed Care Plans and a few of the more expensive Supplemental Insurance Policies cover certain prescription drugs up to a specified dollar limit. In general, the Original Medicare Plan only covers medication while you are in a hospital or skilled nursing facility.

Other Important Things To Think About

In the Original Medicare Plan, Medicare pays doctors and other healthcare providers directly for each service that you receive. For all other Medicare health plans, Medicare pays the health plan a lump sum amount of money; the plan oversees the services you receive. Plan benefits and costs can change each year. These changes are usually effective the first day of the new year.

Medicare health plans may terminate their contract with Medicare at any time. If the plan terminates its contract with Medicare, you would be notified by the plan and automatically returned to the Original Medicare Plan. You may join another plan in the area, but you will be covered by the Original Medicare Plan until the new coverage is in effect.

Except for Medicare MSA Plans, you may leave (disenroll from) most Medicare health plans at any time and either return to the Original Medicare Plan, or switch to another plan. Special rules may apply if you choose to return to your Supplemental Insurance Policy or your employer's health insurance.

As a Medicare beneficiary, you have rights. All Medicare health plans are required to have an appeal and grievance (complaint) process and must respond to your concerns.

* * *

You have a right to appeal many decisions about your Medicare covered services. You have this right whether you are enrolled in a Medicare Managed Care Plan, Private Fee-for-Service Plan, or a Medicare Medical Savings Account Plan. Your health plan must provide you with written instructions on how to appeal. You may file an appeal if your health plan denies a service, or terminates or refuses to pay for services that you believe should be covered. After you file an appeal, the health plan reviews its decision. Then, if your health plan does not decide in your favor, the appeal automatically goes to an independent review organization that contracts with Medicare. You may be eligible for a fast decision (within 72 hours) if your health or ability to function could be seriously harmed by waiting the amount of time needed for a standard decision. See the health plan's membership materials or contact your health plan for details about your Medicare appeal rights. If you believe you are being discharged too soon from a hospital, you have a right to immediate review by the Peer Review Organization (PRO). During the immediate review, you may be able to stay in the hospital at no charge and the hospital cannot discharge you before the PRO reaches a decision.

Questions

What characteristics would describe a person who should stick with traditional Medicare? Why?

Grijalva v. Shalala
152 F.3d 1115 (9th Cir. 1998)

WIGGINS, Circuit Judge:

Medicare beneficiaries enrolled in health maintenance organizations ("HMOs") in Arizona sued the Secretary of Health and Human Services ("Secretary"). Their suit alleged a failure to enforce due process requirements and a failure to monitor HMO denials of medical services to enrolled Medicare beneficiaries. The district court granted Plaintiffs summary judgment, holding that HMO denials of medical services to Medicare beneficiaries constitute state action and that the regulations issued by the Secretary fail to provide due process. The district court issued an injunction mandating certain procedural protections for Medicare beneficiaries enrolled in HMOs. The Secretary appeals. We affirm.

I. Background

Congress passed the Medicare Act, Title XVIII of the Social Security Act, 42 U.S.C. §§ 1395 *et seq.*, in 1965 to provide a federal health insurance program for the elderly and the disabled. Today, a Medicare beneficiary can receive Medicare services in two different ways. The first is to receive Medicare on a fee-for-service basis. Under this option, the beneficiary goes to a health care provider for the necessary covered services; either the provider or the beneficiary will be reimbursed by the government for the cost of the services. The second, newer option is to enroll in an HMO or other eligible organization. *See* 42 U.S.C. § 1395mm(b).

In 1982, Congress authorized the Secretary to enter into "risk-sharing" contracts with HMOs. *See* § 1395mm. Under these contracts, HMOs provide to enrolled Medicare beneficiaries all the Medicare services provided in the statute, *see* § 1395mm(c)(2)(A), in exchange for a monthly flat payment from the Secretary. *See* § 1395mm(a).

The Medicare statute establishes in § 1395mm(c) procedural protections for those beneficiaries that enroll in HMOs. Among these, the HMO must "provide meaningful procedures for hearing and resolving grievances between the organization . . . and members enrolled . . . ." § 1395mm(c)(5)(A). HMO members must also have certain appeal rights:

> A member enrolled with an eligible organization under this section who is dissatisfied by reason of his failure to receive any health service to which he believes he is entitled and at no greater charge than he believes he is required to pay is entitled, if the amount in controversy is $100 or more, to a hearing before the Secretary to the same extent as is provided in [42 U.S.C. § 405(b)], and in any such hearing the Secretary shall make the eligible organization a party. If the amount in controversy is $1,000 or more, the individual or eligible organization shall, upon notifying the other party, be entitled to judicial review of the Secretary's final decision as provided in [42 U.S.C. § 405(g)] . . . .

§ 1395mm(c)(5)(B).

The Secretary created additional appeal protections in subsequent regulations. *See* 42 C.F.R. §§ 417.600-417.638. Under § 417.604, each HMO must establish appeal procedures and ensure that beneficiaries receive written information about the appeal and grievance procedures. *See* § 417.604(a). If the HMO makes an "organization determination" (defined in § 417.606) adverse to the enrollee, "it must notify the enrollee of the determination within 60 days of receiving the enrollee's request for payment for services." § 417.608(a)(1). An example of an adverse organization determination is an HMO's decision that certain medical services are not covered by Medicare. The notice to the beneficiary must "[s]tate the specific reasons for the determination" and inform the enrollee of his or her "right to a reconsideration." § 417.608(b). Failure to provide timely notice is an adverse determination and may be appealed by the enrollee. *See* § 417.608(c).

If the enrollee is dissatisfied with an adverse determination, a request for reconsideration may be filed within 60 days from the date of the notice. *See* §§ 417.614 & 417.616(b). Within 60 days of the request, the HMO may make a decision fully favorable to the enrollee. *See* § 417.620(a). If it decides to make a decision that partially or completely affirms the adverse determination, it must explain its decision in writing and forward the case to the Health Care Financing Administration ("HCFA"). See § 417.620(b). If the enrollee is dissatisfied with the result of the reconsideration, and the amount remaining in controversy is $100 or more, the enrollee has a right to a hearing before an administrative law judge ("ALJ"). See § 417.630. The enrollee can appeal that hearing decision to the Appeals Council and then to the district court. See §§ 417.634 & 417.636.

The Secretary possesses a number of sanctions to ensure HMO compliance with the Medicare statute and the Secretary's regulations. First, the Secretary "may not enter into a contract . . . with an [HMO] unless it meets the requirements of [§ 1395mm(c)] and [§ 1395mm(e)]." 42 U.S.C. § 1395mm(c)(1). The specified sections require the HMO, inter alia, to provide all Medicare services to eligible enrollees, to have particular open enrollment periods, to provide enrollees annually with information on their rights, including appeal rights, to provide covered services "with reasonable promptness," to provide the aforementioned procedural protections, and not to exceed certain limits on rates charged to beneficiaries and the Secretary. §§ 1395mm(c) & 1395mm(e).

Second, the Secretary may terminate any contract with an HMO if she determines that the HMO has not met the terms of the contract or has not satisfied the statutory or regulatory requirements. See § 1395mm(i)(1). If the Secretary determines that an HMO has failed to provide necessary covered services to an enrollee and that failure has adversely affected the individual, the Secretary may seek civil money penalties, suspend enrollment, or suspend payment to the HMO. See § 1395mm(I)(6).

In 1993, five Medicare beneficiaries enrolled in an Arizona HMO sued the Secretary. Among other claims, Plaintiffs alleged that the Secretary "has failed and refused to take effective action to implement beneficiaries' notice and appeal rights when they are denied health care services by their HMOs," and "has failed and refused to provide Medicare beneficiaries enrolled in HMOs with a procedure of obtaining review of HMO denial decisions contemporaneously with the denial decisions." In a decision not on appeal, the district court certified a nationwide plaintiff class.

In October 1996, the district court granted partial summary judgment to Plaintiffs on the claims described above. The court held that the "organization determinations" made by HMOs constitute state action, triggering constitutional due process requirements. The court also held that the regulations promulgated by the Secretary regarding adverse determinations by HMOs fail to provide sufficient due process to enrollees under *Mathews v. Eldridge*, 424 U.S. 319 (1976). In particular, the district court found that the notices issued by HMOs failed to provide adequate notice: they were often illegible, failed to specify the reason for the denial, and failed to inform the beneficiary that he or she had the right to present additional evidence to the HMO. Therefore, "[s]ubsequent due process, available in the administrative review phase of the appeal, comes too late in many cases . . . ." The district court also found that the language of § 1395mm(c)(1) ("The Secretary may not enter into a contract . . . with an eligible organization unless it meets the requirements of this subsection") was mandatory, requiring the Secretary to enforce her regulations by refusing to renew a contract with an HMO if the denial notices of that HMO fail to provide due process.

The district court found that the Secretary violated § 1395mm(c)(1) by entering into a contract with any HMO that failed to provide timely notice for any and all denials of service. The court held that the notice must be legible (at least 12-point type), state clearly the reason for the denial, inform the enrollee of all appeal rights, explain hearing rights and procedures, and provide "instruction on how to obtain supporting evidence, including medical records and supporting affidavits from the attending physician." The district court also held that any hearing must be "informal, in-person communication with the decisionmaker," available upon request for all service denials, and timely. The district court also required expedited hearings for "acute care service denials."

On March 3, 1997, the district court issued an injunction mandating the above requirements. The Secretary appealed the district court's decision in May 1997. The district court granted her a stay of its injunction pending this appeal.

II. Standards of Review

We review a grant of summary judgment de novo. We must determine, viewing the evidence in the light most favorable to the nonmoving party, whether there are any genuine issues of material fact and whether the district court applied correctly the relevant substantive law. We may affirm on any ground supported by the record.

We review the scope of an injunction for an abuse of discretion or application of erroneous legal principles.

III. Discussion

A. State Action Doctrine

The Secretary appeals the district court's holding that HMO denials of medical services to enrolled Medicare beneficiaries constitute state action and therefore invoke constitutional due process protections.

The actions of private parties are not subject to the requirements of constitutional due process unless they can fairly be considered government action. *See Shelley v. Kraemer*, 334 U.S. 1 (1948). We use the same standards to attribute the actions of private actors to the federal government under the Fifth Amendment as we do to attribute private actions to state governments under the Fourteenth Amendment. *See Kitchens v. Bowen*, 825 F.2d 1337, 1340 (9th Cir. 1987).

The actions of private entities constitute state action under particular circumstances. "In order to show that a private action is in fact state action, the plaintiff must show that 'there is a sufficiently close nexus between the State and the challenged action of the regulated entity so that the action of the latter may be fairly treated as that of the State itself.'" *Blum v. Yaretsky*, 457 U.S. 991, 1004 (1982) (quoting *Jackson v. Metropolitan Edison Co.*, 419 U.S. 345, 351 (1974)). The government's regulation of the private actor is insufficient alone to show federal action. *See Blum*, 457 U.S. at 1004; *Jackson*, 419 U.S. at 350. Government action exists if there is a symbiotic relationship with a high degree of interdependence between the private and public parties such that they are "joint participant[s] in the challenged activity." *See Burton v. Wilmington Parking Auth.*, 365 U.S. 715, 725 (1961). Government action exists if the challenged private action occurs under government compulsion. *See Adickes v. S.H. Kress & Co.,* 398 U.S. 144, 170-71 (1970). The government must do more, however, than merely acquiesce in the challenged action. *See Flagg Bros., Inc. v. Brooks,* 436 U.S. 149, 164 (1978) (holding that government inaction is insufficient for state action). A detailed inquiry into the facts of the particular case may be necessary to determine whether there is state or federal action. *See Jackson,* 419 U.S. at 351.

In this case, the question is whether the challenged action—HMO denials of services to Medicare beneficiaries with inadequate notice—may fairly be treated as that of the federal government. We agree with the district court's cogent analysis and conclusion that, in the circumstances of the Secretary's regulation of and delegation of Medicare coverage decisions to HMOs, HMO denials of services to Medicare beneficiaries with inadequate notice constitute federal action.

We find that HMOs and the federal government are essentially engaged as joint participants to provide Medicare services such that the actions of HMOs in denying medical services to Medicare beneficiaries and in failing to provide adequate notice may fairly be attributed to the federal government. The Secretary extensively regulates the provision of Medicare services by HMOs. HMOs are required, by the Medicare statute and their contracts with the Secretary, to comply with all federal laws and regulations. The Secretary is required to ensure, *inter alia*, that HMOs provide adequate notice and meaningful appeal procedures to beneficiaries. The Secretary pays HMOs for each enrolled Medicare beneficiary (regardless of the services provided). The federal government has created the legal framework—the standards and enforcement mechanisms—within which HMOs make adverse determinations, issue notices, and guarantee appeal rights. Medicare beneficiaries enrolled in HMOs may appeal an HMO's adverse determination to the Secretary, who has the power to overturn the HMO's decision. Each of these factors alone might not be sufficient to establish federal action. Together they show federal action. *See Catanzano v. Dowling,* 60 F.3d 113, 117-20 (2d Cir. 1995) (similar analysis in Medicaid context); *J.K. v. Dillenberg,* 836 F. Supp. 694, 697-99 (D. Ariz. 1993) (same).

The Secretary argues that the Supreme Court case of *Blum v. Yaretsky,* 457 U.S. 991 (1982), mandates a finding that HMO adverse determinations are not state action. We disagree.

In *Blum*, the Supreme Court held that nursing home decisions made by doctors and administrators to transfer patients to other facilities, thereby terminating their Medicaid benefits, did not constitute state action. The Court held that the decisions at issue in the case turned "on medical judgments made by private parties according to professional standards that are not established by the State." 457 U.S. at 1008. Because state officials did not have the power to approve or disapprove the nursing home decisions, but just altered the level of Medicaid benefits accordingly, the Court held that the decisions were not state action. *See id.* at 1010.

Unlike the nursing home doctors and administrators in *Blum*, the HMOs in this case are not making decisions to which the government merely responds. HMOs are following congressional and regulatory orders and are making decisions as a governmental proxy—they are deciding that Medicare does not cover certain medical services. In *Blum*, by contrast, the nursing homes decided that certain medical services were no longer medically necessary. While such an inquiry may occur in HMO service denials, the decisions in the case at hand are more accurately described as coverage decisions—interpretations of the Medicare statute—rather than merely medical judgments (particularly when no reason for the denial is given other than that the service does not meet "Medicare guidelines . . . based upon [the HMO's] understanding and interpretation of Medicare . . . coverage policies and guidelines," to quote a typical notice provided by Plaintiffs).

The district court's reasoning and holding that HMO service denials are federal action therefore do not run counter to *Blum*. As noted by the district court, the government cannot avoid the due process requirements of the Constitution merely by delegating its duty to determine Medicare coverage to private entities. *See* 946 F. Supp. at 752; *see also Burton*, 365 U.S. at 725 ("But no State may effectively abdicate its responsibilities by either ignoring them or by merely failing to discharge them whatever the motive may be.").

We hold, therefore, that, when denying medical services to enrolled Medicare beneficiaries, HMOs are federal actors.

B. Due Process and *Mathews v. Eldridge*

The parties agree that the balancing test used by the Supreme Court in *Mathews v. Eldridge*, 424 U.S. 319 (1976), applies to determine the necessary procedural protections to ensure that due process is provided to Medicare beneficiaries enrolled in HMOs.

In *Mathews v. Eldridge*, the Supreme Court considered the sufficiency of the procedures by which Social Security disability benefits were terminated. *See* 424 U.S. 319 (1976). The Supreme Court held that constitutional due process is flexible, demanding particular protections depending on the situation. *See id.* at 334. The requirements of due process in a particular situation depend on an analysis of three factors:

> First, the private interest that will be affected by the official action; second, the risk of an erroneous deprivation of such interest through the procedures used, and the probable value, if any, of additional or substitute procedural safeguards; and finally, the Government's interest, including the functions involved and the fiscal and administrative burdens that the additional or substitute procedural requirements would entail.

Id. at 335.

A court must balance these factors to determine whether the particular additional procedural safeguards sought by a plaintiff are required in a given situation. *See id.*

We agree with the district court's analysis of the *Eldridge* factors and its conclusion that due process requires additional protections for Medicare beneficiaries enrolled in HMOs.

1. Private Interest at Stake

The district court held that the private interest at stake from an HMO's initial denial of Medicare coverage is the potential that medical care will be precluded altogether. The court held that this interest is a substantial private interest in additional protections such as timely and effective notice of service denials. We agree.

In *Eldridge*, the Court held that the private interest at stake was the individual's interest in "uninterrupted receipt" of disability benefits. 424 U.S. at 340. The Court held that this interest was not based on financial need (unlike the situation of the welfare recipient in *Goldberg v. Kelly*, 397 U.S. 254 (1970)) and does not implicate a high degree of potential deprivation. *See id.* at 340-41.

The district court was correct in holding that Plaintiffs' interest in Medicare benefits is greater than the interest of the plaintiff in *Eldridge*. As the district court noted, "[u]nlike *Eldridge*, the deprivation suffered from an HMO denial to provide care cannot so easily be remedied by retroactive recoupment of benefits." 946 F. Supp. at 757. An HMO's denial of coverage is an initial refusal to provide any medical services. The mere fact that the enrollee may be able to go elsewhere and pay for the services herself is of little comfort to an elderly, poor patient—particularly one who is ill and whose skilled nursing care has been terminated without a specific reason or description of how to appeal.

The Secretary argues that the district court erred by "adjudicating a complex procedural scheme as falling short of basic standards of fairness, without conducting the sort of detailed inquiry needed." For example, the Secretary argues, the district court should have distinguished between different types of medical services and their urgency when considering this first *Eldridge* factor, the magnitude of the private interest at stake. The Secretary also argues that the district court's finding that the interests of Medicare HMO enrollees are "especially" great because they may not receive immediate medical care is erroneous because some beneficiaries can seek those services elsewhere (and then seek reimbursement from the HMO) or disenroll from the HMO. The Secretary's arguments fail. Although, in some cases, the effect of service denial may be remedied easily after the fact, the potential for irreparable damage is surely great when it comes to denial of medical services (particularly denial without notice of any reason for the denial), unlike the suspension of disability benefits pending review as in *Eldridge*. In many, if not most, cases, the denial of coverage may result in total failure to receive the services.

The Secretary argues that the district court failed to recognize that the Medicare program is not need-based, a fact which the Secretary argues mandates holding against additional procedural protections. The Secretary cites to *Eldridge* for this proposition. The Court in *Eldridge*, however, discussed the fact that the disability benefits were not need-based in order to distinguish the case from that in *Goldberg v. Kelly*, 397 U.S. 254 (1970), where the Court had held that a hearing was necessary prior to the suspension of welfare benefits. The Court did not hold that a program has to be need-based in order for this factor to weigh in favor of additional protections.

Other courts have found on similar facts that a significant private interest is at stake that weighs in favor of additional protections. *See, e.g., Kraemer v. Heckler*, 737 F.2d 214, 222 (2d Cir. 1984) ("In applying the balancing test, the private interest at stake [in the termination of Medicare coverage] should be weighed more heavily than in *Eldridge* because of the astronomical nature of medical costs."); *Vorster v. Bowen*, 709 F. Supp. 934, 946 (C.D. Cal. 1989) ("The private interest, in this case, is the claimant's need to obtain reimbursement for medical bills that he or she has already paid. That interest is fairly great. Congress enacted the [Medicare] program because of the special coincidence of medical needs and financial problems of the elderly."). The interest of the HMO enrollees in medical services weighs in favor of additional procedural protections beyond that offered by the Secretary's original regulations.

2. Risk of Erroneous Deprivation

The district court also held that factor two weighed in favor of greater procedural protections for Medicare beneficiaries enrolled in HMOs. The court reviewed Plaintiffs' analysis of notice failures and conducted its own review of the notices provided to Plaintiffs. The court held that the notices failed to provide adequate explanation for the denials. *See* 946 F. Supp. at 757-58. We agree. This failure creates a high risk of erroneous deprivation of medical care to Medicare beneficiaries. The appeal rights and other procedural protections available to Medicare beneficiaries are meaningless if the beneficiaries are unaware of the reason for service denial and therefore cannot argue against the denial. "Due process requires notice that gives an agency's reason for its action in sufficient detail that the affected party can prepare a responsive defense." *Barnes v. Healy*, 980 F.2d 572, 579 (9th Cir. 1992). Therefore, inadequate notice creates the risk of erroneous deprivation by undermining the appeal process.

The Secretary attacks the district court's analysis of this factor by arguing that the court simply identified an "arguable problem" faced by enrollees—inadequate notice—rather than address whether that problem actually results in deprivations. The Secretary argues that the district court "simply assumed that the perceived failures of notice resulted in fewer appeals, and that more appeals would diminish erroneous deprivations." The Secretary fails to recognize the real problem: Inadequate notice renders the existence of an appeal process meaningless. Moreover, the question established by *Eldridge* is not whether the inadequate notices actually resulted in erroneous deprivations, but whether the inadequate notices created an unjustifiably high risk of erroneous deprivation. Because due process has at its foundation the notion of adequate notice, the risk of erroneous deprivation caused by ineffective notices points towards the need for added procedural protections for Medicare beneficiaries enrolled in HMOs.

3. The Government's Interest

The Secretary argues that the district court paid only cursory attention to this factor, dismissing the government's concerns. The Secretary argues that the procedures sought by plaintiffs would impose a large burden on HMOs, which would accordingly affect the benefits received by enrollees.

The district court did not engage in as detailed an analysis of this third factor as of the other two. A shorter analysis, however, does not mean the analysis is cursory or dismissive. The Secretary has failed to show that the added procedural protections sought by Plaintiffs would result in significant additional costs to the government. Unlike the plaintiff in *Eldridge*, Plaintiffs do not seek a hearing prior to every denial, which would greatly increase costs. Adequate notices do not impose a burden on HMOs that outweighs the beneficiaries' need for them. "[A] weighing of the *Mathews* [*v. Eldridge*] factors suggests that the administrative burden of providing an explanation for denying a [certain benefit] is minimal in light of the added potential for spotting erroneously withheld [benefits]." *Barnes v. Healy*, 980 F.2d 572, 579 (9th Cir. 1992). The Secretary fails to advance any convincing argument that an additional burden on the government outweighs the effects of the other factors such that additional procedural safeguards are not necessary.

Taken together, the *Eldridge* factors point to a need for additional procedural protections for Medicare beneficiaries enrolled in HMOs, in particular for adequate notice of service denials, including the specific reason for the denial and an explanation of appeal rights, and expedited review for critical care denials. We therefore affirm the district court's holdings on *Eldridge*.

C. The Scope of the Injunction

The Secretary challenges the scope of the injunction issued by the district court. The scope of an injunction is reviewed for an abuse of discretion or application of erroneous legal principles. "When injunctive relief is sought against a state agency or official, such relief 'must be no broader than necessary to remedy the constitutional violation.'" *Barnes v. Healy*, 980 F.2d 572, 576 (9th Cir. 1992) (quoting *Toussaint v. McCarthy*, 801 F.2d 1080, 1086 (9th Cir. 1986)).

The Secretary argues vociferously that the injunction issued by the district court was widely and irrationally broad in scope. For example, the Secretary repeatedly ridicules the district court's requirement of 12-point type for all notices of service denials. The scope of the district court's injunction, however, is not either an abuse of discretion or the result of application of erroneous legal principles.

The district court required legible (which requires 12-point type for senior citizens) and clear notices that adequately explain to beneficiaries the reasons for the denial of services and inform them of their appeal rights. The court required any hearings to be informal and in-person. An abuse of discretion is not apparent in these requirements. Moreover, many of them are already required by the Medicare statute or the Secretary's regulations (which might make them redundant, but does not make them an abuse of discretion). The court also required the Secretary to monitor the behavior of HMOs. This requirement is not an abuse of discretion given that Congress implicitly required such in the Medicare statute by forbidding the Secretary from entering into contracts with HMOs that did not comply with the statute or the regulations and by providing the Secretary with the power to sanction the HMOs.

The Secretary argues that the district court abused its discretion by prohibiting the Secretary from entering into new contracts with HMOs that fail to provide the procedural protections mandated by the court. The Secretary argues that Congress provided the Secretary with a wide range of enforcement mechanisms, and that the district court could not require the Secretary to use the harshest mechanism. This argument fails. The Medicare Act mandated that the Secretary "may not enter into a contract . . . with an [HMO] unless it meets the requirements of [§ 1395mm(c)] and [§ 1395mm(e)]." 42 U.S.C. § 1395mm(c)(1). Under its clear meaning, this provision is not permissive; to the contrary, it is mandatory. The district court did not err or abuse its discretion.

The Secretary notes that, since the district court's summary judgment and injunction in favor of Plaintiffs, she has promulgated new regulations providing additional procedural protections for Medicare beneficiaries enrolled in HMOs. She asks us to review and modify the district court's injunction accordingly. Finding it unnecessary to do so, we decline her invitation. The district court has continuing jurisdiction over the modification of the injunction. The Secretary may move in the district court for a modification of its injunction.

IV. Conclusion

For the foregoing reasons, we AFFIRM the district court's summary judgment and injunction in favor of Plaintiffs.
AFFIRMED.

Questions

1. Do you agree that the HMO acted as a "proxy" for the government?

2. How will a right to a federal remedy impact the trend toward Medicare managed care?

2. Supplemental Health Insurance

a. "Medigap"

Kathy J. Greenlee
Medicare
KANSAS LONG-TERM CARE HANDBOOK 30-44 (1999)[*]

Medicare supplement insurance is designed to cover many, but not all, of the health care costs which are not paid by Medicare. Although Medicare is a federal program, Medicare supplement insurance is private health insurance and is regulated by the insurance department in each state. Medicare supplement insurance is called commonly referred to as "Medigap" insurance or MedSup" insurance. A specific definition of a Medicare supplement policy can be found at 42 U.S.C. § 1395ss(g)(1) . . . .

* * *

The Omnibus Budget Reconciliation Act of 1990 defines ten standard Medicare supplement plans. Only these 10 plans may be sold in the United States. (42 U.S.C. § 1395ss(p)(2).) These plans are labeled with letters, A through J, and every company must use the same letter to label its plan. A company does not have to sell all 10 plans,

---

[*] Copyright © 1999. Reprinted with permission.

but every Medicare supplement company must sell Plan A (basic Coverage). (42 U.S.C. § 1395ss(o).) The other nine plans add different combinations of other benefits to Plan A's basic coverage. These benefits cannot be modified in any way. All 10 plans protect against catastrophic health care costs. The best plan for a particular individual depends on many factors, such as health care needs, type of benefits desired, and price.

* * *

All Medicare supplement policies must contain an identical set of basic benefits. (42 U.S.C. § 1395ss(o).) The plan which contains only these basic benefits is the first plan, Plan A. The following benefits are identical in all 10 plans:

1. Part A: Hospitalization (Per Benefit Period)
   - Days 61-90 Full coinsurance coverage.
   - Days 91-150: Full coinsurance coverage. These are known as "lifetime reserve days."
   - Beyond 150 days: 100% of all eligible Part A charges for 365 lifetime nonrenewable days.
   - First three pints of blood (Part A charges).

2. Part B: Medical Expenses (Per Calendar Year)
   - 20% Coinsurance after the $100 annual deductible.
   - First three pints of blood (Part B charges).

3. Evaluating these Benefits. With just Basic Benefits, the insured person is protected against the costs of an extended hospital stay and physicians' services. However, deductibles, excess charges from non-participating physicians, and services not covered by Medicare are still the responsibility of the insured.

* * *

All Medicare supplement policies issued must be guaranteed renewable. This means that the company cannot cancel the policy, except for failure to pay premiums. (42 U.S.C. § 1395ss(q)(1).)

* * *

A Medicare supplement policy is secondary to Medicare, which means it pays only after Medicare payments have been authorized. Most payments are tied solely to an eligible and approved Medicare charge. Commonly found exclusions are mental or emotional disorders, alcohol and drug addiction, cosmetic surgery, foot care, chiropractic or other care to correct spinal disorders, dental care, eyeglasses, hearing aids, eye exams, rest cures, custodial care, and routine physical exams.

* * *

Insurer must offer a six month open enrollment period to Medicare beneficiaries aged 65 and older. The six month period begins with the first month in which the beneficiary first enrolls in benefits under Medicare Part B. During this open enrollment period the insurance company must accept all individuals who apply. Insurers may apply waiting periods for pre-existing condition. For those persons who work past age 65 and delay enrolling in Medicare Part B, open enrollment starts when Part B coverage begins and continues for six months.

* * *

. . . Insurers that offer Medicare Supplement policies may accept new applications after the open enrollment period has expired. However, at that time, an insurer may reject an applicant based upon the applicant's health condition. As a person ages, they typically develop a more complicated health profile. A Medicare beneficiary is not required to purchase a Medicare supplement policy at the time they [sic] turn 65. If they wait, however, they run the risk of not being able to purchase a Medicare supplement policy in later years.

Questions

1. Why are Medigap policies limited in number and required to be standardized nationwide?

2. Why is the federal government so intimately involved in the regulation of acute care insurance products for the elderly, but not for other population groups and not for long-term health care insurance?

b. Long-Term Care Insurance

Joshua M. Wiener
Long-Term Care Insurance
<http://www.senate.gov/~aging/hr12jw.htm>[*]

The current American system of financing and delivering long-term care for the elderly and the younger disabled population is badly broken. At present, the United States does not have, either in the private or the public sectors, satisfactory mechanisms for helping people anticipate and pay for long-term care. In particular, the disabled elderly and their families find, often to their astonishment, that the costs of nursing home and home care are not covered to any significant extent either by Medicare or their private insurance policies. Instead, the disabled elderly must rely on their own resources or, when those have been exhausted, turn to welfare in the form of Medicaid. Moreover, although the vast majority of disabled elderly live in the community, nearly two-thirds of public expenditures for long-term care for the elderly are for nursing home care.

As the American population ages, demand and expenditures for long-term care are certain to grow. It is projected that nursing home and home care expenditures for

---

[*] Reprinted with permission.

the elderly will increase by 123 percent in inflation-adjusted dollars between 1993 and 2018, public expenditures for Medicare, Medicaid and other public programs will increase by 109 percent over that same time period. Although spending will grow substantially, the burden will not be as heavy as commonly assumed because the economy will be expanding as well. Assuming, that the economy grows at a real rate of 2.5 percent a year, long-term care for the elderly will increase from about 1.21 percent of the gross domestic product in 1993 to about 2.14 percent in 2048 when the baby boom generation hits its stride in needing nursing home and home care services. While a non-trivial additional burden, this level of increase is not the end-of-the-world as some would maintain and by itself would be sustainable without much problem. What makes these expenditures more difficult to finance is that they are on top of additional resources that will inevitably be needed for Medicare and Social Security.

To address the problems of long-term care, a small but growing private long-term care insurance market has developed over the last fifteen years. Although over 95 percent of the elderly have Medicare coverage and about 70 percent have supplemental private insurance policies, insurance against the potentially devastating costs of long-term care is relatively rare. As of the end of 1995, only 4.3 million long-term care policies ever had been sold (although far fewer were in force), overwhelmingly to the elderly on an individual basis rather than to younger people on an employer-subsidized group basis.

By far the greatest impediment is the high cost of good quality policies. Despite the marked improvement in the financial position of the elderly over the past twenty years, long-term care insurance remains unaffordable for most elderly. The average annual premium for policies covering four years of nursing home and home care with inflation protection and non-forfeiture benefits in 1995 was $1,124 per year if purchased at age 50, $2,560 per year if purchased at age 65, and $8,146 a year if purchased at age 75.

The policies are expensive for two reasons: 9 out of 10 are sold individually and, therefore, carry high administrative costs; and, most policies are bought by older people whose risk of needing long-term care is substantial. Consequently, most studies estimate that only 10 to 20 percent of the elderly can afford good-quality private long-term care insurance. Other research has found the percentage of the elderly who can afford private insurance to be higher, but these studies have done so by assuming purchase of policies with limited coverage, by assuming the elderly would use their assets as well as income to pay premiums, or by excluding a large portion of the elderly from the pool of people considered interested in purchasing insurance. Affordability is not likely to dramatically improve in the future.

* * *

The simulations show that the market penetration and ability to finance long-term care of private insurance aimed at the elderly is likely to remain extremely limited.

* * *

Moreover, because private insurance is bought mostly by upper-middle and upper-income elderly with substantial assets, it will have little impact on public spending through Medicaid. For policies sold to the elderly, the projected Medicaid savings are 2-4 percent, basically rounding error for estimates 20 years into the future.

Given the limitations of the current market for private long-term care insurance, public subsidies to promote its purchase are frequently proposed. One approach is to provide employers a tax subsidy for the purchase of long-term care insurance policies for their employees by allowing them to deduct insurance contributions as a business expense. A second strategy is to provide a tax deduction or credit to individuals for purchase of private long term care insurance. Tax incentives for employers and individuals were part of the Health Insurance Portability and Accountability Act of 1996 (the Kassebaum-Kennedy law). A final strategy is to waive some or all of the Medicaid asset depletion requirements for purchasers of qualified private long-term care insurance policies, an approach being tied in several states. The shared intent of these strategies is to induce more people to purchase policies by lowering premium costs through tax breaks or guaranteeing publicly-funded coverage once privately purchased coverage is exhausted. Proponents argue that a key consequence of any of these actions is public endorsement of the importance and desirability of private long-term care insurance.

All of these options will, no doubt, promote the purchase of private long-term care insurance, but to what extent is unclear. Moreover, with the possible exception of easing access to Medicaid by persons who purchase private long-term care insurance, these strategies are not free to the government. All of these options could result in substantial loss of federal revenue, which is spending just as certainly as the direct expenditures of a public insurance program.

Employer Contributions and the Tax Status of Private Insurance

One approach to address the affordability problem is to encourage purchase of private long-term care insurance at younger ages, especially through employers. Since 1987, a tiny but expanding market of employer-sponsored insurance for long-term care has developed. As of 1995, only about 500,000 policies had been sold through 1,260 employees. In a key difference from acute care polices, where most employers pay a large proportion of the cost of insurance, most employer-sponsored long-term care policies are offered on an employee-pay-all basis.

The Advantages of the Employer-Sponsored Market

Theoretically, employer-sponsored plans offered to the nonelderly provide several advantages over those purchased individually. First, premiums for younger policyholders can be substantially lower than those for older policyholders because younger policyholders pay premiums over a longer period of time and because earnings on premium reserves have more time to build. For example, the premiums for a 42-year-old will be approximately on quarter to one-third of the premium for a 67-year-old. Computer simulations suggest that purchase of long-term care insurance by the younger population could largely solve the affordability problem of private long-term care insurance, even without employer contributions. Because of the improved affordability, significant Medicaid savings could be achieved if persons purchased long-term care insurance when they were younger.

Although lower premiums are tied to the age of the purchaser and not necessarily to the fact that the policy is employer-sponsored, the nonelderly are easiest to reach through their place of employment. The workplace is where most health, life, and disability insurance is purchased and most retirement savings through pensions are established.

Lower administrative and marketing costs offer another potential source of savings over individual policies. Administrative and marketing costs are high in individual policies because sales have to be made one at a time. Group markets are able to achieve lower costs through economics of scale. Moreover, in group policies, employers bear many of the costs of administering the policy, such as collecting premium payments through payroll deductions. Employers may also elect to assume part of the costs of marketing the plan to their employees. However, informal discussions with insurance actuaries suggest that most assume only a ten percentage point difference in the anticipated loss ratio between individual and group plans. Thus, although the administrative savings of group policies are desirable and not trivial, they will not dramatically lower premiums.

Enrolling people at younger ages through the workplace also reduces the risk of adverse selection and therefore the need for medical underwriting. Disability is relatively rare at younger ages. The less frequent underwriting typical of employer-based policies is an improvement over the universally strict practices used for purchase of individual insurance policies. However, most younger persons with significant disabilities are not in the work force and would not, therefore, be eligible for these policies.

Finally, advocates of employer-sponsored insurance argue that the quality of policies should improve through the involvement of company benefit manager. Large groups have more market power than individuals to negotiate with insurance carriers for less restrictive policies. with richer benefits and lower prices. In general, the quality of policies in the employer market is quite good, especially in providing home care benefits. On the other hand, most employer-sponsored policies have grossly inadequate inflation protection. Under most policies, the insured must purchase additional coverage from time-to-time to compensate for inflation. but at the new older age and therefore at a substantially higher premium!

Impediments to an Employer-Sponsored Strategy

Despite the potential advantages of selling to the nonelderly population through employer groups, the employer-sponsored market may not expand enough to play a significant role in financing long-term care. Employers are reluctant to offer the policies, and employees are not rushing to purchase them. In particular, employers have been unwilling to contribute to the cost of the policies.

Tax Treatment of Private Long-Term Care Insurance

Employer contributions could make long-term care insurance more affordable by reducing the amount that employees have to pay out-of-pocket and might give employees confidence in the product. Until passage of the Kassebaum-Kennedy bill in 1996, private long-term care insurance was not specifically recognized in the federal tax code. Because of its unique characteristics, long-term care insurance did not fit neatly into the existing tax models of health and accident, life, or disability insurance, pensions or private annuities. As a result, the tax status of employer contributions and of insurance benefits were unclear and this lack of clarity no doubt slowed the growth of long-term care insurance, at least to some extent. The Kassebaum-Kennedy bill clarified that contributions towards the cost of group long-term care insurance policies was a tax-deductible expense for employers (like health insurance) and that benefits (within limits) were not considered income.

A persistent problem with tax incentives is the probability that most of the tax expenditures will be for people who would have purchased policies anyway. As a result, tax subsidies can be very costly ways of promoting private insurance. For example, Wiener, Illston, and Hanley (1994) estimate that the lost revenue to the federal government of allowing employers to deduct the cost of their contribution to private long-term care insurance would be $7,900 to $11,300 per year per additional policy sold.

These tax benefits are also not free to the federal government, producing potentially substantial tax losses. Some advocates argue that reductions in government expenditures for Medicaid nursing home and home care will offset the tax loss because some people who will buy private insurance would otherwise be eligible for Medicaid. At least for a long time period, these offsets are unlikely to occur because the tax loss will happen immediately, because the revenue loss is linked to premium payments, but the savings, if any will not occur until the benefits are used, typically many years into the future. This imbalance in timing guarantees short-term tax losses. Using a computer simulation model, Wiener, Illston, and Hanley (1994) estimate that it could take twenty-five years before the annual tax loss approximately equals the Medicaid savings.

While the uncertain tax status of long-term care insurance has no doubt prevented some employers from offering long-term care insurance policies to their employees, these factors are likely to be overwhelmed by the financial problems facing employer-sponsored acute health insurance benefits for retired employees which supplement the Medicare program. Unlike pensions, virtually all corporations offering post-retirement health benefits have financed them on a pay-as you-go basis rather than prefunding them. Prodded by accounting rules established by the Financial Accounting Standards Board that require companies to disclose their future financial liability for these benefits, corporations are now aware that, collectively, they have an estimated $187 billion to $400 billion in mostly unfunded liabilities.

As a result, large numbers of employers, concerned about health care costs for both their active employees and retirees, are cutting back on retiree benefits, making retirees pay a greater part of the cost or dropping that coverage altogether. For example, data from Foster Higgins' annual survey of mostly large employers found a drop in retiree health benefits between 1988 and 1992. In 1988, 55 percent of responding firms offered retiree health benefits to Medicare eligible retirees; by 1992, only 46 percent of responding firms did so. The percentage of full-time workers in state and local governments with retiree health benefits declined between 1990 and 1992 from 58 percent to 50 percent. A recent study of 50 of the largest companies showed that 31 companies showed increases in retiree cost sharing for medical benefits in 1994. In this environment, it seems unlikely that many additional employers will want to contribute to a new, potentially expensive insurance plan that will primarily benefit retirees twenty to thirty years after they have left the company. Indeed, employers are trying to distance themselves as much as possible from such benefits.

Limited Employee Demand

To date, employee demand has not played a large role in the decision of companies to add long-term care insurance to their benefit package. The desire to maintain a company's image as a leader in employee benefits or a personal sensitivity to the problem by a senior officer or employee benefit manager have been larger factors. Nonetheless, surveys of large employers suggest the possibility of a large increase in the number of companies offering policies, if not paying for them. Employees also have been reluctant to purchase insurance. The Health Insurance Association of America estimates that depending on how the universe of eligibles is defined, only 5.3 percent to 8.8 percent of those offered employer-sponsored long-term care insurance have purchased policies.

Several factors limit employee demand. First, although premiums for policies without inflation adjustment are lower at younger ages, they cost more than many people are willing to pay voluntarily. Moreover, a high quality long-term care insurance policy with a level premium, inflation protection, and nonforfeiture benefits purchased at age 50 can cost more than $1,000 a year. In a survey of nonpurchasers of employer-sponsored policies offered by two major insurers, LifePlans, Inc., reported that 82 percent of respondents felt that the fact that "the policy costs too much" was either "very important" or "important" in their decision not to purchase a policy. Even though economists contend that increased employer contributions for fringe benefits are mostly offset by reduced wages, 90 percent of respondents in this survey said that they would be more willing to purchase a policy if their employer contributed to the cost.

In addition, middle-age workers usually must contend with other, more immediate expenses, such as child care, mortgage payments, and college education for their children. In [a 1992] survey, 80 percent of nonpurchasers stated that "more important things to spend money on at this time" was either "very important" or "important" in their decision not to purchase a policy. The risk of needing long-term care is too distant to galvanize many people into buying insurance.

Finally, selling to the nonelderly population raises difficult considerations of pricing and product design. An actuary pricing a private long-term care, insurance product for a 45-year-old must predict what is going to happen forty years into the future, when the insured is age 85. To say the least, this is difficult. Ironically, although one of the advantages commonly claimed for private insurance is its flexibility to respond to the needs and wants of consumers, policyholders who buy insurance at younger ages could be locked into the existing model of service delivery decades before they use services. Who knows what the optimal delivery system will be a half century from now?

Tax Incentives for Individual Purchase of Private Insurance

Another set of options would improve the affordability of private long-term care insurance by offering direct tax incentives to individuals who purchase policies. For example, the Kassebaum-Kennedy legislation allow individuals to count private long-term care insurance premiums as a health expense. Health care expenses in excess of 7.5 percent of adjusted gross income are tax deductible. As a result of the ability to deduct part of the cost of private long-term care insurance, the net price of insurance policies will be reduced. Some insurance advocates argue that providing a tax benefit have a "sentinel" effect, promoting insurance beyond merely reducing the price. A tax incentive, they contend, will signal potential purchasers that the government thinks private long-term care insurance is a worthwhile product.

The type of tax chosen to provide the tax subsidy defines the scope of who can benefit. Allowing taxpayers to deduct all or part of cost of a private long-term care insurance policy would provide a premium subsidy valued at the marginal tax rate of the household. Since upper-income taxpayers have higher marginal tax rates than lower-income taxpayers, deductions are regressive in nature. That is, they are worth more to upper-income people than to lower-income people. However, for the 72 percent of taxpayers in the 15 percent tax bracket in 1993, this type of tax subsidy would reduce the cost of obtaining long-term care insurance by only about one seventh, probably not enough to motivate very many additional people to purchase polices. The other major drawback is that relatively few taxpayers itemize their deductions. In 1993, only 29 percent of all tax returns included itemized deductions; only 4 percent claimed a deduction for medical expenses.

The other broad approach is to provide a tax credit, which is a direct reduction in the amount of tax owed, for purchase of policies. In theory, tax credits need not be as regressive as deductions. However, as a practical matter, moderate and low-income taxpayers may not have the cash on hand to pay premiums during the year so as to be able to claim a tax credit in the following year. The other problem is that, unless the credit is refundable, it is an ineffective policy for people who do not have a tax liability. This is especially a problem for the elderly; only about half of whom have any federal income tax liability.

* * *

While changing the tax code is the most commonly proposed way of publicly subsidizing private long-term care insurance, the initiatives by Connecticut, Indiana, California, Iowa and New York take a substantially different approach. Commonly referred to as the "Robert Wood Johnson Public-Private Partnerships" (named for the foundation that promoted this strategy), these states provide easier access to Medicaid for persons who purchase a state-approved private long-term care insurance policy. In essence, these states allow nursing home patients with private long-term care insurance to be Medicaid eligible with substantially higher levels of assets than is normally allowed. At present, Medicaid only allows unmarried nursing home patients to retain $2,000 in assets (excluding the home). While employer-paid plans and tax incentives seek to reduce the net cost of insurance, this public-private partnership does the reverse by trying to increase the amount of benefits received per dollar spent.

There are two models of how to link Medicaid and private insurance. In both cases, Medicaid acts as a kind of reinsurance for persons with limited private long-term care insurance.

In one model, used by Connecticut, California, Indiana, and Iowa, the level of Medicaid-protected assets is tied to the amount that the private insurance policy pays out. For example, if a person buys a policy that pays $100,000 in long-term care benefits, then that individual can keep $100,000 in assets and still be eligible for Medicaid. Consumers are able to purchase insurance equivalent to the amount of assets they wish to preserve, potentially reducing the amount of insurance individuals need to buy.

The other model, used by New York, provides protection of an unlimited amount of assets if an individual purchases a policy that meets state standards, including coverage of at least three years of a combination of nursing home and home care, with a minimum $100 per day indemnity payment. The rationale for not requiring an asset test for Medicaid coverage is that nursing home costs are so high in New York that few individuals can avoid Medicaid over an extended period of time. Thus, New York is targeting a higher income population, with potentially more assets, than are the other states.

The key observation supporting the public-private approaches is that long-team care insurance that covers shorter periods of nursing home and home care are cheaper and more affordable then policies that cover longer periods of care. The problem with the current system is that if an individual buys a policy that covers, for example, two years of nursing home care and ends up staying a nursing home for five years, then the insured's assets can still be lost. Thus, under these Medicaid initiatives, it is possible to obtain lifetime asset protection without having to buy an insurance policy that pays lifetime benefits. Proponents of this approach contend that the goal is not asset protection, per se, but rather to preserve financial autonomy toward the end of life.

Supporters assert that by encouraging purchase of insurance, Medicaid long-term care expenditures will possibly be reduced or, at least, will not increase. This argument is probably stronger for the approach used by Connecticut, Indiana, Iowa, and California, where there is a "dollar-for-dollar" correspondence between the amount the insurance pays and the level of Medicaid protected assets. In New York, the ability to protect potentially very large amounts of assets makes this argument weaker, although still possible. To the extent that these systems are budget-neutral, these strategies will be a move toward what economists call "Pareto Optimality," that is, making some people better off without making anybody worse off. Insurance dollars are simply substituted for private asset dollars.

There are two other potential advantages to this approach. First, since only "approved" policies are eligible for the enhanced asset protection, state regulators can use the initiative as a "carrot" to induce insurance companies to upgrade the quality of their policies. Second, by giving the elderly the alternative of protecting their assets by purchasing insurance, legal and illegal transfer of assets for the purpose of obtaining Medicaid eligibility may be reduced.

Despite these arguments, there are several concerns about the equity and efficiency of this option. The first concern is whether it is appropriate to use a means-tested welfare program like Medicaid as a mechanism to protect the assets of upper-middle and upper-income elderly. Indeed, under this approach, it remains an open question how far down the income distribution insurance purchase will go. Computer simulations by Wiener, Illston and Hanley (1994) suggest that the vast bulk of private insurance expenditures will be for the relatively well-to-do elderly.

The second concern is whether providing improved asset protection will actually induce substantial numbers of people to purchase long-term care insurance who would not otherwise have bought it. As of December 1996, participation in partnership plans has been disappointing, with only 22,000 policies in force, over half of which are in New York State. While it is difficult to sift through people's motivations for buying insurance, one recent study of purchasers found that only 23 percent of respondents listed protection of assets as the "most important" reason for buying insurance. Asset protection may have a narrow appeal because most elderly have relatively modest levels of financial wealth.

Even more fundamentally, many elderly do not want easier access to Medicaid. Indeed, one of the major reasons people buy long-term care insurance is to avoid having to apply for welfare. One survey of insurance purchasers found that 91 percent of respondents reported that avoiding Medicaid was an "important" or "very important" reason for buying a policy. Medicaid's relatively low reimbursement rates have led to inadequate access and quality of care problems in nursing homes heavily dependent on Medicaid. In addition, upper-middle and upper income elderly will probably find the $30 a month personal needs allowance of the Medicaid program to be inadequate. Therefore, they would use up at least some of their newly-protected assets for daily living expenses. Avoiding Medicaid is also the principal argument that insurance agents use to market policies; the partnership plans require a radical revision in the agents' "sales pitch." In sum, it is not clear that easier access to Medicaid will be enough of an inducement to get large numbers of additional elderly to purchase private long-term care insurance.

The third concern is whether the public-private partnership will truly be budget-neutral. After all, Medicaid benefits are being offered to people who would otherwise not be eligible. Because most policies probably will be sold to healthy young elderly who are at least 10 to 20 years away from needing nursing home care, even fragmentary evidence as to the effect of the partnership on the public purse will not be available for a decade or two. If additional public expenditures should prove to be required, then one may well ask whether providing asset protection to relatively well-to-do elderly is the best place to put our next long-tem care dollar.

It is also important to realize that an indispensable component for assessing the effect on the Medicaid budget is establishing a comparison level of expenditures. In a world with no private long-term care insurance at all, it is likely, although not certain, that the partnership would be budget-neutral. However, there is likely to be continuing modest growth in the number of private long-term care insurance policies sold. Compared to this scenario, if the partnership does not induce substantial numbers of additional insurance purchasers, then the partnership will require larger Medicaid expenditures than would otherwise be needed. This is because under current Medicaid rules purchasers of insurance who would have bought policies without the public-private partnership would have to spend-down their assets after their insurance benefits have been exhausted before qualifying for Medicaid, something that they are not required to do under the partnership.

In addition, while supporters argue that the partnership offers persons a more appealing alternative to transferring assets as a way to avoid Medicaid's claim on these resources, it is conceivable that it will actually increase the level of premature asset transfer. Current rules prohibit the transfer of assets to other persons at less than fair market value for 36 months prior to application for Medicaid eligibility. Once the partnership has encouraged the elderly to look to Medicaid as a way to protect their assets, some insurance purchasers may only buy the 36 months worth of coverage required to comply with Medicaid rules and then legally transfer the remainder of their financial wealth upon entry to a nursing home. Others may calculate that they can transfer or shelter their assets and obtain Medicaid benefits without purchase of any long-term care insurance policy.

Conclusions and Recommendations

The United States faces major challenges in the way it organizes and finances long-term care for the elderly. The aging of the baby boom generation absolutely guarantees that expenditures for nursing home and home care will grow substantially in the future. Based on the available evidence, the following observations should form the framework for reform.

Although the role of private long-term care insurance. will inevitably grow over time, it is doubtful that it will ever play a major role in the financing of long-term care. Especially for the elderly population, good-quality policies are simply too expensive. Medicaid savings are particularly unlikely because the people who can afford policies are not the people who spend down to Medicaid.

Selling private long-term care insurance to younger people through employers can make policies significantly more affordable. However, policies are still costly and employees have so far been unwilling to buy policies in large numbers. Substantial employer subsidies could make private long-term care insurance more attractive, but even with tax subsidies employers are unlikely to make contributions because of their large unfunded liability for retiree acute care benefits. Employee demand among people in their 40s is low because of competing demand for their spending. As a result, market penetration is likely to be far below the levels projected by simulations (including my own) based solely on upper-bound determined affordability. While some of the tax clarifications for private long-term care insurance enacted in the Health Insurance Portability and Accountability Act of 1996 were desirable, the tax deduction for individual purchase of private long-term care insurance is regressive, primarily benefits the well-to-do, and is a highly inefficient way to encourage the purchase of private long-term care insurance. Most of the subsidy will go to people who would have bought insurance without the tax benefit. Even clarifying the tax treatment of employer contributions will result in federal tax losses that are "spending" as surely as any direct appropriation. Congress should refrain from providing any more tax incentives for the purchase of private long-term care insurance.

While the quality of policies has improved dramatically over the last ten years, the lack of inflation protection and nonforfeiture benefits in most policies are significant deficiencies. Congress lost a major opportunity to upgrade policies when they provided tax breaks to insurance companies without requiring any substantial upgrading in consumer protection.

While a favorite of some policy analysts, the public-private partnerships for long-term care have failed the market test—very few policies have been sold, even in states that have promoted them for several years. Although the reasons are unclear, probably the primary reason is that insurance agents prefer to sell policies by emphasizing the negative aspects of the Medicaid program, a strategy that is inconsistent with a product whose primary benefit is easier access to the program.

Given the limitations of private long-term care insurance, serious long-term care reform that seeks to make life better for the great majority of elderly will require expansions of public programs—Medicare, Medicaid, and others—that currently are the major source of third-party funding. To ignore the public programs in the hope that private insurance will replace them someday is a luxury that the disabled elderly and their families can ill afford.

Recent Long-Term Care Proposals Fail to Address Real Problems
BW HEALTHWIRE, March 11, 1999*

An expert in long-term care issues is telling Congress that recent proposals to help resolve the coming crisis will do nothing to avert it. Robert L. Pearson, president and CEO of CareQuest, Inc. of Madison, Wis. said, "While the attention to the long-term care issue is long overdue, I believe the current initiatives to be misplaced and misdirected. We are sending the wrong messages to employers, caregivers and retirees and its time to set the record straight."

Pearson, whose experience in the long-term care (LTC) industry dates back to consulting on the first generation of insurance policies in 1985, says that the statistics do not support the current movement that encourages employers to purchase LTC insurance for their working age employees, where there will be little or no utilization. Conversely, the caregiving issues that will plague nearly half of those employees in the next few years will find little or no relief with the proposed $1000 tax credit.

He says that employers, who are losing in excess of $29 billion each year in lost productivity due to employees with eldercare responsibilities, are a key factor in the solution. But, we need to step back and look at who really needs to buy the insurance, and who needs assistance with caregiving issues. "We need to start thinking of first things first," Pearson said.

---

* Copyright © 1999. Reprinted with permission.

In a 23-page report to Congress, Pearson raised several issues that he thinks Congress should address immediately.

The first is, Pearson said, that while employers have the advantage of 100 percent tax deductibility on LTC insurance purchased for employees who have little or no chance of ever using it, the program fails to address the people who need it most: pre-retirees, retirees, parents, in-laws and grandparents of employees.

"There should be a 100 percent tax deduction given to all individuals who purchase LTC insurance. This will provide incentive for those who need it to purchase these plans, while making it more affordable."

In tandem with that, Pearson said that employers should be motivated and educated about the real facts and effects of long-term insurance. "They must be encouraged to extend the offer of reduced group rates to those who really need it."

He also believes that government should not be in the caregiving assistance business. "Government will never have enough resources to even start paying for it all," he said. "The best thing they could do is offer employers more incentives to provide a comprehensive caregiving benefit package for their employees."

"With an estimated loss in productivity of $3,142 per year, per caregiver employee, employers have all the justification they need to purchase a comprehensive assistance package for them. These people are faced with the exhausting and disruptive tasks of selecting, contacting, evaluating and negotiating with facilities, providers and insurers, without ever having a true understanding of what their options really are," Pearson said. "Employers will be hard pressed, however, to substantiate offering an LTC insurance benefit that has little or no chance of helping their employees."

Additionally, Pearson said that until LTC insurance evolves into the type of policy that will hold its value for 15-50 years, working Americans should not regard these policies as a retirement investment. "The changes that have taken place in the 10 to 15 year history of LTC insurance policies has been tremendous, and it's going to continue. That's not good news for the young consumer," he said. "Encouraging people in their 20s, 30s, 40s and even 50s to buy LTC insurance today is like telling a 12-year-old to buy automobile insurance now because he's going to be driving when he's 16. It's their parents and grandparents who need to purchase LTC insurance."

Questions

1. Is the comparison with a 12-year-old's need to buy auto insurance a useful analogy?

2. Poll your extended family. Does anyone have long-term care insurance? Has anyone considered its purchase? What reasons did this person give for his or her choice?

3. What level of government involvement in the provision of long-term care services do you think is appropriate? Why?

3. Medicaid and Long-Term Care

Mary Onnis Waid
Health Care Financing Administration
Brief Summaries of Medicare and Medicaid: Title XVIII and Title XIX of the Social Security Act as of June 25, 1998
<http://www.hcfa.gov/medicare/ormedmed.htm>*

Overview of Medicaid

Title XIX of the Social Security Act is a Federal-State matching entitlement program that pays for medical assistance for certain vulnerable and needy individuals and families with low incomes and resources. This program, known as Medicaid, became law in 1965 as a jointly funded cooperative venture between the Federal and State governments (State used herein includes the Territories and the District of Columbia) to assist States furnishing medical assistance to eligible needy persons. Medicaid is the largest source of funding for medical and health-related services for America's poorest people. In 1996, it provided health care assistance to more than 36 million persons, at a cost of $160 billion dollars.

Within broad national guidelines established by Federal statutes, regulations and policies, each State: (1) establishes its own eligibility standards; (2) determines the type, amount, duration, and scope of services; (3) sets the rate of payment for services; and (4) administers its own program. Medicaid policies for eligibility, services, and payment are complex, and vary considerably even among similar-sized and/or adjacent States. Thus, a person who is eligible for Medicaid in one State might not be eligible in another State; and the services provided by one State may differ considerably in amount, duration, or scope from services provided in a similar or neighboring State. In addition, Medicaid eligibility and/or services within a State can change during the year.

* * *

Long term care is an important and increasingly utilized provision of Medicaid—especially as our nation's population ages. Almost 45% of the total cost of care for persons using nursing facility or home health services in the U.S. in recent years is paid for by the Medicaid program. A much larger percentage is paid for by Medicaid, however, for those persons who use more than four months of such long-term care. As Medicaid has continued to provide extensive nursing facility care over the years, the focus has become the struggle to rely more on community-based long term care alternatives. The data for 1996 show that Medicaid payments for nursing facility (excluding ICF/MRs) and home health care totaled $40.5 billion for more than 3.6 million recipients of these services—an average 1996 expenditure of more than

---

* Copyright © 1997. Reprinted with permission. *See* Disclaimer, *supra* p. 321 n.*.

$12,300 per long-term care recipient. With the percentage of our population who are elderly and/or disabled increasing faster than the younger groups, the need for long-term care is expected to increase.

* * *

Medicaid data as reported by the States indicate that more than 36 million persons received health care service through the Medicaid program in 1996. These data show that, in addition to administrative costs, the total outlays for the Medicaid program in 1996 included: direct payment to providers of $122 billion; payments for various premiums (for HMOs, Medicare, etc.) of more than $16 billion; and payments to the disproportionate share hospitals of $15 billion.

The total expenditure for the nation's Medicaid program was $160 billion ($91 billion in Federal and $69 billion in State funds) in 1996. With anticipated impacts from the Balanced Budget Act of 1997, projections now are that total Medicaid outlays may be $250 billion in fiscal year 2003, with an additional $5.8 billion expected to be spent for the new Children's Health Insurance Program.

a. Assistance for Low-Income Seniors

Mary Onnis Waid
Health Care Financing Administration
Brief Summaries of Medicare and Medicaid: Title XVIII and Title XIX of the Social Security Act as of June 25, 1998
<http://www.hcfa.gov/medicare/ormedmed.htm>[*]

The Medicaid-Medicare Relationship

Medicare beneficiaries who have low incomes and limited resources may also receive help from the Medicaid program. For persons who are eligible for *full* Medicaid coverage, the Medicare health care coverage is supplemented by services that are available under their State's Medicaid program, according to eligibility category. These additional services may include—for example—nursing facility care beyond the 100 day limit covered by Medicare, prescription drugs, eyeglasses, and hearing aids. For persons enrolled in both programs, any services that are covered by Medicare are paid for by the Medicare program before any payments are made by the Medicaid program, since Medicaid is always payor of last resort.

Certain other Medicare beneficiaries may receive some help through their State Medicaid program. Qualified Medicare Beneficiaries (QMBs) and Specified Low-Income Medicare Beneficiaries (SLMBs) are the best known and the largest in numbers. QMBs are those Medicare beneficiaries who have resources at or below twice the standard allowed under the SSI program, and incomes at or below 100% of

---

[*] Copyright © 1997. Reprinted with permission. *See* Disclaimer, *supra* p. 321 n.*.

360   ELDER LAW: READINGS, CASES, AND MATERIALS

the FPL. This also includes persons who are eligible for full Medicaid coverage. For QMBs, the State pays the HI and SMI premiums and the Medicare coinsurance and deductibles, subject to limits that States may impose on payment rates. SLMBs are Medicare beneficiaries with resources like the QMBs, yet with incomes that are higher—but still less than 120% of the FPL. For SLMBs, the Medicaid program only pays the SMI premiums. The Medicare law states that disabled and working individuals who previously qualified for Medicare because of disability, but who lost entitlement because of their return to work (despite the disability), are allowed to purchase Medicare HI and SMI coverage. If these persons have incomes below 200% of the FPL, but do not meet any other Medicaid assistance category, they may qualify to have Medicaid pay their HI premiums as Qualified Disabled and Working Individuals (QDWIs).

According to HCFA estimates, Medicaid provided some level of supplemental health coverage for 5.9 million persons who were Medicare beneficiaries in the above three categories for FY 1995. Although they represent only 17% of the total Medicare enrollees, they accounted for 35% of the total Medicaid expenditures ($53 billion in FY 1995)—including $10 billion for Medicare cost-sharing, $5 billion for other acute care services and prescription drugs, and $38 billion and for long-term care.

Health Care Financing Administration
Medicare and You (November 1998)
<http://www.medicare.gov/publications/handbook.html>

Medicare Savings for Qualified Beneficiaries

Help in Paying Medicare Out-of-Pocket Expenses for Some Low-Income People

The Health Care Financing Administration (HCFA), a Federal government agency that administers Medicare and Medicaid, and your State have developed programs that can help pay your Medicare out-of-pocket expenses. These programs help people who have limited resources and income to pay for some Medicare expenses. This could save you hundreds of dollars each year. If you qualify, you may not have to pay for your:
• Medicare premiums, and in some cases, deductibles, and coinsurance.

* * *

Several Programs Offer Help

There are four programs that offer different levels of help. They are:
• Qualified Medicare Beneficiary (QMB)
• Specified Low-income Medicare Beneficiary (SLMB)
• Qualifying Individual-1 (QI-1)
• Qualifying Individual-2 (QI-2)

You may qualify for one of these programs if:

1. You are entitled to Medicare Part A. If you do not have Part A or you are not sure, check your Medicare card or call the Social Security office at 1-800-772-1213 to find out how to get it.

2. Your financial resources, such as bank accounts, stocks, and bonds, are not more than $4,000 for one person or $6,000 for a couple. Some things—like the home you live in, one automobile, burial plots, home furnishings, personal jewelry, and life insurance—usually do not count as resources. (If the combined face value of the life insurance policy is less than $1,500, it is not counted.)

3. Your monthly income is at or below a certain level. Income includes Social Security benefits, pensions, and wages as well as interest payments and dividends on stocks and bonds you may own. The amount of help you can get depends upon your monthly income. The monthly income limits for different levels of help are shown below. If your monthly income changes you may move to a different level of help.

If your monthly income in 1998 is at or below: $691 (individual) $925 (couple), you may qualify for: Qualified Medicare Beneficiary (QMB). This program pays your Medicare premiums, deductibles, and coinsurance.

If your monthly income in 1998 is at or below: $825 (individual) $1,105 (couple), you may qualify for: Specified Low-income Medicare Beneficiary (SLMB). This program pays your Medicare Part B premium.

If your monthly income in 1998 is at or below: $926 (individual) $1,241 (couple), you may qualify for: Qualifying Individual-1 (QI-1).This program pays your Medicare Part B premium.

If your monthly income in 1998 is at or below: $1,194 (individual) $1,603 (couple), you may qualify for: Qualifying Individual-2 (QI-2). This program pays for a small part of your Medicare Part B premium.

Molly M. Wood
Home and Community Based Services
KANSAS LONG-TERM CARE HANDBOOK 1-6 (1999)[*]

I. Introduction

Home and Community Based Services (HCBS) is a less well known Medicaid [waiver] program in which frail or disabled low-income Kansans may receive home based care. Services are intended to provide eligible persons with the least intensive level of care which maintains or improves the overall physical or mental condition of those who would otherwise be placed in a nursing home or hospital. Those age 65 and older may be served under the Frail Elderly HCBS [waiver] program, but those under age 65 will require a disability determination to become eligible. The Division of Assets rules, with some modifications, are applicable to married people, one of whom needs a substantial amount of in-home care.

* * *

---

[*] Copyright © 1999. Reprinted with permission.

II. Eligibility Basics

    A. Medical necessity for nursing home care is per se medical necessity, and the first element of eligibility, for HCBS.

If your client is eligible for Medicaid in the nursing home, elects HCBS, and the Medicaid agency can develop a home care plan, the client is also eligible for HCBS. So, for example, if your client goes from the hospital or rehabilitation center to the nursing home for a period of convalescence, becomes eligible for Medicaid assistance, and the client's care needs would continue to support Medicaid eligibility in the nursing home, it may be possible for the client to return home and shift to HCBS. Moreover, at the time of the assessment screening, whether your client resides in a nursing facility or that move appears imminent, HCBS services should be explored at the same time as Medicaid for nursing home care.

    B. HCBS income mechanics.

If HCBS services are otherwise appropriate, the Medicaid agency will develop a plan of care and determine the cost of services. Unlimited services are not available; the agency has a cost cap which equals the average Medicaid reimbursement for nursing facility or other institutional services. All income received by the HCBS applicant is considered initially, but a portion will be disregarded and not considered available to meet medical expenses:

- The first $20 per month of any income;
- The first $65 per month of gross earned income; and
- One-half of the remainder of earned income are to be disregarded.

Practice Tip: Pension benefits, Social Security, interest income, veteran's benefits, etc. are unearned income. The utility of the disregards of earned income to retired people is, of course, limited.

The HCBS recipient is allowed to protect a "monthly standard"—$671 in 1999—to allow the client to meet his/her maintenance needs, that is, the cost of shelter, utilities, clothing, non-medical transportation, and food. Total income less disregards produces "countable income" from which the monthly standard is deducted to determine the applicant's "monthly client obligation for services." The client obligation represents the amount the HCBS recipient must incur in medical expenses, including HCBS service costs, before Medicaid will pay.

Example: Mrs. McClure, a widow, requires homemaker services, a bath aide, assistance with transferring between her wheelchair and her bed each morning and evening, physical therapy, and medication monitoring. The monthly cost of these services is $1,300. In addition, she has medical insurance premiums of $178 per month and her prescription medications cost $222 per month. Her monthly income consists of $750 of Social Security retirement income and a small pension—$250. Her countable income is $1,000 minus $20 = $980. Countable income less the monthly standard—$980 minus $671—produces a client obligation amount of $309, that is, Mrs. McClure must document that she has incurred $309 in medical expenses applicable to her client obligation before SRS will pick up her HCBS costs. In this hypothetical, proof that she has at least been billed for her prescription medication and her health insurance premiums will allow Medicaid to bear her entire in-home cost of care. In fact, after she pays her health insurance bill, Medicaid will pick up $19 of her prescription medication—$309 less $178 insurance premium less $144 of the medication meets the spenddown. The balance of the spenddown should be borne by Medicaid.

But what if Mrs. McClure's income is considerably more? What if, in addition to her Social Security and pension, she also receives $500 per month in alimony payments and $6,000 per year net crop income from the farm (upon which she lives) which her son cultivates for her? Her monthly countable income is $1,980, minus the $671 monthly maintenance standard, produces a client obligation of $1,309. Even after payment of her medication and health insurance, Mrs. McClure must incur $987 in additional medical expenses, including the HCBS service costs, before Medicaid will cover anything. If her HCBS services only run $1,300 per month, she will receive only $313 per month in assistance.

C. Spousal income mechanics.

1. If the combined total income of the marriage partnership is $1,357 (1998 amount with cost-of-living adjustment of 1.3% effective July 1999) or less, the HCBS spouse's client obligation will be zero and the first dollar of medical expenses incurred will be paid by Medicaid.

2. If the combined total income is more than $1,357 per month, income sufficient to bring the well spouse's gross income up to $1,357 per month can be made available. So if, for example, Mr. Paul's income is $1050 per month, his wife's income is $525, and he is otherwise eligible for HCBS, he would be able to make $832 available to her ($1,357 minus $525), and his countable income for HCBS purposes would be $218. Because his remaining income is less than the monthly standard, his client obligation will be zero. But if Mrs. Paul's income is also $1,050, she would receive an allowance of only $307 ($1,357 minus $1,050), Mr. Paul's remaining income would be $743, and he must incur $72 in out-of-pocket medical expenses before HCBS will cover the cost of his in-home care. If the couple have excess shelter expenses—the amount by which the couple's monthly expense for rent or mortgage payments, including principal, interest, taxes, and insurance (or in the case of a condominium or cooperative, monthly maintenance charges) exceeds $218—he well spouse can receive up to $2,019 per month.

Questions

1. What fundamental differences can you identify between Medicare and Medicaid?

2. What barriers to access to Medicaid are apparent from your reading so far?

b. Nursing Facility Care

Department of Health and Human Services
Americans Less Likely to Use Nursing Home Care Today
HHS News Release (January 23, 1997)

Dramatic changes in the nursing home industry have taken place over the past decade, especially because of growth in home health care, according to findings from the latest survey of nursing homes in America released today by HHS. The 1995 survey shows there are fewer, but larger, nursing homes offering long-term care today than 10 years ago. At the same time, despite the growth in the number of older Americans who make up the largest proportion of nursing home residents, there has been only a slight increase in the number of residents and an actual decline in the occupancy rates.

The 1995 survey also showed that nursing homes are more likely to be operated as part of a chain, when comparing the 1995 survey with the previous survey conducted in 1985.

"Americans who need long-term care have more choices today. Many more are able to stay in their homes and still receive the care they need," said HHS Secretary Donna E. Shalala. She attributed this shift to the rapid growth in home health care as well as the advances in medical technology that permit people to postpone institutional care and opt for less costly home-based alternatives. However, Secretary Shalala said, "Nursing homes remain a critical component of health care in this country and are essential for those who need intensive, 24-hour medical care. Wherever care is provided, we must ensure that it is appropriate and high quality."

Since 1985, the number of nursing homes decreased by 13 percent while the number of beds increased by 9 percent. The number of nursing home residents was up only 4 percent between 1985 and 1995, despite an 18-percent increase in the population aged 65 years and over. Prior to the 1995 survey, utilization rates had kept pace with the increase in the elderly population.

About 1.5 million residents were receiving care in 16,700 nursing homes in 1995. Nearly 1.8 million beds were available for use and these facilities operated at about 87 percent of their capacity. Almost 90 percent of the residents in the 1995 survey were aged 65 years and over. More than 35 percent were aged 85 years and over. Residents were also predominantly white (88 percent) and female (72 percent).

Most nursing homes (66 percent) are operated for profit and over half are operated as part of chains. Chain-affiliated homes increased from 41 to 55 percent between 1985 and 1995. While there was a 23-percent drop in the number of proprietary homes over the past decade, the total number of beds in proprietary homes increased by almost 3 percent, resulting in fewer, but larger, homes. Overall, some 1.3 million full-time equivalent employees (FTE's) were working in nursing homes. The largest single category—almost 1 million FTE's—provide nursing services.

Molly Mead Wood
Medicaid Eligibility for Long-Term Care: The Basics
16 Preventive L. Rep. 8 (1997)*

Seniors seeking assistance with the cost of long-term nursing facility care from Medicaid must meet the following four-part eligibility test:

Medical Need: Nursing home care, whether skilled, intermediate, or custodial, must be the appropriate level of care for the medical assistance applicant. Most states require applicants to complete a screening prior to, or soon after, nursing home admission. Practitioners should be alert to the range of in-home services which would postpone institutionalization.

* * *

The Income Test: Find out if your state has an income cap. For those states, a Medicaid applicant must receive less than the cap to be eligible for assistance. Unfortunately, the maximum cap for these applicants is 300% of the Supplemental Security Income level, which is [$1,500 per month in 1999 (300% of $500)], and some states are lower. It is implausible that anyone could pay his or her cost of care after other resources are exhausted with that level of income, and until October 1, 1993, this requirement produced harsh results.

Part of the Omnibus Budget Reconciliation Act of 1993, however, created a loophole. 42 U.S.C. § 1396p(d)(4)(B) codified the "Miller" trust, so named for the case that launched the legislation. *Miller v. Ibarra*, 746 F. Supp. 19 (D. Colo. 1990). These trusts are appropriate only in income cap states, must contain only the income of the Medicaid recipient, and must include a payback provision upon termination.

[In states without an income cap, i]f the Medicaid applicant's income is less than his/her private pay cost of care, the applicant meets the income test. Attribution of income follows the name on the check, that is, income is attributed to the spouse to whom payment is drawn. Jointly held income producing property is allocated pro rata.

The Resource Test: A Medicaid recipient cannot retain over $2,000 in non-exempt resources.

Exempt resources include:
- A home of any value. An applicant generally is entitled to exempt the home even if these is no real expectation that he or she will be able to return.
- A car of any value;
- Household goods, family keepsakes, memorabilia;
- Life insurance with a death benefit of $1,500 or less;
- Real property, equipment or materials used in an income producing trade or business. (These exceptions help conserve the family farm or other small business); and
- Irrevocable burial plans.

---

* Copyright © 1997. Reprinted with permission.

All other resource are non-exempt, including, but not limited to:
- Cash assets;
- Cash value of life insurance policies of which the applicant or the applicant's spouse is the owner.
- Resource available to the applicant as the beneficiary of a grantor trust established before August 10, 1993 to the extent the trustee has discretion to invade principal for the benefit of the applicant. . . .
- For trusts created after August 10, 1993, assets of a Medicaid applicant conveyed to a trust (other than by will) for the benefit of the individual or the individual's spouse are considered available, regardless of the purposes of the trust, if the trust is revocable, or, if irrevocable, the trustee has any discretion with respect to distributions of principal or income. . . .
- Fair market value of real estate other than the home.

Spousal Impoverishment

Division of assets modifies the resource test in the context of a well spouse remaining in the community. Here, the community spouse retains all the exempt property. All the non-exempt resources of the married couple are pooled, regardless of ownership, and a portion is set aside for the community spouse. The community spouse retains a minimum of $16,382 and a maximum of $81,960 (1999). If the total non-exempt resources of the couple are greater than $32,784 and less than $163,920, the community spouse retains one-half of the couple's non-exempt resources.

After the institutionalized spouse has spent his half down to the protected $2,000 amount, he has met the resource test. Proper spend-down techniques include purchase of prepaid exempt burial plans for both marital partners, improvements and repairs to the exempt home, upgrade of the exempt family car, and, of course, payment of medical and other expenses for both marital partners.

Do not begin to spend down until after institutionalization! Because the allocation of resources takes place at the time the Medicaid applicant enters the nursing home, keeping the couple's total non-exempt resources as high as possible will make the community spouse's protected amount greater.

The community spouse of a Medicaid recipient is also potentially eligible for a spousal income allowance—a sort of "division of income" in which her income can be supplemented to $1,357 (1999) from the income of the institutionalized spouse after the Medicaid applicant has become eligible.

The Transfer Test: Transfers for less than adequate consideration may incur eligibility penalties. These provisions were altered considerably by OBRA '93 and became law on August 10, 1993. *See* 42 U.S.C. § 1396p(c). For transfers occurring after August 10, 1993, the look-back period is increased from 30 to 36 months. The look-back period for transfers to trusts is 60 months.

Just because a gift was made during the look-back period, does not mean the applicant is not eligible. The transfer penalty is calculated by dividing the amount of the gift by the average monthly cost of nursing home care. This dollar amount varies widely by region. In parts of the northeast the divisor ranges as high as $6,000 per month, but a Kansas applicant incurs one month of ineligibility for every

$2,000 of uncompensated value. In Kansas, therefore, a $10,000 gift will incur a 5-month penalty. If the applicant can pay his own way for five months, the penalty will have expired and is not a bar to eligibility.

The penalty period begins on the date of the transfer, and all uncompensated transfers after May 1, 1993 are combined to determine the cumulative penalty. Thus, multiple penalty period will run consecutively rather than concurrently, as was permitted before OBRA. Transfers which may incur a penalty include:
- disclaimer of an inheritance or failure to exercise spousal election which diminishes the applicant's resources;
- a triggering event which makes a revocable trust irrevocable;
- addition of other owner(s) in joint tenancy or as remaindermen to real property; and
- uncompensated transfers by the community spouse after August 10, 1993, if resource eligibility is obtained under the spousal impoverishment provisions.

Questions

1. Why should people buy long-term care insurance if the Medicaid program will pay for their care?

2. Is it ethical for lawyers to explain how to transfer assets to become eligible for Medicaid? Why or why not?

c. Estate Recovery

In re Estate of Thompson
586 N.W.2d 847 (N.D. 1998)

SANDSTROM, Justice.

Lyndon R. Thompson, personal representative of the estate of Victoria Jane Thompson (the personal representative), appealed an order granting the claim of the Department of Human Services (the department) against Victoria Thompson's estate for medical assistance provided to her spouse, Nathaniel M. Thompson. We conclude 42 U.S.C. § 1396p authorizes the department's claim and North Dakota's estate recovery statute was not applied retroactively. We affirm.

I.

Nathaniel Thompson received medical assistance benefits of $58,237.30 between January 1, 1991, and his death on December 20, 1992. His wife, Victoria Thompson, died on September 15, 1995, leaving an estate of $46,507.98. A copy of an application for informal probate and appointment of a personal representative was mailed to the department. Lyndon Thompson was appointed personal representative.

The department filed a claim against Victoria Thompson's estate for $58,237.30 in medical assistance provided to Nathaniel Thompson and $9,356.79 in interest. The personal representative filed a notice of disallowance of the claim. The department petitioned the trial court for allowance of the claim. The personal representative moved for summary judgment, arguing: "The state statute [N.D. CENT. C. § 50-24.1-07] would allow recovery from the estate of a spouse while the federal statute [42 U.S.C. § 1396p(b)(1) and (2)] would not." The department also moved for summary judgment. On January 8, 1998, the court denied the personal representative's motion for summary judgment and granted the department's motion for summary judgment and petition for allowance of its claim. The personal representative appealed.

* * *

II.

The personal representative contends the trial court erred in construing 42 U.S.C. § 1396p(b)(1) to allow the department to recover medical assistance benefits provided to Nathaniel Thompson from the estate of his surviving spouse, arguing the plain meaning of the federal statute prohibits recovery of medical assistance benefits from the estate of a deceased recipient's surviving spouse.

Summary judgment is a procedure for the prompt and expeditious disposition of a controversy without trial if either party is entitled to judgment as a matter of law, if no dispute exists as to either the material facts or the inferences to be drawn from undisputed facts, or if resolving factual disputes would not alter the result. Interpretation of a statute is a question of law, which is fully reviewable by this Court.

The primary objective of statutory construction is to ascertain the Legislature's intent. In ascertaining legislative intent, we look first at the words used in the statute, giving them their ordinary, plain-language meaning. We construe statutes as a whole to give effect to each of its provisions, whenever fairly possible. "If the language of a statute is clear and unambiguous, the legislative intent is presumed clear from the face of the statute." *Medcenter One, Inc. v. North Dakota State Bd. of Pharmacy,* 1997 N.D. 54, ¶ 13, 561 N.W.2d 634. If statutory language is ambiguous, we may resort to extrinsic aids to construe the statute. For an ambiguous statute, "[w]here a public interest is affected, an interpretation is preferred which favors the public. A narrow construction should not be permitted to undermine the public policy sought to be served." 2B Norman J. Singer, *Sutherland Stat. Constr.* § 56.01 (5th ed. 1992).

When Nathaniel Thompson began receiving medical assistance benefits, N.D. CENT. C. § 50-24.1-07 provided, in part:

> On the death of any recipient of medical assistance who was sixty-five years of age or older when he received such assistance, the total amount of medical assistance paid on behalf of the decedent following his sixty-fifth birthday must be allowed as a preferred claim against the decedent's estate. . . . No claim must be paid during the lifetime of the decedent's surviving spouse . . . .

Effective August 1, 1995, N.D. CENT. C. § 50-24.1-07 was amended to provide in part:

1. On the death of any recipient of medical assistance who was <u>fifty</u>-five years of age or older when the recipient received <u>the</u> assistance, <u>and on the death of the spouse of such a deceased recipient,</u> the total amount of medical assistance paid on behalf of the <u>recipient</u> following the <u>recipient's fifty</u>-fifth birthday must be allowed as a preferred claim against the decedent's estate . . . .

2. No claim must be paid during the lifetime of the decedent's surviving spouse, <u>if any</u> . . . .

[Emphasis added.]

When Nathaniel Thompson died on November 20, 1992, 42 U.S.C. § 1396p(b) (1988) provided in part:

(b) Adjustment or recovery of medical assistance correctly paid under a State plan. (1) No adjustment or recovery of any medical assistance correctly paid on behalf of an individual under the State plan may be made, except—

. . . .

(B) in the case of any other individual who was 65 years of age or older when he received such assistance, from his estate.

(2) Any adjustment or recovery under paragraph (1) may be made only after the death of the individual's surviving spouse, if any

. . . .

Effective October 1, 1993, after Nathaniel Thompson's death, but before Victoria Thompson died on September 14, 1995, 42 U.S.C. § 1396p(b) (1994) was amended to provide in part:

(b) Adjustment or recovery of medical assistance correctly paid under a State plan. (1) No adjustment or recovery of any medical assistance correctly paid on behalf of an individual under the State plan may be made, except <u>that the State shall seek adjustment or recovery of any medical assistance correctly paid on behalf of an individual under the State plan in the case of the following individuals:</u>

. . . .

(B) In the case of <u>an</u> individual who was <u>55</u> years of age or older when <u>the individual</u> received such medical assistance, <u>the State shall seek adjustment or recovery</u> from <u>the individual's</u> estate . . . .

. . . .

(2) Any adjustment or recovery under paragraph (1) may be made only after the death of the individual's surviving spouse, if any . . . .

. . . .

<u>(4) For purposes of this subsection, the term "estate", with respect to a deceased individual—</u>

> (A) shall include all real and personal property and other assets included within the individual's estate, as defined for purposes of State probate law; and
> (B) may include, at the option of the State . . . any other real and personal property and other assets in which the individual had any legal title or interest at the time of death (to the extent of such interest), including such assets conveyed to a survivor, heir, or assign of the deceased individual through joint tenancy, tenancy in common, survivorship, life estate, living trust, or other arrangement.

[Emphasis added.]

The personal representative contends the plain meaning rule of statutory construction requires reversal because 42 U.S.C. §1396p(b)(1) does not allow recovery of medical assistance benefits from the estate of a recipient's spouse.

* * *

However, the "plain meaning" of the very broad definition of the recipient's estate in 42 U.S.C. § 1396p(b)(4) must also be considered. That definition gives the State the option to include in the recipient's "estate" from which it may recover medical assistance benefits after the death of the recipient's surviving spouse any "real and personal property and other assets in which the individual had any legal title or interest at the time of death (to the extent of such interest), including such assets conveyed to a survivor, heir, or assign of the deceased individual through joint tenancy, tenancy in common, survivorship, life estate, living trust, or other arrangement."

That expansive definition is broad enough to encompass the department's claim against the estate of a deceased spouse of a deceased recipient of medical assistance benefits for the amount of medical assistance paid out, to the extent the recipient at the time of death had any title or interest in assets which were conveyed to his or her spouse "through joint tenancy, tenancy in common, survivorship, life estate, living trust, or other arrangement."

The court in *In re Estate of Craig*, 604 N.Y.S.2d 908, 911 (N.Y. Ct. App. 1993), has also construed the 1993 amendment to 42 U.S.C. § 1396p(b): "The Omnibus Budget Reconciliation Act of 1993 (Pub.L. 103-66), signed into law on August 10, 1993, amended the estate recovery provisions of the Federal Medicaid law. This Act gives the States, at their option, the power to recover against a spouse's estate, but only against the recipient's assets that were conveyed through joint tenancy and other specified forms of survivorship."

* * *

The personal representative contends use of extrinsic aids in interpreting the federal statute also warrants reversal. The relevant amendment to 42 U.S.C. § 1396p was contained in the Omnibus Budget Reconciliation Act of 1993. The personal representative observed in his brief, "The language that was ultimately passed into law is *not* the language that was originally proposed." Relying on "the original House version of the bill," which specifically provided for recovery of medical assistance benefits "from the estate of the surviving spouse," the personal representative argues: "It may be inferred, therefore, that Congress did *not* intend to allow recovery from the estate of the surviving spouse of a recipient of medical assistance." However, this Court has held "public policy is declared by the action of the legislature not by its failure to act." *James v. Young*, 77 N.D. 451, 460, 43 N.W.2d 692, 698 (1950).

Furthermore, consideration of the purpose of the estate recovery provisions also warrants rejection of the personal representative's construction. "Allowing states to recover from the estates of persons who previously received assistance furthers the broad purpose of providing for the medical care of the needy; the greater amount recovered by the state allows the state to have more funds to provide future services." *Belshe v. Hope*, 38 Cal. Rptr. 2d 917, 925 (Cal. Ct. App. 1995). That broad purpose is furthered more fully by allowing states to trace a recipient's assets and recover them from the estate of a recipient's surviving spouse. Also, Senate and conference committee reports reflect an intent to require states to attempt estate recoveries of medical benefits and to allow states a wide latitude in seeking estate recoveries:

> *Present Law*
>
> States have the option to recover the costs of all Medicaid expenditures from the estates of deceased Medicaid claimants who were at least 65 years old when they were eligible for Medicaid. . . . Current law does not specify a definition of estate.
>
> *Committee Proposal*
>
> Extends current law as a mandate on all states. Provides a minimum definition of estate as including all real and personal property and other assets included within estate as defined by state laws governing treatment of inheritance. Allows states to expand the definition of estate to include other real or personal property or other assets in which the individual had any legally cognizable title or interest at the time of death, including such assets conveyed to a survivor, heir, or assignee of the deceased individual through joint tenancy, survivorship, life estate, living trust or other arrangement.

Senate Report No. 103-36, 103rd Cong., 1st Session (1993).

> *Medicaid Estate Recoveries (Section 13612).*—Requires States to recover the costs of nursing facility and other long-term care services furnished to Medicaid beneficiaries from the estate of such beneficiaries. . . . At the option of the State, the estate against such recovery is sought may include any real or personal property or other assets in which the beneficiary had any legal title or interest at the time of death, including the home.

House Conference Committee Report No. 103-213, 103rd Cong., 1st Session (1993), *reprinted in* 3 U.S.C.C.A.N. 1523-1524 (1993).

The 1993 amendments, and our interpretation of them, reflect the Congressional purpose to broaden states' estate recovery programs, as indicated in the history of amendments incorporated in the present Federal statute.

We conclude consideration of all the relevant statutory provisions, in light of the Congressional purpose to provide medical care for the needy, reveals a legislative intention to allow states to trace the assets of recipients of medical assistance and recover the benefits paid when the recipient's surviving spouse dies.

III.

The personal representative contends, even if the 1993 version of the federal statute is construed to allow recovery from the estate of the surviving spouse, the department's claim in this case is not legally supportable. He argues: "In 1992 even the state statute did not purport to allow recovery of medical assistance from the estate of the surviving spouse of a recipient of such benefits. Therefore, the Department is seeking to apply the post-1995 version of Section 50-24.1-07 to a claim which arose in 1992 (upon the payment of all benefits to Nathaniel Thompson). This is a classic example of an attempted, inappropriate retroactive application of a statute."

However, this Court has said "[a] statute is not retroactive because it draws upon antecedent facts for its operation or because part of the requisites of its action is drawn from time antecedent to its passing." *Public Sch. Dist. No. 35 v. Cass County Bd. of County Comm'rs,* 123 N.W.2d 37, 40 (N.D. 1963). The obligation to repay the medical assistance benefits Nathaniel Thompson received arose when he received them: "[T]he obligation to repay, if any, arises upon receipt of the benefits, i.e., prior to the decedent's death. Although the Department's ability to enforce the claim was tolled until Hooey's death, the obligation was incurred by Hooey during her lifetime." *In re Estate of Hooey,* 521 N.W.2d 85, 87 (N.D. 1994). Thus, the obligation to repay arose before Nathaniel Thompson's death in 1992, although the department's right to recover the benefits paid was suspended until the death of his surviving spouse. We conclude the department's claim is not a retroactive application of the 1995 amendment to N.D.C.C. § 50-24.1-07.

IV.

The order is affirmed.

Questions

1. If Medicaid is a program for low-income people, why would the Congress require the States to recover benefits from the estates of recipients?

2. Do you agree with the public policy arguments underlying *Thompson*? Why or why not?

C. Health-Care Decisionmaking (Short of Ending Life)

We now examine the ways in which the elderly can preserve their ability to make medical decisions, or can have this ability delegated to others, in the face of illness or incapacity. In this chapter, we concentrate substitute decisionmaking that does not involve the imposition of guardianship. Guardianship is covered in Chapter 6. We also focus on medical decisions other than those aimed at ending the patient's life; end-of-life issues are discussed in Chapter 9.

1. The Need for Substitute Decisionmaking

Mark Tanney
The Defense of Marriage Act: "A Bare Desire to Harm" An Unpopular Minority Cannot Constitute a Legitimate Governmental Interest
19 THOMAS JEFFERSON L. REV. 99, 112-13 (1997)[*]

In November 1983, a drunk driver hit Sharon Kowalski's car. She suffered brain damage and debilitating physical injuries, and was unable to act on her own behalf. Sharon had been involved in a committed relationship with her partner, Karen Thompson, for four years. They had exchanged rings, purchased a home, and had named each other as beneficiaries in their life insurance policies.

The hospital denied Karen Thompson visitation rights. Karen wasn't even told for several hours that Sharon was alive. When Sharon's parents arrived, they petitioned the court for guardianship and the right to determine visitation, eventually denying Karen all access to their daughter. During Karen's last allowed visit, Sharon, unable to speak, typed "[H]elp me. Get me out of here. Take me home with you." They would not see each other again for three-and-one-half years.

Birch Bayh
The Twenty-Fifth Amendment: Dealing with Disability
30 WAKE FOREST L. REV. 437, 439 (1995)[**]

The announcement that former President Reagan is suffering from Alzheimer's disease once again reminds us that Presidents, too, are human. They suffer from the same variety of infirmities as the rest of us. Presidents have colon, gall bladder and hemorrhoid surgeries. They are stricken by strokes, heart attacks and, tragically, assailant's bullets. Sometimes their disability is temporary; sometimes chronic or permanent.

Questions

1. What do these excerpts tell you about the need for substitute decisionmaking? Do they illustrate representative cases, or outliers?

2. What steps might Ms. Kowalski and President Reagan have taken to preserve or delegate their decisionmaking capacity?

---

[*] Copyright © 1997. Reprinted with permission.
[**] Copyright © 1995. Reprinted with permission.

2. The Common-Law Background: The Doctrine of Informed Consent

ARTHUR S. BERGER
DYING AND DEATH IN LAW AND MEDICINE:
A FORENSIC PRIMER FOR HEALTH AND LEGAL PROFESSIONALS 95-96 (1993)[*]

The doctrine of informed consent is founded on the common law principle of bodily integrity and the rights of individuals to consent before any contact is made with their bodies. This doctrine forces physicians to make disclosures to patients concerning a proposed treatment or procedure in order that any consent will be based on full medical information. Patients are to be informed about their diagnoses, the nature of the proposed treatment or procedure, its benefits and risks, alternative therapies and their benefits and risks, what may happen during the recuperation process after the procedure or treatment, and what may happen if the proposed course of action is not followed.

* * *

Generally, apart from the element of disclosure of information by the physician, there are three essential components of informed consent: (1) treatment decisions by patients must be free of coercion and voluntary; (2) patients must have the mental capacity to comprehend the nature of their medical conditions, their prognoses, and the risks of death or serious physical harm as well s the benefits of the proposed course of action and the alternative procedures or treatments possible; and (3) patients must have the mental capacity to make rational judgments. The last two factors are all-important.

Schloendorff v. Society of New York Hospital
105 N.E. 92 (N.Y. 1914)

CARDOZO, J.

In the year 1771, by royal charter of George III, the Society of the New York Hospital was organized for the care and healing of the sick. During the century and more which has since passed, it has devoted itself to that high task. It has no capital stock; it does not distribute profits; and its physicians and surgeons, both the visiting and the resident staff, serve it without pay. Those who seek it in search of health are charged nothing if they are needy, either for board or for treatment. The well-to-do are required by its by-laws to pay $7 a week for board, an amount insufficient to cover the per capita cost of maintenance. Whatever income is thus received is added to the income derived from the hospital's foundation, and helps to make it possible

---

[*] DYING AND DEATH IN LAW AND MEDICINE, Arthur S. Berger. Copyright © 1993 by Arthur S. Berger. Reproduced with permission of Greenwood Publishing Group, Inc., Westport, CT.

for the work to go on. The purpose is not profit, but charity, and the incidental revenue does not change the defendant's standing as a charitable institution.

To this hospital the plaintiff came in January, 1908. She was suffering from some disorder of the stomach. She asked the superintendent or one of his assistants what the charge would be, and was told that it would be $7 a week.

She became an inmate of the hospital, and after some weeks of treatment, the house physician, Dr. Bartlett, discovered a lump, which proved to be a fibroid tumor. He consulted the visiting physician, Dr. Stimson, who advised an operation. The plaintiff's testimony is that the character of the lump could not, so the physicians informed her, be determined without an ether examination. She consented to such an examination, but notified Dr. Bartlett, as she says, that there must be no operation. She was taken at night from the medical to the surgical ward and prepared for an operation by a nurse. On the following day ether was administered, and, while she was unconscious, a tumor was removed. Her testimony is that this was done without her consent or knowledge. She is contradicted both by Dr. Stimson and by Dr. Bartlett, as well as by many of the attendant nurses. For the purpose of this appeal, however, since a verdict was directed in favor of the defendant, her narrative, even if improbable, must be taken as true. Following the operation, and, according to the testimony of her witnesses, because of it, gangrene developed in her left arm, some of her fingers had to be amputated, and her sufferings were intense. She now seeks to charge the hospital with liability for the wrong.

Certain principles of law governing the rights and duties of hospitals, when maintained as charitable institutions have, after much discussion, become no longer doubtful. It is the settled rule that such a hospital is not liable for the negligence of its physicians and nurses in the treatment of patients.

* * *

In the case at hand, the wrong complained of is not merely negligence. It is trespass. Every human being of adult years and sound mind has a right to determine what shall be done with his own body; and a surgeon who performs an operation without his patient's consent commits an assault, for which he is liable in damages. This is true, except in cases of emergency where the patient is unconscious, and where it is necessary to operate before consent can be obtained. The fact that the wrong complained of here is trespass, rather than negligence, distinguishes this case from most of the cases that have preceded it. In such circumstances the hospital's exemption from liability can hardly rest upon implied waiver. Relatively to this transaction, the plaintiff was a stranger. She had never consented to become a patient for any purpose other than an examination under ether. She had never waived the right to recover damages for any wrong resulting from this operation, for she had forbidden the operation. In this situation, the true ground for the defendant's exemption from liability is that the relation between a hospital and its physicians is not that of master and servant. The hospital does not undertake to act through them, but merely to procure them to act upon their own responsibility. That view of the relation has the support of high authority.

* * *

The defendant undertook to procure for this plaintiff the services of a physician. It did procure them. It procured the services of Dr. Bartlett and Dr. Stimson. One or both of those physicians (if we are to credit the plaintiff's narrative) ordered that an operation be performed on her in disregard of her instructions. The administrative staff of the hospital believing in good faith that the order was a proper one, and without notice to the contrary, gave to the operating surgeons the facilities of the surgical ward. The operation was then performed. The wrong was not that of the hospital; it was that of physicians, who were not the defendant's servants, but were pursuing an independent calling, a profession sanctioned by a solemn oath, and safeguarded by stringent penalties. If, in serving their patient, they violated her commands, the responsibility is not the defendant's; it is theirs.

* * *

The conclusion, therefore, follows that the trial judge did not err in his direction of a verdict. A ruling would, indeed, be an unfortunate one that might constrain charitable institutions, as a measure of self-protection, to limit their activities. A hospital opens its doors without discrimination to all who seek its aid. It gathers in its wards a company of skilled physicians and trained nurses, and places their services at the call of the afflicted, without scrutiny of the character or the worth of those who appeal to it, looking at nothing and caring for nothing beyond the fact of their affliction. In this beneficent work, it does not subject itself to liability for damages, though the ministers of healing whom it has selected have proved unfaithful to their trust.

The judgment should be affirmed, with costs.

HISCOCK, CHASE, COLLIN, and CUDDEBACK, JJ., concur.

WILLARD BARTLETT, C. J., absent. MILLER, J., not sitting.

Questions

1. Do you agree with the court's opinion in *Schloendorff*? Why or why not?
2. How likely is it that the plaintiff's allegations were true?
3. Why is the doctrine of informed consent such an important part of American health law?

3. The Common-Law Background: Medical Decisionmaking in the Years Before Advance Directives

T.P. Gallanis
Write and Wrong: Rethinking the Way We Communicate Health-Care Decisions
31 Conn. L. Rev. 1015, 1017-18, 1020-22 (1999)[*]

Anglo-American law has long recognized the right of competent adults to accept or reject medical care. It was no less than Judge Benjamin Cardozo who famously observed that "[e]very human being of adult years and sound mind has a right to determine what shall be done with his own body." This right is so firmly established, in fact, that it applies even to patients on the verge of death, who have the option to refuse life-saving treatment. Doctors who violate a patient's right to self-determination expose themselves to liability for damages and, depending on the circumstances, to criminal prosecution.

* * *

In order to understand the development of written advance directives in the United States, we must start by considering two rules governing patient decisionmaking in the Anglo-American common law. First, the common law recognized the right of a competent adult to make medical decisions, but viewed this right as personal to each patient. Put differently, no mechanism existed at common law whereby an adult could delegate to someone else the right to make medical decisions on his or her behalf. The common law did recognize the power of attorney—a written instrument creating an agency relationship between the principal and the attorney-in-fact—but held that the power operated only while the principal was competent. In modern parlance, the power of attorney was not "durable," meaning that it did not survive the incapacity of its creator. Second, the common law contained a firm prohibition against voluntary euthanasia, treating it as suicide by the patient and murder by the assisting physician. The patient's consent provided no defense at common law for the physician, and this was true even if the patient was in extreme pain and was dying anyway. As an English judge explained, the definition of murder did not involve an inquiry into the reason behind the killing but only into the defendant's intention; if the defendant had a "definite intention to kill," then the act of killing constituted a murder.

In reaction to the second of these common-law rules, a movement to legalize voluntary euthanasia began in England in the early twentieth century. Its ideological roots have been traced back to the Renaissance, but the birth of the organized movement in England occurred in 1931, the year in which the president of the Society of Medical Officers of Health, Dr. Killick Millard, used his presidential address to advocate the legalization of euthanasia. This speech galvanized supporters of reform, who quickly organized the Voluntary Euthanasia Legalization Society. With the Society's

---

[*] Copyright © 1999. Reprinted with permission.

lobbying, a bill to permit voluntary euthanasia was introduced in the House of Lords in 1936. The bill would have instituted a four-step procedure for requesting an assisted death. First, the patient would have been required to sign a statutory application in the presence of two witnesses. Second, the patient would have been required to obtain two medical certificates stating that he or she had a terminal illness and was in severe pain. Third, the application and certificates would have been sent to a "euthanasia referee" appointed by the Minister of Health. Fourth, the referee would have interviewed the patient to ensure that the requirements of the legislation had been met and that euthanasia was truly desired. If the referee was satisfied, and if all of the formalities had been observed, then death would have been administered in the presence of an official witness, such as a justice of the peace. Both in spite of these lengthy safeguards and also because of them, the bill generated a heated discussion, with significant opposition coming from the Church of England and some leading members of the medical profession. In December 1936, the bill was defeated by a nearly three-to-one margin.

Two years later, in 1938, the first organization for voluntary euthanasia appeared in the United States. Like its English counterpart, the Euthanasia Society of America drafted a piece of proposed legislation to permit patients to choose their own death. Under the American bill, the patient would have been required to sign a petition in the presence of two witnesses and then file it, along with a physician's certificate attesting to the petitioner's severe pain and terminal illness, with a state supreme court justice or county court judge. The judge or justice would then have appointed a committee of three persons, two of whom were required to be physicians, to examine the patient and make a recommendation. If the recommendation favored euthanasia, the judge or justice would have been required to grant the petition "unless there is reason to believe that the [committee's] report is erroneous or untrue." After the granting of the petition, euthanasia would have been administered in the presence of at least two members of the examining committee. As in England, however, attempts at reform in the United States proved unsuccessful. Efforts to introduce this legislation in New York, for example, failed repeatedly for lack of a sponsor; and in Nebraska, a bill with some important differences from the Society's proposal was soundly defeated.

For the next forty years, advocates of voluntary euthanasia continued unsuccessfully to press for change in England and in the United States. They also petitioned the United Nations to recognize euthanasia for the terminally ill as a human right, but this endeavor likewise failed.

Questions

1. Why did the common law permit delegation only by competent principals?
2. Why is the history of the movement for legalized euthanasia relevant to the development of advance directives?

4. The Rise of Advance Medical Directives

a. The Three Types of Advance Directives

T.P. Gallanis
Write and Wrong: Rethinking the Way We Communicate Health-Care Decisions
31 CONN. L. REV. 1015, 1018-19 (1999)[*]

Today, the law provides various documentary mechanisms, known collectively as advance medical directives, by which patients can preserve or delegate their authority to make health-care decisions in the event of incapacity. These mechanisms, which are creatures of state rather than federal law and thus vary from jurisdiction to jurisdiction, fall into three broad categories. First, *instructional directives* allow people to put their wishes into writing for future reference. These directives are frequently, but confusingly, called "living wills." Second, *health-care proxies* allow people to appoint in writing surrogate decision-makers, typically spouses or close relatives, to act on their behalf. These proxy documents are often known by their longer name: durable powers of attorney for health care. Third, *combined directives* contain both instructional and delegational elements; they name a health-care proxy but also explain the patient's wishes, usually about the application of life-sustaining treatment.

Questions

Do you understand the differences among these three types of directives? What are their respective advantages and disadvantages?

b. Luis Kutner and the Birth of the Living Will

George J. Annas
The Health Care Proxy and the Living Will
324 NEW ENG. J. MED. 1210, 1210 (1991)[**]

The term "living will" was coined by Luis Kutner in 1969 to describe a document in which a competent adult sets forth directions regarding medical treatment in the event of his or her future incapacitation. The document is a will in the sense that it spells out the person's directions. It is "living" because it takes effect before death.

---

[*] Copyright © 1999. Reprinted with permission.
[**] Copyright © 1991 Massachusetts Medical Society. All rights reserved.

Luis Kutner
Due Process of Euthanasia: The Living Will, A Proposal
44 IND. L.J. 539, 550-52 (1969)*

Where a patient undergoes surgery or other radical treatment, the surgeon or the hospital will require him to sign a legal statement indicating his consent to the treatment. The patient, however, while still retaining his mental faculties and the ability to convey his thoughts, could append to such a document a clause providing that, if his condition becomes incurable and his bodily state vegetative with no possibility that he could recover his complete faculties, his consent to further treatment would be terminated. The physician would then be precluded from prescribing further surgery, radiation, drugs or the running of resuscitating and other machinery, and the patient would be permitted to die by virtue of the physician's inaction.

The patient may not have had, however, the opportunity to give his consent at any point before treatment. He may have become the victim of a sudden accident or a stroke or coronary. Therefore, the suggested solution is that the individual, while fully in control of his faculties and his ability to express himself, indicate to what extent he would consent to treatment. The document indicating such consent may be referred to as "a *living will*," "a declaration determining the termination of life," "testament permitting death," "declaration of bodily autonomy," "declaration for ending treatment," "body trust," or other similar reference.

* * *

The document would be notarized and attested to by at least two witnesses who would affirm that the maker was of sound mind and acted of his own free will. The individual could carry the document on his person at all times, while his wife, his personal physician, a lawyer or confidant would have the original copy.

* * *

The individual could at any time, before reaching the comatose state, revoke the document. Personal possession of the document would create a strong presumption that he regards it as still binding.

* * *

A *living will* could only be made by a person who is capable of giving his consent to treatment. A person who is a minor, institutionalized, or adjudged incompetent could not make such a declaration. A guardian should not be permitted to make such a declaration on behalf of his ward nor a parent on behalf of his child.

* * *

The *living will* is analogous to a revocable or conditional trust with the patient's body as the *res*, the patient as the beneficiary and grantor, and the doctor and hospi-

---

* Copyright © 1969. Reprinted with permission.

tal as the trustees. The doctor is given authority to act as the trustee of the patient's body by virtue of the patient's consent to treatment. He is obligated to exercise due care and is subject to liability for negligence. The patient is free at any time to revoke the trust. From another perspective, the patient in giving consent to treatment is limiting the authority the doctor and other medical persons may exercise over his body. The patient has the ultimate right to decide what is to be done with him.

T.P. Gallanis
Write and Wrong: Rethinking the Way We Communicate Health-Care Decisions
31 CONN. L. REV. 1015, 1023 (1999)[*]

From the beginning, Kutner's proposal attracted significant interest. But legislative reform seemed impossible until 1975, when the case of Karen Ann Quinlan captured America's attention.

Questions

1. How does a living will work?
2. How apt are Mr. Kutner's analogies to trusts and testamentary wills?

c. **The *Quinlan* Case and its Aftermath**

T.P. Gallanis
Write and Wrong: Rethinking the Way We Communicate Health-Care Decisions
31 CONN. L. REV. 1015, 1023-24 (1999)[**]

[On April 15, 1975,] the 21-year-old Quinlan was admitted to a New Jersey hospital in a coma. She was unable to breathe on her own and was put on a mechanical respirator. All attempts to revive her were unsuccessful, and her doctors described her as being in a persistent vegetative state. Five months later, seeing no improvement in her condition, Quinlan's parents filed an action for guardianship, for the express purpose of turning off the respirator and allowing their daughter to die. In the documents submitted to the Chancery court, Quinlan's parents emphasized their daughter's previous expressions of intention: on two separate occasions, she had allegedly mentioned that "she would not wish her life to be prolonged through the futile use of extraordinary medical measures." The Chancery court nevertheless rejected their petition, holding that "the act of removing Karen from the respirator . . . would be a homicide." But the New Jersey Supreme Court disagreed. In a unanimous opinion

---

[*] Copyright © 1999. Reprinted with permission.
[**] Copyright © 1999. Reprinted with permission.

rendered in March 1976, the justices held that Quinlan's right to privacy included the right to terminate extraordinary medical treatment; that this right could legally be asserted by her guardian; and that Quinlan's father was best suited to serve in that position.

That same year, and in response to the Quinlan litigation, California became the first state to pass legislation authorizing the use of a living will. The California Natural Death Act of 1976 explicitly recognized "the right of an adult person to make a written directive instructing his physician to withhold or withdraw life-sustaining procedures in the event of a terminal condition." The statute contained a form to be used and required it to be signed by the patient in the presence of two attesting witnesses. The statute also provided that each form would be valid only for five years, after which time a freshly-executed form would be needed. Although the California legislation was not adopted elsewhere verbatim, the passage of the Natural Death Act quickly spurred developments in other states. In the three years between 1977 and 1979, for example, Arkansas, Kansas, New Mexico, North Carolina, Texas, and Washington each enacted its own version of a living will statute.

Questions

1. Why was the *Quinlan* litigation so influential?

2. Read, in the statutory supplement, § 7186.5 of the current version of the California Natural Death Act. Has the five-year recertification requirement, present in the 1976 Act, been retained? Do you agree with the California legislature's decision on this point?

d. The Living Will Today

T.P. Gallanis
Write and Wrong: Rethinking the Way We Communicate Health-Care Decisions
31 CONN. L. REV. 1015, 1025-26 (1999)[*]

[Living wills] are currently authorized in 49 states and the District of Columbia, with variations in the law from state to state. In each jurisdiction, however, the central purpose of an instructional directive is the same: to enable the written preservation of patient preferences for future reference.

* * *

The one state missing from that list is Massachusetts, which has neither living will legislation nor any reported cases in which the validity of a living will has been litigated.

---

[*] Copyright © 1999. Reprinted with permission.

Question

What accounts for the widespread enactment of living-will legislation?

e. The Rise of Health-Care Proxies

T.P. Gallanis
Write and Wrong: Rethinking the Way We Communicate Health-Care Decisions
31 CONN. L. REV. 1015, 1024-25 (1999)*

In the 1980s . . . there was developing an alternative to the living will, namely the durable power of attorney. Unlike powers of attorney at common law, these durable powers created an agency relationship that remained in force even if the principal later became incapacitated. As originally designed, durable powers of attorney dealt with financial matters and allowed an agent to transact business on the principal's behalf. Questions arose about whether these powers might be used for medical decision-making, and these questions prompted a number of jurisdictions to enact legislation specifically authorizing durable powers for health care. The movement in favor of such powers received a considerable boost in 1990, when Justice O'Connor praised them as "a valuable additional safeguard to the patient's interest in directing his medical care."

* * *

The first state to permit durable powers of attorney for health care was Delaware in 1982. Other states quickly followed Delaware's lead.

Cruzan v. Director, Missouri Department of Health
497 U.S. 261, 290-92 (1990)

O'CONNOR, J., concurring.

Delegating the authority to make medical decisions to a family member or friend is becoming a common method of planning for the future. Several States have recognized the practical wisdom of such a procedure by enacting durable power of attorney statutes that specifically authorize an individual to appoint a surrogate to make medical treatment decisions. Some state courts have suggested that an agent appointed pursuant to a general durable power of attorney statute would also be empowered to make health care decisions on behalf of the patient. Other States allow an individual to designate a proxy to carry out the intent of a living will. These procedures for surrogate decisionmaking, which appear to be rapidly gaining in acceptance, may be a valuable additional safeguard of the patient's interest in directing his

---

* Copyright © 1999. Reprinted with permission.

medical care. Moreover, as patients are likely to select a family member as a surrogate, giving effect to a proxy's decisions may also protect the "freedom of personal choice in matters of . . . family life."

Questions

1. What is a health-care proxy? How does it differ from a living will?

2. Why might a patient choose to execute a proxy rather than a living will, or vice versa?

f. Health-Care Proxies Today

T.P. Gallanis
Write and Wrong: Rethinking the Way We Communicate Health-Care Decisions
31 CONN. L. REV. 1015, 1029 (1999)[*]

Today . . . all fifty states and the District of Columbia authorize the use of written proxies, which are often known more formally as durable powers of attorney for health care. The law governing these proxies varies from state to state, but all of the statutory schemes enable people to execute documents transferring decision-making authority to representatives of their choosing.

Question

What accounts for the universal acceptance in the United States of health-care proxies, given that they were not permitted at common law?

5. Drafting Written Directives: The Use of Statutory Forms

In Chapter 5, we saw that many states have a statutory form for powers of attorney for property. The same is true with respect to living wills and powers of attorney for health care. Lawyers drafting advance directives in these states must be attentive to whether the statutory form is presented merely as a model, or whether substantially the same language must be used. In either case, tracking the language of the statutory form (to the extent that it represents the wishes of the client) will ensure the directive's validity.

To answer the following questions, read in the statutory supplement: (a) Hawaii Revised Statutes § 551D-2.6; and (b) Oregon Revised Statutes § 127.531.

---

[*] Copyright © 1999. Reprinted with permission.

Questions

Is the statutory form in Hawaii merely a suggested model, or should all forms track the language of the statute? What about the statutory form in Oregon?

6. The Uniform Health-Care Decisions Act

In connection with the following excerpt, skim through the provisions of the Uniform Health-Care Decisions Act ("UHCDA"), in the statutory supplement.

Uniform Health-Care Decisions Act (1993), Historical Notes[*]

The Uniform Health-Care Decisions Act was approved by the National Conference of Commissioners on Uniform State Laws in 1993.

* * *

Since the Supreme Court's decision in *Cruzan v. Commissioner, Missouri Department of Health*, 497 U.S. 261 (1990), significant change has occurred in state legislation on health-care decision making. Every state now has legislation authorizing the use of some sort of advance health-care directive. All but a few states authorize what is typically known as a living will. Nearly all states have statutes authorizing the use of powers of attorney for health care. In addition, a majority of states have statutes allowing family members, and in some cases close friends, to make health-care decisions for adult individuals who lack capacity.

This state legislation, however, has developed in fits and starts, resulting in an often fragmented, incomplete, and sometimes inconsistent set of rules. Statutes enacted within a state often conflict and conflicts between statutes of different states are common. In an increasingly mobile society where an advance health-care directive given in one state must frequently be implemented in another, there is a need for greater uniformity.

The Health-Care Decisions Act was drafted with this confused situation in mind. The Act is built around the following concepts. First, the Act acknowledges the right of a competent individual to decide all aspects of his or her own health care in all circumstances, including the right to decline health care or to direct that health care be discontinued, even if death ensues. An individual's instructions may extend to any and all health-care decisions that might arise and, unless limited by the principal, an agent has authority to make all health-care decisions which the individual could have made. The Act recognizes and validates an individual's authority to define the scope of an instruction or agency as broadly or as narrowly as the individual chooses.

---

[*] Copyright © 1993. Reprinted with permission.

Second, the Act is comprehensive and will enable an enacting jurisdiction to replace its existing legislation on the subject with a single statute. The Act authorizes health-care decisions to be made by an agent who is designated to decide when an individual cannot or does not wish to; by a designated surrogate, family member, or close friend when an individual is unable to act and no guardian or agent has been appointed or is reasonably available; or by a court having jurisdiction as decision maker of last resort.

Third, the Act is designed to simplify and facilitate the making of advance health-care directives. An instruction may be either written or oral. A power of attorney for health care, while it must be in writing, need not be witnessed or acknowledged. In addition, an optional form for the making of a directive is provided.

Fourth, the Act seeks to ensure to the extent possible that decisions about an individual's health care will be governed by the individual's own desires concerning the issues to be resolved. The Act requires an agent or surrogate authorized to make health-care decisions for an individual to make those decisions in accordance with the instructions and other wishes of the individual to the extent known. Otherwise, the agent or surrogate must make those decisions in accordance with the best interest of the individual but in light of the individual's personal values known to the agent or surrogate. Furthermore, the Act requires a guardian to comply with a ward's previously given instructions and prohibits a guardian from revoking the ward's advance health-care directive without express court approval.

Fifth, the Act addresses compliance by health-care providers and institutions. A health-care provider or institution must comply with an instruction of the patient and with a reasonable interpretation of that instruction or other health-care decision made by a person then authorized to make health-care decisions for the patient. The obligation to comply is not absolute, however. A health-care provider or institution may decline to honor an instruction or decision for reasons of conscience or if the instruction or decision requires the provision of medically ineffective care or care contrary to applicable health-care standards.

Sixth, the Act provides a procedure for the resolution of disputes. While the Act is in general to be effectuated without litigation, situations will arise where resort to the courts may be necessary. For that reason, the Act authorizes the court to enjoin or direct a health-care decision or order other equitable relief and specifies who is entitled to bring a petition[.]

Questions

1. What improvements on earlier legislation does the UHCDA make?

2. Is the form in UHCDA § 4 optional or mandatory? Do you agree with the drafters' decision on this point?

7. Encouraging the Use of Advance Directives: The Patient Self-Determination Act

In connection with the following excerpt, read in the statutory supplement: the Patient Self-Determination Act ("PSDA") (Pub. L. 101-508, §§ 4206, 4751), which was passed as a part of the Omnibus Budget Reconciliation Act of 1990.

Edward J. Larson & Thomas A. Eaton
The Limits of Advance Directives: A History and Assessment of the Patient Self-Determination Act
32 WAKE FOREST L. REV. 249, 250, 256-58, 260-61, 269-71, 274, 276-79, 281-85 (1997)[*]

Society's preference for advance directives is reflected in the Patient Self-Determination Act (PSDA). This federal statute requires certain health care facilities receiving Medicare or Medicaid funds to advise patients of their rights under state law to execute advance directives. It was enacted by Congress [in 1990] with little fanfare as a budget amendment and, consequently, has little formal legislative history. On the one hand, the PSDA is a relatively simple law. It only requires health care facilities to distribute information about rights existing under state law. On the other hand, the PSDA is remarkably ambitious in that it envisions the education of millions of people about complex legal rights. Proponents of the PSDA believed that if given information, more people would execute advance directives and thereby reduce the number of difficult ethical and legal issues presented when treatment decisions are made regarding incompetent patients.

The PSDA has now been in effect for more than five years and has been the subject of much study. Has the PSDA been a success? This article examines this question in three parts. In Part I, we discuss the history of the PSDA and identify the goals and concerns expressed by significant players in the legislative process. In Part II, we summarize studies that directly or indirectly measure the extent to which the PSDA advances its goals or produces the feared concerns. Our overall conclusion is that although the PSDA has produced little measurable harm, it has achieved only limited success in advancing its goals. The empirical literature convinces us that the PSDA and the strategy of relying on advance directives cannot completely address the problem of treatment decisionmaking for incompetent patients. We conclude in Part III with a brief discussion of additional measures that might be taken to deal with this problem

* * *

Our review of the legislative history reveals that the principal proponents of the PSDA expressed six clearly distinguishable goals for the Act. Of course, both sup-

---

[*] Copyright © 1997. Reprinted with permission.

porters and opponents of the PSDA occasionally alluded to other purposes for the legislation, and all proponents did not share the same objectives. Nevertheless, we will identify the six goals that feature prominently in the legislative history.

1. *"Empower people"*

Throughout the course of congressional consideration of the PSDA, [one of the Act's sponsors, U.S. Representative Sander Levin] repeatedly asserted that his sole purpose was to "empower people" by informing them of their legal rights.

* * *

2. *More advance directives*

Naturally, most proponents of the PSDA believe in the value of people executing advance directives, and hoped that the legislation would lead to greater use of such documents.

* * *

3. *Honoring advance directives*

The original Senate version of the PSDA states: "It is the purpose of this Act to ensure that a patient's right to self-determination in health care decisions be communicated and protected."

* * *

4. *More state advance directive statutes*

A stated objective of [the] original Senate bill was to require that every state enact "legislation recognizing the validity of advance directives." Even though the state-law mandate did not survive, [Senator John Danforth, one of the Act's sponsors] hoped to achieve this objective through the alternative requirement that each state "develop a written description of the law of the State (whether statutory or as recognized by the courts of the State) concerning advance directives."

* * *

5. *Less treatment*

When Elizabeth McCloskey [one of the staffers who worked on the bill] arrived for her first day of work for Senator Danforth in 1989, she was assigned responsibility for the PSDA and was greeted by a letter from her new boss asking: "Is it good to extend the life of a senile 90 year old who wears diapers?" Clearly Danforth believed that the correct answer to this question was no, and hoped that the PSDA would lead to less medical treatment being given at the end of life.

* * *

6. *Medical cost control*

A legislative goal of less terminal medical treatment inevitably suggests the aim of reduced health care spending, especially since the federal government pays for most end-of-life treatment through Medicare.

* * *

[T]he PSDA has been successful in generating uniform and consumer-friendly statements of law for patients in the vast majority of states. This, of course, is but the first step in empowering patients. We now turn to the method and manner by which this information is conveyed to patients.

* * *

The method and manner of conveying information can affect how well it is understood. Studies suggest that presentation of PSDA materials varies according to the type of health care facility. Hospitals tend to implement the PSDA in a perfunctory manner. Most patients are simply given a pamphlet or sheet of paper when they are admitted to the hospital.

* * *

Nursing homes, by contrast, appear to make a more comprehensive effort at educating their residents about advance directives. Nursing homes are more likely than hospitals to have clear institutional policies and a designated person who implements the PSDA.

* * *

Although the public is generally familiar with advance directives, the depth of knowledge is suspect. In one study, ninety-four percent of hospital patients who had previously received PSDA materials professed to know what a living will was, but only forty-one percent could correctly define the term and only thirty-two percent could correctly identify the clinical circumstances in which the document would take effect. Fewer than half of these patients even claimed to be familiar with a durable power of attorney. The authors [of the study] conclude that levels of understanding of living wills and durable powers of attorney for health care were not affected by materials distributed pursuant to the PSDA. Other studies suggest that elderly patients have difficulty understanding the terminology of advance directives, often confuse living wills with testamentary wills, and demonstrate confusion over the concept of a power of attorney. Moreover, one study found that "patients who said they had completed a living will did not understand this document's definition or its clinical application better than patients who said they had not completed one."

* * *

The absence of active physician participation in the process may seriously limit the effectiveness of the PSDA. Many studies report that patients want information about advance directives and would prefer to receive it in face-to-face discussions with their physicians prior to admission to a hospital or other health care facility. Prior to the enactment of the PSDA, doctors rarely initiated such discussions. Although the PSDA does not impose any obligation on physicians to discuss advance directives with their patients, and the AMA made clear its opposition to any such mandate, proponents of the legislation hoped it would lead to better doctor-patient communications. The available evidence suggests that it has not.

* * *

The PSDA is perceived by some as reflecting a European-American cultural prototype that may not be sensitive to the values of other ethnic groups. The assumptions that individuals should be empowered to direct end-of-life treatment decisions is not necessarily shared by all communities. Many Asian and Hispanic-Americans, for example, are reported to believe that medical decisions should be made by the family rather than the individual patient.

* * *

The substantive goals of the PSDA are relatively straight-forward. Key proponents of the legislation hoped that the PSDA would cause more people to execute advance directives, which would be honored by treating physicians. They hoped that more advance directives would therefore lead to less aggressive end-of-life treatment, resulting in a reduction of medical costs. As discussed below, the available evidence does not indicate that the Act has achieved much with regard to these goals.

* * *

1. *The impact of the PSDA on the number of advance directives*

The impact of the PSDA on the number of advance directives is fairly easy to measure. Before the enactment of the PSDA, researchers estimated that between four and twenty-eight percent of the population had advance directives, with the most common estimates being in the range of fifteen to twenty percent. Numerous studies have concluded that the PSDA has not produced a significant increase in these numbers.

* * *

2. *Honoring advance directives*

The extent to which medical decisionmaking is influenced by advance directives is more difficult to determine . . . . The available evidence suggests, however, that most end-of-life treatment decisions are not significantly driven by advance directives.

* * *

3. *The impact of advance directives on treatment and cost of end-of- life medical care*

As previously discussed, some proponents of the PSDA believed that the legislation would bring about a greater use of advance directives which, in turn, would produce less aggressive end-of-life treatment and substantial cost savings.

* * *

Several studies report substantial differences in the intensity and cost of medical care received by patients with advance directives when compared to patients without advance directives.

* * *

Other studies, however, conclude that advance directives have little or no impact on the intensity or cost of terminal medical care.

* * *

[The authors conclude:] Our review of the empirical literature convinces us that the PSDA has been only a modest success. It has resulted in the drafting of relatively simple and uniform statements of state laws regarding advance directives and patients' rights to accept or refuse medical treatment. This information appears to be routinely distributed to virtually all hospital patients and nursing home residents upon admission. Nursing homes appear to take an active role in attempting to educate their residents about advance directives, while hospital compliance with the PSDA appears to be limited to distributing a piece of paper during the admissions process. There is little evidence that distribution of PSDA materials produces undue anxiety or that vulnerable populations are being coerced into executing advance directives.

We characterize these successes as modest, however. Most studies suggest that the distribution of PSDA materials has done little to increase the public's level of understanding of advance directives. Doctor-patient communication about advance directives and end-of-life medical decisionmaking continues to be quite poor. Although there has been a small increase in the percentage of the public who have executed an advance directive, a large majority of the population has not done so. Several studies suggest that we have reached a "ceiling" on the percentage of people we can expect to have signed advance directives. Even for the minority of patients who have an advance directive, these documents often do not appear to influence actual treatment decisions. Moreover, the impact of advance directives on the level and cost of end-of-life treatment is not clear. Even under optimal circumstances, potential cost savings appear to be much less than first suggested by proponents of advance directives.

Questions

1. To what extent do you agree with the objectives of the PSDA?
2. Why was the PSDA not more successful at achieving these objectives? What might have been done differently?

8. Alternatives to Written Directives

T.P. Gallanis
Write and Wrong: Rethinking the Way We Communicate Health-Care Decisions
31 CONN. L. REV. 1015, 1026-33 (1999)[*]

Given the attractiveness in principle of instructional directives, one would expect them to have been executed by a significant percentage of the population; but there is growing evidence to the contrary. A recent study of terminally ill patients—a group particularly likely to have considered the question—revealed that less than 15 percent had executed an advance directive of any sort. A different study, focusing on instructional directives (and excluding health-care proxies) but sampling the population at large, yielded a smaller percentage: just under 10 percent of a random sample of the population had executed a living will.

This reticence on the part of the American public is well-founded, because instructional directives as currently conceived pose at least four difficulties, which I have labeled "the four uncertainties." The first of these is *uncertainty of preparation*. Like most legal documents, instructional directives are complicated; preparing and executing them is difficult without legal knowledge. Self-help resources, in paper and electronic formats, are available, but these require a moderate level of skill to find and interpret; they also demand a high level of consumer confidence in their quality. People unsure about the reliability of this information, or hesitant about their ability to understand and use it, are not likely to prepare and sign documents having legal effects. In this regard, it is instructive to contrast the creation of a trust with the making of an anatomical gift. People rarely create trusts without legal counsel, in part because the documents governing the transaction are complicated; but people routinely make anatomical gifts using their driver's licenses without consulting a lawyer, because the legal formalities can be easily understood and met. In terms of their complexity, instructional directives today are more like trust declarations than anatomical gifts. In order for these directives to increase substantially in use, they need to become easier for members of the public to understand and execute without professional assistance.

The second problem with written instructional directives is *uncertainty of execution*. It is not enough simply to execute a directive; the directive must also be communicated to medical personnel. In practice, health-care workers often do not know whether a given patient has executed an instructional directive. This problem is particularly acute for paramedics, and it is easy to understand why. Upon arriving at the scene, they are legally bound to take all reasonable steps to bring an unconscious patient back to life. In these circumstances, a directive containing provisions to the contrary is of value only if it can be produced quickly. But like other documents, a written directive is rarely kept on the person of its creator. In order for these directives to become more effective, it is essential that they be more easily and reliably communicated to the personnel they are designed to direct.

---

[1] Copyright © 1999. Reprinted with permission.

The third problem with documentary instructional directives is *uncertainty of revocation*. Even if a patient has executed a directive of which the relevant health-care workers are aware, there is still the lingering possibility that the directive has been modified or revoked. The Uniform Health-Care Decisions Act, which on this point is typical of state legislation, allows instructional directives to be revoked or modified by subsequently-executed writings. Without any guarantee that they have been given a patient's most recent documents, health-care providers must therefore act, or refrain from acting, based on their own judgments about the ongoing validity of the directives presented to them. There are, to be sure, legal protections for health-care workers who rely in good faith on directives that later turn out to have been revoked, but these *ex post* immunities are a second-best solution. A better approach would eliminate the problem entirely by making it simple to determine whether or not a given directive remains in force.

Finally, the fourth problem with instructional directives is *uncertainty of interpretation*. A validly-executed directive, promptly communicated and unrevoked, is worthwhile only to the extent that it can be interpreted easily and accurately by medical personnel. Recent studies suggest that most instructional directives fail this test. The study of terminally ill patients referred to earlier, for example, revealed that out of 688 directives, only 22 contained instructions that were sufficiently specific to guide medical care. General commands, such as "no heroic measures," do not give doctors enough information about how to respond to particular circumstances that may or may not have been foreseen by the patient. To be fully effective, instructional directives should contain detailed directions covering a range of possible contingencies. Yet here is where the first and fourth uncertainties work against each other; the more skill it takes to draft a useful directive, the less likely it becomes that a non-lawyer can, with any confidence, prepare it.

* * *

In their current form, health-care proxies suffer from the first three of the four uncertainties mentioned earlier. They suffer from uncertainty of preparation, because the rules governing their creation and execution are complicated and unfamiliar to non-professionals (although probably to a lesser degree than living wills, because proxies need not contain medical instructions). Written proxies also suffer from uncertainty of execution, particularly in emergencies, because they are rarely kept on hand and often cannot be quickly communicated to medical personnel. Finally, written proxies suffer from uncertainty of revocation, because all 51 jurisdictions in which they exist permit them to be modified or annulled by subsequent writings.

What about the fourth uncertainty, uncertainty of interpretation? On this point, health-care proxies, unlike instructional directives, present relatively few difficulties. It is easy to see why. By naming a substitute decision-maker rather than attempting to spell out the patient's wishes, proxies by their nature contain fewer potential ambiguities and thus raise fewer interpretive problems than living wills. The trade-off, however, is that proxies raise an uncertainty of their own, which might be termed *uncertainty of agent location*. Health-care agents (the surrogates named in the proxies) do not always accompany their principals and thus can be difficult to locate.

It is remarkable that, of the 39 state statutes that contain proxy forms, not one explicitly requests the addresses and telephone numbers of both the agent's residence and workplace. A health-care proxy, although easier than a living will to interpret, is of little value if the agent it names cannot be timely reached.

* * *

In order to make advance directives work better, the law must stop thinking of them merely as written instruments analogous to wills and common-law powers of attorney. This will not be easy to do, however; such analogies, as we have seen, have been an important part of these documents' history. Yet in many respects it is precisely these analogies that have created the barriers to their widespread and effective use.

* * *

The exact form the new advance directives should take is an open question, and the answer will change as technology develops. But three possible options should be mentioned here. The first option, which is currently being tested, is the use of engraved bracelets worn on the wrist. These bracelets are analogous to the well-known "Medic Alert" jewelry that some people wear to inform health-care workers about life-threatening allergies or other unusual medical conditions. The use of such bracelets to communicate information about medical *decisions* may well prove promising. At the moment, however, the bracelets are so new that it is difficult to judge their appeal and effectiveness. A second option, now only in the experimental stages, is a military "dog tag" that would contain "a computerized version of the wearer's current health status, medical history, . . . [and] other data of use to physicians." This device is under development for members of the armed forces; but if the technology works well, the use of the dog tag could easily spread to the civilian community. Also on the drawing board is the third option that should be mentioned: a so-called "smart" identification card that would carry financial and medical data on a computer chip. Experimental and relatively limited versions of smart cards are now being tested around the globe, dealing with everything from the purchase of fast food on Long Island to the processing of health insurance claims in Germany. In the not-too-distant future, according to some analysts, each smart card will contain its owner's complete medical dossier, which could readily include any advance directives he or she may have executed.

Questions

1. Do you agree that written directives pose inherent difficulties?
2. What are the advantages and disadvantages of the alternatives?

9. Decisionmaking in the Absence of an Advance Directive: Surrogacy Statutes

Christine H. Nooning
Surrogate Health Care Decision Making: The Pennsylvania Supreme Court Recognizes the Right of an Individual in a Permanent Vegetative State to Refuse Life-Sustaining Measures Through a Surrogate Decision Maker
35 Duq. L. Rev. 849, 870-72 (1997)[*]

Although Pennsylvania has yet to enact legislation setting forth a procedure for a surrogate to follow when making a health care decision on behalf of another, at least eighteen states and the District of Columbia have passed legislation governing the issue of surrogate health care decision making. The following is a survey of these nineteen jurisdictions.

All nineteen of the jurisdictions have provided by statute a list of persons who may act as a surrogate for an incompetent patient. Those persons authorized by statute to make a health care decision (if no guardian has been appointed) generally include the patient's spouse, adult child, parent, adult sibling, grandparent and/or adult grandchild. Several jurisdictions additionally provide that either a competent relative of the patient or the patient's nearest living relative may make the health care decision. Four states, including Arizona, Idaho, Oregon and South Carolina also allow the attending physician to make the decision if no other person on the list can be located. Finally, Connecticut alone authorizes only the incompetent patient's attending physician to make [a] health care decision to terminate life-sustaining treatment.

Richard S. Saver
Critical Care Research and Informed Consent
75 N.C. L. Rev. 205, 266 (1996)[**]

A more troubling problem of increased use of surrogate consent mechanisms is the danger that surrogates will substitute their own interests for the patient's. As already noted, family members may have conflicts of interest when acting as surrogates. Equally problematic is that even when acting with the best of intentions, surrogates may simply not be accurate predictors of what the patient wanted because of the inherent subjectivity of the factors and judgments involved. Relying upon intuitive, subjective decision-making by surrogate family members makes judicial reviewability of such decisions nearly impossible and thus offers little protection to patients who do not have idealized "selfless, loving families" to rely upon. Studies indicate that surrogates, even close family members, often do not adequately understand the preferences of the patients for whom they are acting.

---

[*] Copyright © 1997. Reprinted with permission.
[**] Copyright 1996 by the North Carolina Law Review Association. Reprinted with permission.

Questions

1. In the statutory supplement, read § 25 of the Illinois Health Care Surrogate Act (755 Illinois Compiled Statutes 40/25). Compare its list of potential surrogates with the list in § 5 of the UHCDA. Are there ways in which either list is under- or over-inclusive?

2. What are the advantages and disadvantages of having statutorily-designated surrogates make medical decisions?

10. The Standard(s) for Substitute Decisionmaking

Norman L. Cantor
Discarding Substituted Judgment and Best Interests: Toward a Constructive Preference Standard for Dying, Previously Competent Patients Without Advance Instructions
8 RUTGERS L. REV. 1193, 1200-02, 1205, 1208, 1210-11,
1220-23, 1225, 1241-42 (1996)[*]

In 1983, when a presidential commission studied medical decisionmaking, the prevailing standards for incompetent patients seemed fairly straightforward to the commissioners. A surrogate's initial focus would be substituted judgment, seeking to replicate what the now-incompetent patient would have decided, if competent. The commission also mentioned an "objective" best interests standard aimed at promoting the incompetent patient's well being without reference to that patient's previous preferences. The commission apparently viewed the best interests test as applicable to never-competent patients, or to previously competent patients whose actual preferences could not be discerned using a substituted judgment approach.

In the thirteen years since the President's Commission reported, the picture regarding decisionmaking criteria has become more nuanced and complicated. It is now clear that there is more than one version of the substituted judgment standard. Each version has generated some dissatisfaction and criticism. Dispute also exists regarding when the best interests standard prevails, the soundness of a best interests standard, and the factors that comprise such a standard.

* * *

An incompetent person, by definition, lacks capacity to understand and weigh the available options regarding critical medical decisions. A surrogate decisionmaker must employ some standard in making such decisions on behalf of the patient. One possible standard is to seek to replicate the decision that the now-incompetent patient would make if that patient were somehow competent and aware of all the circumstances. This general approach is known as substituted judgment though, as will be seen, the substituted judgment concept is subject to several variations. [These vari-

---

[*] Copyright © 1996. Reprinted with permission.

ations (discussed next) exist primarily with respect to end-of-life decisionmaking, and are thus more relevant to the material in Chapter 9 than to the material discussed here.—Eds.]

* * *

In a few jurisdictions, courts have conditioned removal of life support from an incompetent patient on a demonstration that the patient, while competent, clearly indicated a preference for that course of action in the circumstances now confronted.

* * *

Several jurisdictions accept the . . . emphasis on determining the genuine wishes of the now-incompetent patient, but also allow a range of evidentiary material (beyond just the patient's prior expressions) regarding life-sustaining treatment.

* * *

The final version of substituted judgment allows for a wide range of evidence in determining an incompetent patient's putative preference regarding life and death issues. Moreover, it authorizes a surrogate to interpret that evidence and make the best approximation of what the patient would want. Under this approach, "clear and convincing evidence" of the patient's wishes is not demanded.

* * *

As in the case of substituted judgment, a best interests of the patient standard for surrogate decisionmaking is susceptible to multiple visions or variations. One disputed issue is whether best interests is an entirely discrete standard, independent of substituted judgment, or if it is rather just part of a continuum in which the best interests approach succeeds the substituted judgment approach when the latter fails due to insufficient indicia of patients' preferences.

Some commentators view the best interests approach as free-standing and distinct from substituted judgment, asserting that the best interests approach is exclusively focused on the contemporaneous well-being of the now-incompetent patient. That well-being, in turn, is measured by present patient interests such as physical pain, emotional suffering, and pleasure from interaction with the patient's environment. According to this version of the best interest approach, the patient's prior values, wishes, and beliefs are essentially irrelevant to the patient's current best interests.

Another school of thought interprets the best interests standard as free-standing and discrete, but also as unconfined to the immediate, tangible interests of the now-incompetent patient. Perhaps in deference to the respect for self-determination . . . this alternative approach to best interests brings the now-incompetent patient's prior values and beliefs into consideration.

* * *

The notion of a continuum—beginning with substituted judgment and culminating in best interests as a fallback position—has struck a responsive chord.

* * *

Legislative developments in a number of states also give impetus to a continuum approach culminating in a best interests of the patient standard. An example can be found among the numerous statutes, sometimes called "durable power of attorney" acts authorizing an individual's designation of a health care agent to make post-competence decisions on behalf of the appointing individual. Many of these enactments provide that the agent must follow the wishes of the now-incompetent patient, but when that patient's wishes are unclear, the best interests of the patient standard governs. A similar statutory instruction is contained in some surrogate decision-making statutes which establish a hierarchy of decisionmakers in the absence of a patient's prior specification of an agent. Among the approximately twenty-six existing statutes, at least four provide that if the now-incompetent patient's wishes are unclear, the surrogate must act according to the best interests of the patient.

* * *

Rather than impose the preferences of medical personnel, surrounding family, or government, American society has opted to allow people to shape their own medical fates in the context of death and dying. With regard to competent patients, both the common law doctrine of informed consent and the constitutional right to reject life-sustaining treatment reflect society's abiding solicitude for autonomous choice. As to incompetent patients, the societal acceptance of advance medical directives confirms the role of autonomy in the context of end-stage medical decisionmaking. The function of such directives is to implement people's personal preferences in post-competence, end-of-life medical care. Even in the absence of actual patient choice, much of the jurisprudence of surrogate decisionmaking is geared toward discernment of what the patient probably would have wanted if competent.

* * *

Unfortunately, both the substituted judgment and best interests approaches, as currently constituted, are inadequate guides to effectuation of likely patient preferences in instances when no advance instructions exist. Substituted judgment fails (in the absence of articulated patient choice) because of its recourse to indeterminate indices, such as patient lifestyle and character, that do not usually answer the critical question of when the patient would prefer death to his or her deteriorated existence. A best interests approach fails both in reliance on immeasurable elements, such as burdens and benefits of a gravely demented patient, and in its reference to inadequately defined notions of quality of life.

I propose a "constructive preference" approach to guide surrogates in making end-of-life medical decisions for formerly competent patients who have left no instructions. The object of constructive perference—as in the case of much of substituted judgment and best interests doctrine—is to give now-incompetent patients the medical treatment they probably would have desired had they spoken, while competent, to that issue. At the same time, I would not disturb the current jurisprudence giving binding effect to patients' explicit advance instructions. Constructive preference [would apply], therefore, only to those formerly competent patients who never issued intelligible instructions.

Questions

1. What are the differences among the three standards described by Professor Cantor?

2. Which standard is adopted by §§ 2(e) and 5(f) of the UHCDA?

3. Of the possible standards, which is the best one? Why?

FURTHER READING. ALISON BARNES ET AL., COUNSELING OLDER CLIENTS chs. 11-14, 16-18, 28 (1997); PETER J. STRAUSS & NANCY M. LEDERMAN, THE ELDER LAW HANDBOOK chs. 1-2, 5-10 (1996); PETER J. STRAUSS ET AL., AGING AND THE LAW, chs. 14-17, 36 (1996).

CHAPTER 8

Housing

A. Home Ownership and "Aging in Place" 402
B. The Elderly Tenant 417
C. Retirement Communities and Assisted Living 424
D. Nursing Facilities 433

Many of us come to fear dependency, and, for some, the most punishing lack of independence occurs if we lose our ability to stay at home—where the heart is. This chapter will review the "continuum of care" response to this challenge, from the single family home to the nursing facility, and the legal issues which arise in consequence.

Lawrence A. Frolik
The Special Housing Needs of Older Persons: An Essay
26 STETSON L. REV. 647 (1996)*

When we think about the challenges that face older members of our society, we are likely to think of problems such as paying for medical care, mental capacity, economic insecurity, and end-of-life health care decisionmaking. One issue that does not often come to mind is housing. Yet, housing, where the older person lives, is one of the key determinants of the quality of life for older Americans. Along with good health and economic security, appropriate housing that meets the needs of the older resident is surely necessary if an older person is to have a comfortable and satisfying life. Housing that is adequate for old age, however, does not just happen. Older persons who are happy with their housing (at least within the limits of what they can afford) usually are not just lucky. Rather, they have housing they like because they, and those who advised them, took stock of their needs, values and capabilities and selected a housing option that was right for them.

---

* Copyright © 1996. Reprinted with permission.

A. Home Ownership and "Aging in Place"

American Bar Association
National Handbook on Laws and Programs Affecting Senior Citizens (1998)
<http://www.abanet.org/srlawyers/handbook.html>*

Sale of Principal Residence

The Taxpayer Relief Act of 1997 repealed the one-time $125,000 exclusion of income from the sale of a principal residence by taxpayers age 55 or over. The Taxpayer Relief Act replaces this provision with an exclusion of up to $250,000 (or $500,000, in the case of married taxpayers filing a joint return) of income realized on sale or exchange of a principal residence by taxpayer regardless of age.

To be eligible for the exclusion, a taxpayer must have owned the residence and occupied it as a principal residence for at least two years before the date of sale. The exclusion is not a one-time exclusion, but is generally available no more frequently than once every two years.

American Association of Retired Persons
What Housing Options Do You Have?, Housing (1995)**

You do *not* have to choose between your current unaltered home or a nursing home. There are many other housing options available. Listed below are just a few:

If you own your home, you may be able to adapt it. Door knobs, bathtubs, stairs, lighting—and much more—can all be adapted for easier and safer use.

Accessory apartments are created by making a separate apartment in your home with one or more rooms and a separate kitchen, a conversion allowing you to live independently without living alone.

ECHO (Elder Cottage Housing Opportunity) homes are small, portable units that you can place in the back or side yard of your single-family house, enabling you to live close to family or friends who will provide the support necessary for you to live independently. You'll need to check local zoning laws to make sure these units are permitted in your area.

Purchasing a manufactured or "mobile" home is a low-cost alternative. The term "mobile" is misleading because the homes usually only make one trip to a permanent stopping place. These homes have a relatively low purchase price, and are usually kept in a mobile home park.

Modular, panelized, and prefabricated homes, and their contents, are shipped from the factory direct to your property. This low-cost alternative is used mainly by

---

* Copyright © 1998 American Bar Association. All rights reserved. Reprinted by permission. This handbook is based on the *Senior Citizens Handbook: Laws & Programs Affecting Senior Citizens in Virginia,* copyright © 1996, The Virginia State Bar, 707 East Main Street, Suite 1500, Richmond, VA 23219-2803

** Copyright © 1995. Reprinted with permission.

those who already own land, but maybe don't need as large a home as they needed earlier in their lives.

*   *   *

Community services can help too. Home repair programs, property tax rebates, adult day care, paratransit systems, and friendly visiting programs can be just what a person needs to stay in their own home.

H.E.L.P.
Think Twice (or More) Before Giving Away Your Home
<http://www.palosverdes.com/helpcorp/news.htm#thinktwice>*

Many people, as they grow older, consider giving away their homes during their lifetimes. We call this "lifetime transfer" and contrast it with a transfer to heirs that becomes effective at death. When thinking about a lifetime transfer of their homes, people often consider things like avoiding probate, having someone else take responsibility for upkeep, helping a family member, or encouraging someone to live with them and provide care to them. Sometimes they believe that if they need nursing home care, [Medicaid] will take their homes from them.

Things to Consider

If you are thinking about making a lifetime transfer of your home, there are many things to consider first.

Loss of Control: If you transfer your home, you will lose control over it. You will have no say in whether it is sold, mortgaged or used for purposes you don't like. You may lose your right to live in your home or to rent it out.

Creditors: If you transfer your home, you may create problems if a creditor has a lien on it or if you file for bankruptcy. Also, the new owner of the home may have creditors who are able to make claims against the home.

Impact on SSI Benefits: If you receive SSI (Supplemental Security Income), transfer your home and continue to live there without paying rent, your SSI benefits will likely be reduced. Also, giving your home to someone who receives SSI and already owns a home will likely cause that person to lose SSI benefits.

Questions

1. What other legal issues weigh against a lifetime transfer of the home?
2. What alternatives could you offer a client who was considering transfer of the home to a family member in exchange for personal care?

---

* Reprinted by permission of H.E.L.P., A Non-Profit Information Resource for Older Adults, Torrance, California, (310) 533-1996, <http://www.palosverdes.com/helpcorp/>.

3. How would the availability of Medicaid (*see* Chapter 7, *supra*) for the expense of nursing home care impact your advice?

Estate of Furgason v. DHSS
566 N.W.2d 169 (Wis. App. 1997)

DYKMAN, P.J.

The estates of Mildred and John Furgason appeal from a judgment affirming a decision of the Wisconsin Department of Health and Social Services (DHSS). DHSS concluded that the Furgasons were ineligible for medical assistance (MA) benefits because the farm that they placed in a revocable trust did not qualify as an exempt asset. We conclude that the farm held in trust was an exempt homestead, and therefore DHSS erred in denying the Furgasons MA benefits. Accordingly, we reverse.

Background

John Furgason applied for and began to receive MA as a nursing home resident on March 12, 1990. On April 16, 1991, John and his wife, Mildred, transferred their farm into the Furgason Family Trust. Mildred continued to live on the farm until July 1995, when she entered the nursing home. Her application for MA benefits was denied on September 6, 1995. Furthermore, on September 6, 1995, the county notified John that his MA benefits would be discontinued effective October 1, 1995.

The basis for both the denial of Mildred's benefits and the termination of John's benefits was that each had excess assets. The asset that caused their ineligibility was the corpus of the trust. The farm was the only asset transferred to the trust. John and Mildred were the original settlors, trustees and primary beneficiaries of the trust, and the trust was fully revocable by either one of them.

On September 13, 1995, the Furgasons petitioned DHSS to review the county's determination. The DHSS hearing examiner upheld the county's decision, and on May 29, 1996, the circuit court affirmed DHSS's decision. The estates of Mildred and John were subsequently substituted as the proper parties because Mildred died on March 14, 1996 and John on March 17, 1996. The estates appeal.

Standard of Review

We review DHSS's decision, not the decision of the circuit court. We review an agency's conclusions of law under one of three levels of deference—great weight, due weight, or *de novo*. In *Behnke v. DHSS*, we concluded that we should give deference to DHSS's decisions on MA eligibility: DHSS is the agency charged with the administration of the medical assistance program. Determination of eligibility or benefits is uniquely reserved to DHSS. This process invokes the agency's expertise. Such a determination, we conclude, represents a value judgment to which we must give appropriate deference and weight.

Here, DHSS's decision is not entitled to great weight because the agency's interpretation is not one of long standing. Therefore, we will give its interpretation due weight. Under this standard, we will not defer to an agency's interpretation, although reasonable, when we consider a different interpretation to be the best and most reasonable.

Discussion

Medical Assistance, also known as "Medicaid," is a joint state and federal program intended to provide medical services to the poor and needy. To be eligible to receive MA benefits, an individual must meet strict income and asset limits.

Because George and Mildred were over sixty-five years of age, they were eligible for MA benefits if they met the financial conditions of eligibility. MA applicants are ineligible for benefits if their non-exempt assets exceed a certain level. Both the Furgasons and the DHSS agree that revocable trusts are considered a resource available to the applicant in determining MA benefit eligibility. They disagree, however, as to whether the corpus of the trust—the Furgasons' farm—is exempt from consideration.

Section 49.47(4)(b)1, Stats., provides that an MA applicant is eligible for benefits "if the applicant's property does not exceed," among other things, "[a] home and the land used and operated in connection therewith if the home is used as the person's or his or her family's place of abode." Similarly, Wis. Adm. Code provides that "[a] home owned and lived in by an applicant or recipient is an exempt asset." A home is exempt as long as the applicant resides in it, or intends to return to it. Wis. Adm. Code Section HFS 103.06.

DHSS argues that the farm is owned by the trust, not the Furgasons, and therefore the trust property does not qualify for this homestead exemption. The Furgasons argue that they have a sufficient ownership interest in the trust property to make the farm exempt from consideration.

The Furgasons were the settlors of the trust and its trustees and primary beneficiaries during their lifetimes. Section 701.05(1), Stats., provides that "[u]nless the creating instrument expressly limits the trustee to a lesser title or to a power, *the trustee takes all title of the settlor.*" (Emphasis added.) In addition, Section 701.05(2) provides that "[i]f a trustee of a private trust has title to the trust property, a beneficiary has an equitable interest, present or future, in the trust property." Furthermore, *Becker v. Becker,* 56 Wis. 2d 369, 373, 202 N.W.2d 688, 690 (1972), states that "[w]hen a settlor creates a trust by declaration naming himself as sole trustee, no transfer of ownership occurs."

Accordingly, under Section 701.05, Stats., and *Becker* the Furgasons continued to have an ownership interest in the farm as the trustees and beneficiaries of the trust. Because the Furgasons continued to own the farm, the farm was exempt under Section 49.47(4)(b)1, Stats., as long as either John or Mildred or both intended to return there. The State apparently concedes that such intent to return to the farm did exist. Therefore, DHSS erred in denying the Furgasons MA benefits.

DHSS argues that the Furgasons were ineligible for benefits because Section 49.45(23), Stats., 1991-92, and Section 49.454, Stats., which expressly govern the treatment of trusts under the MA program, take precedence over Section 701.05, Stats., a general trust law provision. In support of its argument, DHSS cites *City of Muskego v. Godec,* 167 Wis. 2d 536, 546, 482 N.W.2d 79, 83 (1992), which provides that "[w]hen we compare a general statute and a specific statute, the specific statute takes precedence."

We reject DHSS's argument because we do not see a conflict between the MA statutes and the general trust statutes. "The rule of statutory construction that favors the specific over the general statutory provision applies only where there is a conflict between the two provisions." *Novak v. Madison Motel Assocs.*, 188 Wis. 2d 407, 416, 525 N.W.2d 123, 126 (Ct. App. 1994). The MA statutes do not provide that anyone with access to revocable trust assets is ineligible for MA benefits. Rather, the statutes provide that the assets in a revocable trust are considered "available" to the MA applicant. Trust assets available to the applicant are still subject to the property exemptions of Section 49.47(4)(b), Stats. *See, e.g., Zimmerman v. DHSS*, 169 Wis. 2d 498, 485 N.W.2d 290 (Ct. App. 1992) (applying Section 49.47(4)(b)3g liquid asset exemption to trust assets). The Furgasons have an ownership interest in the trust assets under Section 701.05, Stats., and therefore the farm is an exempt homestead under Section 49.47(4)(b)1. This result is not inconsistent with the MA statutes which provide that the trust assets are "available" to the Furgasons.

Finally, DHSS argues that by placing the farm in trust, the Furgasons are shielding their property from the lien and estate claim recovery remedies otherwise available to the government against an MA recipient's home. For example, Section 49.496(2), Stats., provides that DHSS may obtain a lien on an MA recipient's home "if the recipient resides in a nursing home and cannot reasonably be expected to be discharged from the nursing home and return home," and Section 49.496(3) provides that DHSS must file a claim against an MA recipient's estate for benefits paid while the recipient resided in a nursing home. Because the trust owns the farm and trust property may be passed to heirs outside of probate, DHSS argues that neither the lien recovery nor estate claim recovery remedies of Section 49.496 are available against the Furgasons' farm. DHSS contends that if we consider the farm as an exempt homestead, we would place the Furgasons at an advantage over other MA recipients who simply own their homes.

We do not see how DHSS's ability to recover benefits paid from the trust assets is relevant to whether the Furgasons may receive MA benefits in the first place. The statutes provide the eligibility requirements for MA benefits. The statutes also provide the situations in which a settlor's creditor may reach trust assets. If the legislature believes that it is inequitable to allow MA applicants to place their homes in revocable trusts and still receive MA benefits, it can change the statutes accordingly. But it is for the legislature, not this court, to make such a policy determination. *See State v. Richards*, 123 Wis. 2d 1, 12-13, 365 N.W.2d 7, 12 (1985).(4) We cannot rewrite the statutes to meet DHSS's desired construction.

Judgment reversed.

Question

When public policy and the long-standing laws governing trusts collide, which should take precedence?

1. Adaptations

**National Resource and Policy Center on Housing and Long Term Care
(USC Andrus Gerontology Center)
Housing Highlights: *Accessory Units* (January 13, 1998)**[*]

What Are Accessory Units?

"Accessory units" are private housing arrangements in, or adjacent to, existing single family homes. There are two types:

Accessory Apartments, created within single family homes, are complete living units including a private kitchen and bath.

Elder Cottage Housing Opportunity Units are complete, portable, small homes installed in back or side yards of single family house lots.

Why Are Accessory Units Important?

Accessory units are a source of affordable housing for small households.
Accessory units adapt existing housing stock.
Installation upgrades and improves the property.
Accessory units make efficient use of land and existing infrastructure.
Accessory units may encourage economic and personal support between two separate households.
Accessory units generate rental income for home owners.

* * *

Legal Restrictions:

1) Zoning Ordinances
Explore with local zoning commission the procedure for securing a "conditional" or "special use" permit.
2) Covenants
These conditions written into deeds are generally difficult to change and costly to fight.

NIMBY (Not In My Backyard), Neighbors May Object to a Multifamily Setting:

Inform neighbors and neighborhood associations about your building plans.
Meet with local officials and neighbors to address concerns.

Costs and Tax Issues:

Determine the economic feasibility and availability of home remodeling loans with your accountant or bank loan officer.

Consult with a tax advisor or benefits specialist to determine the impact renting [or purchasing] an accessory unit will have on your tax situation or eligibility for public programs.

---

[*] Copyright © 1998. Reprinted with permission.

Total general costs for accessory apartments can cost $20,000 or more. ECHO units may cost $30,000 or more.

2. Home Equity Conversion Mortgages

Jean Reilly
Reverse Mortgages: Backing into the Future
5 ELDER L.J. 17, 17, 19 (1997)[*]

In 1995 there were 2.89 million households headed by persons sixty-five years of age or older. The median income of these seniors was $18,500, while the median value of their homes was $70,000. Thus, many seniors find themselves in the position of being house rich, but cash poor. They find it increasingly difficult to meet home maintenance expenses, energy costs, property taxes, insurance premiums, health care bills, and even subsistence needs. Yet, according to a survey by the American Association of Retired Persons, 86% of seniors indicated that they wanted to live in their homes for the rest of their lives. For those older homeowners faced with the dilemma of wanting to stay in their homes and yet not having enough income to meet their expenses, reverse mortgages may be the answer.

* * *

Although reverse mortgages have been nationally available since 1988, they have not widely caught on. Indeed, as of March 5, 1996, only 30,000 seniors had taken out a reverse mortgage.

Department of Housing and Urban Development
Top Ten Things To Know If You're Interested In A Reverse Mortgage
<http://www.hud.gov/rmtopten.html>

Reverse Mortgages are becoming popular in America. The U.S. Department of Housing and Urban Development (HUD) created one of the first. HUD's Reverse Mortgage is a federally-insured private loan, and it's a safe plan that can give older Americans greater financial security. Many Seniors use it to supplement social security, meet unexpected medical expenses, make home improvements, and more. You can receive free information from HUD about Reverse Mortgages by calling 1-888-466-3487, toll-free.

Since your home is probably your largest single investment, it's smart to know more about reverse mortgages, and decide if one is right for you!

---

[*] Copyright © 1997 by the Board of Trustees of the University of Illinois. Reprinted with permission.

1. *What is a reverse mortgage?*

A reverse mortgage is a special type of home loan that lets a homeowner convert the equity in his or her home into cash. The equity built up over years of home mortgage payments can be paid to the homeowner: in a lump sum, in a stream of payments, or as a supplement to Social Security or other retirement funds. But unlike a traditional home equity loan or second mortgage, no repayment is required until the borrowers no longer use the home as their principal residence. HUD's reverse mortgage provides these benefits, and it is federally-insured as well.

2. *Can I qualify for a HUD reverse mortgage?*

To be eligible for a HUD reverse mortgage, HUD's Federal Housing Administration requires that you are a homeowner 62 years of age or older; have a very low outstanding mortgage balance or own your home free and clear; and that you meet with a HUD-approved counseling agency—to make sure you understand what a HUD Reverse Mortgage will mean for you. Call 1-888-466-3487, toll free, for more information.

3. *Can I apply if I didn't buy my present house with FHA mortgage insurance?*

Yes. While your property must meet FHA minimum standards, it doesn't matter if you didn't buy it with an FHA-insured mortgage. Your new HUD reverse mortgage will be a new FHA-insured mortgage loan.

4. *What if I own a condominium, not a single-family home?*

You can still qualify for HUD's reverse mortgage program. An eligible property must be your principal residence, but can be a single-family residence; a one- to four-unit dwelling with one unit occupied by the borrower; a manufactured home (mobile home); a unit in FHA-approved condominiums; and Planned Unit Developments. Your property must meet FHA minimum property standards, but you can fund repairs from your reverse mortgage.

5. *What's the difference between a reverse mortgage and a bank home equity loan?*

With a traditional second mortgage, or a home equity line of credit, you must have sufficient income to qualify for the loan, and you are required to make monthly mortgage payments. A reverse mortgage works very differently. The reverse mortgage pays you, and it is available regardless of your current income. You don't make payments, because the loan is not due as long as the house is your principal residence. Like all homeowners, you still are required to pay your real estate taxes and other conventional payments like utilities, but with an FHA-insured HUD Reverse Mortgage, you cannot be foreclosed or forced to vacate your house because you "missed your mortgage payment."

6. *Can the lender take my home away if I outlive the loan?*

No! You cannot outlive the loan agreement, and no debt from a Reverse Mortgage will passed along to the estate or heirs. You cannot be forced to sell your home to pay off the mortgage loan even if the loan balance grows to exceed the value of the property. And, HUD's Federal Housing Administration guarantees that you'll receive all the payments that are owed to you.

7. *Will I still have an estate that I can leave to my heirs?*

When you sell your home or no longer use it for your primary residence, you or your estate will repay the cash you received from the reverse mortgage, plus interest and other finance charges, to the lender. All proceeds beyond what you owe belong to you or your estate. This means the remaining equity in your home can be passed on to your heirs. None of your other assets will be affected by HUD's reverse mortgage loan. No debt will ever be passed along to the estate or heirs. You retain ownership of your home, and may sell or move at any time.

8. *How much money can I get from my home?*

A borrower who uses an FHA-insured HECM will receive a reverse mortgage amount based on a formula which includes a Maximum Claim Amount. In general, this means the maximum amount you can receive will be determined by factors including the age of the borrower(s), and the appraised value of the property (or the maximum FHA mortgage amount for your area, if lower). For example, based on a loan at recent interest rates, a 65-year-old could borrow up to 26 percent of the home's value, a 75-year-old could borrow up to 39 percent, and an 85- year-old could borrow up to 56 percent. You should discuss the formula with your lender and your HUD-approved housing counselor.

9. *What if I want to take out more equity from my home than the FHA-insured mortgage limits for my area?*

Like FHA's home mortgage programs, HUD's reverse mortgage is primarily intended for low- and moderate-income families. For instance, FHA maximum home mortgage amounts range from $78,660 to $155,250, depending whether the home is in a standard housing-cost area, or an area determined by FHA to be a high-cost area. An owner with a property valued well beyond the FHA mortgage limits, and who has a large amount of equity, will not receive as much cash from a HECM as they might from another reputable private or public agency. Reverse mortgage programs are available in most states of the nation, including the District of Columbia and Puerto Rico, through HUD-approved lenders or highly regarded organizations like Fannie Mae. However, anyone interested in a reverse mortgage is encouraged to speak with a HUD-approved housing counseling agency first.

10. *Should I use an estate planning service to find a reverse mortgage? I've been contacted by a firm that will give me the name of a lender for a "small percentage" of the loan?*

HUD does NOT recommend using an estate planning service, or any service that charges a fee just for referring a borrower to a lender! HUD provides this information without cost, and HUD-approved housing-counseling agencies are available for free, or at minimal cost, to provide counseling and free referral to a list of HUD-approved lenders.

Department of Housing and Urban Development
How HUD's Reverse Mortgage Program Works
<http://www.hud.gov.reverse.html>

Homeowners 62 and older who have paid off their mortgages or have only small mortgage balances remaining are eligible to participate in HUD's reverse mortgage program. The program allows homeowners to borrow against the equity in their homes.

Homeowners can receive payments in a lump sum, on a monthly basis (for a fixed term or for as long as they live in the home), or on an occasional basis as a line of credit. Homeowners whose circumstances change can restructure their payment options.

Unlike ordinary home equity loans, a HUD reverse mortgage does not require repayment as long as the borrower lives in the home. Lenders recover their principal, plus interest, when the home is sold. The remaining value of the home goes to the homeowner or to his or her survivors. If the sales proceeds are insufficient to pay the amount owed, HUD will pay the lender the amount of the shortfall. The Federal Housing Administration, which is part of HUD, collects an insurance premium from all borrowers to provide this coverage.

The size of reverse mortgage loans is determined by the borrower's age, the interest rate, and the home's value. The older a borrower, the larger the percentage of the home's value that can be borrowed.

For example, based on a loan at today's interest rates of approximately 9 percent, a 65-year-old could borrow up to 26 percent of the home's value, a 75-year-old could borrow up to 39 percent of the home's value, and an 85-year-old could borrow up to 56 percent of the home's value.

There are no asset or income limitations on borrowers receiving HUD's reverse mortgages.

There are also no limits on the value of homes qualifying for a HUD reverse mortgage. However, the amount that may be borrowed is capped by the maximum FHA mortgage limit for the area, which varies from $81,548 to $160,950, depending on local housing costs. As a result, owners of higher-priced homes can't borrow any more than owners of homes valued at the FHA limit.

HUD's reverse mortgage program collects funds from insurance premiums charged to borrowers. Senior citizens are charged 2 percent of the home's value as an up-front payment plus one-half percent on the loan balance each year. These amounts are usually paid by the lender and charged to the borrower's principal balance.

FHA's reverse mortgage insurance makes HUD's program less expensive to borrowers than the smaller reverse mortgage programs run by private lenders without FHA insurance.

Donna G. Klein
Reverse Mortgages
THE COMPLEAT LAWYER—GENERAL PRACTICE, SOLO, AND SMALL FIRM SECTION
AMERICAN BAR ASSOCIATION (Spring 1998)
<http://www.abanet.org:80/genpractice/lawyer/complete/sp98reverse.html>[*]

If Social Security, pensions, and savings fail to provide enough retirement income, elders may also rely upon the equity in their home. Home equity is the largest unaccessed financial resource for the elderly, and reverse mortgages allow elders to take advantage of this resource.

A reverse mortgage is a non-recourse loan that is secured by the borrower's principal residence. Reverse mortgages are tailored to fit the needs of elderly clients. For instance, elderly people are typically unable to afford the cost and interest associated with additional debt. However, through the reverse mortgage, a borrower may obtain credit with very little expense and without having to satisfy an income requirement.

Although title to the residence remains in the name of the borrower, reverse mortgages attach as a first lien on the residence. The amount of funds available pursuant to reverse mortgages are calculated using formulas analyzing the borrower's age, the proposed schedule of fund distribution, the interest rate, and the equity in the home. The more equity the borrower has in her home, the greater the amount of funds available to her. Funds are distributed to the borrower in one of several ways, including lump sum payments, monthly payments, or a line of credit. The IRS does not consider the advances received to be gross income.

Significantly, complete payoff of the debt is not required until the end of the term, which occurs when the owner sells or vacates his home or, in a minority of situations, on a fixed repayment date. Until the end of the term, no payments are due. This aspect of reverse mortgages satisfies the elderly person's wish to live in his home for his entire life.

Any interest accrued pursuant to reverse mortgages is not deductible until the end of the term. However, because the end of the term cannot be definitively defined, the debt may often grow larger than the value of the residence. Nevertheless, since reverse mortgages are non-recourse loans, the lender is not entitled to receive the deficiency from the borrower. However, if the value of the house at sale is more than the amount of the debt, the borrower's estate is entitled to the excess proceeds.

Reverse mortgages can significantly improve the life of an elderly person. It is beneficial due to its non-recourse nature, the diversity of disbursement alternatives, and the fact that payment is not due until the end of the term.

Question

What barriers to wider use of reverse mortagages can you identify?

---

[*] Copyright © American Bar Association. All rights reserved. Reprinted with permission.

Jean Reilly
Reverse Mortgages: Backing into the Future
5 ELDER L.J. 17, 20-21 (1997)*

I. Obstacles Impeding Acceptance of Reverse Mortgages by Borrowers and Lenders

Litigation surrounding reverse mortgages and tales of predatory lending have made borrowers wary of this complex financial instrument. The growth of the reverse mortgage market has been further hindered by lenders' aversion to the perceived risks and delays inherent in these mortgages.

A. Litigation and "Predatory Lending"

Beginning in 1999 there have been a series of lawsuits by disappointed reverse mortgage borrowers who accuse lenders of defrauding them out of the equity in their home. The suits, all against private lenders, have generated bad press and have scared potential borrowers away from even the relatively safe government-backed reverse mortgages. *Barron's*, the well-respected financial publication, trumpeted in an article, "Reverse mortgages can be a nightmare . . . . Some retirees have seen their home equity completely wiped out in five years or less." The magazine further stated, without differentiating among reverse mortgage lenders, that reverse mortgages "can leave people shell-shocked, with little or no money to pay for expensive stays in nursing homes during their final years of life—or to pass on to their heirs." Similarly, the headline of a *Worth* article discussing charges that some reverse mortgage lenders "bilked millions of dollars from trusting senior citizens" gave potential borrowers the generic warning: "Beward Reverse-Mortgage Mania: Don't Let A Bad Deal Burn Up Your Home Equity." The legal profession also has warned of predatory lending, high interest rates, and unconscionable terms in reverse mortgage transactions. The result has been to make the public wary of reverse mortgages. This public distrust is best exemplified by a woman who wrote into the Newark *Star-Ledger's* Question and Answer Financial Column asking, "It is my belief that many senior citizens have obtained reverse mortgages without knowing the actual cost of such borrowing, because the mortgage lenders did not reveal those costs. Am I correct?" The answering columnist confirmed her perceptions: "These is little doubt that some unscrupulous lenders did not reveal the true cost of reverse mortgages to gullible seniors."

Question

To what extent should senior citizens be shielded from the consequences of their own unwise choices?

---

* Copyright © 1997 by the Board of Trustees of the University of Illinois. Reprinted with permission.

Jean Reilly
Reverse Mortgages: Backing into the Future
5 ELDER L.J. 17, 26-28 (1997)*

B. Lenders: "Headaches" and Hesitation

Financial institution managers, despite their constant search for additional sources of loan volume and their long-held interest in the potential benefits of leveraging the equity of elderly homeowners, have nevertheless been hesitant to enter the reverse mortgage market. . . . [F]inancial institutions are reluctant to offer reverse mortgages because of four perceived risks: value risk, reputation risk, tort risk, and demand risk.

With value risk, the concern is that the mortgage might accrue interest and principal that will eventually exceed the value of the house. Such fate befell Providential, the lender that was the defendant in the fraud and misrepresentation lawsuit [*McCarthy v. Providential Corp.*, No. C94-0627FMS, 1994 WL 387852 (N.D. Cal. July 19. 1994)]. Providential got in trouble partly because it made loans at the top of the California real estate market, based on expectations that property prices would continue to appreciate at a 5% rate. Instead, California home prices declined at a 5% annual rate from 1988 to 1994. The result was that Providential's reverse mortgage portfolio, which was listed as having a carrying value of $51 million, received a $33 million write-down in 1994. The write-down cut the value of Providential reverse mortgage holdings by 65% and caused shares of stock in the company to plummet to $5 per share from a high of $16. Providential subsequently sold off all of its loans and liquidated itself. Capital Holding, Providential's closest competitor, also withdrew from the reverse mortgage market in 1993 because it did not believe it could make any money. . . .

With reputation risk, lenders are worried about how their image may be affected in the event of foreclosure due to default. . . .

Moral hazard describes the tendency of borrowers to act against the interests of lenders. For example, when it becomes apparent to an elderly person that she will have to vacate the home by the end of the year because she needs to enter a nursing home, she may cease maintaining the home. This is particularly likely to be true if all the equity in the house has been used up by the reverse mortgage. . . .

Tort risk involves the possibility of claims by the borrowers or their heirs and relatives that the borrower was deceived by the bank regarding the material terms of the reverse mortgage. . . .

Lenders also face an interest rate risk with reverse mortgages. In a rising rate environment, a fixed rate investor normally has the benefit of reinvesting cash flows into higher yielding investments. This benefit is not available to the reverse mortgage lender, however, because reverse mortgages do not result in any intermediate cash flows to the lender. A fixed rate, reverse mortgage lender is helplessly locked into a

---

* Copyright © 1997 by the Board of Trustees of the University of Illinois. Reprinted with permission.

rising rate environment. Although an adjustable-rate reverse mortgage is certainly more attractive to the lender with regards to interest rate, it is not risk-free. In a rising rate environment, an adjustable-rate reverse mortgage accrues increasing amounts of interest. Thus, the lender faces risk from negative amortization; that is to say, the possibility increases that the accrued interest and principal will exceed the resale value of the home.

Campaign to Keep America Warm
Save LIHEAP–Overview
<http://www.save-liheap.org/c_overview.htm>[*]

Meeting the Energy Needs of the Poor In an Era of Welfare Reform and Utility Restructuring

The Low Income Home Energy Assistance Program (LIHEAP) is one of the most critical components of the social safety net. The program provides heating and cooling assistance to almost 5 million low-income households, including the working poor, those making the difficult transition from welfare to work, disabled persons, elderly and families with young children.

Without energy assistance, many low-income households would have to choose between heating and eating or other vital necessities. This is especially true during the peak winter heating season when energy bills can frequently reach up to 30 percent of a low-income household's income, especially in substandard housing.

* * *

Experience has demonstrated that pressures to pay energy bills and the inability to pay have resulted in increased medical expenses for the elderly, malnutrition for infants and homelessness. Food, water, shelter and heat are equals in the social safety net.

* * *

Although the nature of the marketplace has changed sharply during the 15-year history of the program, one constant remains. The percentage of disposable income spent by low-income households on energy has remained at a high level throughout this period. Fully two-thirds of the households receiving heating assistance or winter/year-round crisis assistance from LIHEAP make under $8,000 per year. In winter, these same households spend up to 30 percent of their monthly income on heating.

* * *

---

[*] Reprinted with permission.

III. Background and Current Situation

The purpose of the Low Income Home Energy Assistance Program block grant . . . is to "assist low-income households, particularly those with the lowest income, that pay a high proportion of household income for home energy, primarily in meeting their immediate home energy needs." Created in response to the energy crisis of the late 1970s and early 1980s, LIHEAP was designed to provide assistance to low-income households with a minimum of government bureaucracy and a maximum of involvement by civic institutions.

Federal dollars for LIHEAP are allocated by the U.S. Department of Health and Human Services to the states as a block grant and are disbursed under programs designed by the individual states. Program funds are distributed by a formula, which is weighted towards relative cold-weather conditions and households living in poverty.

The program is administered at the state and county levels by governmental agencies and implemented primarily at the local level by community action programs (CAPS), local welfare agencies and area agencies on aging. LIHEAP funds are supplemented to a limited extent by additional state appropriations, programs from energy suppliers and utilities, church donations and local charitable "fuel funds" administered by the Salvation Army, Catholic Charities and other organizations.

* * *

Federal funds for LIHEAP peaked in FY 1986 at $2.1 billion . . . and then declined to $1.3 billion in 1995 and to $1.0 billion in FY 1997. The impact of these budget cuts has been severe. The total number of recipient households has declined from 6.0 million in 1994 to 5.5 million in 1995 to 4.3 million in 1996, as states have had to restrict eligibility to the neediest of the needy. Only 19 percent of households who are eligible receive LIHEAP assistance.

The residential energy burden (including heating, cooling and all other energy uses in the home) for all U.S. households in 1995 was $1,247 per household, or 6.8 percent of income. For LIHEAP recipient households, the respective figures are $1,089 and 17.4 percent, *two and one half times the average burden*. At this level, many poor and elderly, including households with children, are forced to choose between heating their homes and purchasing important medications.

* * *

Weatherization.

States may allocate up to 15 percent of their basic grant allocation for low-cost residential weatherization or other energy-related home repair and to 25 percent if they meet certain conditions and obtain a waiver from HHS. In 1995, 45 states allocated almost $160 million for this purpose. The program reduces the heating costs for low-income families by improving the energy efficiency of their homes and thereby improves their health and safety.

* * *

Elderly, Disabled, Children.

Many households receiving heating assistance include elderly residents, disabled residents and children. In 1995, the percentage of households with at least one member who was elderly was 30 percent, and with one disabled person, 24 percent. Most states reported 25-40 percent of the assisted households had young children.

Questions

1. Are there no prisons? Are there no workhouses?

2. To what extent should government be involved in ameliorating the hardships endured by the elderly poor?

B. The Elderly Tenant

1. Protection from Discrimination

**National Resource and Policy Center on Housing and Long Term Care
(USC Andrus Gerontology Center)
Housing Highlights: What Are Your Rights (January 13, 1998)***

Why Are The Rights Of Tenants With Disabilities Important To Older Persons?

Many older people are unable to manage daily activities as well as they once did. They may have difficulty walking, seeing, hearing, taking care of personal or health needs or doing household chores. Landlords may refuse to rent to them, or ask them to move, simply because they need assistance with certain activities. These rejections or evictions of older people are illegal under the Fair Housing Amendments Act of 1988, and other federal and state laws.

What is the Fair Housing Amendments Act?

The Fair Housing Amendments Act of 1988 is a federal statute that protects frail or disabled persons against discrimination in housing.

What It Does:
- Extends civil rights protection in the housing area to people with disabilities.
- Requires new construction of dwellings with four or more units to include features such as wheelchair accessibility, reinforced walls to accommodate later installation of grab bars.
- Requires landlords to treat people with disabilities just like they treat everyone else.

---

* Copyright © 1998. Reprinted with permission.

- Prohibits landlords from asking current tenants or people applying for housing questions about their age, health or ability to live independently, unless this information is necessary for a special program.
- Requires landlords to make reasonable accommodations in rules and procedures, and to allow reasonable modifications to the premises, at the request of tenants with disabilities.

What It Does Not Do:
- Does not apply to rental buildings which contain fewer than four units, where the owner also lives in the building.
- Does not require a landlord to rent to current users of illegal drugs.
- Does not require a landlord to rent to a person who is a threat to the safety or health of other tenants, or whose tenancy would result in substantial damage to property of others.
- Does not require a landlord to provide services to a tenant with disabilities, unless the housing program already includes services.
- Does not require a landlord to change the basic nature of the housing program.

What Changes Can Be Made?

Reasonable Accommodations: Changes in rules or procedures which (1) are reasonable under the circumstances, and (2) give a disabled tenant equal opportunity to use and enjoy the residence. Examples include:
- waiving a no-pets rule for a tenant with a mental disability who is emotionally dependent on their pet.
- waive a no-guest rule for a tenant who needs a live-in aide.
- changing the due date for rent to allow a tenant time to deposit their disability check and avoid late charges.
- arranging to have a staff person pick up the trash from the apartment of a tenant who is ill and cannot carry the bag to the trash disposal.
- providing large print notices for a vision-impaired tenant.

Reasonable Modifications: Changes to the physical structure of the premises, which (1) are reasonable and (2) give a tenant with disabilities equal access to residence. A tenant has the right to make reasonable modification at his or her own expense, but may be required to restore the premises to the original condition upon moving out. The landlord must pay for the costs of modification to common areas of the building. Examples include:
- installing grab bars in the bathroom and replacing doorknobs with lever handles.
- widening doorways for wheelchair access.
- installing a ramp at the entrance to the building.
- replacing small floor numbers with large numbers which contrast with the wall so that tenants can read them more easily.

2. Rental Subsidies

National Resource and Policy Center on Housing and Long Term Care
(USC Andrus Gerontology Center)
Housing Highlights: Government Assisted Housing (January 13, 1998)[*]

What Is Government Assisted Housing?

Government housing assistance is available to low-income older persons through three major programs: public housing, Section 8, and Section 202. Public housing and Section 8 programs are managed by local housing authorities, and Section 202 housing is sponsored on a complex-by-complex basis by non-profit companies. Most of these programs are over-subscribed, with waiting lists that vary in length. This fact sheet is designed to provide basic information about housing programs and the procedures for obtaining housing assistance.

What Type Of Housing Assistance Is Available?

Three basic types of government housing assistance are:

Public housing—low cost housing in multi-unit complexes that are available to low-income families, including the elderly and disabled, typically requiring tenants to pay no more than 30 percent of their monthly income for rent. Eligibility: Public housing authorities that receive funding from the federal government own and operate public housing complexes, available to applicants that do not exceed published income levels (dependent on the size of the household).

Section 8 rental certificates—allows very low-income families (including the elderly and disabled) to choose where they want to live, subject to HUD standards, by providing rental certificates that limit tenants' rent to 30 percent of their adjusted monthly income. Eligibility: Very low-income families with incomes not exceeding 50 percent of the median income for the area.

Section 202 housing—senior citizen housing, usually with supportive services such as meals, transportation, and accommodations for the disabled. Eligibility: Private, nonprofit organizations and consumer cooperatives. Occupancy is open to very low-income households with at least one person 62 years of age or older, and the disabled.

Why Do Older People Apply For Housing Assistance?

Some of the reasons that older people apply for government housing assistance include:
- Want lower housing costs
- Want a safer neighborhood
- Want a better quality home
- Want to live with other seniors

---

[*] Copyright © 1998. Reprinted with permission.

- Have difficulty climbing stairs in present residence
- Want services (meals, transportation)

* * *

Federal Preference Rules: Should You Apply Or Shouldn't You?

Federal Law requires that housing applicants who meet certain criteria be given preference for admission to government assisted housing. These applicants are placed higher on the waiting list, and should receive assistance before those who do not meet federal housing preferences.

Preference for admission is extended to applicants who:
- have severe rent burden; that is, pay housing costs (rent or mortgage plus utilities) that exceed 50 percent of monthly income.
- are being involuntarily displaced (by fire, threat of violence, or government action); or
- live in substandard housing (severe plumbing, electrical, or structural problems).

Because of the shortage of government assisted housing, it is difficult for applicants not meeting federal housing preferences to receive assistance. However, availability of housing assistance may vary from area to area. Most local housing authorities have long lists of persons waiting for government assisted housing. Check with your local housing authority to determine conditions where you want to live.

3. Legal Remedies

Williams v. Hanover Housing Auth.
113 F.3d 1294 (1st. Cir. 1997)

CAMPBELL, Senior Circuit Judge.

At issue in this appeal is whether the plaintiffs in an action they brought under 42 U.S.C. § 1983 are entitled to recover attorneys' fees under 42 U.S.C. § 1988.

In the course of plaintiffs' § 1983 action, the district court determined an underlying state law issue in plaintiffs' favor. Because federal and state officials thereupon accepted the district court's interpretation reversing a former interpretation challenged by plaintiffs the § 1983 action became moot. The district court denied attorneys' fees, ruling that fees under § 1988 were improper as plaintiffs had vindicated no federal right. The court also declined fees as a matter of discretion. We conclude, notwithstanding plaintiffs failure to prevail on specifically federal grounds, that they are nonetheless prevailing parties under § 1988, and entitled to fees.

I.

The disputed fees claim arises in the following circumstances. The plaintiffs-appellants were receiving federal housing subsidies under Section 8 of the United States Housing Act of 1937, as amended. In April of 1993, they brought an action under 42 U.S.C. § 1983 against the Arlington and Danvers, Massachusetts, Public

Housing Authorities (the "Authorities"), as well as against the Hanover, Massachusetts Public Housing Authority and the Secretary of the Department of Housing and Urban Development ("HUD"). Plaintiffs-appellants alleged that the Authorities, with HUD's approval, were illegally and unconstitutionally preventing them from using their Section 8 subsidies for housing outside the geographical limits of the city or town within which the Authority issuing the subsidy was located.

* * *

Fearing the loss of their Section 8 subsidies if they could not immediately find housing within the municipal boundaries of the Authority that issued their respective Section 8 certificates, the plaintiffs moved for a preliminary injunction that would toll or freeze the subsidies' expiration dates. The need for preliminary relief ceased, however, when defendants agreed not to terminate the plaintiffs' subsidies while the case was pending.

After reviewing submissions and hearing arguments, the district court issued an oral opinion on September 9, 1993, followed by a written decision on December 12, 1994. The district court stated in both that, in its view, Massachusetts law permitted state public housing authorities to contract with landlords owning dwellings outside their municipal boundaries.

Less than a month after the district court's oral opinion, HUD issued a directive to the Massachusetts public housing authorities informing them that all Section 8 tenants could henceforth use their housing subsidies anywhere in the Commonwealth. HUD, as the district court later declared, treated the district court's ruling as an authoritative declaration of state law, superseding the contrary opinion of the EOCD. The Authorities also went along. . . .

At a November 30, 1995 hearing in the district court to determine the status of the case, HUD assured the district court that, in spite of its changed regulations, it would continue to instruct all Massachusetts public housing authorities to abide by the court's oral and written decisions issued in plaintiffs' § 1983 case. The district court thereupon dismissed the § 1983 action as moot and plaintiffs petitioned, unsuccessfully, for their attorneys' fees.

II.

In its opinion denying to plaintiffs attorneys' fees under 42 U.S.C. § 1988, the district court stated that, to receive fees, the plaintiffs had to be prevailing parties in their § 1983 action. In that action, the court continued, plaintiffs claimed to have been deprived of "rights secured by federal statutes, regulations and the United States Constitution." In the court's view, plaintiffs never became entitled to fees because the court never found that they "had a right under federal law to have the Authorities contract outside of their political boundaries for Section 8 housing." Rather the import of the court's ruling was that state, not federal law allowed the Authorities to contract outside of their political boundaries. As plaintiffs did not vindicate a federal right, the district court believed that § 1988 provided no right to fees.

The court also stated, as a separate ground for decision, that it would refrain from awarding attorneys' fees as a matter of discretion, even assuming plaintiffs could be said to have prevailed on a federal right.

* * *

III.

We think the district court's analysis is unsupported by Supreme Court precedent and that of this and other circuits. The clear tendency of the courts has been to apply the fees statute in a more practical and less restrictive way. . . . And fees can be allowed only to a prevailing party. But the attorneys' fees being requested here are for services in an action to enforce a provision of § 1983 and (as further discussed below) plaintiffs have, in every practical sense, prevailed having, as a result of their lawsuit, achieved precisely the end-relief they wanted, namely the right to use their Section 8 housing subsidies outside the political boundaries of the Authority providing the subsidy.

To uphold the district court's rationale, we would have to read into §1988 an implied further requirement that, to be a prevailing party, it is necessary not only to have secured a significant objective of one's federal lawsuit, but to have done so by obtaining a favorable ruling on some federal legal or constitutional claim advanced in the suit. A theory akin to this was rejected seventeen years ago in *Maher v. Gagne*, 448 U.S. 122 (1980), the Supreme Court saying, "The fact that respondent prevailed through settlement rather than through litigation does not weaken her claim to fees. Nothing in the language of § 1988 conditions the District Court's power to award fees on full litigation of the issues or on a judicial determination that the plaintiffs' rights have been violated."

* * *

We, therefore, reject the district court's reasoning that plaintiffs are not entitled to attorneys' fees because their success did not derive from the vindication of any specifically federal right.

We add that it is well-settled in this circuit that a § 1983 plaintiff seeking attorneys' fees under § 1988 may establish "prevailing party" status under a "catalyst" as well as a "merits" analysis. Plaintiffs argue that they win under either approach. Because the "catalyst" formulation is so plainly dispositive we need not determine whether plaintiffs sufficiently prevailed on the merits of their claims to be entitled to fees under a "merits" analysis also. Their action under § 1983 was at least a "catalyst," which resulted in their achieving precisely the result they sought by bringing the action.

Before this action was filed, both HUD and the Authorities had taken a firm position towards the plaintiffs' plight: for the first twelve months of the Section 8 tenancy, the plaintiffs were only entitled to housing located within the municipal boundaries of the public housing Authority issuing their Section 8 certificates. It was only in the wake of the district court's announced decision to the contrary that HUD reversed this policy by notifying all Massachusetts public housing authorities that their "jurisdiction," for purposes of Section 8, extended to any community within the Commonwealth, and by granting the plaintiffs full portability rights under § 1437f(r)(1). There is no suggestion that without the filing of the underlying action, and the proceedings spawned by it, this change in Section 8 portability policy would have occurred. Plaintiffs' lawsuit was not only a "necessary and important factor" in achieving the desired result, it seems to have been the key factor.

While acknowledging that the plaintiffs got what they wanted in their lawsuit, the Authorities attribute this "practical" success to HUD's "voluntary" agreement to change its Section 8 portability policy, a "gratuitous gesture" by the fee-target. But for reasons already stated, there is no reasonable way that HUD's and the defendant Authorities' change of heart can be disassociated from the lawsuit. We accept that HUD and the Authorities were cooperative once the court had expressed its interpretation of state law. They might have continued to fight. One may applaud their good sense and good will. Still, a ruling even as to state law by an experienced district judge is a significant matter, as these events showed, and the court's ruling was backed by the pending certification to the highest state court. HUD and the Authorities would hardly have accepted the ruling had they doubted its correctness. The filing of this case triggered a process before the district court (i.e. the submission of papers, the holding of hearings, the presentation of arguments, etc.) that led to the district court's decision. It was in response to that decision that HUD, and the Authorities, changed their Section 8 portability policy in Massachusetts. Plaintiffs are thus prevailing parties as that term is used in 42 U.S.C. § 1988.

IV.

Having found that the plaintiffs are "prevailing parties" for purposes of § 1988, we now turn to the second issue presented for review, to wit, whether there were "special circumstances" in this case meriting the district court's denial of attorneys' fees on discretionary grounds....

Although the defendants' good faith, in and of itself, was not enough to justify the denial of attorneys' fees, the district court found "something more" in this case, to wit, the defendants' good faith reliance on the EOCD's interpretation of Massachusetts law.... The Civil Rights Attorney's Fees Awards Act is not meant as a "punishment" for "bad" defendants who resist plaintiffs' claims in bad faith. Rather, it is meant to compensate civil rights attorneys who bring civil rights cases and win them. The need for such law suits, and such payment, may well be greatest in just those instances in which lawyers and officials, in totally good faith, have opposing views about what state and federal law requires of them."

* * *

V.

For all of the foregoing reasons, we vacate the district court's order denying the plaintiffs' motion for attorneys' fees under § 1988. We remand the case to the district court for consideration of the fee application in a manner not inconsistent with this opinion.

It is so ordered. Costs for appellant.

C. Retirement Communities and Assisted Living

American Association of Retired Persons
What Housing Options Do You Have?, HOUSING (1995)[*]

Continuing Care Retirement Communities (CCRC) or Retirement Communities allow you to live on your own with a minimum of assistance, providing shelter, social, health care, and support services under a contractual arrangement.

Assisted living facilities are residential group facilities that are not licensed as nursing homes, providing personal care to those who need assistance with daily activities. These facilities can also respond to emergency needs and provide some related services.

National Center on Assisted Living
Key Concepts Of Assisted Living (September 1998)
<http://www.ncal.org/about/concepts.htm>[**]

Definition

While assisted living is the most common term used in the nation, assisted living settings may be known by as many as 26 different names, including residential care, personal care, adult congregate care, boarding home and domiciliary care. Common to all these terms, however, is the understanding that an assisted living setting is:
- a congregate residential setting that provides or coordinates personal services, 24-hour supervision and assistance (scheduled and unscheduled), activities, and health-related services;
- designed to minimize the need to move;
- designed to accommodate individual residents' changing needs and preferences;
- designed to maximize residents' dignity, autonomy, privacy, independence, choice and safety; and
- designed to encourage family and community involvement.

Size

An assisted living residence is not defined by its capacity for residents, but by the scope of the services it provides. The size and configuration of each assisted living residence should be determined by consumer demand and the types of services provided. Services to individuals with mental illnesses, developmental disabilities, Alzheimer's disease, other forms of dementia or disabilities requiring specialized services, must be delivered in an appropriate and safe setting in compliance with state and federal regulations.

---

[*] Copyright © 1995. Reprinted with permission.
[**] Copyright © 1998. Reprinted with permission.

Physical Plant

An assisted living residence should be designed, operated, and maintained in a manner appropriate to the special needs of the population served. The residence should be located, constructed, and equipped in compliance with all applicable local codes and state and federal regulations. An assisted living setting should be designed in a way that maximizes the quality of life, independence, autonomy, safety, dignity, choice and privacy of residents. Settings should also be designed in a manner that encourages family and community involvement.

Move-In and Occupancy Agreements

New residents and/or their family members should receive an orientation about the services the assisted living residence offers.

Individuals should not be allowed to move into an assisted living residence that is unable to meet the full scope of their needs.

Occupancy agreements should clearly specify what services can and will be provided, the facility's rates for all services and payment structure, the facility's occupancy criteria, and relocation criteria.

Service Agreements

When moving into an assisted living setting, each resident should be evaluated or assessed to determine how his or her need for services can best be met. A service agreement should be developed indicating what services will be delivered to meet particular needs based on the individual's physical, psychosocial and cognitive capabilities. The individual, family, or a responsible party should assist in the development of the service agreement, which should be reviewed and updated regularly or as needed.

An assisted living service coordinator should be designated to be responsible for developing, implementing, and evaluating the progress of the service agreement.

A copy of the agreement should be given to the resident or his or her legal guardian.

Health Needs

The assisted living residence should provide daily supervision or assistance with activities of daily living and instrumental activities of daily living, coordinate services by outside agencies, and monitor the activities of the resident to ensure his or her health, safety, and well being. Daily assistance with activities may include the administration, supervision and/or assistance with self administration of medication by a qualified staff person, and other health care services as permitted by state laws, rules and regulations.

An emphasis on wellness should be part of each setting's approach toward health care delivery. In addition, staff should assure that prompt and appropriate medical, health, and dental care services are obtained when required. The health care of each resident will be under the supervision of a physician of his/her choice.

Residents with temporary periods of incapacity due to major illness, injury, or recuperation from surgery should be allowed to remain in the facility or be readmitted from a hospital if appropriate services can be provided. If possible, the facility should help residents remain in the facility when death is imminent if appropriate palliative services can be provided in the setting.

* * *

Staffing Patterns

Assisted living facilities should offer 24-hour protective supervision and oversight of residents. Assisted living residences should embrace the philosophy of "aging in place" which allows individuals to remain at the residence as long as staff can properly provide for residents' health, safety and well being.

The number and type of staff employed by an assisted living facility should depend on a number of factors, including state regulations, the number of people living in the facility, each resident's service requirements, and the range of services offered.

The assisted living residence should employ adequate staff to maintain the facility in a manner that promotes the safety, health, and well-being of residents and staff.

Resident Rights

The philosophy of assisted living emphasizes the right of the individual to choose the setting for care and services. Resident rights should include the right to:
- Privacy;
- Be treated at all times with dignity and respect;
- Control personal finances;
- Retain and have use of personal possessions;
- Interact freely with others both within the assisted living residence and in the community;
- Practice religion or abstain from religious practice;
- Control receipt of health-related services;
- Be free from abuse and neglect; and
- Organize resident councils.

Upon move-in, all residents should be given a copy of their rights and responsibilities and should be encouraged to ask questions or discuss their rights with staff or the administrator at any time. A copy of those rights and responsibilities should be posted in a conspicuous place at all times.

Assisted living administrators should also:
- Permit access to the facility and to residents (with the individual resident's permission) by approved advocates and community organizations at reasonable times;
- Ensure that an informal or formal communications process is in place between the residence administration, residents and families;
- Establish residence rules governing visitors, usage of tobacco and alcohol and the use of personal property; and
- Ensure each resident is free from discrimination as provided by local, state and federal law.

Licensure and Certification

In most states assisted living residences are licensed or certified by an appropriate department or agency of the state that should have a process for issuance of initial licenses and for renewing existing licenses. A variance or waiver should be available to allow an individual facility to seek an exception to a requirement of the licensure or certification rules.

The state should maintain an aggressive program to seek out unlicensed or uncertified facilities and bring them into compliance with applicable licensure or certification standards. The health, safety, and well being of the residents should be the primary consideration when a state determines if a facility can be brought into compliance in a reasonable period of time or if closure is necessary. In addition, poor performing facilities that refuse to correct incidences of abuse and neglect should not be allowed to continue to operate.

Each state should also establish a program to reward—through public recognition, incentive payments, or both—assisted living residences that provide the highest quality care to residents.

Measuring and Improving Quality

The National Center for Assisted Living (NCAL) strongly believes that placing assisted living on a parallel regulatory track with nursing homes would be a mistake. Such a regulatory model would stifle the very spirit that led to the creation of assisted living. Instead of following the nursing home regulatory model, a quality assurance system for assisted living that focuses on customer satisfaction and actual outcomes should be designed and built. Such a system could be utilized by providers, consumers, managed care entities, and governments to ensure that quality services and care are being maintained. More important, such a system would better serve the interests of assisted living customers by providing them with powerful input into the quality evaluation process and the delivery of services.

Question

Why does NCAL resist the notion of regulation similar to that required for nursing facilities?

American Bar Association
Continuing Care Retirement Communities, in NATIONAL HANDBOOK ON LAWS AND PROGRAMS AFFECTING SENIOR CITIZENS (1998)
<http://www.abanet.org/srlawyers/handbook.html>[*]

Introduction

Also known as life care retirement communities, these facilities have been in existence for over 60 years; however, the industry has greatly expanded in the last two decades. Although the vast majority of Continuing Care Retirement Communities (CCRCs) are run by nonprofit organizations, a number of major corporations have entered the market. The number of these communities is expected to double by the year 2000. The typical CCRC serves between 200 and 300 residents.

What is a Continuing Care Retirement Community?

A Continuing Care Retirement Community is a financially self-sufficient residential community for senior citizens that offers medical care and nursing services in addition to independent living. Continuing Care Retirement Communities vary in the image they wish to project. Some are closely aligned with a particular religious denomination. Some seek to cover the basics in a simple community setting, while others attempt to create a country club or resort atmosphere.

Type A Facility: Extensive Plan

CCRCs differ in the amount of health care they offer their residents. What is sometimes referred to as a "Type A" or "extensive" facility will provide food, housing, medical services and nursing care, and assisted living care for the remainder of the retiree's life, frequently even after you have exhausted your financial resources. It can be thought of as a form of self-insurance, spreading the risk of catastrophic health care costs among all residents in the CCRC so that no one will face financial ruin. Because of the guaranteed health care, Type A facilities are the most expensive.

Type B Facility: Modified Plan

"Type B" or "modified" retirement communities offer the same services as the Type A facilities but without the health care guarantee. For example, a Type B facility may provide 15 days of nursing care per year. After you use up your 15 days, you must pay a daily charge for the nursing care. In the event you run out of money, the facility is not contractually obligated to provide for your care.

Type C Facility: Fee for Service Plan

In the "Type C" or "fee for service" community, residents have priority access to the nursing unit, but they must pay for the services received. Moreover, Type C facilities generally do not include meals or personal care assistance as part of their package. Consequently, they are the least expensive.

---

[*] Copyright American Bar Association. All rights reserved. Reprinted by permission.

CCRC Fees

A Continuing Care Retirement Community charges two fees—a onetime entry fee followed by a monthly maintenance fee. The entry fee may currently range anywhere from $38,000 to $400,000 depending on whether it is a Type A, B, or C facility, the size of the living unit, and the amenities associated with the community (such as swimming pool or golf course). The monthly maintenance fee usually ranges from $650 to $3,500 and may be increased from year to year as inflation dictates. Residents meet the monthly fee with social security and pension income, while the funds for the entry fee are often obtained from the sale of the retiree's home. An alternative used by some CCRCs is to offer a reduced entry fee which is accompanied by proportionally higher monthly fees.

Pros and Cons

Security and flexibility are two reasons for joining a CCRC. With increased life expectancies brought about by modern medicine, many elderly persons experience two stages in their retirement years. The younger elderly are capable of independent living and community involvement. For this age group, the social and recreational features are attractive. Dependency and declining health characterize the second stage of retirement. The CCRC is equipped to keep you in your apartment as long as possible. Housekeeping and dietary services (offered by the Type A and B facilities) handle the day-to-day living activities you may no longer be able to do for yourself. Transportation to shopping areas is often provided. Most importantly, a nursing facility is located on the premises if and when skilled or custodial care becomes necessary. The support systems of a CCRC enable various gradations of living along the independent/dependent continuum tailored to the individual's needs. In addition, some life care contracts (Type A) promise to care for you even after you exhaust your financial resources.

There are some drawbacks to living in a Continuing Care Retirement Community. The most obvious is the cost. The entry fees are so expensive that should you join a CCRC and later find you do not like it, the bulk of your life savings is gone and you cannot afford to move elsewhere. Some senior citizens do not desire a community as homogeneous as CCRCs tend to be. Finally, there have been a few instances where, due to fraud or mismanagement, CCRCs have gone bankrupt.

Choosing a Continuing Care Retirement Community

Initially, you must determine whether or not communal living is for you. The book "If I Live to be 100" by Vivian Carlin and Ruth Mansberg is very helpful in this regard. Free from technical language, the book describes the day-to-day lives of residents in a retirement community. The authors address management/resident relations, the nursing unit, recreational activities, and the relationship between the retirees and the townspeople.

Once the decision is made to pursue this form of housing, you should visit each CCRC you are considering and determine what the entrance requirements for each are. You should also inquire about rules and policies. A visit ought to include a night in the guest house as well as a couple of meals in the dining room. Ask questions about the services available. How many meals are included in the contracts? Is service available to the resident's apartment if it is needed? Is the kitchen willing to prepare meals to fit a prescribed diet?

You should tour the grounds and buildings, paying close attention to the layout, appearance, upkeep, and security. Within the apartment you should look for the usual features which concern prospective renters or homeowners, along with looking for an emergency call system. You should engage the residents and staff in conversation. Are the people friendly? How do they interact? Are there many social activities? Is there a library? Are there recreational facilities?

You should insist upon visiting the nursing unit. This is essential for the Type A facilities as health care constitutes a significant portion of the services you will be purchasing. Does the health care facility provide a full range of services, such as annual or routine physical exams, dental care, physical/occupational/speech therapy, prescription drugs and/or eyecare? What is the limit to the health and medical care coverage that is included in the regular fees? What is the community's policy for transferring residents from apartment and independent living units to nursing home facilities? What is the policy for returning residents to their apartments or independent living units? You should observe the manner of the staff. Are they calm or frantic? What about the patients? Are they groomed and dressed? Are the halls clean and free of odor? Finally, the visit should include a trip into town to see the nearby churches, stores and recreational opportunities.

Seek Professional Advice

More important than the physical layout of a retirement community is the insurance/services package you will be buying. You must remember that you are buying a contract and not real estate. To this end, you should carefully read the contract and have your lawyer read it. You should have in writing all fees and the corresponding services to be rendered by the provider. Clarify whether services such as housekeeping, linens and personal laundry, telephones, parking and transportation are included. You should ask the facility for its fee-hike history. You should see what the refund policy is in the event a resident dies prematurely or chooses to leave the community. Nonrefundable entry fees tend to be lower. However, retirees wishing to leave an estate for their heirs may want to look for a CCRC offering a refundable (or partially refundable) entry fee.

You and your lawyer should also scrutinize several annual reports and balance sheets of the CCRC. You should ask if an actuarial study has been done and request a copy of the report. Even more so than a financial disclosure statement, an actuarial study will reveal whether the facility will be able to meet its obligations several years down the road. In addition, you might inquire if the CCRC has been accredited by the American Association of Homes and Services for the Aging (AAHSA). As of January 1996, this group has inspected and accredited over 180 CCRCs in 24 states.

Continuing Care Retirement Communities are increasing in popularity as evidenced by the long waiting lists for admission at some of the more established facilities. Careful planning, coupled with wise shopping, can make this form of housing and health care a successful alternative for many senior citizens.

American Bar Association
Adult Day Care in NATIONAL HANDBOOK ON LAWS AND PROGRAMS
AFFECTING SENIOR CITIZENS (1998)
<http://www.abanet.org/srlawyers/handbook.html>[*]

Introduction

Adult day care programs provide a variety of daytime services for impaired older adults. Individuals who participate in adult day care programs attend on a regular, planned basis. Most adult day care centers are open 8-10 hours a day on weekdays and there is a trend toward weekend service as well. Adult day care centers work to assist the older adult to remain living in the community at the highest level of independence possible. Many participants and their family caregivers are able to delay or avoid use of more costly in-home and nursing home care by using adult day care. Admission requirements and procedures vary somewhat across centers, but all require that the applicant have a personal physician or clinic with whom care can be coordinated.

Services Provided

Adult day care services are designed to assist both the participant and the family. Adult day care centers provide health maintenance services, therapeutic activities, personal care, and emotional support to participants. Older persons may benefit from the special care if they are:
- physically impaired
- socially isolated
- in need of personal care help
- mentally confused
- limited in their ability to function independently in the community
- in need of supervision

Family caregivers benefit from adult day care as well. Knowing their family member is safe at the day care center gives employed caregivers peace of mind while at work.

Paying for Adult Day Care

Although many adult day care participants pay for care out-of pocket, almost all centers have provisions such as sliding fee scales or scholarships, to serve those who need financial assistance. Most long-term care insurance policies cover adult daycare, and worker's compensation policies have paid adult daycare costs for those with work-related disabilities. Medicare, however, does not pay for adult day care or other long-term care services (nursing home, adult home, in-home companions.) Medicaid may pay for adult day care and transportation if the person meets financial and nursing home pre-admission screening criteria.

---

[*] Copyright American Bar Association. All rights reserved. Reprinted by permission.

Stephanie Edelstein, Vicki Gottlich, Dorothy Siemon & Bruce Vignery
Housing Rights of Group Home and Nursing Facility Residents
29 CLEARINGHOUSE REV. 664 (October 1995)[*]

I. Introduction

Housing options for persons who are unable to live independently include a variety of supervised living programs, ranging from small board-and-care programs to continuing care facilities, nursing facilities, and, the most recent trend, assisted living. Residents may encounter discrimination if the form of zoning and land-use restrictions, licensing, or health and safety regulations. This article discusses the ways in which federal civil rights laws are being used to challenge this discrimination in the context of group house and nursing facilities.

A. Overview of Relevant Statutes

Section 504 of the Rehabilitation Act of 1973 prohibits discrimination on the basis of disability or perceived disability in any program or activity that receives federal financial assistance, including public and subsidized housing programs and nursing facilities that receive Medicare or Medicaid funding. Section 504 requires that such programs be accessible to and usable by persons who are "handicapped" or who have disabilities. (29 U.S.C. § 794, as amended.) The Fair Housing Amendments Act of 1988 (FHAA) prohibits discrimination in almost all housing activities or transactions, whether in the public or private sector; in the provision of services or facilities in connection with a dwelling; and in the application of zoning, land use, or health and safety regulations. (42 U.S.C. § 3601 *et seq.*) These laws are complemented by the Americans with Disabilities Act (ADA). (42 U.S.C. § 12101 *et seq.*; 28 C.F.R. pt. 36, app. B.) Although Title II (state and local programs) and III (public accommodations) of the ADA do not specifically cover housing (and indeed specifically exclude entities covered by the FHAA), they apply to nonhousing function of a facility, such as meeting rooms, meal sites, adult day care, or long-term care. Under all three statutes, discrimination includes a refusal to make resonable accommodations (adjustments to rules or procedures) or modifications (changes in the physical premises) upon request.

The three statutes use virtually the same definition of "handicap" or "disability." Individuals are protected if they (1) have a physical or mental impairment that substantially limits one or more major life activities, such as performing manual tasks, walking, seeing, hearing, speaking, or personal care; (2) have a record of having such an impairment, whether or not the impairment still exists; or (3) are regarded as having such an impairment, whether or not the perception is accurate.

While age alone does not equal disability, the symptoms and conditions of the aging process may cause an individual to meet these definition. The protections extend to persons who are "frail," described in the Older Americans Act as being 60

---

[*] Copyright © 1995. Reprinted with permission.

years of age or older and unable to perform without assistance (i.e., visual reminder, physical cue, or supervision) at least two activities of daily living. (42 U.S.C. § 3002.) The protections also extend to persons who, due to a cognitive or other mental impairment, require substantial supervision because of behavior that poses a serious health or safety hazard to themselves or others.

D. Nursing Facilities

1. Nursing Home Residents' Rights

a. Nursing Home Reform Act of 1987

Margaret Farley
Adult Care Homes
KANSAS LONG-TERM CARE HANDBOOK 1-11 (1999)[*]

I. Nursing Home Reform Act of 1987 and Amendments

This section concerns the federal and state laws which govern the specific type of adult care home known as nursing homes. Most nursing homes participate in the federal Medicare or Medicaid program and are therefore subject to the Nursing Home Reform Act of 1987, its amendments (the NHRA), and certain federal regulations. . . .

A. Overview of the Nursing Home Reform Act of 1987 and Amendments

1. Introduction

In 1995 about 1.5 million Americans spent some time in a nursing home. Ninety (90) percent of these nursing home residents were 65 years of age or older; over thirty-five (35) percent were age 85 or older. Most nursing homes are freestanding, but can also be long-term care units in hospitals or continuing care retirement communities. In 1995, about 96% of all nursing homes were Medicaid- or Medicare-certified, or both.

2. The Nursing Home Reform Act of 1987

The NHRA became law with the passage of the Omnibus Budget Reconciliation Act of 1987. Consequently, for many years the NHRA was more commonly known as OBRA87. Public pressure for significant federal nursing home legislation grew out of nursing home scandals, state studies and Congressional hearings on the quality of nursing home care in the 1970s and early 1980s. In 1984, the Tenth Circuit ruled in the landmark *Estate of Smith v. Heckler*, that the Department of Health and Human Services (DHHS) had a legal duty to assure quality care for Medicaid recipients in

---

[*] Copyright © 1999. Reprinted with permission.

nursing homes but had failed in that duty. The federal appeals court directed DHHS to implement systemic changes to remedy the breach.

When the Reagan administration instead proposed regulations for survey and enforcement systems in the early 1980s which many believed were too weak, Congress objected and placed two moratoria on the regulations and threatened a third. A compromise was reached between the executive and legislative branches by an agreement that the DHHS commission a comprehensive study of nursing home issues.

In 1986, the Committee on Nursing Home Regulation of the Institute of Medicine (IoM) published the resulting study, "Improving the Quality of Care in Nursing Homes." The IoM report was comprehensive and largely critical of a system of regulations and enforcement which failed to protect nursing home residents from poor care and rights violations. A pivotal document with clear recommendations for improvement, it became a blueprint for legislative reform. In the following year the NHRA was passed with remarkable consensus from the industry and consumer advocates and contained many of the IoM recommendations.

B. Sources of the Federal Law

Medicare requirements for certified facilities are located at 42 U.S.C. § 1395i-3; Medicaid requirements are found at 42 U.S.C. § 1396r. The implementing regulations for both programs are found at 42 C.F.R. § 483. Interpretive guidelines published by the Health Care Financing Administration (HCFA) assist federal surveyors in applying the federal regulations and are a good research aid in understanding how the regulations are applied. Such guidelines are not legally enforceable standing alone, but are highly influential.

C. Key Provisions of the NHRA

1. Medicare Skilled Nursing Facilities

The Medicare portion of the NHRA defines a Medicare facility and sets out the requirements for, and assuring quality of care in, skilled nursing facilities, as follows:

> A Medicare skilled nursing facility (SNF) is defined as an institution which is primarily engaged in providing skilled nursing care (direct supervision or direct care by an RN) and related services for residents who require medical or nursing care, or rehabilitation services for the treatment of injured, disabled, or sick persons, and which is not primarily for the care and treatment of mental diseases.

A typical stay in a SNF is about 20 days, but at least partial Medicare coverage can last up to 100 days. Common qualifying conditions are those which may benefit from short term physical and occupational or speech therapies, such as stroke, cardiac rehabilitation or fractured hip. Otherwise, persons admitted to SNFs must require at least daily skilled nursing care such as, e.g., intravenous antibiotic administration, assessment and stabilization of complex medical conditions, or wound care.

2. Medicaid Nursing Facilities

The statutory definition for Medicaid NFs follows:

> ... an institution ... which is primarily engaged in providing to residents (A) skilled nursing care and related services for residents who require medical or nursing care, (B) rehabilitation services for the rehabilitation of injured, disabled, or sick persons, or (C) on a regular basis, health-related care and services to individuals who because of their mental or physical condition require care and services (above the level of room and board) which can be made available to them only through institutional facilities, and is not primarily for the care and treatment of mental disease.

Notice that, except for subsection C above, the definitions for Medicare and Medicaid facilities are the same. Medicaid nursing facilities provide general nursing home care, above the level of room and board, in addition to the skilled nursing and rehabilitative services. Before the NHRA there were two separate levels of care in Medicaid-certified nursing homes, intermediate and skilled. Some facilities still characterize the level of care they provide as intermediate, but Medicaid certification no longer provides for this distinction. All Medicaid facilities are held to the same statutory and regulatory standards, i.e., there is no lesser standard for Medicaid certified care simply because a facility purports to provide intermediate care.

As noted above, facilities may be both Medicare- and Medicaid-certified. By far the majority of nursing homes are Medicaid-certified. Reference will be made to NFs throughout; all of the rules which follow in this discussion apply equally to Medicare SNFs unless specifically noted otherwise. Where applicable, footnote citations will be made to both the Medicare and Medicaid sections of the Social Security Act. Finally, these laws and regulations create duties and responsibilities for the entire certified facility. Thus the law, with rare exception noted below, protects all residents in any certified facility. Persons who pay for their care entirely from their own private funds or insurance benefit from the laws the same as persons receiving Medicare or Medicaid assistance.

3. Required Nursing Facility Services

Requirements relating to the facilities' services set out standards for targeted outcomes, process and structure, to achieve the goals of quality of care, quality of life and protecting residents' rights. Specific areas include quality of life, care planning, resident assessment, ancillary services, training of nurse aides and physician services. The cornerstone provision of the NHRA requires nursing homes to "provide services to attain or maintain the highest practicable physical, mental, and psycho-social well-being of each resident." An NF must also "care for its residents in such a manner and in such an environment as will promote maintenance or enhancement of the quality of life of each resident." And, facilities must establish an internal quality assurance committee which meets at least quarterly.

The NHRA requires the development of a standardized, comprehensive resident assessment coordinated by an RN within the first two weeks of admission, updated quarterly and "promptly after a significant change in the resident's physical or mental condition." The assessment becomes a part of the resident's medical record and the basis for comprehensive care planning. Prior to the NHRA, each facility used its own assessment form; many were cursory. Baseline data to evaluate a resident's progress or decline was scarce and updates were even rarer. The NHRA standardized form currently known as the Minimum Data Set for Nursing Home Resident Assessment and Care Screening, or MDS, is now used in all certified nursing homes.

Certain services must be available for residents. These include nursing and rehabilitative services, under the cornerstone standard "to attain or maintain the highest practicable physical, mental, and psycho-social well-being of each resident." Also required are social, pharmaceutical, dietary, activities program, and routine and emergency dental services. Nursing facilities are required to comply fully with all applicable federal, state and local laws and regulations and with accepted professional standards and principles which apply to professionals providing services in such facilities.

Implementing the statutory requirement to "attain or maintain the highest practicable" condition of residents, the HCFA also specified outcome standards in major quality of care areas. Specific standards addressed in the regulations include but are not limited to the following:

- activities of daily living, including toileting, ambulation, dressing;
- vision and hearing;
- pressure sores (also known as decubitus ulcers);
- urinary incontinence;
- limb range of motion;
- mental and psychosocial functioning;
- naso-gastric tube feedings;
- prevention of accidents, including falls;
- nutritional status;
- hydration;
- respiratory care;
- care of prostheses;
- ostomy care; and
- proper medication.

The facility must carry out an appropriate plan of care based upon a comprehensive interdisciplinary assessment to prevent each resident's condition from deteriorating unnecessarily. Most residents in nursing facilities have more than one disease or condition. The statute and regulations aim to prevent decline due to poor nursing and rehabilitative care or neglect. For example, concerning pressure sores, the regulations provide:

> Based upon the comprehensive assessment of a resident, the facility must ensure that; (1) a resident who enters the facility without pressure sores does not develop pressure sores unless the individual's clinical condition demonstrates that they were unavoidable; and (2) a resident having pressure sores receives necessary treatment and services to promote healing, prevent infection and prevent new sores from developing.

Thus, the HCFA developed a straightforward statement of the expected outcome of proper professional care based upon a comprehensive assessment and care planning. Minimal professional nursing services are required. An LPN or RN must be on duty 24 hours a day, and a supervisory RN must be on duty 8 hours a day, 7 days a week. Each nurse aide on duty must complete a training and competency evaluation program within 4 months of employment. Residents' medical care must be under the supervision of a physician, emergency medical care must be available and detailed clinical records must be kept on each resident. Physicians must provide basic medical oversight of the quality of medical and other care of all residents in the facility and at least one physician must be a member of the quality assurance committee.

4. Express Resident Rights

The NHRA sets out the following explicit rights for each resident. Again, all resident rights apply equally to Medicare- and Medicaid-certified facilities. Other rights are set out in other specific sections of the law and will be discussed elsewhere in this section, e.g., management of personal funds. The rights of adjudicated incompetent residents devolve to, and may be exercised by, their state-appointed guardians, or their legally designated agents. Upon admission to the nursing facility, residents or their legal agents must be given specific notice of the delineated rights. Such notice must include, for example, the facility's procedure for handling personal funds, and its policy for implementing residents' advance directives.

a. Free Choice

Each resident must have a personal attending physician, and each resident has a right to choose his or her physician. The difficulty is that many physicians frequently decline to follow the care of their patients once they move to a nursing home. A Medicaid-certified facility is required to make transportation available for necessary medical appointments, so some residents may continue to see their physician in the office, but that is not always feasible or recommended. In practice, if a resident does not have a physician, the facility will offer the services of the "house physician," usually the medical director, as the resident's attending physician.

Freedom of choice includes the right to advance, informed consent to all care and treatment, including advance informed consent to changes in care and treatment which may affect the resident's well-being and the right to participate in care planning, unless a resident is an adjudicated incompetent. Even if a person has been adjudicated incompetent, it may be advisable to attempt to ascertain the person's wishes to the extent possible.

b. Freedom from Restraints and Abuse

i. Background

Before the implementation of the NHRA, the use of inappropriate physical and chemical restraints on residents in nursing homes was widespread. For many years restraints were a well-established intervention to prevent accidents, i.e., to keep residents from falling and injuring themselves or others, or from eloping and to con-

trol behavioral symptoms. The use of restraints is now closely controlled through NHRA provisions. Probably the most dramatic effect of the NHRA was an overwhelming reduction of the use of physical and chemical restraints within the first few years of the implementation of the law. Across the nation by 1992 (the NHRA became effective in 1990) the use of physical restraints had declined by at least 25%.
. . .

Medical and nursing literature now abounds with the benefits of eliminating the use of restraints, i.e., eliminating the common negative side effects of inappropriate physical and chemical restraints (depression, physical injuries, decreased mobility and socialization, decubitus ulcers, dehydration, inactivity, muscle and bone loss, weight loss and malnutrition, to name a few). Contemporary lawsuits against nursing homes have successfully argued the negligence of facility staff for applying physical restraints when residents are injured or strangled to death struggling to free themselves from, for example, a vest restraint. Even side rails can kill.

ii. Definition of Physical and Chemical Restraints

Physical restraints are "defined as any manual method or physical or mechanical device, material, or equipment attached or adjacent to the resident's body that the individual cannot remove easily which restricts freedom of movement or normal access to one's body." A chemical restraint is "a psycho-pharmacologic drug that is used for discipline or convenience and not required to treat medical symptoms." "Discipline" is punishing or penalizing a resident; "convenience" is a facility action to control resident behavior not in the best interest of the resident and with a lesser amount of facility effort.

According to the interpretive guidelines, physical restraints include, but are not limited to, leg restraints, arm restraints, hand mitts, soft ties or vests, and wheelchair lap trays. Certain other facility practices are considered physical restraints, such as using bed rails to keep a resident from getting out of bed (as opposed to enhancing mobility), tucking a sheet so tightly that a bed-bound resident cannot move or placing a resident in a chair that prevents rising. Orthotic devices used as restraints are expressly prohibited in the guidelines.

* * *

c. Privacy

A resident has the right to privacy in accommodations, medical treatment, written and telephone communications, visits and meetings of family and resident groups. Thus, the facility must furnish a telephone in a private area for the use of residents and a private meeting room for a resident or family group, if requested.

d. Confidentiality

All personal and clinical records must be kept confidential. Within 24 hours (excluding weekends and holidays) upon a written request, a resident or his legal agent must be given access to current clinical records. The facility must provide, at a reasonable rate, copies of resident's records within two working days of such a request by the resident or the resident's legal representative.

e. Accommodation of Needs

Facilities must reasonably accommodate residents' individual needs and preferences, except where the health or safety of the resident or other residents would be endangered. This is a quality of life issue and requires facilities to be more "resident-centered." Also, residents must receive notice before a facility changes his or her room or roommate. In itself, the latter is largely an empty right, as there is no time requirement for advance notice and no explicit right to oppose the transfer.

However, many residents are frail, become attached to their room or roommate, and may be at risk to decline in health with a room transfer. Opposition to the change of room can be rested upon the duty to accommodate the individual needs and preferences of the resident, or to help him or her "maintain the highest practicable physical, mental, or psycho-social well-being." Concerning the change of roommate, obviously the rights and preferences of both residents would need to be taken into consideration.

f. Grievances

Residents have the right to voice grievances about treatment or care. The facility must make prompt efforts to resolve those grievances. The law prohibits reprisal and discrimination against residents for voicing grievances. Enforcing this provision is difficult, at best. Very few citations in surveys for retaliation can be found. Frail residents in nursing homes are completely dependent upon their care-givers. They cannot always vote with their feet; another nursing home may not be available. Many residents do not speak out for fear of retaliation despite this paper protection.

Anecdotally, many family members acting as residents' legal representatives have reported that they are asked to leave after they voice a grievance "if they are not satisfied with the care." Most would consider this a form of retaliation; yet, it is a tactic commonly enlisted without reproach from regulators. If it works, the resident leaves of his or her own volition, and transfer and discharge rights are effectively nullified. See section III on transfer and discharge rights.

g. Participation Resident and Family Groups

Residents have the right to organize themselves and to meet privately in the nursing home with other residents. Families are frequently the chief advocates for residents, and NHRA granted them the same right. Commonly called resident and family councils, respectively, these groups have the right to submit complaints and recommendations for change to the administration. If a complaint is submitted in writing to the facility, the staff must consider it and respond, without necessarily making the recommended change, of course.

h. Participation in Other Activities

Nursing homes must allow residents to participate in social, religious and community activities that do not interfere with the rights of other residents in the facility.

* * *

j. Access and Visitation Rights

Before the NHRA, a resident's contact with persons outside the nursing home was largely controlled by whether facility staff would permit access to the resident. The NHRA reversed that order and explicitly rested the right of granting and denying access to outside visitors with the resident. The resident's right of association thus takes precedence over the property rights of the facility operator, as follows: An NF must allow the resident immediate access to his or her physician and family, and a representative of the state, including an ombudsman. Friends and other visitors, including the resident's attorney must be granted immediate access, subject to reasonable restrictions. Outside service providers must be granted "reasonable access" to the resident. All visitors, except the state authorities, are subject to the resident's right to decline their visit.

5. Protection Against Medicaid Discrimination

An NF must establish and maintain identical policies and practices concerning transfer and discharge and services, regardless of whether the resident is receiving Medicaid assistance or paying privately. A facility may not require prospective residents to waive their rights to Medicaid benefits. Nor may the facility require oral or written assurance that individuals are not eligible for or will not apply for Medicaid benefits.

However, many facilities require a financial statement from prospective residents, which effectively allows a facility to calculate the length of time a prospective resident will remain on private pay. If the time is too short, the facility simply denies the resident admission. HCFA has failed to enforce discrimination prohibitions with regard to financial screening, and it is freely exercised.

In addition, facilities cannot require a third party guarantee of payment to the facility as a condition of admission or continued stay in the facility. Before the NHRA facilities frequently obtained assurances from family members signing as the "responsible party," that they would guarantee payment of the resident's bill. Facilities would then hold family members accountable for unpaid bills. That practice is now illegal.

6. Protection of Resident Funds

A nursing facility, upon written authorization by the resident, must hold, safeguard and account for the resident's personal funds, but cannot require residents to deposit personal funds with the facility. Any amount held by the facility for the resident in excess of one hundred (100) dollars may be placed in an interest bearing account separate from the facility's operating account. Amounts less than one hundred dollars must be maintained in a petty cash fund or non-interest bearing account. Separate written accounts must be maintained and residents must be given "reasonable access" to such records. Medicaid residents must be notified when their accounts are within two hundred (200) dollars of the Supplemental Security Income resource limit for one person and of the consequences of reaching such an amount. A nursing facility must promptly convey a deceased resident's personal funds and final accounting to the administrator or executor of the resident's estate within thirty days.

Medicaid residents' personal funds may not be charged in excess of the Medicaid or Medicare reimbursement for nursing facility services covered by the Medicaid state plan or the Medicare per diem rate.

Questions

1. Would physical restraints be appropriate when a mentally impaired resident has a history of elopement? Chemical restraints? Why or why not?

2. What restrictions on a resident's ability to leave the facility "at will" would be appropriate under the NHRA?

b. Other Remedies

Stephanie Edelstein, Vicki Gottlich, Dorothy Siemon & Bruce Vignery
Housing Rights of Group Home and Nursing Facility Residents
29 CLEARINGHOUSE REV. 664 (October 1995)[*]

Nursing Facilities as Entities Subject to Section 504 and the Americans with Disabilities Act

Nursing facilities must comply with federal laws that prohibit discrimination on the basis of disability. In fact, several common nursing facility practices, including admission and discharge, use of special care units, eligibility for activities and services, imposition of additional costs, and retaliation, may be redressable under the ADA (42 U.S.C. § 12101 *et seq.*) and Section 504 (29 U.S.C. § 794) in combination with or in lieu of other laws, such as the Nursing Home Reform Law. (42 U.S.C. §§ 1395r-i(3)(a), 1396r(a)-(h).)

All facilities that receive Medicaid and/or Medicare funds are subject to Section 504. Facilities run by state or local governments are subject to Title II of the ADA, regardless of whether they receive federal funding. Privately operated nursing facilities are subject to Title III of the ADA, which prohibits discrimination by public accommodations that fall within one of the 12 enumerated categories. (Health care providers and social service establishments.) Depending on their operating structure, nursing facilities controlled by religious organizations may not be covered under Title III of the ADA, since religious entities are specifically exempt from the statute. (29 U.S.C. § 12187.)

A nursing facility may not discriminate by (1) denying an individual the opportunity to participate in its services becaue of the person's disability; (2) segregating

---

[*] Copyright © 1995. Reprinted with permission.

the person by providing services in a segregated setting; (3) applying eligibility criteria that serve to screen out individuals or classes of persons with disabilities, in considering whether the ADA applies to a particular situation, it is important to keep in mind three questions: What is the service being denied? What is the nature of the discrimination? Against whom is the facility discriminating?

Question

Given the difficulty of the task, that is, caring for a group of extremely frail people, many of whom have significant mental impairments, is the application of the ADA and Section 504 of the Rehabilitation Act fair to facilities?

Wagner v. Fair Acres Geriatric Center
49 F.3d 1002 (3d Cir. 1994)

MANSMANN, Circuit Judge.

The general issue we address is whether Fair Acres Geriatric Center, a county-operated intermediate care nursing facility, violated Section 504 of the Rehabilitation Act of 1973, 29 U.S.C. § 794, when it denied admission to Margaret C. Wagner, a 65 year old woman afflicted with Alzheimer's disease. Although Fair Acres admits Alzheimer's patients, it denied admission to Mrs. Wagner because it determined that its facility and staff could not accommodate the behavioral manifestations of her disease.

The jury was asked to decide whether, despite her handicap of Alzheimer's disease, Mrs. Wagner was "otherwise qualified" for admission to Fair Acres within the meaning of section 504, including any reasonable accommodation Fair Acres was required to make. Following the jury verdict in favor of Mrs. Wagner, the district court granted Fair Acres' motion for judgment as a matter of law and conditionally granted its motion for a new trial.

We find that there was legally sufficient evidence to support the jury's verdict. Thus, we will vacate the district court's grant of judgment as a matter of law for Fair Acres. We are uncertain, however, that given the correct legal standards, the district court would have exercised its discretion in finding that the verdict was against the great weight of the evidence. Thus we will also vacate the district court's conditional grant of Fair Acres' motion for a new trial and remand for reconsideration of this motion.

I.

In 1988, at age 58, Margaret Wagner was diagnosed as suffering from Alzheimer's disease, a chronic degenerative neurological disorder that impairs intellectual functioning. Alzheimer's is associated with and has a devastating effect on intellectual functions including memory, recognition, comprehension and basic functional ability. As the disease progresses, basic skills are lost, such as the ability to feed, dress, groom or bathe oneself. Mrs. Wagner suffers from a particularly difficult, but not unique, form of Alzheimer's disease which is characterized by screaming, agitation and aggressive behavior. Initially, Mrs. Wagner was cared for by her husband, assisted by his two adult daughters and by visiting nurses supplied through the County Office of Services to the Aging, who provided care approximately 27 hours a week. In the summer of 1992, however, Mrs. Wagner suffered a marked deterioration in cognitive functioning and behavior associated with her dementia.

As a result, her family could no longer satisfactorily care for her at home. On August 23, 1992, Mrs. Wagner was admitted to Dowden Nursing Home, a private facility located in Newton Square in Delaware County, Pennsylvania. On September 2, 1992, she was transferred from Dowden to the Wills Geriatric Psychiatry Program operated by Thomas Jefferson University Hospital, due to Mrs. Wagner's severe episodes of agitated behavior and confusion. On September 16, 1992, Wills made an initial referral for Mrs. Wagner to be admitted to Fair Acres Geriatric Center. Fair Acres is a 900-bed skilled intermediate nursing facility operated by the Delaware County Board of Institutional Management, licensed by the Pennsylvania Department of Health and certified under Titles 18 and 19 of the Social Security Act. Fair Acres receives county, state and federal funding, including Medicare and Medicaid funding. At least 98% of its patients are admitted under medical assistance.

Fair Acres' stated mission and goal is to provide care primarily for the geriatric community. Approximately 60% of its patients suffer from Alzheimer's disease or some other form of dementia. Although it has a staff-to-patient ratio of one to eight, it is not staffed or equipped to handle psychiatric residents. Accordingly, if an applicant for admission poses a threat of injury to himself or others, the application is rejected. An applicant's psychiatric history is reviewed to determine (1) if the applicant's primary diagnosis is medical, warranting nursing home placement and (2) if the applicant can be absorbed comfortably and appropriately into Fair Acres' geriatric population. *See* Fair Acres' admission's guidelines containing its "Psychiatric Policy."

On September 16, 1992, upon receiving Mrs. Wagner's application for admission, Fair Acres' Admissions Committee made an initial determination that Mrs. Wagner was not then suitable for admission, but placed her application on "hold" pending further information regarding her condition. The Committee met again on October 8, 1992 and designated Mrs. Wagner's application as "medically disapproved," acting on the recommendation of its psychiatric consultant, Dr. Satyendra Diwan, that Mrs. Wagner was not appropriate for admission due to the behavioral problems she was exhibiting at Wills.

Between Mrs. Wagner's second and third evaluations, Linda Hadfield, Fair Acres' admissions RN, visited Wills to speak with Mrs. Wagner's nurses and staff and to observe Mrs. Wagner firsthand. Mrs. Wagner was put on "hold" again after the third admissions committee meeting on October 29, 1992. Dr. Diwan's notes in the "comments" area of Mrs. Wagner's October 29th evaluation form indicated that Mrs. Wagner "needs more time" and was "not appropriate for Fair Acres."

On December 30, 1992, due to contradictions in the documentation from Wills that had been submitted to Fair Acres, Ms. Hadfield made a second visit to Wills and on January 6, 1993, Dr. Diwan evaluated Mrs. Wagner for a fourth time. After reviewing Wills' progress reports, Dr. Diwan noted that Mrs. Wagner was still agitated, confused and irritable as late as December 29, 1992, but recommended a further evaluation in six to eight weeks. Finally, on February 17, 1993, a fifth evaluation took place. Although Wills' hospital records indicated that Mrs. Wagner's behavioral problems had improved slightly, the records showed that she continued to experience episodes of combativeness, agitation and assaultiveness on a daily basis. Under "comments," Dr. Diwan noted that Mrs. Wagner was a "borderline case and will not fit into our milieu." Accordingly, Mrs. Wagner was again denied admission to Fair Acres.

On April 12, 1993, approximately two months after her last evaluation by Fair Acres, Mrs. Wagner was admitted to Easton Nursing Center. Easton Nursing Center is located approximately 85 miles from the home of Mrs. Wagner's husband and children. Because this represents a commute by car of one and one-half hours each way, the number of visits between Mrs. Wagner and her husband and children was severely curtailed. While Mrs. Wagner was at Wills, she was visited by her husband on a daily basis unless he was ill. Due to the fact that her husband has vision only in one eye, he was unable to make the trip to Easton independently. Consequently, while Mrs. Wagner was at Easton, her family was only able to visit her twice a week.

On May 21, 1993, Margaret Wagner, by her next friend George Wagner, filed a two count complaint in United States District Court for the Eastern District of Pennsylvania. Count One alleged that Fair Acres had discriminated against Mrs. Wagner on the basis of her handicap, the behavioral aspects of her dementia, in violation of section 504 of the Rehabilitation Act of 1973, 29 U.S.C. § 794, by refusing to admit her to its nursing facility. Mrs. Wagner sought a declaration that the acts of Fair Acres had violated her rights under section 504 of the Rehabilitation Act and sought injunctive relief enjoining Fair Acres from unlawfully excluding her from its facility and directing Fair Acres to admit Mrs. Wagner to its first available bed. She also sought damages and an award of attorney's fees and costs.

* * *

At trial, Mrs. Wagner introduced the testimony of three expert witnesses to support her claim that she was qualified for admission to Fair Acres in spite of the behavioral manifestations of her Alzheimer's disease. Dr. Gary L. Gottlieb, a geriatric psychiatrist and the director of the geriatric psychiatry program at the University of Pennsylvania School of Medicine, testified, based on his review of Mrs. Wagner's medical records, that as early as September, 1992, Mrs. Wagner was appropriate for the type of care provided by a nursing facility such as Fair Acres.

Dr. Edward Kim, Mrs. Wagner's treating physician at Wills, testified that Mrs. Wagner could have been accommodated by a nursing home around the third week of October. Finally, Mrs. Wagner introduced the testimony of Dr. Bijan Etemad, a psychiatrist at Easton Nursing Center (where Mrs. Wagner resided at the time of trial), that in his judgment, Mrs. Wagner was appropriate for nursing home care.

Fair Acres argued that Mrs. Wagner's "sustained combative and assaultive behavior distinguished her from Fair Acres' patients and prevented her from being qualified for admission," because its guidelines prohibited it from admitting psychiatric patients. Challenging Mrs. Wagner's expert witnesses' lack of consideration for her need for one-on-one supervision, Fair Acres contended that it is not equipped, due to its staff to patient ratio, to provide one-on-one supervision for prolonged periods of time. It further asserted that Dr. Kim's testimony was at odds with and often contradicted his own progress notes, which indicated that Mrs. Wagner was still exhibiting symptoms of agitation and combativeness at the time when he claimed she became suitable for transfer to a nursing facility.

On September 22, 1993, at the close of all the evidence, Fair Acres moved for judgment as a matter of law pursuant to Fed. R. Civ. P. 50. The court reserved its judgment on this motion and submitted the case to the jury on one issue—whether Margaret Wagner was "otherwise qualified" for admission into Fair Acres within the meaning of section 504. After deliberating, the jury returned a verdict in favor of Mrs. Wagner.

On October 5, 1993, Fair Acres renewed its motion for judgment as a matter of law, or in the alternative for a new trial pursuant to Fed. R. Civ. P. 50(b), asserting that Mrs. Wagner was not "otherwise qualified" within the meaning of section 504 because she did not meet all of Fair Acres requirements for admission. Fair Acres also contended, for the first time, that Mrs. Wagner had not been discriminated against "solely by reason of handicap."

On October 7, 1993, Mrs. Wagner filed a motion for a new trial limited to damages only. On February 15, 1994, the district court entered its order granting Fair Acres' motion for judgment as a matter of law and conditionally granting its motion for a new trial. The district court found that Mrs. Wagner was not an "otherwise qualified" handicapped individual who had been denied a benefit solely by reason of her handicap, because according to the court, she "sought admission to Fair Acres because of her handicap and not in spite of it." *Wagner v. Fair Acres Geriatric Center*, 859 F. Supp. 776, 782 (E.D. Pa. 1994). According to the court, the decision not to admit Mrs. Wagner was a medical treatment decision made by Fair Acres' medical and health care professionals, and medical treatment decisions are generally immune from scrutiny under section 504. Observing that Fair Acres admits patients suffering from Alzheimer's disease, the court also held that section 504, by its very terms, does not cover discrimination among similarly handicapped persons. Finally, the court concluded that Mrs. Wagner was not "otherwise qualified" for admission to Fair Acres based on the evidence introduced at trial, because "it was not the function of Fair Acres to provide psychiatric services for persons with disruptive psychotic disorders." *Wagner v. Fair Acres*, 859 F. Supp. at 783. Accordingly, the court concluded that Mrs. Wagner failed to establish a case for relief under section 504.

* * *

II.

Section 504 of the Rehabilitation Act of 1973, 29 U.S.C. § 4, prohibits a federally funded state program from discriminating against a handicapped individual solely by reason of his or her handicap. Section 504 of the Rehabilitation Act reads in pertinent part:

No otherwise qualified handicapped individual in the United States, as defined in section 706(7) of this title shall, solely by reason of his handicap, be excluded from participation in, be denied the benefits of or be subjected to discrimination under any program or activity receiving Federal financial assistance . . . .

A "handicapped individual" for purposes of the Act is defined as "any person who (i) has a physical or mental impairment which substantially limits one or more of such person's major life activities, (ii) has a record of such impairment, or (iii) is regarded as having such an impairment." 29 U.S.C. § 706(7)(B). In order to establish a violation of the Rehabilitation Act, a plaintiff must prove (1) that he is a "handicapped individual" under the Act, (2) that he is "otherwise qualified" for the position sought, (3) that he was excluded from the position sought "solely by reason of his handicap," and (4) that the program or activity in question receives federal financial assistance. *Strathie v. Department of Transp.*, 716 F.2d 227 (3d Cir. 1983); *Nathanson v. Medical College of Pennsylvania*, 926 F.2d 1368, 1380 (3d Cir. 1991). It is undisputed that Mrs. Wagner is a handicapped individual within the meaning of the Act and that Fair Acres is a recipient of federal assistance. Indeed, the only issue submitted to the jury was whether Mrs. Wagner was "otherwise qualified" for admission to Fair Acres.

In *Southeastern Community College v. Davis*, 442 U.S. 397 (1979), the Supreme Court held that an "otherwise qualified" handicapped individual is one who can meet all of a program's requirements in spite of his handicap. *Id.* at 406. Significantly, the Court indicated that an individual may be otherwise qualified in some instances even though he cannot meet all of a program's requirements. In *Strathie*, we observed that "this is the case when the refusal to modify an existing program would be unreasonable and thereby discriminatory." 716 F.2d at 230.

Further interpreting the Supreme Court's decision in *Davis*, we held in *Strathie* that two factors pertain to the reasonableness of a refusal to accommodate a handicapped individual. First, requiring accommodation is unreasonable if it would necessitate modification of the essential nature of the program. Second, requiring accommodation is unreasonable if it would place undue burdens, such as extensive costs, on the recipient of federal funds. *Davis*, 442 U.S. at 412; *Strathie*, 716 F.2d at 230. *See also Easley by Easley v. Snider*, 36 F.3d 297 (3d Cir.), *reh'g denied*, (Oct. 18, 1994). In *Easley*, we held, "It follows, of course, that if there is no factual basis in the record demonstrating that accommodating the individual would require a fundamental modification or an undue burden, then the handicapped person is otherwise qualified." *Id.* Thus, in looking at whether an individual is otherwise qualified, we must analyze whether the person would be otherwise qualified if reasonable accommodations are made for his/her handicap.

A.

The district court reviewed these same cases and concluded that Mrs. Wagner was not an otherwise qualified handicapped individual because Mrs. Wagner "sought admission to Fair Acres because of her handicap and not in spite of her handicap, and thus she is not an 'otherwise qualified' handicapped individual who has been denied a benefit solely by reason of handicap." The district court concluded:

> ... [I]n the absence of the Alzheimer's disease, Mrs. Wagner would not need the nursing home care she sought at Fair Acres. Clearly she sought a benefit because of her handicap and not in spite of it. Unlike the plaintiff in *Nathanson* [*Nathanson v. Medical College of Pennsylvania*, 926 F.2d 1368 (3d Cir. 1991)] who sought admission to medical school in spite of her back problem, not because of it, and the plaintiff in *Strathie* who sought a school bus driver's license in spite of his deafness, not because of it, Mrs. Wagner sought admission to an institution capable of caring for Alzheimer's sufferers because she also suffers from Alzheimer's.

859 F. Supp. at 782-83.

We believe that in focusing on why Mrs. Wagner sought access to Fair Acres, the district court's analysis is misplaced. It is irrelevant why a plaintiff sought access to a program, service or institution; our concern, for purposes of section 504, is why a plaintiff is *denied* access to a program, service or institution. Obviously, everyone that applies for admission to a nursing home does so because of his or her disabilities. Indeed, no one would be able to meet a nursing home's admissions requirements in the absence of some handicapping condition necessitating nursing home care. Further, if the district court's analysis is taken to its logical extreme, no program, service or institution designed specifically to meet the needs of the handicapped would ever have to comply with section 504 because every applicant would seek access to the program or facility *because* of a handicap, not in spite of it. This result would contradict both the statutory and regulatory framework of section 504.

The legislative history of section 504 indicates that Congress clearly contemplated that section 504 would apply to nursing homes that receive federal funding. The Senate Committee Report that introduced the Rehabilitation Act stated, "[T]he bill further proclaims a policy of nondiscrimination against otherwise qualified individuals with respect to participation in or access to any program which is in receipt of federal financial assistance." S. Rep. No. 1135, 92 Cong., 2d Sess. 49. *See also* 118 Cong. Rec. 32294. The Report identified examples of the types of programs that section 504 was designed to cover: housing, transportation, education and health services. Since the primary purpose of the Rehabilitation Act as enacted in 1973 was to extend and expand the 53-year old federal-state vocational rehabilitation program, Congress initially defined the phrase "handicapped individual" in terms of employment and employability. However, because it was clearly the intent of Congress in adopting section 504, which Congress labeled "nondiscrimination in federal grants", the term "handicapped individual" was no longer to be narrowly limited to employment. As the Senate Report accompanying the 1974 amendments to the Rehabilitation Act elaborated: Section 7(6) of the Rehabilitation Act of 1973 defines "handicapped individual." That definition has proven to be troublesome in its application to provisions of the Act such as sections 503 and 504 because of its orientation toward employment and its relation to vocational rehabilitation services. It was clearly the intent of the Committee and of Congress in adopting section 503 (affirmative action) and section 504 (nondiscrimination) that the term "handicapped individual" in those sections was not to be narrowly limited to employment (in the case of section 504), nor to the individual's potential benefit from vocational rehabilitation services under Titles I and III (in the case of both sections 503 and 504) of the Act.

* * *

The Committee substitute adds a new definition of "handicapped individual" for the purposes of titles IV and V of the Act in order to embody this underlying intent.

Section 504 was enacted to prevent discrimination against all handicapped individuals, regardless of their need for, or ability to benefit from, vocational rehabilitation services, in relation to Federal assistance in employment, housing, transportation, education, *health services*, or any other Federally-aided programs. *Examples of handicapped individuals who may suffer discrimination in the receipt of Federally-assisted services but who may have been unintentionally excluded from the protection of section 504 by the references to enhanced employability in section 7(6) are as follows*: physically or mentally handicapped children who may be denied admission to Federally-supported school systems on the basis of their handicap; *handicapped persons who may be denied admission to Federally-assisted nursing homes on the basis of their handicap*; those persons whose handicap is so severe that employment is not feasible but who may be denied the benefits of a wide range of Federal programs; and those persons whose vocational rehabilitation is complete, but who may nevertheless be discriminated against in certain Federally-assisted activities.

S. Rep. No. 1297, 93d Cong., 2d Sess., *reprinted in* [1974] U.S. Code Cong. & Ad. News 6376, 6388-89. (Emphasis added.)

We interpret this legislative history as indicating that Congress contemplated that section 504 would apply to nursing home admissions decisions. Thus, we conclude that Mrs. Wagner was not prevented from seeking the protection of section 504 even though she was motivated to make application to Fair Acres because of her disability. The district court erred, as a matter of law, in holding to the contrary.

B.

In addition to finding that Mrs. Wagner was not "otherwise qualified" on the ground that she sought admission to Fair Acres because of her handicap and not in spite of it, the district court also found that she was not otherwise qualified because Fair Acres' decision was a "medical treatment" decision. Citing *Bowen v. American Hosp. Ass'n*, 476 U.S. 610 (1986) and *United States v. University Hosp., State University of New York at Stony Brook*, 729 F.2d 144 (2d Cir. 1984), the district court concluded that "medical treatment decisions are generally immune from scrutiny under section 504." We disagree with the district court's characterization of this case.

In *Bowen* and *University Hospital*, the applicability of section 504 to the withholding of heroic medical treatment to profoundly handicapped infants was at issue. In *University Hospital*, the United States sought an order directing University Hospital to provide the Department of Health & Human Services with access to the medical records of a handicapped infant whose parents had refused to consent to corrective surgical procedures but, rather, had opted for conservative treatment of their infant's disabilities. The Court of Appeals for the Second Circuit held that the "otherwise qualified" criteria of Section 504 cannot be meaningfully applied to such medical treatment decisions. The court observed,

> ... [w]here medical treatment is at issue, it is typically the handicap itself that gives rise to, or at least contributes to the need for services. ... As a result, the phrase cannot be applied in the comparatively fluid context of medical treatment decisions without distorting its plain meaning. In common parlance, one would not ordinarily think of a newborn infant suffering from multiple birth defects as "otherwise qualified" to have corrective surgery performed. ... If Congress intended section 504 to apply in this manner, it chose strange language indeed. ... The legislative history, moreover, indicates that Congress never contemplated section 504 would apply to treatment decision of this nature.

729 F.2d at 156.

Similarly, the issue in *Bowen* was whether the Secretary of Health & Human Services had authority under the Rehabilitation Act to regulate medical treatment decisions concerning handicapped newborn infants. The Supreme Court, however, did not reach the issue of whether a medical treatment decision made on the basis of handicap is immune from scrutiny under section 504, because the Court held there was no evidence that the hospitals had denied treatment on the basis of handicap. Rather, treatment was denied because of the absence of parental consent. Accordingly, the Supreme Court concluded, "A hospital's withholding of treatment from a handicapped infant when no parental consent has been given cannot violate Section 504, for without the parent's consent the infant is neither 'otherwise qualified' for treatment nor has he been denied care solely by reason of his handicap." 476 U.S. at 610.

Unlike these medical treatment cases involving handicapped infants which necessitate complex assessments of the medical needs, benefits and risks of providing invasive medical care, the issue we confront here concerns the "essential nature" of the service that Fair Acres provides and involves an assessment of whether providing the skilled nursing care, which no one disputes Mrs. Wagner required, would alter the essential nature of Fair Acres' program or impose an undue burden in light of its program. *See, e.g., Easley by Easley v. Snider*, 36 F.3d at 305. A decision of this type, regarding whether an institution can provide certain services without a modification of the essential nature of its program or imposition of an undue burden, involves administrative decision-making and not medical judgment. For example, here Fair Acres must determine whether it is able to provide the requisite staff (*i.e.*, nurses and nurses aids to care for, *i.e.*, feed, bathe, and occupy Mrs. Wagner) as well as the appropriate physical accommodations without incurring extensive cost. These are decisions that administrators routinely make.

III.

Applying these legal principles, we now review the record to determine whether Mrs. Wagner presented legally sufficient evidence that she was "otherwise qualified" for admission to Fair Acres. . . . When reviewing the jury's finding that Mrs. Wagner was "otherwise qualified" for admission to Fair Acres, we give to her, as the verdict winner, the benefit of all logical inferences that could be drawn from the evidence presented, resolve all conflicts in the evidence in her favor and, in general, view the record in the light most favorable to her. *See Williamson v. Consolidated Rail Corp.,* 926 F.2d at 1348 (3d Cir. 1991).

A.

In support of her assertion that there was a legally sufficient basis for the jury's determination that she was an "otherwise qualified individual," Mrs. Wagner points to the testimony of her three expert witness. Dr. Gottlieb reviewed Mrs. Wagner's medical records of her psychiatric hospitalization at Wills from September 2, 1992 until April 12, 1993. Based upon his review of these records, it was his opinion that Mrs. Wagner's behavior was consistent with a large proportion of people suffering from Alzheimer's disease. Dr. Gottlieb testified that the largest proportion of people in nursing home settings have Alzheimer's disease and that Mrs. Wagner was appropriate or qualified for the services and type of intermediate care provided by Fair Acres Nursing home. Based on a reasonable degree of medical certainty, he believed it appropriate to transfer Mrs. Wagner back to a nursing home setting sometime between the end of September and the end of October of 1992.

Dr. Gottlieb also testified regarding the type of accommodations that Fair Acres would have to make in order to care for Mrs. Wagner. He testified that Mrs. Wagner's combative assaultive behavior occurred relatively infrequently, rarely more than once a day, and often it was predictable as to when this behavior would occur. Thus, he concluded that she would need one-to-one supervision infrequently.

Dr. Kim, Mrs. Wagner's treating psychiatrist at Wills testified that she did not require one-to-one supervision for extended periods of time and could be redirected easily. It was his opinion that about the third week of October, 1992, Mrs. Wagner could have been managed and accommodated by a nursing home. Indeed, on October 23, 1992, Dr. Kim had written a letter to the administrator of Fair Acres stating that should Mrs. Wagner experience a deterioration in her mental status requiring rehospitalization, he would be willing to readmit her to Wills for further treatment and stabilization.

Dr. Etemad, the staff psychiatrist at Easton Nursing facility, testified that Easton Nursing Home is a regular nursing home that has patients at different levels of functioning. Although Dr. Etemad did not review the Wills records, he reviewed a final summary by a psychiatrist who was sent to Easton Nursing Home when Mrs. Wagner was transferred. Dr. Etemad evaluated Mrs. Wagner on April 14, two days after her admission to Easton and again around May 18, 1992. He testified that he saw her one time after that, and then there were no more requests by the staff for him to see her. During the five months preceding trial that Mrs. Wagner spent at Easton, Dr. Etemad informed the court that it was not necessary for her to be referred to an inpatient psychiatric hospital and that Easton was able to accommodate her and meet her needs. In his judgment, she is most appropriately classified as a nursing home patient.

Fair Acres' defense consisted of Mrs. Wagner's medical records and progress notes from her hospitalization at Wills, and the testimony of various members of Fair Acres' admissions committee who evaluated Mrs. Wagner's application for admission. R.N. Mimi Huver-Delaney, the Admissions Director at Fair Acres since 1982, testified that up to February 19, 1993, Fair Acres would not have been staffed to handle the kind of treatment that Mrs. Wagner required. Admissions case worker Amy Thomas testified that Mrs. Wagner was not admitted to Fair Acres because they could not meet her needs.

Dr. Satyendra K. Diwan testified that, as a consultant to Fair Acres since 1981, he did not examine Mrs. Wagner personally but instead reviewed Mrs. Wagner's records with respect to her admission at Fair Acres. He is not board certified in either psychiatry or geriatric psychology. Dr. Diwan testified that he does not rely on any written criteria in order to evaluate whether someone is appropriate for admission. His own personal criterion is that the patient be symptom-free of agitation for a 3-4 week period. [The reasonableness of this requirement for admission was called into question by Mrs. Wagner's experts. Dr. Kim testified that, by and large, a three week period without any symptoms of agitation is uncommon in many Alzheimer's patients and that it would be fairly common that a patient would exhibit some form of agitation on a daily basis. Dr. Etemad testified that it was not reasonable medical practice to look for symptom free behavior, *i.e.*, no agitation for a 3-week period, as a precondition of admission to a nursing home. In his practice, he has never seen a patient who was totally asymptomatic before transfer to a nursing home.] Dr. Diwan testified that Mrs. Wagner was inappropriate for care at Fair Acres the five times he reviewed her, mainly because of her dangerousness towards herself and others.. He was not aware that, prior to her last review, she was not ambulating as her physical condition had weakened, nor was he aware of the fact that she was spending approximately 80% of her day confined in a geri-chair.

Linda Hadfield, admissions coordinator at Fair Acres, testified that she visits almost every patient before admission to Fair Acres. She visited Mrs. Wagner on October 23, immediately prior to the third review. She discussed the techniques employed by Wills to calm Mrs. Wagner: they would put her in a quiet room, massage her feet, play soft music for her—techniques Fair Acres would not provide. On October 29th, the third meeting, Fair Acres put Mrs. Wagner on "for hold" status. Hadfield visited Wills again on December 30, between the third and fourth evaluation of Mrs. Wagner's application for admission. She observed that Wills was still using the quiet room and inapsine to calm Mrs. Wagner. She testified that the nurse's notes did not always reflect what the psychiatric doctor wrote.

B.

Based upon its review of this evidence, the district court held that there was no legally sufficient basis for the jury's determination that Margaret Wagner was an "otherwise qualified" individual for purposes of section 504, because the court found that she did not meet Fair Acres' requirements for admission. The district court opined, "It was not the function of Fair Acres to provide psychiatric services for persons with disruptive psychotic disorders." Further, the court opined, "Nor is it a case of Fair Acres making a reasonable accommodation." 859 F. Supp. at 783. The district court's conclusions, in these regards, are erroneous. Because the district court arrived at these conclusions based upon the application of incorrect legal precepts, our review is plenary. *Griffiths v. CIGNA Corp.*, 988 F.2d 457, 462 (3d Cir.), *cert. denied*, 114 S. Ct. 186 (1993).

IV.

The inquiry into whether an applicant is otherwise qualified necessarily involves a determination of whether the applicant could have gained access to the program if the recipient of funds had made reasonable accommodations. *Alexander v. Choate*, 469 U.S. 287, 301 (1985). In the unanimous decision in *Alexander*, the Supreme Court stated:

> *Davis* . . . struck a balance between the statutory rights of the handicapped to be integrated into society and the legitimate interests of federal grantees in preserving the integrity of their programs: while a grantee need not be required to make "fundamental" or "substantial" modifications to accommodate the handicapped, it may be required to make "reasonable"ones.
>
> The balance struck in *Davis* requires that an otherwise qualified individual must be provided with meaningful access to the benefit that the grantee offers. The benefit itself, of course, cannot be defined in a way that effectively denies otherwise qualified individuals the meaningful access to which they are entitled; to assure meaningful access, reasonable accommodations in the grantee's program or benefit may have to be made.

Alexander, 469 U.S. at 300 (citation and footnotes omitted).

As the Court of Appeals for the Fifth Circuit observed in *Brennan v. Stewart*, 834 F.2d 1248 (5th Cir. 1988), "After *Alexander*, it is clear that the phrase 'otherwise qualified' has a paradoxical quality; on the one hand, it refers to a person who has the abilities or characteristics sought by the grantee; but on the other, it cannot refer only to those already capable of meeting *all* the requirements—or else no reasonable requirement could ever violate section 504, no matter how easy it would be to accommodate handicapped individuals who cannot fulfill it." 834 F.2d 1248 (5th Cir. 1988). We agree with the Court of Appeals for the Fifth Circuit: "The question after *Alexander* is the rather mushy one of whether some 'reasonable accommodation' is available to satisfy the legitimate interests of both the grantee and the handicapped person." 834 F.2d at 1262.

In light of *Alexander* and our decision in *Strathie*, we are required to review the record to determine additionally if there was a factual basis in the record demonstrating that Fair Acres' refusal to accommodate Mrs. Wagner was unreasonable. *See Strathie*, 716 F.2d at 230 (a section 504 claim could be defeated "if there is a factual basis in the record reasonably demonstrating that accommodating the individual would require either a modification of the essential nature of the program or impose an undue burden on the recipient of federal funds.") *See also School Bd. of Nassau County, Fla. v. Arline*, 480 U.S. 273 (1987) (determinations regarding whether plaintiffs are "otherwise qualified" will generally require an individualized inquiry and appropriate findings of fact). Here there was ample evidence that Mrs. Wagner's aggressive behaviors associated with her Alzheimer's disease clearly rendered her, as amicus curiae characterizes her, "a challenging and demanding patient." We find that this fact alone cannot justify her exclusion from a nursing home that receives federal funds. Otherwise nursing homes would be free to "pick and choose" among patients, accepting and admitting only the easiest patients to care for, leaving the more challenging and demanding patients with no place to turn for care. [Dr. Gottlieb testified at trial that currently approximately four million Americans have been diagnosed with Alzheimer's disease and it is estimated that this disease affects 11 percent of all Americans who are over the age of 65. Moreover, the number of Americans afflicted with Alzheimer's disease is expected to increase with the size of the burgeoning elderly population. Consequently, many people who suffer from Alzheimer's will be forced to seek nursing home placement. Because Mrs. Wagner's plight is typical of a growing number of others, the issue of whether Fair Acres was required, in keeping with section 504, to make reasonable accommodations to care for Mrs. Wagner should have been, but was not, addressed. . . .The Alzheimer's Disease and Related Disorders Association of Greater Philadelphia points out in its amicus brief that "Contrary to the commonly held belief that nursing homes are 'genteel rest homes for elderly people, the prevalence of psychiatric behavioral disorders in nursing homes has been estimated to range from 68 to 94 percent,'" citing Grossberg, *Psychiatric Problems in the Nursing Home,* 38 J. of the American Geriatrics Sec. 907 (1990). . . .]

Indeed, the evidence introduced at trial confirmed that Mrs. Wagner was a difficult patient, one for whom the ravages of Alzheimer's disease were manifested in a myriad of extremely unpleasant ways—by mood swings, periods of combativeness, and outbursts of shouting. However, as Mrs. Wagner's expert witness, Dr. Gottlieb, pointed out, "the fact that she had agitated behavior does not contradict that she could be managed in a nursing home."

Our review of the record reveals that Fair Acres presented little or no evidence about the type of accommodations it would have needed to make in order to provide care for Mrs. Wagner. While Fair Acres made general allegations that it could not adequately care for Mrs. Wagner or meet her needs due to her aggressive behavior, it failed to offer any factual basis demonstrating that the admission of Mrs. Wagner to Fair Acres would have changed the essential nature of the facility as a nursing home or imposed an undue burden on the facility, economically or otherwise. Larry Rendin, the medical director at Fair Acres for the past fifteen years, testified that of the 900 patients at his facility, some 64 to 70% are afflicted with Alzheimer's or dementia-related disease, that is, organic brain syndrome of one type or another. Mr. Rendin agreed that some of the characteristics of the Alzheimer's patients at Fair Acres included screaming, yelling, confusion, agitation, combativeness and aggression on occasion and that "Fair Acres takes care of them and the staff is equipped to deal with that." He agreed that some patients require one-to-one care for certain periods of time, and many times Fair Acres has two or three staff members providing care to one patient. His facility is equipped to provide that level of care. Rendin also testified that between 20-25 times a year it is necessary to transfer a patient from Fair Acres to an in-patient psychiatric facility. Most are returned to Fair Acres after a few weeks and Fair Acres is then able to accommodate their needs. Thus the record reveals Fair Acres is clearly capable of providing and, in fact, has provided the kinds of services that Mrs. Wagner required, although she may have needed them on a more frequent basis.

Linda Hadfield, Fair Acres' admissions coordinator, discussed the techniques employed by Wills to calm Mrs. Wagner during her disturbances. These techniques included putting Mrs. Wagner in a "quiet room," massaging her feet, talking to her and playing soft music. Although Ms. Hadfield testified that Fair Acres did not provide these services, there was no evidence that these were calming techniques that Fair Acres could *not* provide, or that to do so would change the essential nature of Fair Acres as a nursing home into an acute psychiatric facility or impose an undue burden on Fair Acres.

Ms. Hadfield opined that Mrs. Wagner was also not suitable for admission to Fair Acres because she had been receiving injections of Inapsine at Wills, a drug that Fair Acres had not previously administered. Dr. Kim testified that he prescribed Inapsine for Mrs. Wagner while she was at Wills because Inapsine is a neuroleptic, or tranquilizing agent, which is very short acting and is available in vials and ampoules. It is administered by intramuscular injection. Notwithstanding the fact that Inapsine had not been administered at Fair Acres before, Dr. Gottlieb testified that Inapsine could be administered in a nursing home setting and that roughly 25 percent of the people in nursing homes receive supertrophic, sedating drugs on a daily basis. Dr. Gottlieb's testimony was further supported by Larry Rendin when he testified that many of the patients at Fair Acres are administered Haldol. Thus, based on this evidence, a jury could reasonably conclude that the accommodations Fair Acres would need to make to care for Mrs. Wagner were not unreasonable.

Fair Acres also contended that accommodating Mrs. Wagner would have created a health and safety risk to the staff and patients at Fair Acres. Dr. Diwan testified that "each time I concluded that she is not appropriate because mainly of her dangerousness towards others and herself." Our review reveals that Dr. Diwan's testimony was contradicted by the testimony of Mrs. Wagner's treating physician at Wills, Dr. Kim. Dr. Kim testified that he did not view Mrs. Wagner as creating a health or safety risk. With respect to the references in her chart that she was combative and assaultive, Dr. Kim testified that, "[W]e describe being combative or assaultive as any behavior that is resistive or aggressive. . . . But this is all [done by] someone who is essentially bedridden and can barely [sic] walk and is more or less slapping out like a child." Dr. Kim also testified on cross-examination that at the time of Mrs. Wagner's final evaluation in early February, she was spending 60-80% of her waking hours in a geri-chair, and that she needed 80% support by staff to remain upright. Thus, there was sufficient evidence presented from which a reasonable jury could conclude that Mrs. Wagner, at least by February, posed little threat to anyone's health or safety due to her extremely weakened physical condition.

Finally, by the later dates on which Mrs. Wagner was denied admission to Fair Acres, the jury could infer from the evidence that Mrs. Wagner would not have needed a quiet room or much of anything in the way of reasonable accommodation. For example, Dr. Kim testified that, "We noted that progressively she became more and more physically handicapped. She needed increasing assistance to walk, she needed to be spoon-fed, by the end of her stay, she became incontinent, needed to be in a diaper, and spent most of her days sitting in a chair staring off into space, occasionally making semi-coherent expressions, sometimes crying. But for the most part staring blankly off into space for a majority of that time."

Based on our review of the evidence, we find that a jury could have determined that at some point during the period from September 1992 to February 1993, Mrs. Wagner was "otherwise qualified" for admission to Fair Acres in accordance with section 504 because Fair Acres could have cared for her if it made reasonable accommodations. Thus, we must reverse the district court's order granting summary judgment as a matter of law.

V.

Concurrent with its motion for judgment as a matter of law, Fair Acres moved in the alternative for a new trial. The district court conditionally granted Fair Acres' motion for a new trial on the grounds that: (1) it was prejudicial error to fail to instruct the jury that administrators of Fair Acres were entitled to "some measure of deference," and (2) the verdict was against the great weight of the evidence.

The authority to grant a new trial resides in the exercise of sound discretion by the trial court, and will only be disturbed if the court abused that discretion. *Allied Chemical Corp. v. Daiflon, Inc.*, 449 U.S. 33, 36 (1980); *American Bearing Co. v. Litton Industries, Inc.*, 729 F.2d 943, 948 (3d Cir.), *cert. denied*, 469 U.S. 854 (1984). We are cognizant that a new trial may be granted even when judgment as a matter of law is inappropriate. *Roebuck v. Drexel University*, 852 F.2d 715, 735 (3d Cir. 1988); *American Bearing Co.*, 729 F.2d at 948 n.11. *See also Rousseau v. Teledyne Movible Offshore, Inc.*, 812 F.2d 971, 972 (5th Cir.) (affirming grant of new trial even though there was "legally sufficient evidence to support the verdict, thus foreclosing a j.n.o.v."), *cert. denied*, 484 U.S. 827 (1987). With these principles in mind, we review the district court's conditional grant of Fair Acres' alternative motion for a new trial.

A.

At the close of all the evidence, Fair Acres submitted the following instruction for inclusion in the court's points for charge:

> Administrators from Fair Acres Geriatric Center are entitled to some measure of judicial deference in this matter, by reason of their experience with and knowledge of the administrative procedures in question.

Defendants' proposed points of charge No. 6.

Counsel for Mrs. Wagner objected to this point for charge because counsel did not believe the charge to be a correct statement of the law. The district court sustained Mrs. Wagner's objection and decided not to include this point in its charge to the jury. In ruling on the motion for a new trial, the district court found its refusal to give this charged constituted prejudicial error. We disagree.

We addressed the issue of the deference to be given the judgment of program administrators in cases arising under section 504 in our decision in *Strathie v. Dept. of Transp.*, 716 F.2d 227 (3d Cir. 1983). There we rejected the notion that broad judicial deference was required, and instead we observed,

> Notably absent from the Supreme Court's opinion in *Davis*, however, is any discussion of the scope of judicial review with regard to the reasonableness of a refusal to accommodate a handicapped individual. Program administrators surely are entitled to some measure of judicial deference in this matter, by reason of their experience in question. *On the other hand, broad judicial deference* resembling that associated with the "rational basis" test *would substantially undermine Congress' intent* in enacting section 504 that stereotypes or generalizations not deny handicapped individuals access to federally-funded programs.

716 F.2d at 231 (citations omitted) (emphasis added). We then held that "the following standard effectively reconciles these competing considerations: a handicapped individual who cannot meet all of a program's requirements is not otherwise qualified if there is a factual basis in the record reasonably demonstrating that accommodating that individual would require either a modification of the essential nature of the program, or impose an undue burden on the recipient of federal funds." 716 F.2d at 231. We observed that the Court of Appeals for the Second Circuit has also applied this "factual basis" standard, although it did not designate it as such. *See New York State Ass'n for Retarded Children, Inc. v. Carey*, 612 F.2d 644, 650 (2d Cir. 1979) (section 504 prevented a city board of education from excluding from its regular classrooms mentally retarded children who were thought to be carriers of hepatitis, when the board was unable to demonstrate that the health hazard posed by the children was anything more than a remote possibility).

In the present case, there was no factual basis demonstrating that accommodating Mrs. Wagner would require Fair Acres to modify the essential nature of its program, or impose an undue burden upon it. In the absence of such a factual basis, Fair Acres' request that the jury be instructed that Fair Acres administrators be accorded "some" deference cannot be justified. Accordingly, the district court's failure to give an instruction that Fair Acres administrators were entitled to some measure of deference by reason of their experience with and knowledge of the procedures in question, was not legal error. Clearly it would not then rise to the level of fundamental error.

Here the district court's instructions to the jury in this regard struck the appropriate balance between deference to program administrators and the anti-discrimination mandate of section 504. The district court informed the jury that while Fair Acres was required to make reasonable accommodations, it was not required to make fundamental or substantial modifications to its program. Additionally, the district court instructed the jury that it must consider the views and evaluation process of Fair Acres. The court instructed the jury that it "must take into account the evaluation made by the institution itself in the absence of a showing that its standards and its application of those standards serves no purpose other than to deny access to handicapped persons."

B.

Finally, the district court conditionally granted Fair Acres' motion for a new trial on the grounds that the verdict was against the great weight of the evidence. The district court found "the evidence, as demonstrated by the Wills records, incontrovertibly and overwhelmingly showed that at the time Fair Acres made the decision that Mrs. Wagner was not appropriate for placement in its nursing home she was suffering from the same psychotic symptoms that caused her transfer from the Dowden Nursing Home to Wills Psychiatric Hospital." Under these circumstances, "a final determination that Fair Acres violated section 504 of the Rehabilitation Act would result in a miscarriage of justice." 859 F. Supp. at 785.

The authority to grant a new trial, as previously stated, is confined to the trial court. Thus, our review is extremely deferential. We have held that "[s]uch deference is peculiarly appropriate in reviewing a ruling that a verdict is against the weight of the evidence because the district court was able to observe the witnesses and follow the trial in a way that we cannot replicate by reviewing a cold record." *Roebuck, supra,* 852 F.2d at 735.

We have reviewed the record for evidence that is legally sufficient to support the jury's verdict. We find that Mrs. Wagner presented sufficient evidence to preclude the district court's granting judgment against her as a matter of law. Given, however, the district court's application of incorrect legal standards regarding the applicability of section 504 to the facts in this case, we are uncertain as to whether the court would have granted a new trial under the appropriate legal standards. Consequently, we will vacate the court's order granting a new trial and remand to the district court for reconsideration of this motion.

Questions

1. Does the *Wagner* ruling mean that nursing facilities must take all comers? Could Fair Acres exclude those with a primarily psychiatric diagnosis after *Wagner*?

2. Why doesn't Fair Acres' denial of admission to Mrs. Wagner fall under the "medical treatment decision" exception to section 504?

3. If Mrs. Wagner was your grandmother, would you fight for her admission even though Fair Acres didn't want her? Why or why not?

2. Involuntary Transfer and Discharge

Stacey Gunya
Adult Care Homes
KANSAS LONG-TERM CARE HANDBOOK 28-34 (1999)*

III. Long-Term Care Facility Transfer and Discharge

... Long-term care facilities ... are governed by a complex set of federal laws regarding involuntary transfer and discharge. These laws, as they relate to Medicare certified facilities, are found at 42 USC §1395i-3, *et seq.* The laws relating to Medicaid certified facilities are found at 42 U.S.C. §1396r, et seq. While the sources of law come from a Medicare section and a Medicaid section, it is important to remember that facilities must maintain identical policies and practices for residents regardless of source of payment.

The Health Care Financing Administration has codified these statutes as requirements for states and long-term care facilities at 42 C.F.R. § 483. ....This section discusses the federal laws regarding involuntary transfer and discharge, how to initiate an involuntary transfer and how to defend a proposed transfer.

A. Intra-Facility Transfer

An intra-facility transfer is a transfer within the physical plant of the long-term care facility. Often a transfer occurs when a resident's Medicare days have ended. The facility may seek to move the resident to a distinct part of the facility that is not certified for Medicare. Transfers may also occur when the resident's care needs change or to accommodate roommate preferences.

The nursing facility is obligated to provide notice of the intended intra-facility transfer. The notice must be given to the resident and the legal representative or family member. The regulations do not specify any other requirements of the notice.

A resident has a general right to refuse a transfer. Additionally, a resident has an absolute right to refuse a transfer to a distinct part of the facility that is not a skilled nursing facility. The skilled nursing facility is the portion of the long-term care facility that is certified for Medicare. It may be advisable to refuse a transfer from the Medicare section of the facility if the resident is particularly frail. Transfers of any kind may be particularly traumatic to very frail residents.

If the facility fails to honor the residents refusal to transfer, then the resident has several choices. All residents have a right to file a grievance with the facility.

* * *

B. Inter-Facility Transfer and Discharge

Transfer and discharge generally involve the desire by the long-term care facility to remove the resident permanently. An inter-facility transfer may involve transfer to a psychiatric facility for evaluation or transfer to a hospital for treatment. A

---

* Copyright © 1999. Reprinted with permission.

transfer or discharge may also involve admission to a different long-term care facility. Federal and state laws establish the requirements for an involuntary discharge.

Nursing facilities are generally charged with the duty to "ensure safe and orderly transfer" of a resident in all situations. The facility is not relieved of this duty in the involuntary discharge situation. Nursing facilities need to take care that the resident is not discharged into an unsafe environment.

For example, a resident might come to the facility after having been abused and neglected by a family member. Unless the resident should prefer to return to that home, it would not be appropriate to discharge that resident back to his family. Instead, the facility may need to contact other community resources about other safe locations to discharge that resident.

1. Therapeutic Transfers

Nursing home residents are often transferred to the hospital for treatment and/or evaluation. In these situations the resident needs to be concerned about holding a bed in the facility. Nursing homes are required to have a bed hold policy. Federal regulations give particular protection to the Medicaid resident. The bed hold policy must allow for readmission of the resident to the first available semi-private room. Notice of the policy is to be made available to the resident and family prior to the transfer and at the time of transfer. . . . Additionally, private pay residents would have a contractual right to return to the bed they have paid for.

2. Involuntary Discharge (Eviction)

Involuntary discharge or eviction from a nursing facility is a serious matter. Frail and elderly residents are likely to suffer life threatening consequences from transfer trauma. Medicaid residents generally face difficulty in choosing a facility and will want to fight to stay in their facility. A facility seeking to discharge a resident involuntarily will want to follow the statutory requirements carefully. Failure to follow the statutory requirements may mean the facility would face citation and fines from [the state regulatory agency] and litigation from the resident.

a. Notice

The statutory requirements for notice of involuntary discharge are found at 42 U.S.C. § 1395i-3(c)(2)(B), 42 U.S.C. § 1396r(c)(2)(B), and 42 C.F.R. 483.12(a). The facility is required to provide written notice to the resident and/or his legal representative. The reasons for the discharge must be recorded in the resident's clinical record. The notice must be given 30 days in advance of discharge unless:

- The safety of other residents is at issue;
- The facility ceases to operate;
- The resident's health has improved so that care is no longer needed;
- The resident has an urgent medical need; or
- The resident has not resided in the facility for at least 30 days.

Contents of the notice are also governed by statute. The notice must contain the following information.

- The grounds for discharge;
- The location of the intended discharge;
- The right to appeal the discharge; and
- The name, address and telephone number of the state Long-Term Care Ombudsman.

b. Grounds

A long-term care facility is limited on the grounds that may be used to discharge a resident involuntarily. Only five (5) reasons are recognized as permissible grounds for involuntary discharge. Statutes also state how these grounds must be substantiated. The five permissible grounds are:

1. The discharge is necessary to meet the resident's welfare and resident's welfare cannot be met by the facility. This must be documented in the resident's clinical record by the resident's physician.
2. The resident's health has improved sufficiently so that the resident no longer needs the services provided by the facility. This must also be documented in the clinical record by the resident's physician.
3. The safety of individuals in the facility is endangered. The safety threat must be documented in the clinical record.
4. The health of individuals in the facility is endangered by the resident. Again, the health threat must be documented in the clinical record by the resident's physician.
5. The resident has failed after reasonable notice to pay for the stay in the facility.

* * *

d. Defending an Involuntary Discharge

A resident who wishes to defend an involuntary discharge will want to involve as many agencies as possible. The advocate should request [a Medicaid agency administrative] hearing as well as an investigation by [other state regulatory agencies]. Also, the advocate should contact the state Long-Term Care Ombudsman for assistance in resolving the dispute. The advocate should require the long-term care facility to produce all the resident's medical and social service records.

Typically the [Medicaid agency administrative] hearing will not take place before the date of intended discharge of the resident. If the facility will not voluntarily agree to postpone the discharge until after the . . . hearing, then the advocate will want to take steps to restrain the facility from transferring the resident. [Generally, none of the regulatory state agencies] have the power to stop a facility from transferring a resident. In exigent circumstances, a petition for injunctive relief and motion for temporary restraining order should be filed with the district court. . . . For the court to issue the temporary restraining order and the injunction, the resident must establish:

1. The applicant is likely to prevail when the court finally disposes of the matter;
2. Without relief the applicant will suffer irreparable injury;
3. The grant of relief to the applicant will not substantially harm other parties to the proceedings; and

4. The threat to public health, safety, or welfare relied on by the agency is not sufficiently serious to justify the agency's action in the circumstances.

* * *

e. Special Situations

i. Involuntary Discharge for Behavior Problems

A common reason for involuntary discharge is that the resident's behavior has become objectionable to the facility. For example, a resident with dementia may become violent or develop other difficult to manage behaviors. The resident may have a habit that is dangerous, like smoking. In either case where the behavior or condition of the resident is at issue, it is important to look at the care plan. Each resident should have an individual care plan. When a problem arises, there should be a multi-disciplinary team approach to dealing with the problem. Also, facilities have promised as part of their Medicare and Medicaid certification that they have staff trained to provide care to a variety of resident conditions including dementia.

Practice Tip: In defending a behavior-based discharge, the key is generally the physician. The opinion of the physician is required in three of the five specified grounds for involuntary discharge. The physician is almost always an employee of the nursing facility or may see most of the facility's residents. Because of the close relationship between the long-term care facility and the physician it may be difficult for the physician to take the side of the resident. The resident, however, is always free to choose his own physician. A change of treating physician, therefore, may be necessary to successfully defend the discharge.

Additionally, an advocate should keep in mind other sources of law that may extend protections to the resident. In other jurisdictions, judges have extended the protections of the Americans with Disabilities Act, Section 504 of the Rehabilitation Act of 1973 and the Fair Housing Amendment's Act of 1978 to residents of long-term care facilities. These acts prohibit discrimination in the provision of services and housing to persons who are disabled.

A hypothetical example may help explain how all these regulations work. Suppose that Ruth is a nursing home resident. She has dementia and low vision. She has begun to spit at staff when they approach her to care for her. The nursing facility has decided to discharge Ruth claiming that the spitting is a health risk for the staff and other residents. In order to support this ground for discharge the medical record would need to reflect that there is indeed a medical risk as documented by the treating physician. Also, the problem should be addressed in a care plan meeting. The medical record should show attempts by the facility to try to deal with the problem. And finally, if discharge cannot be supported the facility will need to find an appropriate location to transfer Ruth.

Ruth's advocates will want to make sure that the notice is technically correct and carefully review the supporting documentation for the discharge. Any mistake by the facility should be promptly reported to [the relevant regulatory agency]. Her advocates should also contact their [State] Long-Term Care Ombudsman for assistance resolving the dispute and contact Social and Rehabilitation Services about requesting an appeal. It is also important to contact the treating physician about whether Ruth's behavior cannot be ameliorated in some way.

If Ruth's advocates cannot persuade the nursing home to keep Ruth until the appeal is heard, they will want to go to district court to try to enjoin the facility from transferring her. They may also want to bring a separate cause of action against the facility for discriminating against her because of her disability. Such litigation can be exhausting and financially costly for all parties. Hopefully, a case like Ruth's would be resolved before it reaches the courts.

ii. Involuntary Discharge for Non-Payment

Non-payment is not as simple as it may appear. Non-payment extends only to non-payment of "covered services." Each state defines what constitutes "covered services" in their Medicaid plan. Only non-payment of those services is considered grounds for discharge. Non-payment of a Medicare co-pay is not considered non-payment and is not grounds for discharge. If the resident's stay is paid by Medicaid it is not considered non-payment. The state reimbursement rate for Medicaid is considerably lower than the private pay rate. The long-term care provider, however, in its contract with the State . . . has agreed to accept Medicaid as full payment of the resident's long-term care nursing bill. Additionally, the submission of a Medicaid application is sufficient to avoid discharge for non-payment.

Finally, the long-term care facility should be sensitive to whether financial exploitation is the reason for non-payment. If a family member or other fiduciary is controlling the resident's finances, but not paying for the resident's care, this may be financial exploitation. Medicaid may be denied because of malfeasance by the fiduciary. For example, an attorney in fact may have transferred property into his own name or have persuaded the resident to do so. This may make the resident ineligible for Medicaid. It also is a breach of fiduciary duty, and should be reported to [the state regulatory agency] as financial exploitation.

Attempting to discharge a resident for non-payment, while not exploring the issue of financial exploitation may expose the facility to other liabilities. Long-term care facility administrators and staff are mandatory reporters of abuse, neglect, and exploitation. Failure to report abuse and exploitation may be charged as a class B misdemeanor. Financial exploitation should be reported to [the state regulatory agency]. The appointment of a guardian and/or conservator may be necessary to protect the resident.

C. Conclusion

Transfer or discharge of a resident from a long-term care facility is carefully regulated by the state and federal government. The long-term care facility should take care to follow the requirements during any transfer and discharge. Residents should remember that they are not powerless when confronted with an unwanted transfer or discharge. Federal and state laws give residents recourse in these situations. Residents may also look to various state agencies . . . for assistance in resolving their disputes with a long-term care facility.

Questions

1. Why should a facility be required to keep a resident whose unacceptable behavior cannot be controlled?

2. Why would a family insist on such a resident staying in a facility which apparently cannot meet his or her needs?

3. What solutions to the problem of Ruth's spitting can you think of, short of involuntary discharge?

FURTHER READING. ALISON BARNES ET AL., COUNSELING OLDER CLIENTS chs. 22-25 (1997); LAWRENCE A. FROLIK, RESIDENTIAL OPTIONS FOR OLDER AND DISABLED CLIENTS (1996); Carolyn H. Sawyer, *Reverse Mortgages: An Innovative Tool for Elder Law Attorneys*, 26 STETSON L. REV. 617 (1996); PETER J. STRAUSS ET AL., AGING AND THE LAW, chs. 22-24 (1996).

CHAPTER 9

End of Life Issues

A. Viatical Settlements 465
B. The Right to Die 472
C. Anatomical Donations 505

As we age, our tendency as human beings is to begin thinking about death—what it means biologically and metaphysically, its inevitability, how it occurs. For an older person who has been diagnosed with a progressive or terminal disease, concerns about pain, the financial costs of a major illness, and religious issues may become a central focus of her thoughts and actions. The elder law attorney must, accordingly, be educated about the various ethical, legal, and medical issues that are associated with the concept and process of "death." This section considers three substantive areas that might be described as end-of-life issues: viatical settlements, the right to die, and anatomical donations.

A. Viatical Settlements

A viatical settlement is, in essence, a contractual arrangement by which a person who is near death due to old age or a terminal illness can sell a life insurance policy for a portion of its face value, paid either in installments or as a lump sum. By "accelerating" death benefits in this manner, the owner of the life insurance policy can access financial resources that would not normally be available until after death. Although the premise of the viatical settlement seems reasonable enough, the actual process of obtaining such a settlement, and the substance of such a contract, may present legal and ethical concerns for the attorney and her client.

1. Introduction

Federal Trade Commission
Consumer Publication: Viatical Settlements (May 1998)
<http://www.ftc.gov/bcp/conline/pubs/services/viatical.htm>

If you have a terminal illness—or if you are caring for someone who is terminally ill—chances are you're giving a great deal of thought to time and money. You may be thinking about life insurance, too. It's in that context that you may hear the phrases "accelerated benefits" and "viatical settlements." Accelerated benefits sometimes are called "living benefits." They are the proceeds of life insurance policies that are paid by the insurer to policy holders before they die. Occasionally, these benefits are included in policies when they are sold, but usually, they are offered as riders or attachments to new or existing policies.

Viatical settlements involve the sale of a life insurance policy. If you have a terminal illness, you may consider selling your insurance policy to a viatical settlement company for a lump sum cash payment. In a viatical settlement transaction, people with terminal illnesses assign their life insurance policies to viatical settlement companies in exchange for a percentage of the policy's face value. The viatical settlement company, in turn, may sell the policy to a third-party investor. The viatical settlement company or the investor becomes the beneficiary to the policy, pays the premiums, and collects the face value of the policy after the original policyholder dies.

Decisions affecting life insurance benefits can have a profound financial and emotional impact on dependents, friends, and care-givers. Before you make any major changes regarding your policy, talk to your friends and family as well as to someone whose advice and expertise you can count on—a lawyer, an accountant, or a financial planner.

Investigating Your Options

Many options exist for people with terminal illnesses when financial needs are critical. For example, you may consider a loan from someone such as the original beneficiary of your life insurance policy. Or, if you've already ruled out less expensive alternatives to raise cash, you might sell your life insurance policy through a viatical settlement.

Many life insurance policies in force nationwide now include an accelerated benefits provision. Companies offer anywhere from 25 to 100 percent of the death benefit as early payment, but policyholders can collect these payments only under very specific circumstances. The amount and the method of payment vary with the policy.

If you own a life insurance policy, call your state Insurance Commissioner or your company's Claims Department to find out about alternatives. Ask whether your life insurance policy allows for accelerated benefits or loans, and how much it will cost. Some insurers add accelerated benefits to life insurance policies for an additional premium, usually computed as a percentage of the base premium. Others offer the benefits at no extra premium, but charge the policyholder for the option if and when it is used. In most cases, the insurance company will reduce the benefits advanced to the policyholder before death to compensate for the interest it will lose on its early payout. There also may be a service charge.

In addition, you may consider selling your life insurance policy to a viatical settlement company, a private enterprise that offers a terminally ill person a percentage of the policy's face value. It is not considered an insurance company.

The viatical settlement company becomes the sole beneficiary of the policy in consideration for delivering a cash payment to the policyholder and paying the premiums. When the policyholder dies, the viatical settlement company collects the face value of the policy.

Viatical settlements are complex legal and financial transactions. They require time and attention from physicians, life insurance companies, lawyers, and accountants or financial planners. The entire transfer process can take up to four months to complete.

Eligibility for Viatical Settlements

Each viatical settlement company sets its own rules for determining which life insurance policies it will buy. For example, most viatical companies will require that:

- you've owned your policy for at least two years;
- your current beneficiary sign a release or a waiver;
- you are terminally ill. Some companies require a life expectancy of two years or less, while others may buy your policy even if your life expectancy is four years;
- you sign a release allowing the viatical settlement provider access to your medical records.

Most companies will require that the company issuing your life insurance policy be financially sound. If your life insurance policy is provided by your employer, purchasers will want to know if it can be converted into an individual policy or otherwise be guaranteed to remain in force before it can be assigned.

Financial Implications

Because the decision to sell your life insurance policy is a very complex matter, you should consult a tax advisor before doing so. Generally, if you sell your policy to a viatical settlement company, the proceeds are tax-free if you have a life expectancy of less than two years. You still may owe state tax, although a number of states, including New York and California, have made these settlements tax-free. Collecting accelerated benefits or making a viatical settlement also may affect your eligibility for public assistance programs based on financial need, such as Medicaid. The federal government does not require policyholders either to choose accelerated benefits or cash in their policies before qualifying for Medicaid benefits. But once the policyholder cashes in the policy and receives a payment, the money may be counted as income for Medicaid purposes and may affect eligibility.

In 1997, Congress changed the tax code so that proceeds from accelerated benefits and viatical settlements are tax-exempt. Under the law, proceeds from accelerated benefits and viatical settlements are tax-exempt as long as your life expectancy is less than two years and the viatical settlement company is licensed—if you live in a state that requires licensing. If your state does not require viatical settlement companies to be licensed, state law will still require that these companies meet other standards and make certain other disclosures.

Most states have declared that payments of accelerated benefits or viatical settlements are exempt from state taxes. Some states, however, do not give these payments tax-free status. Because of the complexity of the situation, seek professional tax advice from a lawyer, an accountant, or a financial planner.

Guidelines for Consumers

The daily physical and emotional demands of a terminal illness can be overwhelming, and financial burdens can seem insurmountable. If you are considering making a viatical settlement on your life insurance policy—or if you are helping someone with this decision—these consumer guidelines should help you avoid costly mistakes and make the choice that's right.

- Contact two or three viatical settlement companies to make sure offers are competitive, and be aware of prevailing discount rates. A viatical settlement company may pay 80 percent of the face value of a policy to a person whose life expectancy is six months or less.
- Check with your state insurance department to see if viatical settlement companies or brokers must be licensed. If so, check the status of the companies with whom you are considering doing business.
- Don't fall for high pressure tactics. You don't have to accept an offer, and you can change your mind. Some states require a 15-day cooling off period before any viatical settlement transaction is complete.
- Verify that the investor or the company has the money for your payout readily available. Large companies may have cash on hand; smaller ones may have uneven cash flows or may be "shopping" the policy to third parties.
- Insist that the company set up an escrow account with a reputable, independent financial institution before the company sends the offer papers for your signature. An escrow account will let you be sure that the funds are available to cover the offer.
- Insist on a timely payment. Once the insurance company has made the necessary changes, you should get your money within two to three business days from the escrow agent. No more than a few months should go by from the initial contact with the company to the closing. Check with your state Attorney General's office or department of insurance to see if there are complaints against the company before you do business.
- Ask the company about possible tax consequences and implications for public assistance benefits. Some states require viatical settlement companies to make these disclosures and tell you about other options that may be available from your life insurance company.

- Ask about privacy. Some companies may not protect a policyholder's privacy when they act as brokers for payouts from potential investors. Contact a lawyer to check on the possible probate and estate considerations. If you make a viatical settlement, there will be no life insurance benefits for the person you originally designated as beneficiary.

* * *

Jim Mechler
Annotated Bibliography: Viatical Settlements (December 1996)
<http://www.ink.org/public/keln/bibs/mechler2.html>*

vi-at-i-cal *adj.* [Lat. viaticus<via, road.] *Of or relating to travel, a road, or a way.*

* * *

Viatical Settlements—History and Mechanics

For many years, the traditional use of a life insurance policy was to bestow financial benefits on a survivor. In most instances this beneficiary was the purchaser's spouse, children, or parent. With improved medical technology though, people have been allowed to live longer, but for a price. With the high costs of medical treatment, many people have needed money to pay for procedures. This is the [rationale for] a viatical settlement.

Under the conventional "whole life' policy, the insured can cash in the policy while living, but will only receive the cash value of the policy—usually much less than if the death benefits were paid out. Because this cash value payout often did not cover costly experimental procedures, it offered a poor solution to the problem. Largely in response to the AIDS epidemic of the 1980's, the insurance industry created viatical settlements and accelerated death benefits.

In a viatical settlement, the insured assigns the proceeds of [her] life insurance policy to an investor. The insured receives a cash settlement for less than the value of the death benefit. The cash settlement is computed based upon the life expectancy of the insured, with a higher percentage payout for those closer to death. In return, the investor pays the premiums and when the insured dies, receives the death benefit value of the policy. Like any investment, the investor is speculating upon the happening of an event. In this case, that event is the death of the insured. If the insured dies before the date predicated by the investor, then the return on the policy will be greater than the payout.

. . . With the advent of recent drug therapies which have increased the life expectancy of AIDS patients, the viatical settlement industry has begun cultivating a new type of seller. This new market includes those who suffer from cancer, ALS, Alzheimer's, or any other disease or condition that has resulted in a terminal diag-

---

* Copyright © 1995-97. Reprinted with permission.

nosis. Each viatical settlement company sets its own rules regarding which life insurance policies it will buy. Some considerations that the viatical settlement company will take into consideration include:

- that the individual has owned the life insurance policy for 2 years.
- that the individual is terminal (defined as death expected within six months).
- that the insured has a waiver from the current beneficiary of the policy.
- that the policy has a "large" value.
- that the policy is issued from a "well-known" insurance company.

The insured will probably also be asked to release his/her medical records to the viatical settlement firm.

* * *

Accelerated Death Benefits

Accelerated Death Benefits provisions are of two varieties. The first variety, known as the "lien" model, leaves the underlying policy untouched. The insured is paid a percentage of the policy's death benefit, with the remaining percentage for the policy's beneficiaries. The remaining percentage is reduced by the amount of premium paid by the insurer until the insured's death.

The second model, the "proceeds" model, is similar to a viatical settlement. Death benefits for a beneficiary are not preserved, with the insured receiving a discounted percentage of the policy's death benefit. Usually Accelerated Death Benefits are available only if the original policy provided for them. In addition, Accelerated Death Benefits are more restrictive than viatical settlements. ADB's usually require a note from the insured's physician stating that the insured has less than twelve months to live. Viatical settlements do not usually require such a prognosis. Accelerated Death Benefits offer an alternative to viatical settlements that allow the insured, in some cases, to retain death benefits while still receiving a portion of the benefits in advance.

Legal Issues Pertaining to Viatical Settlements

For several years the principal legal issue surrounding viatical settlements was whether viatical settlements constituted a security transaction as defined by the Securities Act of 1933. The 1933 Act expressly exempts insurance contracts from the definition of a "security." But viatical settlements, though tied to the proceeds of insurance policies, probably cannot be described as insurance contracts.

In 1992, two viatical brokers were issued cease-and-desist orders by North Dakota's Securities Commissioner. The Commissioner charged that what the brokers were engaging in was an "unregistered sale of securities." The SEC soon began its own investigation.

The SEC's investigation led it to file suit against Life Partners, the largest viatical settlement company, in August of 1994. The SEC claimed that viatical settlements are security transactions and must be registered. Life Partners claimed that viatical settlements are not securities and are required to be registered. A year later, the federal district court for the District of Columbia concluded that viatical settlements are subject to federal securities laws and issued a preliminary injunction against Life Partners.

The decision was appealed to the Court of Appeals for the District of Columbia. The D.C. Circuit reversed the decision of the District Court. In *SEC v. Life Partners, Inc.* [7 F.3d 536 (D.C. Cir. 1996), the Court held that viatical settlements are not securities within the Securities Act of 1933 because there is no "venture" associated with ownership of a fractional interest in an insurance contract from which the investor's profit depends entirely on the mortality of the insured. The Court also found that the post-purchase activities of the viatical settlement company are ministerial in nature and do not have a material impact on the profits of the investors.

A second legal issue concerning viatical settlements is their proper tax treatment. Generally, neither the states or the federal government tax life insurance proceeds after the insured has died. But on the federal level, no such benefit exists for pre-death life insurance proceeds received from a viatical settlement.

In a 1994 private letter ruling, the IRS stated that viatical settlements are taxable income. The IRS has not issued any rulings concerning the tax treatment of accelerated benefits. This issue was finally resolved with the passage of legislation in 1995 that specifically exempts both viatical settlements and accelerated death benefits from federal income tax.

Questions

1. Why might the elderly be special targets of the sellers and brokers of viatical settlement agreements?

2. Read 26 U.S.C. § 101(g) in the statutory supplement. Do you approve of the tax provisions that exempt viatical settlements and accelerated death benefits from the federal income tax?

2. Regulatory Issues

The relative lack of regulation of the viatical settlement/accelerated death benefit industry is aggravated by the fact that many companies operate over the Internet and thus can appeal directly to potential viators. One viator advocate has estimated that "tens of dozens" of these organizations hawk their wares on-line. It may be difficult for a terminally-ill consumer to make rational choices about what type of contract, and what provider, is in the viator's best interests. Find and visit the website of at least one for-profit viatical company or broker (and don't assume that because the company's uniform resource locator ends in ".org" that the company is a non-profit entity). Does the company provide sufficient information to allow a potential viator to make a decision informed by the considerations listed by the FTC, above? Does the risk of fraud or overreaching justify special regulation of viatical settlement transactions carried out in whole or part over the Internet?

Question

Read the Viatical Settlements Model Act in the statutory supplement. Does this proposed model act resolve some of the problems associated with viatical settlements?

B. The Right to Die

1. Introduction: Constitutional Considerations

The law has long recognized the right of competent persons to refuse medical treatment. In *Cruzan v. Director, Missouri Dep't of Health*, 497 U.S. 261 (1990), the United States Supreme Court implicitly acknowledged that this right, and a corollary "right-to-die," are protected by the Fifth and Fourteenth Amendment due process clauses. In *Cruzan*, the Court upheld a state evidentiary rule requiring that, before nutrition and hydration may be withdrawn from a person in a persistent vegetative state, it must be demonstrated by "clear and convincing evidence" that such action is consistent with the patient's previously manifested wishes. In that case, the family of Nancy Cruzan, who was in a persistent vegetative state as a result of an automobile accident, asked hospital employees to terminate the artificial nutrition and hydration procedures after it had become apparent that Nancy Cruzan had virtually no chance of regaining her mental faculties. The hospital employees refused to do so without court approval, and the state of Missouri intervened in behalf of Nancy to prevent withdrawal of the feeding tube.

The Court said in *Cruzan* that the Due Process Clause does not require that the state rely on the judgment of the family, the guardian, or "anyone but the patient herself" in making a medical decision of this nature. Unless clear and convincing evidence exists that the patient herself had expressed an interest not to be sustained in a persistent vegetative state, or that she had expressed a desire to have a surrogate make such a decision for her, the state may refuse to allow withdrawal of nutrition and hydration. "A State is entitled to guard against potential abuses" that can occur if family members do not protect a patient's best interests, and "may properly decline to make judgments about the 'quality' of life that a particular individual may enjoy, and [instead] simply assert an unqualified interest in the preservation of human life to be weighed against the . . . interests of the individual."

The *Cruzan* decision was a narrow one in the sense that it held only that Missouri's evidentiary requirement did not violate the due process clauses. The Court's opinion in *Cruzan*, however, assumes that a competent person has a constitutionally protected right to refuse lifesaving hydration and nutrition. More important, a majority of Justices declared in a separate opinion that such a liberty interest exists. Thus, the Court appears committed to the position that the right to refuse nutrition and hydration—or other life sustaining measures—is subsumed in the broader right to refuse medical treatment, and is a right of constitutional dimension. Although *Cruzan* involved a young person, the decision has had a profound impact on public policy and how lawyers help their older clients plan for death.

Sarah E. Ubel
Living Wills: An Annotated Bibliography (May 1998)
<http://www.ink.org/public/keln/bibs/ubel.html>*

"Just as I choose a ship to sail in or a house to live in, so I choose a death for my passage from life."

—*Seneca (4 B.C.–65 A.D.)*

* * *

Definitions and Explanations

Agent: A health care proxy appointed through a Durable Power of Attorney for Health care.

Artificially Administered Nutrition and Hydration (Tube Feeding): This does not mean food and water taken by mouth—eating and drinking. Tube feeding means providing nutrients and fluids through tubes that are inserted into a person's stomach through the nose (nasogastric or NG tube) or surgically inserted into the stomach (gastrostomy) or, less frequently, into the small intestine (jejunostomy). As a rule, tube feeding decisions are not about intravenous (IV) administration of fluids, nutrients, and medications. See Total Parenteral Nutrition (TPN) and Intravenous Nutrition and Hydration (IV)

Autonomy: The principle that a person has the ethical, legal, and medical right of self-determination to consent or refuse to consent to medical treatment, based on the moral principle of respect for person.

Brain Death: Characteristics of brain death consist of:

1) unreceptivity and unresponsiveness to externally applied stimuli and internal needs;
2) no spontaneous movements or breathing;
3) no reflex activity; and
4) a flat electroencephalograph reading after 24 hour period of observation. The brain death determination is used when a person is on a respirator and the usual determination of death, that there is neither cardiac (heart) nor respiratory (breathing) activity, cannot be applied.

Cardiopulmonary Resuscitation (CPR): Restoring breathing or heartbeat after either cardiac or respiratory arrest. CPR methods range from basic mouth to mouth breathing and chest compression to more advanced methods such as administration of electric shock to the heart, drugs and other mechanical or chemical agents.

Death: The cessation of life; permanent cessations of vital functions and signs. Numerous states have enacted statutory definitions of death which include brain related criteria. For example, many states have adopted, sometimes with variations, the Uniform Determination of Death Act definition: "An individual who has sustained

---

* Copyright © 1998. Reprinted with permission.

either 1) irreversible cessation of circulatory and respiratory function, or 2) irreversible cessation of all functions of the entire brain, including the brain stem, is dead. A determination must be made in accordance with accepted medical standards."

Do Not Intubate Order (DNI Order): This means that a tube should not be inserted in the throat for purpose of putting someone on a respirator to maintain breathing indefinitely. In an emergency, paramedics may insert a tube into the throat for the purpose of resuscitation—to attempt to establish breathing—and a decision must be made later to withdraw it.

Do Not Resuscitate Order (DNR Order): Resuscitation includes various means of attempting to restart or to strengthen weak and irregular heartbeat and breathing. Neither of these two functions, breathing or heartbeat, can continue unassisted for many minutes without the other . . . Many people have taken basic CPR courses and learned how to do mouth-to-mouth breathing and apply pressure to the chest . . . Resuscitation may involve applying a bag, a type of mask, over the person's mouth to assist in breathing, or intubation, which means inserting a tube into the person's throat so that mechanically assisted breathing can be started. Intubation requires placing the person on a respirator, sometimes called a ventilator. Resuscitation may involve injecting drugs or applying electric shock, or both, and then transporting the person to a hospital emergency room. A DNR order directs medical personnel NOT to resuscitate using one or more of these methods. Also see: Do Not Intubate Order.

Durable Power of Attorney for Health Care: A means by which one person, the principal, can appoint, by a written document, a second person, the attorney in fact or agent, to make health care decisions when the principal is unable to do so.

Intravenous (IV) Nutrition and Hydration : IV administration is usually short-term, because most people's veins will not tolerate long term use; IVs are not usually used for nutritional purposes in nursing homes or home health care.

Life Sustaining Procedures: Such procedures which may be suspended on a court order or pursuant to a living will in case of, for example a comatose and terminally ill individual, are medical procedures which utilize mechanical or other artificial means to sustain, restore, or supplant a vital function, which serve only or primarily to prolong the moment of death, and where, in the judgment of the attending and consulting physicians, as reflected in the patient's medical record, death is imminent if such procedures are not utilized.

Living Will: A document that governs the withholding or withdrawal of life-sustaining treatment from an individual in the event of an incurable or irreversible condition that will cause death within a relatively short time, invoked when such person is no longer able to make decisions regarding his or her medical treatment.

Medical Power of Attorney: An instrument in writing whereby one person, as principal, appoints another as his or her agent and confers authority to make medical decisions on behalf of the principal. The agent is attorney in fact and his or her power is revoked on death of the principal by operation of law or upon the revocation of the principal.

Natural Death: A death which occurs by the unassisted operation of natural causes.

Natural Death Acts: Such statutes authorize an adult to make a written directive instructing his or her physician to withhold life-sustaining procedures in the event of a terminal condition. In the directive, which is to be executed in a prescribed manner and made a part of the patient's medical records, the declarant directs that if he or she has been certified by two physicians as being afflicted with a terminal condition, he or she is to be permitted to die naturally. Such laws relieve from civil or criminal liability physicians who act in accordance with its provisions. . . .

No CPR Order: See Do Not Resuscitate Order

Patient Self-Determination Act: A federal law, effective December 1991, that requires hospitals, nursing homes, home health and hospice care providers, and health maintenance organizations (HMOs) to ask persons admitted for care if they have an advance directive. If so, the directive must be placed in the person's medical record. These health providers must also provide information about state law on advance directives and about their own policies related to patients' rights to make medical decisions, and provide community education about advance directives. They cannot discriminate on the basis of whether a person has or does not have directive.

Persistent Vegetative State (PVS): A condition caused by disease or injury in which the upper portion of the brain has been destroyed. A person in a PVS has lost all conscious function but may still have sleep/wake cycles, and there can be involuntary, repetitive arm and leg movements. The lower part of the brain, the brainstem, still functions, so breathing and heartbeat continue.

Respirator: These machines, sometimes called ventilators, are devices that either assist or take over the exchange of air for people who, because of disease, injury, or death (brain only) cannot breathe for themselves. A person is connected to the respirator by a tube that enters the body either through the nose and mouth or through a surgical incision in the throat (tracheostomy).

Right to Die Laws: Cases and statutes which recognize in some instances the right of a dying person to decline extraordinary treatment to prolong life, or the right of the person's guardian to request such . . . .

Substituted Judgment: A term used when making medical decisions for another, based on the principle of autonomy. It means to decide as the person would have decided for himself or herself, if he or she were able to do so. By honoring an advance directive, the health care proxy is exercising substituted judgment and respecting the declarant's right of self-determination.

Terminal Condition/Illness: An illness or injury from which there is no hope of recovery and for which death is the expected result. A living will does not go into effect until a person is in a terminal condition, which is defined differently in the various state living will laws.

Total Parenteral Nutrition (TPN): This is a type of tube feeding or artificially administered nutrition and hydration. Tubes are inserted into a large vein in the chest or neck for longer-term use than an IV. TPN is rarely used in terminal care, because it is more expensive and requires more intensive nursing care than NG and gastrostomy feedings.

Questions

1. Why might a person choose to execute a DNR or DNI order?

2. Should health care providers be liable to an individual or her family members for failing to comply with a DNR order?

2. Statutory Considerations

Read the Patient Self-Determination Act of 1990, Pub. L. 101-408 § 4206(a)(2), in the statutory supplement (now codified at 42 U.S.C. § 1395cc(f)(1)-(4).

Memorandum from Walter S. Wheeler III
Bureau of Health Systems, Department of Public Health, State of Michigan, to Administrators/Managers of Hospitals, Nursing Home, Hospice Programs, Home Health Agencies, and Health Maintenance Organizations
(November 25, 1991)
<http://www.msu.edu/~iphh/mnp.htm>

The Federal Omnibus Budget Reconciliation Act of 1990 (OBRA) contains a section we now refer to as the "Patient Self-Determination Act" (PSDA) which imposes new responsibilities on certain providers of Medicare and/or Medicaid services. Effective December 1, 1991, hospitals, nursing homes, certain HMO agencies, home health agencies and hospice programs are required to develop policies and programs on advance directives and those programs must:

- Provide written information to patients/residents at admission regarding their rights under State law to make decisions regarding medical care and on the programs' policies governing implementation of those rights.
- Document in the patient/resident medical record whether or not he/she has executed an advance directive.
- Ensure compliance with the requirements of Michigan law respecting advance directives at the institution.
- Provide, individually or with others, education for staff and the community on issues concerning advance directives.
- Not condition the provision of care or otherwise discriminate against an individual based on whether or not the individual has executed an advance directive.

In addition to this memorandum, this mailing contains a reprinting of the federal statutory change along with a short article on practical considerations regarding implementation that should be shared with your legal advisor and those responsible for implementation of this new requirement.

To assist you in explaining patients' rights under Michigan law, the Michigan Department of Public Health convened a panel of experts who were responsible for drafting and finalizing the enclosed guide entitled "MICHIGAN NOTICE TO PATIENTS." While you are required to provide the information contained in this guide to your patients at the time of admission, you are not required to use the document provided by the State. You may photocopy the material (with or without your own logo) or you may elect to include the contents of the guide in other material you are preparing to fulfill this new regulatory requirement.

Long-term care providers (nursing homes) will notice that the "MICHIGAN NOTICE TO PATIENTS" differs from the memorandum we issued in February 1991, which implied that a guardian was needed if a resident was no longer "able" to make his/her treatment decisions and that resident had not previously appointed a surrogate decision maker consistent with Michigan law. Our panel of experts considered this matter carefully and concluded that it is not always necessary to seek guardianship appointments when residents are "unable" to exercise their treatment decision options.

We believe this material will be of considerable assistance as your program changes to meet new federal requirements. We understand that several provider organizations are working with their members to assist in implementation. Questions specific to a type of provider should be referred to that organization. In addition, the legal community has expressed significant interest in this subject and is available for consultation. Many State Senators and Representatives have available in their office material describing the process for the appointment of a surrogate decision maker consistent with Michigan law.

Michigan Department of Public Health, Bureau of Health Systems
Michigan Notice to Patients Required by the
Patient Self Determination Act ("PSDA")
(November 1991)

Your Rights to Make Medical Treatment Decisions

We are giving you this material to tell you about your right to make your own decisions about your medical treatment. As a competent adult, you have the right to accept or refuse any medical treatment. "Competent" means you have the ability to understand your medical condition and the medical treatments for it, to weigh the possible benefits and risks of each such treatment and then to decide whether you want to accept treatment or not.

Who Decides What Treatment I Will Get?

As long as you are competent, you are the only person who can decide what medical treatment you want to accept or reject. You will be given information and advice about the pros and cons of different kinds of treatment and you can ask questions about your options. But only you can say "yes" or "no" to any treatment offered. You can say "no" even if the treatment you refuse might keep you alive longer and even if others want you to have it.

What If I'm In No Condition to Decide?

If you become unable to make your own decisions about medical care, decisions will have to be made for you. If you haven't given prior instructions, no one will know what you would want. There may be difficult questions: for instance, would you refuse treatment if you were unconscious and not likely to wake up? Would you refuse treatment if you were going to die soon no matter what? Would you want to receive any treatment your care givers recommend? When your wishes are not known, your family or the courts may have to decide what to do.

What Can I Do Now to See That My Wishes Are Honored in the Future?

While you are competent, you can name someone to make medical treatment decisions for you should you ever be unable to make them for yourself. To be certain that the person you name has the legal right to make those decisions, you must fill out a form called either a durable power of attorney for health care or a Patient Advocate Designation. The person named in the form to make or carry out your decisions about treatment is called a Patient Advocate. You have the right to give your Patient Advocate, your care givers and your family and friends written or spoken instructions about what medical treatment you want and don't want to receive.

Who Can Be My Patient Advocate?

You can choose anyone to be your Patient Advocate as long as the person is at least 18 years old. You can pick a family member or a friend or any other person you trust, but you should make sure that person is willing to serve by signing an acceptance form. It's a good idea to name a backup choice, too, just in case the first person is unwilling or unable to act when the time comes.

Where Can I Get a Patient Advocate Designation Form?

Many Michigan hospitals, health maintenance organizations, nursing homes, homes for the aged, hospices and home health care agencies make forms available to people free of charge. Many senior citizens' groups and church and civic groups do, too. You can also get a free form from various members of the Michigan legislature. Many lawyers also prepare Patient Advocate Designations for their clients. The forms aren't all alike. You should pick the one which suits your situation the best.

How Do I Sign a Patient Advocate Designation Form So That It's Valid?

All you have to do is fill in the name of the advocate and sign the form in front of two witnesses. But that's not as simple as it sounds, because under this law some people cannot be your witnesses. Your spouse, parents, grandchildren, children, and brothers or sisters, for example, cannot witness your signature. Neither can anyone else who could be your heir or who is named to receive something in your will, or who is an employee of a company that insures your life or health. Finally, the law disqualifies the person you name as your Patient Advocate, your doctors and all employees of the facility or agency providing health care to you from being a witness to your signature.

It is easier to make a Patient Advocate Designation before you become a patient or resident of a health care facility or agency. Friends or co-workers are often good people to ask to be witnesses, since they see you often and can, if necessary, swear that you acted voluntarily and were of sound mind when you made out the form.

Do I Have to Give My Patient Advocate Instructions?

No. A Patient Advocate Designation can be used just to name your Patient Advocate, the person you want to make decisions for you. But written instructions are generally helpful to everybody involved. And, if you want your Patient Advocate to be able to refuse treatment and let you die, you have to say so specifically in the Patient Advocate Designation document itself. Any other instructions you have you can either write down or just tell your Patient Advocate. Either way, the Patient Advocate's job is to follow your instructions.

Can I Just Give Instructions and Not Name a Patient Advocate?

Yes, you can simply tell somebody, for example, your care giver or your family and close friends, what your wishes are. Better yet, you can write what is called a "Living Will," which is a written statement of your choices about medical treatment. Even though there is not yet a [Michigan] Living Will law, courts and health care providers still find Living Wills valuable. Those taking care of you will pay more attention to what you have written about your treatment choices, whether in a Patient Advocate Designation or a Living Will, because they can be more confident they know what you would have wanted. Most doctors, hospitals and other health care providers will also pay attention to what you've said to others, especially your family, about medical treatment. But again, it's better for everyone involved if you write your wishes down.

Do I Have to Make a Decision Now About My Future Medical Treatment?

No. You don't have to fill out a Patient Advocate Designation or a Living Will and you don't have to tell anybody your wishes about medical treatment. You will still get the medical treatment you choose now, while you are competent. If you become unable to make decisions, but you've made sure that your family and friends know what you would want, they will be able to follow your wishes. Without instructions from you, your family or friends and care givers may still be able to agree how to proceed. If they don't, however, a court may have to name a guardian to make decisions for you.

If I Make Decisions Now, Can I Change My Mind Later?

Yes. You can give new instructions in writing or orally. You can also change your mind about naming a Patient Advocate at all and cancel a Patient Advocate Designation at any time.

You should review your Patient Advocate Designation or Living Will at least once a year to make sure it still accurately states how you want to be treated and/or names the person you want to make decisions for you.

What Else Should I Think About?

Treatment decisions are difficult. We encourage you to think about them in advance and discuss them with your family, friends, advisors and care givers. You can and should ask your facility or agency about their treatment policies and procedures to be sure you understand them and how they work.

If you want more information about a Patient Advocate Designation or Living Wills, or sample forms, please ask your care givers for assistance. Many facilities and agencies have staff available who can answer your questions. Additional materials may be available from your state representative or senator.

Questions

1. Is a national policy favoring execution of advance directives, living wills, or health care powers of attorney really justified? Are hospitals and other health care providers the best purveyors of information on such legal documents?

2. Imagine that a seventy-three year old woman arrives at the emergency room in suffering from shortness of breath and chest pains. Immediately upon her admission, she is given the Michigan Notice to Patients reprinted above. What message might this convey to the patient, who is already distraught? Is there a better way to address the concerns implicit in the Patient Self-Determination Act?

3. Read the Uniform Health-Care Decisions Act in the statutory supplements. In what ways does this statute go beyond the requirements of the Patient Self-Determination Act? Consider this question again after you read the materials in subsection 3, *infra*.

3. Advance Directives, Living Wills, and Health Care Powers of Attorney

Charles P. Sabatino
10 Legal Myths About Advance Medical Directives
ABA Commission on Legal Problems of the Elderly
<http://www.abanet.org/elderly/myths.html>[*]

Myth 1: Everyone should have a Living Will.

False. A Living Will, without more, is not the document most people need. As a threshold goal, most people should have a Health Care Power of Attorney (or Health Care Proxy) that names a trusted person as agent or proxy. A still better alternative is to execute both documents or a single, combined "Advance Directive" that names a proxy and provides guidance about one's wishes. Unfortunately, because of statu-

---

[*] Copyright © American Bar Association. All rights reserved. Reprinted with permission of the American Bar Association.

tory restrictions or inconsistencies within state law, many practicing attorneys advise clients to execute separate rather than combined documents. State advance directive laws are slowly moving toward acceptance of flexible, combined advance directives, but the states differ significantly in this regard.

The reason for the primary importance of the proxy appointment is simple. Most standardized living will forms are quite limited in what they can accomplish and what conditions they cover. For example, most provide instructions that apply only if the individual is in a terminal condition or permanently unconscious, yet the majority of health care decisions that need to be made for patients lacking capacity concern questions about day-to-day care, placement options, and treatment options short of "pulling the plug."

Moreover, most boilerplate instructions express fairly géneral sentiments about not wanting treatments that serve only prolong the dying process. Relatively few people disagree with this sentiment. However, applying it to a particular set of facts is more difficult than at first meets the eye. . . . Any intervention can produce multiple consequences, some predictable, some not so predictable. If an aggressive and possibly painful course of treatment will give the patient a 1 in 3 chance of recovering to the point of being able to converse again with loved ones for a least a few more months, is that hope enough to treat aggressively? What if the odds were 1 in 25?

Living will instructions always need interpretation, even when the terminal nature of an illness is clear. An agent or proxy under a health care power of attorney can do precisely that. The proxy, who should know the patient's values intimately, can respond to the actual facts and variables known when an actual health care decision needs to be made. Short of possessing a crystal ball, no one can anticipate the specific and often complicated circumstances fate will place them in. The proxy acts not only as legal decisionmaker, but also as spokesperson, analyzer, interpreter, and advocate.

One caveat: if there is no one close to the individual whom he or she trusts to act as health proxy, then the health care power of attorney should not be used. In this circumstance, the Living Will is safer, despite its limitations.

Myth 2: Written Advance Directives are not legal in every state.

False. Every state recognizes both the proxy and living will type advance directives, although the laws of each state vary considerably in terminology, the scope of decisionmaking addressed, restrictions, and the formalities required for making an advance directive.

A more frequently raised question is whether an advance directive written in one state will be recognized in other states. In other words, is the directive portable across state lines? Many states expressly recognize out-of-state advance directives if the directive meets either the legal requirements of the state where executed or the state where the treatment decision arises. Several states are silent on this question. If there is doubt, the rules of the state where treatment takes place, not the state where the advance directive was signed, will normally control. [E]ven if an advance directive fails to meet technicalities of state law, health providers still should value the directive as important, if not controlling, evidence of the patient's wishes.

The threshold problem with most state provisions addressing portability is that they presumably require providers to be fully knowledgeable of the other state's law.

Most use language derived from the Uniform Probate Code and similar to the following provision included in the now defunct Uniform Rights of the Terminally Ill Act:

> A declaration executed in another state in compliance with the law of that state or of this State is validly executed for purposes of this [Act].

Colorado and Utah offer a more user-friendly approach to recognizing out-of state directives:

> Unless otherwise provided therein, any medical power of attorney or similar instrument executed in another state shall be presumed to comply with the provisions of this [Act] and may, in good faith, be relied upon by a health care provider or health care facility in this state.

Thus, in these, states providers may assume that the out-of-state directive is valid unless they have actual knowledge to the contrary.

Myth 3: Just telling my doctor what I want is no longer legally effective.

False. While it is better to have a written Advance Directive, oral statements remain important both on their own and as supplements to written directives.

Oral instructions may take many forms. A person physically unable to execute an advance directive may provide oral instructions that are reduced to writing by the doctor or another person, acting for the patient. Several states treat such statements as formal Advance Directives if witnessed properly. Less formal instructions in the nature of conversations with family, friends, or physicians will not have the same legal status of a written Advance Directive.

Nevertheless, informal oral statements have two important attributes. First, good health care decisionmaking requires good communication among all interested parties, and oral communication is our most natural and, indeed, primary mode of communication. Ideally, a formal advance directive serves to aid this kind of communication, not to replace it. Second, oral statements constitute important evidence of one's wishes and help expand upon, clarify, and reinforce individual preferences. The contents of the written Advance Directive should reflect a continuing conversation among the individual, physician, family, and close friends.

Myth 4: An Advance Directive means "Don't treat."

False. While it is true that most people use Advance Directives to avoid being kept alive against their wishes when death is near, it is a mistake to assume that the existence of an advance directive means, "Don't treat." Advance directives are also used to say that the individual wants all possible treatments within the range of generally accepted medical standards. What is said depends upon one's particular wishes and values. Moreover, even when an advance directive eschews all life-sustaining treatments, one should always assume (and insist upon) continuing pain control, comfort care and respect for one's dignity.

Myth 5: When I name a proxy in my Advance Directive, I give up some control and flexibility.

False. An individual gives up no authority or choice by doing an Advance Directive. As long as the person remains able to make decisions, his or her consent must be obtained for medical treatment. Health care providers cannot legally ignore the patient in favor of one's agent or written instruction. Indeed, in most states, health care advance directives are "springing." That is, they have no legal effect unless and until the patient lacks the capacity to make a health care decision. In a minority of states, immediately effective directives are permissible, but the maker always retains a right to override the proxy or revoke the directive.

There are situations in which a competent patient abdicates decisionmaking by saying, for example, "Do whatever my daughter thinks is best." However, this form of delegation of decisionmaking is effective only from moment to moment and needs to be rechecked at every significant decision point. Neither the proxy nor a written instruction can override one's currently expressed choice.

Myth 6: I must use a prescribed Advance Directive form for my state.

Usually false. In most states, you do not have to use a specific form. About 37 state statutes include forms for appointing proxies or for creating comprehensive advance directives. In the majority of these, the forms are optional. In about 18 states, the forms must be "substantially followed" or certain information disclosure language must be included in the form. Even with these requirements, changes and additions to standard language are permissible. Indeed, any form can and should be personalized to reflect the individual's particular values, priorities, and wishes. If you do not agree with language contained in an approved form, change the language. If changing the language creates any doubt about the validity of the form, then further legal consultation is in order. Above all, it is a mistake to pick up an "official" form and just sign it unchanged, without first being sure that it truly reflects one's specific wishes.

Myth 7: I need a lawyer to do an Advance Directive.

No, a lawyer is not needed. Yes, a lawyer is a helpful resource, but not the only resource, nor necessarily the best resource for all persons. Advance directives are not difficult to complete, but they require a few steps to do well. Try these steps for yourself, even if you already have an advance directive.

First, obtain an "official" or generally accepted form for your state, plus at least one or two additional advance directive forms from other sources.... This helps you see the variations in topics different advance directives cover and the alternative instructions they provide. The form-publishing business may be burgeoning, but most are inadequate in one respect or another. Even with the best drafting, there is no perfect form for everyone. People are different.

Second, discuss the contents of the forms with your physician, close family, and the person you may name as proxy. Most people find these discussions difficult to initiate, but they are extremely important. Gather information about your current medical condition and its implications for future medical problems; clarify your own values and wishes; and ask your physician, close family, and proxy if they are willing to support you in the way you want.

Third, complete the form you choose, being sure to add or modify language to reflect your wishes more accurately. Be sure to follow the witnessing instructions for your state exactly. Most, but not all states, require two completely disinterested witnesses. If you have a potential family conflict, special legal concern, or unusual request, additional legal drafting help may be needed. These circumstances call for consultation with a lawyer experienced in personal planning.

Myth 8: Doctors and other health care providers are not legally obligated to follow my Advance Directive.

Legally false, but as in many endeavors, reality muddies the waters. As a matter of law, it is clear that medical providers cannot treat an individual against his or her wishes. Consequently, if a physician acts contrary to a patient's clear instruction directive or contrary to the decision of the patient's authorized proxy, the physician risks the same liability he or she would face if the physician were to ignore a refusal of treatment by a fully competent patient. Treatment would constitute a battery. However, a few factors complicate the situation.

First, the doctor or health facility sometimes do not know about the existence of an advance directive. While federal law requires hospitals, nursing homes, and home health agencies to ask about and to document your Advance Directive, the document often does not make it into the appropriate record. It is up to the patient and those close to the patient to ensure that everyone who might need a copy of the directive in fact has a copy.

Second, as noted earlier, people often do not express their wishes very clearly or precisely in advance directives. Simply using general language that rejects "heroic measures" or "treatment that only prolongs the dying process" does not give much guidance. Therefore, interpretation problems may arise. Giving a proxy broad authority to interpret one's wishes will help avoid this problem, except that sometimes proxies themselves are not quite sure what the patient would want done. This fact underscores the importance of discussing one's wishes and values with the intended proxy.

Third, in most states, if a physician or facility objects to an Advance Directive based on reasons of conscience, state law permits the physician or facility to refuse to honor it. However, facilities must notify the patient of their policies regarding advance directives at the time of admission. If a refusal occurs, the physician and facility should provide assistance in transferring the patient to a provider that will comply with the directive.

Fourth, persons who are dying, but living in the community, may face problems in having an advance directive followed if a crisis occurs and emergency medical services (EMS) are called (for example, by calling "911"). EMS personnel are generally required to resuscitate and stabilize patients until they are brought safely to a hospital. States are beginning to address this situation by creating procedures that allow EMS personnel to refrain from resuscitating terminally ill patients who are certified as having a "do not resuscitate order" and who have an approved identifier (such as a special bracelet).

Myth 9: If I do not have an Advance Directive, I can rely on my family to make my health care decisions when I am unable to make decisions for myself.

This is only partly true. If an individual does not have an advance directive naming a health decisions agent or proxy, several states expressly designate default "surrogates," typically family members in order of kinship, to make some or all health care decisions. Only a few of these statutes authorize a "close friend" to make decisions, and then normally only when family members are unavailable.

Even without such statutes, most doctors and health facilities routinely rely on family involvement in decisionmaking, as long as there are close family members available and there is no disagreement. However, problems can arise because family members may not know what the patient would want in a given situation, or they may disagree about the best course of action. Disagreement can easily undermine family consent. A hospital physician or specialist who does not know you well may become the default decisionmaker.

In these situations, patients risk having decisions made contrary to their wishes or by persons whom they would not choose. Moreover, family members and persons close to patients experience needless agony in being forced to make life and death decisions without the patient's clear guidance. It is far better to make one's wishes known and to appoint a proxy ahead of time through an Advance Directive.

Myth 10: Advance Directives are a legal tool for old people.

False. Don't think of this as an "old" people's issue. It may be natural to link death and dying issues with old age, but that is a mistake when it comes to advance directives. Consider that perhaps the most well known landmark court cases those of Nancy Cruzan and Karen Ann Quinlan involved individuals in their 20's. The stakes are actually higher for younger persons in that, if tragedy strikes, they might be kept alive for decades in a condition they would not want. An Advance Directive is an important legal planning tool for all adults.

Questions

1. What is the difference between a living will and an advance directive? Why might a client prefer one to the other?

2. Does the Uniform Health-Care Decisions Act adequately address the choice-of-law isssue suggested by the Sabbatino article?

AARP, ABA Commission on Legal Problems of the Elderly, and American Medical Association
Shape Your Health Care Future with Health Care Advance Directives (1995)
<http://www.ama-assn.org/public/booklets/livgwill.htm>[*]

What Is A Health Care Advance Directive?

A health care advance directive is a document in which you give instructions about your health care if, in the future, you cannot speak for yourself. You can give

---

[*] Copyrighted in 1995, American Association of Retired Persons, ABA Commission on Legal Problems of the Elderly, and the American Medical Association. All rights reserved under International and Pan American Copyright Conventions. Reprinted with permission.

someone you name (your "agent" or "proxy") the power to make health care decisions for you. You also can give instructions about the kind of health care you do or do not want.

In a traditional Living Will, you state your wishes about life-sustaining medical treatments if you are terminally ill. In a Health Care Power of Attorney, you appoint someone else to make medical treatment decisions for you if you cannot make them for yourself.

The Health Care Advance Directive in this booklet combines and expands the traditional Living Will and Health Care Power of Attorney into a single, comprehensive document.

Why Is It Useful?

Unlike most Living Wills, a Health Care Advance Directive is not limited to cases of terminal illness. If you cannot make or communicate decisions because of a temporary or permanent illness or injury, a Health Care Advance Directive helps you keep control over health care decisions that are important to you. In your Health Care Advance Directive, you state your wishes about any aspect of your health care, including decisions about life-sustaining treatment, and choose a person to make and communicate these decisions for you.

Appointing an agent is particularly important. At the time a decision needs to be made, your agent can participate in discussions and weigh the pros and cons of treatment decisions based on your wishes. Your agent can decide for you wherever you cannot decide for yourself, even if your decision-making ability is only temporarily affected.

Unless you formally appoint someone to decide for you, many health care providers and institutions will make critical decisions for you that might not be based on your wishes. In some situations, a court may have to appoint a guardian unless you have an advance directive.

An advance directive also can relieve family stress. By expressing your wishes in advance, you help family or friends who might otherwise struggle to decide on their own what you would want done.

Are Health Care Advance Directives Legally Valid In Every State?

Yes. Every state and the District of Columbia has laws that permit individuals to sign documents stating their wishes about health care decisions when they cannot speak for themselves. The specifics of these laws vary, but the basic principle of listening to the patient's wishes is the same everywhere. The law gives great weight to any form of written directive. If the courts become involved, they usually try to follow the patient's stated values and preferences, especially if they are in written form. A Health Care Advance Directive may be the most convincing evidence of your wishes you can create.

What Does A Health Care Advance Directive Say?

There are two parts to the Health Care Advance Directive . . . . The most important part of the advance directive is the appointment of someone (your agent) to make health care decisions for you if you cannot decide for yourself. You can define how much or how little authority you want your agent to have. You also can name persons to act as alternate agents if your primary agent cannot act for you, and disqualify specific persons whom you do not want to make decision for you.

If there is no one whom you trust fully to serve as your agent, then you should not name an agent. Instead, you can rely on the second part of the Advance Directive to make your wishes known.

In the second part of the Advance Directive, you can provide specific instructions about your health care treatment. You also can include a statement about donating your organs. Your instructions in the second part provide evidence of your wishes that your agent, or anyone providing you with medical care, should follow. You can complete either or both parts of the Health Care Advance Directive.

How Do I Make A Health Care Advance Directive?

The process for creating a Health Care Advance Directive depends on where you live. Most states have laws that provide special forms and signing procedures. Most states also have special witnessing requirements and restrictions on whom you can appoint as your agent (such as prohibiting a health care provider from being your agent). Follow these rules carefully. Typically, states require two witnesses. Some require or permit a notarized signature. Some have special witnessing requirements if you live in a nursing home or similar facility. Even where witnesses are not required, consider using them anyway to reinforce the deliberate nature of your act and to increase the likelihood that care providers in other states will accept the document.

If you use the form included here, you should be able to meet most states' requirements. However, you may want to check the rules in your state.

If I Change My Mind, Can I Cancel Or Change A Health Care Advance Directive?

Yes, you can cancel or change your Health Care Advance Directive by telling your agent or health care provider in writing of your decision to do so. Destroying all copies of the old one and creating a new one is the best way. Make sure you give a copy of the new one to your physician and anyone else who received the old one.

What Do I Need To Consider Before Making A Health Care Advance Directive?

There are at least four important questions to ask yourself:

First—What Are My Goals for Medical Treatment? The Health Care Advance Directive may determine what happens to you over a period of disability or at the very final stage of your life. You can help others respect your wishes if you take some steps now to make your treatment preferences clear.

While it is impossible to anticipate all of the different medical decisions that may come up, you can make your preferences clear by stating your goals for medical treatment. What do you want treatment to accomplish? Is it enough that treatment could prolong your life, whatever your quality of life? Or, if life-sustaining treatment could not restore consciousness or your ability to communicate with family members or friends, would you rather stop treatment?

Once you have stated your goals of treatment, your family and physicians can make medical decisions for you on the basis of your goals. If treatment would help achieve one of your goals, the treatment would be provided. If treatment would not help achieve one of your goals, the treatment would not be provided.

In formulating your goals of treatment, it is often helpful to consider your wishes about different end-of-life treatments and then asking yourself why do you feel that way. If you would not want to be kept alive by a ventilator, what is it about being on a ventilator that troubles you? Is it the loss of mobility, the lack of independence, or some other factor? Would it matter if you needed a ventilator for only a few days rather than many months? The answers to these kinds of questions will reflect important values that you hold and that will help you shape your goals of treatment.

Another way to become clear about your goals of treatment is to create a "Values History." In doing a Values History, you examine your values and attitudes, discuss them with loved ones or advisors and write down your responses to questions such as:

- How do you feel about your current health?
- How important is independence and self-sufficiency in your life?
- How do you imagine handling illness, disability, dying, and death?
- How might your personal relationships affect medical decision-making, especially near the end of life?
- What role should doctors and other health professionals play in such decisions?
- What kind of living environment is important to you if you become seriously ill or disabled?
- How much should the cost to your family be a part of the decision-making process?
- What role do religious beliefs play in decisions about your health care?
- What are your thoughts about life in general in its final stages: your hopes and fears, enjoyments and sorrows?

Once you have identified your values, you can use them to decide what you want medical treatment to accomplish.

Second—Who Should Be My Agent? Choosing your agent is the most important part of this process. Your agent will have great power over your health and personal care if you cannot make your own decisions. Normally, no one oversees or monitors your agent's decisions.

Choose one person to serve as your agent to avoid disagreements. If you appoint two or more agents to serve together and they disagree, your medical caregivers will have no clear direction. If possible, appoint at least one alternate agent in case your primary agent is not available.

Speak to the person (and alternate agents) you wish to appoint beforehand to explain your desires. Confirm their willingness to act for you and their understanding of your wishes. Also be aware that some states will not let certain persons (such as your doctor) act as your agent. If you can think of no one you trust to carry out this responsibility, then do not name an agent. Make sure, however, that you provide instructions that will guide your doctor or a court-appointed decision-maker.

Third—How Specific Should I Be? A Health Care Advance Directive does not have to give directions or guidelines for your agent. However, if you have specific wishes or preferences, it is important to spell them out in the document itself. Also discuss them with your agent and health care providers. These discussions will help ensure that your wishes, values and preferences will be respected. Make sure to think about your wishes about artificial feeding (nutrition and hydration), since people sometimes have very different views on this topic.

At the same time, be aware that you cannot cover all the bases. It is impossible to predict all the circumstances you may face. Simple statements like "I never want to be placed on a ventilator" may not reflect your true wishes. You might want ventilator assistance if it were temporary and you then could resume your normal activities. No matter how much direction you provide, your agent will still need considerable discretion and flexibility. Write instructions carefully so they do not restrict the authority of your agent in ways you did not intend.

Fourth—How Can I Make Sure That Health Care Providers Will Follow My Advance Directive? Regardless of the laws about advance directives in your state, some physicians, hospitals or other health care providers may have personal views or values that do not agree with your stated desires. As a result, they may not want to follow your Health Care Advance Directive.

Most state laws give doctors the right to refuse to honor your advance directive on conscience grounds. However, they generally must help you find a doctor or hospital that will honor your directive. The best way to avoid this problem is to talk to your physician and other health care providers ahead of time. Make sure they understand the document and your wishes, and they have no objections. If there are objections, work them out, or change physicians.

Once you sign a Health Care Advance Directive, be sure to give a copy of it to your doctor and to your agent, close relatives, and anyone else who may be involved m your care.

What Happens If I Do Not Have An Advance Directive?

If you do not have an advance directive and you cannot make health care decisions, some state laws give decision-making power to default decision-makers or "surrogates." These surrogates, who are usually family members in order of kinship, can make some or all health care decisions. Some states authorize a "close friend" to make decisions, but usually only when family members are unavailable.

Even without such statutes, most doctors and health facilities routinely consult family, as long as there are close family members available and there is no disagreement. However, problems can arise because family members may not know what the patient would want in a given situation. They also may disagree about the best course of action. Disagreement can easily undermine family consent. A hospital physician or specialist who does not know you well may become your decision-maker, or a court proceeding may be necessary to resolve a disagreement.

In these situations, decisions about your health care may not reflect your wishes or may be made by persons you would not choose. Family members and persons close to you may go through needless agony in making life and death decisions without your guidance. It is far better to make your wishes known and appoint an agent ahead of time through a Health Care Advance Directive.

Who Can Help Me Create A Health Care Advance Directive?

You do not need a lawyer to make a Health Care Advance Directive. However, a lawyer can be helpful if your family situation is uncertain or complex, or you expect problems to arise. Start by talking to someone who knows you well and can help you state your values and wishes considering your family and medical history.

Your doctor is an important participant in creating your Health Care Advance Directive. Discuss the kinds of medical problems you may face, based on your current health and health history. Your doctor can help you understand the treatment choices your agent may face. Share your ideas for instructions with your doctor to make sure medical care providers can understand them.

* * *

If your state has a statutory form, remember that preprinted forms—including the one contained in this booklet—may not meet all your needs. Take the time to consider all possibilities and seek advice so that the document you develop meets your special needs.

If you want legal help, contact your state or local Office on Aging. These offices usually are quite familiar with health care issues and local resources for legal assistance. You also can contact the bar association for your state or locality. Its lawyer referral service may be able to refer you to an attorney who handles this type of matter. Finally, organizations that deal with planning for incapacity, such as your local Alzheimer's Association chapter, may be able to provide advice or referrals.

[Sample]

Health Care Advance Directive
FORM AND INSTRUCTIONS

CAUTION: This Health Care Advance Directive is a general form provided for your convenience. While it meets the legal requirements of most states, it may or may not fit the requirements of your particular state. Many states have special forms or special procedures for creating Health Care Advance Directives. Even if your state's law does not clearly recognize this document, it may still provide an effective statement of your wishes if you cannot speak for yourself.

Section 1—HEALTH CARE AGENT

Print your full name here as the "principal" or creator of the health care advance directive.

Print the full name, address and telephone number of the person (age 18 or older) you appoint as your health care agent. Appoint only a person with whom you have talked and whom you trust to understand and carry out your values and wishes.

Many states limit the persons who can serve as your agent. If you want to meet all existing state restrictions do not name any of the following as your agent, since some states will not let them act in that role:

—your health care providers, including physicians;
—staff of health care facilities or nursing care facilities providing your care;
—guardians of your finances (also called conservators);
—employees of government agencies financially responsible for your care;
—any person serving as agent for 10 or more persons.

Section 2—ALTERNATE AGENTS
It is a good idea to name alternate agents in case your first agent is not available. Of course, only appoint alternates if you fully trust them to act faithfully as your agent and you have talked to them about serving as your agent. Print the appropriate information in this paragraph. You can name as many alternate agents as you wish, but place them in the order you wish them to serve.

Section 3—EFFECTIVE DATE AND DURABILITY
This sample document is effective if and when you cannot make health care decisions. Your agent and your doctor determine if you are in this condition. Some state laws include specific procedures for determining your decision—making ability. If you wish, you can include other effective dates or other criteria for determining that you cannot make health care decisions (such as requiring two physicians to evaluate your decision—making ability). You also can state that the power will end at some later date or event before death.

In any case, you have the right to revoke or take away the agent's authority at any time. To revoke, notify your agent or health care provider orally or in writing. If you revoke, it is best to notify in writing both your agent and physician and anyone else who has a copy of the directive. Also destroy the health care advance directive document itself.

Health Care Advance Directive
Part I
Appointment of Health Care Agent

1. HEALTH CARE AGENT

I, _____ hereby appoint:
PRINCIPAL

_____
AGENT'S NAME

_____
ADDRESS

_____
HOME PHONE# WORK PHONE#

as my agent to make health and personal care decisions for me as authorized in this document.

2. ALTERNATE AGENTS
   IF
   —I revoke my Agent's authority; or
   —my Agent becomes unwilling or unavailable to act; or
   —if my agent is my spouse and I become legally separated or divorced,
I name the following (each to act alone and successively, in the order named) as alternates to my Agent:

A. First Alternate Agent _____
   Address _____
   Telephone _____

B. Second Alternate Agent _____
   Address _____
   Telephone _____

3. EFFECTIVE DATE AND DURABILITY
By this document I intend to create a health care advance directive. It is effective upon, and only during, any period in which I cannot make or communicate a choice regarding a particular health care decision. My agent, attending physician and any other necessary experts should determine that I am unable to make choices about health care.

Section 4—AGENT'S POWERS

This grant of power is intended to be as broad as possible. Unless you set limits, your agent will have authority to make any decision you could make to obtain or stop any type of health care.

Even under this broad grant of authority, your agent still must follow your wishes and directions, communicated by you in any manner now or in the future.

To specifically limit or direct your agent's power, you must complete Section 6 in Part II of the advance directive.

4. AGENT'S POWERS

I give my Agent full authority to make health care decisions for me. My Agent shall follow my wishes as known to my Agent either through this document or through other means. When my agent interprets my wishes, I intend my Agent's authority to be as broad as possible, except for any limitations I state in this form. In making any decision, my Agent shall try to discuss the proposed decision with me to determine my desires if I am able to communicate in any way. If my Agent cannot determine the choice I would want, then my Agent shall make a choice for me based upon what my Agent believes to be in my best interests.

Unless specifically limited by Section 6, below, my Agent is authorized as follows:

A. To consent, refuse, or withdraw consent to any and all types of health care. Health care means any care, treatment, service or procedure to maintain, diagnose or otherwise affect an individual's physical or mental condition. It includes, but is not limited to, artificial respiration, nutritional support and hydration, medication and cardiopulmonary resuscitation;

B. To have access to medical records and information to the same extent that I am entitled, including the right to disclose the contents to others as appropriate for my health care;

C. To authorize my admission to or discharge (even against medical advice) from any hospital, nursing home, residential care, assisted living or similar facility or service;

D. To contract on my behalf for any health care related service or facility on my behalf, without my Agent incurring personal financial liability for such contracts;

E. To hire and fire medical, social service, and other support personnel responsible for my care;

F. To authorize, or refuse to authorize, any medication or procedure intended to relieve pain, even though such use may lead to physical damage, addiction, or hasten the moment of (but not intentionally cause) my death;

G. To make anatomical gifts of part or all of my body for medical purposes, authorize an autopsy, and direct the disposition of my remains, to the extent permitted by law;

H. To take any other action necessary to do what I authorize here, including (but not limited to) granting any waiver or release from liability required by any hospital, physician, or other health care provider; signing any documents relating to refusals of treatment or the leaving of a facility against medical advice; and pursuing any legal action in my name at the expense of my estate to force compliance with my wishes as determined by my Agent, or to seek actual or punitive damages for the failure to comply.

Section 5—MY INSTRUCTIONS ABOUT END-OF-LIFE TREATMENT

The subject of end-of-life treatment is particularly important to many people. In this paragraph, you can give general or specific instructions on the subject. The different paragraphs are options choose only one, or write your desires or instructions in your own words (in the last option). If you are satisfied with your agent's knowledge of your values and wishes and you do not want to include instructions in the form, initial the first option and do not give instructions in the form.

Any instructions you give here will guide your agent. If you do not appoint an agent, they will guide any health care providers or surrogate decision—makers who must make a decision for you if you cannot do so yourself. The instruction choices in the form describe different treatment goals you may prefer, depending on your condition.

Directive In Your Own Words. If you would like to state your wishes about end-of-life treatment in your own words instead of choosing one of the options provided, you can do so in this section. Since people sometimes have different opinions on whether nutrition and hydration should be refused or stopped under certain circumstances, be sure to address this issue clearly in your directive. Nutrition and hydration means food and fluids given through a nasogastric tube or tube into your stomach, intestines, or veins, and does not include non-intrusive methods such as spoon feeding or moistening of lips and mouth.

Some states allow the stopping of nutrition and hydration only if you expressly authorize it. If you are creating your own directive, and you do not want nutrition and hydration, state so clearly.

Health Care Advance Directive
Part II
Instructions About Health Care

5. MY INSTRUCTIONS ABOUT END-OF-LIFE TREATMENT
(Initial only ONE of the following statements)
_____ NO SPECIFIC INSTRUCTIONS. My agent knows my values and wishes, so I do not wish to include any specific instructions here.

DIRECTIVE TO WITHHOLD OR WITHDRAW TREATMENT. Although I greatly
value life, I also believe that at some point, life has such diminished value that medical treatment should be stopped, and I should be allowed to die. Therefore, I do not want to receive treatment, including nutrition and hydration, when the treatment will not give me a meaningful quality of life. I do not want my life prolonged...
_____ ... if the treatment will leave me in a condition of permanent unconsciousness, such as with an irreversible coma or a persistent vegetative state.
_____ ... if the treatment will leave me with no more than some consciousness and in an irreversible condition of complete, or nearly complete, loss of ability to think or communicate with others.
_____ ... the treatment will leave me with no more than some ability to think or communicate with others, and the likely risks and burdens of treatment outweigh the expected benefits. Risks, burdens and benefits include consideration of length of life, quality of life, financial costs, and my personal dignity and privacy.
_____ DIRECTIVE TO RECEIVE TREATMENT. I want my life to be prolonged as long as possible, no matter what my quality of life.
_____ DIRECTIVE ABOUT END-OF-LIFE TREATMENT IN MY OWN WORDS:

SECTION 6—ANY OTHER HEALTH CARE INSTRUCTIONS OR LIMITATIONS OR MODIFICATIONS OF MY AGENT'S POWERS
In this section, you can provide instructions about other health care issues that are not end-of-life treatment or nutrition and hydration. For example, you might want to include your wishes about issues like non-emergency surgery, elective medical treatments or admission to a nursing home. Again, be careful in these instructions not to place limitations on your agent that you do not intend. For example, while you may not want to be admitted to a nursing home, placing such a restriction may make things impossible for your agent if other options are not available.

You also may limit your agent's powers in any way you wish. For example, you can instruct your agent to refuse any specific types of treatment that are against your religious beliefs or unacceptable to you for any other reasons. These might include blood transfusions, electro-convulsive therapy, sterilization, abortion, amputation, psychosurgery, or admission to a mental institution, etc. Some states limit your agent's authority to consent to or refuse some of these procedures, regardless of your health care advance directive.

Be very careful about stating limitations, because the specific circumstances surrounding future health care decisions are impossible to predict. If you do not want any limitations, simply write in "No limitations."

SECTION 7—PROTECTION OF THIRD PARTIES WHO RELY ON MY AGENT
In most states, health care providers cannot be forced to follow the directions of your agent if they object. However most states also require providers to help transfer you to another provider who is willing to honor your instructions. To encourage compliance with the health care advance directive, this paragraph states that providers who rely in good faith on the agent's statements and decisions will not be held civilly liable for their actions.

SECTION 8—DONATION OF ORGANS AT DEATH
In this section you can state your intention to donate bodily organs and tissues at death. If you do not wish to be an organ donor, initial the first option. The second option is a donation of any or all organs or parts. The third option allows you to donate only those organs or tissues you specify. Con-

sider mentioning the heart, liver, lung, kidney, pancreas, intestine, cornea, bone, skin, heart valves, tendons, ligaments, and saphenous vein in the leg. Finally, you may limit the use of your organs by crossing out any of the four purposes listed that you do not want (transplant, therapy, research or education). If you do not cross out any of these options, your organs may be used for any of these purposes.

6. ANY OTHER HEALTH CARE INSTRUCTIONS OR LIMITATIONS OR MODIFICATIONS OF MY AGENTS POWERS

_____
_____

7. PROTECTION OF THIRD PARTIES WHO RELY ON MY AGENT

No person who relies in good faith upon any representations by my Agent or Alternate Agent(s) shall be liable to me, my estate, my heirs or assigns, for recognizing the Agent's authority.
Upon my death: (Initial one)

_____ I do not wish to donate any organs or tissue, OR

_____ I give any needed organs, tissues, or parts, OR

_____ I give only the following organs, tissues, or parts:

(please specify)

_____
_____

My gift (if any) is for the following purposes: (Cross out any of the following you do not want)

—Transplant

—Research

—Therapy

—Education

SECTION 9—NOMINATION OF GUARDIAN

Appointing a health care agent helps to avoid a court-appointed guardian for health care decision-making. However, if a court becomes involved for any reason, this paragraph expressly names your agent to serve as guardian. A court does not have to follow your nomination, but normally it will honor your wishes unless there is good reason to override your choice.

SECTION 10—ADMINISTRATIVE PROVISIONS

These items address miscellaneous matters that could affect the implementation of your health care advance directive.

SIGNING THE DOCUMENT

Required state procedures for signing this kind of document vary. Some require only a signature, while others have very detailed witnessing requirements. Some states simply require notarization.

The procedure in this booklet is likely to be far more complex than your state law requires because it combines the formal requirements from virtually every state. Follow it if you do not know your state's requirements and you want to meet the signature requirements of virtually every state.

First, sign and date the document in the presence of two witnesses and a notary.

9. NOMINATION OF GUARDIAN

If a guardian of my person should for any reason need to be appointed, I nominate my Agent (or his or her alternate then authorized to act), named above.

10. ADMINISTRATIVE PROVISIONS

(All apply)

—I revoke any prior health care advance directive.

—This health care advance directive is intended to be valid in any jurisdiction in which it is presented.

—A copy of this advance directive is intended to have the same effect as the original.

SIGNING THE DOCUMENT

BY SIGNING HERE I INDICATE THAT I UNDERSTAND THE CONTENTS OF THIS DOCUMENT AND THE EFFECT OF THIS GRANT OF POWERS TO MY AGENT.
I sign my name to this Health Care Advance Directive on this

    ____ day of _____ , 19 ____.

    My Signature _____

    My Name _____

    My current home address is _____

Your witnesses should know your identity personally and be able to declare that you appear to be of sound mind and under no duress or undue influence.

In order to meet the different witnessing requirements of most states, do not have the following people witness your signature:

—Anyone you have chosen to make health care decisions on your behalf (agent or alternate agents).
—Your treating physician, health care provider, health facility operator, or an employee of any of these.
—Insurers or employees of your life/health insurance provider.
—Anyone financially responsible for your health care costs.
—Anyone related to you by blood, marriage, or adoption.
—Anyone entitled to any part of your estate under an existing will or by operation of law, or anyone who will benefit financially from your death. Your creditors should not serve as witnesses.

If you are in a nursing home or other institution, a few states have additional witnessing requirements. This form does not include witnessing language for this situation. Contact a patient advocate or an ombudsman to find out about the state's requirements in these cases.

Second, have your signature notarized. Some states permit notarization as an alternative to witnessing. Doing both witnessing and notarization is more than most states require, but doing both will meet the execution requirements of most states. This form includes a typical notary statement, but it is wise to check state law in case it requires a special form of notary acknowledgment.

WITNESS STATEMENT

I declare that the person who signed or acknowledged this document is personally known to me, that he/she signed or acknowledged this health care advance directive in my presence, and that he/she appears to be of sound mind and under no duress, fraud, or undue influence.

I am not:
—the person appointed as agent by this document,
—the principal's health care provider,
—an employee of the principal's health care provider,
—financially responsible for the principal's health care,
—related to the principal by blood, marriage, or adoption, and,
—to the best of my knowledge, a creditor of the principal/or entitled to any part of his/her estate under a will now existing or by operation of law.

Witness # 1:
    Signature _____ Date_____
    Print Name_____
    Telephone_____
    Residence Address_____
    _____

Witness #2:
    Signature _____ Date_____
    Print Name_____
    Telephone_____
    Residence Address_____
    _____

[Formalities for notarization omitted]

Questions

1. Compare the explanations of living wills, advance directives, and health care powers of attorney offered by the ABA's document on the one hand, and the document authored by AARP, the AMA, and the ABA on the other. Is the information they contain consistent? How might the ABA's perspective on end-of-life issues differ from the AMA's?

2. Find a state statute that articulates the requirements for a valid living will or health care power of attorney in that state. Does the "sample" form above comport fully with this statute?

3. Are there any circumstances in which you would advise a client NOT to execute a health care power of attorney?

4. Physician Assisted Suicide

Leslie Joan Harris
Semantics and Policy in Physician-Assisted Death: Piercing the Verbal Veil
5 ELDER L.J. 251, 251, 264-71 (1997)[*]

During the last twenty years, courts and legislatures have developed principles that allow individuals and their surrogates to refuse medical care, even when refusal will lead to death. This article traces these developments, from early cases concerning withdrawal of respirators and decisions not to treat fatal illnesses through withdrawal or refusal of artificial nutrition and hydration to the current debate over physician-assisted death. Throughout these developments, those who believed that the law should allow refusal of care have characterized the issue as a matter of personal autonomy, while their opponents have called refusal of care "suicide" and denial of care "homicide." This article traces the rhetorical battle from the early cases through the most recent Supreme Court decisions on physician-assisted death, showing that the rhetoric predicts outcomes but does not explain them. The rhetoric reveals one important set of issues that are at stake in these decisions—who should choose among the varying definitions of respect for human life and the role that law should place in this debate. However, the language obscures other important issues that should be figured heavily in deciding whether to allow refusal of treatment, as well as physician-assisted death. These issues include how power should be distributed between doctors and their patients and how much of society's resources should be allocated to health care.

In *Vacco v. Quill* [117 S. Ct. 2293 (1997)] and *Washington v. Glucksberg* [117 S. Ct. 2258 (1997)] the Supreme Court reversed decisions from the Second and Ninth Circuits which held that the Constitution requires that terminally ill people be

---

[*] Copyright © 1997 by the Board of Trustees of the University of Illinois. Reprinted by permission.

allowed to seek the assistance of physicians in ending their lives. In *Vacco* and *Glucksberg*, the Court found that legislation in the area of physician-assisted death does not violate equal protection or due process, leaving the continuing debate over physician-assisted death to the various state legislatures. Legislation to allow physician-assisted death has been introduced in more than fifteen states, though only Oregon has enacted this type of legislation. The Oregon statute survived an effort to repeal it by popular initiative in November 1997.[8]

* * *

B. "Killing" Versus "Letting Die"—Passive and Active Euthanasia, Acts, Omissions, and Causation

A variety of terms in ethical and legal discussions have been used to draw a line between "killing" and "letting die" and between "committing suicide" and "escaping from suffering."

1. Active Versus Passive Euthanasia

The ethical terms with the oldest and most elaborate lineage are "passive" and "active" euthanasia. The distinction is typically made in this way: "Passive euthanasia involves allowing a patient to die by removing her from artificial life support systems such as respirators and feeding tubes or simply discontinuing medical treatments necessary to sustain life. Active euthanasia, by contrast, involves positive steps to end the life of a patient, typically by lethal injection."

When Glanville Williams proposed in the late 1950s to allow doctors to end the lives of terminally ill, competent, suffering patients at their request, he used these terms. In 1975, near the time of the *Quinlan* decision, when the moral and legal acceptability of withdrawing respirators and other sorts of life support was still disputed, a famous ethical debate over the topic was carried out in terms of "active" versus "passive" euthanasia. James Rachels argued that the distinction is not morally sustainable, asking "what is the point of drawing out the suffering" of a person who will die anyway? In reply, Tom Beauchamp argued that the distinction is morally significant and should be maintained because of the slippery slope problem, that

---

[8] The state legislature referred the Death with Dignity Act back to the voters recommending that they repeal it. H.R. 2954, 69th Leg. (Or. 1997). The electorate rejected this request and upheld the act by a margin of nearly 60%-40%. Suicide Law Stands, Portland Oregonian, Nov. 4, 1997, A, at 1. The Oregon Death with Dignity Act was successfully challenged in the federal district court on the basis that it denied them from protection against incompetent doctors and their own mental incapacity. *Lee v. Oregon,* 891 F. Supp. 1429 (D. Or. 1995). However, the Ninth Circuit reversed because the challengers lacked standing. *Lee v. Oregon,* 107 F.3d 1382 (9th Cir.), cert. denied, 118 S. Ct. 328 (1997). . . . In *Compassion in Dying v. Washington,* the Ninth Circuit, sitting en banc, sharply criticized the district court opinion in Lee. 79 F.3d at 838 n.139. On appeal, the Supreme Court commented, "*Lee*, of course, is not before us, any more than it was before the Court of Appeals below, and we offer no opinion as to the validity of the *Lee* courts' reasoning. In *Vacco v. Quill,* however, . . . we hold that New York's assisted-suicide ban does not violate the Equal Protection Clause." *Glucksberg,* 117 S. Ct. at 2262 n.7. The constitutional challenge in *Lee* is quite different from those in *Glucksberg* and *Quill.* The Supreme Court's holding in those cases—that the Constitution does not require states to allow physician-assisted suicide—does not mean that legislation allowing and regulating physician-assisted suicide is unconstitutional.

"active" killing may lead to programs to exterminate people regarded as socially undesirable. Because the term "euthanasia" has become associated with this slippery slope, those who support actions that allow patients to die have largely quit using the term, while opponents continue to use the term for exactly the same reason.

2. Acts Versus Omissions and Legal Causation

On the legal side, early proponents of allowing withdrawal of life support confronted the legal distinction between acts and omissions. In most American jurisdictions, criminal liability for "omissions" is more limited than for acts, because a person is not legally liable for failure to act unless that person has a legal duty to act, and the sources of legal duty are limited. Writing in 1967, George Fletcher argued that a doctor who turned off the ventilator of a person with no brain activity should be treated as having "omitted" to care for the patient rather than having affirmatively "acted" to kill the patient and that the doctor "permitted death to occur" rather than "caused death." In *Barber v. Superior Court*, a 1983 criminal prosecution of a doctor for turning off the respirator of a patient in a persistent vegetative state, the court reversed the conviction, accepting the argument that the doctor had omitted to act when he had no duty to do so.

In other cases courts relied on principles of legal causation to preclude criminal liability for withdrawing life support. For example, in 1985, in *In re Conroy*, one of the most important and famous cases concerning withdrawal of feeding tubes, the New Jersey court relied in part on a causation argument, saying that refusal of treatment is not suicide because the person's underlying medical condition was not self-inflicted and the person dies from nature "taking its course."

3. Criticisms of the Distinctions as Artificial

Although the distinction between "killing" and "letting die" seems clear with regard to the newest issue, physician-aided death, both supporters and opponents of the practice have denied that the distinction is morally significant. For example, Yale Kamisar, who opposed withdrawal of treatment as well as physician-assisted death, wrote:

> Many who support the "right to die" say they are strongly opposed to active euthanasia. I must say I do not find the arguments made by proponents of this distinction convincing. Least persuasive of all, I think, are the arguments that lifting the ban against active euthanasia would be "to embrace the assumption that one human being has the power of life over another" (the withholding or withdrawal of life-sustaining treatment embraces the same assumption) and that maintaining the prohibition against active euthanasia "prevents the grave potential for abuse inherent in any law that sanctions the taking of human life" (passive euthanasia, at the very least, presents the same potential for abuse).
>
> Indeed I venture to say that a law that sanctions the "taking of human life" indirectly or negatively rather than directly or positively contains much more potential for abuse. Because of the repugnance sur-

rounding active euthanasia—because it is what might be called "straightforward" or "out in the open" euthanasia—I think it may be forcefully argued that it is less likely to be abused than other less readily identifiable forms of euthanasia.

Similarly, Tom Beauchamp, who originally championed the distinction between "killing" and "letting die," has more recently argued that the distinction is difficult to make and creates moral and conceptual confusion. He argues that the right to autonomy which justifies allowing patients to refuse treatment seems in principle to extend to a patient's request for physician-assisted death.

C. Intent to Die Versus Intent to Relieve or Escape Suffering

Although some definitions of "suicide" include all voluntary acts that result in the ending of one's life, the actor's intent has commonly been used to limit the scope of the term. In *Satz v. Perlmutter*, a 1978 Florida case involving the request of a competent man with amyotrophic lateral sclerosis (Lou Gehrig's disease) to turn off his respirator, the court denied that Abe Perlmutter wanted to commit suicide. The court said that Perlmutter wanted to live, but not with assistance. A Florida trial court recently made a similar distinction in *McIver v. Krischer*, stating that a man who made a request for physician-assisted death "is not suicidal, but merely wishes to end what is to be a painful and protracted dying period."

The cases involving withdrawal of tube-feeding evoked some of the most spirited discussion about what kind of intention counted as "suicidal" and, by implication, homicidal, because the patients involved were not at immediate risk of dying from their underlying disease or condition, but rather perished most directly from lack of nutrition and hydration. Yet most courts, like the court in *In re Conroy*, which involved termination of tube-feeding, said that patients who decline treatment are not suicidal, in part because they do not have the specific intent to die.

As this discussion shows, at each of the major steps in the development of the legal "right to die"—withdrawing or withholding lifesaving treatments such as respirators, and withdrawing artificial nutrition and hydration—the ethical and legal debate has used remarkably similar terminology. Opponents of legalization call actions "euthanasia," "killing," and "suicide." Proponents accept that such categories exist but deny that the action currently under scrutiny fits into the category, relying on the distinction between acts and omission and the principles of causation and intention.

Those who seek to extend the legal right to die avoid these terms because they connote illicit choices. This pattern of debate continues, as illustrated in the Supreme Court's recent decisions about physician-assisted death.

* * *

Statement of Thomas Reardon, M.D.
Chair, American Medical Association Board of Trustees
AMA Reaction to Oregon Decision to Allow Physician-Assisted Suicide Law
(AMA Press Release, November 5, 1997)
<http://www.ama-assn.org/advocacy/statemnt/1105oreg.htm>

The announcement today of the decision by the citizens of Oregon to let stand its "Physician-Assisted Suicide Law," is a serious blow to their health and safety. Further, it sets a dangerous precedent for other states considering similar initiatives that physician-assisted suicide is an acceptable option for patients in the last phase of life.

We all have rights at the end of life that preclude us from having to resort to physician-assisted suicide. Not only is it our duty to educate ourselves, our loved ones and the public regarding these existing rights, it is our obligation to ensure that these rights are honored.

The American Medical Association is committed to making sure that the wishes of individuals with terminal and advanced chronic illness are carried out with compassion, comfort and dignity. In June, 1997, the American Medical Association affirmed "The Elements of Quality Care at the End of Life," a set of eight principles that all patients should reasonably expect when faced with death.

As the beacon for protecting patients and the ethics of the medical profession, the AMA will continue its unyielding opposition to physician-assisted suicide. We will do everything in our power to see that this practice never becomes a generally-accepted option to quality patient care.

Statement of the American Medical Association
to the Subcommittee on the Constitution
Committee on the Judiciary
U.S. House of Representatives
RE: Physician-Assisted Suicide
Presented by: Lonnie R. Bristow, MD
April 29, 1996
<http://www.house.gov/judiciary/2170.htm>

My name is Lonnie R. Bristow, MD. I practice internal medicine in San Pablo, California, and I also serve as President of the American Medical Association (AMA). On behalf of the AMA, I appreciate the opportunity to present our views on physician-assisted suicide to this Subcommittee.

For nearly 2,500 years, physicians have vowed to "give no deadly drug if asked for it, [nor] make a suggestion to this effect." What has changed, that there should be this attempt to make "assisted suicide" an accepted practice of medicine? Certainly the experience of physical pain has not changed over time. Yet the blessings of medical research and technology present their own new challenges, as our ability to delay or draw out the dying process alters our perceptions and needs.

Our efforts in this new paradigm must recognize the importance of care that relieves pain, supports family and relationships, enhances functioning, and respects spiritual needs. Calls for legalization of physician-assisted suicide point to a public perception that these needs are not being met by the current health care system. In addition, society has not met its responsibility to plan adequately for end-of-life care. It is this issue—how to provide quality care at the end of life—which the AMA believes should be our legitimate focus.

The AMA believes that physician-assisted suicide is unethical and fundamentally inconsistent with the pledge physicians make to devote themselves to healing and to life. Laws that sanction physician-assisted suicide undermine the foundation of the patient-physician relationship that is grounded in the patient's trust that the physician is working wholeheartedly for the patient's health and welfare. The multidisciplinary members of the New York State Task Force on Life and the Law concur in this belief, writing that "physician-assisted suicide and euthanasia violate values that are fundamental to the practice of medicine and the patient-physician relationship."

Yet physicians also have an ethical responsibility to relieve pain and to respect their patient's wishes regarding care, and it is when these duties converge at the bedside of a seriously or terminally ill patient that physicians are torn.

The AMA believes that these additional ethical duties require physicians to respond aggressively to the needs of the patients at the end of life with adequate pain control, emotional support, comfort care, respect for patient autonomy and good communications.

Further efforts are necessary to better educate physicians in the areas of pain management and effective end-of-life care. Patient education is the other essential component of an effective outreach to minimize the circumstances which might lead to a patient's request for physician-assisted suicide: inadequate social support; the perceived burden to family and friends; clinical depression; hopelessness; loss of self-esteem; and the fear of living with chronic, unrelieved pain.

ETHICAL CONSIDERATIONS

Physicians' Fundamental Obligation: The physician's primary obligation is to advocate for the individual patient. At the end of life, this means the physician must strive to understand the various existential, psychological, and physiological factors that play out over the course of terminal illness and must help the patient cope with each of them. Patients who are understandably apprehensive or afraid of their own mortality need support and comforting, not a prescription to help them avoid the issues of death. Patients who believe sudden and "controlled" death would protect them from the perceived indignities of prolonged deterioration and terminal illness must receive social support as well as the support of the profession to work through these issues. Providing assisted suicide would breach the ethical means of medicine to safeguard patients' dignity and independence.

Pain Management and the Doctrine of Double Effect: Many proponents of assisted suicide cite a fear of prolonged suffering and unmanageable pain as support for their position. For most patients, advancements in palliative care can adequately control pain through oral medications, nerve blocks or radiotherapy. We all recognize, however, that there are patients whose intractable pain cannot be relieved by treating the area, organ or system perceived as the source of the pain. For patients for whom pain cannot be controlled by other means, it is ethically permissible for physicians to administer sufficient levels of controlled substances to ease pain, even if the patient's risk of addiction or death is increased.

The failure of most states to expressly permit this practice has generated reluctance among physicians to prescribe adequate pain medication. Additional uncertainty is produced by the potential for legal action against the physician when controlled substances are prescribed in large amounts to treat patients with intractable pain. This uncertainty chills physicians' ability to effectively control their terminally ill patients' pain and suffering through the appropriate prescription and administration of opiates and other controlled substances. In this area, states such as California and Texas have developed clear legislative guidance that resolves these concerns for most physicians. The AMA is developing similarly structured model legislation for state medical societies to pursue with their state legislatures and medical licensing boards.

In some instances, administration of adequate pain medication will have the secondary effect of suppressing the respiration of the patient, thereby hastening death. This is commonly referred to as the "double effect." The distinction between this action and assisted suicide is crucial. The physician has an obligation to provide for the comfort of the patient. If there are no alternatives but to increase the risk of death in order to provide that comfort, the physician is ethically permitted to exercise that option. In this circumstance, the physician's clinical decision is guided by the intent to provide pain relief, rather than an intent to cause death. This distinguishes the ethical use of palliative care medications from the unethical application of medical skills to cause death.

Distinction Between Withholding or Withdrawing Treatment and Assisted Suicide: Some participants in the debate about assisted suicide see no meaningful distinction between withholding or withdrawing treatment and providing assistance in suicide. They argue that the results of each action are the same and therefore the acts themselves carry equal moral status. This argument largely ignores the distinction between act and omission in the circumstances of terminal care and does not address many of the principles that underlie the right of patients to refuse the continuation of medical care and the duty of physicians to exercise their best clinical judgment.

Specifically, proponents who voice this line of reasoning fail to recognize the crucial difference between a patient's right to refuse unwanted medical treatment and any proposed right to receive medical intervention which would cause death. Withholding or withdrawing treatment allows death to proceed naturally, with the underlying disease being the cause of death. Assisted suicide, on the other hand, requires action to cause death, independent from the disease process.

The "Slippery Slope": Physician-assisted suicide raises troubling and insurmountable "slippery slope" problems. Despite attempts by some, it is difficult to imagine adequate safeguards which could effectively guarantee that patients' decisions to request assisted suicide were unambivalent, informed and free of coercion.

A policy allowing assisted suicide could also result in the victimization of poor and disenfranchised populations who may have greater financial burdens and social burdens which could be "relieved" by hastening death. As reported two years ago by the New York State Task Force on Life and the Law (composed of bioethicists, lawyers, clergy and state health officials), "[a]ssisted suicide and euthanasia will be practiced through the prism of social inequality and prejudice that characterizes the delivery of services in all segments of society, including health care."

Recent studies documenting reasons for patient requests for physician-assisted suicide speak to our "slippery slope"concerns. Patients were rarely suffering intractable pain. Rather, they cited fears of losing control, being a burden, being dependent on others for personal care and loss of dignity often associated with end-stage disease.

The Case of the Netherlands: While euthanasia and assisted suicide are not legal in the Netherlands, comprehensive guidelines have been established which allow physicians to avoid prosecution for the practice. Despite this environment, Dutch physicians have become uneasy about their active role in euthanasia, prompting the Royal Dutch Medical Association to revise its recommendations on the practice.

Findings of more than 1,000 cases of involuntary euthanasia in the Netherlands should raise hackles in the United States, particularly given the stark societal differences between the two countries. Health coverage is universal in the Netherlands, the prevalence of long-term patient-physician relationships is greater and social supports are more comprehensive. The inequities in the American healthcare system, where the majority of patients who request physician-assisted suicide cite financial burden as a motive, make the practice of physician-assisted suicide all the more unjustifiable. No other country in the world, including the Netherlands, has legalized assisted suicide or euthanasia. This is one movement in which the United States should not be a "leader."

EDUCATING PHYSICIANS AND PATIENTS

At its last meeting in December of 1995, the AMA House of Delegates adopted recommendations from a report issued by its Task Force on Quality Care at the End of Life. The report identified issues involved with care of the dying, including the need to develop a definition of "futility," provision of optimal palliative care, legislation ensuring access to hospice benefits, and the importance of advance care planning as a part of standard medical care. Based on the report's recommendations, the AMA is coordinating its current efforts and developing a comprehensive physician and patient education outreach campaign regarding quality of care at the end of life.

The AMA is uniquely capable of educating physicians and other caregivers, legislators, jurists, and the general public as to end of life care issues. Recognizing the profession's desire to structure discussions of end-of-life care and maintain an active and improved role in the care of dying patients, the AMA is currently designing a comprehensive physician education outreach to instruct physicians in conducting advance care planning and managing palliative care with their patients. In fostering such communication, the AMA is particularly concerned with enabling physicians to support patient autonomy, providing patients with sufficient background and support to make informed decisions regarding their end-of-life treatment.

In October of 1995, the AMA, with the American Bar Association (ABA) and the American Association of Retired Persons (AARP), jointly published the booklet "Shaping Your Health Care Future," which offers information about advance care planning and a portable model advance directive for physicians and their patients. The guide also provides explicit instructions for including expressed wishes in the patient's record to ensure that they will be honored. A copy accompanies this testimony. The AMA is working with [the Health Care Financing Administration] to facilitate distribution of this valuable resource to Medicare enrollees. We are also in discussion with the U.S. Consumer Information Center to promote broader public distribution of the booklet.

In supporting professional education, the AMA's continuing medical education division, in cooperation with the United States Air Force Reserve, produced a four-part video series, "The Ethical Question: Decisions Near the End of Life." The videos include discussions of patient autonomy, awareness of legal requirements, allocation of scarce resources and emphasis on compassionate care. Such videos are valuable educational tools, stimulating thoughtful discussion physician to patient or with groups of either patients or physicians. The AMA was also actively involved in the development of the Education Development Corporation workshop, "Decisions Near the End of Life," an institution-based program to train caregivers facing ethical decisions regarding dying patients.

Through continued educational efforts, physicians are committed to demonstrating their enduring commitment to providing the best patient care during every stage of life. Furthermore, provided the tools to facilitate improved terminal care, physicians can readily answer many of the arguments of assisted suicide's proponents.

MEDICARE AND MEDICAID COVERAGE

A significant portion of end-of-life care is provided under Medicare and Medicaid, with estimates showing that Medicare and Medicaid beneficiaries account for 65% of all deaths that occur each year in the United States. Based on the patient populations served by these two programs—the elderly, the disabled, the poor, and the bulk of the nation's nursing home patients—this is not surprising. While these programs have supported the establishment and expansion of the hospice benefit, end-of-life care for most Medicare and Medicaid patients is provided in hospitals. Under Medicare, hospital coverage is provided through the prospective pricing system based on the appropriate Diagnosis Related Group (DRG) payment amount. HCFA has announced that it is working with the Milbank Memorial Fund to explore the possibility of establishing a DRG for hospital inpatient care services related to palliative care for "final" illnesses. Consistent with this direction, AMA is asking the Current Procedural Terminology (CPT) Editorial Panel to consider the potential for development of CPT codes to identify physician services for palliative care.

* * *

CONCLUSION

The movement for legally sanctioning physician-assisted suicide is a sign of society's failure to address the complex issues raised at the end of life. It is not a victory for personal rights. We are equipped with the tools to effectively manage end-of-life pain and to offer terminally ill patients dignity and to add value to their remaining time. As the voice of the medical profession, the AMA offers its capability to coordinate multidisciplinary discourse on end-of-life issues, for it is essential to coordinate medical educators, patients, advocacy organizations, allied health professionals and the counseling and pastoral professions to reach a comprehensive solution to these challenging issues. Our response should be a better informed medical profession and public, working together to preserve fundamental human values at the end of life.

Questions

1. When, if ever, would it be appropriate for an attorney to advise a client to seek assistance in actively terminating her own life?

2. Could an attorney ethically withdraw from representing a client who wished to assert a statutory right to physician-assisted suicide?

3. Should the American Bar Association, like the American Medical Association, adopt an "official" position on physician-assisted suicide?

C. Anatomical Donations

For many reasons, a client may wish to ensure that, upon her death, organs or tissue are donated to individuals in need or the medical profession. Indeed, in some circumstances, organ and tissue donations may be made by living persons. Although the tendency may be to think that an older person's anatomical gift may be less "useful" than that of a younger person, this is not the case. Statistics compiled by the United Network for Organ Sharing show that in 1997, persons age 50 and older accounted for 28% of all organ donations by non-living donors, up from 11.6% in 1988, and 17.3% of all living-donor donations, up from 12.8% in 1988. Moreover, future anatomical gifts can be made as part of the larger process of planning for death, an activity in which older persons and their attorneys regularly engage. Finally, older persons are often *in need of* organ or tissue donations. A number of ethical issues, both theoretical and pragmatic, arise in connection with anatomical gift-giving. Anticipating these problems, federal and statute statutes extensively regulate the area of organ and tissue donation. In this section, we look at some of these statutes and selected legal questions that are associated with their interpretation.

1. Introduction

National Organ and Tissue Donation Initiative
Frequently Asked Questions About Organ and Tissue Donation
<http://www.organdonor.gov/faq.html>

Who can become a donor?

All individuals can indicate their intent to donate. Medical suitability for donation is determined at the time of death.

Are there age limits for donors?

There are no age limitations on who can donate. The deciding factor on whether a person can donate is the person's physical condition, not the person's age. Newborns as well as senior citizens have been organ donors. Persons under 18 years of age must have parent's or guardian's consent.

How do I express my wishes to become an organ and tissue donor?

1. Indicate your intent to be an organ and tissue donor on your driver's license. Look here for driver's licensing information for your state.
2. Carry an organ donor card.
3. Most importantly, DISCUSS YOUR DECISION WITH FAMILY MEMBERS AND LOVED ONES.

If I sign a donor card, or indicate my donation preferences on my driver's license, will my wishes be carried out?

Even if you sign a donor card it is ESSENTIAL THAT YOUR FAMILY KNOWS your wishes. Your family will be asked to sign a consent form in order for your donation to occur.

What organs and tissues can I donate?

Organs: heart, kidneys, pancreas, lungs, liver, and intestines
Tissue: cornea, skin, bone marrow, heart valves, and connective tissue

If I sign a donor card, will it affect the quality of medical care I receive at the hospital?

No! Every effort is made to save your life before donation is considered.

Will donation disfigure my body? Can there be an open casket funeral?

Donation does not disfigure the body and does not interfere with funeral plans, including open casket services.

Why should minorities be particularly concerned about organ donation?

Some diseases of the kidney, heart, lung, pancreas and liver are found more frequently in racial and ethnic minority populations than in the general population. For example, African Americans, Asian and Pacific Islanders and Hispanics are three times more likely to suffer from end-stage renal disease than Whites. Native Americans are four times more likely than Whites to suffer from diabetes. Some of the these diseases are best treated through transplantation; others can only be treated through transplantation. Successful transplantation often is enhanced by the matching of organs between members of the same ethnic and racial group. For example, an African American patient is often less likely to reject a kidney if it is donated by an individual who is genetically similar. Generally, people are genetically more similar to people of their race than to people of other races. A shortage of organs donated by minorities can contribute to death and longer waiting periods for transplants for minorities.

* * *

Are there any costs to my family for donation?

The donor's family does NOT pay for the cost of the organ donation. All costs related to donation of organs and tissues are paid by the recipient, usually through insurance or Medicare.

Can I sell my organs?

No! The National Organ Transplant Act (Public Law 98-507) makes it ILLEGAL to sell human organs and tissues. Violators are subject to fines and imprisonment. Among the reasons for this rule is the concern of Congress that buying and selling of organs might lead to inequitable access to donor organs with the wealthy having an unfair advantage.

How are organs distributed?

Patients are matched to organs based on a number of factors including blood and tissue typing, medical urgency, time on the waiting list, and geographical location.

* * *

Can I be an organ and tissue donor and also donate my body to medical science?

Total body donation is an option, but not if you choose to be an organ and tissue donor. If you wish to donate your entire body, you should directly contact the facility of your choice to make arrangements. Medical schools, research facilities and other agencies need to study bodies to gain greater understanding of disease mechanisms in humans. This research is vital to saving and improving lives.

United Network for Organ Sharing
Critical Data: U.S. Facts About Transplantation
<http://www.unos.org/Frame_default.asp?Category=Newsdata>[†]

On April 7, 1999, the UNOS National patient waiting list for organ transplant included the following:

Type of Transplant	Registration for Transplant	Patients Waiting for Transplant
kidney transplant	43,151	41,302
liver transplant	12,850	12,648
pancreas transplant	457	447
pancreas islet cell transplant	119	119
kidney-pancreas transplant	4,226	1,821
intestine transplant	120	120
heart transplant	4,226	4,209
heart-lung transplant	248	244
lung transplant	3,242	3,191
Totals	**Total Registrations: 66,297**	***Total Patients: 62,260**

NOTE: UNOS policies allow patients to be listed with more than one transplant center (multiple-listing), thus the number of registrations is greater than the actual number of patients.

*Some patients are waiting for more than one organ, therefore the total number of patients is less than the sum of patients waiting for each organ.

Number of Donors Recovered, 1997*	
Type of Donation	Number
cadaveric	5,478
living	3,820
Total	**9,298**

*Based on UNOS Scientific Registry data as of January 4, 1999. Double kidney, double lung, and heart-lung transplants are counted as one transplant. NOTE: Data subject to change due to future data submission or correction.

[†] Copyright © 1999. Reprinted with permission.

CHAPTER 9: END OF LIFE ISSUES   509

2. The Uniform Anatomical Gift Act

Read the Uniform Anatomical Gift Act in the statutory supplement. The Uniform Anatomical Gift Act has been adopted in every state and the District of Columbia.

Questions

1. What problems of interpretation does the language of the UAGA suggest?

2. Does the UAGA create an unacceptable risk of overreaching by potential beneficiaries of an anatomical gift?

a. Counseling the Client

```
UNIFORM DONOR CARD OF
_____
Print or type name of donor

In the hope that I may help others, I hereby make this anatomi-
cal gift, if medically acceptable, to take affect upon my death.
The words and marks below indicate my desires.

I give (a) _____ any needed organs or parts

        (b) _____ only the following organs or parts.
_____
Specify the organ(s) or part(s)

For the purposes of transplantation, therapy, medical research or
education.

   (c) _____ my body for anatomical study if needed

Limitations or special wishes, if any
_____

                          Fold

Signed by the donor and the following two witnesses in the
presence of each other:
_____
Signature of Donor           Date of Birth of Donor

__/__/__  _____
Date Signed                  City & State
_____
Witness      Witness
```

This is a legal document under the Uniform Anatomical Gift Act or similar laws.

Questions

1. What considerations are likely to be relevant to a client's decisions concerning after-death organ donation?

2. How proactive should the attorney be in encouraging organ donation by her clients as part end-of-life planning process?

b. Problems of Interpretation

Daniel G. Jardine
Comment: Liability Issues Arising out of Hospitals' and Organ Procurement Organizations' Rejection of Valid Anatomical Gifts: The Truth and Consequences
1990 WIS. L. REV. 1655, 1657-58[*]

Surprising as it may seem, despite the UAGA's unequivocal declaration that a decedent's written directive makes the donation of his organs a valid gift effective upon death, and that persons who accept such gifts in good faith are insulated from civil and criminal liability, the gifts are almost always rejected by attending physicians, hospitals and organ procurement organizations (OPOs). Though contrary to the clear language of the UAGA and the presumed intent of the state legislatures that have adopted it, healthcare officials will not accept organs donated by a decedent unless they obtain "consent" from the next of kin. However, it is clear that "consent" is a misnomer. In the eyes of the law, health care officials actually first reject the gift of the decedent, then look to the next of kin to make an anatomical gift (which is allowed by the UAGA when there is no indication of contrary intention by the decedent).

Questions

Why would potential beneficiaries or medical professionals reject a facially valid anatomical gift? Is this consistent with, for example, the medical profession's self-described duty to "do no harm"?

Alcor Life Extension Foundation, Inc. v. Mitchell
9 Cal. Rptr. 2d 572 (Cal. App. 1992)

JUDGES: Opinion by GATES, Acting P. J., with NOTT, J., and MANELLA, J., concurring

Appealing from the judgment entered in favor of Alcor Life Extension Foundation, Inc. (Alcor), and two of its members, the Department of Health Services, its Office of the State Registrar and their respective heads (referred to collectively as DHS unless otherwise indicated), seek a determination from this court "that death cer-

---

[*] Copyright 1977 by The Board of Regents of the University of Wisconsin System; reprinted by permission of the Wisconsin Law Review.

tificates and disposition permits cannot be issued for bodies of persons who have designated Alcor as a donee pursuant to the Uniform Anatomical Gift Act [Health and Safety Code section 7150 et seq.] and have directed Alcor to store their bodies in cryonic suspension."

As set forth in Alcor's first amended complaint, "Cryonic suspension (also known as cryogenic suspension) is a process by which the legally dead but biologically viable body of a person who has been ill or injured is preserved at low temperatures until such time as medical science may be capable of reviving the person and implementing effective cure or treatment of the illness or injury. Since 1964, the practice of cryonic suspension has become widespread, with organizations formed in major cities to provide cryonic suspension for their members. The first reported cryonically suspended person has been maintained in that state since 1967."

The question here tendered is peculiarly unique and extremely narrow in scope and, hopefully, our affirmance of the challenged judgment will completely preclude this particular issue from arising again in the future. That is to say, we merely examine the propriety of the trial court's decision concerning DHS's recent actions which have resulted in the denial of death certificates (Health & Saf. Code, § 10375) and disposition permits (Health & Saf. Code, § 10376) to Alcor members who have been placed in cryonic suspension. Neither side contends these individuals are not legally dead (Health & Saf. Code, § 7180) and otherwise entitled to death certificates. Their conflict relates solely to the obtainment of disposition permits.

The trial court has expressed no opinion on the validity of cryonics or the manner in which it should be regulated, nor do we. The initial determination of such issues, at least in the absence of any conflict, is clearly an administrative or legislative function.

Even DHS, despite its determined efforts to render Alcor's operations illegal, asserts "this case is not an attempt to prohibit cryonic suspension activity." In fact, until questioned by us, in both its opening and closing briefs, DHS expressed a willingness to grant Alcor all necessary documentation if it would but utilize subterfuge to disguise its actual structure and the true nature of its operations. By way of example, although subsequently recanted, DHS in its reply brief had stated: "The Department has encouraged Alcor to obtain a license as a cemetery or mausoleum or appoint another entity, such as a research institute, hospital, or physician, as the donee under the U.A.G.A. so that Alcor's members can have their bodies or body parts cryonically suspended legitimately. However, Alcor has refused to do so."

Turning to the specific contention at hand, section 10375 of the Health and Safety Code provides: "No person shall dispose of human remains unless (a) there has been obtained and filed with a local registrar a death certificate, as provided in chapter 5 (commencing with Section 10200) of this division [division 9, Vital Statistics], and (b) there has been obtained from a local registrar a permit for disposition."

Appellant Office of the State Registrar is charged with executing the state's vital statistic statutes (Health & Saf. Code, § 10000 et seq.), including those pertaining to disposition permits. (Health & Saf. Code, § 10375 et seq.) It also has supervisory power over local registrars to insure uniform compliance with the requirements of vital statistics laws. (Health & Saf. Code, § 10026.)

Health and Safety Code section 10376 identifies three permissible methods of treating human remains for the purpose of the disposition permit: interment in a cemetery; cremation; and burial at sea. Viewed merely semantically, under the Health and Safety Code's circular definitions (*see* Health & Saf. Code, §§ 7003, 7005, 7009, 7012, 7015) Alcor might possibly be said to be operating a mausoleum. However, such statutory language was aptly characterized in *Cemetery Board v. Telophase Society of America* (1978) 87 Cal.App.3d 847, 855 [151 Cal.Rptr. 248], as "virtually nonsensical," and neither party, albeit for different reasons, now wishes Alcor to be so considered.

DHS has also recognized "scientific use," a disposition associated with the Uniform Anatomical Gift Act as an additional means of legally dealing with human remains. An anatomical gift of all or part of an individual's body may be made to the following donees:

(1) A hospital, physician, surgeon, or procurement organization, for transplantation, therapy, medical or dental education, research, or advancement of medical or dental science.
(2) An accredited medical or dental school, college, or university for education, research, or advancement of medical or dental science.
(3) A designated individual for transplantation or therapy needed by that individual." (Health & Saf. Code, § 7153, subd. (a).)

For a number of years Alcor was apparently permitted to operate under that act. However, in March 1988, the Chief of the Office of the State Registrar, David W. Mitchell, in a letter making explicit reference to Alcor, advised the Riverside County Coroner that burial permits may not be issued for cryonic suspension. Mitchell further admonished that state law provides for "storage" of a dead body only if it is used "for scientific purposes or qualifies as a gift under the Anatomical Gift Act" and pointed out that disposing of a dead body anywhere in the city or county, except within a cemetery, is a misdemeanor.

Three months later, in response to an inquiry from the Riverside County Department of Health, Mitchell stated if Alcor was storing bodies or body parts in its facility, it would be "guilty of a misdemeanor" and "should be reported to the local District Attorney for investigation and prosecution as appropriate."

Shortly thereafter, DHS, through its Office of the State Registrar and pursuant to its supervisory authority over local registrars, issued a "Handbook for Local Registrars of Birth and Death" which instructed local registrars that disposition of human remains by cryonic suspension does not constitute "scientific use" within the meaning of the Uniform Anatomical Gift Act. The 1990 version of this book, the most recent one available at the time the instant summary judgment motion was heard, similarly specified: "The holding of human bodies in cryonic suspension does not constitute the operation of a cemetery, nor does arranging to have one's body so placed meet the scientific use requirements of the Uniform Anatomical Gift Act."

The authority cited for this statement was 63 Ops.Atty.Gen. 879 (1980). In its representation of DHS on this appeal, the Attorney General still purports to rely upon that opinion despite making suggestions which are totally inconsistent with the views it expressed there. Of course, such an opinion, even when correct, a debatable proposition here, would not be binding on this court. (*California Assn. of Psychology Providers v. Rank* (1990) 51 Cal.3d 1, 17 [270 Cal.Rptr. 796, 793 P.2d 2].)

DHS now advises that it subsequently has altered its posture, concluding "it does not have the authority to determine whether or not cryogenic suspension of dead bodies or body parts constitutes valid science research and that such question should appropriately be decided by the Legislature." However, this shift in position does not aid Alcor since DHS refuses to recognize Alcor as a "procurement organization" for purposes of the Uniform Anatomical Gift Act, the donee category into which Alcor might possibly fit.

A procurement organization is defined as "a person licensed, accredited, or approved under the laws of any state or by the State Department of Health Services for procurement, distribution, or storage of human bodies or parts." (Health & Saf. Code, § 7150.1, subd. (j).)

DHS points out that Alcor has not been "licensed, accredited or approved" to function as a procurement organization, though obviously Alcor could not possibly have done so since DHS has not established any procedure or mechanism which would permit Alcor or any other organization even to make application therefor. DHS then announces its intention to await "further guidance from the Legislature prior to even considering Alcor as a possible procurement organization." It argues that Health and Safety Code section 7150.1 is merely a definitional provision.

Understandably, the trial court declined to accept this "catch-22" approach which exposes Alcor to potential criminal liability. Therefore, it "permanently enjoined and . . . ordered [DHS] to desist from prohibiting, instructing or directing against, or otherwise interfering with, the registration of deaths or the issuance of disposition permits for the bodies of persons who have designated Alcor as a donee pursuant to the Uniform Anatomical Gift Act (Health and Safety Code § 7150 et seq.) and who have directed that Alcor place their bodies in cryonic suspension, provided that . . . in the event and at such time as [DHS] implements an otherwise lawful licensing and registration system for procurement organizations pursuant to the Uniform Anatomical Gift Act, plaintiff Alcor will be subject to lawful and reasonable licensing and registration requirements."

Under the circumstances, particularly in the absence of any evidence that Alcor's operations pose an actual threat to the public health, we agree with the injunctive relief ordered by the trial court. We need not determine whether each of the court's individual findings was correct. It is enough that we agree DHS's sudden and unexplained about-face with respect to Alcor's status as a donee under the Uniform Anatomical Gift Act cannot be premised upon Alcor's failure to secure a license as a procurement organization when DHS has failed to establish a mechanism for obtaining such a license. Such conduct is, at the very least, inconsistent with DHS's basic duty to administer and enforce the statutes pertaining to the registration of death certificates and issuance of disposition permits.

In that regard, DHS frankly acknowledges that its "Office of the State Registrar [is] charged with the duty . . . of registering births, deaths, marriages, etc." but declares it is "at [a] loss as to how to register the status" of cryonically suspended persons without first receiving "specific guidance from the Legislature." However, like the trial court, we take a more sanguine view of appellants' abilities. In any event, if, in carrying out the trial court's mandate DHS proceeds in a fashion contrary to that envisioned by the Legislature because of the lack of statutory guidance, that body will no doubt take corrective action.

DHS also poses a number of what it characterizes as "serious questions," e.g.: "Should cryonically suspended people be considered 'dead' or should a separate category of 'suspended' people be created? How should such people be registered in official records? . . . What happens to the estate and the assets of the 'decedent' after the decedent is put in cryonic suspension? . . . What would happen to such estate and assets if and when cryonic suspension is successful and the decedent is restored to life? Whose identity is the person to assume or be assigned and what of the record of the person's death? Alcor also stores body parts, such as human heads and hands. In such cases, whose identity will the suspended heads and hands assume upon their restoration; the identity of the original owner of the body part or the identity of the new body to which the body part will be attached?"

These are, of course, but a few of the presently imaginable conundrums which could arise should Alcor at some future time actually succeed in reviving the currently dead. Nonetheless, we are confident that those persons who will then head our various branches of government will be far wiser than we and entirely capable of resolving such dilemmatic issues without our assistance.

The judgment is affirmed.

NOTT, J., and MANELLA, J., concurred.

Questions

1. How vulnerable is the senior population to the activities of organizations such as Alcor?

2. How might an attorney, without patronizing her client, "protect" a client from unscrupulous offers of "immortality"?

Rahman v. The Mayo Clinic
578 N.W.2d 802 (Minn. App. 1998)

SHORT, Judge

Marilyn Rahman brought suit against The Mayo Clinic after discovering it had retained her deceased son's pelvic block. On appeal from a grant of summary judgment in favor of the Clinic, Rahman argues the trial court erred in granting summary judgment under the Uniform Anatomical Gift Act's (UAGA) good faith immunity provision, Minn. Stat. § 525.9221(c) (1996).

Facts

On March 17, 1994, Christopher Rahman (the decedent) was admitted to Saint Mary's Hospital, as the result of a self-inflicted gunshot wound to the head. The decedent was placed in the intensive care unit, where he was treated by Dr. Marc Goldman (treating physician), the chief resident associate of the Clinic's neurosurgery department. The following day, the treating physician determined the decedent's neurologic condition was "very poor" and concluded the gunshot wound would prove fatal. The treating physician informed the decedent's mother, Marilyn Rahman (Rahman), of his prognosis and that she had a right to make a donation of organs and tissue pursuant to the Uniform Anatomical Gift Act (UAGA), Minn. Stat. § 525.9214(a) (1996). Elizabeth Gayner, an employee of Life Source, a tissue and organ procurement agency, also spoke with Rahman at the Clinic to explain organ and tissue donation.

That same day, the decedent was declared brain-dead. Rahman again spoke with the treating physician and agreed to make a donation of organs and tissue. Rahman and the treating physician completed part of the organ donation permission form, which stated:

> Permission is granted for organ or tissue donation for transplantation, research or education purposes (subject to restrictions indicated below)
> Yes No.
> Restrictions :

The treating physician checked the "yes" box, wrote "none" on the restrictions line, and signed the form and placed it back into the decedent's medical charts. Rahman told the treating physician that she did not want a postmortem examination.

Subsequently, Rahman had a second conversation with Gayner. Rahman told Gayner that the decedent's organs were not to be used for medical research or education. Based on this conversation, Gayner wrote "no research" above the restriction area and added the phrase "heart, heart for valve, lungs, liver, pancreas, [k]idneys, long bones of lower extremities" to the restrictions line on the original organ donation permission form. Gayner failed to write "no education purposes" on the form. The treating physician was not present during Gayner's second conversation with Rahman, was unaware of Rahman's intentions to impose restrictions, and did not see the revised permission form.

After some of the decedent's organs were harvested for transplant purposes, the body was taken to an autopsy suite. Despite Rahman's objections, the coroner ordered an autopsy pursuant to Minn. Stat. § 390.11, subd. 2 (1996), due to the violent nature of the decedent's death. An autopsy was performed by a Clinic pathologist and pathology resident. As a standard part of the autopsy procedure, the decedent's pelvic block, which consists of the prostate, seminal vesicles, urinary bladder, and rectum, was removed and examined. The pathologist, who had read a copy of the revised organ donation permission form prior to performing the autopsy, decided to retain the pelvic block for educational use in the Mayo Medical School. The pelvic block, which would eventually be mounted in Plexiglass for use in the medical school, was placed into a container with fixative fluid for preservation and kept in a locked storage room, known as the "museum," at the Clinic.

Shortly thereafter, Rahman brought an unrelated suit against the decedent's life insurance carrier regarding death benefits. This suit was settled. During a review of her attorney's files, Rahman read that the decedent's urinary bladder, prostate, and seminal vesicles had been "preserved with [his] pelvic block for [the] museum." Rahman retained new counsel, who contacted the Clinic and discussed Rahman's concerns. The Clinic informed Rahman's counsel the pelvic block had not yet been used for research or educational purposes, and sought further instructions. Rahman commenced this lawsuit against the Clinic, Mayo Foundation, Mayo Group Practices, Mayo Foundation for Medical Education and Research, and Mayo Medical Services, Ltd. (collectively "the Clinic"), alleging it: (1) violated the UAGA, Minn. Stat. § 525.9212 (1996); (2) intentionally, recklessly, or negligently removed, withheld, mutilated, or operated upon the decedent's body; and (3) intentionally or unintentionally caused Rahman emotional distress.

Issue

Did Rahman present any evidence to defeat the Clinic's claim it acted in good faith under the UAGA?

Analysis

On appeal from a grant of summary judgment, we must determine whether any genuine issues of material fact exist and whether the trial court erred in applying the law. Minn. R. Civ. P. 56.03; *State by Cooper v. French*, 460 N.W.2d 2, 4 (Minn. 1990). While we view the evidence in the light most favorable to the nonmoving party, the nonmovant must produce specific facts to create an issue for trial. We need not defer to the trial court's decision on purely legal issues.

Minnesota has adopted, without substantial modification, the UAGA. *See* Minn. Stat. §§ 525.921-.9224 (1996) (providing method of making anatomical gifts). The UAGA establishes a statutory scheme which outlines the means of effecting an anatomical gift, the classes of individuals entitled to effect such a gift, and the circumstances under which such a gift must be deemed null and void. The UAGA was enacted in response to the need for more family donations of organs and to the medical profession's uncertainty about whose consent was necessary for donations. *Perry v. Saint Francis Hosp. & Med. Ctr.*, 886 F. Supp. 1551, 1557 (D. Kan. 1995); *see* Unif. Anatomical Gift Act (1968) Prefatory Note, 8A U.L.A. 64-65 (1993) (recognizing need for comprehensive act addressing organ donation and concluding UAGA, wherever enacted, will eliminate uncertainty and protect all parties); *see also* Gloria J. Banks, *Legal and Ethical Safeguards: Protection of Society's Most Vulnerable Participants in a Commercialized Organ Transplantation System,* 21 AM. J.L. & MED. 45, 67 (1995) (stating UAGA amended in 1987 to better address issues, such as concern over providing "encouraged volunteerism" system with teeth needed to increase supply of transplantable organs); E. Blythe Stason, *The Uniform Anatomical Gift Act,* 23 BUS. LAW 919, 921-24 (1968) (recognizing legal uncertainties of organ donation laws during pre-UAGA era as providing major basis for adoption of model act).

In furtherance of its goals, the UAGA provides, in pertinent part:

> (a) If, at or near the time of death of a patient, there is no documentation in the medical record that the patient has made or refused to make an anatomical gift, the hospital administrator or a representative designated by the administrator shall discuss with the patient or a relative of the patient the option to make or refuse to make an anatomical gift and may request the making of an anatomical gift pursuant to section 525.9211 or 525.9212. The request must be made with reasonable discretion and sensitivity to the circumstances of the family. * * * An entry must be made in the medical record of the patient, stating the name of the individual making the request, and the name, response, and relationship to the patient of the person to whom the request was made.

Minn. Stat. § 525.9214 (a). The UAGA further provides:

> An anatomical gift by a person authorized * * * must be made by (i) a document of gift signed by the person, or (ii) the person's telegraphic, recorded telephonic, or other recorded message, or other form of communication from the person that is contemporaneously reduced to writing and signed by the recipient.

Minn. Stat. § 525.9212(c).

The Clinic moved for summary judgment arguing: (1) it had permission to retain the decedent's pelvic block for educational purposes, and in the alternative; (2) it was immune from liability under the UAGA's good faith immunity provision. In granting the Clinic's motion, the trial court concluded Rahman "failed to provide *any* evidence that the [Clinic] acted in deliberate contravention of [Rahman's] wishes." (Emphasis in original.) We are asked whether the Clinic's actions fall within the UAGA's good faith immunity provision.

The UAGA insulates individuals involved in the organ procurement process from civil and criminal liability, so long as they act in good faith. *See* Minn. Stat. § 525.9221(c) (providing hospital or person, acting in accordance with UAGA or with applicable anatomical gift law of another state or foreign country or attempting in good faith to do so, is not liable for that act in civil action or criminal proceeding). That statute provides immunity from suit, not simply a defense to liability. Whether actions constitute good faith is a question of law, properly resolved on summary judgment.

Neither the Minnesota legislature nor Minnesota courts have defined good faith in the context of the UAGA. However, other jurisdictions consistently define this statutory good faith requirement as activity involving an "honest belief, the absence of malice, and the absence of design to defraud or to seek an unconscionable advantage." In keeping with the UAGA's goal of providing uniformity among states, we adopt that definition of good faith. *See Perry*, 886 F. Supp. at 1558 (adopting same general definition of good faith in order to assure uniformity in enforcement and interpretation of UAGA among different states).

Both the treating physician and Gayner discussed organ donation with Rahman. Both completed parts of the organ donation permission form under Rahman's direction. With Gayner, Rahman expressed her desire that the decedent's organs not be used for medical research or education. Thus, the question of the Clinic's immunity turns on whether Rahman's instructions to Gayner are sufficient to negate the Clinic's claim that it acted out of an honest belief, and in the absence of fraud or design to seek an unconscionable advantage.[5] *See, e.g., Lyon*, 843 F. Supp. at 534 (concluding issue of hospital's good faith turns on whether everyone at hospital relied on signed form or whether hospital arranged for enucleation despite fact someone in authority knew family did not consent).

The undisputed facts are critical to our analysis. Despite Rahman's instruction that the decedent's organs not be used for medical research or education, Gayner only wrote "no research" on the permission form, and "heart, heart for valves, lungs, liver, pancreas, kidneys, long bones of lower extremities" on the restrictions line. Therefore, the revised organ donation permission form did not prevent the use of organs for educational purposes. The Clinic's pathologist read that form and decided to retain the pelvic block for educational use at the Mayo Clinic School. However, after learning Rahman's true intentions, the Clinic immediately attempted to correct the error.

Viewing the evidence in the light most favorable to Rahman, we conclude Rahman's conversation with Gayner is insufficient to negate the Clinic's claim that it acted in good faith because the Clinic pathologist relied on a facially valid organ donation permission form and, unaware of Rahman's actual wishes, acted out of an honest belief that retention of the decedent's pelvic block was in accordance with those wishes. *See Perry*, 886 F. Supp. at 1559 (concluding court can find as matter of law that hospital's actions were taken in good faith even when person in authority had actual notice of contrary indications); *see also Nicoletta*, 519 N.Y.S.2d at 931 (concluding Eye Bank entitled to good faith immunity when agent acted in justified reliance on written permission form that complied with requirements of UAGA and plaintiff failed to present any evidence Eye Bank had actual notice of any opposition to gift); *see, e.g., Lyon*, 843 F. Supp. at 535-36 (concluding hospital entitled to good faith immunity despite one doctor's knowledge of plaintiffs' contrary intentions where hospital employees relied on organ donation form and were unaware of plaintiffs' wishes).

Rahman also argues the good faith immunity provision of the UAGA is inapplicable because the Clinic removed the decedent's pelvic block during an autopsy, after the organ donation process was complete. *See* Minn. Stat. § 525.9221(c) (providing good faith immunity only to individuals acting in accordance with UAGA). However, the UAGA does not require organs to be harvested before an autopsy is performed; the statute specifically permits harvesting any time after death, and prior to embalming. *See* Minn. Stat. § 525.9217(a) (providing donee, upon death of donor and

---

[5] Rahman alleges Gayner was a designee of the Clinic because she: (1) spoke with Rahman; (2) completed organ donation forms; and (3) oversaw the organ donation process. *See* Minn. Stat. § 525.9214(a) (providing hospital administrator or representative designated by administrator shall discuss with patient or relative option to make or refuse to make anatomical gift). Due to the posture of this case, we must assume Gayner is a designee of the Clinic.

before embalming, shall cause body part donated to be removed without unnecessary mutilation); *see also* Minn. Stat. § 525.9213(a) (providing coroner or medical examiner may release and permit removal of body part within official's custody for transplantation or therapy under certain circumstances). Here, the Clinic's actions were taken pursuant to the UAGA. The Clinic's organ donation permission form, which places no time restrictions on the organ donation process, accompanied the decedent's body to the autopsy suite. The organ donation permission form was relied on by the pathologist, who decided to retain the decedent's pelvic block for educational purposes. Moreover, Rahman's lawsuit is based on her belief that, in retaining the decedent's pelvic block, the Clinic exceeded its authority under the UAGA. Under these circumstances, the UAGA, not the autopsy statute, is controlling. Thus, we conclude the Clinic's retention of the pelvic block after an autopsy does not prevent application of the UAGA's good faith immunity provision.

Rahman finally argues the Clinic may not use its own ambiguous forms to justify exceeding a patient's consent. However, the revised organ donation permission form unambiguously permits retention of organs for educational purposes. Even assuming an ambiguity existed, it would be insufficient to overcome the Clinic's claim of good faith immunity unless Rahman demonstrated the Clinic failed to act out of an honest belief that its actions were in accordance with Rahman's wishes. *See, e.g., Perry*, 886 F. Supp. at 1559-60 (concluding hospital not entitled to summary judgment based on good faith immunity where there was evidence of conscious or intentional wrongdoing carried out for dishonest purposes or furtive design).

Decision

Rahman failed to allege any facts that demonstrate the Clinic acted dishonestly, maliciously, fraudulently, or unconscionably. There are no genuine issues of material fact to preclude summary judgment in favor of the Clinic.

Affirmed.

Jacobsen v. Marin General Hospital
963 F. Supp. 866 (N.D. Cal. 1997), *aff'd*, C.A. No. 97-16139
(9th Cir. Feb. 3, 1999), 1999 U.S. App. LEXIS 1595

PATEL, District Judge.

Memorandum and Order

Plaintiffs Karen and Hardy Jacobsen (collectively, "plaintiffs") brought this action against defendants Marin General Hospital ("Hospital"), California Transplant Donor Network, Inc. ("Network") and Marin County Coroner's Office ("Coroner") alleging various claims under California law arising from the harvesting of organs from the body of their son Martin Jacobsen ("Martin"). This case is before the court pursuant to the court's diversity jurisdiction. 28 U.S.C. § 1332. Now before the court are separate motions to dismiss submitted by all three defendants in this action.

520   ELDER LAW: READINGS, CASES, AND MATERIALS

Having considered the parties' arguments and submissions and for the reasons stated below, the court now issues the following memorandum and order.

Background

Plaintiffs are citizens and residents of the Kingdom of Denmark and the parents of Martin Jacobsen, also a Danish citizen. Martin was visiting the United States as a tourist when he was found unconscious and suffering from head trauma in the early morning hours of October 4, 1995 on Northbound 101, south of the Waldo Tunnel in Sausalito, California. The parties do not know how this occurred. Martin was taken to defendant Hospital and admitted at 4:05 a.m. on October 4. At this time, Dr. Morris, the attending physician, presumed he was homeless and indicated that no identification had been made. At 8:25 a.m., defendant Network contacted defendant Coroner requesting organ donation; Coroner denied this request. At 9:00 a.m. on October 4, a search began for Martin's next of kin or other persons authorized to make an anatomical gift.

At 9:30 a.m. on October 4, photos were taken by the Marin County Sheriff's Office ("Sheriff") and the Coroner, where a blue card stating "Jacobsen, M" and "10/4/95" was displayed with the body. At 12:25 p.m., another request for organ donation was made, but Dr. Morris indicated that Martin was not brain dead at that time. At 2:00 p.m., Network called the Sheriff who revealed that the patient had been identified by the FBI as Martin Jacobsen from New York City.

The following day, on October 5, 1995 at 9:00 a.m., Network spoke with the Sheriff who stated that he felt "9/10" sure that the patient was Martin Jacobsen. At 9:40 a.m., Dr. Ramirez made a clinical determination of brain death. At 3:00 p.m., another determination of brain death was made by Dr. Nisam who stated in his report that the patient was being maintained pending identification of next of kin and that an extensive forty hour search by the Sheriff, Coroner, and FBI to find any family member or identification of the patient had been unsuccessful. His report also indicated that the body was "officially released" to Network for organ donation.

On October 6, 1995 around 9:00 a.m., the Sheriff reported to Network that they were unable to locate the identification of "this John Doe." At 10:13 a.m., Network requested authorization from Coroner to recover the organs of "John Doe." Coroner consented. Martin's kidney, liver, pancreas and heart were removed and the harvesting was completed at 2:16 a.m. on October 7, 1995.

Neither Martin nor plaintiffs would have consented to the maintenance of Martin's body or the removal of his organs for the purposes of making an anatomical gift. Plaintiffs filed their original complaint on October 4, 1996 and an amended complaint on January 22, 1997. Defendants Hospital, Network and Coroner subsequently filed separate motions to dismiss pursuant to Federal Rule of Civil Procedure 12(b)(6).

Legal Standard

A motion to dismiss for failure to state a claim will be denied unless it appears that the plaintiff can prove no set of facts which would entitle him or her to relief. All material allegations in the complaint will be taken as true and construed in the light most favorable to the plaintiff. Although the court is generally confined to consideration of the allegations in the pleadings, when the complaint is accompanied by attached documents, such documents are deemed part of the complaint and may be considered in evaluating the merits of a Rule 12(b)(6) motion.

Discussion

Plaintiffs' various claims are rooted in the sequence of events culminating in the harvesting of Martin's organs in October 1995. They argue that defendants mutilated his body by maintaining it for harvesting, which was done without their consent. In their first amended complaint, plaintiffs bring the following six separate causes of action against all three defendants: (1) negligent search; (2) negligence in procuring injury-producing conduct of another; (3) intentional mutilation of a corpse and infliction of emotional distress; (4) negligent mutilation of a corpse and infliction of emotional distress; (5) joint enterprise liability; and (6) violation of equal protection under the fourteenth amendment.

In response, defendants argue that they were complying with the provisions of the Uniform Anatomical Gift Act, adopted by the California legislature in 1988, when they maintained Martin's body and harvested organs from it. Accordingly, they argue that plaintiffs do not state any claims in their first amended complaint for which relief may be granted.

I. The Uniform Anatomical Gift Act

Although all fifty states have adopted the Uniform Anatomical Gift Act (the "Gift Act") in some form, there is very little case law interpreting its provisions. *See Kelly-Nevils v. Detroit Receiving Hospital*, 207 Mich. App. 410, 526 N.W.2d 15, 17 (Mich. App. 1994). The Gift Act is intended to "make uniform the law with respect to [organ donation] among states enacting it" and is codified in California in the Health and Safety Code. Cal. Health & Safety Code § 7156.5. The Gift Act provides that several classes of people may authorize an anatomical gift: the decedent's (1) attorney-in-fact with power of attorney; (2) spouse; (3) adult son/daughter; (4) either parent; (5) adult brother/sister; (6) grandparent; or (7) guardian/conservator (collectively "next of kin"). *Id.* § 7151(a). If the next of kin, as defined in section 7151(a), cannot be located to provide consent, the coroner or hospital, whichever entity has custody of the body at the time the consent is given, may authorize the anatomical gift so long as several criteria are met, including a reasonable "search" for persons listed in section 7151(a).[6] *Id.* §§ 7151.5(a)-(b).

II. Equal Protection Claim

In their sixth claim, plaintiffs allege that while implementing the provisions of the Gift Act pertaining to the search for next of kin, defendant Coroner discriminated against plaintiffs because of their alien status. They assert that as foreign nationals, they were discriminated against because they were:

---

[6] As Danish citizens, plaintiffs allege that in Denmark, no organs are harvested without the consent of the decedent's next of kin and if no next of kin can be found, Danish law does not permit harvesting in the manner described in the Gift Act.

more likely to have a relative of theirs have his or her organs harvested without consent to the detriment of the relatives' right to custody and possession of a decedent. In conducting a search for next of kin, the class of aliens are thus treated differently from the class of non-aliens.

[Complaint at 82.]

In their opposition papers, plaintiffs concede that their constitutional claim for violation of their fourteenth amendment rights implicates only defendant Coroner, not defendants Hospital and Network. In response to this claim, defendant Coroner argues that plaintiffs have not properly pleaded an equal protection claim because they do not allege any claim under 42 U.S.C. section 1983 as required in this Circuit. Coroner is correct. The Ninth Circuit has clearly stated that "a litigant complaining of a violation of a constitutional right must utilize 42 U.S.C. § 1983." *Azul-Pacifico, Inc. v. City of Los Angeles*, 973 F.2d 704, 705 (9th Cir. 1992), *cert. denied*, 506 U.S. 1081, 122 L. Ed. 2d 357, 113 S. Ct. 1049 (1993). Plaintiffs have not done this and therefore have not properly stated a claim for equal protection in their amended complaint.

Although plaintiffs could readily cure this defect if given leave to amend, the claim is so fundamentally futile that leave could not cure its substantive defects. As Coroner argues, plaintiffs lack standing to bring an equal protection claim because the clause applies only to persons within the territorial jurisdiction of the United States. In this case, plaintiffs were in Denmark when the events underlying their complaint took place.

The Fourteenth Amendment explicitly states "nor shall any state deprive any person of life, liberty, or property without due process of law; nor deny to any person within its jurisdiction the equal protection of the laws." U.S. Const. amend. XIV. In interpreting this language, the Supreme Court has stated that the provisions of the Fourteenth Amendment "are universal in their application, to all persons within the territorial jurisdiction, without regard to any differences of race, of color, or of nationality." *Plyler v. Doe*, 457 U.S. 202, 212, 72 L. Ed. 2d 786, 102 S. Ct. 2382 (1982). Here, it is undisputed that plaintiffs were not in United States territory when the events giving rise to their complaint occurred. Accordingly, plaintiffs have no standing to invoke the protections of the Fourteenth Amendment and their equal protection claim against defendant Coroner must be dismissed.

III. Remaining State Law Claims

Having dismissed the only federal claim in plaintiffs' complaint, the court now considers plaintiffs' remaining state law claims under the court's diversity jurisdiction.

A. Claims Against Coroner

Defendant Coroner argues that plaintiffs' failure to file a claim under the California Tort Claims Act bars all of plaintiffs' state law claims against them. Under the California Tort Claims Act, a plaintiff seeking money damages from local public entities is required to file a claim against such entities not later than six months after the accrual of the action causing personal injury. Cal. Gov't Code §§ 905, 905.2, 910, 911.2. The Ninth Circuit has found that "failure to comply with state imposed procedural conditions to sue the State bars the maintenance of a cause of action based upon these pendent State claims." *Ortega v. O'Connor*, 764 F.2d 703, 707 (9th Cir. 1985), *rev'd in part on other grounds,* 480 U.S. 709 (1987).

At oral argument, plaintiffs admitted that they had not filed a claim as required under the Tort Claims Act. Plaintiffs offer no excuse for this non-compliance. Instead, they argue that the Tort Claims Act is inapplicable to them because it only applies where a federal court maintains supplemental jurisdiction over state claims, whereas here, the court maintains original jurisdiction over plaintiffs' state law claims under its diversity jurisdiction. In support of this contention, plaintiffs apparently rely on the fact that *Ortega* specifically discussed the Tort Claims Act in the context of pendent state claims.[7] *Id.* at 707. If true, plaintiffs' proposition would eviscerate state law requirements whenever parties filed their claims in federal court under diversity. Certainly, plaintiffs' misperception is incorrect. Because plaintiffs failed to file a claim with the State Board of Control pursuant to the California Tort Claims Act, plaintiffs are barred from bringing any claims against Coroner in this action.

The court will now consider the substance of plaintiffs' remaining claims against all of the defendants, including Coroner, assuming arguendo that plaintiffs could bring a claim against Coroner.

B. Negligent Search Claim

Plaintiffs argue that the defendants acted negligently in searching for persons authorized to provide consent for an anatomical gift. The Gift Act authorizes a coroner, medical examiner, hospital, or local public health official to release and permit removal of a body part where that institution has custody of a body and after a "reasonable effort has been made to locate and inform" next of kin of their option to make, or object to, an anatomical gift. Cal. Health & Safety Code §§ 7151.5(a)-(c). The court must determine whether the actions taken to locate plaintiffs, as described in the complaint, were reasonable under the requirements of the Gift Act.

Neither the parties nor the court has identified California cases interpreting what constitutes a "reasonable" search for next of kin under the Gift Act. Nevertheless, the Gift Act itself provides the court with some guidance. Where a coroner has custody of a body, the Gift Act states that "a reasonable effort [to locate next of kin] shall be deemed to have been made when a search for the persons has been underway for at least 12 hours." *Id.* § 7151.5(a)(2). Similarly, where a hospital has custody of a person who is still alive but expected to die, a reasonable search "may be initiated in

---

[7] Plaintiffs also argue that the state law requirement that parties exhaust administrative remedies under the California Tort Claims Act only applies to pendent claims, and not to those claims before the court under supplemental jurisdiction. Plaintiffs apparently perceive a substantive distinction between "pendent" and "supplemental" jurisdiction. This misperception is presumably derived from *Ortega,* which describes "pendent" state law claims. *Ortega,* 764 F.2d at 707. Plaintiffs are mistaken. In federal court, the change from "pendent" to "supplemental" jurisdiction over state law claims is procedural, rather than substantive, in nature. Congress would certainly be surprised to find that by making this procedural change, they had eviscerated state sovereign immunity.

anticipation of death, but . . . the determination [to release a body for an anatomical gift] may not be made until the search has been underway for at least 12 hours." *Id.* § 7151.5(b). This search

> shall include a check of local police missing persons records, examination of personal effects, and the questioning of any persons visiting the decedent before his or her death or in the hospital, accompanying the decedent's body, or reporting the death, in order to obtain information that might lead to the location of [next of kin].

Id. These provisions suggest that when the legislature adopted the Gift Act, the legislature considered and accepted that some searches for next of kin would be unsuccessful, and that where the next of kin could not be located in twelve hours, other institutions would be empowered to release a body in order to fulfill the underlying purposes of the Gift Act. In adopting the Gift Act, the California legislature likely recognized that "time is usually of the essence in securing donated organs at the time of the donor's death." *Lyon v. United States*, 843 F. Supp. 531, 536 (D. Minn. 1994).

By adopting a twelve hour search period and stating that a reasonable search "shall be deemed to have been made" once this amount of time has passed, it is clear that the California legislature contemplated (1) a relatively short period of time in which to conduct a search for next of kin and (2) the possibility that such a search might be unsuccessful. Therefore, the court must consider what actions could have reasonably been taken in a twelve hour period to determine whether a reasonable search for plaintiffs was conducted.

In plaintiffs' complaint, they state that a search for next of kin began at 9:00 a.m. on October 4 and continued until October 6 between 9:00 and 10:13 a.m., when Coroner released the body for harvesting. Martin had no identification on his person when he was found and brought to the hospital. As alleged in the complaint, the search for plaintiffs lasted about forty-eight hours, but was ultimately unsuccessful. The complaint discloses that the Sheriff was notified and involved in the search efforts, that five hours after the search had begun the FBI identified the body as belonging to Martin Jacobsen from New York City, and that a doctor's report described an extensive forty hour search conducted by the Sheriff, the Coroner and the FBI.

Plaintiffs argue that defendants search was negligent because they should have known he was from Denmark when they found a ring inscribed with Danish writing on Martin's finger and a Danish poem in his pocket. These facts do not establish that the search was unreasonable. It is quite possible that the hospital and police did not know that the language was Danish. Moreover, even if they could identify the language, these items alone do not immediately suggest nor create the inference that Martin was a Danish citizen.[8] Accordingly, the search for plaintiffs was not negligent

---

[8] For example, a person may enjoy reading French poems so much that she keeps a copy of her favorite poem in her wallet. It is absurd to think that the mere fact she has a French poem in her wallet suggests that she is a citizen or resident of France. Similarly, here, the Sheriff and the Hospital had no reason to think that simply because Martin carried a Danish poem and other items inscribed in Danish, that he was a Danish citizen from Denmark.

CHAPTER 9: END OF LIFE ISSUES   525

simply because defendants did not assume, on the basis of these items, that Martin was from Denmark.

Plaintiffs also argue that the search was negligent because the Sheriff knew that Martin was a tourist and that based on this information, they should have checked the records of the Immigration and Naturalization Service ("INS") during their search for next of kin. The fact that the INS records were not checked during the search does not establish that it was unreasonable. The court notes that a person's status as a tourist in the San Francisco area does not immediately suggest that the person is from a foreign country. Many tourists from all over the United States and the world visit this area. Accordingly, the Sheriff's failure to check INS records upon discovering that Martin was a tourist provides little to support plaintiffs' negligent search claim.

Plaintiffs' description of the search suggests that all reasonable acts were taken to locate plaintiffs and obtain their consent prior to releasing Martin's body for harvesting. The complaint describes a search lasting over forty hours and involving the efforts of the Marin County Sheriff as well as the FBI; such a search is "reasonable" as contemplated by the legislature in adopting the Gift Act. Before Martin's body was released, defendants Hospital and Coroner complied with the Gift Act's provisions and conducted a reasonable, although ultimately unsuccessful, search to locate plaintiffs and obtain their consent.[9] Accordingly, the court finds that plaintiffs have failed to state a claim for negligent search against defendants Hospital and Coroner.

As for defendant Network, under the provisions of the Gift Act, Network had no legal duty to search for Martin's next of kin or obtain their consent for an anatomical gift. *See* Cal. Health & Safety Code § 7151.5 (placing this duty on other entities including coroners and hospitals). Plaintiffs urge the court to impose this duty on Network based on unspecified "common law" duties for which plaintiffs have provided no authority. The court has found no California cases supporting plaintiffs' position and declines the opportunity to create such a duty here. Accordingly, the court finds that plaintiffs have not stated a claim against Network for negligent search.

C. Remaining State Law Claims

Plaintiffs' remaining claims for negligence in procuring injury-producing injury, joint enterprise and negligent and intentional infliction of emotional distress are based on plaintiffs' allegation that defendants mutilated Martin's body by maintaining it prior to harvesting and actually harvesting organs from it. Plaintiffs' contend that all three defendants acted in concert to mutilate the body of their son and obtain organs for transplantation, thereby causing them injury.

---

[9] The court notes that defendant Hospital had no legal duty under the provisions of the Gift Act to conduct a search for plaintiffs because defendant Coroner was the entity that ultimately gave the final consent and release of the body for harvesting. *See* Cal. Health & Safety Code § 7151.5. However, the Gift Act contemplates that a hospital might be required to conduct a reasonable search where it has custody of a body prior to its release. *Id.* § 7151.5(b). Here, plaintiffs' complaint clearly states that defendant Coroner released the body; accordingly, only defendant Coroner had a duty to search for next of kin prior to releasing the body. Defendants make much of this statutory distinction in their papers. However, this point is immaterial in light of the court's finding that the search for plaintiffs was reasonable under the provisions of the Gift Act.

Defendants' behavior, as described in plaintiffs' complaint, is consistent with the provisions of the Gift Act. As discussed above, defendants' search for Martin's next of kin complied with the provisions of the Gift Act and constituted a reasonable search. Defendants also acted in compliance with other sections of the Gift Act. For example, hospitals are required to "cooperate in the implementation of the anatomical gift or release and removal of a part." Cal. Health & Safety Code § 7152.5(d). The Gift Act also states that "each hospital in this state, after consultation with other hospitals and procurement organizations, shall establish agreements or affiliations for coordination of procurement and use of human bodies and parts." Id. § 7154.5. When identifying potential organ and tissue donors, hospitals must comply with laws requiring that the coroner be notified of all reportable deaths. Id. § 7184(a) (referenced in section 7152.5 of the Gift Act). Prior to harvesting, a donor must be determined to be dead pursuant to the Uniform Determination of Death Act (the "Death Act"). Id. §§ 7180-82. Death is "determined by determining that the individual has suffered an irreversible cessation of all functions of the entire brain, including the brain stem" and "there shall be an independent confirmation of death by another physician" before harvesting can take place. Id. § 7182. Furthermore, hospitals may contact organ and tissue procurement organizations when a potential donor is identified and ask them to assist in locating the potential donor's next of kin as required under section 7151 of the Gift Act. Id. § 71849(c) (referenced in section 7152.5 of the Gift Act).

These provisions suggest that defendants acted in compliance with the Gift Act when they maintained Martin's body and harvested organs from it. Defendants were required, under the provisions of the Gift Act, to cooperate with one another to maintain the body and its organs for transplantation purposes. In accordance with the Gift Act and the Death Act, defendants maintained Martin's body and did not release it for harvesting until after there had been a determination of brain death that was confirmed by another physician. Plaintiffs have not alleged any facts showing that defendants violated the provisions of the Gift Act or acted contrary to the purposes for which it was enacted by the California legislature. Defendants' efforts to comply with the provisions of the Gift Act may not serve as a basis for tort liability. Therefore, plaintiffs can prove no set of facts entitling them to relief on any of their remaining claims. *Conley*, 355 U.S. at 45-56. Accordingly, plaintiffs' remaining state claims against all three defendants must be dismissed.

Conclusion

For the foregoing reasons, defendants Coroner, Hospital and Network's motions to dismiss are granted and all claims in plaintiffs' first amended complaint are dismissed with prejudice.
IT IS SO ORDERED.

Questions

1.   Does the result in *Rahman* encourage or discourage organ donation?

2. Should the standard of liability for misinterpreting the scope of an anatomical gift be different than the standard articulated in these two cases?

3. In a world that is growing increasingly smaller due to technological advances, how might international organizations work together to avoid the situation that occurred in *Jacobsen*?

3. The National Organ Transplant Act

Read the National Organ Transplant Act in the statutory supplement.

Questions

1. Why should the federal government prohibit the sale of organs?

2. Does the National Organ Transplant Act reflect an appropriate balancing of the various interests affected by the shortage of organs for transplant?

a. Allocation of Donated Organs

Read 42 C.F.R. 121.1 et seq. (1998) in the statutory supplement. Section 213(a) of P.L. 105-277 provides that this regulation may take effect no earlier than October 21, 1999.

**Organ Procurement and Transplantation Network Final Rule
Supplementary Information
Federal Register: April 2, 1998 (Volume 63, Number 63)
<http://www.hrsa.gov/News-PA/ruletxt.htm>**

Over the past two decades, the safety and survival rates for transplantation of human organs have improved markedly, and the number of transplants has increased. In 1996, about 20,000 transplants were performed in the United States. At the same time, the rapid development of transplant techniques and the growth of the Nation's transplant system present new challenges:

1. The demand for organs for transplantation exceeds the supply, and this gap is growing. About 4,000 persons died in 1996 while awaiting transplantation.

2. The Nation's organ allocation system remains heavily weighted to the local use of organs instead of making organs available on a broader regional or national basis for patients with the greatest medical need consistent with sound medical judgment. Technological advances have made it possible to preserve organs longer and share them more widely, but the allocation system does not yet take full advantage of this capacity. Instead, some patients with less urgent medical need receive transplants before other patients with greater medical need whether listed locally or away from home.

3. The criteria used in listing those who need transplantation vary from one transplant center to another, as do the criteria used to determine the medical status of a patient. This lack of uniform, medically objective criteria make it difficult to compare the medical need of patients in different centers.

4. As a result of both the local preference in allocation and the lack of standard medical criteria, waiting times for organs are much longer in some geographic areas than in others. The statute envisions a national allocation system, based on medial criteria, which results in the equitable treatment of transplant patients. But equitable treatment cannot be assured if medical criteria vary from one transplant center to another and if allocation policies prevent suitable organs from being offered first to those with the greatest medical need.

5. Useful, current, transplant-center specific data for patients and health care providers are not available, despite information technology advances that make more current reporting feasible.

Efforts are needed to address these challenges in the areas of both donation and allocation.

In order to bring about substantial increases in the number of organ donors and the number of transplants performed each year, a new national Organ and Tissue Donation Initiative has been launched. Working in partnership with national and local organizations, the Department of Health and Human Services (HHS) seeks to increase donation through encouraging more individuals to chose to be organ donors and that share that decision with their families; through improved performance by hospitals and organ procurement organizations toward ensuring that the families of potential donors are given the opportunity to allow donation; through higher consent rates by families, especially by encouraging those who elect to be organ donors to inform their families of their decision; and through new research on enhancing donation . . .The Department expects that the supply of organs may be raised by about 20 percent through this initiative, which would greatly alleviate organ shortages.

In order to improve allocation of organs for transplantation, this final rule establishes performance goals to be achieved by the OPTN. Actions already underway in the OPTN are consistent with several of these goals. The rule does not establish specific allocation policies, but instead looks to the organ transplant community to take action to meet the performance goals. The goals include:

• *Minimum Listing Criteria*—The OPTN is required to define objective and measurable medical criteria to be used by all transplant centers in determining whether a patient is appropriate to be listed for a transplant. In this way, patients with essentially the same medical need will be listed in the same way at all transplant centers.

• *Status Categories*—The OPTN is required to determine objective medical criteria to be used nationwide in determining the medical status of those awaiting transplantation. This will provide a common measurement for use by all transplant centers in determining the urgency of an individual's medical condition, and it will facilitate OPTN efforts to direct organs to those with greatest medical need, in accordance with sound medical judgment.

- *Equitable Allocation*—The OPTN is required to develop equitable allocation policies that provide organs to those with the greatest medical urgency, in accordance with sound medical judgment. This increases the likelihood of patients obtaining matching organs, and gives all patients equal chances to obtain organs compared to other patients of equal medical status, wherever they live or list. By requiring common criteria for listing eligibility and medical status, and by requiring that organs be directed so as to equalize waiting times, especially for those with greatest medical need, this rule is designed to provide patients awaiting transplants with equal access to organs and to provide organs to sickest patients first, consistent with sound medical judgment. While present OPTN policies give weight to medical need, the "local first" practice thwarts organ allocation over a broad area and thus prevents medical need from being the dominant factor in allocation decisions.

Under the provisions of this rule, it is intended that the area where a person lives or the transplant center where he or she is listed will not be primary factors in how quickly he or she receives a transplant. Instead, organs will be allocated according to objective standards of medical status and need. In this way, suitable organs will reach patients with the greatest medical need, both when they are procured locally and when they are procured outside the listed patients' areas. This objective reflects the views of many commenters on the proposed regulations, as well as the finding of the American Medical Association in its Code of Medical Ethics: "Organs should be considered a national, rather than a local or regional resource. Geographical priorities in the allocation of organs should be prohibited except when transportation of organs would threaten their suitability for transplantation."

The OPTN is required to develop proposals for the new allocation policies (except for livers) within a year of the effective date of the final rule. In the case of liver allocation policies, where policy development work has been underway for several years, the OPTN is required to develop a new proposed allocation policy within 60 days of the effective date.

Other provisions of this rule include requirements that the OPTN make more current data available for the public, including measures of performance of individually identified transplant centers. This information is needed by patients, families, physicians, and payers in choosing a course of action and is needed as a quality measurement instrument.

In addition, the rule defines the governing structure of the OPTN and outlines procedures for the establishment of policies by the OPTN that include appropriate participation by transplant professionals and families, with oversight by HHS. The rule also includes a requirement that the OPTN develop a "grandfathering" proposal for patients currently awaiting liver transplantation so that these patients are treated no less favorably under the new allocation policies than they would have been under current allocation policies. The OPTN also is required to develop proposed transition policies for the initial changes required by this rule to its allocation policies for other organs.

The National Organ and Tissue Donation Initiative and this final rule build on more than a decade of experience, including improving medical technology, to create a national community of organ sharing and to save and improve more lives through transplantation. The rule defines Federal expectations, based on the role given to the Secretary under the statute, but looks to the OPTN to propose policy choices that meet those expectations.

* * *

Questions

1. Does the proposed federal regulatory scheme for regulating organ transplants adequately protect the interests of senior citizens as donors *and* as donees?

2. What role should the elder law attorney play respecting living donor organ donations by older clients?

3. To what extent might a person's religious or moral beliefs affect her views on organ donation? *See* <gopher://info.med.yale.edu:70/00/Disciplines/Disease/ Transplant/religion.txt>.

b. Problems of Interpretation

Wheat v. Mass
994 F.2d 273 (5th Cir. 1993)

DUHE, Circuit Judge.

Background

In November 1989, Margaret Gordon underwent tests by Dr. Joseph Mass at Our Lady of the Lake Regional Medical Center (OLOL) after she complained to him of abdominal pain. After the tests revealed severe liver disfunction, Mrs. Gordon was admitted to OLOL and was treated there by Drs. Joseph Mass, John Hoppe, and William Anderson. Mrs. Gordon's condition deteriorated, and she was transferred to Ochsner Hospital (Ochsner) in New Orleans to undergo evaluation by Dr. Luis Balart for a possible liver transplant.

At Ochsner, Mrs. Gordon's condition stabilized temporarily until December 10, when Ochsner physicians determined that she needed a liver transplant. Because Mrs. Gordon's medical insurance did not cover transplants, her family was contacted by Ochsner's social worker on December 11 and informed that a $175,000 down payment must be raised for the transplant. At the social worker's suggestion, Mrs. Gordon's family contacted the Louisiana state government for assistance and was subsequently informed on December 13 that funding for the transplant may be available from the state. Mrs. Gordon was immediately placed on the national transplant waiting list, but before an organ match was made, she passed away at 10:00 p.m. that night. In December 1990, Appellants sued Drs. Mass, Hoppe, OLOL, Ochsner, and Drs. Balart and Head, alleging that they discriminated against Mrs. Gordon on the basis of age, sex, and poverty while providing her medical services, in violation of the Civil Rights Act, Title VII, the U.S. Constitution, and the Louisiana Constitution. The district court dismissed the complaint, upon Appellees' motions, for failure to state a claim. The court also denied Appellants' motion to amend the petition. Appellants appeal both the dismissal and the district court's refusal to allow an amendment to the complaint.

Discussion

I. Dismissal of Complaint.

    A. Standard of Review.

Dismissal cannot be upheld unless it appears beyond doubt that Appellants would not be entitled to recover under any set of facts that could be proved in support of their claims.

    B. Alleged causes of action.

Appellants' 42 U.S.C. § 1983 claim states that "Ochsner and its doctors, as well as proposed defendant state officials," are state actors who violated Mrs. Gordon's civil rights under the equal protection clause of the Fourteenth Amendment. Ochsner is not a state actor, and cannot be considered as such solely because it receives medicare and medicaid funds and is subject to state regulation. *Daigle v. Opelousas Health Care, Inc.*, 774 F.2d 1344, 1349 (5th Cir. 1985). Because no state action was involved, this claim was properly dismissed.

Appellants next argue that Ochsner violated Mrs. Gordon's equal protection rights under the Fifth Amendment by discriminating against her on the basis of sex. A Fifth Amendment claim is cognizable only against a federal government actor, and Appellants argue that Ochsner is such an actor by virtue of its membership in the United Network for Organ Sharing (UNOS).[1] Ochsner's receipt of federal funds by virtue of its participation in UNOS does not make Ochsner a federal actor. *See Wahba v. New York University*, 492 F.2d 96, 102 (2d Cir. 1974), *cert. denied*, 419 U.S. 874, 95 S. Ct. 135, 42 L. Ed. 2d 113 (1974) (private university's administration of public health service grants pursuant to statute does not make the university a federal actor); *Greenya v. George Washington University*, 167 U.S. App. D.C. 379, 512 F.2d 556, 559-60, (D.C. Cir. 1975), *cert. denied*, 423 U.S. 995, 96 S. Ct. 422, 46 L. Ed. 2d 369 (1975) (university's receipt of federal funding and exemption from taxation does not make university a government actor for purposes of a Fifth Amendment claim); *Fidelity Financial Corp. v. Federal Home Loan Bank of San Francisco*, 792 F.2d 1432, 1435 (9th Cir. 1986), *cert. denied*, 479 U.S. 1064, 107 S. Ct. 949, 93 L. Ed. 2d 998 (1987) (extensive and detailed regulation does not render business a government actor). Furthermore, Appellants have failed to allege any facts demonstrating that Mrs. Gordon was discriminated against on the basis of her sex. This claim was properly dismissed.

---

    [1] The United Network for Organ Sharing has an exclusive contract with the Department of Health and Human Services to serve as the national organ procurement and transplant network under the National Organ Transplant Act of 1984, 42 U.S.C. § 273.

Third, Appellants argue that "Louisiana finances liver transplants with Medicaid funds on an arbitrary and political rather than reasonable and equitable basis" in violation of 42 U.S.C. § 1396b(i), which provides that states must distribute organ transplant funds equally to similarly situated individuals. This claim only applies to Ochsner, because Ochsner is the only Appellee that performs liver transplants or is involved in Louisiana's funding of transplants. We held in *Stewart v. Bernstein,* 769 F.2d 1088, 1092-94 (5th Cir. 1985), that the Medicaid Act does not furnish substantive rights enforceable in civil suits between private parties. The court's power to enforce this statute is limited to adjudication of whether a state properly administers federal medicaid funds, and therefore this claim against Ochsner was properly dismissed.

Fourth, Appellants argue that a cause of action exists under the Age Discrimination Act, 42 U.S.C. § 6101, which prohibits discrimination on the basis of age in federally assisted programs. Appellants argue that the organ transplant program is a federally assisted program because it is heavily subsidized and funded with federal Medicare and Medicaid funds. Again, this claim can only be asserted against Ochsner as Ochsner is the only Appellee involved in organ transplants. This Court has not considered whether a private cause of action exists under the Age Discrimination Act, nor has the Court considered whether such an action may be brought by a Plaintiff's survivors; we need not address these issues now. Appellants have made no showing whatsoever that Ochsner discriminated against Mrs. Gordon on the basis of her age, and for that reason the claim was properly dismissed.

Appellants next argue that Ochsner violated Title IX of the Education Amendment of 1972, 20 U.S.C. § 1681 which prohibits sexual discrimination in education programs receiving federal funding. Appellants argue that Ochsner is within the purview of Title IX because it has educational programs and receives federal funds through medicare and medicaid. Appellants then state that Ochsner discriminated against Mrs. Gordon on the basis of sex in violation of Title IX. This claim was properly dismissed because Appellants have made no showing that Mrs. Gordon's gender was a factor in her not receiving a liver transplant, or in any other decision involving her medical care.

Finally, Appellants argue that they are entitled to show that UNOS and its members such as Ochsner maintain a monopoly on organ transplants and create market harm by restricting the availability of such services and charging prohibitively high prices in violation of the Sherman Anti-Trust Act, 15 U.S.C. §§ 1, 2. Appellants have failed to state a claim under § 1 of the Sherman Act because they have failed to allege any effect on interstate commerce, and have failed to show Ochsner's requisite market power or intent to monopolize the market. Appellants have also failed to state a claim under § 2 of the Sherman Act because they have not shown an agreement between two or more economic entities, a specific intent to monopolize, or any overt act in furtherance of the conspiracy. These claims are frivolous, and were properly dismissed.

* * *

Conclusion

For the foregoing reasons, the district court's dismissal of Appellants' complaint and refusal to allow an amendment are AFFIRMED.

Question

Are there any grounds upon which to challenge the national organ allocation system?

4. Defining Death

Read the Uniform Determination of Death Act in the statutory supplement. The Act has been adopted, with some modifications, in every state and the District of Columbia.

David DeGrazia
Biology, Consciousness, and the Definition of Death: Report from the Institute for Philosophy and Public Policy (Winter 1998)
<http://www.puaf.umd.edu/ippp/winter98/biology_consciousness.htm>[*]

When does a human life end? This question used to be answered quite easily. According to the traditional standard, which has only recently been questioned, a human being is dead when her heart and lungs have irreversibly ceased to function. In some cases, permanent loss of consciousness may precede cardiopulmonary failure. But the interval between these two events has typically been a matter of hours or days, and the traditional standard regards only the latter event as definitive. Today, however, the development of mechanical respirators, electronic pacemakers, and other medical technologies has created the possibility of a greater temporal separation between various system failures—a patient may lose consciousness a decade or more before his heart and lungs fail, for example. Meanwhile, interest in the availability of transplantable organs has provided an incentive not to delay unnecessarily in determining that a person has died. (Current law, it need hardly be said, embraces the so-called "dead-donor rule": organs necessary for life may not be procured before donors are dead, since the removal of such organs would otherwise cause death—that is, kill the donors—violating laws against homicide.)

Two landmark reports helped to generate a movement away from exclusive reliance on the traditional standard: the 1968 report of the Harvard Medical School Ad Hoc Committee and a 1981 presidential commission report, Defining Death. This second document included what became the Uniform Determination of Death Act (UDDA). Today all fifty states and the District of Columbia follow the UDDA in rec-

---

[*] Copyright © 1998. Reprinted with permission.

ognizing whole-brain death—irreversible cessation of all functions of the entire brain—as a legal standard of death. The UDDA doesn't jettison the cardiopulmonary standard, however. Instead, it holds that death occurs whenever either standard (whichever applies first) is met. One important consequence of this change is that an individual can be legally dead even if her cardiopulmonary system continues to function. If a patient's entire brain is nonfunctioning, so that breathing and heartbeat are maintained only by artificial life-supports, that patient meets the whole-brain standard of death.

Some philosophers and scientists have argued that the whole-brain standard does not go far enough. Several leading authors on the subject have advocated a higher-brain standard, according to which death is the irreversible cessation of the capacity for consciousness. This standard is often met prior to whole-brain death, which includes death of the brainstem—that part of the brain which allows spontaneous respiration and heartbeat but is insufficient for consciousness. Thus, a patient in a permanent coma or permanent vegetative state (PVS) meets the higher-brain, but not the whole-brain, standard of death. Should society embrace the higher-brain standard? Should laws be changed so that permanently unconscious patients can legally be declared dead? This essay offers both conceptual and pragmatic grounds for rejecting such a change. However, it will also argue that the linkage between definitions of death and policies regarding life-supports and organ procurement is less strict than some observers might suppose. In other words, a rejection of the higher-brain standard does not imply an endorsement of policies that would prolong life at any cost.

Questions

1. Do you believe the typical layperson understands "death" to mean the condition described in the UDDA?

2. How might an attorney help a client to articulate her understanding of "death"? Might the word "death" have different meanings for a person depending on whether, for example, the issue is when to withdraw life support on the one hand, and when organs may be harvested on the other?

Further Reading. Peter J. Strauss & Nancy M. Lederman, The Elder Law Handbook ch. 10 (1996); Peter J. Strauss et al., Aging and the Law, ch. 36 (1996); Melvin I. Urofsky & Philip E. Urofsky, The Right to Die: A Two-Volume Anthology of Scholarly Articles (1996).

CHAPTER 10

Estate Planning: An Overview

A. State Property Law 536
B. The Law of Federal Transfer Taxation 552
C. A Note on State Death Taxes 559

This chapter provides a brief overview of the law of estate planning for students who have not yet taken the basic courses in this area. The chapter is divided into three parts. Part A examines aspects of state property law, Part B considers aspects of the law of federal transfer taxation, and Part C offers a brief discussion of death taxes imposed by state law.

Part A begins with the law of intestacy, which controls to the extent that there is not a valid will disposing of all of the decedent's probate property. It then explores the law of wills and will substitutes, focusing on three important points: the formal requirements for a validly executed will, the main grounds upon which a will's validity can be contested, and the alternatives to wills that have arisen because of the fundamental distinction between probate and nonprobate transfers. It then examines an important protection for surviving spouses, namely the elective share, which limits the power of decedents to transfer property outside the marital unit. Finally, it considers the procedures used by probate courts to distribute property to the appropriate beneficiaries.

Part B turns to the law of federal transfer taxation. It begins by exploring the federal estate tax, which is imposed on the transmission of property at death. It then examines the federal gift tax, which is imposed on transfers made inter vivos. Finally, it considers the comparatively recent federal generation-skipping transfer tax, which is designed, as its name suggests, to impose an excise tax on transfers that pass over one or more generation(s) of potential recipients.

Part C concludes the chapter with a brief discussion of the death taxes imposed at the state level. These taxes are largely but not exclusively patterned after the federal estate tax. State taxes are not as significant as federal taxes for estate planning purposes, and only a short overview of state taxation is offered in this book.

A. State Property Law

1. Intestacy

a. Terminology

Carolyn S. Bratt
A Primer on Kentucky Intestacy Laws
82 Ky. L.J. 29, 30-31 (1993/1994)[*]

Every state has a system of inheritance created by statute and by case law. State inheritance laws contemplate that the owner of property has died in one of two ways—"testate" (with a will) or "intestate" (without a will). A majority of all Americans die intestate without any directions as to the disposition of their property. Consequently, the legislature of every jurisdiction has adopted statutes governing intestate succession.

* * *

Today, there are few significant distinctions between intestate succession to real and personal property. At the common law, however, different laws determined the identity of the intestate takers of real property and the intestate takers of personalty. Thus, distinct, but parallel, technical vocabularies developed to describe succession based on the characterization of the decedent's property as real or personal. For example, "descent" refers to the devolution of intestate real property, while "distribution" denominates the intestate succession to personalty. Those to whom the decedent's real property descends are "heirs," and those who take the decedent's personal property are "next of kin" or "distributees."

Question

In addition to learning the terms mentioned above, you should also become familiar with the following: partial intestacy, testator, decedent, devise, legacy, bequest, devisee, legatee, personal representative, executor, and administrator. What do these terms mean?

---

[*] Copyright © 1994. Reprinted with permission.

b. Purposes Behind Intestacy Statutes

Mary Louise Fellows et al.
Committed Partners and Inheritance
16 L. & INEQ. 1, 11-13 (1998)*

[The drafting of the Uniform Probate Code ("UPC") in 1969 and its revision in 1990] have served as catalysts for reexamination of existing intestate succession laws. The UPC pattern of distribution inevitably is a product of the tradition and history that has influenced other intestacy statutes. The drafters of the UPC, however, were careful not to perpetuate historical rules that they found to be inconsistent with modern attitudes. Their goal was to design a statute that reflects the donative intent of persons who die without wills. By reflecting probable donative intent of those likely to die without a will, the intestacy statute furthers testamentary freedom because it gives persons the right not to have to execute wills to assure that accumulated wealth passes to their intended takers.

Effectuating probable intentions of decedents, however, is not the only objective of intestacy statutes. A second objective of intestacy statutes is to produce a pattern of distribution that the recipients believe is fair and thus does not produce disharmony among expectant takers or disdain for the legal system. Rooted in a patriarchal tradition, historically inheritance laws were not concerned with principles of equality. Today, however, it is no longer acceptable to treat an eldest son as more deserving of the family's wealth than his siblings, nor is it acceptable to treat adopted children differently than biological children, or nonmarital children differently than marital children.

The question of fairness goes beyond issues of equality. Fairness also includes equity considerations of financial dependence, reliance, unjust enrichment and trust. Based on these considerations, there is widespread acceptance of the right of a surviving legal spouse to receive a substantial share of a decedent's estate, even when the decedent is survived by children. A final objective of intestacy laws is to promote and encourage the nuclear family. Historically, the family has been a highly valued institution viewed as of great benefit to a stable and productive society. Indeed, the safeguarding of families and family life is a value that continues to shape policy and political debate today.

The difficulty, of course, arises in defining family.

Questions

Professor Fellows has described several different objectives of a well-drafted intestacy statute. Which of these objectives is the most important? Why?

---

* Copyright © 1998. Reprinted with permission.

c. Sample Intestacy Laws

In the statutory supplement, read the Statute of Distribution 1670, Ohio Revised Code § 2105.06, Pre-1990 UPC §§ 2-102 and 2-103, and 1990 UPC §§ 2-102 and 2-103.

Comment to Pre-1990 UPC § 2-102

This section gives the surviving spouse a larger share than most existing statutes on descent and distribution. In doing so, it reflects the desires of most married persons, who almost always leave all of a moderate estate or at least one-half of a larger estate to the surviving spouse when a will is executed. A husband or wife who desires to leave the surviving spouse less than the share provided by this section may do so by executing a will[.]

Comment to Pre-1990 UPC § 2-103

This section provides for inheritance by lineal descendants of the decedent, parents and their descendants, and granparents and collateral relatives descended from grandparents; in line with modern policy, it eliminates more remote relatives tracing through great-grandparents.

Comment to 1990 UPC § 2-102

This section is revised to give the surviving spouse a larger share than the pre-1990 UPC.

Questions

In light of the text of these statutes and the commentary reprinted above, what features of intestacy law have changed over time, and why?

2. Wills and Will Substitutes

a. Wills: Formalities of Execution

i. Formal Requirements

In the statutory supplement, read the Statute of Frauds 1677, the Statute of Wills 1837 (known colloquially as the "Wills Act"), Ohio Revised Code § 2107.03, Pre-1990 UPC §§ 2-502 and 2-503, and 1990 UPC § 2-502.

Questions

1. Historically, state laws governing the execution of wills were modeled either on the Statute of Frauds or the Statute of Wills. Which of these two was the model for Ohio Revised Code § 2107.03?

2. How has the UPC departed from older legislation (here exemplified by the Ohio Revised Code)?

ii. Purposes of Wills Act Formalities

John H. Langbein
Substantial Compliance with the Wills Act
88 HARV. L. REV. 489, 492-96 (1975)*

Several discrete functions can be identified and ascribed to the formalities . . . .

1. *The Evidentiary Function.*—The primary purpose of the Wills Act has always been to provide the court with reliable evidence of testamentary intent and of the terms of the will; virtually all the formalities serve as "probative safeguards." The requirement of writing assures that "evidence of testamentary intent [will] be cast in reliable and permanent form." The requirement that the testator sign the will is meant to produce evidence of genuineness. The requirement that he sign at the end prevents subsequent interpolation.

The attestation requirement, the distinguishing feature of the so-called formal will, assures that the actual signing is witnessed and sworn to by disinterested bystanders. When the statute directs the testator to publish his will to the witnesses, he is made to announce his testamentary intent to the persons who may later "prove" the will. Those who survive the testator are available to testify in probate proceedings. The requirement that they be competent, meaning disinterested, produces witnesses whose testimony is not self-serving.

* * *

2. *The Channeling Function.*—What Fuller calls the "channeling" function of legal formalities in contract law is also an important purpose of the Wills Act formalities. Fuller likens the channeling function to the role of language: "One who wishes to communicate his thoughts to others must force the raw material of meaning into defined and recognizable channels . . . ."

* * *

Standardization of wills is a matter of unusual importance, because unlike contracts or conveyances, wills inevitably contemplate judicial implementation,

---

* Copyright © 1975 Harvard Law Review Association. Reprinted by permission.

although normally in nonadversarial litigation resembling adjudication less than ordinary governmental administration.

* * *

The standardization of testation achieved under the Wills Act also benefits the testator. He does not have to devise for himself a mode of communicating his testamentary wishes to the court, and to worry whether it will be effective.

* * *

3. *The Cautionary Function.*—A will is said to be revocable and ambulatory, meaning that it becomes operative only on death. Because the testator does not part with the least incident of ownership when he makes a will, and does not experience the "wrench of delivery" required for inter vivos gifts, the danger exists that he may make seeming testamentary dispositions inconsiderately, without adequate forethought and finality of intention. Not every expression that "I want you to have the house when I'm gone" is meant as a will. One purpose of many of the forms is to impress the testator with the seriousness of the testament, and thereby to assure the court "that the statements of the transferor were deliberately intended to effectuate a transfer." They caution the testator, and they show the court that he was cautioned.

* * *

4. *The Protective Function.*—Courts have traditionally attributed to the Wills Act the object "of protecting the testator against imposition at the time of execution." The requirement that attestation be made in the presence of the testator is meant "to prevent the substitution of a surreptitious will." Another common protective requirement is the rule that the witnesses should be disinterested, hence not motivated to coerce or deceive the testator.

Questions

How well do the formalities imposed by non-UPC jurisdictions, such as Ohio, serve these four purposes? How about the formalities imposed by the UPC?

iii. Loosening the Formal Requirements

In conjunction with the following excerpt, read 1990 UPC § 2-503 in the statutory supplement.

John H. Langbein
Substantial Compliance with the Wills Act
88 HARV. L. REV. 489, 498-99, 515-16, 531 (1975)*

What is peculiar about the law of wills is not the prominence of the formalities, but the judicial insistence that any defect in complying with them automatically and inevitably voids the will. In other areas where legislation imposes formal requirements, the courts have taken a purposive approach to formal defects. . . . The essential rationale of . . . [this purposive approach, which Professor Langbein calls in this context "substantial compliance"—Eds.] is that when the purposes of the formal requirements are proved to have been served, literal compliance with the formalities themselves is no longer necessary.

* * *

The substantial compliance doctrine would admit to probate a noncomplying instrument that the court determined was meant as a will and whose form satisfied the purposes of the Wills Act.

* * *

The rule of literal compliance with the Wills Act is a snare for the ignorant and the ill-advised, a needless hangover from a time when the law of proof was in its infancy. In the three centuries since the first Wills Act we have developed the means to adjudicate whether formal defects are harmless to the statutory purpose.

Questions

1. Do you agree with Professor Langbein about the defects of strict compliance with Wills Act formalities?

2. How well does § 2-503 of the 1990 UPC respond to the perceived problem with strict compliance?

b. Wills: Grounds for Contest

In this section, we consider the four main grounds for contesting a will: lack of testamentary intent, lack of testamentary capacity, undue influence, and fraud.

i. Lack of Testamentary Intent

In connection with the following excerpts, read 1990 UPC § 2-502(c) in the statutory supplement.

---

* Copyright © 1975 Harvard Law Review Association. Reprinted by permission.

In re Kauffman's Estate
76 A.2d 414, 416-417 (Pa. 1950)

That the paper offered for probate was actually written and signed by the decedent is not seriously disputed. The main question for our decision is, Did she write it with testamentary intent? *i.e.,* Did she intend that the paper so written by her should be her will?

* * *

In all cases of this kind where a paper is proposed for probate and its testamentary character is denied, it becomes the duty of the Court in the first instance to examine the paper, its form and its language, and therefrom determine as a matter of law whether it shows testamentary intent with reasonable certainty. If testamentary intent is satisfactorily revealed from such an examination by the Court, the paper should be probated as a will.

On the other hand, if, from such examination, the paper is shown not to be a testamentary disposition, but is shown to be a document of another type, then it is not to be probated as a will. But, if, from such an examination, the Court should determine that a real doubt or ambiguity exists, so that the paper offered for probate might or might not be testamentary, . . . [then] the document presents an ambiguity which will permit the use of extrinsic evidence.

Mallory v. Mallory
862 S.W.2d 879, 881 (Ky. 1993)

An expression of testamentary intent has been uniformly held to require 1) a disposing of property 2) which takes effect after death.

* * *

There must be a contemporaneous intention thereby to create a revocable gift of property to take effect at death, and not merely to declare a purpose to make a gift in praesenti or a bequest by some other paper, or to speak of such action as already done by some other instrument. If the writer does not intend the letter or other document to take effect as a will but intends to execute another instrument to that effect, it is not a will.

* * *

It is familiar law that no particular form or special language is required for a will. It is sufficient if it shows an intention that it shall be so regarded.

Question

How might one establish testamentary intent, or the lack of it?

ii. Lack of Testamentary Capacity

RESTATEMENT (SECOND) OF PROPERTY (Donative Transfers)
§ 34.5, comment a[*]

Who is mentally incompetent. A person is mentally incompetent to make a donative transfer if such person is unable to understand fully the significance of such transfer in relation to such person's own situation. Stated another way, to be mentally competent a person must know and understand the extent of his or her property, comprehend to whom he or she is giving his or her property, and know the natural objects of his or her bounty. A slightly different statement of what constitutes mental capacity is that the person must understand the nature and extent of his or her property, know and recall the natural objects of his or her property, and be able to determine and understand how he or she wishes to dispose of his or her property. A person who is mentally incompetent part of the time but who has lucid intervals during which he or she comprehends fully the significance of a donative transfer can, in the absence of an adjudication or statute that has contrary effect, make a valid will or a valid inter vivos donative transfer, provided such will or transfer is made during a lucid interval.

Williams v. Vollman
738 S.W.2d 849, 850-51 (Ky. Ct. App. 1987)

[This test] does not require that the testator have actual knowledge of the objects of his bounty. Rather, the [test] requires that the testator have "sufficient mind to know" the objects of his bounty.

Lawrence A. Frolik
The Biological Roots of the Undue Influence Doctrine: What's Love Got to Do With It?
57 U. PITT. L. REV. 841, 849 (1996)[**]

This is a minimum level of capacity, far less than is required for many other acts. For example, an individual may have testamentary capacity even though he or she was previously declared incompetent and placed under a guardianship. Even if a conservatorship is necessary to protect the property while the individual is living (it must be conserved to support the individual), permitting a testator with greatly diminished capacity to execute a will does him or her no harm since the gift does not take effect until death. The relatively low level of capacity required to execute a will

---

[*] Reprinted with permission.
[**] Copyright © 1996. Reprinted by permission.

reflects the judicial concern that individuals be given every opportunity to direct who shall take their property after they die.

Questions

1. Why is lack of testamentary capacity a particular problem for the elderly?

2. If you were a lawyer representing an elderly client, what steps might you take to reduce the likelihood of a will contest on the ground of lack of capacity?

iii. Undue Influence

Lawrence A. Frolik
The Biological Roots of the Undue Influence Doctrine:
What's Love Got to Do With It?
57 U. Pitt. L. Rev. 841, 843, 850-51, 853-54, 857-58 (1996)[*]

The doctrine of undue influence permits an otherwise valid will or testamentary gift to be overturned on the basis that the testamentary bequest represented not the will of the testator, but that of the influencer.

* * *

... [T]oday almost all jurisdictions recognize five elements or variants on them as being the necessary components of a cause of action[.]

* * *

1. Susceptibility

For any claim of undue influence to succeed, it must be proven that the testator was susceptible to the will of the influencer, and so it is very difficult to successfully claim undue influence if the testator is physically robust and mentally alert. Usually the claimants must show that the testator was physically ill, had diminished capacity, suffered from dementia, was under the influence of drugs or alcohol, or suffered some mental impairment, and as a result, he or she was susceptible to the destruction of his or her free will and the substitution of the influencer's desires.

* * *

2. Confidential Relationship

The great majority of, though not all, jurisdictions require that a confidential relationship exist between the testator and the influencer. A confidential relationship is close to, but not quite the same as a fiduciary relationship and is defined as a relationship in which there is a special trust and confidence between the parties. As a

---

[*] Copyright © 1996. Reprinted by permission.

result, the testator does not "hold[] the influencer at arms length," which permits the influencer to artfully insinuate his or her desires into the mind of the testator and thereby replace the testator's testamentary intent with his or her own.

* * *

3. Active Procurement

The third element of undue influence is a requirement of proof of active procurement of the challenged will by the influencer. Active procurement can be proven by actions such as being present at the execution of the will, being present at the time when the testator expressed a desire to make a will, recommending an attorney to draw up the will, instructing the attorney as to the contents of the will, paying the attorney for preparing the will, securing the witnesses to the will, or safekeeping the will after its execution.

* * *

A showing of active procurement of the will must be demonstrated because undue influence must be something more than merely currying favor or playing up to the testator. That is, the influence must be direct and part of a plan or design. Otherwise, undue influence is difficult to distinguish from simply being solicitous to the testator.

* * *

4. Change of the Dispository Plan

Proof of undue influence requires that the testator actually changed the will in favor of the influencer, or if the will was the first one executed, that the contents of the will differed from earlier oral statements of how the testator intended to dispose of his or her property. As with the requirement of active procurement, the change in distribution plan requirement demonstrates that the undue influence was actively directed at modifying the will, and was not just excessive involvement in the testator's life.

5. Unconscionable Gift

Finally, a successful claim of undue influence must show that the testator made an unconscionable change in plans or an unnatural devise. Typically this means disinheriting or greatly decreasing the shares of children or other blood relatives in favor of the influencer.

Questions

1. Of the five elements discussed by Professor Frolik, which one is likely to be the easiest to prove? The most difficult to prove? The most significant in a court's analysis?

2. How would the age of the testator affect your answers to the above questions?

3. If you were a lawyer representing an elderly client, what steps might you take to reduce the likelihood of a will contest on the ground of undue influence?

iv. Fraud

John A. Warnick
The Ungrateful Living: An Estate Planner's Nightmare—
The Trial Attorney's Dream
24 LAND & WATER L. REV. 401, 44-45 (1989)*

A will purportedly executed by an individual with sufficient testamentary capacity may still fail if a contestant can show that it is the product of duress or forgery. Provisions of a properly attested will, or the will itself, may fail if they are the product of fraud.

Fraud occurs where there is an intentional, deceitful misrepresentation made with the purpose of altering the testamentary disposition. The fraud may be in the inducement or in the execution. The outcome of the will contest will vary according to the nature of the fraud and its pervasiveness.

When a person misrepresents facts and the testator is influenced thereby in making or revoking a testamentary disposition there has been fraud in the inducement. Courts will strike down the fraudulently induced inheritance if the testator would not have left the inheritance or made the bequest if he had known the true facts. The balance of the will stands unless it is shown that fraud affects the entire will or the fraudulently induced bequest cannot be separated from the rest of the will.

Fraud in the execution occurs when someone misrepresents the contents or nature of a will and in reliance on that representation the testator signs the instrument. For example, if the testator signs a will, a portion of which was prior to execution removed without the testator's knowledge and another portion inserted, this would constitute fraud in the execution. In this case the balance of the document will stand and a constructive trust will be imposed on the interest received by the wrongdoer as a result of the fraud. This must be distinguished from the case where the testator, without another's intervention, executes a different person's will. In that case, the will generally will not be admitted to probate.

Questions

What explains the use of the constructive trust as a remedy for fraud? Why do probate courts not simply give effect to the testator's true desires?

---

* Copyright © 1989. Reprinted by permission.

c. Will Substitutes and the Distinction Between Probate and Non-Probate Transfers

John H. Langbein
The Nonprobate Revolution and the Future of the Law of Succession
97 HARV. L. REV. 1108, 1108-09 (1984)*

Over the course of the twentieth century, persistent tides of change have been lapping at the once-quiet shores of the law of succession. Probate, our court-operated system for transferring wealth at death, is declining in importance. Institutions that administer non-court modes of transfer are displacing the probate system. Life insurance companies, pension plan operators, commercial banks, savings banks, investment companies, brokerage houses, stock transfer agents, and a variety of other financial intermediaries are functioning as free-market competitors of the probate system and enabling property to pass on death without probate and without will. The law of wills and the rules of descent no longer govern succession to most of the property of most decedents. Increasingly, probate bears to the actual practice of succession about the relation than bankruptcy bears to enterprise: it is an indispensable institution, but hardly one that everybody need use.

* * *

Four main will substitutes constitute the core of the nonprobate system: life insurance, pension accounts, joint accounts, and revocable trusts. When properly created, each is functionally indistinguishable from a will—each reserves to the owner complete lifetime dominion, including the power to name and to change beneficiaries until death. These devices I shall call "pure" will substitutes, in contradistinction to "imperfect" will substitutes (primarily joint tenancies), which more closely resemble lifetime transfers. The four pure will substitues may also be described as mass will substitutes: they are marketed by financial intermediaries using standard form instruments with fill-in-the-blank beneficiary designations.

The typical American of middle- or upper-middle-class means employs many will subsitutes. The precise mix of will and will substitutes varies with individual circumstances—age, family, employment, wealth, and legal sophistication. It would not be unusual for someone in mid-life to have a dozen or more will substitutes in force, whether or not he had a will.

Questions

1. What does Professor Langbein mean by the distinction between pure and impure will substitutes?

2. To what extent are will substitutes governed by Wills Act formalities?

---

* Copyright © 1984 Harvard Law Review Association. Reprinted by permission.

3. What changes in current law might be suggested by your answer to the preceding question?

3. Protecting the Surviving Spouse Against Disinheritance

a. Background on Elective Share Statutes

Susan N. Gary
Share and Share Alike?: The UPC's Elective Share
PROB. & PROP. 19, 19 (March/April 1998)*

An elective share statute allows a decedent's surviving spouse either to elect to receive the assets given to the spouse under the decedent's will or to take a statutory percentage of the estate. Traditionally, only the decedent's probate estate was subject to the elective share. Limiting the elective share to the probate estate, however, creates many potential inequities. If the decedent transfers assets by a will substitute to someone other than the surviving spouse, the decedent can significantly reduce or completely defeat his or her spouse's elective share. If the decedent transfers assets by a will substitute to the surviving spouse or if each spouse holds title to a share of the marital assets and the surviving spouse also takes an elective share of the probate estate, beneficiaries other than the surviving spouse may suffer.

Question

In the statutory supplement, examine Ohio Revised Code § 2106.01. This statute is an example of non-UPC legislation. To what extent does it suffer from the defects Professor Gary has described?

b. The Elective Share: Incorporating Nonprobate Transfers and Spousal Assets

Susan N. Gary
Share and Share Alike?: The UPC's Elective Share
PROB. & PROP. 19, 20 (March/April 1998)*

In 1969 the UPC attempted to create a more equitable elective share by applying the spouse's elective share to the decedent's "augmented" estate. The augmented estate included assets transferred by most will substitutes but, notably, excluded

---

* Copyright © 1998 by the American Bar Association. Reprinted by permission.

insurance, annuities and pension benefits. The augmented estate also included assets that the decedent gave to the surviving spouse but did not include other assets owned by the surviving spouse.

* * *

[The 1990 UPC is based in part upon a] marital partnership theory, [which] views marriage as an economic partnership to which both spouses contribute productive effort. . . . To implement the partnership theory, the 1990 UPC creates an augmented estate that includes property owned and controlled by both spouses—probate property and property passing under will substitutes. The guiding principle of giving each spouse one-half of the marital property made it necessary to look at the assets owned by both spouses and not just property controlled by the decedent. [Furthermore,] [i]n contrast to the prior UPC, the 1990 UPC makes no exceptions for insurance, annuities and pensions.

Question

Examine Pre-1990 UPC §§ 2-201 and 2-202 and 1990 UPC §§ 2-202 and 2-203 in the statutory supplement. Do you see the improvements discussed by Professor Gary?

c. The Elective Share: Responding to a Multiple-Marriage Society

Lawrence W. Waggoner
The Multiple-Marriage Society and Spousal Rights Under the Revised Uniform Probate Code
76 Iowa L. Rev. 223, 239, 247-49 (1991) (reprinted with permission)[*]

Under typical American elective-share law, including the elective share provided by the pre-1990 UPC, a surviving spouse is granted a right to claim a one-third share of the decedent's estate, not a right to claim the fifty percent share of the couple's combined assets that the partnership theory would imply. The redesigned elective share promulgated in the 1990 UPC is intended to bring elective-share law into line with the partnership theory of marriage.

* * *

[One way in which] the UPC drafters decided to implement the marital-partnership theory [is] by means of a mechanically determined approximation system, which the drafters call an accrual-type elective share. Under the accrual-type elective share, there is no need to identify which of the couple's property was earned during

---

[*] Copyright © 1991. Reprinted by permission.

the marriage and which was acquired prior to the marriage or acquired during the marriage by gift or inheritance.

[Instead, the UPC's approach] . . . has three essential features. The first, implemented by section 2-201(a), establishes a schedule under which the elective share adjusts to the length of the marriage. The longer the marriage, the larger the "elective-share percentage." The "elective-share percentage" is initially small and increases annually according to a graduated schedule until reaching a maximum rate of fifty percent.

* * *

The second feature of the UPC's redesigned system is that the "elective-share percentage" is applied to the value of the "augmented estate," as defined in section 2-202(a). The augmented estate includes the couple's combined assets, not merely the value of assets nominally titled in the decedent's name.

* * *

The third feature implemented by section 2-207 is that the surviving spouse's own assets are counted first when determining the spouse's ultimate entitlement, so that the decedent's assets are liable only to make up the deficiency, if any.

Questions

1. Examine §§ 2-202, 2-203 and 2-207 of the 1990 UPC in the statutory supplement. Do you see the changes described by Professor Waggoner?

2. Do you agree that the elective share in the 1990 UPC reflects a marital-partnership theory?

4. The Probate Process

a. Terminology

John H. Langbein
The Nonprobate Revolution and the Future of the Law of Succession
97 Harv. L. Rev. 1108, 1108 n.1 (1984)[*]

The term "probate" originally applied only to the proceedings used to prove (*probare*) a will; it stood in contrast to "administration," which comprehended all subsequent proceedings winding up the estate. In modern American usage, "probate" embraces "administration" and hence extends to the administration of both testate and intestate estates.

---

[*] Copyright © 1984 Harvard Law Review Association. Reprinted by permission.

b. Functions of Probate

John H. Langbein
The Nonprobate Revolution and the Future of the Law of Succession
97 HARV. L. REV. 1108, 1117, 1120-21 (1984)[*]

Probate performs three essential functions: (1) making property owned at death marketable again (title-clearing); (2) paying off the decedent's debts (creditor protection); and (3) implementing the decedent's donative intent respecting the property that remains once the claims of creditors have been discharged (distribution).

* * *

The probate court is empowered to transfer title to a decedent's real property and thereby to restore it to marketability under the recording system. The cautious procedures of probate administration have seemed especially appropriate for realty, because the values tend to be large and the financing complex. In theory, the probate court should exercise a similar title-clearing function for all personalty, down to the sugar bowl and the pajamas, because only a court decree can prefect a successor's title in any item of personalty. Of course, ordinary practice quite belies the theory. Beyond the realm of vehicles and registered securities, which are covered by recording systems and thus resemble realty in some of the mechanics of transfer, formal evidence of title is not required to render personalty usable and marketable.

* * *

The other set of changes that underlie the nonprobate revolution concerns another great mission of probate: discharging the decedent's debts. Many of the details of American probate procedure, as well as much of its larger structure, would not exist but for the need to identify and pay off creditors. These procedures are indispensible, but—and here I am asserting a proposition that has not been adequately understood—only for the most exceptional cases. In general, *creditors do not need or use probate.*

* * *

In the vast majority of cases, survivors pay off decedents' debts voluntarily and rapidly.

Questions

1. How necessary is probate in today's society?
2. Which of the three functions of probate is the most important?

---

[*] Copyright © 1984 Harvard Law Review Association. Reprinted by permission.

c. Summary of the Probate Process

The rules governing probate and the administration of estates vary widely from state to state. It is therefore crucial to become familiar with the rules of the state(s) in which you practice. However, the following excerpt is presented as a general overview.

Max Rheinstein & Mary Ann Glendon
The Law of Decedents' Estates 478-79 (1971)[*]

In any legal system in which individual ownership of property exists, some person must be charged with the task of seeing to it that upon an owner's death the transfer of his assets to new owners is performed in an orderly fashion and that the obligations left behind by the dead man are properly paid. . . . [U]nder the system that originated in England and was taken over in the United States and other countries of the Common Law, a special functionary is interposed, who is called executor or administrator, as the case may be, or, comprehensively, personal representative. As a temporary manager he winds up the affairs of the decedent. In particular, he pays the debts of the decedent and ascertains the identity of the distributees and the terms under which they are entitled. In connection with these tasks he must collect the assets of the estate, and then inventory and appraise them. Next he must provide for their temporary care and management; give public notice to persons who may have claims; have, insofar as necessary, these claims authoritatively passed upon by a court; prepare a plan for the distribution of the net assets remaining after payment of the claims; and ultimately distribute the assets under the plan as finally determined. As the manager of another person's property he occupies a fiduciary position; he has to account for his management and he is not relieved from his responsibilities until he has been formally discharged.

B. The Law of Federal Transfer Taxation

We now turn to the law of federal taxation, focusing on the estate, gift, and generation-skipping transfer taxes.

---

[*] Copyright © 1971. Reprinted with permission.

1. The Federal Estate Tax

Robert B. Smith
Should We Give Away the Annual Exclusion?
1 FLA. TAX REV. 361, 367-73 (1993)[*]

The federal estate tax, originally adopted in 1916, is an excise tax imposed upon the transfer of property at death. A major reason for taxing estates, in addition to generating revenue, was breaking up concentrations of wealth. Subject to the exceptions discussed below, the tax is imposed on the transfer of all property owned by an individual at death, and on other property as to which the decedent, either at death or within the three years preceding death, had certain types of control or from which the decedent benefited either at death or within the three years preceding death. The tax is calculated on the basis of the fair market value of the property transferred determined as of the date of death or, in some circumstances, as of the date six months after death.

The estate tax applies only to persons who make cumulative transfers, during life and at death, in excess of $600,000. The maximum estate tax rate currently is fifty percent. There is an additional five percent tax, imposed on the portion of an estate between $10 million and $18.34 million, which operates to deny large estates the benefit of both (i) a $192,800 credit against transfer tax available to all other taxpayers, and (ii) the lower estate tax rate brackets applicable to the first $2.5 million in an estate.

The potential impact of the estate tax on those to whom it applies has increased because it has been supplemented by the other two elements of the transfer tax system: (i) the federal gift tax, enacted in 1932, which applies to lifetime gratuitous transfers of property; and (ii) the generation skipping transfer tax, enacted in 1986, which applies to transfers benefiting more than one generation of a family. As is discussed below, each of these other transfer taxes makes it more difficult to avoid transfer tax.

The potential bite of the transfer tax on transfers of substantial amounts of wealth, and particularly on multigenerational transfers, is fearsome. Amounts in excess of $600,000 which do not qualify for any exception are subjected to tax at a rate of thirty-seven percent and the rate increases to fifty percent for taxable transfers over $2.5 million. Accordingly, the rate of tax imposed on those estates that actually incur it is immediately substantial and can be as much as one-half of the aggregate property. When imposed in conjunction with the generation-skipping transfer tax (discussed below), the rates can reach seventy-five percent. This makes avoidance of estate tax a highly desirable goal for those with considerable amounts of wealth.

* * *

---

[*] Copyright © 1993. Reprinted with permission.

There are four significant exceptions to the estate tax. First, testamentary transfers of property to the transferor's surviving spouse, or to certain types of trusts for the lifetime benefit of the surviving spouse, are free of estate tax. This is referred to as the "marital deduction." However, property transferred under the marital deduction is ultimately subject to estate tax when the surviving spouse dies, assuming it is not consumed by the survivor. Thus, the marital deduction defers the estate taxation of property, but it does not allow avoidance of estate tax.

Second, testamentary transfers for charitable purposes are free from federal estate tax. However, the property which escapes tax under this exception is usually paid to charity and is not available to the transferor's family or to other individual beneficiaries. Hence, the family wealth is reduced by such transfers.

A third major exception to the application of the estate tax under current law is the unified credit—a $192,800 credit provided to all taxpayers. Like all credits, it applies to reduce the tax due dollar for dollar. It thus reduces any estate tax due to the extent it has not been consumed through lifetime transfers. Based on the present estate tax rate tables, the credit of $192,800 permits $600,000 worth of property to be transferred at death without estate tax. One function of the credit is to remove most individuals from the reach of the estate tax and to permit all of their property to pass free of estate tax. With proper planning, each spouse in a married couple can utilize his or her unified credit and thus pass to their beneficiaries $1.2 million worth of property and not incur estate tax. As noted above, an add-on rate of five percent is applied to estates over $10 million, which serves to phase out the benefit of the credit.

The fourth method of reducing or avoiding estate tax is to make a gift of property. While the gift may be subject to gift tax, that tax is imposed on the value of the gift at the time of the transfer. If the property that is the subject of the gift appreciates after the date of the gift, the appreciation is subject to neither gift tax nor estate tax vis-a-vis the donor. Accordingly, a gift under the annual exclusion is an especially attractive way to avoid estate tax because it incurs no gift tax, uses none of the donor's unified credit, and, if the annual exclusion gift appreciates, the appreciation also escapes gift and estate tax. Gift tax is also calculated in a way different than estate tax, and in some instances this difference makes it advantageous to make a taxable gift rather than hold the property until death.

Questions

1.   Examine Internal Revenue Code § 2001 in the statutory supplement. What is the current maximum rate of estate taxation?

2.   Examine Internal Revenue Code § 2010 in the statutory supplement. What has happened to the $600,000 credit shelter amount in the years after 1997?

2. The Federal Gift Tax

Robert B. Smith
Should We Give Away the Annual Exclusion?
1 FLA. TAX REV. 361, 373-78 (1993)[*]

When the federal estate tax was first introduced in 1916, no federal tax on gratuitous lifetime transfers was enacted with it. Presumably, it did not take long for advisors to those subject to the new estate tax to urge their clients to make lifetime gifts of substantial amounts of property. Since lifetime gifts were not subject to any federal transfer tax and property owned at death was subject to such a tax, gifts were an easy way to reduce the federal estate tax liability. Between 1916 and 1932 a couple of interim measures were used in an effort to limit the use of gifts as an estate tax avoidance technique, but neither proved workable. In 1932, Congress finally decided to narrow this estate tax escape hatch with a comprehensive set of provisions, the federal gift tax.

The principal purpose of the federal gift tax is to "back-up" the estate tax and prevent the avoidance of estate tax by lifetime transfers. Like the estate tax, the federal gift tax is an excise tax on the transfer of property. Its purpose suggests, of course, that the gift tax and estate tax should be so integrated that the use of a lifetime gift to transfer property does not provide any transfer tax savings as compared to a testamentary transfer of the same amount. Accordingly, all gratuitous transfers by one donor should be aggregated and taxed under a single set of rates. The transfers may be made at different times during the course of the donor's life and at death, but the total tax collected on the aggregate transfers should be the same as if all the transfers were made at one time and the tax collected then.

Consistent with this notion, from its inception in 1932, the federal gift tax has required that the tax due on any gift be calculated on an aggregate basis. This is accomplished by aggregating all prior taxable gifts made by the same donor with any current taxable gift, calculating the gift tax due on the total, and reducing the amount so determined by the tax that would have been paid on the previous gifts using the existing rate schedule.

Notwithstanding the central purpose of having both a gift and estate tax, the gift tax as originally enacted, and for nearly forty-five years thereafter, had its own rate structure which was separate from the estate tax rate structure and under which each rate applicable to a taxable gift amount was lower than the corresponding estate tax rate on the same amount passing at death. Further, from 1932 until 1977, lifetime gifts were not taken into account in determining the tax rate applicable to testamentary transfers.

* * *

---

[*] Copyright © 1993. Reprinted with permission.

In the Tax Reform Act of 1976, Congress took several steps to integrate the estate and gift tax systems. First, it repealed the separate estate and gift tax rates and adopted a single set of rates to be imposed on all taxable gifts and testamentary transfers. Second, it ordained that the value of all taxable lifetime gifts made by an individual after 1976 should be taken into account in determining the transfer tax rate applicable to the same person's estate at death. Thus, under the post-1976 system, all of an individual's taxable lifetime gifts (except for those made before the change in the law) are added to the value of the property that the individual transfers at his death in order to determine the rate of tax applicable to the property transferred at death.

* * *

There are several exceptions to the gift tax which correspond to the exceptions to estate tax discussed above and which can be used to avoid or postpone transfer tax. Gifts to charity are not subject to gift tax, gifts to spouses or into certain types of trusts for spouses are not subject to gift tax, and the first $192,800 of gift tax due is offset by the unified credit. Thus, due to the unified credit, an individual may make taxable gifts of $600,000 without paying any tax out-of-pocket. If the credit is used to offset tax due on lifetime transfers, it will not be available to reduce estate taxes due at death. In addition to these exceptions, which are similar to the exceptions to the estate tax, amounts paid on behalf of any other person as tuition to educational institutions that meet certain criteria (meant to ensure that the institutions are bona fide) are not subject to gift tax. Neither are amounts paid to a medical care provider for the medical care of any other person.

Finally, there is the annual exclusion from gift tax. Under the annual exclusion, an individual may make annual gifts of property to any number of persons of up to $10,000 each without incurring any gift tax, so long as the gift is not a gift of a future interest in property.

* * *

Because the exclusion is calculated on a per year, per donee basis, an individual who has the resources can transfer substantial amounts of wealth under the exclusion. For example, if the individual has nine donees, the individual can give $10,000 to each donee each year, thus transferring a total of $90,000 a year. If the individual is married, the individual and the individual's spouse can each give $10,000 to each donee each year, for a combined gift of $20,000 per donee. If one of the two spouses has $20,000 to give away and the other has no property to give away, the one with the $20,000 can make the gift and the couple can treat the $20,000 gift as a $10,000 gift from each.

Question

Examine Internal Revenue Code § 2503(b) in the statutory supplement. What has happened to the annual exclusion in the years after 1998?

3. The Federal Generation-Skipping Transfer Tax

John A. Miller & Jeffrey A. Maine
Fundamentals of Estate Tax Planning
32 IDAHO L. REV. 197, 236-240 (1996)[*]

Like the estate and gift taxes, the generation-skipping transfer ("GST") tax is an excise tax. It is a tax on the gratuitous transfer of property to a person who is more than one generation below the generation of the transferor. Succinctly put, it taxes transfers which skip a generation, forcing every generation to pay a transfer tax even if the generation did not get the benefit of the property transferred. The GST tax mainly is a device for closing the loophole which exists in the estate and gift taxes for transfers of property from one generation to another without any tax. For example, assume Grandfather dies, leaving $1,000,000 to Father who lives off the income but not the principal; Father dies, leaving the $1,000,000 to Granddaughter. In this scenario, the transfer to Father is subject to estate tax because the property is included in Grandfather's gross estate, and the transfer to Granddaughter is subject to estate tax because the property is included in Father's gross estate. The property benefited two generations, and there were two transfer taxes. Assume, however, that Grandfather leaves $1,000,000 in trust to Father for life, remainder to Granddaughter. In this scenario, the transfer to the trust is fully taxed to Grandfather or his estate; when Father dies, however, there is no further tax because Father's interest terminated at death. Thus, the property benefited two generations, but there was only one transfer tax. The GST tax is a device for closing this opportunity.

The GST tax is triggered by any one of three events: (1) a taxable distribution, (2) a taxable termination, or (3) a direct skip. All involve transfers of property to "skip persons." A skip person is one who is two or more generations below the transferor. The generation to which a transferee belongs is determined in accordance with mechanical rules.

* * *

The direct skip is perhaps the easiest triggering event to comprehend. A direct skip is a transfer, subject to estate or gift tax, to a skip person. To illustrate a direct skip, assume that Grandfather dies leaving $1,000,000 to Grandchild. This transfer is a direct skip because it is subject to the estate tax, and it is a transfer to someone two generations below the transferor.

Taxable terminations are terminations of any interest held in trust (1) unless after the termination the interest is held by a non-skip person, or (2) unless after the termination there can be no distributions from the trust to a skip person. To illustrate, Father establishes a lifetime trust, with income to be paid to himself for life, then Son for life, and then remainder to Grandson. At Father's death, with Son surviving, enjoyment of the property shifts to Son who is a non-skip person. Therefore, termi-

---

[*] Copyright © 1996. Reprinted with permission.

nation of Father's interest is not a taxable termination. However, at Son's death, with Grandson surviving, enjoyment of the property shifts to Grandson, who is a skip person (one who is more than two generations below Father's). This shift constitutes a taxable termination subject to the GST tax.

Taxable distributions are distributions from a trust to a skip person. When a trust distributes to someone assigned to two or more generations below the generation of the transferor (usually the settlor of the trust), there is a taxable distribution. For example, in a transfer of property to Child and Grandchild for the life of Child, remainder to Grandchild, the distribution of income to Grandchild is a taxable distribution.

The amount against which the GST tax is levied (the "taxable amount") varies depending upon several factors, including whether it arises out of a direct skip, taxable termination, or taxable distribution. In general, the taxable amount is the fair market value of the property interest passing to the skip person, valued at time of the transfer. The tax is computed by multiplying the "taxable amount" by the "applicable rate." This is not as simple as it appears, because the applicable rate must be derived through a number of computational steps.

The GST tax is designed to be a powerful impediment to the use of transfers which skip generations for tax avoidance purposes. There are several tools which ameliorate this effect in some cases. Of significance to the estate planner is a $1,000,000 dollar GST exemption per transferor, which the transferor may allocate to any particular transfers as she chooses. There are special rules for designating how the exemption is used in the absence of a specific allocation by the transferor. If the GST transfer is a gift for which the transferor and her spouse have elected to use the gift-splitting device under section 2513, they also are allowed to split the transfer for GST tax purposes. In this way, one spouse can take advantage of another spouse's GST exemption. It should be noted further that inter vivos GSTs also receive the benefit of the annual gift tax exclusion and the exclusion for certain qualified educational and medical expenditures.

* * *

This article simplifies many aspects of the GST tax, as its operation is quite complex.

Question

Examine Internal Revenue Code § 2631(c) in the statutory supplement. What has happened to the GSTT exemption in the years after 1998?

C. A Note on State Death Taxes

We now turn from the transfer taxes imposed by the federal government to the death taxes imposed by the several states. As we mentioned at the beginning of this chapter, state taxes are less important than their federal counterparts in estate planning practice, but state death taxes nonetheless deserve a brief overview.

In conjunction with the following excerpt, read Internal Revenue Code § 2011 in the statutory supplement.

Louis S. Harrison & John M. Janiga
Maximizing the Use of the State Death Tax Credit
19 EST. PLAN. 104, 104-05 (March/April 1992)[*]

States impose death taxes pursuant to one of three general death tax schemes. The dominant scheme, used by 27 states and the District of Columbia, developed in response to the state death tax credit [available under Internal Revenue Code § 2011. These states impose an estate tax equal to the maximum allowable state death tax credit on the Federal estate tax return. This taxing scheme is referred to as a "pick-up" tax because it picks up the credit for state death taxes allowed by the Federal estate tax.

The second most popular scheme, used by 18 states, involves a combination of an inheritance tax [paid by the recipients of the property rather than by the decedent's estate] and an additional estate tax [paid by the decedent's estate].

The typical inheritance tax statute divides beneficiaries into various classes, depending on how closely related to the decedent, and assigns different exemptions and tax rates to each class. States that have an inheritance tax also levy an additional estate tax designed to absorb the maximum state death tax credit allowed. That tax generally equals the amount, if any, by which the maximum allowable state death tax credit exceeds the state inheritance tax (and the total of estate and inheritance taxes paid to all states).

The least used tax scheme, adopted by five states, provides for an initial estate tax plus, if necessary to maximize fully the state death tax credit, an additional estate tax. Generally, the estate tax levy is similar in mechanics to the Federal estate tax, but the amount of the tax varies considerably because of different tax rate schedules and exemption amounts. The additional estate tax is the excess, if any, of the maximum state death tax credit allowable over the initial estate tax.

Payment due dates for death taxes vary among states, but generally, the original due date is no later than the due date of the Federal estate tax return (i.e., nine months after death). In addition, there are substantial differences among states regarding deferred tax payments. A few states provide no extensions for payment of

---

[*] Copyright © 1992. Reprinted with permission.

death taxes. Several states tailor their laws to mirror payment extensions provided by Federal law. Yet other states allow extensions if certain conditions or requirements are met (e.g., "good cause shown" or "undue hardship").

State laws regarding payment of state death taxes are important for two reasons. First, the timing of state death tax payments may have an impact on the availability of the state death tax credit. Second, to the extent a state permits (e.g., pursuant to discretion granted by statute) or provides alternative payment methods, an issue arises as to whether it is more advantageous to pay state death taxes in a lump sum or by the installment method.

* * *

State death tax laws have not remained static. The most dramatic recent change has been the shift to a pick-up tax scheme. Because this trend is likely to continue and because of the ambulatory nature of clients and their changes in domicile, practitioners should be aware of the status of the death tax laws in various states.

Questions

Having read Internal Revenue Code § 2011, do you understand how the state death tax credit works? Why do you think the federal government has included this provision in its laws?

FURTHER READING. ROGER W. ANDERSEN, UNDERSTANDING TRUSTS AND ESTATES (1994); THOMAS E. ATKINSON, HANDBOOK OF THE LAW OF WILLS (2d ed. 1953); DOUGLAS A. KAHN ET AL., FEDERAL TAXATION OF GIFTS, TRUSTS, AND ESTATES (3d ed. 1997); W. LESLIE PEAT & STEPHANIE J. WILLBANKS, FEDERAL ESTATE AND GIFT TAXATION: AN ANALYSIS AND CRITIQUE (2d ed. 1995); LAWRENCE W. WAGGONER ET AL., FAMILY PROPERTY LAW (2d ed. 1997).